FROMMER'S
MEXICO ON $20 A DAY

by Tom Brosnahan and
Jane Kretchman

1983-1984 Edition

Copyright © 1962, 1964, 1966, 1968, 1970, 1971, 1973, 1975, 1977, 1979, 1981, 1983
by Simon & Schuster

All rights reserved
including the right of reproduction
in whole or in part in any form

Published by Frommer/Pasmantier Publishers
A Simon & Schuster Division of
Gulf & Western Corporation
1230 Avenue of the Americas
New York, NY 10020

ISBN 0-671-45297-5

Manufactured in the United States of America

*Although every effort was made to ensure the accuracy
of price information appearing in this book,
it should be kept in mind that prices
can and do fluctuate in the course of time.*

CONTENTS

Introduction	**MEXICO ON $20 A DAY**	1
	1. A Brief History	2
	2. The $20-a-Day Way	7
	3. Preparing for Your Trip	10
	4. About This Book	16
Chapter I	**GETTING THERE**	19
	1. By Air	20
	2. By Train	21
	3. By Bus	23
	4. By Car	24
Chapter II	**HEADING SOUTH OVERLAND**	30
	1. The West Coast Route: Hermosillo to Culiacan	30
	2. The El Paso Route: Chihuahua to Fresnillo	37
	3. The Eastern Route via Monterrey and Saltillo	46
Chapter III	**PACIFIC COAST RESORTS**	65
	1. Mazatlán	65
	2. San Blas and Tepic	75
	3. Puerto Vallarta	79
	4. San Patricio and Barra de Navidad	87
	5. Manzanillo to Playa Azul	89
	6. Ixtapa—Zihuatanejo	95
	7. Acapulco	100
	8. Puerto Escondido and Puerto Angel	116
Chapter IV	**GUADALAJARA AND NEARBY CITIES**	119
	1. Guadalajara	119
	2. Lake Chapala	134
	3. Colima	137
	4. Uruapan	138
	5. Patzcuaro	141
	6. Morelia	146
Chapter V	**THE COLONIAL SILVER CITIES**	151
	1. Zacatecas	152
	2. Aguascalientes	155

	3. San Luis Potosí	158
	4. Guanajuato	164
	5. San Miguel de Allende	174
	6. Querétaro	180
Chapter VI	**MEXICO CITY: BASIC ORIENTATION**	185
	1. Arriving in Mexico City	186
	2. Public Transportation	192
	3. Organized Tours	194
	4. Tourism Information	194
Chapter VII	**MEXICO CITY: ROOMS ON A BUDGET**	196
	1. Getting the Most for Your Money	196
	2. Choosing a Hotel Location	197
	3. Hotels in the Zona Rosa	197
	4. Hotels Near Jardín del Arte	200
	5. Hotels Near Revolución Monument	201
	6. Hotels Near Alameda Central	204
	7. Hotels Near the Zócalo	205
	8. Hotels Near Bus, Train, and Air Terminals	210
	9. Apartment Hotels	211
Chapter VIII	**MEXICO CITY: MEALS ON A BUDGET**	213
	1. About Mexican Restaurants	213
	2. In and Near the Zona Rosa	214
	3. Near Jardín del Arte / Revolución	219
	4. Near the Alameda and Bellas Artes	221
	5. In the Zócalo Area	225
Chapter IX	**MEXICO CITY: DAYTIME ACTIVITIES**	228
	1. A Walk Around Town	228
	2. Museums in the Downtown Area	234
	3. Outdoor Markets	236
	4. Arts and Crafts Shops	238
	5. Chapultepec Park and Its Museums	240
	6. Attractions on the Outskirts	246
	7. The Bullfights and Horse Races	255
Chapter X	**MEXICO CITY: BUDGET NIGHTTIME ACTIVITIES**	257
	1. Nightlife in the Zona Rosa	257

	2. Mariachis, Music, and Margaritas	258
	3. Movies and Theaters	260
	4. The Ballet Folklorico	261
	5. Jai Alai	262
	6. The National Lottery Drawing	262
Chapter XI	**ONE-DAY TRIPS FROM THE CAPITAL**	**264**
	1. Pyramids of San Juan Teotihuacán	264
	2. Tula	269
	3. Toluca	270
	4. The Volcanoes	271
	5. Cuernavaca	272
	6. Taxco	279
Chapter XII	**TO THE GULF**	**285**
	1. Orizaba and Cordoba	285
	2. Jalapa	286
	3. Veracruz	288
	4. Tuxpan and Tajin	297
	5. Lake Catemaco	299
Chapter XIII	**SOUTH OVER THE MOUNTAINS**	**302**
	1. Puebla	303
	2. Tehuacan	312
	3. Oaxaca	314
	4. Tehuantepec	333
Chapter XIV	**THE ISTHMUS AND CHIAPAS**	**335**
	1. Acayucan	336
	2. Villahermosa	337
	3. Palenque	340
	4. Tuxtla Gutierrez	345
	5. San Cristóbal de las Casas	347
	6. Tapachula	353
Chapter XV	**THE YUCATÁN AND MEXICO'S CARIBBEAN**	**355**
	1. Merida	356
	2. Uxmal and Nearby Ruins	368
	3. Campeche	375
	4. Chichén-Itzá and Valladolid	377
	5. Cancún	382
	6. Isla Mujeres	391

	7. Cozumel	**396**
	8. Xel-ha, Tulum, and Cobá	**403**
	9. Carrillo Puerto and Chetumal	**406**
	10. Travel to Belize and Guatemala	**410**
Chapter XVI	**LATIN LISTINGS**	**411**
	1. The ABCs of Life South of the Border	**411**
Appendix	**FOR YOUR INFORMATION**	**425**
	1. Shopping Guide	**425**
	2. Basic Vocabulary	**427**
	3. Useful Phrases	**429**
	4. Menu Terms	**430**

MAPS

Mexico	2
Chihuahua	39
Monterrey	49
Mazatlán	66
Puerto Vallarta	81
Zihuatanejo	94
Acapulco Bay Area	103
Downtown Acapulco	104
Guadalajara	121
Greater Guadalajara	129
Patzcuaro	142
Aguascalientes	157
San Luis Potosí	160
Guanajuato	165
San Miguel de Allende	175
Mexico City	187
Mexico City Metro	191
Reforma and Zona Rosa	198
Revolucíon and Alameda	202
Zócalo and Merced	206
Chapultepec Park	241
Cuernavaca	273
Taxco	280
Veracruz	289
Puebla	305
Oaxaca	315
Merida	358
Campeche	375
Ciudad Cancún	384
Cancún's Zona Turística	389

To Anita Papafrita and Estebanito Bandido

Important Notes

In previous years, this guide included copious information for travelers going to Guatemala and Belize, as well as to Mexico. The political and social climate in Guatemala and Belize is not conducive to tourism as of this writing, and I cannot in good conscience include them here. As these are two of the most fascinating countries I've ever visited, I'm hopeful that things will get better so that they can be included in the next edition of this guide. It would be a shame for you to miss two such beautiful and interesting places. For an update on Travel Advisories to these two countries, you can call the U.S. Department of State's Citizens' Emergency Center at 202/632-5225 during business hours (Eastern time).

Important to remember: In Mexico, the dollar sign is used to denote pesos, and a Mexican sign reading "$5" means 5 pesos, not 5 dollars. To eliminate confusion, the dollar sign in this book is used only to indicate U.S. dollars.

It's good to have $25 or so in cash dollars of small denominations with you at all times for emergencies (most places will take them if you don't have the proper local currency).

Mexico now has a Value Added Tax ("Impuesto de Valor Aggregado," or "IVA") of 10% on almost everything, including hotel rooms and restaurant meals. In the prices I quote for rooms in my recommended hotels, the tax is *included.*

Mexico's 10% IVA tax in *not* included in the prices given for any other items—such as meals or souvenirs—unless I specifically note that it has been included.

The $20 daily budget, which provides the title for this book, is intended to cover only the cost of your hotel room and three meals, and not your entertainment and transportation expenses. As a result, the accommodations listed in this book are, in my opinion, generally moderately priced, and not rock-bottom. The book can be used with safety by persons of both sexes and of all ages.

Although every effort is made to ensure that the information given is accurate and up-to-date at press time, keep in mind that some transportation schedules, museum opening hours, telephone numbers, and *prices* (in this age of inflation) may change by the time you reach Mexico. Mexico's economic situation is chaotic these days, with inflation running near 100% a year. But foreign tourists going to Mexico benefit from the frequent devaluations of the peso, so a trip to Mexico is now more of a bargain than ever.

As of this writing, the rate of exchange in Mexico is between 85 and 120 pesos for U.S. $1. This may well change by the time you visit Mexico, but any bank will be glad to provide you with the current rate.

Introduction

MEXICO ON $20 A DAY

**1. A Brief History
2. The $20-a-Day Way
3. Preparing for Your Trip
4. About This Book**

EVERYONE NORTH OF THE RIO GRANDE has at least some idea (usually an old-fashioned one) about what Mexico is like, but only those who go there can know the real Mexico, for the country is undergoing fast-paced and far-reaching change, as are most countries touched by modern technology. Being so close to the United States and Canada, she is so forcefully affected by what goes on in her neighboring countries to the north that the Old Mexico of cowboy songs and movies has long ago been replaced by a land full of the familiar signs of 20th-century life. But this does not mean that a trip to Mexico will reveal people, sights, and sounds just like home, for Mexico is very much her own country, the result of a particular blending of the land itself and of ancient Indian, colonial European, and modern industrial influences. These three elements have produced a tradition and a culture unique in all the world.

To discover this unique Mexico you must look beyond the many modern conveniences—good roads, luxury hotels, frequent air and bus service, and the like—back to the basis of the culture. First there is the land: seemingly trackless desert, thousands of miles of lush seacoast, tropical lowland jungle, snow-capped mountains; from the breathtaking gorges of Chihuahua to the flat coastal plain of Yucatán, from the Pacific at California to the Caribbean at Quintana Roo, Mexico stretches 2000 miles from sea to sea. Then there are the peoples: Indians descended from the founders of many civilizations—Olmec, Toltec, Mayan, Aztec; the Spanish Conquistadores; Africans brought as slaves; European merchants and soldiers of fortune; a French influence left from the time of the abortive venture at New World empire by Maximilian of Habsburg and Napoléon III. All these influences have combined to create a particularly Mexican cast of mind, which you will see revealed in the architecture of the cities and towns, the cuisine, the costumes and habits of the people.

Mexican history goes back over 10,000 years, and is crucial to your understanding of the country and its people. To whet your appetite, here follows a summary of those 10,000 years.

1. A Brief History

The earliest "Mexicans" were Stone Age men and women, descendants of the race which had crossed the Bering Strait and reached North America prior to about 10,000 B.C. These were *Homo sapiens* who hunted mastodons, bison, and the like, and gathered other food as they could. Later (Archaic Period, 5200–1500 B.C.), signs of agriculture and domestication appear: baskets were woven; corn, beans, squash and tomatoes were raised; turkeys and dogs were kept for food. By 2400 B.C. the art of potting had been discovered (the use of pottery was a significant advance). Life in these times was still very primitive, of course, but there were "artists" who made clay figurines for use as votive offerings or household "gods." Actually, goddesses is a better term, for all the figurines found so far have been female, and are supposed to be symbols of Mother Earth or Fertility in a very primitive sense. (Use of these figurines predates any belief in well-defined gods.)

THE PRECLASSIC PERIOD: It was in the Preclassic Period (2000 B.C.–A.D. 300) that the area known by archeologists as Middle America (from the northern Mexico Valley through Guatemala) began to show signs of a farming culture. They farmed either by the "slash-and-burn" method of cutting grass and trees, then setting fire to the area to clear it for planting; or by constructing terraces and irrigation ducts, this latter method being the one used principally in the highlands around Mexico City, where the first large towns developed. At some time during this period, religion became an institution as certain men took the role of *shaman,* or guardian of the magical and religious secrets. These were the predecessors of the folk healers and nature priests still to be found in modern Mexico and Guatemala.

The most highly developed culture of this Preclassic Period was that of the Olmecs, flourishing a full millennium before that of the Mayas. From 1200 to 400 B.C. the Olmecs lived in what is today the state of Tabasco, south of Veracruz, and it was to this coastal land that they tranported colossal 40-ton blocks of basalt, carved as roundish heads. These sculptures still present problems to archeologists: How were they cut and carved with only the primitive implements the Olmecs had? How and why were they transported the many miles from the source of the basalt to the Gulf Coast at La Venta (near Villahermosa)? What do they signify? The heads seem infantile in their roundness, but all have the peculiar "jaguar mouth" with a high-arched upper lip which is the identifying mark of the Olmecs, and which was borrowed and adapted by many later cultures. The artists seemed obsessed with deformity, and many smaller carved or clay figures are of monstrosities or misshapen forms. Besides their achievements in sculpture, the Olmecs were the first in Mexico to use a calendar of 365 days.

THE CLASSIC PERIOD: Most of the real artistic and cultural achievement came during the Classic Period (A.D. 300–900), when life was no longer centered in the villages but rather in cities. Class distinctions, absent from village life, arose as the military and religious aristocracy took control, a class of merchants and artisans grew, and the farmer who had been independent became the serf under a landlord's control. The cultural centers of the Classic Period were the Yucatán and Guatemala (home of the Maya), the Mexican Highlands at Teotihuacán, the Zapotec cities of Monte Alban and Mitla (near Oaxaca), and the Totonac cities of Tajin and Zempoala on the Gulf Coast.

The Mayas are at the apex of pre-Columbian cultures. Besides their superior artistic achievements, the Mayas made significant discoveries in science, including the use of the zero in mathematics and their famous, complex calendar with which their priests could predict eclipses and the movements of the stars for centuries to come. The Mayas were warlike, and although one group or another might raid its neighbors from time to time, their sacrifices—some of them human—were on a very small scale compared to those of their successors, the bloodthirsty Aztecs. All considered, the Mayas seem to have been an admirable people: fairly peaceable, artistically gifted, imaginative, although also conservative and superstitious.

Teotihuacán is thought to have been a Toltec city of 85,000 inhabitants. At its height, Teotihuacán was the greatest cultural center in Mexico. Its layout is certainly of religious significance; on the tops of its pyramids consecrated to the sun and moon, high priests performed human sacrifices, attended but not observed by the masses of the people at the foot of the pyramid. Some of the magnificent reliefs and frescoes which decorated the religious monuments can be seen in Mexico City's museums.

The Zapotecs, influenced by the Olmecs, raised an impressive culture in the region of Oaxaca. Their two principal cities were Monte Alban, inhabited by an elite of merchants and artisans, and Mitla, reserved for the high priests. Both cities exhibit the artistic and mathematical genius of the people: characteristic geometric designs, long-nosed gods with feathered masks, hieroglyph stelae, a bar-and-dot numerical system, and a 52-cycle calendar. Like the Olmecs, the Zapotecs favored grotesque and fantastic art, of which the frieze of the "Danzantes" at Monte Alban—naked figures of distorted form and contorted position—is an outstanding example.

Of these important Classic Period cultures, perhaps least is known of the Totonacs, a small tribe centered in Tajin and Zempoala on the Gulf Coast. The Pyramid of the Niches which they built at Tajin is unique of its kind, and the numerous clay figures they crafted of men at play, smiling, dancing, and clowning, bespeak a joyfulness best described by a 16th-century Spaniard: "They were fun-loving with no affront of words, no ugly or unjust thing." Be sure to see their art in the museum at Villahermosa.

THE POSTCLASSIC PERIOD: In the Postclassic Period (900–1520), warlike cultures in time developed impressive societies of their own, although they never surpassed the Classic peoples. All paintings and hieroglyphs of this period show war, migration, and disruption. Somehow the glue of society became unstuck, people wandered from their homes in search of a better life, the religious hierarchy lost influence over the people.

Finally, in the 1300s, the most warlike people of all, the Aztecs, settled in the Mexico Valley on Lake Texcoco (site of Mexico City), with the island city of Tenochtitlán as their capital. Legend has it that as the wandering Aztecs were passing the lake they saw a sign which their prophets had told them to look for: an eagle perched on a cactus plant with a snake in its mouth. They built their city where they saw the sign, and in time it grew to become a huge (pop. 300,000) and impressive capital. The empire which grew up with it was a more or less loosely united congeries of states and territories of great size. The high lords of the capital became fabulously rich in gold, stores of food, cotton, and perfumes; the artisans were skilled and prosperous; events of state were occasions of elaborate ceremony. But the other part of the picture was that of the victorious Aztecs returning from battle to sacrifice thousands of captives on the altars atop the pyramids, cutting their chests open with stone knives and ripping the living hearts out to offer to their gods.

QUETZALCOATL: The legend of Quetzalcoatl, a holy man who appeared during the time of troubles at the end of the Classic Period, is one of the most important tales in Mexican history and folklore. Quetzalcoatl means "feathered serpent," but seems to have been a religious title during later Maya times. Like the young Jesus, wise and learned beyond his years, he became the high priest and leader of the Toltecs at Tula, and did a good deal to "civilize" them and stop or ameliorate the bad effects of sacrifice. He stopped human sacrifice altogether. His influence completely changed the Toltecs from a group of spartan warriors to peaceful and fabulously productive farmers, artisans, and craftsmen. But his success upset the old priests who had depended on human sacrifice for their own importance, and they called upon their ancient god of darkness, Texcatlipoca, to degrade Quetzalcoatl in the eyes of the people. One night the priests conspired to dress Quetzalcoatl in a ridiculous garb, get him drunk, and tempt him to break his vow of chastity. The next morning they offered him a mirror, and the horror of what he saw after this night of debauch drove him in shame out of his own land and into the wilderness, where he lived for 20 years. He emerged in Coatzacoalcos, in the Isthmus of Tehuantepec, constructed a boat of feathers, bade his few followers farewell, and sailed away, having promised to return in a future age. But artistic influences noted at Chichén-Itzá in the Yucatán suggest that in fact he landed there and began his "ministry" again, this time with much success among the peaceable Mayas. He died there, but the legend of his return in a future age remained.

THE SPANISH CONQUISTADORES: When Hernan Cortes and his men landed in 1519 in what would become Veracruz, the Aztec empire was ruled by Moctezuma (also, misspelled, Montezuma) in great splendor. The emperor thought the strangers might be Quetzalcoatl and his followers, returning at last, in which case no resistance must be offered; on the other hand, if the strangers were not Quetzalcoatl, they might be a threat to his empire. Moctezuma tried to bribe them with gold to go away, but this only whetted their appetites. Despite the fact that Moctezuma and his ministers received the Conquistadores with full pomp and glory when they reached Mexico City, Cortes pronounced the Aztec chief to be under arrest and had him tortured. Moctezuma never did reveal where he had hidden his fabulous treasure, which had been seen by a Spaniard earlier.

Actually the Spaniards were living on bravado at this point, for they were no match for the hundreds of thousands of Aztecs; but they skillfully kept things under their control until a revolt threatened Cortes's entire enterprise. He retired to the countryside, made alliances with non-Aztec tribes, and finally marched on the empire when it was governed by the last Aztec emperor, Cuauhtémoc. He was victorious; Cuauhtémoc defended himself and his people furiously, but was finally captured, tortured, and made a prisoner. He was ultimately executed.

The Spanish conquest had started out as an adventure by Cortes and his men, unauthorized by the Spanish crown or its governor in Cuba, but the conquest was not to be reversed and soon Christianity was being spread through "New Spain." Guatemala and Honduras were explored and conquered, and by 1540 the territory of New Spain included Spanish possessions from Vancouver to Panama. In the two centuries that followed, Franciscan and Augustinian friars converted great numbers of Indians to Christianity, and the Spanish lords built up huge feudal estates on which the Indian farmers were little more than serfs. The silver and gold which Cortes had sought made Spain the richest country in Europe.

INDEPENDENCE: Spain ruled Mexico through a viceroy until 1821, when Mexico finally gained its independence after a decade of upheaval. The independence movement had begun in 1808 when a priest, Fr. Miguel Hidalgo, cried from his pulpit "Mexicans, long live Mexico!" With the help of a military officer named Ignacio de Allende, who had had revolutionary thoughts even earlier

6 MEXICO ON $20 A DAY

than had Hidalgo, the priest assembled a mob army and sought redress of grievances against the Spanish. The revolt soon became a revolution, and Hidalgo and Allende were joined by another priest, Father Morelos, as their "army" threatened Mexico City. Ultimately the revolt failed, and Hidalgo was executed, but he is honored as Mexico's foremost patriot, "the Father of Modern Mexico." Morelos kept the revolt alive until 1815 when he, too, was caught and executed. When independence finally came, one Agustín Iturbide was ready to take over. Iturbide founded a short-lived "empire" with himself as emperor in 1822. The next year it fell and was followed by the proclamation of a republic with Gen. Guadalupe Victoria as first president. A succession of presidents and military dictators followed Guadalupe Victoria until one of the most bizarre and extraordinary episodes in modern times: the French intervention.

In the 1860s, certain factions among the Mexican upper class offered the Habsburg Archduke Maximilian the crown of Mexico, and with the support of the ambitious French emperor, Napoléon III, the young Austrian actually came to Mexico and "ruled" for three years (1864–1867) while the country was in a state of civil war. This move for European interference in New World affairs was not welcomed by the United States, and as Napoleon's support became more and more extensive without good results, the French emperor finally withdrew his troops, leaving the brave but misguided Maximilian to be captured and shot in Querétaro. His adversary and successor (as president of Mexico) was a Zapotec Indian lawyer named Benito Juarez, one of the most powerful and heroic figures in Mexican history. After victory over Maximilian, Juarez did his best to unify and strengthen his country, but it was not long before the stresses of the struggle gave him a heart attack. He died in 1872. His effect on the future of Mexico was profound, however, and his plans and visions continued to bear fruit for decades to come.

From 1877 to 1911 the prime role in the drama of Mexico was played by one of Juarez's generals, an emotional strongman named Porfirio Díaz. Hailed by some as a modernizer, he was a terror to his enemies and to anyone who stood in his way or challenged his absolute power. He was finally forced to step down in 1911 by Francisco Madero and the greater part of public opinion.

The fall of the Porfirist dictatorship only led to more trouble, however. The country was split among several factions, including those led by "Pancho Villa" (real name Doroteo Arango), Alvaro Obregon, Venustiano Carranza, and Emiliano Zapata. The turbulent era from the fall of Porfirio Díaz through the next ten years is referred to as the Mexican Revolution. Drastic reforms were proposed and carried out by the leaders in this period, and the surge of vitality and progress from this exciting if turbulent time has inspired Mexicans down to the present day. Succeeding presidents have invoked the spirit of the Revolution, and it is still studied and discussed.

MEXICO TODAY: The United Mexican States today is headed by an elected president and a bicameral legislature. It's divided into 30 states, plus the Federal District (Mexico City) and a national territory. The population of about 60 million is 15% white (descendants of the Spaniards); 60% mestizo, or mixed Spanish and Indian blood; and 25% pure Indian (descendants of the Mayas, Aztecs, and other tribes). Although Spanish is the official language, about 50 Indian languages are still spoken, mostly in the Yucatán Peninsula and the mountainous region of Oaxaca. Economically, Mexico is not by any means a poor country. Only about a sixth of the economy is in agriculture. Mining, which made the Spanish colonists and their king fabulously rich, is still fairly important. Gold and silver account for some of it, and there are many other important minerals still mined, but the big industry today is oil. In the last several years fields which promise to make Mexico the world's sixth-richest oil nation have been opened up in Chiapas, on the Guatemalan border, supplementing Mexico's already sizable income from oil. Mexico is also well industrialized, manufacturing textiles, food products, everything from high-quality auto parts to tape cassettes.

In short, Mexico is well into the 20th century, with all the benefits and problems which contemporary life brings, and although vast sums are spent on education and public welfare (much, much more than is spent on implements of war), a high birth rate and unequal distribution of wealth show that much remains to be done.

This is the Mexico you'll get to know.

2. The $20-a-Day Way

Although Mexico is no longer the ultra-cheap place it once was, a trip to Mexico can be the most reasonably priced foreign vacation you'll ever experience if you abide by the philosophy and recommendations of this book. As a reader of this book you'll have a better chance to discover the truly fascinating Mexico, for many times the guests at the posh hotel are tempted to stay there and not risk discomfort or inconvenience, while the readers of *Mexico on $20 a Day* will have at their fingertips the information needed to get the basics of travel—hotels, meals, and transportation—out of the way as quickly and as cheaply as possible so they can plunge into the Mexico of the Mexicans. In fact, it's amazing how much of a country you can miss by going through it luxury class. The luxurious hotel room, the taxi or chauffeur-driven car, the plush restaurant with "local and international cuisine" all cater to an imaginary wealthy stereotype who, it seems, is always pleased to live in the midst of smiling and subservient staff, bland meals, canned music, and picturesque sights kept at a respectful distance—all at a greatly padded price. Think of the difference if you can say "Buenos dias!" to the cheerful señora who runs your pension, happy in her work and confident of her position in society; eat in local restaurants where the cuisine is designed to please residents of the neighborhood, and presents the outsider with new delights (and some perils!); rub shoulders with the real Mexican, the man in the street, in the subway, on buses or in *peseros* (shared taxis). What you give up is standardization: rooms are different in each hotel and pension, whereas Hilton will give you almost exactly the same room, in Baghdad or Bombay. The staff in a small hotel can be super-friendly or indifferent, whereas in the big places they are always polite but distant.

Our $20-a-Day budget is intended to cover only the expenses of room and three meals each day. Thus, I will recommend hotels where you will be able to stay for about $10 per person per night, and restaurants in which it will be possible to have three meals for the other $10: breakfast for about $2.50, lunch (the largest meal in the Mexican's day) for about $4.50, and supper for about $3. Spend a few dollars more, and you can live a good deal more comfortably—even luxuriously—for $25 a day.

In fact, your vacation to Mexico may cost you well over $20 a day, but that will be your choice, and will be much affected by your personal preferences: if you like air travel, expect to pay a good deal more; if you don't mind buses (and in Mexico they are the easiest and cheapest way to go), your extra cost for transportation will be minimal. Add a few dollars a day for entertainment if you're a nightclub fan, but add only a quarter or two if you are satisfied

8 MEXICO ON $20 A DAY

with going to museums and exhibitions. Of course there are those who want to do Mexico as cheaply as possible and will gladly pass up comforts rather than part with dollars, so under my "Starvation Budget" heading I'll give some tips on how to do it as cheaply as possible short of sleeping in cornfields, bumming rides, and singing for supper. Therefore, the hotels generally recommended in this book will be clean, respectable places, sometimes with some comforts and conveniences such as multilingual staff, swimming pools, or bathrooms in the rooms, suitable for any traveler except the luxury-minded. You will not find these hotels standardized into sterility, as are many luxury places; each will have its own special treats—and surprises—and as some readers may like certain features more than others, descriptions of each establishment are given. Let's say you want a room with a view over the lovely *zócalo* in the center of Queretaro. Then you must next consider, as you look over the hotel descriptions and also when you look at the hotel itself, how seriously you might be bothered by motorcycles buzzing under your window. If motor noise is your weak point, it'd be best to look into someplace on a side street, perhaps with rooms around an inner court; or even a motel on the outskirts of town, which may not have a view and which may be slightly more expensive but will be easier on your nerves.

There will be times when you'd like to get away from it all, when the buses and motorcycles (most of which have no mufflers in order to save gas) so assault your ears and nose that the scented, soundproofed, air-conditioned, and be-Muzak'ed halls of a Hilton or a Sheraton seem like a piece of heaven, or when the 25¢ "calculation error" on your budget lunch bill makes you wish the proprietor would simply charge an extortionate rate at the start (as luxury places do) and get it over with. These are the daily fatigues that go with strenuous travel in a strange land, and for those times when you want to escape to cushioned comfort I have included hotel and restaurant choices under the heading "The Big Splurge." American-style eateries are also noted now and then so you may, if you wish, give your stomach a respite from unfamiliar food. But the reason you bought this book is so that you can live closer to things authentically Mexican, and have a memorable trip at a reasonable price, so travel the way I do.

MONEY-SAVING TIPS, OR HOW TO STRETCH YOUR $$$: What you spend on your trip to Mexico depends a lot on how you operate. Here, first, are some tips to save you money on hotel bills. At the outset, remember that rooms with bath or air conditioning are always more expensive. Don't deny yourself these comforts if you want them, but ask yourself "Do I really want/need it today?" Second, in many hotels rooms in the back of the hotel with no view (except of an airshaft) are cheaper *and quieter* than rooms with a view of the street. How much time will you be spending looking out your hotel window at the street? Third, two people sharing a room always pay less than two people in single rooms, and two people sharing a double bed (called a *cama matrimonial* in Mexico) pay least of all. When the desk clerk asks "How many beds?" don't necessarily answer "Two." Or if the clerk shows you a room with two beds, ask if he has one with a double bed. Save a buck—sleep with a friend. Fourth, often the price the desk clerk quotes you for a room *won't* be the cheapest room he has available, but rather what he thinks to be the most desirable—which is bound to be more expensive. Ask to see a cheaper room (*"Quiero ver un cuarto mas barato, por favor"*)—it can't hurt, and if the cheap room turns out to be a dungeon you can always take the more expensive room.

Saving on Food

More money can be saved by how you eat than on any other expense of your trip, but I rush to add that eating well is one of the most important things you can do to make your trip enjoyable. Wholesome food—good bread, milk, meat, fish, fresh vegetables, and fruit—is always a bargain, because you get your money's worth in nutrition. If a Coke costs 10 pesos and an equal amount of milk costs 12, get in the habit of drinking the milk—it'll keep you going longer. Avoid snacky "junk" foods, a luxury item in Mexico, and eat nuts or fruit instead. This pays off not only in having to eat less, but also in getting sick less, as good nutrition is one of the keys to avoiding or mitigating the dread "Turista" diarrhea (see below under "Health").

Breakfast: Now some specifics on eating cheaply. Breakfast is the most overpriced meal in the world for travelers, and in Mexico it is no exception. Big-breakfast eaters should not refrain from buying the bacon and eggs they want, but if you can exist until lunchtime on a light breakfast, consider this. In most Mexican cities you can drop by a *panaderia* or *pasteleria* (bakery or pastry shop) and get delicious rolls and sweet rolls or pastry for incredibly cheap prices, and a few of these, plus perhaps a glass of milk or a piece of cheese (available in the markets), can keep you going until you have your big lunch at noon. Also, a $2 immersion coil, plus a heat-resistant plastic cup, a jar of instant coffee or a tea bag, and some powdered milk will enable you to make your own coffee or tea in the morning at a cost of about 16¢ a cup. Coffee in Mexico normally costs 40¢ to 50¢ a cup. The electrical current throughout Mexico is 110-volt and the plugs and sockets are American style. Some of my more fanatic money-saving readers pack small, lightweight aluminum percolators in their bags, with which they can brew fresh coffee, make soup or even pork and beans! Having a coil or a hot pot is also very handy if you come down with diarrhea and can only stomach tea, herb tea (camomile tea is a specific for queasy stomach), or bouillon. Coffee, ground or instant, teabags, powdered milk *(leche in polvo),* and bouillon cubes are all readily available in Mexico, and I've indicated the whereabouts of pastry shops in most cities covered in this book.

Lunch: Now for lunch. Your best value by far will be to eat a big meal at noon, and if you're not inflexible it shouldn't be too hard to fit in the rest of the day around this meal rather than vice-versa. For instance, most parts of Mexico that you will be visiting will be warm or hot during most of the day, so plan to be up early and out to the things you want to see early in the morning after a light breakfast. Then, after some exercise, relax and collect your thoughts over a largish lunch at about one o'clock, amble back to your hotel for a nap (or escape to a shady place if your hotel's a good distance away), and take it easy during the hottest part of the day. Then, rested and replenished, set out again in the late afternoon and evening for more exploration, and have a light supper before returning to your hotel. This is what Mexicans invariably do, and so most restaurants offer a *comida corrida,* or special lunch of several courses at a special, low price, served between about 1 and 4 p.m. Usually the meal will be of soup, pasta, a main course, dessert, and coffee, and will cost anywhere from $1 to $4, depending on the class of the restaurant, but it will always be much cheaper than the total for the individual items offered. Often there is some choice of soup and entree. Many of the cheaper restaurants will advertise their comida corrida on blackboards hung by the door, and that will be your only look at a menu; slightly more expensive places will attach a slip to the menu listing the comida and its price. The comida corrida is the biggest meal bargain in Mexico, so you should try to take advantage of it.

Dinner: For dinner you'll want to eat lightly, having eaten heavily at one o'clock, and if you can make do on a good bowl of soup and a plate of enchiladas you will need to spend very little. Avoid by all means the long, luxurious dinners so popular in Europe and the U.S., unless you've decided to splurge or are celebrating a special occasion. Such evening meals are not truly Mexican, and are therefore more expensive.

Markets: Some other eating tips: Every town in Mexico has a market, the ones in the cities being fabulous affairs, often modern, in which the full range of local produce, cheese, eggs, bread, etc., is for sale. I've bought pineapples for as little as 20¢, bananas for a song. The location of the market (indicated by "M" or "Market" on my city maps) is given for most towns covered in this book; if in doubt, ask for the *mercado*. Avoid milk and cream in open containers. In most places you should be able to find modern factory-packaged milk; if not, the powdered whole milk sold everywhere is almost as good, much more delicious than the powdered skim milk available at home.

THE WAGES OF CHANGE: On the subject of money, it might be good to put in a word about prices and inflation. Back in the halcyon days (several decades ago) when prices throughout the world changed at a rate of about 3% a year, a traveler could take dad's copy of a good travel book abroad and make a mental adjustment for a small price rise. But recently the inflation rate for Mexico has been in the neighborhood of 100% per annum; some businesses (hotels and restaurants included) will hold off as long as they can, perhaps two years, and then raise prices by even more than this factor to compensate for *future* inflation! Every effort is made to provide the most accurate and up-to-date information in this book, even to the point of predicting price increases which I feel are on the way and which will arrive before the book reaches the reader's hands; but changes are inevitable and uncontrollable with inflation. Keep in mind when you look at price lists that even though the price may have risen over that given in the book, *the establishments recommended will still be the best value for the money.*

Speaking of currency, don't forget that the dollar sign ($) is used by Mexicans and some other Latin Americans to denote their own national currencies, and thus a Mexican menu will have "$30" for a Coke and mean 30 pesos. To avoid confusion I will use the dollar sign in this book *only* to denote U.S. currency. Peso prices will be listed merely with figures or with the qualifying word "pesos."

3. Preparing for Your Trip

Preparation means information—you must know what you're preparing for. Below are some hints on how to get ready, so you can avoid unpleasant surprises when you arrive. Keep in mind the entire time you're reading this book that there is a wealth of classified information at your fingertips in Chapter XVI, "Latin Listings." When you have a question, look there first.

WHERE SHOULD I GO? People often ask me, "Where should I go in Mexico? It's so big, and I've heard so much about it, but what places are really worth visiting?" Here's what I tell them:

You have to travel as much as 1000 miles south of the border to find the "real" Mexico of your dreams: gorgeous colonial mountain towns, bustling modern cities, sleek coastal resorts. Northern Mexico is arid but rich, hard-working, vast, and heavily influenced by its great neighbor to the north.

ADVANCE PREPARATIONS

The Mexico of the travel brochures begins south of the Tropic of Cancer. Of the resorts, Puerto Vallarta is without doubt my favorite. Of the major cities, Guadalajara is nice, but is a pale second to the great capital, Mexico City, which you definitely should see. The silver mining towns of the northern Mexico Valley are the undiscovered treasures of Mexican tourism: Guanajuato is a spellbinding place, San Miguel de Allende is charming, Queretaro and San Luis Potosí clean and pleasant, with a wealth of colonial architecture. Zacatecas, at the border of the desert, has a rugged charm enhanced by great palaces and churches from centuries ago.

Between Mexico City and Guadalajara, Patzcuaro is the town to visit, as close to an authentic, remote Spanish mountain town as you'll find north of Central America.

South of Mexico City, Taxco is a must-see, Oaxaca too. You can spend a day in Veracruz pleasantly enough if you're passing through. Puerto Escondido and Puerto Angel, south of Oaxaca on the Pacific Coast, are the relatively undiscovered coastal hideaways which, in a decade, will be the new Acapulco and Puerto Vallarta. See them before it's too late.

East of the Isthmus of Tehuantepec, everybody wants to see San Cristóbal de las Casas. It's cool up there in the mountains, the wild scenery is beautiful, and the Indians largely retain their traditional way of life.

And then there's Yucatán. For my money, Yucatán—along with the Valley of Mexico—represents the most fascinating area to visit. Perfect beaches, ancient ruins, interesting local cuisine, friendly people—Yucatán has it all. You must see Palenque (near Villahermosa), Merida, Uxmal, and Chichén-Itzá. Cancún is for the charter-group sun-seekers, although you might try out the beaches for a day or two. Much more interesting resorts, in my way of thinking, are Isla Mujeres and Cozumel.

How long will it take? You could see a lot in two weeks, based in Mexico City or Merida, traveling by bus. To see all of these favorite places you'd need a month at least, for Mexico is a huge and mountainous place, and the twisty roads take much longer to negotiate than do Interstate highways. If you can afford the occasional airplane ride, you'll be able to fit more sightseeing into your vacation.

A NEWSLETTER: Lloyd Wilkins, a keen and witty observer of the Mexican scene, publishes a bimonthly newsletter called *AIM* (*"Adventures in Mexico"*), directed at those who may be planning to retire south of the border. But the contents prove useful—and entertaining—to just about anyone planning more than a short trip to Mexico. The current price for a year's subscription is U.S.$10; send it to AIM, Apdo. 31-70, Guadalajara, Jalisco, México.

BOOKS: "What you take away from a country depends on what you bring," so you may want to do some reading before you go. There are endless numbers of books written on the history, culture, and archeology of Mexico and Central America. I have listed those which I especially enjoyed or those that have been recommended by readers.

History: *A Short History of Mexico* by J. Patrick McHenry (Doubleday), a concise historical account. *The Conquest of New Spain* by Bernal Diaz (Penguin), the famous story of the Mexican conquest written by Cortes's lieutenant. *The Crown of Mexico* by Joan Haslip, a biography of Maximilian and Carlotta that reads like a novel. *Sons of the Shaking Earth* by Eric Wolf, the best single-volume introduction to Mexican history and culture of which I know.

Culture: *Five Families* and *Children of Sanchez* by Oscar Lewis, a sociological study written in the late 1950s of a typical Mexican family (somewhat outdated but still a very valuable source of information to understand the Mexican culture). *Mexican and Central American Mythology* by Irene Nicholson (Paul Hamlyn, 1973). *The People's Guide to Mexico* by Carl Franz, a mine of information and helpful hints, and very entertaining to read. *A Guide to Tequila, Mescal and Pulque* by Virginia B. de Barrios (Minutiae Mexicana), a very interesting account of the agave agriculture which includes the history and culture surrounding this industry. Three more specialized works devoted to art are: *My Art, My Life* by Diego Rivera; *Mexican Muralists* by Alma Reed; *Mexico South* by Miguel Covarrubias.

Archeology: *The Ancient Sun Kingdoms of the Americas* by Victor Wolfgang Von Hagen (Paladin), an easy-to-read, concise account of Mexican cultures from the Maya to the Aztec—recommended! *Tikal, Copan Travel Guide* by Nicholas Helmuth (Latin American Anthropological Research, 6 Conway Lane, St. Louis, MO 63124). A must for any traveler visiting the Mayan ruins is *The Maya* by Michael Coe (Praeger); it is easy to understand and will help the archeology buff to relate art and architecture with the different periods of Maya life. *National Geographic* subscribers who save back copies should look up the December 1975 (vol. 148, no. 6) edition for the interesting articles on the Maya, as well as the society's book, *Discovering Man's Past in the Americas.* C. Bruce Hunter's *A Guide to Ancient Maya Ruins* (University of Oklahoma Press) covers most of the major Maya sites in Mexico and Central America. Last, a book recommended by the Chennells of Santa Barbara, California, *The Mexican Codices and Their Extraordinary History* by Maria Sten (Ediciones Lara).

On Yucatán: Anyone heading for Yucatán should first read the wonderfully entertaining accounts of travel in that region by the 19th-century Yucatán traveler, New York lawyer, and amateur archeologist John L. Stephens. His books, *Incidents of Travel in Central America, Chiapas and Yucatan,* and also the account of his second trip, *Incidents of Travel in Yucatan,* have been reprinted by Dover Publications, Inc. (180 Varick St., New York, NY 10014). Stephens's adventures are part of Dover's fascinating series of reprints on Mayan archeology, history, and culture, which are available at bookstores or from Dover by mail.

The series also includes Friar Diego de Landa's *Yucatan Before and After the Conquest,* written in the 1560s. Friar Diego's account is a detailed description of Maya daily life, much of which has remained the same from his time until today. Dover even has a book on learning to read Maya hieroglyphs.

LEGAL DOCUMENTS: You'll need a Mexican Tourist Card, issued free, available at the border, at a Mexican consulate, or at any of the Mexican National Tourist Council offices listed below. Those flying to Mexico can ask their travel agent to get them a Tourist Card; most agents will do so at no extra charge.

The Tourist Card is more important than a passport in Mexico, so hold onto it carefully—if you lose it, you may not be able to leave the country until you can replace it, and that bureaucratic hassle takes several weeks at least.

Important Note: A Mexican Tourist Card can be issued for up to six months, and although your stay south of the border will doubtless be less than that, you should get the card for the maximum time, just in case. When the official who fills out your card asks you how long you intend to stay, say "six months," or at least *twice* as long as you really plan to be there. Who knows?

ADVANCE PREPARATIONS 13

You may find the perfect stretch of beach and not want to leave, or you may have to stay for some reason, and you'll save yourself *a lot* of hassle if you don't have to renew your papers. This hint is especially important for people who take cars into Mexico.

Mexican National Tourist Council offices in North America include those in the following cities:

Atlanta: Peachtree Center, Cain Tower, Suite 1201, Atlanta, GA 30303 (tel. 404/659-2409).

Chicago: John Hancock Center, Suite 3612, Chicago, IL 60611 (tel. 312/649-0090).

Dallas: Two Turtle Creek Village, Suite 1230, Dallas, TX 75219 (tel. 214/526-6950).

Denver: The Forum at Cherry Creek, 425 S. Cherry St., Suite 640, Denver, CO 80222 (tel. 303/355-0517).

Houston: C. E. Lummus Tower, Suite 1370, 3000 S. Post Oak Rd., Houston, TX 77056 (tel. 713/840-8332).

Los Angeles: 9701 Wilshire Blvd., Suite 1201, Beverly Hills, CA 90212 (tel. 213/274-6315).

Miami: 100 N. Biscayne Blvd., Suite 2804, Miami, FL 33132 (tel. 305/371-8037).

Montréal: 1 Place Ville-Marie, Suite 2409, Montréal H3B 3M9 (tel. 514/871-1052.)

New Orleans: One Shell Square Bldg., Suite 1515, New Orleans, LA 70139 (tel. 504/525-2783).

New York: 405 Park Ave., Suite 1203, New York, NY 10022 (tel. 212/755-7212).

San Antonio: GPM South Tower, Suite 240, 800 N.W. Loop 410, San Antonio, TX 78216 (tel. 512/341-6212).

San Diego: San Diego Federal Bldg., Suite 1220, 660 "B" St., San Diego, CA 92101 (tel. 714/236-9314).

San Francisco: 50 California St., Suite 2465, San Francisco, CA 94111 (tel. 415/986-0992).

Toronto: 101 Richmond St. West, Suite 1212, Toronto M5H 2E1 (tel. 416/364-2455).

Tucson: 5151 E. Broadway, Suite 1535, Tucson, AZ 85711 (tel. 602/745-5055).

Vancouver: 700 W. Georgia St., Vancouver V7Y 1B6 (tel. 604/682-0551).

Washington, D.C.: 1156 15th St. NW, Suite 329, Washington, DC 20005 (tel. 202/296-2594).

To get your Tourist Card, be sure to bring along a birth certificate, passport, or other proof of citizenship when you apply, and when you travel in Mexico. Minors under the age of 18 when traveling alone must have a notarized statement of parental consent *signed by both parents* before they can get a permit. One parent entering Mexico with a minor child must have written consent from the other parent. Check with the nearest Mexican tourist office for details.

Special Note for Car Drivers: Those who have visited Mexico before by car know that a car driver is issued a Temporary Importation Permit for his car. It used to be that this document was issued in addition to the Tourist Card, also required; but now there's a new procedure by which a car driver turns in his Tourist Card as he enters Mexico, and is issued a *single document* which serves as both Tourist Card and Temporary Importation Permit. When you

14 MEXICO ON $20 A DAY

walk out of the border station, don't think you've lost your Tourist Card, or that the officials have forgotten to give it back to you: the one-page document you're carrying does double duty.

RESERVE IN ADVANCE FOR HOLIDAYS: Those planning to be in resort areas like Mazatlán, Acapulco, Puerto Vallarta, Manzanillo, Cozumel, Isla Mujeres, and similar spots should definitely write ahead for hotel reservations on major holidays (Mexican as well as international). Christmas and New Year's are the worst for crowding. If you discover you're up against a holiday when you're almost there, plan to arrive in the resort early in the day—before noon—and see what you can find.

Several readers have written to say that they've encountered difficulties in making reservations by mail, and even by toll-free reservation number: no answer, no record of their request (or deposit check) when they've arrived, and such like. I've experienced the same frustrations. Here's a suggestion: write for reservations in plenty of time, saying in your letter that you'll forward a deposit upon receipt of a confirmation. Or, instead, place a telephone call to the hotel concerned, make the reservation, get the name of the person who takes the reservation, and then send your deposit by registered mail, return receipt requested. Remember that the process can take a good deal of time.

WEATHER, CLOTHING, PACKING: As for your clothing needs, Mexico City is high up, and so you'll need a topcoat in winter and preferably a couple of sweaters. In summer, it gets warm during the day and cool, but not cold, at night. It also rains almost every afternoon or evening between May and October (this is common all over Mexico)—so take a raincoat.

In sea level areas, there is considerable difference between climates on the Gulf and West Coast. This is particularly true in winter. The tropic latitude zone of the Pacific Coast, bounded on the north by Puerto Vallarta and south by Puerto Angel, Oaxaca, furnishes one of the world's most perfect winter climates—dry, balmy, with temperatures ranging from the 80s by day to the 60s at night. (Although geographically within the tropic zone, Mazatlán is excluded from this perfect weather belt. From Puerto Vallarta south you can swim year round; in Mazatlán you'll encounter winter days when dips would appeal only to the hardiest.) But it's an entirely different scene on the gulf. While high mountains shield Pacific beaches from *nortes* (freezing blasts out of Canada via the Texas Panhandle), the gulf enjoys no such immunity. The most disconcerting thing about nortes is that they strike so suddenly. You can be luxuriating on a Veracruz beach, enjoying Montego Bay weather, when all of a sudden you'll notice a slight haze obscuring the sun. That's all the warning you'll get. Within an hour it's like March in New York—gray skies, a boisterous wind, chilly rain whipping your cheeks. In that brief hour the temperature will have dropped as much as 40 degrees. But here's an interesting twist. While nortes hit Veracruz (latitude 19) with vicious intensity, their sting is far less severe in the most northerly Yucatán Peninsula. This is because these gales hit Veracruz overland and Merida over water, the gulf having a warming effect.

So much for winter climate. In summer the difference between West Coast and Gulf Coast temperatures lessens considerably, both areas becoming warm and rainy. Of the two regions the gulf is far rainier, particularly in the states of Tabasco and Campeche.

Here's a handy temperature scale so you can convert easily between the degrees Celsius used in Mexico, and the degrees Fahrenheit used in the U.S.:

ADVANCE PREPARATIONS 15

°Fahrenheit	°Celsius
10	−12
20	−7
32	0
40	4
50	10
60	16
70	21
80	27
90	32
100	38
212	100

When packing your bag, put in some tissues, and keep them handy. Other things various readers have not found easily (or cheaply) in Mexico include: deodorant, vitamins, cosmetics, emery boards, razor blades (except standard blue-blade type), washbowl drainstopper (the rubber disc type is preferred), suntan lotion, and film. Bring your own washcloth if you use one regularly—you'll never find one in a hotel room. If you plan on visiting archeological sites, a small flashlight will aid you in seeing the interior parts of the ruins.

HEALTH AND MEDICAMENTS: Of course, the very best ways to avoid illness or to mitigate its effects are to make sure that you're in top health and that you *don't overdo it*. Travel, strange foods, upset schedules, overambitious sightseeing tend to take more of your energy than a normal working day, and missed meals provide less of the nutrition you need. Make sure you get three good, wholesome meals a day, get *more* rest than you normally do, don't push yourself if you're not feeling in top form, and you'll be able to fight off the "turista." This is the name given to the pervasive diarrhea, often accompanied by fever, nausea, and vomiting, which attacks so many travelers to Mexico on their first trip. Doctors say it's not just one "bug," or factor, but a combination of different food and water, upset schedules, overtiring, and the stresses that accompany travel. I've found that I get it when I'm tired and careless about what I eat and drink. A good high-potency (or "therapeutic") vitamin supplement, and even extra vitamin C, is a help; yogurt is good for a healthy digestion, but it is not available everywhere in Mexico. Should you come down with "turista," the first thing to do is go to bed, stay there, and don't move on until it runs its course. Traveling with the illness only makes it last longer, whereas you can be over it in a day or so if you take it easy. Drink lots of liquids: tea without milk or sugar, or the Mexican *te de manzanilla* (camomile tea), is best. Eat only *pan tostada* (dry toast rusks), sold in grocery stores and *panaderias* (bakeries). Keep to this diet for at least 24 hours, and you'll be well over the worst of it. If you fool yourself into thinking that a plate of enchiladas can't hurt, you'll be back at square one as far as the turista is concerned.

A drug recommended by your doctor is good to have along, although you should realize that no drug can restore your digestive tract to smooth functioning in an hour or two. Only time, rest, and careful eating can do that. Many *norteamericanos* have found that Pepto-Bismol, taken when turista hits, or even beforehand as a preventative, is a helpful, safe, and inexpensive medicine (available without prescription both at home and in Mexico).

Another thing you should consider is the bugs and bites. Mosquitos and gnats are quite prevalent along the coast and in the lowlands of Yucatán. Insect repellent is a must, and it's not always available in Mexico. Also, those sensitive

16 MEXICO ON $20 A DAY

to bites should pick up some antihistamine cream from a drugstore at home ("Di-Delamine" is available without a prescription). Rubbed on a fresh mosquito bite, the cream keeps down the swelling and reduces the itch. In Mexico, ask for "Camfo-Fenicol" (Camphofenique), a second-best remedy.

Most readers won't ever see a scorpion, but they are found in most parts of Mexico. Stings can be painful to dangerous (if you're particularly sensitive to the venom), and it's best to go to a doctor if you get stung. Also, in several locations on the southern Pacific coast of Mexico (Puerto Angel, Puerto Escondido), malaria has been found, so should you want to visit these areas you should take quinine tablets, available from your doctor at home or at public clinics in many Mexican cities.

4. About This Book

THE FUTURE OF THIS BOOK: *Mexico on $20 a Day* has become a clearinghouse for the low-cost hotel and restaurant "finds" discovered by its readers. If you have come across any particularly appealing hotel, restaurant, store, beach, you-name-it, don't keep it to yourself. I'll send free copies of the next edition of *Mexico on $20 a Day* to all readers whose suggestions are used in future printings of this book. Send your find to Frommer/Pasmantier Publishers, Simon & Schuster Bldg., 1230 Avenue of the Americas, New York, NY 10020.

By the way, I *personally* read every single letter sent in, although it is sometimes impossible to answer every letter. Be assured: I'm listening!

Besides the army of readers whose letters have given me the important feedback I need to make sure this guide is doing its job, I'd like to express special thanks to my wife, Jane Kretchman, for her valuable help on earlier editions of this book.

How to Save Money on All Your Travels—The $15-a-Day Travel Club

In just a few paragraphs, you'll begin your exploration of Mexico. But before you do, you may want to learn how to save money on all your trips and travels by joining the widely known $15-a-Day Travel Club, now in its 20th successful year of operation.

The Club was formed at the urging of readers of the $-a-Day Books and the Dollarwise Guides, many of whom felt that such an organization could bring continuing travel information and a sense of community to economy-minded travelers in all parts of the world. And so it does!

In keeping with the budget concept, the membership fee is low and is immediately exceeded by the value of your benefits. Upon receipt of U.S. $14 (U.S. residents), or $16 (Canadian, Mexican, and foreign residents) to cover one year's membership, we will send all new members by return mail (book rate) the following items:

(1) The latest edition of any *two* of the following books (please designate in your letter which two books you wish to receive).

Europe on $20 a Day
Australia on $20 a Day
England and Scotland on $25 a Day
Greece on $20 a Day

THE TRAVEL CLUB 17

Hawaii on $25 a Day
Ireland on $25 a Day
Israel on $25 & $30 a Day
Mexico on $20 a Day
New Zealand on $20 & $25 a Day
Scandinavia on $25 a Day
South America on $25 a Day
Spain and Morocco (plus the Canary Is.) on $25 a Day
Washington, D.C. on $25 a Day

Dollarwise Guide to the Caribbean (including Bermuda and the Bahamas)
Dollarwise Guide to Canada
Dollarwise Guide to Egypt
Dollarwise Guide to England and Scotland
Dollarwise Guide to France
Dollarwise Guide to Germany
Dollarwise Guide to Italy
Dollarwise Guide to Portugal (plus Madeira and the Azores)
Dollarwise Guide to California and Las Vegas
Dollarwise Guide to Florida
Dollarwise Guide to New England
Dollarwise Guide to the Southeast and New Orleans
(Dollarwise Guides discuss accommodations and facilities in all price ranges, with emphasis on the medium-priced.)

How to Beat the High Cost of Travel
(This practical guide details how to save money on absolutely all travel items—accommodations, transportation, dining, sightseeing, shopping, taxes, and more. Includes special budget information for seniors, students, singles, and families.)

The New York Athlete
(The ultimate guide to all the sports facilities in New York City for jocks and novices.)

Museums in New York
(A complete guide to all the museums, historic houses, gardens, zoos, and more in the five boroughs. Illustrated with over 200 photographs.)

The Speak Easy Phrase Book
(The four most useful languages—French, German, Spanish, and Italian —all in one convenient, easy-to-use phrase guide.)

Where to Stay USA
(By the Council on International Educational Exchange, this extraordinary guide is the first to list accommodations in all 50 states that cost anywhere from $3 to $25 per night.)

(2) A one-year subscription to the quarterly 8-page tabloid newspaper— **The Wonderful World of Budget Travel** which brings you the latest money-saving travel information—the kind of information you'd have to pay over $25 a year to obtain elsewhere. This consumer-conscious publication also provides special services to readers: **The Traveler's Directory** (a list of members all over the world who are willing to provide hospitality to other members as they pass

through their home cities), **Share-a-Trip** (offers and requests from members for travel companions who can share costs and help avoid the burdensome single supplement) and **Readers Ask ... Readers Reply** (true questions from members to which other members reply with authentic firsthand information.)

(3) A copy of **Arthur Frommer's Guide to New York,** a newly revised pocket-size guide to hotels, restaurants, nightspots, and sightseeing attractions in all price ranges throughout the New York area.

(4) Your personal membership card, which, once received, entitles you to purchase through the Club all Arthur Frommer publications for a third to a half off their regular prices during the term of your membership.

So why not join this hardy band of international budgeteers and participate in its exchange of travel information and hospitality? Simply send your name and address, together with your membership fee of $14 (U.S. residents), or $16 (Canadian, Mexican, and other foreign residents) in U.S. currency to: $15-a-Day Travel Club, Inc., Frommer/Pasmantier Publishers, 1230 Avenue of the Americas, New York, NY 10020. Remember to specify which *two* books in section (1) above you wish to receive in your initial package of members' benefits. Or, if you prefer, use the last page of this book, simply checking off the two books you want and enclosing $14 or $16 in U.S. currency.

Chapter I

GETTING THERE

1. By Air
2. By Train
3. By Bus
4. By Car

YOU'RE PAYING FOR TIME SAVED when you travel to Mexico, so if time is not so important to you the trip to the border needn't be very expensive. If, on the other hand, you only have a week or two and yet you want a good Mexican experience, you'll have to pay for air travel. Remember that Mexico City is a thousand miles south of the border (at El Paso), and so to get to the hub of the country you'll have a lot of traveling to do even after you reach Mexico, unless you fly. Perhaps the best deal for someone with limited time would be a round-trip excursion air ticket (discussed below), which costs slightly more than a one-way fare but much less than the regular round-trip fare. From Canada or the northern U.S., this is a very practical way to get there.

If you live in any of the southern states, your transportation problem is that much simpler. Domestic flights in Mexico itself are reasonably priced, and so one way to combine both speed and economy is to take a bus or drive to the Texas border towns of El Paso, Eagle Pass, Laredo, or Brownsville, cross the border, and then fly into Mexico City from there.

To cut your expenses even further, consider the first-class buses from the Mexican border. In Mexico, everybody uses the buses: the first-class ones are fast, comfortable, and very cheap, and as satisfactory as their North American counterparts. As for the second-class ones, the less said the better (don't use them for long trips, at any rate, unless you have nothing but time on your hands and don't mind finding goats and chickens in your lap).

On the basis of reports from friends, I wouldn't recommend taking the bus all the way to Mexico City from any northern part of the United States. It's a long, long trip and by the time all expenses of meals, at least one stopover, and other sundries have been added to the fare, the saving over the air fare doesn't seem to merit the discomfort and time spent.

As for rail travel, that's a matter of time and personal preference. Very often it's cheaper and faster to go by bus, but if buses give you that claustrophobic feeling then you might find the train a better way. Personally, I find train travel relaxing, and when possible I pay for a sleeping compartment and relax for several days in the lap of luxury rather than going through the rush-rush routine of airports and transfers. But that's the point; it costs about the same to fly as it does to go first class deluxe on the train, and the train takes longer—which means more meals and thus more expense. And when you get to the Mexican border you still have that long trip south to Mexico City.

To sum up: (1) Drive down if you have plenty of time, taking along company to share the expenses. (2) Combine a bus trip to the border with a flight from there to Mexico City if you live within a couple of days' journey from southern Texas. (3) Fly at least one way if you don't have time for anything else.

In the sections that follow, you'll find these alternative methods of transportation discussed separately and in greater detail. This information is meant to serve as a helpful guide, not as a timetable. Let us emphasize that it is important to check schedules *every* time you plan to travel. They change often and without notice.

1. By Air

TO MEXICO: Air fares to Mexico are an indisputable bargain. Many airlines run frequent flights from New York, Los Angeles, Chicago, New Orleans, Dallas/Fort Worth, and Miami. Excursion and package plans proliferate, getting cheaper and cheaper as the Mexican peso continues its inexorable fall in value.

So much depends on where you fly from, where you fly to, when you fly, how long you stay, etc., that it's essential to visit a good travel agent. The agent will work out your itinerary at no cost to you, and a good agent will get you the lowest fare possible.

In these days of airline deregulation, new airlines and routes are popping up literally overnight, keeping costs low and convenience high.

The Mexican national carriers, AeroMéxico and Mexicana, are merging. They now share the same executive structure, and are both owned by the Mexican government, but it will take some time before all routes, schedules, equipment, and sales offices are under one rubric. The name of the new superairline may be AeroMéxico, or it may not. As the final form is still unclear, and as sales offices still exist for both airlines, I've continued to treat them as two separate entities in these pages. Keep in mind, though: if you can't find the Mexicana office, go to the AeroMéxico office instead, and they'll deal with your problem.

Important Note

Mexico charges an airport tax *on every airport takeoff*. When it comes time to leave the country, you'll need 300 pesos *in cash pesos* to get out of the country, so don't spend every last centavo until you have your boarding pass and have paid the tax. As for internal flights, a 100-peso tax applies *on every takeoff*. Thus, if you fly from Guadalajara to Veracruz via Mexico City, you pay 200 pesos, 100 pesos for each of two takeoffs.

RETURN FROM MEXICO CITY: For the return trip from Mexico City, check as early as possible with the airline that brought you. Here are their Mexico City addresses and telephone numbers:

AeroMéxico, Reforma 64 (tel. 566-0800 or 592-0711)
American Airlines, Reforma 314 or Juarez 117 (tel. 566-2500)
Canadian Pacific, Reforma 87 (tel. 546-9540)
Eastern Airlines, Reforma 30 (tel. 535-7850)

Mexicana, Juarez and Balderas (tel. 585-2666)
Pan American, Reforma 35 (tel. 566-2600)
Western Airlines, Reforma 51 (tel. 533-2000)
Hughes Air West, Reforma 155 (tel. 592-3655)
Texas International, Reforma 325–11 (tel. 533-1605)
TWA, Reforma 195 (tel. 566-9944)

TO MEXICO CITY FROM THE BORDER: In addition to the flights to Mexico City from U.S. cities, there are flights from border cities on the Mexican side by Mexican airlines. Many people, particularly those living in the southern and western parts of the United States, find it convenient to take a bus or to drive to border towns, cross the border into Mexico, and then fly to the capital from there. This can be a considerable money-saver, because domestic Mexican air fares may be lower than their U.S. counterparts.

2. By Train

TO MEXICO: What condition are you in when you start your vacation? If you've been under a great deal of pressure or stress, consider this: you can make a phone call and get a reservation on a train departing from a nearby major city; and if you're on a main line you might be able to climb into a sleeping car and into your own little compartment, and for several days do nothing but unwind, look at the scenery, and every now and then amble on down to the dining car or bar for sustenance. Personally, I think it's a piece of heaven, not claustrophobic like the bus, not hectic like the plane, not tiresome like a car. But it is not cheap. To get a sleeper (called in the trade a "roomette"), you will have to travel first class and pay a supplement—but the point is you're buying a piece of limbo so you can get it together and begin your vacation in the right frame of mind. Should you want some adventure on the way, you may be eligible for stopovers at no extra charge (ask about the requirements when you buy your ticket). In fact, several New York-to-Los Angeles express trains spend part of a day and a night in New Orleans, and if you have a sleeper the car becomes your hotel at no extra charge. You can buy a through ticket to Mexico City (see below for train travel in Mexico), or you can get off at a border town, cross the border, and take a bus or plane to Mexico City. This sort of luxury train travel is similar in price to air fare, and remember that you have the cost of meals to consider.

Call Amtrak (in the white pages of your phone book) toll free for fares, information, and reservations.

IN MEXICO: Train travel is a matter of economics or personal preference; for although it is safer and also cheaper than going by bus (in some cases *half* the very reasonable bus fare), it is slower and schedules are liable to be a bit more inconvenient. I would not recommend train travel east of the Isthmus of Tehuantepec, or traveling *segunda* (second class) anywhere as it is usually hot, overcrowded, dingy, and generally unpleasant. *Primera* (first class) can be the same way unless you are sure to ask for *primera especial:* that is, a first-class reserved seat which you buy a day or so in advance if possible. In primera especial there is rarely the crowding and disorder of other classes. The top-of-the-line accommodations on trains, cheaper than flying but more expensive than the bus, are Pullman compartments for overnight travel.

Sleeping cars are called *coche dormitorio,* and have several different types of accommodation. Cheapest is the upper berth *(cama alta),* next is the lower berth *(cama baja),* then a private compartment for one or two persons *(camarín),* and finally larger, more deluxe compartments for two, three, or four *(alcoba* and *gabinete).* You must make sure in advance that the specific train you plan to take hauls sleeping cars on the date you want to take it. You should reserve your accommodations a day or more in advance if you can. You must have a first-class sleeping car ticket *(primera dormitorio),* which costs slightly more than a first-class coach seat ticket *(primera coche), plus* you must have a ticket for the sleeping accommodations you desire.

More detailed information on trains from the border is given in Chapter II, "Heading South Overland." From Nuevo Laredo, it's a 25-hour, 735-mile ride to Mexico City. Other border towns are farther from the capital, though. The trip from Ciudad Juarez, across from El Paso, takes over 35 hours to Mexico City. There is a daily train from Matamoros, across from Brownsville, Texas, to Monterrey. This trip takes eight hours and then a change of trains is made. There is an overnight (6 p.m. to 9 a.m.) sleeper train daily between Monterrey and Mexico City.

In addition to the Mexican National Railways (Ferrocarriles Nacionales de México), there's the Pacific Railroad Company (Ferrocarriles del Pacifico), which operates daily service between the border and Guadalajara. From Nogales, the trip takes 26 or 36 hours, depending on which train you take. From Mexicali, the fast train takes 30 hours to Guadalajara, 45 to Mexico City, and is several hours faster on the northbound run. It leaves Mexicali around noon daily, connecting later with the train from Nogales. Reservations can be made directly with Sonora Baja Calif. Railway (Ferrocarril Sonora–Baja Calif.) by mail: P.O. Box 231, Calexico, CA 92231 (tel. 903/767-2101; (there's an English-speaking clerk generally available from 9 a.m. to 1 p.m.). You can either ask to pay for the ticket when you arrive at the station, or send money (money order or cashier's check only), and tickets will be mailed to you in about two weeks.

Information, Tickets, Schedules, Stations

If you plan to travel by train into Mexico from one of the border towns, it would be advisable to check the schedules first. The Mexican National Railways has offices at 489 Fifth Ave., Room 2601, New York, NY 10017 (tel. 212/682-1494). The New York office is for information only.

The Pacific Railroad Company maintains its headquarters at Tolsa 336, Guadalajara, Jal., but has branch offices both in Mexico City (Avenida Lázaro Cárdenas 13–701) and in Nogales. For information, contact the New York office of the Mexican National Railways.

Mexico City has a modern railroad station, Estación Buena Vista, on Avenida Insurgentes Norte at Mosqueta, eight blocks north of the Insurgentes–Reforma intersection.

Note: If you want train fares and schedule information in Mexico City, just phone 547-6593 or 547-1084.

You can also get fairly reliable schedule information by consulting the passenger travel edition of the *Official Railway Guide.* Better travel agents will have a recent edition.

3. By Bus

TO MEXICO: Traveling to Mexico by bus is a long, tiring trip from northern cities and is economical only at first glance. From New York, for example, you could be on the bus three days and three nights if you rode straight through, closer to a week if you spent the nights in hotels. Add the price of hotels, meals, and incidentals (think of how many newspapers, magazines, books, and snacks you'll need on that ride!), and that "expensive" plane fare looks a lot more reasonable.

Advantages of bus travel are that you do get to see the countryside, and you can usually make any stopovers you want along the way for no extra charge. Those out to make their vacation a Pan-American one, seeing both Mexico and U.S., will appreciate this feature.

A bus operated by a U.S. company (mostly Greyhound and Trailways) will take you to the border, where you change to a Mexican bus for the remainder of the trip to your Mexican destination. Greyhound has offices in Mexico City, and will book you straight through to a Mexican destination (i.e., you needn't buy another ticket at the border) in some cases.

As for fares, the two big U.S. companies' rates are controlled by the Interstate Commerce Commission, and are therefore liable to be exactly the same for any given journey. In addition, Greyhound and Trailways are usually neck-and-neck when it comes to special promotional fares, but it's advisable to call both and see what's currently being offered. Some of the short-term special fares are incredible bargains: as of this writing, the one-way fare from New York City or Chicago to the border at Laredo, Texas, is only $99 from either company; from Los Angeles to El Paso it's a mere $79. But these fares change all the time, so call to keep current. Here is the essential data:

From New York City

Both companies operate out of the Port Authority Bus Terminal at Eighth Avenue and 41st Street (tel. Greyhound, 212/635-0800; Trailways, 212/564-8320). Each company has a daily bus headed for the border at Laredo; the trip takes around 60 hours, depending on the route.

From Chicago

Greyhound is at Clark and Randolph Streets (tel. 312/781-2882), with daily service to Laredo. The trip takes about 55 hours, straight through. Trailways, at 20 E. Randolph St. (tel. 312/726-9500), has similar service in a similar number of hours.

From Los Angeles

Greyhound is at 6th and Los Angeles Streets (tel. 213/620-1200), and has frequent daily buses to the border at El Paso, as well as frequent service to Tijuana and Laredo. Trailways, again, has similar service; they're located at 601 S. Main St. (tel. 213/742-1200). The trip from Los Angeles to El Paso takes about 50 hours.

Remember that in summer U.S. buses (Mexican ones, too) tend to be powerfully air-conditioned, and so a sweater or warm jacket is essential even in the blazing heat of the Texas desert.

Take along things to eat and to read for the Mexican part of the journey especially. Also toilet paper—because the area you're passing through is one of the most sparsely populated in the whole country, and the rest stops aren't exactly up to Howard Johnson standards. Also don't forget that tickets on a Mexican bus entitle you to a specific seat; you don't just sit anywhere. Keep your eye on your luggage and stay in sight of the bus driver at meal stops, because when he's finished eating he'll go—in spite of what he says about stopping for 20 minutes.

Good luck! You'll need it for this usually exhausting trip.

IN MEXICO: Within Mexico, large air-conditioned Greyhound-type buses operated by a dozen private companies roll over the intercity routes at a very reasonable cost, working out to only 3¢ or 4¢ a mile. No longer is bus travel the *mañana* pastime of Malcolm Lowry's day when the village bus growled and wheezed into motion as soon as it was sufficiently overloaded. Today it's best to buy your reserved-seat ticket (all seats are reserved) a day in advance, and to be at the terminal on time for departure, as schedules are fairly dependable. Many Mexican cities now have new central bus stations rather than the bewildering and constantly changing array of tiny private company offices scattered all over town. For long trips, carry some food and a sweater for overpowering air conditioning, and always a good amount of toilet paper.

Where feasible in this book I've included information on bus routes along our suggested itineraries. Keep in mind that routes, times, and prices are liable to change, and as there is no central directory of schedules for the whole country, current information must be obtained from local bus stations or travel offices.

4. By Car

TO MEXICO: The cheapest way to get to Mexico from one of the northern U.S. states or Canada is to drive, taking along a couple of other people in the car to share the driving and expenses. The total cost for the 3000-mile trip from New York, for example, will be about $220 for gas and tolls, plus whatever expenses are incurred by staying overnight and eating. Several American motel chains offer good, clean, air-conditioned double rooms for about $20. The **Motel 6, Susse Chalet,** and **Days Inn** chains are examples I've found well worth the money.

From New York, I'd suggest traveling via New Orleans and Laredo. This route is about 2850 miles and can be done, without stops, in four days. It is more reasonable to allow six. From Los Angeles via Nogales is about 2100 miles. From Chicago via San Antonio and Laredo is about 2250 miles.

IN MEXICO: Using your own car in Mexico is no longer the cheapest, or even best way to see the country. Insurance costs are now very high (about $100 for two months of the minimum liability coverage—collision coverage is extra, a lot extra), although gas is a bit cheaper than at home, and parking is a problem in the cities (isn't it everywhere?). Unless you have a full carload, the bus and train come out cheaper per person, and with public transport you don't have to undertake the tedious amount of driving needed to see a country this big. More and more North Americans are using public transport in Mexico, but if you cherish the privacy and independence only a private automobile can give you, and are willing to pay for it, by all means take your car.

But one last note: Should you want to drive to the Mexican border, but not *into* Mexico, several readers have had good luck in striking bargains with garage and parking lot managers in U.S. border towns such as El Paso and Nogales. They paid a small sum to leave their cars in a lot or garage while they were seeing Mexico by bus or train, and then picked up their cars upon leaving Mexico for the drive home.

Mexican Roads

Most Mexican roads, although quite sufficient, are not up to northern standards of smoothness, hardness, width of curve or grade of hill, or safety marking. You will have to get used to the spirited Latin methods which tend to depend more on flair and good reflexes than on system and prudence. Be prepared for new procedures, as when a truck flips on his left-turn signal when there's not a crossroad for miles. He's probably telling you that the road's clear ahead for you to pass—after all, he's in a position to see better than you are. How do you tell that's what he means, and not that he intends to pull over on the left-hand shoulder? Hard to say. More about trucks: They're very important to the country's economy, but the government is only in the first stages of building a system of divided, limited-access highways so that truck and car traffic is easy for both. You may follow trucks without mufflers and pollution-control devices for miles. Under these conditions it's best to drop back and be patient, take a side road, or stop for a break when you feel tense or tired.

Your Car

It's important to know the condition of your car before you cross the border. Parts and service in Mexico, while often of the very best quality, are usually a good deal more expensive than at home. Your cooling system should be in good condition, with the proper mixture of coolant and water, and no old radiator hoses. Carry a spare fan belt. In summer for long drives an air conditioner is not a luxury but nearly a necessity. You might want a spare belt for this, too, just in case. Remember that Mexico is a big country, and that you may put several thousand miles on your tires before you return home—can your tires last a few thousand on Mexican roads? Mexican gasoline is not up to high standards, even the best of it, so it's good to be sure your car's in tune to handle it. By the way, Mexican filling stations are not as frequent as those up north, but we've never run out of gas. Plan ahead: don't leave a city for a long drive through the mountains or the desert with a half-full tank. Take simple tools along if you're handy with them, also a flashlight or spotlight, a cloth to wipe the windshield, toilet paper, and a tire gauge (saves tread wear to have the pressure right).

Car Papers

You will have to provide proof that you own the car, of course. Registration papers are sufficient for this. Then, you will turn in your Tourist Card and an official will type out a new document which serves as a Temporary Import Permit for your car, and also as your Tourist Card. *You do not receive two separate documents,* as in years past. The car papers will be issued for the same length of time as your Tourist Card was issued for. It's a very good idea to greatly overestimate the time you'll spend in Mexico, *when applying for your Tourist Card,* so that if something unforeseen happens and you have to (or want to) stay longer, you don't have to go through the long, long hassle of getting your papers renewed. The maximum term for Tourist Card and Temporary

Importation Permit is six months. When the official who is filling out your Tourist Card asks how long you intend to stay, tell him six months.

Mexican Auto Insurance

You might want to buy your Mexican auto insurance before you cross the border. It costs no more on the American side, and the various agencies which handle it are often helpful in handing out free travel literature or in changing small amounts of dollars to pesos. You must purchase Mexican insurance, as U.S. or Canadian insurance is not valid in Mexico, and any party involved in an accident who has no insurance is automatically clapped into jail and his car is impounded until all claims are settled. Those with insurance are assumed to be good for claims and are released. The agency will show you a full table of current rates and will recommend the coverage it thinks adequate. The policies are written along lines similar to those north of the border. The agents usually tell you that it's best to *overestimate* the amount of time you plan to be in Mexico, for should you plan to stay longer than originally expected, it's a real runaround to get your policy term lengthened in Mexico; whereas any part of the term unused will be prorated and that part of your premium refunded to you in cash at the office on the American side as you come out, or by mail to your home.

Another hint on saving money: If you go through Guatemala and Belize, you'll have to pick up local insurance there as well—your Mexican insurance isn't good in these countries—so as you leave Mexico, have the Customs official stamp your policy with the date and time of exit from Mexico. When you reenter, have the official stamp you in again, and the portion of your time spent out of the country will be refunded to you.

After you cross the border into Mexico from the U.S., stop at the first Customs post you come to. If you don't have a Tourist Card, you'll have to pick one up here. Then you may be told to proceed down the road a ways (depending on the border crossing point) to the auto inspection station. Here you must park and lock your car and go into the office. Forms will be filled out, you wait your turn to be called, the car will be registered on the driver's Tourist Card, a sticker will be put on the window, and an inspection will be carried out. Theoretically the Tourist Card, the auto permit, and the inspection are not subject to charge, but how you say no to the uniformed officer when he says politely, "That will be one dollar, please," I don't know. See Chapter XVI, "Bribes."

Remember that the driver of the car will not be able to leave the country without the car (even if it's later wrecked or stolen) unless he or she satisfies Customs that the import duty will be paid. This means that if you must suddenly fly home, you've got to go through the procedure at the airport of putting the car under Customs seal and having your tourist permit stamped to that effect. There may be storage fees. Check into it.

A last word: Mexican border officials are human, and I've found that if you look presentable (from a Mexican point of view, which means neat and clean), and are friendly and patient, the officials will treat you the same and make it all as easy as possible. Incidentally, when you cross back into the U.S. after an extended trip in Mexico, the American Customs officials will more often than not inspect *every* nook and cranny of your car, your bags, even your person, all very quickly, efficiently, and politely. They're looking for drugs, of course.

Driving in Mexico

Cardinal rule: **Never drive at night if you can avoid it.** The roads aren't good enough, the trucks and carts and pedestrians and bicycles usually have no lights, you can hit potholes, animals, rocks, dead ends, bridges out with no warning. Enough said.

Indeed, get used to the fact that people in the countryside are not good at judging the speed of an approaching car, and often panic in the middle of the road even though they could easily have reached the shoulder. It's not rude to use your horn if it may save someone from injury.

Road Signs

Here are the most common ones:

Camino en Reparación	Road Repairs
Conserva Su Derecha	Keep Right
Cuidado con el Ganado, el Tren	Watch Out for Cattle, Trains
Curva peligrosa	Dangerous Curve
Derrumbes	Earthquake Zone
Despacio	Slow
Desviación	Detour
Disminuya Su Velocidad	Slow Down
Entronque	Highway Junction
Escuela	School (Zone)
Grava Suelta	Loose Gravel
Hombres Trabajando	Men Working
No Hay Paso	Road Closed
Peligro	Danger
Puente angosto	Narrow Bridge
Raya Continua	Continuous (solid) White Line
Tramo en Reparación	Road Under Construction
Un Solo Carril a 100 m.	One-lane Road 100 Meters Ahead
Zona Escolar	School Zone

Also *Topes,* or a sign with a drawing of a row of little bumps on it, means that there's a row of bumps across the road placed there by the authorities to slow you down through towns or villages. Slow down when coming to a village whether you see the sign or not—sometimes they install the bumps, but not the sign!

Kilometer stones on main highways register the distance from local population centers. There is always a shortage of directional signs, so check quite frequently that you are going on the right road.

The Green Patrols

The Mexican government sponsors an admirable service whereby green, radio-equipped repair trucks manned by uniformed, English-speaking officers patrol the major highways during daylight hours to aid motorists with troubles. Minor repairs and adjustments should be free of charge, although you pay for parts and materials if you have need of these "Green Angels."

Minor Accidents

Most motorists think it best to drive away from minor accidents if possible. You are at a distinct disadvantage without fluent Spanish when it comes to describing your version of what happened. Sometimes the other descriptions border on mythology, and you may end up spending days straightening out things that were not even your fault. In fact, fault often has nothing to do with it.

Parking

I use pay parking lots in cities, especially at night, to avoid annoyances such as broken antennas, swiped emblems, or break-ins. Never leave anything within view inside your locked car on the street (day or night), for Mexico has thieves like everyplace else. Another good reason to use pay parking lots is that you avoid parking violations, and when a cop in Mexico finds you parked illegally, and knows you may ignore a ticket, he'll take out his pliers and screwdriver and remove your license plate and take it to the station house. When pay lots are not available, dozens of small boys will surround you as you stop, wanting to "watch your car for you." Pick the leader of the group, let him know you want him to guard it, and give him a peso or two when you leave. Kids may be very curious about the car and may look in, crawl underneath, or even climb on top, but they rarely do any damage.

Getting Gas

Check that the pump is wound back to zero; check that the oil can the attendant tips into your engine is indeed a full one; check your change; make sure your gas cap is back in place. I've found that these days almost all attendants are honest and helpful but once in a while may be forgetful. It's wise to keep the gas tank pretty full at all times. All gasoline in Mexico is sold by the government-owned **Pemex** (Petroleras Mexicanas) company. There are two grades: Nova (81 octane) for about 65¢ per gallon, and Extra (94 octane) for 92¢ a gallon. Nova is leaded gasoline *(con plomo)*, and comes from the blue pump; Extra is a high-octane unleaded *(sin plomo)* gasoline, from the silver pump; the red pump is for diesel fuel, which costs about 15¢ a gallon. In Mexico fuel and oil are sold by the liter, so, a liter being slightly more than a quart, 40 liters equal about 10½ gallons.

No credit cards are accepted for gas purchases, so be prepared to pay in cash.

CAMPING: The *Rand McNally Campground and Trailer Park Guide: United States/Canada/Mexico* (New York, published every year) covers camping areas in Mexico, with full descriptions of facilities. Sanborn's, which sells Mexican insurance in the U.S., also hands out a list of camping places, free, to its insurance customers.

THE AVAILABLE ROUTES: Depending on where you live in the United States, you will drive to Mexico by one of four basic routes.

Approaching from the West, the most likely border-crossing towns are either Nogales or El Paso; approaching from the East, the most popular entry point is Nuevo Laredo. This latter town also draws much of the traffic from the Chicago area and the Midwest. The fourth route is a relatively new one and just recently completed all the way from Mexico City to the border. Your point of entry here is Eagle Pass, Texas, just across the border from Piedras Negras in the Mexican state of Coahuila. This route to Mexico City travels one of the country's newest and best roads (Route 57), and you won't have to contend with either hot weather or dizzying mountain passes.

The following chapter deals with all four of these routes, first the West Coast route, entering at Nogales, then the route from El Paso, and finally the Laredo and Eagle Pass routes.

Chapter II

HEADING SOUTH OVERLAND

1. The West Coast Route: Hermosillo to Culiacan
2. The El Paso Route: Chihuahua to Fresnillo
3. The Eastern Route via Monterrey and Saltillo

ALTHOUGH AIR TRAVEL IS a very popular way to get to Mexico, and although flying is a good choice because of the great distances to be covered, the traveler who enters Mexico by road sees parts of the country and ways of life which the air traveler will miss for good. The northern regions of the country, while only sparsely furnished with what might be called "tourist attractions," are of critical importance to Mexico's economy. Mining, fishing, manufacturing, farming, and cattle ranching make these vast semi-arid regions among the wealthiest in the country.

The scenery and customs of the people change gradually as the kilometers click by. Soon the tall buildings of Americanized Chihuahua, the farmers in cowboy hats and pickup trucks, the fuming smokestacks of Monterrey give way to the lusher country of the Valley of Mexico or to the incredibly fertile tropics of the Gulf and Pacific Coasts.

Herewith I provide hints for stops along the way south, no matter what route you take, no matter whether your destination is Acapulco, Mexico City, Veracruz, or beyond.

1. The West Coast Route: Hermosillo to Culiacan

If you're coming to Mexico from the western United States, you'll probably cross the border at Nogales, near the Gulf of California. This west coast route to Mexico's capital is an attractive one, as it heads straight down to Mexico's Pacific beach resorts (see Chapter III). Well traveled by Mexican and American tourists, truckers and locals, the route poses no problems—if you stick to the route. But you should know that the Pacific Coast state of Sinaloa has long been known as a center of drug trafficking and other unsavory activities. You won't see any of this if you stick to the beaten path and the main highway, with no adventurous side trips to little out-of-the-way villages.

Coming from California, it's not really worth it to cross the border at Tijuana and drive over bad roads through the desert to pick up Mexican Route 15. Take my word for it, you'd be much better off taking I-10 or I-8 to Tucson and then I-19 to Nogales.

After crossing at Nogales, your first major destination is the coastal resort city of Mazatlán, 735 miles to the south. Much of this stretch is desert country, boiling hot in the summer. Here first are the towns you'll pass through en route, with suggestions for food and lodging.

Remember to stop at the border station and pick up your Tourist Card, if you don't already have one. The cars that are zipping right through the border station are not heading south, but are just crossing over into Nogales for the day—that's why they don't have to stop. A few miles farther along the road south, Customs officials will check your Tourist Card, car entry permit (if you have a car), and will inspect your luggage.

HERMOSILLO: This city (altitude: 720 feet; pop. 300,000), capital of the state of Sonora, is the center of a fruit and vegetable farming area. You enter on a lovely tree-lined boulevard, which in summer is vibrant with the orange flowers of the yucateros.

Where to Stay and Eat

Highway 15 goes straight through the center of Hermosillo, becoming Avenida Rosales and passing the university. At the corner of Serdan and Rosales you'll see the **Hotel San Alberto** (tel. 621/2-1800), on the right-hand side as you come from the north, across the street from the Telegraph Office. It's an older, five-story structure on the outside, but a warm and well-run hotel on the inside. Comfy rooms with private bath in this prime downtown location cost 990 pesos single, 1225 pesos double.

Although it's somewhat difficult to see from the street, the **Hotel Washington**, at Dr. Noriega Pte. 68 (tel. 621/3-1183), is worth looking for as it is one of the few budget-priced places in this surprisingly expensive city. Simple but acceptable rooms are stacked along narrow courts. All are air-conditioned and equipped with clean bathrooms, and cost 525 pesos single, and 725 pesos double. For those sharing a room but not a bunk, there are two double beds in each room.

If you have no luck at the Washington, an excellent choice is the **Hotel Monte Carlo** (tel. 621/2-0853), at the corner of Juarez and Sonora. You can save yourself some steps by telephoning first to see if there is a vacancy at this very busy hotel. The 24 units are all air-conditioned and bright for the most part. Adjoining the Monte Carlo is a corner restaurant that is simple, inexpensive, and jammed with hungry Mexicans who know a good deal at lunchtime. If you need some help or information, ask for Sr. Gilberto Villa Martinez, who speaks a little English and who has infinite patience with those who speak only a little Spanish.

Another establishment offering similar rates to the Monte Carlo's is the **Hotel America Colonial** (tel. 621/2-2448), where single rooms are 630 pesos and doubles are 770 pesos (with one bed). Rooms here are dark and housekeeping standards a bit less stringent than at the places recommended above, but the air conditioners are powerful and the people at the front desk very friendly and helpful. The lobby has a TV and supply of good cold drinking water; there's off-street parking in front of the hotel. To get to the Colonial, follow Highway 15 through town and turn left on the "Bulevar Transversal," a divided road. Look for Avenida Juarez; turn left on Juarez and go nine blocks to no. 171 Sur (which is in the direction of the mountains). **Note:** The **bus station** is on Juarez as well.

You will note that there are many expensive hotels in Hermosillo, as befits a state capital, and in extreme cases you may have to search one of them out.

As for meals, the **El Rodeo Rosticeria**, Dr. Noriega Pte. 92, is a fine choice for dinner, or just for a fruit juice or bottle of *cerveza* as you wander around town. Muzak caresses your eardrums as you order from a bilingual menu: a quarter chicken served any one of several ways costs 200 pesos, avocado dip (guacamole) is 65 pesos, refried beans are 85 pesos. The specialty of the house is broiled beef served hot at your table on a Mexican "hibachi" for 325 pesos.

About my favorite snack in Hermosillo—or in all of the state of Sonora for that matter—is a chili dog from the vendor who spends his evenings at the university. He always seems to be there, in the little park near the intersection of Rosales and Bulevar Transversal, selling hot dogs on steamed buns topped with onions, tomatoes, beans, mayonnaise, mustard, and hot sauce for a mere 35 pesos.

Another good choice, this time for breakfast, is the **Cafe San Cesar**, Plutarco Elias Calles Pte. 71. Ham and eggs will cost 100 pesos; two pork chops with potatoes, just a bit more. For dinner, the seafood dishes are priced at around 185 pesos each, but Mexican specialties are only half that.

An interesting place to stop for a refreshing glass of fruit juice is a juice bar called **El Oasis**, on Aquiles Serdan across from the Gon-Pard shoe store. Here 50 pesos will buy a very large glass of any of the 12 flavors offered. Very clean.

Side Trips

Sixty-seven miles west of Hermosillo on a fairly good road lies **Kino Bay**. Actually there are two Kinos: **Kino Viejo**, a somnolent fishing village with no recommendable hotels, and **Kino Nuevo**, an area which has become popular with wealthy Americans and condominium owners. Part of the attraction is due to the good fishing, and in June the International Sport Fishing Tournament draws crowds. The beach, too, is pleasant, with gorgeous houses lining it, and many public beach shelters along the shore.

Unfortunately, all of Kino's hotels are out of our price range, but you can dine without too much damage at the **Marlin Restaurant** in Kino Viejo, a low white building next to the trailer park called Islandia Marina. The house specialty is a seafood platter at 675 pesos—a bit steep, I admit—but for this you receive lobster, shrimp, turtle, crab, and octopus. You may request substitutes. Otherwise, turtle steak is 345 pesos, seafood cocktails cost half that, and a good sandwich is only 90 pesos. All the seafood is certifiably fresh: ask the bilingual waiter to show you one of the live sea turtles out back, and you'll get to know what fresh is.

Occasionally a group of Seri Indians will be camped beyond the end of the road in Kino Nuevo on their way to or from Desemboque. The Seri are known for their ironwood carvings; you can find them at work in Kino Viejo as well. Today, the ancient tool kit contains power carving tools as well.

For nondrivers there are daily second-class buses from Hermosillo to Kino Bay. The line is **Autobuses Castellanos**, Juarez Sur 9, and departures are at 7 a.m. and 3 p.m. Travel time is roughly two hours. If you can't afford the motel, there's nothing to prevent you from getting an early start, making a day of it at the beach, and returning to Hermosillo in the later afternoon. Warning: Be sure to plan your return on the *next-to-last* bus, which leaves the bay area between 4 and 5. The driver of the final run spends the night in Kino and so will you if you're counting on him for return transportation.

GUAYMAS: Guaymas (pronounced WHY-mass; pop. 152,000), on the coast, owes its reputation to fishing, both commercial and sport. Runs of marlin and sailfish generally occur between February 15 and August 15. Lobster, sea turtles, and clams abound in nearby waters as well.

The town is divided by a hilly range, the port on one side and the resort plus Miramar Beach on the other. Unfortunately, it's not much of a resort. The beach is unexceptional and the majority of the hotels and motels in the area customarily charge *more* in the scorching off-season summer months than they do in winter. Explanation: You pay extra for the electrical current used by the air conditioner (which you must take advantage of).

The town's Tourism Office (tel. 622/2-0848) is at Avenida Miguel Aleman 290.

The bus station here is right downtown and there are taxis available to take you anywhere in the city.

Where to Stay and Eat

With exurban motels very much in vogue it's getting increasingly hard to find a decent centrally located hotel. However, there are a few that are acceptable. The **Del Puerto Motel** (tel. 622/2-3408) is right downtown at the corner of Yanez and Calle 19, in the market ("Mercado") area. From Calle 19, the Del Puerto's facade is quite deceiving: the massive cement walls and small "porthole" windows make it look more like a prison than a hotel, but a turn around the corner reveals a beautiful ground-floor patio and a parking area. Flowering bushes, banana plants, and mango trees provide welcome shade, even on the third-floor walkways. The 40 rooms are all air-conditioned and have hot-water showers and even telephones. The rates are a bit high, but only a bit: singles are 495 pesos and doubles are 770 pesos. For the double-room price you get two beds, a single and a double.

The **Malibu Motel,** operated by the same people as the Del Puerto, has phones and TVs with similar accommodations and rates. It's located north of the city on Highway 15. Also up this way is the **Motel Armida,** with singles for 880 pesos, doubles for 990 pesos.

A good all-purpose restaurant in downtown Guaymas is the **Restaurant El Paradise,** Rodriguez 30, right across from the ancient Hotel Impala and one block from the market. In Paradise you'd expect to find those little extra touches (to say the least): English menu, waiters who can speak your lingo, air conditioning, big portions. What I'd want from Paradise is seafood, and they have it here, fresh from Guaymas harbor. The simple, modern businesslike decor allows you to concentrate on the fish, shrimp, chowders, and cocktails. You can spend 400 or 500 pesos for a big meal here, or even less.

On Playa Miramar

Guaymas's resort area, north of town across the hills is called Playa Miramar, on Bocochibampo Bay. A flyover whisks you from Highway 15 the mile or so down to the beach. The city bus ("Miramar") will do the same, turning right (north) and finally terminating at a beachfront complex of shops, little restaurants, a trailer park, and **Leo's Inn** (tel. 622/2-1337). Leo's is a nice, modern little place with a verdant garden on one side and two floors of tidy air-conditioned rooms with bug screens and even screen doors. Rooms with a sea view cost 800 to 900 pesos. The official address is Calle 28 no. 133.

In the beachfront complex right next to Leo's is the **Restaurant La Bocana,** an airy glassed-in room with a view of the sea, an informal ambience, and seafood: cheapest and best is the filete de pescado al mojo de ajo (fish filet in garlic sauce) for 195 pesos. Choicer cuts, such as huachinango (red snapper) a la Veracruzana (in tomato sauce) cost more. For a meal from the sea, figure to spend 350 to 450 pesos; for Mexican "antojitos" such as enchiladas or tacos, only half that much; even less for just a sandwich, dessert, and beverage. La Bocana is open from 8 a.m. to 10 p.m. daily.

Side Trip to San Carlos

About 12 miles north of Guaymas off Highway 15 is the new resort area of San Carlos. The beaches are nice, for sure, but the hotels and restaurants are pretty expensive. You drive east seven miles from the highway through a riot of billboards advertising house lots for sale, condos, time-sharing, trailer parks, and all types of *bienes raices* (real estate).

Set in the midst of striking scenery—pinnacled mountains on a beautiful bay—San Carlos is not at all like Puerto Vallarta or Acapulco. Rather, it's new, growing, and aimed not at the casual tourist but at the condo crowd. Restaurants, besides being expensive, tend to be undependable and very changeable.

CIUDAD OBREGON: The best way to describe Ciudad Obregon (pop. 168,000) is by asking the reader to picture a typical old colonial hill town with narrow cobblestone streets—and then imagine the polar opposite. Ciudad Obregon, a model city founded in 1928, has probably the flattest location, widest streets, and least colonial atmosphere of any community in Mexico. With 20th-century buildings, and oozing modernity at every pore, it differs from such settlements as San Cristóbal de Las Casas and Guanajuato as the Yukon does from the Congo.

Best choice in Obregon is the **Hotel Imperial** (tel. 641/3-5062), on the corner of Sinaloa and Guerrero, a pastel-green tile edifice located unfortunately at the opposite side of town from the bus station. The Imperial is rather large, and is graced with a cool central court and simplistic modern curved stairway. The reception desk is enclosed in a refrigerated glass box, but the amiable gentleman behind the desk will be happy to come out into the sticky heat and show you one of the simple air-conditioned rooms. They all have bath, telephone, bare walls, and venetian blinds, and are blessedly cool. Singles are 440 pesos; doubles, 550 pesos.

Lower prices can be found at the little **Hotel Jardín** (tel. 641/3-5490), Galeana Ote. 411, which is only about half the distance from the bus station as the aforementioned Imperial. The lobby is no great shakes, but you'll probably forget what it looked like once you settle into one of the air-conditioned rooms. Rooms are small with multicolored baths with walls that go only two-thirds of the way to the ceiling! Singles are 550 pesos; doubles 660 pesos.

The **Hotel Kuraica** (tel. 641/3-5047), Calle 5 de Febrero no. 211 Sur, is a good low-budget choice. The clean, absolutely naked lobby attracts the local neighborhood residents because of its TV set. Rates for the air-conditioned rooms are 325 pesos single, 455 pesos double with two double beds. The two-story blue-and-white building would be easy to miss, as one must stand in the street and look straight up to see the hotel's sign. But it's pretty much back-to-back with the aforementioned Hotel Imperial.

Side Trip to Alamos

About 42 miles south of Ciudad Obregon is the town of Navojoa, and it is here that you will find the road (east on Calle Abasolo) to visit the old colonial city of Alamos. This is a tourist town, so there are no cheap accommodations: I recommend you make it a daytime trip and stay in either Obregon or Los Mochis.

At the turnoff from Route 15, it is 33 miles on a dead-end road to reach the ancient silver city of Alamos. This city was already more than a century old when the king of Spain sent out a surveyor-general to plan out the main streets in 1750. Early Catholic missions were maintained in this isolated valley as early as 1613, and by 1685 some of the richest silver mines in the world were operating nearby.

Before the year 1800, the population had increased to 14,000 and Spain was benefiting by millions of pesos worth of silver each year from the city and its industrious workers. Beautiful homes and government buildings were erected, and although the city changed hands many times in subsequent wars and the silver finally gave out (around 1900), there were very few physical changes. Today, Alamos is a National Monument and cannot be altered. It is an impressive sight.

Cobbled streets wind aimlessly around arcaded porticos, and the visitor quickly becomes affected by the isolation. Because of the valley's sheltered location, 1400 feet above sea level, it has an excellent climate and flowers are abundant. There is a branch of the National Museum of Arts and Crafts and a small American colony of enterprising souls who have bought old houses for a song and remodeled them into mansions.

As this is a tourist town, most hotels are expensive. But you can stay at the **Hotel Enriquez** (no phone), next to the Hotel Los Portales on the main square, for 440 pesos double. Besides the town's expensive restaurants, there are snack shops and burger stands to keep down the cost of sustenance.

LOS MOCHIS: Los Mochis, Sinaloa (alt. 243 feet; pop. 85,000), is in a fertile agricultural area and, aside from the enormous sugar mill at the northwest end of town, there is not much of note. It is from here that you can board the Ferrocarril Chihuahua al Pacifico, which makes the 13-hour trip through the spectacular Copper Canyon to Chihuahua (see Part 2 of this chapter, under Chihuahua).

Where to Stay and Eat

A good place to stay is the two-story, 42-room **Hotel America** (tel. 681/2-1355), two blocks south of Obregon on Allende Sur, at no. 655. The second floor has an open sitting area furnished with chairs, purified water, and an ice-making machine. Rooms are all air-conditioned and telephone equipped, and are priced at 475 pesos single, 585 pesos double (with one bed). The hotel has off-street parking. It's clean, friendly, and central, being only a half block south of the Tres Estrellas de Oro bus station (with other bus stations nearby), and two blocks from the Hotel Catalina, which is pretty much the center of town. The America is operated by the same people who run the Hotel Beltran (see below).

Attached to the Hotel America is a restaurant with the same name. Most entrees are in the 100-peso range, while the comida corrida costs 140 pesos. Open 7 a.m. to 11 p.m.

The **Hotel Catalina** (tel. 681/2-1240), Obregon Pte. 36 at Allende Sur, is another possibility. All 50 rooms show signs of wear. Singles go for 500 pesos; a double with one bed, 660 pesos. The lobby is spartan but functional, and includes a restaurant specializing in Oriental food. And there's air conditioning throughout.

The three-story **Hotel Beltran** (tel. 681/2-0092), Hildago and Zaragoza, has had its ups and downs in this book, but is now very much on the up. The 42 rooms, some with views of the city, all have air conditioners and telephones. Singles are 475 pesos; doubles 585 pesos. Purified water and an ice-making machine can be found on each floor, along with pleasant sitting rooms complete with rocking chairs.

One-half block north of the Beltran at Zaragoza Sur 356 is **El Gordo y El Flaco** ("The Fat and the Thin"), where the comida corrida is only 125 pesos (150 on Sunday) and brings you a choice of three soups, a main dish, and dessert or coffee. (It's good to remember that the comida corrida is usually only served from about 1 to 4 p.m., throughout Mexico.) From the à la carte menu, you could choose soup, meat, and dessert for about 350 pesos, all in. They feature no fewer than nine set-price breakfasts, ranging from 50 to 245 pesos.

If your budget can stand a small splurge, try the finest restaurant in Los Mochis, **El Farallon**, on Obregon (no. 495—if it had a number) at Flores, down the block from the Restaurant Madrid (see below). The walls are painted with murals depicting the wealth of the Sea of Cortes and also the new agricultural pride of the area: the dam on the Fuerte River. Fish nets strung about, seashells, sharks' jaws, and glass fishing floats complete the nautical decor. The restaurant is air-conditioned and holds about 40 tables. For a seafood dinner of soup, fish or shrimp, dessert, and coffee, you pay about 400 pesos. For dessert, try the fresh fruit displayed in the refrigerated case near the front door. An alternative, melon with ice cream, will cool you on even the hottest summer day.

The **Restaurant Madrid**, Obregon 414 at Leyva, is plain but nice, its tables covered with white cloths, and the white cloths thriftily covered with plate-glass tops. The air conditioning is powerful, the food is good, the portions are big, and the prices are low: a large lunch or dinner need cost only 175 to 300 pesos.

Side Trips

The Ferrocarril Chihuahua al Pacifico station is about three miles from the center of town on a street with the unpronounceable name of Netzahualcoyotl. Trains leave from here daily for Copper Canyon and Chihuahua at 7 a.m., Mountain Time. Take note: The railroad runs on Central Time, although Los Mochis is on Mountain Time! (See Part 2 of this chapter, on Chihuahua, for more details.) The best way to get to the station is to board a green bus at the bus station across from the Hotel Catalina on Obregon. Get your place on the bus early as the taxi ride will cost you 125 pesos or more, while the bus is only a few pesos.

Buses also trundle down to Topolobampo (get a bus by that name) on the coast, almost continuously throughout the day. From Topolobampo, a ferryboat leaves for La Paz, Baja California Sur, three times a week.

CULIACAN: Almost equidistant between Los Mochis and Mazatlán (130 miles from the former, 140 miles from the latter) is Culiacan, capital of Sinaloa. The surrounding region, located between the foothills of the Sierra Madre and the Pacific, is a rich agricultural one abounding in cotton, peanuts, and some of the world's finest tomatoes. The last are regularly exported to the U.S., as is that illegal commodity derived from the sector's abundant poppy fields.

Along with Turkey and Southeast Asia, the Culiacan area is one of the world's greatest producers of crude opium.

On a happier note, Culiacan itself is a humming, progressive city of 358,000, where modern buildings stand cheek-by-jowl with structures dating back to colonial times. Examples of both can be seen on Plaza Obregon, where a lovely old cathedral looks across the park at some of the most futuristic architecture in Mexico.

Where to Stay and Eat

The bus station is about a mile from the center of town, but right across the street from the first-class station is the **Hotel Salvador** (tel. 671/3-7466), Boulevard L. Solano (the main highway) at Corona. There are 50 rooms here, all with air conditioning and TV for 770 pesos single, 990 pesos double.

A block along the street from the Salvador is the snazzier **Hotel del Valle** (tel. 671/3-9020), Boulevard L. Solano (no number). It's right at a traffic circle, an odd mod-colonial building with spikes along the top of the facade as the colonial touch, but lush carpeting and air conditioning inside. Prices for rooms are higher, of course: 960 pesos single, 1175 pesos double.

Just a bit farther along Boulevard L. Solano is the **Restaurant El Farallon**, on the opposite side of the street from the two aforementioned hotels. With a big dining room overlooking the street and a park with a fountain, background music, and air conditioning, it's one of the city's nicer spots. Lunch and dinner are served, and a decent meal will cost in the range of 350 pesos from soup to nuts. El Farallon is less than a block from the Hotel del Valle.

Onward to the Resorts

From Culiacan it's an easy three-hour drive to Mazatlán, the most northerly of Mexico's fabulous Pacific resorts. Pretty country separates the two cities, with rolling uplands gradually yielding to fertile tropic savannahs.

Not far to the south of where you are now, some of Mexico's most exciting attractions await you. Refer to Chapter III for the rundown on the resort towns along the coast, from Mazatlán all the way to Puerto Angel in the state of Oaxaca. Chapter IV is devoted to Guadalajara, Mexico's second-largest city, and the towns and sights around it. From Guadalajara you can journey to the fascinating Silver Cities of the northern Valley of Mexico (Chapter V), or on to the largest (and in my opinion also the greatest) city in the world—México, D.F. (Chapters VI through XII).

2. The El Paso Route: Chihuahua to Fresnillo

An alternate route to the Valley of Mexico from the southwestern U.S. is through El Paso, Texas (Ciudad Juarez on the Mexican side), and down either Highway 45 through Durango or Highway 49 through Torreon. The Durango way offers no particular advantage unless you're heading for Mazatlán and the Pacific Coast resorts. Highway 49 via Torreon, on the other hand, takes you straight into the Colonial Silver Cities (see Chapter V) in the northern part of the Valley of Mexico. The bus will undoubtedly follow 49 to Fresnillo, near where the two highways merge to become Highway 45/49, parting ways again east of Zacatecas.

Although the range of the Sierra Madre Occidental divides this route from the one in the previous section, there are several points at which it is practical to cross over. The Chihuahua al Pacifico Railroad (described below) will take you from Chihuahua to Los Mochis, and will take your car as well, for a price.

38   MEXICO ON $20 A DAY

You can drive or bus over the mountains from Durango if your goal is Mazatlán.

Border formalities at the Ciudad Juarez Customs and Immigration station take between 30 minutes and an hour, the longer period if you're bringing in a car. Then it's a four-hour ride along a straight, fast road to Chihuahua, 230 miles to the south.

READER'S TIP ON BUS TRANSPORTATION: "It's best to get your bus south in either of the two bus stations in El Paso. Omnibus de México buses depart from the Trailways terminal, Transportes Chihuahuenses depart from the Greyhound terminal. You will be assured of a reserved seat, assistance at Mexican Customs and Immigration, and fewer problems this way than if you cross into Juarez and go to the bus station, which is often crowded to capacity" (Ms M. Terrazas, Chihuahua, Chih., México).

CHIHUAHUA: This American-style city (alt. 4700 feet; pop. 700,000) is the capital of the state of Chihuahua, the largest and richest state in Mexico. The money comes from mining, timber, and cattle-raising besides the industry in the city, and you'll notice lots of well-dressed businessmen striding purposefully through its streets. Somehow, they manage to impart their aura of hardworking prosperity to the rest of the city.

Aside from its industry, Chihuahua boasts a modern university, a museum in the house where Pancho Villa lived, and those tiny, hairless Chihuahua dogs. According to many Chihuahuans, the little dogs are rapidly becoming extinct around here, but a few kennels still raise them and sell them in the Sunday market.

Where to Stay

As you bypass the town, coming in from the north on Route 45, you'll see the **Santa Rita Motel (1)**, P.O. Box 507 (tel. 141/3-2411), whose 32 roomy units are nestled among shade trees and flowering plants. Rates are average (singles, 660 pesos; doubles, 880 pesos), and a bonus is the convenience of staying right on the highway. There's a pool and a lively little colony of retired American couples living here, and the rooms are very large and pleasant. The adjoining and similarly named restaurant, actually a separate entity, has moderately priced à la carte entrees and soup-and-sandwich meals.

The **Motel Nieves** on Route 45 (tel. 141/3-2516), just a few blocks south of the older, aforementioned Santa Rita, is another good on-the-highway choice. Despite its arctic name (*nieves* could mean "snow" or "ice cream"), you will find no polar bears at the Nieves, but after a hot drive across the state of Chihuahua the clean, air-conditioned rooms and the very pretty swimming pool will do very nicely. You will pay 550 to 875 pesos single, 660 to 995 pesos double to stay here, but that includes a staff which speaks some English, a nice shady poolside copse, and 62 rooms to choose from. The motel has a restaurant, and smaller, less expensive eateries are nearby. For campers, the motel provides a bare but hookup-equipped lot in the rear.

Halfway between in-town and on-the-road is the grand and pleasant **Hotel Victoria** at the corner of Avenidas Juarez and Colon (tel. 141/2-8893), only a few blocks from the highway and ten blocks from the main plaza. The Victoria is a substantial place richly decorated with colored tiles, run by a soft-spoken and attentive staff, and patronized by well-to-do Mexican businessmen who drive big cars. Room doors open onto mezzanine-like walkways which tower in tiers above the lobby-courtyard, an early version of the Hyatt Regency design. The entire place is air-conditioned, and rooms cost 1000 pesos

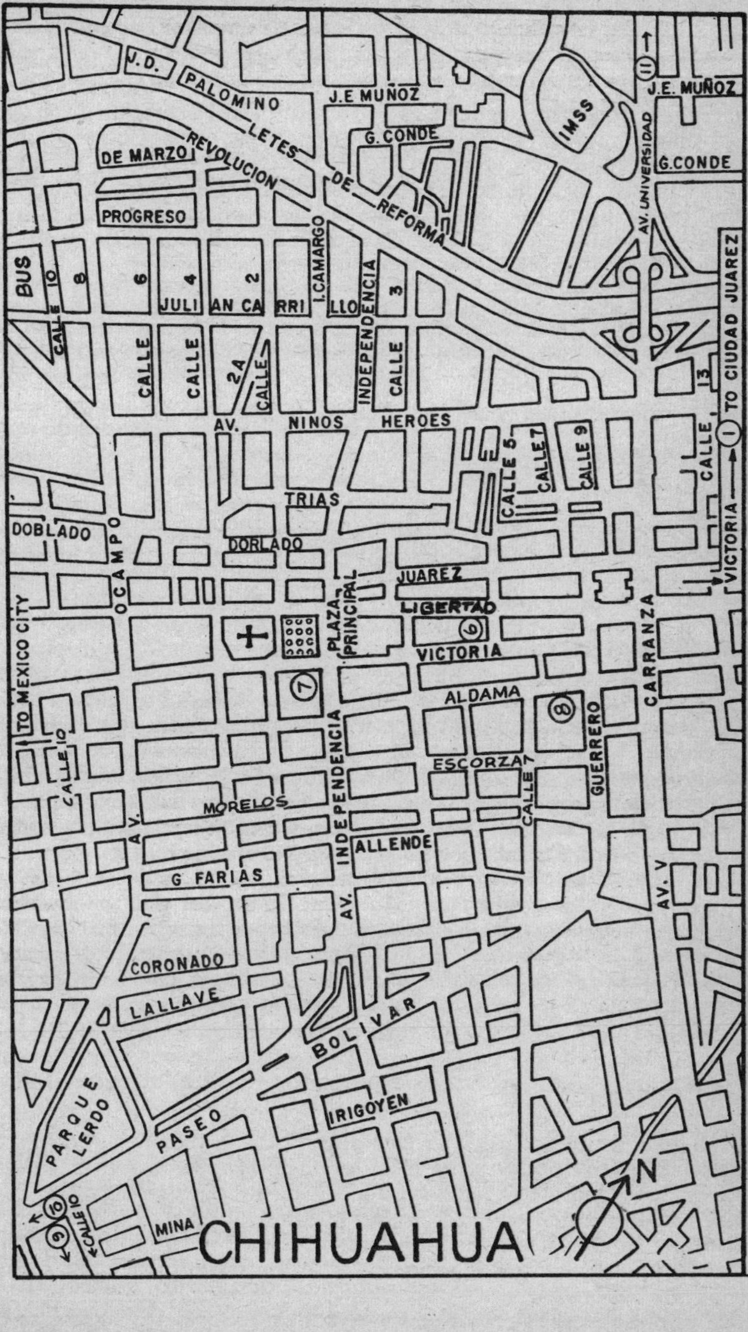
J.D. PALOMINO
J.E MUÑOZ
J.E. MUÑOZ
LETES DE REFORMA
REVOLUCION
DE MARZO
G. CONDE
G.CONDE
IMSS
AV. UNIVERSIDAD
PROGRESO
I. CAMARGO
BUS
CALLE 10
8
6
4
2
3
JULIAN CARRILLO
CALLE
CALLE
2A
CALLE
INDEPENDENCIA
CALLE
AV. NINOS HEROES
TRIAS
DOBLADO
DORLADO
OCAMPO
CALLE 5
CALLE 7
CALLE 9
CALLE 13
TO CIUDAD JUAREZ
VICTORIA
JUAREZ
LIBERTAD
PLAZA PRINCIPAL
VICTORIA
TO MEXICO CITY
CARRANZA
ALDAMA
CALLE 10
ESCORZA
GUERRERO
CALLE
MORELOS
AV. INDEPENDENCIA
ALLENDE
G FARIAS
AV. V
CORONADO
LALLAVE
BOLIVAR
IRIGOYEN
PASEO
PARQUE LERDO
MINA
CALLE 10
N
CHIHUAHUA

single, 1200 pesos double, with bath. A bar, restaurant, disco, and private parking lot fill out the services. You can drive, or take a bus or cab straight down Juarez into the heart of town.

From the Central Camionera (bus station, "BUS" on map), you can see the several tall buildings which mark Chihuahua's center. For the amount of time you'll spend here you might as well stay at the del Cobre; but if you feel like going downtown, I recommend taking a taxi to one of the restaurants listed below. City buses easily bring you *back* to the Central Camionera (look for "C. Camionera" in white paint on the bus windshield) from downtown, but for some reason it's not so easy to go from the bus station to the city's center.

READERS' HOTEL SELECTIONS: "An exceptional bargain is the **Hotel Avenida** at the corner of Avenida Juarez and Carranza (tel. 141/5-2891). Rooms are clean, large, carpeted, and with plenty of windows. The desk clerk Sr. Adolfo Rios speaks English. There is a color TV in the lobby. Cost is 440 pesos single, 550 pesos double, plus tax. Credit cards are accepted" (Aline Erwin, Benton, Ark.).... "I arrived late at night, and ended up staying in the overpriced Motel Mirador. But hotels with good prices, recommended by people I met, were the **Maria Dolores**, the **El Dorado**, the **Pacifico**, the **Estrella**, and the **Apollo** (the old one)" (Arlene R. Alexandrovitch, Victoria, B.C., Canada).

Where to Eat

The cafeteria in the **Central Camionera** is as good a place as any to have an informal lunch or dinner or some quick breakfast eggs. Prices are kept at a reasonable level because you do the serving (it's a real cafeteria line) and the problem of choosing unfamiliar dishes from a foreign-language menu is not present—you choose the unfamiliar dishes by sight from the hot table in the line. (When in doubt, ask *"Es piquante?"*—eys-pee-kahn-teh—"Is it spicy?") Prices are marked near the dishes: stews and soups are 45 to 80 pesos, carne asada (a serving of roast meat) is 150 pesos. Free seconds on coffee.

Those out for a walk in the center of the city should try the **Cafeteria Liveer (6)**, Libertad 318 between Calles 3 and 5, another American-style cafeteria. Bright and clean, it serves hamburgers for 65 to 95 pesos, delicious and filling burritos (large wheat tortillas rolled and stuffed with such things as chicken, pork, refried beans, eggs, etc., and garnished with lettuce and tomato) for only 44 pesos, depending on stuffing. A breakfast of juice, eggs, toast, and coffee costs 100 pesos, a bit more with bacon.

A few blocks east of the main plaza is the **El Herradero (8)**, on the corner of Aldama and Calle 7a. It is a pleasant enough restaurant: clean, modern, with American music. They offer 120- or 150-peso comidas for lunch and dinner which include a soup, a choice of ten entrees (biftek with guacamole, filete of fish with potatoes), and a dessert. The menu is in Spanish only. For a light meal or snack, try one of the *licuados* whipped up (literally) next door.

What to Do

For a diversion in Chihuahua, take a drive past the statue of Pancho Villa at Division del Norte and Avenida Universidad. To your right, you'll see **Chihuahua University**, a series of rather unimaginative modern buildings against a backdrop of dry, rocky mountains. Note the cattle-raising school and meteorological institute—evidences that Mexico is well aware of the importance of its money-making industries and of the necessity for systematizing knowledge that once passed informally from generation to generation. The university also has an extensive "sports city," whose special pride is the basketball court (basketball's popular in these parts); it includes a swimming pool, baseball stadium, and, to relieve your fears of too much Americana, a jai alai court.

The **Museum of Pancho Villa (9)**, Calle 10 no. 3014, is located in Villa's former house on what was once the outskirts of the city. Villa's legitimate wife (he had others, they say) still lives in the house and will show you around—or will have one of the other relatives do so—for a small fee. Exhibits include Villa's weapons, some personal effects, lots of period photos, and the car in which he was shot in 1923, complete with bullet holes. Open 9:30 a.m. to 6 p.m. every day. To get to the Villa house, first thing to do is to ignore the street address, for Calle 10 is not simply one street but in fact a discontinuous assortment of streets, alleys, thoroughfares, etc., now on the west side of Ocampo, later on the southeast side. Do this: drive or take a bus up Avenida Independencia or Paseo Bolívar to the Parque Lerdo. One block east of the intersection of Bolívar and Ocampo is a largish unmarked street going up a short grade to the south. This is the local incarnation of Calle 10 and if followed for five blocks will bring you to no. 3014 and the museum, on the right-hand side as the street heads downhill.

The Chihuahua Al Pacifico Railroad

If you're headed west from Chihuahua rather than south, you have a scenic treat in store for you on one of the world's most unique train rides. Five days a week (Wednesday and Sunday excepted), the Ferrocarril Chihuahua al Pacifico runs luxurious, smooth-riding autovias (Fiat-built diesel cars) from Chihuahua to Los Mochis. The distance covered is 406 miles and the trip, taking about 12½ hours, is as fascinating culturally as it is scenically. The high spot, literally and figuratively, is a 9000-foot elevation called **Divisadero** where the train makes a 15-minute stop and passengers are allowed to get off and take pictures. Divisadero is in the heart of the Tarahumara country, land of those cave-dwelling Indians who wear a costume resembling a diaper and are world-famous long-distance runners. It also overlooks the incredible **Barranca de Cobre**, 1500 feet deeper than the Grand Canyon and four times as wide. Citizens who painfully scrimp for that jet vacation in the Caribbean would envy the way the Tarahumaras "go south" for the winter. Leaving the snowy pine forests of the rimrock country, they simply descend to the base of the canyon where orchids bloom and the climate is balmily subtropical. The train leaves Chihuahua at 8 a.m. and makes the return trip from Los Mochis the same time (7 a.m. Mountain Time, 8 a.m. Central Time) daily, except Monday and Thursday.

A newer train, the Vista Dome (not an autovia) is a bit more comfortable (with a dining/bar car) than the somewhat compact autovias. These leave Chihuahua on Monday, Thursday, and Saturday at 8:20 a.m., arriving in Los Mochis about 12 hours later. The return trip also starts at 8:20 from Los Mochis on Tuesday, Friday, and Saturday.

A conventional train runs on Tuesday and Friday, leaving Chihuahua at 9:50 p.m. and arriving at the Divisadero at 5:57 a.m. (make sure you'll be in daylight then—it depends on the time of year). This trip takes about 16 hours and costs less than the scenic day train, unless you want a sleeping compartment, which, of course, is always more expensive than a coach seat. The train stops at the Divisadero for 25 minutes during the summer months only (May to September).

You can take the same line to or from the U.S.–Mexico border at Ojinaga-Presidio, Texas. Trains run between Ojinaga and Chihuahua every day but Thursday and Saturday.

42   MEXICO ON $20 A DAY

Note that the entire railroad operates on Central Time, despite the fact that Los Mochis is in the Mountain Time Zone.

Note, too, that the Ferrocarril de Chihuahua al Pacifico has its own stations (no. 10 on map) in both Chihuahua and Los Mochis—their trains do *not* leave from the "main" stations. Tickets are available at the stations (in Chihuahua at the station in the southern part of town, behind the penitentiary; go out Paseo Bolívar to the intersection with Boulevard Diaz Ordaz and turn left; the station is a few blocks ahead) or by writing Superintendent General de Trafico, F. C. Chihuahua al Pacifico, Apdo. Postal 46, Chihuahua, Chih., México (tel. 141/2-2284 or 2-3867). The Tourism Office and your hotel will also be helpful in making arrangements for your trip. I must warn you that several readers have written to say that ticketing on this railroad is a hassle, especially the purchase in advance of round-trip, reserved-seat tickets. Particularly, the Santa Anita Hotel in Los Mochis, which sells some tickets, has met with displeasure. Best to get your tickets at the station or from the Tourism Office.

Two hotels in Creel, some 30-odd miles from the Divisadero, put up passengers wishing to explore the country more thoroughly. The **Copper Canyon Lodge** is quite expensive, but the **Hotel Nuevo** charges 1000 pesos per person, three meals included.

READER'S TRAVEL TIP: "The Vista train is in effect a local passenger train with a few tourist cars attached. It tends to run two to three hours late, by which time it is dark when passing over the most spectacular section of the Divisadero. I recommend taking the Fiat train. In either case I would reserve reclining seats since the crowding in the unreserved section is not worth the few dollars saved. Food on the train is high priced and terrible. It is best to buy some bread and Chihuahua cheese (fabulous stuff) before boarding" (Arlene Alexandrovich, Victoria, B.C., Canada).

READER'S HOTEL SELECTION: "When we rode the exciting Chihuahua al Pacifico Ferrocarril through Copper Canyon, we stayed at the **Hotel Korachi,** across from the train station in Creel. There are eight clean rooms with two double beds; rates are 440 pesos double, 650 pesos for four. Write to David Herandez, owner" (James Fasselman, Fresno, Calif.).

Getting To and From Chihuahua

There's air service from Mexico City, but if you're going through Chihuahua you're undoubtedly going by land.

By Bus: Transportes Chihuahuenses is the big local line, but Omnibus de México and Autobuses Estrella Blanca also run big buses from the border through Chihuahua to points south. Check with them at the Central Camionera, mentioned above.

By Train: Three daily trains in each direction connect Chihuahua and Cuidad Juarez, at the border, departing Juarez at 8 a.m., 5 p.m., and 7:10 p.m., arriving Chihuahua at noon, 9 p.m., and 11:50 p.m. From Chihuahua to Juarez the trains leave at 50 minutes past midnight, 8 a.m., and 5 p.m., arriving in Juarez at 5:35 a.m., noon, and 9 p.m. Trains from Chihuahua south to Mexico City depart at 20 minutes past midnight and 8 a.m. The main station (11) in Chihuahua is at the northeastern end of Avenida Division del Norte. Leave the center of town by Avenida Universidad (going northwest), and turn right at Avenida Division del Norte.

Back on the Highway

At the bifurcation of Highways 45 and 49 is the small city of **Jimenez**, about 140 miles south of Chihuahua. If you want an overnight stop away from the big cities, the best you can do is the **Motel Florido**, with a swimming pool and a good restaurant. It is located at Avenida Juarez and 20 de Noviembre, on a tree-shaded street, only five blocks or so from Highway 45. As you enter Jimenez the motel is to the right (follow the signs). Rates are 575 pesos single, 655 pesos double. They also have camping. The restaurant does a big business and it's no wonder, as the prices are very good. For 85 pesos you can get four delicious chicken burritos (wheat tortillas), and for just a few pesos more, enchiladas. They also serve breakfast.

HIDALGO DEL PARRAL: Hidalgo del Parral (alt. 5430 feet; pop. 41,474), on the way to Durango, was the spot where the famous revolutionary Pancho Villa was ambushed and killed. For centuries before that, it was famous as a rich mining area.

DURANGO: Durango (alt. 6210 feet; pop. 150,000) was at the time of the conquest the land of the Chichimecas. In 1562 an expedition under the direction of Francisco de Ibarra went in search of minerals and by 1563 a rich mining center had been established at Durango. It is still a mining town today but in recent years its claim to fame has been as a mecca for Mexican and American western-movie makers. This town is fairly modern and there are some interesting 16th-century churches, convents, and houses.

You needn't make a special trip to Durango, but if you are here for an overnight stay, head for the **Tourism Office** and pick up their mimeographed information sheet and map. It's on 5 de Febrero at the corner of B. Martinez, very near to the main plaza, Quatro Centenario. It's open from 9 a.m. to 2 p.m. and 4 to 7 p.m. Monday to Friday, 4 to 7 p.m. on Saturday; closed Sunday.

Next door to the Tourism Office is the **Government Palace**, which was built as a private residence in the 17th century. In the courtyard are some very fine murals painted by Montoya de la Cruz.

If you are arriving by bus you'll be on the northeast end of town near the junction of Routes 40 and 45; if by train you'll be north of town on Avenida Felipe Pescador. From the bus station you can take the Central Camionera bus, which will take you to the intersection of 20 de Noviembre and Juarez, right on the zócalo. Any bus traveling down Constitucion, which is the street directly in front of the railroad station, will also take you to the main plaza.

Where to Stay and Eat

On 20 de Noviembre, at no. 811, is the **Hotel Casablanca** (tel. 181/1-3599), two blocks from the main plaza. It's the town's top budget hotel, modern and comfortable, and just within our budgetary limits. The 45 rooms are spacious and colorful and most cost 330 to 525 pesos single, 575 to 695 pesos double. The hotel's restaurant is small and pleasant, and offers quite adequate meals from a menu that lists filet mignon down to vegetable salad. Best thing here is probably the succulent beefsteak and bacon with french fries and bread for 165 pesos. This is probably your best bet for dining. Open 8 a.m. to midnight daily.

Next best choice in town is the old **Posada San Jorge,** Constitucion Sur 102 (tel 181/1-4866), a sturdy forest-green colonial inn which you enter through a handsome 20-foot stone gate. Inside is a large stone court decorated with iron railings and good-looking leather furniture. The San Jorge is clean—and singles run 510 pesos; doubles, 725 pesos. Some rooms have balconies, all have baths.

The **Posada Duran** (tel. 181/1-2412), on the corner of 20 de Noviembre and Juarez, is a small, simple but elegant hotel. There are 15 rooms, all with beautiful tiled baths and tasteful decorations, and price tags of 460 to 580 pesos single, 550 to 895 pesos double.

Eating in Durango is not easy, for most of the restaurants I checked out were either way overpriced or dumpy. One place to try is the **Restaurant Mansion** at Juarez 315, on the east side of the plaza. Downstairs they have a very popular coffeehouse that serves only coffee and cake. Upstairs is a formal dining area and the prices here are high, with most entrees between 160 and 210 pesos.

The **Cafe Neveria "La Bohemia"** suggests Central European cuisine, but in fact the menu turns out to be quite international, with spaghetti, German-style sausage with potatoes and cabbage, various traditional Mexican dishes, and even vegetarian salads. Prices range from 95 to 185 pesos per entree, with hamburgers priced at only about 68 pesos. La Bohemia is open every day until midnight. Look for it at no. 907 on Avenida 20 de Noviembre.

TORREON: Torreon, Coahuila (alt. 3700 feet; pop. 300,000), is a modern city, built less than a century ago. Although there is an unremarkable museum in an inconvenient location, Torreon offers little else—no old churches, historic houses, battlegrounds, or bridges. By admission of the locals, in fact, there is absolutely nothing to see in Torreon. This is mainly a businessman's city.

Though there's nothing to see, there's certainly something to read about Torreon. One Patrick O'Hea, an Englishman who dropped out of Cambridge, came to Mexico in 1905 just in time to witness the end of the Porfiriato (reign of dictator Porfirio Díaz) and the conflagrations of the Mexican Revolution. He managed a country hacienda near Torreon, and wrote an account of the tragicomic events of that turbulent period, entitled *Reminiscences of the Mexican Revolution* (London: Sphere Books, 1981). The book is not for sale in the United States, but if you see a copy in Mexico, grab it—particularly if you can read it while whizzing through Torreon.

The city does have a pretty main plaza, though, lined with the tall, slender royal palm trees usually found only in Acapulco or other coastal towns. The city is also a center for mining, smelting, and viniculture. The Mexican wine industry, all but nonexistent a decade ago, is now flourishing and producing enjoyable vintages and drinkable brandies. Tours of Torreon's wineries can be arranged by asking at the town's tourist Information Office (actually a desk) in the lobby of the Río Nazas Hotel, Morelos and Trevino.

Where to Stay

The aforesaid **Hotel Río Nazas** (tel. 171/6-1212) is Torreon's old reliable hostelry, and as it towers above the intersection of Morelos and Trevino it is visible from practically the entire city. All the standard luxuries are to be found in its 170 modern rooms: air conditioning, wall-to-wall carpeting, telephones, and TVs; and big hotel services, such as a garage, laundry, bar and restaurant, are all available. Rates are not wildly unreasonable for all this plushness: 1050 pesos single, 1250 pesos double.

The new and modern **Hotel Plaza** (tel. 171/6-0616), Rodriguez Sur 153 (between Morelos and Matamoros), has 30 rooms with bath and telephone, and central air conditioning, for which you pay 440 to 495 pesos single, 550 to 630 pesos double; a few rooms cost a bit more than this. The rooms are perhaps a bit claustrophobic, having few windows, but this is more or less typical of Mexican hotels and in fact helps to keep rooms quiet. To find the Plaza, walk from the main plaza one block west on Morelos to Rodriguez, turn left, and the hotel will be half a block down the street on the right-hand side.

The **Hotel Savoy** (tel. 171/2-5745), Manuel Acuna Sur 257, is close to the main Plaza, between Morelos and Juarez. Its spare, modern lobby leads to 80 rooms, the decor of which is a bit on the wild side—one wall brick red, one dull blue, one pink, etc.—but otherwise not unpleasant. All rooms are light and clean, and they have tiled bathrooms. Singles cost 580 pesos; doubles are 670 pesos. All rooms are air-conditioned.

The **Hotel Galicia** (tel. 171/6-1111), on the main plaza at Cepeda Sur 273, was for many years my budget favorite, but is now a bit behind the times in everything but price. Still, it's a fascinating place to stay: the lobby is full of old leather chairs, stained-glass windows, and fanciful carved animals at the foot of the stairs. The decor may be straight out of *Alice in Wonderland,* but the little rooms are clean, if very basic, and all have baths. Design allows for good cross-ventilation—the Galicia is clearly a pre-air conditioning establishment. Rooms cost 400 pesos single, 450 to 550 pesos double.

Where to Eat

For those of you in town at lunchtime, I can recommend an excellent restaurant that attracts totally by word of mouth: there is no sign, and in fact from the outside it looks like a rundown old mansion. It is located at Matamoros 1094, on the corner of Rodriguez (one block east and north of the plaza). Called the **Casa Dona Julia**, it's owned and supervised by the señora herself. The restaurant has four cozy rooms, all always filled with hungry, happy customers. Open every day from 1 to 6 p.m. only, the restaurant serves only a set lunch, which changes in price according to what is served. The specialty is Spanish cooking, and it is tasty. The afternoon I was there they served a choice of soups, paella with shrimp, chicken, and pork (a meal in itself), a choice of entrees served with pasta and vegetables, a choice of dessert, and coffee. The cost was 290 pesos per person and well worth it. The service was some of the best I've had in Mexico and, all in all, it was a lovely dining experience. Highly recommended.

For more general fare at various times of the day, try the **Cafe Los Globos**, at the northeast corner of the main plaza (Cepeda 193). Almost always bustling with hungry-but-busy types, Los Globos is the perfect place for a light meal served quickly in modern, air-conditioned surroundings. The fixed lunch (comida corrida) is set at 165 pesos, but a plate of enchiladas costs even less. For dessert a variety of sweets cost 50 pesos, but for a bit more you can savor a banana split.

Also on the main plaza, on Calle V. Carillo Sur, is the **Apolo Palacio,** a large air-conditioned restaurant with leather booths, tables, and a cheerful cartoon-style painting of a Spanish conquistador to enliven one wall. Service is good, and so are the ten varieties of eggs priced from 44 to 86 pesos. You might want something more substantial, in which case the pork chops or liver (175 pesos) will fill the bill. Open from 6 a.m. to midnight, they serve a luncheon special for 180 pesos.

Torreon Miscellany

The city of Torreon is easy to get around if you orient yourself by the main plaza (zócalo), which is bounded on the south by Juarez and on the north by Morelos. . . . There is a good market on Juarez, two blocks east of the plaza between Acuna and Blanco. . . . The **post office** is located nine blocks east of the plaza on Juarez and Galeana. It's open from 9 a.m. to 5 p.m. daily except Sunday. . . . The **bus** stations (A.D.O., Estrella-Blanca, Omnibus de México, Trailways, Chihuahuenses, Transportes del Norte) are located two blocks west of the plaza between Zaragoza and Lafuente. . . . The town closes down between 2 and 4 p.m. for siesta.

The bank on the southeast corner of the main plaza will change your money for you Monday through Friday between 9 a.m. and 1:30 p.m. Should you be stuck in Torreon for a few days with car troubles or ticket difficulties, wander down to the Casa de la Cultura, Morelos 639, and see what's doing in the way of art exhibits, recitals, and other cultural offerings.

On your way out of town, follow Morelos heading west to regain the highway.

FRESNILLO: Heading south from Torreon you cross the Tropic of Cancer just before arriving in Fresnillo, Zacatecas (alt. 7370 feet; pop. 110,000). This is a silver-mining town at the northern edge of the Valley of Mexico, not quite so fancy or attractive as many of the other silver towns in the region (see Chapter V), but good for an overnight stay after a long day on the road. Try the **Hotel del Fresno,** Avenida Hidalgo 411, which is filled with sunlight, clean, and (dare I say it?) a little stylish. There are 36 rooms stacked above the breezy stone lobby and cactus garden, and they cost 295 pesos single, 385 pesos double. Much older and not nearly so pleasant is the **Hotel Casa Blanca,** Garcia Salino 503, next to the Omnibus de México depot. The long, narrow lobby leads to relatively clean rooms which tend to be dark and cost 260 pesos single, 300 to 400 pesos double. A bar, restaurant, and garage are on the premises.

3. The Eastern Route via Monterrey and Saltillo

The two Texas towns of Eagle Pass and Laredo are only about 120 miles apart on the Rio Grande, and the Mexican highways which run southward from them are roughly parallel, running down either side of a mountain range, and offer several opportunities for crossover from one to the other, first at Saltillo–Monterrey, then at San Roberto–Linares, later on at Huizache and Antigua Morelos, and finally at San Luis Potosí–Ciudad Valles. The route from Laredo (85) is one of the most popular for visitors from the north because it can be reached conveniently from the northern and eastern United States via Interstate highways and also because it goes directly to the large Mexican city closest to the border: Monterrey.

You might try this if you enter at Laredo: go to Monterrey, then take Mex. 40 to Saltillo and then go south on Mex. 57 to San Luis Potosí; the towns along 85 south of Monterrey are not of great interest, and if you go via San Luis Potosí you can stop in Guanajuato, San Miguel de Allende, Queretaro, and Tula ruins before entering Mexico City (see Chapter V). This is by far a more interesting route.

If you cross at Eagle Pass you can take a shortcut to Monterrey via Mex. 53 south of Monclova, then return via Mex. 40 to Saltillo and Mex. 57 south. I'll describe Monterrey, Saltillo, and the preferred Route 57 first, and then tell you what's in store on the alternate road, Route 85.

MONTERREY

READER'S TRAVEL TIP—LEAVE YOUR CAR IN LAREDO: "We drove to Laredo and found an excellent place to leave the car: the **Hamilton Hotel Garage** (tel. 512/723-3833), 1211 Houston St., is about four blocks west of the end of I-35, very near the International Bridge. The garage is open Monday through Saturday from 8 a.m. to 7 p.m. Rates are $15 per week or $40 per month for dead storage. The garage is covered, locked at night, and attended during the day. If you already have your Tourist Cards, a taxi will take you across the bridge to the train station for $3 per person" (Dr. Irwin Rovner, Raleigh, N.C.).

Taking the Train

Though the bus offers many advantages (speed, more departure times), you may want to take the train. Here are some tips.

You can make advance reservations by calling the Mexican National Railways (Ferrocarriles Nacionales de México) in Nuevo Laredo, Tamaulipas, at 871/2-8097. They will quote you prices for a first-class sleeping-car ticket, and for the sleeping-car supplement. Find out the current exchange rate for the peso, compute the prices, and then send two cashier's (bank) checks for the two amounts. For the ticket, the check should be made out to National Railways of Mexico; for the sleeping-car supplement, it must be made out to Sleeping Car Service, Mexican Railways. Mail the checks to National Railways of Mexico, P.O. Box 595, Laredo, TX 78040. Having done all this, you will have had your first encounter with Mexican bureaucratic ways.

Now for some more useful details: Trains run on Central Standard Time, *all year.* Daylight Saving Time is never used. The ticket window at the station is open from 10:50 to 11:50 a.m. and from 5 to 6:50 p.m., Monday through Saturday, closed Sunday and holidays. Go to the "Dormitorio" window if you're going to buy a sleeping-car ticket.

Dr. Irwin Rovner, of North Carolina State University has written and provided lots of helpful tips on train travel. For instance, renting a *camarín* sleeping compartment on the train works out to be the cheapest and best way to move a family from the border to Mexico City (if you don't plan to drive). Have reservations, if possible. Also, pack food *and beverages* (as I advised in Chapter I, Section 2), and toilet paper. Be advised that the air conditioning and the electrical outlets on the train may not work. The trip between Nuevo Laredo and Mexico City takes about 25 hours.

By the way, the train is not the best way to get to Monterrey, since you arrive late in the evening, leaving little time to find a hotel. It's better to spend the night in Laredo (there are many motels in town, including an inexpensive Motel 6) and start out early the next morning.

If you go by road, it takes no more than three hours to cover the 146 miles (235 kilometers) between Nuevo Laredo and Monterrey, once you've cleared the various Customs (*Aduana*) and Immigration (*Migración*) stops.

MONTERREY: This city, capital of the state of Nuevo León, is Mexico's third-largest city (alt. 1770 feet; pop. 1,500,000) and its main industrial center. Its setting is spectacular: hemmed in by towering, craggy mountains, one of which (Cerro de la Silla, "Saddle Mountain") has become a symbol of the city. They seem to make everything here: steel, beer, cement, glass, cigarettes, chemicals, textiles, building materials, and on and on. With the industrial sprawl has come serious noise and air pollution, the latter often in the form of a pall that hangs in the valley 24 hours a day. But Monterrey, named in 1596 for the Count of Monterrey, Viceroy of New Spain, retains some colonial touches among its shiny new buildings and factories: the town hall, the Government Palace (state house of Nuevo León), mansions and hotels, churches and monasteries, and the parks and squares which the colonial planners always put into the new towns they laid out.

I might mention that Monterrey is hardly the best introduction to Mexican urban life. Crowded, polluted, noisy, and expensive, it's hardly the sterotypical Mexican town: laid back, charming, colonial, filled with flowers all year and mariachis each evening. Monterrey is Monterrey, a raw, muscular city which produces a great deal of Mexico's wealth. Save your visions of charm for Guanajuato, Zacatecas, and Querétaro, which have it in abundance.

Now before you start, hotel hunters take note: the interesection of **Juarez** and **Aramberri** divides Monterrey's street addresses. All numbers north or south of Aramberri are norte (north) and sur (south) respectively. All numbers east or west of Juarez are oriente (east) and poniente (west) respectively; and the numbers *start* at this intersection (you might call it the "zero point") and go up.

Getting Around

For most travel between downtown (Plaza Zaragoza) and the region of Avenida Madero—including the bus and train stations—catch either a no. 1 or no. 4 bus. These two buses travel the same circle route through the inner city, the no. 1 going counterclockwise, the no. 4 going clockwise. For instance, to get from the Central de Autobuses to the Plaza Zaragoza, just go a block south from the Central and catch the no. 1. Other convenient lines heading south are nos. 17 and 18, which leave from the corner of Amado Nervo and Madero, just a few steps south of the Hotel Nuevo León, and go directly down Avenida Juarez to the center of the downtown district. To return to the northern part of town, catch a no. 1 bus at the Plaza Zaragoza, going up Zuazua. It'll take a frighteningly convoluted route, and at some point you're sure to think the driver has gone berserk, but rest assured (if that's possible in a Monterrey city bus). Soon he'll head west on Reforma, a narrow street between Madero and Colón, and you'll be able to tick off the streets he passes on our map. Stay on to the bus station if you like.

Lots and lots of buses throng Avenida Juarez going north, to Madero and back to the Central de Autobuses. Catch them at the corner of Juarez and Padre Mier. The no. 39 is a good one; any others heading north and bearing "Central de Autobuses" signs in the windshield will do just as well.

Where to Stay

Unfortunately for those on a tight budget, the cheaper hotels in Monterrey are a good distance from the center of the town's culture and nightlife. In fact, as the city grows and prospers it gets harder and harder to find good, clean hotels within our budget range. As this is one of the three largest cities in Mexico and thus relatively high priced (compared to a provincial town) you may want to allow yourself a splurge for a day or two here, and plan to make up the deficit in a smaller, cheaper city later on in your trip. The prime area for accommodations for those who really want to enjoy their stay in Monterrey is in and around the Zona Rosa ("Pink Zone"), the plush downtown district centered on the Plaza Zaragoza, Monterrey's main square, and the Plaza Hidalgo, a small but very lovely park nearby. I'll give the low-down on places to stay in and around the Zona Rosa, and will then list the cheaper hotels near the bus and train stations, 20 blocks north of downtown.

Zona Rosa Area: Monterrey's top downtown hotel, the **Hotel Ambassador** (tel. 83/42-2040) is one of those plush places which can drain one's pockets

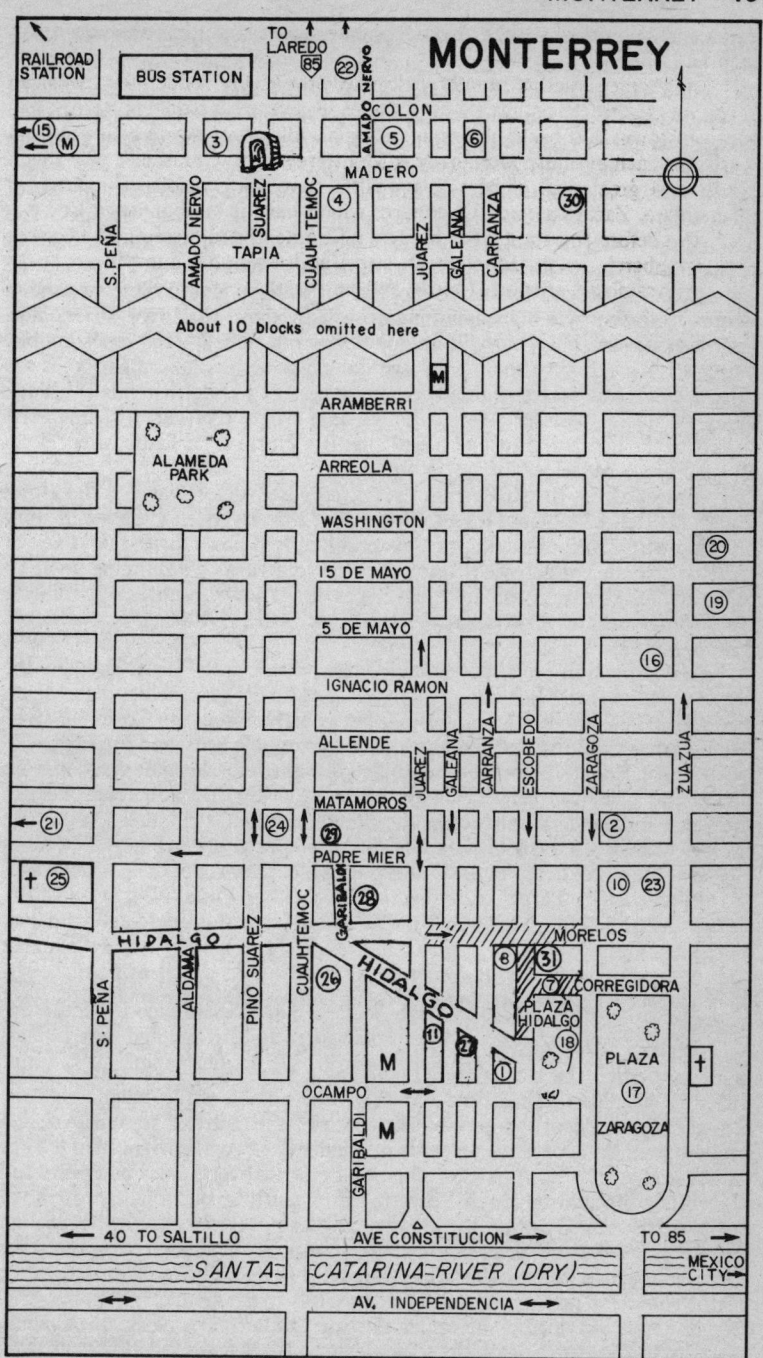

MONTERREY 49

MONTERREY

RAILROAD STATION
BUS STATION
TO LAREDO 85
AMADO NERVO
COLON
MADERO
S. PEÑA
AMADO NERVO
SUAREZ
TAPIA
CUAUHTEMOC
JUAREZ
GALEANA
CARRANZA

About 10 blocks omitted here

ARAMBERRI
ALAMEDA PARK
ARREOLA
WASHINGTON
15 DE MAYO
5 DE MAYO
IGNACIO RAMON
ALLENDE
JUAREZ
GALEANA
CARRANZA
ESCOBEDO
ZARAGOZA
ZUAZUA
MATAMOROS
PADRE MIER
GARIBALDI
MORELOS
HIDALGO
ALDAMA
PINO SUAREZ
CUAUHTEMOC
HIDALGO
CORREGIDORA
PLAZA HIDALGO
S. PEÑA
PLAZA ZARAGOZA
OCAMPO
GARIBALDI

← 40 TO SALTILLO
AVE CONSTITUCION
TO 85 →
MEXICO CITY

SANTA CATARINA RIVER (DRY)

AV. INDEPENDENCIA

with astonishing speed—a double room here costs a terrifying 3600 pesos per night. The Ambassador's courtly and dignified neighbor on the Avenida Hidalgo is the **Gran Hotel Ancira (1)** (tel. 83/43-2060), and the last time I passed by, the Ancira's graceful old rooms were going at 3000 pesos double. In any case, it's well out of our budget. But keep it in mind until you've seen what else downtown Monterrey's Zona Rosa has to offer.

A few blocks from the Plaza Hidalgo are two high-rise hotels with less of the snazz of the two top places, but with all of the luxury facilities. The mammoth 17-story **Hotel Río (28)** (tel. 83/42-2190) is a block long, has 344 rooms, and a garage for 400 cars, plus central air conditioning, TV sets in the rooms, tile baths with tubs, nice modern furnishings, and a large swimming pool surrounded by a big sunbathing area, high above the street. Prices have just risen substantially, but will no doubt stay put now at 2100 pesos double, but this is for a luxury room with two double beds; less luxurious rooms are often available at correspondingly lower prices. The Hotel Río fills the block along Garibaldi between Morelos and Padre Mier; there are two high-rise towers to the hotel, and two lobbies: Hotel Río Norte is on Padre Mier, Hotel Río Sur is on Morelos.

Almost across the street from the Río's Padre Mier entrance is the **Hotel Jolet (29)** (tel. 83/40-5504), Padre Mier Pte. 201, a very modern seven-story building with 100 rooms and prices several hundred pesos lower than those at the Río, the one big difference being that the Jolet lacks a swimming pool. To make up for the lack, the Jolet has a bar in its lobby, and also a toll-free reservations number for use in the U.S. (tel. 800/238-5000; in Canada, tel. 800/261-3333).

Going down in price, but actually going closer to the Plaza Hidalgo, the **Hotel Colonial (13),** Hidalgo Ote. 475 (tel. 83/43-6791), is an older place which has been redecorated in an interesting but ghastly imitation of colonial style. Rooms are air-conditioned and many have two double beds, and prices are 770 pesos single, 990 pesos double—but there's a catch: housekeeping standards are pretty low. They can get away with it because of their location right next to the Plaza Hidalgo and right across the street from the Gran Hotel Ancira. The trick is to take a good look at a few rooms before you move in.

One hotel still in our budget range, three blocks north of the Plaza Zaragoza on the Avenida Zaragoza, is the Spanish-looking **Posada Garza Nieto (2),** Zaragoza Sur 827 (tel. 83/43-0616), with lush foliage in the colonial patio, and a brisk but amiable señorita at the main desk. She speaks very little English but tries hard to understand; the owner of the hotel speaks excellent English. The 25 rooms here are a bit dark, but they're big and cost 400 pesos single, 560 pesos double.

Avenida Madero Area: If you arrive in Monterrey by bus or train you'll come into either the train station on Avenida Reyes or the Central de Autobuses on Avenida Colón, about 20 blocks to the north of the downtown Zona Rosa. The bus depot is a few blocks south of the railroad station; Avenida Madero, with its Independence Arch monument, is two blocks south of the bus station and parallel to Avenida Colón. Madero is a lively, noisy boulevard full of outdoor life and once replete with cheap, fairly good hotels. Most hotel business has moved downtown, however, and so proximity to the bus station and the city's cheapest eateries are about your only advantages here. But since decent and cheap hotel rooms are getting hard to find all over Monterrey, this is still your best bet if you must stick rigidly to your budget.

If you're staying in this older part of Monterrey, a walk up Avenida Madero, starting at the arch that commemorates Mexico's independence from Spain, is a good way to start your day. The street is one of the liveliest in

Mexico—girls will be furiously washing windows . . . music will blare at you from all sides . . . briefcased businessmen will pause to admire the prettier señoritas . . . the current total of Monterrey's car accidents will be inscribed on the arch. It's a capsule view of Mexican life.

Cheapest, newest, and best choice in the area, only two blocks from the bus station, is the **Hotel Nuevo León (3)**, on a quietish side street called Amado Nervo Nte., at no. 1007 (tel. 83/74-1900). Walk out the front center door of the Central de Autobuses, take the left-hand pedestrian bridge over Avenida Colón, and you'll find Amado Nervo a bit more to the left; the hotel is a block down on the left-hand side. The 38 rooms are all doubles with bath, are clean and modern if a bit small, and come without air conditioning. Rates are 350 pesos single, 375 to 460 pesos double, tax included. No English is spoken. The emphasis is on cleanliness with taste of a sort; although the lobby and reception desk sport a lot of whitish Formica, the hallways have brick accents that make the place very attractive. Make sure you get a room off the street. This is my first choice in the area.

Compact but clean and neat is the **Hotel Patricia (5)**, Madero Ote. 123 (tel. 83/75-0750), on the other side of Avenida Juarez and therefore in the "oriente" numbering (zero's at Juarez). If you don't mind somewhat cramped quarters, you'll find their tidy rooms are quite serviceable and not impossibly priced: 435 pesos single, 585 pesos double. All 30 rooms have baths; most have ceiling fans.

Also on the oriente portion of Madero, at no. 245 Ote. (corner of Galeana), is the **Hotêl 5a Avenida (6)** (tel. 83/75-6565), which has been here some years but is still one of the most respectable places in the neighborhood. All the rooms upstairs have fairly modern furniture, private baths, and telephone, and all 70 of them rent for 575 pesos single, 745 to 885 pesos double; but this includes all taxes *and* air conditioning—not available in most of the rooms recommended above. This would make the 5a Avenida a "weather choice," and you might head for it in the scorching days of summer. Commercial travelers make up most of the 5a Avenida's clientele.

Just south of Madero on Calle Zaragoza is the 11-story **Gran Hotel Yamallel (30)**, Calle Zaragoza Nte. 912 (tel. 83/75-3598), a big modern place with its own garage and pretensions to plushness that make it seem a good bargain, in a way. Perhaps the hotel was built before the Zona Rosa became the fashionable area to stay in. In any case, it was built for luxury, although it's a bit faded now; and it offers good value: singles are 585 to 795 pesos; doubles, 755 to 965 pesos. With 11 floors of rooms to choose from, get one with a good view and not much noise. All rooms are air-conditioned.

The **Hotel Madero (4)**, Madero Pte. 428 (tel. 83/75-5471), is a half block from the Independence Arch on Avenida Madero. It's my last choice because it's older, because it's right on the main drag, and because they have a good number of quiet rooms. The Madero has a plain lobby decorated with red leather chairs and star-painted walls. The rooms have a good coat of paint and decent furniture—not brand-new, but serviceable, and the rates are reasonable: singles with bath for 310 pesos, doubles for 380 pesos; several rooms with air conditioning go for 100 pesos more.

Where to Eat

Most of the fun, adventurous, and reasonably priced dining—and there's lots of it—is to be found in the Zona Rosa. As Monterrey is a cosmopolitan city, you'll find all kinds of restaurants: Mexican, American, and some with a European flair.

With a name like **Stop, Eat, Go (7),** you might think a restaurant would serve the fastest and most basic foods to be eaten on-the-run, but in fact the customers who come to this pretty spot on the Plaza Hidalgo come to stay a while. Although the food is an attraction, with "Herefordburgers" for 80 pesos, many other sandwiches for about the same, and desserts for 28 to 50 pesos, the ambience is what packs 'em in. Café tables shaded by Martini & Rossi umbrellas are set up on the Corregidora (north) side of the plaza, the waiters all have top hats and striped aprons, and a full-size traffic light adds visual effect as the restaurant's namesake. Inside, both upstairs and downstairs, the decor is darkish Old West. The crowd is young and mod. Most expensive thing on the menu is the Emparedado Especial ("Special Sandwich"), a Fresser's Dream packed with all sorts of things for 120 pesos.

At **Los Candiles (31),** the specialty is coffee and cake, but don't let this fool you into thinking you can only get dessert here. In fact, this small and congenial café serves an interesting variety of familiar and exotic dishes such as a German sausage plate, crêpes, and the house specialty, carnes a la Plancha, for 140 to 195 pesos. As for dessert, the coffee comes in 17 styles, the pies, cakes, and pastries almost as many. Coffee and dessert will cost you about 85 pesos, depending on what you choose. The restaurant takes its name from the chandeliers and sconces which abound, adding to the French-antique-à-la-Monterrey decor. Note that Los Candiles is open for breakfast, lunch, and dinner, that there is an upstairs seating area as well, and that you can enter at Morelos 546, corner of Escobedo.

There are numerous American-type eateries in the Zona Rosa where you can find tacos, hamburgers, and fried chicken at a reasonable price. Off the Plaza Hidalgo at Corregidora 511 is the **El Corral (7),** a small, clean place with bright-red booths and a few fake arches. Tacos hover around 20 to 30 pesos, frijoles cost 22 pesos, and the specialty, alhambre de filete (charcoaled steak), goes for 190 pesos.

For those of you who want to feel at home, go around the corner to Escobedo 920 where you'll find a branch of **Sanborn's (8),** a large store with cosmetics, magazines, bric-a-brac, etc., as well as a restaurant and coffeeshop. The restaurant is always full so you may have to wait if you are there during peak periods. The menu (same in the restaurant and at the lunch counter) offers a variety of items priced from 150 to 200 pesos, but that's for a very full platter, with drink and tip included. There is also an entrance to Sanborn's at Morelos 464.

Kentucky Fried Chicken (10) has opened about five branches in Monterrey, one in the Zona Rosa on the corner of Padre Mier and Zaragoza, across from the Hotel Monterrey.

A good cheap seafood restaurant is **La Pesca (11),** Hidalgo 126, about a block west of the elegant Ambassador Hotel. Although the place is totally unpretentious (something of a cafeteria ambience), it's clean and very easy on the budget. Have a shrimp cocktail and a fish filet, and the bill will be about 225 pesos.

The little restaurant adjoining the Hotel 5a Avenida (6) seems to be the hotel restaurant (you can enter from the hotel lobby). Clean and shiny, with stainless steel and red equipment and a big refrigerator case at the rear, it's alright for a quick but pleasant breakfast (75 to 100 pesos), perhaps an egg dish for lunch, a sandwich or a hamburger steak (160 pesos) for supper. They have more expensive things, like T-bone steak, but I'd save the money for a splurge, as the prices for these items are almost the same wherever you go, and this is quintessentially a light-lunch place.

Walking down Calle Zaragoza, you'll find the **Restaurant Merida (16)**, Zaragoza Norte 522, a very attractive modern restaurant, with a huge mosaic of the Chichén-Itzá pyramids—and napkin holders in the form of little pyramids. A popular place for businessmen, it offers soup, Mexican plates, meats, and a whole page of Yucatán specialties. You can have a drink here, too, if you like, and a full meal need cost only 200 pesos.

For the Local Specialty: The local specialty, cabrito (roast kid), is to be found in many places around town. Usually restaurants serving it will have a fire of glowing coals in the window, with the meat stretched out on spits.

One of the first restaurants in Monterrey to serve cabrito is still one of the best—as evidenced by the lunchtime family crowds that keep the friendly waiters scurrying back and forth. This is **El Pastor (15),** Madero Pte. 1067, at Alvarez (five blocks west of Pino Suarez). It's a cool corner place, whose window is filled with kid roasting over glowing coals. El Pastor is thoroughly unclassy and democratic. Sit anywhere and order cabrito in any of a dozen ways (*al pastor* is roasted). There's no menu, but a price card is by the kitchen, so no need to worry about excessive charges; it comes, depending on what part of the animal you eat, to around 180 to 300 pesos per order.

What to Do

Much of Monterrey's colonial heritage has been overshadowed, or even replaced, by the more modern and less interesting buildings of our time, but you will be able to spend a pleasant day or two seeing the monuments that remain.

Begin your look around at the **Plaza Zaragoza,** the main square in the center of which is the **Tourist Office (17),** a single-story glass building open (so they say) 8:30 a.m. to 6 p.m. on weekdays, 8:30 to 1 on Saturday, although in practice they're usually closed for an hour or so around lunchtime. Closed Sunday. The staff is very helpful and even knowledgeable, and can give you brochures and information on all the sights in and around Monterrey.

On the west side of the plaza is the town's **cathedral,** begun in 1600 but not finished until 150 years later. The lavish paintings, sculpture, and decoration inside are typical of colonial Catholicism, and, if you think it over, give some insight into the function and position of the church in the colonial period.

Across the plaza from the cathedral is the **City Hall (18)** (Palacio Municipal), where the mayor has his office. The building has a beautiful 16th-century courtyard complete with well, wrought-iron wall lamps, and tiled arches. It's in this lovely setting that the city government stages a variety of free concerts during the spring and summer. One I heard was a Dixieland recital by "El Club de Jazz" of Monterrey, a copy of the Louis Armstrong trumpet, clarinet, sax, drums, and piano group complete with imitation-Satchmo vocals. A real treat!

A block west of the Plaza Zaragoza is the **Plaza Hidalgo,** the center of the Zona Rosa (Pink Zone). If you're just wandering around town and are hot, or maybe want to write a few postcards, drop into the stately **Gran Hotel Ancira (1)** on the southwest corner of Jardín Hidalgo. The ceiling is about 60 feet high, the floor is alternating squares of black and white marble, and the place is filled with patio-style tables and chairs giving it a French-café atmosphere. In the center of all is a magnificent grand staircase that coils down from an ornate gallery on the mezzanine. Both food and lodging here are expensive but this is certainly the prime place to write postcards.

Head north of Zaragoza Plaza to the corner of Zaragoza and Allende and be sure not to miss the lovely fountain and waterfall resplendent with colored lights and little bridges. Farther north at Zaragoza and 15 de Mayo is the

Palacio del Gobierno (19) (actually the capital building of the state of Nuevo León). At Washington and Zaragoza, one block up, is the **Federal Palace and Post Office (20)** where, by climbing the stairs and looking out one of the windows, you can get a good view of the city.

The best view of Monterrey is from the Bishop's Palace, **El Obispado (21)** —perched atop a hill at the western end of Avenida Padre Mier. Built in the late 18th century to provide employment for the poor during a famine, it has played a part in almost every aspect of Monterrey's history. It has been, at various times, a bishop's palace, a fort, a hospital, and now it is a museum. During the Mexican-American war, it served as a barracks for U.S. troops until their exodus from Mexico. During the yellow fever epidemics of 1898 and 1901, it was used as a hospital. In 1913, Pancho Villa stormed it and it was used again as a fort. It's in a commanding position, and the cannons mounted around it emphasize how easy it must have been to defend in those days of small arms. Many historical objects, including the first printing press brought to northern Mexico, in 1813, have been moved here. There is a small admission charge. Its chief asset, however, is its view of the city—excellent.

When approaching El Obispado by car, head west on Padre Mier to the end of the street. Turn right, go one block, turn left, and follow the signs to El Obispado. Bus 1 from in front of the cathedral on Zaragoza Plaza will also take you there.

Another thing to do in town: Go on a free tour of the **Cuauhtemoc Brewery (22)**, Avenida Universidad Nte. 2202, Tuesday through Sunday from 10 a.m. to 6 p.m. You can reach the brewery by taxi, or you can take bus 14 from Alameda Park on Pino Suarez.

Bullfights can be seen on Sunday at the **Plaza Monterrey**, southwest of the city off Avenida Chapultepec. Tickets can be bought from the Tourist Office in Zaragoza Square. The **Charras Rodeo**, every Sunday at 11 a.m., is held in Villa de Guadalupe, off Route 85. You can take a bus, which will leave you in the town plaza. From there it's a bit of a walk to the Charras, but worth it to see cowboys pulling steers off their feet by galloping past and grabbing their tails!

READER'S TOURING TIP: "A must in Monterrey is a trip to the **Carta Blanca brewery**. You should get there by noon and sit in the garden for an hour and consume their wonderful brew; then if you're able, go around the brewery" (Derek Freer, Fort Walton Beach, Fla.).

Markets

There are three main markets in Monterrey that are open every day of the week. They are all similar in terms of merchandise and prices, although bargaining is a bit easier at the Indian Market. The **Colón Market (M)** is a large, semicovered bazaar extending several blocks from Juarez and Hidalgo south to Avenida Constitucion. The **Juarez Market (M)** is a closed market at the corner of Aramberri and Juarez. The **Indian Market (M)**, is outside the downtown area at Simon Bolívar and Madero. You can get there by taking bus 4 from Plaza Zaragoza.

Lest you head off to market with visions of the wealth of the Indies in your head, I hasten to mention that Monterrey's markets are pretty uninspired collections of the mundane and the ridiculous. They have their moments, of course: an artist's stall from which you can buy a recently completed oil painting (if you like the style), or the shop of the *bruja* ("witch," or, more nicely, "herbal healer") in which you can buy an aerosol can of African Power Oil—guaranteed to give you all sorts of powers and bottled in Connecticut. But for a truly superb collection of Mexican arts and crafts, stop in and browse through the shop called **Carapan,** Hidalgo Ote. 305, not far from the Plaza Hidalgo. Antiques and modern items, silver and tin, glass and pottery, textiles and toys—the collection is eclectic and obviously done with an expert's eye. Sr. Humberto Arellano, the owner, has created a work of art—his shop—from works of art—the best of Mexican crafts—and I would be remiss if I didn't mention it. I must add that prices are fairly high, and if you expect to head farther south and you want to buy in quantity, you may decide to put off your purchases until later. It's a gamble: if you find an item you may find it cheaper —but then again you may not be able to find it at all.

One-day Trips from the City

About 25 miles south of Monterrey, on Route 85, are **La Boca Dam** (near the little village of Santiago) and **Horsetail Falls (Cola de Caballo).** La Boca has facilities for waterskiing, swimming, and boating, and features boat races almost every Sunday. There are picnic areas and restaurants nearby. Horsetail Falls (small fee to enter) is located on a private hacienda named Vista Hermosa. Turn right off Route 85 to the village of El Cercado, and travel about four miles up a rough but passable road. The road winds around for about three miles from the main road (making the falls accessible only by car or taxi), and leads to a car park where horses and burros can be hired for the final half mile to the falls. If you walk it, it's hard to resist the blandishments of the children who accompany you on burros, making reduced offers all the way until, when you're nearly there, they start bargaining about the return trip. I walked both ways and found it no particular strain.

On the road to Saltillo, there are several more things to see. Taking Highway 40 in the Saltillo direction, you'll find **Chipinque Mesa** about 13 miles from Monterrey. Turn left at Colonia del Valle, pay a toll of 10 pesos per person, and you're on your way. The trip is up the pine-covered slopes of the Sierra Madre and culminates in a breathtaking view of Monterrey from a 4200-foot plateau. The **Motel and Restaurant Chipinque** here is a very glamorous place, with volleyball courts, badminton, archery range, Ping-Pong, croquet, and expensive rooms; and guided excursions by horseback, burro, or on foot to **Los Manantiales** (The Springs), **Bosque Encantado** (The Enchanted Forest) or into the Sierra Madre Mountains.

You can also travel 15 miles along the road to Saltillo until you reach the village of Santa Catarina. Turn left here, go two miles more, and you'll find yourself at **Huasteca Canyon,** a massive rock formation framing dangerously deep ravines. This trip can be hazardous to the car as well as the nerves.

On the road to Saltillo, too, about 27 miles from Monterrey, are the **Garcia Caves (Grutas de Garcia),** with the usual stalactites and stalagmites, huge chambers, and a subterranean lake.

Monterrey Nightlife

The Zona Rosa tends to be the center of Monterrey's social life. This being a big college town, you'll see lots of students as well as nonscholarly types hanging around, leaning on cars, filling store doorways, and winking, whistling, and flirting. On Sunday in summer there are band concerts in Hidalgo Plaza and other days of the week there are night concerts at City Hall.

Most of the bars in town discourage women—it's a real "macho" man's world in there. For men alone, Monterrey offers good opportunities to practice that old Spanish custom of bar-hopping—whose popularity is best evidenced by the fact that there are at least three colloquial ways of saying "bar-hopping." Of course, to really *ir de tascas* in proper style, one should plan a visit to at least five places, have a drink and some tapas (hors d'oeuvres) in every one, make sure you're seen, greet everybody, and then plow on to the next. The casual tourist, however, will find this ritual rather trying if not impossible, so you can consider yourself excused.

One of the more convenient "men's bars" in town is the **Bar Reforma (23)**, Zaragoza Sur 914, near Padre Mier, a clean, cheerful place with the inevitable domino players and a better dressed clientele than most of the other cantinas.

There are a few places where women, in groups or alone, are perfectly welcome. One such place is **La Cabana (24)**, down Pino Suarez at the corner of Matamoros (P. Suarez 703). It's a very nice, air-conditioned beer garden with wooden booths and woven grass-seated chairs. Beer is 28 to 40 pesos and they also serve food; a light meal goes for about 125 to 175 pesos. They are open from 9 a.m. to 1 a.m. every day of the week with the exception of Saturday when they keep the beer flowing until 3 a.m.

A word about **Purisima Square (25)**: This used to be the place where young people gathered for the nighttime paseo; on my last visit there seemed to be little going on in this neighborhood. It's worth a visit, however, preferably in daylight, to see the famous modernistic **Purisima Church,** built in 1946, with parabolas of concrete and an adjoining tower of brown stone topped with a blue neon cross. The church facade is decorated with a crucified Christ and 12 stone Apostles.

Cinemas: Luckily for gringos (and gringas), most foreign films screened in Mexico are in the original language. This doesn't help you if the movie was made in Spain, but if it was made in Hollywood you'll be able to catch the original English soundtrack. They turn the sound down in some places, though, so don't sit too far back.

Monterrey's cinemas are dotted throughout the city, but there are three movie houses on the Avenida Zaragoza within six blocks of the Plaza Zaragoza, and these three tend to show recent first-run American films. Seven and nine o'clock are common screening times, but take your stroll up Zaragoza slightly earlier, just to be sure.

Monterrey Miscellany

Guided Tours: Walk down along Hidalgo near the Plaza Hidalgo, and every taxi driver you encounter will offer to take you on a tour of Monterrey's sights—for a price. The way to handle it is to talk for a while and see how good his English is, and whether his personality appeals or not. Then, set down exactly what the tour will cover. A good city tour should take you to the Palacio del Gobierno, the Palacio Federal, Purisima Church, El Obispado, University City, and perhaps to the markets, all in about three hours. Offer 800 or 900 pesos for the carload, and then see if you can round up several people to share the cost. It's good to compare prices with several drivers before making a commitment. There should be an easier way to do this, but there isn't.

Taxi tours to points father out of town like Horsetail Falls, Chipinque Mesá, and Garcia Caves will be correspondingly more expensive. Test your bargaining powers, get a lower price.

Sports: The state government has ingeniously converted the dry bed of the Santa Caterina River, which runs through the center of the city, into over two miles of playing fields of every conceivable type: soccer, baseball, tennis, track —you name it, it's there.

SALTILLO

Further Information: Pick up a copy of "Where to Go, What to Know," a tourist publication available for free in tourist offices, hotels, and bus depots; there's much useful information in it, and you can't beat the price.

Bus Information: Your best source of up-to-date information is, of course, the Central de Autobuses (main bus depot) on the Avenida Colón, roughly two blocks north of the Independence Arch; but Transportes del Norte maintains an information office downtown at the intersection of Pino Suarez and Hidalgo (open weekdays 9 a.m. to 1 p.m. and 3 to 7 p.m., on Saturday from 9 a.m. to 2 p.m.; closed Sunday).

Getting to and from Monterrey

The country's third-largest city is easily reached by all means of transportation. Check times and fares, and make reservations at least a day in advance, no matter how you plan to travel.

By Bus: Autobuses Anáhuac, in the Central de Autobuses, will get you to Mexico City in 10½ hours; they also run to San Luis Potosí, as does Transportes del Norte. Tres Estrellas de Oro also operates from Monterrey to points all over Mexico, and, like Transportes del Norte, connects with Greyhound at the Texas border. Autobuses Blancos and Transportes Frontera, too, operate from Monterrey to points south and west. Drop by the Central de Autobuses a day before you plan to leave and arrangements to almost anywhere will be a snap to make.

By Rail: The way to get to Mexico City by rail is to catch **El Regiomontano,** an express leaving Monterrey every day at 6 p.m., arriving in the capital at 9 a.m. the next morning. Times for the Mexico City to Monterrey train are the same. El Regiomontano will drop you in Saltillo at 7:53 p.m., in San Luis Potosí at 1:50 a.m. You can take a slower day train to get to San Luis Potosí, leaving Monterrey at 10:33 a.m. daily, arriving in Saltillo at 1:30 p.m., and in San Luis Potosí at 10 p.m. (the train goes on to Mexico City, arriving at 8:42 a.m.). There's another night train, leaving Monterrey daily at 11:25 p.m., arriving in San Luis Potosí the next morning at 10:40 a.m., and in Mexico City at 8:04 p.m. Between Monterrey and the U.S. border (Nuevo Laredo) there are two trains a day, leaving Monterrey at 1:50 a.m. and 7 a.m., arriving in Nuevo Laredo at 6:25 a.m. (to connect with Amtrak's thrice-weekly train to San Antonio, Dallas, and St. Louis), and 12:20 p.m. From Nuevo Laredo to Monterrey, daily trains run at 2:20 and 7:10 p.m.

By Air: Monterrey has good air connections with Mexico City (seven flights a day), a daily flight to Chihuahua, and two flights daily to Guadalajara. Texas International Airlines runs daily flights between Monterrey and Dallas/Fort Worth and Houston. AeroMéxico has three flights a week between Monterrey and Los Angeles, California. Look into excursion fares on the Dallas/Fort Worth and Houston flights. AeroMéxico as at Padre Mier and Cuauhtémoc (tel. 83/40-8760); Mexicana is at Padre Mier Pte. 1243 (tel. 83/44-1122).

The **Mexicana airport car** remains the cheapest way to get to and from the airport; cost is 100 pesos. A cab may cost you as much as 800 pesos if you're not careful; the airport is a long way away.

SALTILLO: This is the mile-high capital (alt. 5280 feet; pop. 286,000) of the state of Coahuila, and holds both the State College of Coahuila and also the International University, both of which attract American students during the summer. The climate is excellent, with gentle breezes that sweep down from the mountains to dispel lingering heat and humidity in midsummer; in winter, it's chillier than you'd expect—note that most of the budget hotels are not heated.

The main tower of the two-century-old cathedral, on the Plaza de Armas, offers a good view of the city, but this, together with the tree- and-lake filled Alameda Park, present just about the only diversions for the wanderer in this once-colonial-now-industrial city. Sadly, noise and air pollution have become quite a problem.

If you visit Saltillo in August, you may be in time for the big fair and exposition, an annual event to display local achievements in agriculture and industry.

The **Transportes del Norte bus station** is just off one of the town's main streets, Boulevard Allende (Highway 85), at the north end of town. As for the **railroad station,** it's at the southwest corner of town on Avenida Carranza (Highway 57), which runs parallel to Allende. To get to Allende from Carranza, walk along the latter to Ramos Arizpe and turn right, going until you abut on Allende, the town's main axis.

Where to Stay

The hotel situation in Saltillo is bad—and getting worse. The half-dozen downtown hostelries which once surrounded guests with at least a modicum of colonial charm—at low prices—have lost business to the new Rodeway Inn and Camino Real hotels on the outskirts of town. As the trade moved out, downtown hotels got careless with housekeeping and service. Short of settling into one of the out-of-town hotels at exorbitant prices, here's what you can check out downtown:

To guide you to our hotel and restaurant choices, I'll use the lively **Plaza Acuna,** next to the market, as a central point, as it's within easy walking distance of all the places listed below. The plaza is bounded by Allende, Aldama, Padre Flores, and the market.

The **Hotel Urdinola** (tel. 841/3-8140) has been one of Saltillo's better budget lodging choices for many years. Originally built in colonial style many years ago, it has undergone periodic renovation to keep it presentable. Some of its nicer features have escaped the ravages of modernization, though: the huge white granite stairway which leads to the second floor, a lovely long sunny patio onto which the rooms open, and a fine tiled fountain at the patio's end. All rooms have baths and telephones and are priced at 660 pesos single, 770 pesos double. The Urdinola's location at Calle Victoria 427 is ideal: Victoria is the city's main shopping street for handicrafts, and it's only two blocks from the Plaza Acuna.

At Victoria 418 you'll find the rather elegant **Hotel Arizpe-Sainz** (tel. 841/3-8000), right across the street from the Urdinola. Not among the lowest priced of budget choices, the Arizpe-Sainz charges 1000 to 1250 pesos single, 1175 to 1350 pesos double, plus tax, but for this price you get a delightful and well-maintained colonial-style building with two pretty courtyard patios, big and old-fashioned but fairly luxurious rooms, a good (if pricey) restaurant, a coffeeshop, and a bar. Again, the location on Calle Victoria is ideal. The Arizpe-Sainz's famed set-price lunch is now pegged at 275 pesos.

Lower down the budget list is the 20-room **Hotel Poza Rica,** Allende Nte. 436 (tel. 841/3-6596), which from the street looks much like a marble shoebox. In fact, this is a facade in the full sense of the word, for the hotel behind is a sort of "cutaway," with rooms along the north wall only, the rest of the space wide open to the sun. The whole place looks like a Hollywood set in a way, but the rooms will do in a pinch, and all come with shower. Prices are 370 pesos single, 520 pesos double. The Poza Rica is a block north of the market (two blocks north of the Plaza Acuna), on the right-hand side of Allende.

In keeping with the bad reputation of downtown Saltillo hotels, the **Hotel Premier** (tel. 841/2-1050), Allende at Muzquiz, just down the hill from the Hotel Poza Rica, charges a bit too much for what you get: single rooms with bath here run 885 pesos, doubles are 1025 pesos.

Where to Eat

A record for name-changing among Mexican restaurants must be held by **Los Cazadores,** next door to the Urdinola. Previously it was the Roma, before that the Janitzio Cafeteria and before that Los Globos. But appellative confusion doesn't diminish the restaurant's attractiveness or economy. A good comida goes for 170 pesos, set breakfasts start at 76 pesos, sandwiches are slightly less, and à la carte entrees run about 215 pesos. They're big on charcoal broiling here.

For the local specialty, cabrito (roast kid), the best place around is the **Restaurant Principal,** Allende Nte. 710, on the corner of Allende and Alessio Robles, four blocks north (down the hill) from the Plaza Acuna on the right-hand side. Bright and modern, with brick arches and a tiled kitchen open to view, it's a pleasant place to try the succulent (although a bit greasy) kids cooking over coals in the window. The price for a portion is a standard 195 pesos, and while you can have other things here (chicken, for instance, is 170 pesos), you should come here to have the specialty of the house.

Saltillo has a seafood restaurant, an odd place which serves up marine delicacies for moderate prices. The **Boca del Río,** at Allende Nte. 605, has tremendous high ceilings, funny high-backed chairs, white tablecloths, and black-and-white-clad waiters who are out to please. A delicious fish cocktail (ceviche) costs 90 pesos; octopus with shrimp and rice is a moderate 165 pesos, and is very good, if somewhat spicy. Most entree plates are in the same general price range as the octopus, but the Boca del Río's star performance is the jumbo shrimp en brochette, a tremendous helping of food which is almost heavenly, and might well be for 340 pesos. Large portions are the rule here. Open every day, the Boca del Río is only a short walk down Allende from the Plaza Acuna.

What to Do

The **Plaza Acuna** might be called the "People's Park" of Saltillo, for all throughout the day there's action: sellers of boiled corn, tacos, candies and other treats; an army of shoeshine boys; a car being raffled; a public photographer with an antediluvian camera; another man with a more modern camera taking pictures of children astride a plaster horse; a kiddie's rocketship ride; old men sunning on benches; young men checking out the hotrods and the girls; pitchmen selling gizmos of every conceivable type. Don't miss this microcosm.

The "formal" park is all that Acuna is not. This is the **Plaza de Armas,** bounded on one side by the government palace, on the opposite side by the 17th-century cathedral, and on a third by the local headquarters of the PRI, Mexico's leading political party. A graceful fountain plays in the evening when Saltillo's more sedate citizens fill the wrought-iron benches to take the air. Take a close look at the **cathedral,** actually two separate naves with a facade that's truly an eyeful. The style is churrigueresque, a 17th-century Spanish mutation of baroque that carries the style to even more ornate extremes than usual. The nave on the left is quite impressive, but walk all the way to the altar in the nave on the right to see the elaborate side altars of gilded wood. You can climb the cathedral's main tower for a good view of the city.

Saltillo's third park is the **Alameda**, a tree-and-pond oasis at the opposite (west) end of Victoria from Allende, a good place for a late afternoon stroll.

Shopping

The town's main market, **Mercado Juarez**, next to the Plaza Acuna, has been modernized and is hardly worth more than a quick stroll these days. Rather, direct your steps to the main shopping street, the **Calle Victoria**. Next to the town's **post office** (at no. 453, open every day including Sunday) are two big stores which sell the products that give Saltillo its claim to fame, namely the colorful wool or cotton serapes. In my opinion the better of the stores is the one called **El Saltillero**, at Victoria 469, where the serapes (in a back room) come in every shape, size, and pattern, and are very reasonably priced. The store also holds an amazing assortment of other handicrafts including embroidered blouses and shirts, articles in painted paper-mâché (including intricate candelabra), things made from copper, brass, alabaster, leather, glass, and tin. One of the wildest offerings is a row of milk cans decorated with scenic views—heaven knows what you'd use them for. Some of the staff speak English, and all are very helpful and polite.

A new competitor to El Saltillero is the attractive store called **El Sarape de Saltillo**, right next door. Take a look in here as well.

One store you shouldn't miss, even if you're not in a buying mood, is the **Saltillo Silver Factory**, located near the Hotel Arizpe-Sainz at Calle Victoria 404, and offering some of the finest handicrafts in all of Mexico. Prices even by U.S. standards are rather high, but you can admire wares that include huge, striking paper flowers in every color from turquoise to black; papier-mâché bracelets; oddly shaped wall decorations; wrought-iron chandeliers; sculptured candles; and almost every other imaginable objet d'art. You can see the same type of things elsewhere (at San Angel's Bazar Sabado in Mexico City, for instance) but these are done with special skill and imagination.

The last shopping area to look at is on Allende near the market, especially if you're in the market for a fine pair of boots at a reasonable price. The ones I liked best were in the shoe store *(zapatería)* at no. 348.

BACK ON THE HIGHWAY: Off to Monterrey? By road it's about an hour and a half over a divided highway with beautiful mountain vistas. Those going south to Mexico City via Highway 57 will first go through Matehuala.

Matehuala

There's desert almost all the way from Saltillo to San Luis Potosí, but the town of Matehuala, San Luis Potasí (alt. 5085 feet; pop. 50,000) almost halfway, is a welcome oasis. Matehuala is the second-largest city in the state of San Luis Potosí but it's hard to believe it's more than a small town. If you're looking for a quiet, nontouristy, south-of-the-border town, this is it! Nothing happens here, but that's why I like it.

There is a very inexpensive hotel near a quiet plaza, the **Hotel Matehuala**, Bustamente 134. From Route 57 bear to the right under the arch that leads into town. Follow this road until you come to the zócalo, go right, and continue on this road until you come to Hidalgo (about four blocks). Turn left and the hotel is straight ahead. The hotel is a plain, ancient yellow and looks worse on the outside than it does on the inside. There is a mammoth court furnished with

MATEHUALA/CIUDAD VICTORIA 61

kitchen furniture and absolutely quiet. There are 40 rooms on two levels off the court. They are plain, with high ceilings and bare walls. With bath, rooms are 330 pesos single, 400 to 480 pesos double; without bath, even less.

If you're looking for creature comforts, try the **Motel Oasis** (tel. 488/2-0742), on Route 57 just north of Matehuala, next to the large "Gasolinera" sign. The rates are reasonable—singles are 500 pesos; doubles, 650 pesos—and the situation is beautiful, with lots of grass and trees and a refreshing pool. The clientele is mostly Mexican, which tends to keep the rates reasonable. They also have a restaurant on the premises; a full meal costs 180 pesos with tacos or 275 pesos with grilled meat. All in all, a good bet for the weary traveler.

The **Restaurant Tokio** is off the plaza, two blocks from the hotel Matehuala, on the street to the right of the church on the main plaza. It is bright and modern and offers a good comida corrida for 100 pesos.

HIGHWAY 85, THE ALTERNATIVE ROUTE: As mentioned above, the route due south of Monterrey following Highway 85 is not so interesting as the aforementioned trip via Highway 57, but if you decide that Highway 85 is for you, here's what you'll encounter:

Montemorelos

You'll see the name of Montemorelos, Nuevo León (alt. 1609 feet; pop. 18,000), described in large metal letters on an arch above the highway as "Naranjiera Capital" (Orange Capital). Montemorelos is hot in summer and doesn't ever have too much to offer, except the mid-July fiesta, the pecan fair in mid-September, and the sight of the orange and lemon trees in bloom from February to March.

Linares

Fifty-one kilometers (30 miles) south of Montemorelos is Linares, Nuevo León (alt. 1272 feet; pop. 50,000), a clean, pleasant town which is the center of a farming area and some small industry (bricks, furniture). There's a motel on the north side of town, the **Escondido Courts**, with rooms at 580 pesos single, 725 pesos double, all air-conditioned. The rooms are clean, and overlook a pretty courtyard with small swimming pool. The señora serves light meals in a cozy restaurant from 7 a.m. to 7 p.m. If you come late there's a café next door (turn right as you walk out the entrance).

Right in the center of downtown Linares is the **Hotel Ramal**, on the main street and only a block from the first-class bus station. Rooms at the Ramal were redecorated—virtually rebuilt—during 1978 and now have piped-in music (who needs it?), new tiled baths, and shiny air conditioning units. Prices reflect this luxury: singles cost 650 pesos; doubles 770 pesos.

Between Linares and Ciudad Victoria the road is mostly straight and fast, with plenty of greenery and the majestic Sierra Madre range towering up on the right (west). There's little else to be seen, however, except an occasional passing car, bus, or cyclist, and lazy cattle grazing by the road. This is sugar-cane country.

Ciudad Victoria

Victoria (alt. 1471 feet; pop. 125,000), capital of the state of Tamaulipas, was named in 1825 for Mexican revolutionary Guadalupe Victoria, who became the country's first president. Today, far from being a one-burro town, it has modern architecture, open-air snackbars, and a town square complete with fountain.

On the northern edge of town is the 70-room **San Antonio Motel** (tel. 131/2-0311), which has a large modern dining room with glass doors facing a swimming pool. Rooms are simple, clean, and bright, and cost 675 pesos single, 765 pesos double. Quiet, plenty of shade trees, a good place. You might have a bite to eat here (sandwiches are 60 to 110 pesos, most entrees in the 125- to 175-peso range).

The town's main plaza holds three major hotels. Most modern and suitable is the **Hotel Everest** (tel. 131/2-4050) which, like its mountain namesake, is blissfully air-conditioned. All rooms have private baths, of course. Prices are not all that bad: 880 pesos single, 1100 pesos double. The Everest's official address is Hidalgo 9 and Colón 126.

The **Hotel Sierra Gorda** (tel. 131/2-2280) used to hold the place of Victoria's prime hostelry, but has lost it to the Everest. Even so, this seems not to have affected the Sierra Gorda'a high prices, which were an astonishing 990 pesos single, 1300 pesos double, when I checked. One gets the distinct feeling that these prices are only for those who will pay them, however, and that a bit of bargaining will get very dramatic reductions. Once you've bargained for a price, your room will have a private bathroom, piped-in music, a telephone, and (for a bit more) air conditioning and even a TV set. Parking costs extra.

Right next door, still on the plaza, is the **Hotel Los Monteros,** a simple gem of colonial architecture with rooms for half the price. The Monteros' lobby is a vast symmetrical court, edged with pillars and dominated by a sweeping stone staircase; fortunately no one seems to have considered "modernizing" the place, because its downstairs is lit by graceful old chandeliers instead of the standard neon. The rooms are super-clean and face a series of bright interior courts which are bordered by elaborate iron balconies; all have comfortable beds, carved wooden bedsteads, and private baths. The price is the best part: 420 pesos single, 650 pesos double. The big difference in price between the Sierra Gorda and the Monteros comes from the difference in climate control: the Sierra Gorda has air conditioning, while the Monteros has only fans.

Adjoining the Hotel Los Monteros is a good restaurant where prices run 100 pesos or less for a sandwich and drink, or 300 for a more substantial tuck-in. Many of the locals gather, however, at a strange restaurant which looks to be a disused service station. **Restaurant La Tía** is right on the main square, and offers chicken cooked up several ways for 180 pesos, and the northern specialty of cabrito (roast kid) for half again as much. Tacos, enchiladas, and other Mexican antojito delights can make a filling lunch for only about 135 pesos. La Tía has a machine which makes a noise like an air conditioner but seems somehow to contribute little to lowering the temperature of the air.

Twenty-four miles south the road starts to drop considerably; before Ciudad Mante, 85 miles south of Victoria, it falls 1000 feet. Watch for a place to pull off on the left-hand side of the road, and stop for the magnificent views across a miles-wide canyon with startling rock buttes like those in Colorado. Giant cactus and tropical fruit grow all around this tropical area (you're in the Tropic of Cancer now). Continue for another 56 miles (94 kilometers) and you'll reach Ciudad Valles.

Ciudad Valles

This town, in the state of San Luis Potosí (pop. 24,000), doesn't have much to recommend it in my view, for it's dusty in spring and muddy the rest of the year. But if you're looking for a place to spend the night, there are several hotels on Route 85 in Ciudad Valles. The best is the **Hotel Valles** (tel. 138/2-0050), an elaborate hacienda-style motor hotel garnished with quantities of palm trees and gardens and a splendid 100-foot swimming pool. Rooms are large and comfortably furnished; prices are a little high for its being out in the middle of nowhere—singles run 695 to 995 pesos; doubles, 1200 to 1500 pesos; air conditioning is in only the more expensive rooms. But equivalent accommodations in Mexico City would probably cost twice as much. The Valles also has a thatched cathedral-ceilinged restaurant-bar which is nice to look at but expensive. You can camp here for 325 pesos if you have the necessary equipment.

A few blocks south on Route 85 is the **Hotel Casa Grande**. It's a quiet stucco building built around a cobbled court, busy with conscientious gardeners at work on the flowering plants and trees. Rooms are pretty big, very clean but dark, and the trick is to take one without air conditioning, which can add as much as 250 pesos to the cost of the room. Singles without air conditioning cost 580 pesos; doubles 780 pesos. With air conditioning singles cost 660 to 990 pesos; doubles cost 880 to 1100 pesos. The hotel also has a fine pool with very clear water and a tree growing up through a cement island in the middle. Extensive renovations were carried out as recently as 1980.

The **Restaurant Principal,** a short walk from the aforementioned hotels, is downtown at Avenida Miguel Hidalgo 217. Plain but clean, it's run by an engaging man of Chinese descent who cooks up mostly Mexican food: enchiladas and sandwiches for 60 to 95 pesos, grilled meats for 125 to 200 pesos. Walk down the main drag from the Casa Grande to the Pemex station (on the same side of the street), and turn right—you'll be on Avenida Miguel Hidalgo.

Heading West: Going west to San Luis Potosí? The road is wonderfully scenic, even magnificent, joining 9000-foot highlands to tropics but the 170 miles of road are full of twists and turns and rough-ish pavement, so allow about four hours to drive it unless you plan to push hard. See Chapter V for details of San Luis Potosí and other Silver Cities.

Heading South: For a real treat, make sure to be alert for the stretch of road south of Ciudad Valles. From Valles to Mexico City, you pass about 250 miles of unusually beautiful sights, and the trip should definitely be made in daylight. The hillsides are a patchwork quilt of fields, patterned irregularly with different crops and colors. In late summer and fall, clouds of tiny yellow butterflies fill the road and the sun sets early and plays tricks with your eyes.

Heading East to Tuxpan: You can drive to Tuxpan from Ciudad Valles, taking a pretty but fantastically misshapen roadbed from Tamuin through Tancuayalab to El Higo. Before you get to the Río Tampaon you'll have to leave the paved road and turn left onto a dirt track which goes through a village and then descends to a little rickety toll ferry. No sign marks the turnoff. El Higo has a big sugar mill, and so the road surface between the town and the intersection with Highway 105 is pretty beat-up. Turn left onto Highway 127 after Tempoal, and head for Tuxpan. This interesting trip is full of surprises and bone-jaggles, and takes about 4½ hours. Don't expect deliverance from rough roads when you reach Highway 105, 127, and 180. Most of the mileage all the way to Tuxpan is similar to a minefield after the war.

Pachuca

Pachuca, the last major stop before the capital (alt. 8000 feet; pop. 110,000), is an attractive old town which is swept by cooling breezes. The women selling socks, handkerchiefs, and scarves in the plaza are constantly having to get up to retrieve items of clothing blown into the street by sudden gusts of wind. In the hills around the town, silver has been mined for at least five centuries, and is still produced in large quantities.

It is well worth the effort to climb one of the narrow, precipitous streets up the hillside, from which there is an excellent view not only of the forest of TV aerials, but of the irregular surrounding terrain.

Pachuca has a small, clean **market** through which it is pleasant to stroll. One section appears to specialize in making funeral wreaths with dozens of different white flowers woven into the greenery. There are many **bake shops** with appetizing cookies and pastries on show.

First choice for a room is the **Hotel Noriega,** Calle de Matamoros 305, just a few minutes' stroll from the main plaza. A dazzlingly rich old colonial place, the Noriega boasts lots of gleaming glass, red tiles, and carved wood, but also lays on the modern comforts: all rooms come with radio and TV. Prices are 600 pesos single, 800 pesos double. Expect to see a huge rubber tree in the courtyard.

Very near the Noriega is the old but well-kept **Hotel de los Banos,** Calle de Matamoros 205, two blocks from the main plaza. Here one finds a vast, tiled court for a lobby, guarded by sturdy wooden gates. The central court has several tiers of balconies leading to the rooms, some with elaborately carved Spanish furniture, Oriental rugs, and chandeliers; other rooms have modernish, functional hotel furniture. It's a business-like place, kept quite clean. Rooms come in two price ranges, with doubles for either 650 pesos or 925 pesos.

There is no lack of good restaurants in town; you'll find most either on the plaza or the Calle de Matamoros. The **Restaurant La Fogata,** Calle de Matamoros 203, has a comida corrida which includes soup, entrees, dessert, and beverages for 170 pesos. On the same street, the **Restaurant La Blanca,** Calle de Matamoros 201, offers sandwiches, chicken, steak, and two comidas for 95 and 125 pesos. The **Casino Español,** Calle de Matamoros 207, which is classier and looks rather like a gilded men's room, serves broiled chicken for 185 pesos, and a filet mignon for quite a bit more. Finally, right on the main plaza is the **Restaurant Kiko,** a clean and busy place with sandwiches for 45 to 65 pesos and a comida corrida for 100 pesos.

Chapter III

PACIFIC COAST RESORTS

          1. Mazatlán
         2. San Blas and Tepic
          3. Puerto Vallarta
     4. San Patricio and Barra de Navidad
      5. Manzanillo to Playa Azul
        6. Ixtapa–Zihuatanejo
           7. Acapulco
      8. Puerto Escondido and Puerto Angel

  MEXICO'S PACIFIC COAST is over 2000 miles long. Although the northern reaches of the coast are the western edges of the Sonoran Desert, once you get south of Culiacan the lush tropical climate takes over and provides the perfect milieu for beach resorts.
  Visitors from North America discovered how perfectly this stretch lent itself to sunning and swimming and a general laid-back lifestyle long before their Mexican neighbors did. A half-century ago Acapulco was a sleepy fishing port with only a few renegade *norteamericanos* living on low budgets and doing odd things such as lying on the beach half-naked for hours.
  Since then, things have changed. Although the small fishing ports still exist, you have to forge ever southward to find them. The more northerly ones have come of age as glittering resorts served by jet aircraft and guarded from the sea by towering walls of high-rise luxury hotels. But for all this modernity each resort retains an older downtown section of reasonably priced hotels and restaurants.
  Each of Mexico's fabled Pacific resorts has its own special *ambiente*, which you will discover more readily by traveling on $20 a day than if you zip in by Lear-Jet and stay at El Presidente. Here, then, is this fabulous lineup, starting with the most northerly of the resort cities—Mazatlán—and continuing all the way down to the tiny tropical hideaways of Puerto Escondido and Puerto Angel, in the state of Oaxaca.

1. Mazatlán

  Mazatlán, Sinaloa (pop. 200,000), was once best known as a resort for sportsmen who came to hunt sailfish and marlin, some weighing hundreds of pounds. You can still hire a boat for big-game fishing (at $200-plus per day), or guns and guide for a game expedition to the countryside, but Mazatlán today makes its living from industry and resort hotels. Once almost the exclusive

66 MEXICO ON $20 A DAY

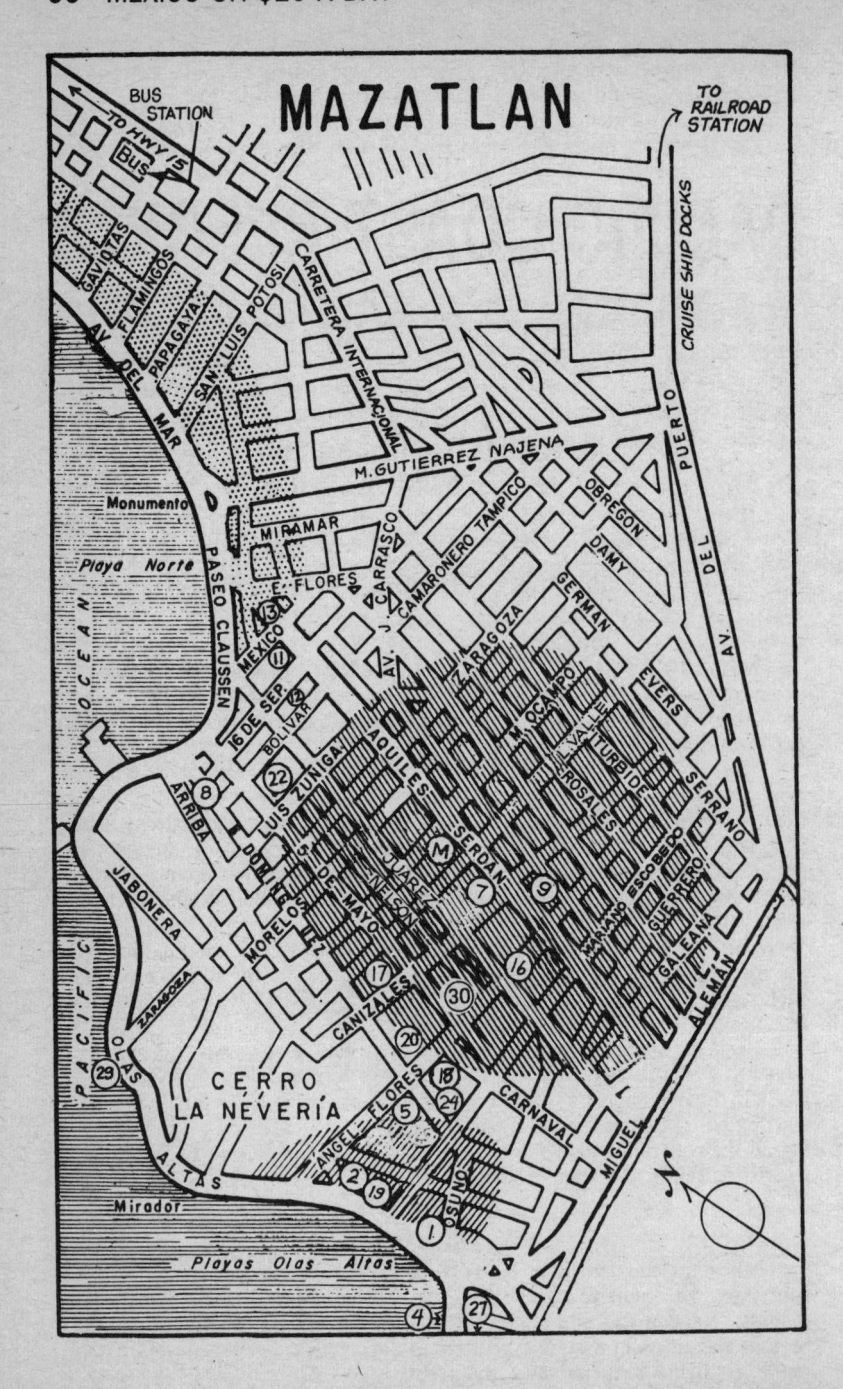

MAZATLÁN

preserve of visitors from California, Mazatlán, with its beaches and resort ambience, has been promoted by the Mexican government into an international attraction. Still, you'll see lots of recreational vehicles with California plates under the palms which shade the local trailer parks.

Travel writers have been kind to Mazatlán, dreaming up such sugary phrases as "jewel of the West," "pearl of the Pacific," and "place of the deer" (this last being a literal translation of the Nahuatl word). The beaches aren't as big and beautiful as Acapulco's, but they are nice enough, especially Sabalo Beach, to the north of the town and accessible by bus from the zócalo. The beach right downtown is good for watching sunsets but not so good for swimming, which might explain why Mazatlán is more popular with souvenir-hunters, window-shoppers, diners-and-dancers than it is with swimmers. In fact, it's good for all these activities.

ORIENTATION: From being just a small port town on a peninsula, Mazatlán has spread northward along the coast for miles. The older part, **downtown,** has several good budget hotel and restaurant choices, and it is also the center of daily life for the townfolk. From the center, a **waterfront drive** heads northward, starting out as Avenida Olas Altas, changing names to Paseo Claussen, Avenida del Mar, Avenida Camaron-Sabalo, and Avenida Sabalo-Cerritos. The bus station (Central Camionera) is about 2½ miles from downtown, but only a few blocks from the waterfront drive and the Hotel Sands.

Four miles north of downtown is a **traffic circle** at Punta Camaron, a restaurant (El Camaron) built on a rocky outcrop over the water, and the Motel Mazatlán. From this point, the resorts continues to spread ever northward. Between the traffic circle and the huge **El Cid** Touristic Complex you'll find the American Express office, rental car offices, a golf course, several trailer parks, and Sabalo Beach, one of Mazatlán's best.

It's another five miles north to **Los Cerritos** (or El Cerrito, the Little Hill[s]), the northern limit of the resort. The northern limits are still under development, and fancy hotels alternate with older trailer parks, vacant lots, the rubble of construction, and a few posh private homes.

Keep in mind, then, that this resort is fully ten miles long, and use the landmarks of downtown, Sabalo traffic circle, El Cid, and Los Cerritos to find your way. Street numbers are of little practical use.

GETTING AROUND: Buses run along the waterfront drive, and since virtually the entire resort is right on the water, they provide easy transport to any point.

Besides taxis, Mazatlán has a moderately priced alternative. Little three-wheel, open-air motorscooters putt and sputter along the waterfront, carrying up to four passengers anywhere for less than taxi fare. Called *pulmonías* (pneumonias), they have a surrey-like top to protect you from the beating sun, but no sides to keep off the cool night breezes. Be sure to haggle for a good price *before* you clamber in the back of the pulmonía.

The downtown transportation center, for buses, taxis, and pulmonías, is the main square with its basilica (look for "Basilica" on bus signboards, if you want to get downtown.)

INFORMATION AND EMERGENCY HELP: The **Federal Tourism Office (29)** (tel. 678/1-4966) is on the waterfront drive, Olas Altas, open from 9 a.m. to 2 p.m. and 4 to 7 p.m. daily except Sunday.

68 MEXICO ON $20 A DAY

The **Municipal Tourism Office (30)** (tel. 678/2-2111) is in the Palacio Municipal on Angel Flores, downtown, one block from the main plaza.

The **post office** (Correos) is on the east side of the main plaza, on Calle Juarez just off Angel Flores.

There's an **American Consulate** (tel. 678/1-2685) in town, on Carranza near the Hotel La Siesta.

Mazatlán's central **market (M)** is located in the block between Aquiles Serdan and Juarez, and Ocampo and Leandro Valle.

By the way, if you arrive in Mazatlán in the week before Lent, carnival will be in full swing. It's barrels of fun—so long as you already have a room reservation locked up tight. Beware: pressure on rooms, and their prices, is intense at this time.

HOTELS IN MAZATLÁN: The hotels in Mazatlán are of two types, generally speaking: those downtown, which are older, cheaper, and some of which are suitable; and those along the beachfront heading north, most of which are new, flashy, and expensive, though others fit our budget nicely. These latter extend in an almost unbroken row for miles and miles. The hotels downtown are in two areas, the Downtown Seafront and the Midtown areas.

Hotels—Downtown Seafront

The **Hotel Belmar (1)**, Olas Altas Boulevard 166 (tel. 678/1-4299), is right on the waterfront drive, and is actually two hotels in one. A recent addition of air-conditioned deluxe rooms is out of our budget range, but the older rooms, which the management refers to rather grandly as the "colonial section," are within our range: singles are 582 pesos and doubles are 695 pesos, without air conditioning but with bath. The hotel is very pleasant, built around a central court and entered through huge wooden gates. A new pool, tennis court, and lots of tiles, color, and colonial effect make it a pleasant place to stay—try here first.

The next block north houses the huge, squat, cement **Hotel La Siesta (2)**, Olas Altas Boulevard 11 (tel. 678/1-2640), one of the most attractive hotels in the area. Tasteful and well-appointed rooms open onto a lush central palm court lined with green balconies. The court, which is long and narrow, sports both a jungle of colorful umbrellas and the restaurant El Shrimp Bucket, which I'll mention later. Singles run from 650 pesos, doubles from 875 pesos. All rooms are air-conditioned and telephone equipped.

Continuing along the coastline and a few blocks up the hill brings you to the 30-room **Hotel Olas Altas (4)** (tel. 678/1-3192), Calle Centenario 14. The upstairs lobby, with white wicker chairs and an airy balcony overlooking the ocean, is a cool delight. The rooms are a bit worn and have no air conditioning, but the hotel's prices sell the rooms. Singles are 338 to 408 pesos; doubles, 455 to 540 pesos. High-priced rooms have an ocean view, and perhaps two double beds; extra persons pay 150 pesos, and there's a 10% discount for weekly stays.

Hotels—Midtown

The largest shaded area on our map comprises the center of the town and its southern limits (as far as hotels are concerned). This area includes the commercial hub of the town with bustling streets, countless shops, chronic parking problems, and continued activity, music and shouting, seasoned with exotic aromas that waft into the streets from a hundred little Mexican restaurants.

Try the **Hotel Central (5)** (tel. 678/2-1888), three very long blocks from the ocean at B. Dominguez Sur 2, near the corner of Calle A. Flores. The prices are a bit steep, but such is fate in a resort town, and the rooms are all very nice, with good beds, air conditioning, and phone: singles are 475 pesos; doubles with two doubles beds, 640 pesos. The upstairs lobby shares space with a small café.

Nearby is the **Hotel Milan (7)** (tel. 678/1-3588), Canizales Pte. 717, corner of Flores. Rooms here aren't quite as good, tend to be dark, but are adequate and each has a private bath. Downstairs there's a lunch counter in the lobby and an amiable staff with a *mañana* outlook on life.

There are two more places which are in a location roughly between the Midtown area and the Northern Beach area. The first is **Joncol's Hotel (8)**, Belisario Dominguez Nte. 2701 (tel. 678/1-2431), a big (36-room) modern multiwindowed place about a block from the ocean. Rooms are quite adequate: large, clean, all with private balconies and sea view, and well-appointed furnishings. Rates are not bad—480 pesos single, 545 pesos double, plus 100 pesos for air conditioning—but Joncol's is highly recommended mainly because of its consistent performance.

In spite of its beachy name, the 22-room **Hotel Villa del Mar (9)**, Aquiles Serdan Nte. 1506, near the corner of 31 de Mayo (tel. 678/1-3426), is about as dead center in town as you can get. But motorists will be pleased to know that they have parking space for seven cars. Nor will lobby sitters be disappointed; they go in for rocking chairs here and cursory inspection revealed no fewer than six of these comfortable accessories. Rooms are adequate, and all have ceiling fans and hot water. Singles are 410 pesos, doubles are 560 pesos, with a 20% discount if you stay longer than three days. Be sure to ask for it.

There are quite a few small, acceptable, less-than-top-notch hotels in the midtown area. Generally speaking, each shares a typical description: small but clean rooms, lazy ceiling fans, and intermittent service.

The **Hotel Beltran (11)** (tel. 678/2-2776), A. Serdan Nte. 2509, is the cheapest of these with singles at 350 pesos, doubles at 480 pesos. Enter the Beltran through the archway and choose a room from among the 28 along the long open patio.

Next in price is the **Hotel Santa Barbara (12)** (tel. 678/2-2120), on the corner of Juarez and 16 de Septiembre. The homey lobby with a piano on one side and a group of avid television viewers on the other is perhaps a more comfortable place to sit than in the tiny rooms. Singles here are 350 pesos; doubles 485 pesos.

One block from the ocean on A. Serdan at 2710 Nte. is the **Hotel San Jorge (13)** (tel. 678/1-3695). The only real problem here is the private bath arrangement—it is possible (just about) to use all of the bathroom facilities at once, the room is so small. Rooms are tidy, but the ones on the street may be noisy. Singles are 285 pesos and doubles run 395 pesos. The "Sabalo" to the beach goes by on the next block.

Hotels—Northern Beach

Finally, there's the Northern Beach area, an elegant arc of golden sand serviced by a palm-lined, dual-lane boulevard and bordered by flashy hotels and a sprinkling of elaborate beach houses complete with high walls and watchdogs. In winter this is Mazatlán's reason for existence, and charter flights fill the big hotels with eager sun-seekers from colder climates. Prices, in winter, are high with little compromise. In summer and in the neither-here-nor-there months of May and September, some of the more modest hotels along this beach cut their prices, usually advertising the fact boldly by a signboard on the sidewalk—customers before pride.

Here's the rundown of the affordable places, starting from downtown and heading north. Street numbers are little help in finding a place, so I'll mention landmarks and prominent establishments so you can spot your chosen hotel as you whiz along the waterfront.

The **Hotel Aqua Marina** (tel. 678/1-7080 or 1-3748) is at Avenida del Mar 110 (Apdo. Postal 301); and you'll recognize it as a two-story motel-type structure with a parking lot, palm trees, and little pool in front. The beach is right across the street, and if you get a room on the preferable second floor of the motel, you'll be able to sit out on a little private terrace and enjoy the view. Prices for the 50 air-conditioned rooms are 880 pesos single, 1125 pesos double. The Aqua Marina has a restaurant and bar.

Not far along is the **Hotel Cabinas al Mar** (tel. 678/1-5752), Avenida del Mar 123 (Apdo. Postal 444), a little five-story building with a thatched palapa on top, a good place from which to watch the sunsets. Rooms on the front have little balconies, sea views, and higher price tags. Other rooms come in a variety of sizes and shapes, tend to be darker, but quieter and cheaper. Several rooms have one double bed and two singles, perfect for a family. Basic prices are 495 pesos single, 685 pesos double.

The **Hotel Sands** (tel. 678/2-0000 or 2-0600) is right between the bus station and the beach, and right next door to Señor Frog's restaurant (see below) and an outlet for Kentucky Fried Chicken. With three stories, balconies with a sea view, air conditioning, a pool, and private baths, it's an excellent choice in all regards. The prices aren't bad, either: 630 pesos single, 800 pesos double, 900 pesos triple.

The **Motel del Sol** (tel. 678/1-4712) is a modernistic brown place with shuttered windows. It looks small from the street, but actually extends a way back, sheltering a warren of various rooms, most of which are modern, small, and nice. Many have kitchenettes; all have air conditioning, private baths, and use of the swimming pool and restaurant. The last time I visited I was quoted a price of 660 pesos, single or double. By the way, there's a Pizza Hut just past the Motel del Sol.

For a bit of a splurge, you can stay in the imposing 100-room **Posada de Don Pelayo** (tel. 678/3-1977), Avenida del Mar 1111 (Apdo. Postal 1088), a few blocks south of the traffic circle. Every room has a king-size bed or two double beds, a telephone, private bath, and air conditioning, and those on the front have sea views. The price for two, three, or four people is the same: 1050 pesos. There's a swimming pool here, too.

The budget choice in the area is on the traffic circle about four miles along the waterfront drive toward Sabalo Beach. It's the **Motel Mazatlán** (tel. 678/3-5703), mailing address Apdo. Postal 295. Take a "Sabalo" bus from the zócalo, midtown at the cathedral, and get off at the circle where you'll see the motel on your right. The ten rooms are clean, comfortable, and feature exposed stone walls in the rooms. You can park for free under the palms in front. Rates for the ground-floor are 425 pesos single, 425 to 575 pesos double (with two double beds), and that includes a ceiling fan. You can walk to beach areas from here, and although you'll still have to take the bus to get to Sabalo, you have only half as far to go as if you'd stayed downtown.

Hotels—Near the Bus Station

If you've just arrived by bus, the aforementioned **Hotel Sands** is the one you want to look at first. It's only one (long) block from the Central Camionera.

EATING IN MAZATLÁN: Sad to say, prices for seafood in this seaside town have kept up with the rise of seafood prices the world over. As in most Mexican towns, Mexican plates (enchiladas, burritos, tacos, etc.) are your best bargain, but those are available anywhere. I'll give you some hints on where to find the most reasonably priced fish dishes.

The **Restaurant Mamucas (22)** (tel. 1-3490), Simon Bolívar Pte. 404, is 1½ short blocks from Joncol's Hotel. Behind a modest entrance is a big, interesting dining room, with the kitchen to one side. White-clad señoras cook away, waiters scurry here and there, and a mariachi band trumpets above the clatter of dishes and silverware. The specialty here is seafood, good and fresh, at moderate prices, and the restaurant keeps busy from 10 a.m. to 10 p.m. every day serving it up. Have a feast beginning with shrimp cocktail or oysters, then grilled fish, coffee, and dessert, and you'll pay about 400 pesos. With beer or wine (bottles reasonably priced), it may be a bit more.

Next choice is **Restaurant Doney (17)**, at the corner of Canizales (no. 408) and 5 de Mayo, a bit higher in price, but then you can enjoy the cool comfort of air conditioning. They have an extensive menu at Doney with delicious enchiladas suizas for 75 pesos, guacamole for 45 pesos, a Mazatlán home-style stew for 105 pesos. The comida corrida is 150 pesos Monday through Saturday, a bit more on Sunday, and is a delectable meal centered on an expensive entree such as shrimp, ham, or fish. Menu in English.

Another air-conditioned restaurant, which is one of the older establishments with a tried-and-true clientele, is **Joncol's (18)**, located two blocks inland on Angel Flores at no. 608. They have a comida for 125 pesos, three courses and good. Meat and fish entrees range from 95 to 145 pesos. They are open for breakfast, and if you want an afternoon *refresca,* stop here for ice cream (28 pesos). *Note:* There have been a few complaints about the service.

The **Madrid (19)**, Olas Altas Boulevard 25, is a Spanish restaurant, with stucco walls and arches. A few outdoor tables overlook the Malecon and the ocean. This restaurant is in the older section of town. Bullfight posters decorate the walls, ceiling fans keep the air moving, and waiters will bring you, say, a nice fruit salad and a garnished platter of fried fish, plus a soft drink, for 225 pesos. The Madrid is one in a row of restaurants.

Another in the row is the **Restaurant Fito's (19)**, Olas Altas 166D, to the right of the Restaurant Madrid. Smaller and less fancy, with only two rows of tables plus a few out on the sidewalk, Fito's is ruled by a señora busy in the kitchen. Prices are similar to those at the Madrid, but Fito's also offers an afternoon comida corrida of soup, fish, dessert, and coffee for 115 pesos. The clients are mostly Mexican families, who know a bargain when they see one.

On North Beach

North Beach is crowded with eateries, everything from elegant places specializing in shrimp to Pizza Hut and Colonel Sanders'. You'll do better for seafood downtown, where the local people go.

A block from the Hotel Sands, and thus near the bus station as well, is **Los Norteños.** A shaded patio overlooks the street, and a glassed-in, air-conditioned dining room is behind that. It's not fancy, but serves good food at good prices: a varied plate of Mexican delicacies, or a fried filet of fish, for 200 pesos or so. They feature exotic repasts as well, like cabrito al pastor (roast kid), partridge, and lobster, for a good deal more. You can spend over 750 pesos if you go exotic, less than half that if you don't.

You'll spot **La Parrillada** on the Avenida del Mar (no. 1004) because it's a small corner place with a square, tile-roofed grill-cum-kitchen surrounded by high stools. A dozen little umbrella-shaded tables surround the grill area. The specialty here is grilled meat, served in soft tacos. Order bistek (steak) or chuletas (chop) tacos, some frijoles, and a beer; or perhaps quesadillas (melted cheese in a grilled, folded tortilla) or sinchronizadas (cheese-and-meat tacos). You can eat well here for less than 150 pesos.

Splurge and Specialty Restaurants

Now for a few places that will cater to your need, every now and then, for a nicer dinner in a nicer place.

Everyone has a good time at Señor Frog's (tel. 1-4367), next to the Hotel Sands. A sign over the door says "Just Another Bar & Grill," but the line waiting to get in says just the opposite. It's a Carlos Anderson restaurant of course, and one cannot help but wonder where he got all those little panes of beveled glass for the front windows. The decor is similarly interesting, original, and expensive; the food and music are great, the company is upbeat and cheerful. The price is not low, but it's good for what you get. Seafood, meat, whatever—expect to pay something like 750 pesos per person for dinner, somewhat less for lunch. Open till midnight.

Casa de Bruno Restaurant is another great place to dine. The ambience of this stucco and brick establishment is created by the friendly staff, wandering minstrels, and lively clientele, whether you choose to sit indoors or outside. Lobster is guaranteed to be fresh. Shrimp entrees are priced from 375 to 425 pesos and fish is 200 to 295 pesos. Specialties are the barbecue dishes, priced in between. In addition, Mexican dishes are available, including a fabulous combination plate for 245 pesos. If Bruno, the owner, is around (you'll know him by the apron bearing his name), ask him to mix up his special concoction called "Bruno's Kiss for the Ladies"—I leave you to take care of it after that. Bruno's is open from noon to 1 a.m. at the intersection of Sabalo and Loaiza.

For the real bullfight aficionado, El Camaron is the place to eat. The indoor dining room is the traditional rendezvous of matadores and aficionados after the bullfights. The dining area is actually a display of hundreds of items of bullfight memorabilia. Oceanside dining is the real treat, and you are liable to have a beautiful view of the beach from your table. Food is excellent, in the range of, say, 375 pesos for shrimp—figure 750 pesos for the full dinner. El Camaron is also a good place just for a drink. It's across from the Motel Mazatlán on the Avenida del Mar at the traffic circle.

Starvation Budget

If you're really low on bucks, try one of Mazatlán's most popular downtown taco houses, La Chiripa (24), located on the corner of Dominguez and Escobedo. Guests enter this restored colonial mansion through wrought-iron gates to have plates of traditional food for about 85 pesos, complete. The bean soup is justly famous. La Chiripa is open only in the evenings, from 7 p.m. to 3 a.m.

Los Comales (16), Angel Flores 908 right downtown, is an odd old place with high ceilings, funky down-home decor, and local cooking that couldn't be called fancy but could be called good. The daily comida corrida goes for just 110 pesos, and a plate of enchiladas is only half that reasonable price. They serve a decent fish soup. Order Pacifico, the local beer, and you'll save a few pesos over national brands. Open most of the time.

An alternative to restaurant-eating is to stop at one of the many *loncherías* scattered throughout downtown Mazatlán. Here, one can purchase a torta (sandwich) for about 35 pesos. Tortas come stuffed with a variety of meats, cheese, chilis, tomatoes, onions, etc.

WHAT TO DO IN MAZATLÁN: Mazatlán is a beach resort so most of the entertainment is along these lines. Herewith, a rundown of the beaches.

The Beaches

Right downtown is the rocky, pebbly **Playa Olas Altas,** not the best for swimming when the northern beaches are so much better. Around a rocky promontory to the north of Olas Altas is **Playa Norte,** several miles of good sand beach.

At the traffic circle, a point (Punta Camaron) juts into the water, and on either side of the point is **Playa Las Gaviotas. Playa Sabalo** is yet farther north, and is perhaps the very best of all. The next point jutting into the water is Punta Sabalo, past which is a bridge over the channel which flows in and out of the lagoon. North of the bridge, even more beach, all the way to Los Cerritos. Enjoy! And remember that *all* beaches in Mexico are public property, so feel free to wander where you like.

Cruises and Rentals

The **Fiesta Yacht Cruise (27)** runs a large double-deck boat every morning at 10:30 a.m., leaving from the south beach near the lighthouse. You can purchase your tickets from any of the big hotels. The cruise is three hours around the harbor and bay; they have bilingual guides to explain the marine activity as well as a musical group to entertain. They stop for a short swim at one of the small islands so be sure to bring your suit.

You can **rent a fishing boat (27)** on the south side of town, at the base of the 515-foot hill which supports the lighthouse. Rates range from $200 and up a day for deep-sea cruises including all equipment. A fishing license is necessary; you can write to Unifleet, P.O. Box 1035, Mazatlán, Sinaloa, México, or call 678/1-5121 for information. There are also places that rent skindiving and waterskiing equipment, but the prices vary from shop to shop so be sure to check around for the lowest offer (bargaining may be necessary).

If you want to **rent bicycles, motor scooters, sailboats,** or take a flying leap over the Pacific on a **parachute,** go to the Hotel Playa Mazatlán, four miles north of downtown, past the traffic circle.

Arrangements for city tours, or tours to any part of Mexico, can be made at the front desk of any major hotel.

A good place to go for primitive camping, unspoiled beaches, and pleasant picnics, is the **Isla de la Piedra (27).** From the center of town, board a *circunvalación* bus from the north side of the zócalo for the ride to the boat landing. Talk to the pilot of a small launch for the trip to the island. Take whatever you'll need on the island as there are no services at all.

Other Things to Do

There is a bullring in town where they have scheduled bullfights every Sunday, but *only* in the winter. The rest of the year, the ring is used for rodeos, an equally interesting spectacle.

Looking for a disco? Those out for dining-and-dancing need only take a stroll along the northern beach to run into the city's assorted discos, all fun, new, loud, and relatively expensive: **Elephant, La Jirafa, Ney's,** are only a few.

The **Arts and Crafts Center,** north of the traffic circle at Punta Camaron, is a modern bazaar with numerous artists' stalls. They sell all types of crafts from all over Mexico. Open daily from 9 a.m. to 6 p.m.

Activities for Children

Mazatlán has two outstanding attractions for children. Besides the beaches, children interested in the sea will love the **Acuario Mazatlán** (the aquarium), a brand-new government-run building one block of Avenida del Mar (look for the turn near the Motel del Sol and the Pizza Hut). Open 10 a.m. to 6 p.m. Tuesday through Sunday, closed Monday, the admission charge is 50 pesos for adults, half price for kids aged 3 to 14.

Still in the realm of the aquatic, Mazatlán has a water slide called **Aqua Sport,** north of El Cid and just before the Holiday Inn, on the waterfront drive. You'll see a low hill, and lots of kids milling about on top, carrying plastic mats. They'll plop down their mats in the chute and come slushing down into the three-foot-deep pool at the base. Here's how it works: you pay 100 pesos for a 30- or 40-minute period, and your child receives a mat of a certain color. The color identifies the period, so the kid shouldn't swap mats with anyone. Shady chairs and a refreshments stand cater to waiting parents while the kids glide down from the hilltop, past bushes and around boulders, to the little pool. Aqua Sport is open daily from 10 a.m. to 8 p.m.

GETTING TO AND FROM MAZATLÁN: Almost any land transport coming down the Pacific coast goes by Mazatlán, and there are many direct flights from various Mexican cities and from several in the United States.

By Bus

Transportes del Norte, Tres Estrellas de Oro, Autobuses Estrella Blanca, Transportes Norte de Senora, Transportes del Pacifico—all these major lines have service to and from Mazatlán; most of them touch here on their way to and from the U.S.–Mexico border at Nogales or Mexicali. All these lines have onward service from Mazatlán to Guadalajara and Mexico City as well. Reserve in advance and you'll have no trouble finding space.

By Train

Ferrocarriles del Pacifico runs two trains a day through Mazatlán on the Nogales–Guadalajara run (see map for station location). Trains arrive from Nogales at 4 a.m. and 8:25 a.m., leaving for Guadalajara at 4:30 a.m. and 8:35 a.m. The trip to Guadalajara takes 13½ hours on the earlier train, 11 hours on the later one (named *El Costeno*). Trains heading north to Nogales and Mexicali depart from Mazatlán at 1 a.m. (the slower) and 6:05 p.m. (the faster, *El Costeno*). Remember when figuring schedules that there's a time zone change between Mazatlán and Guadalajara. For information (and to check these changeable times) call 678/1-2036.

By Air

From Mazatlán there are three or four flights a day to Mexico City, three a week to Ciudad Júarez (El Paso), and daily flights to Monterrey and Guadalajara, all run by AeroMéxico and Mexicana airlines. Hughes Air West runs two flights a day each from San Francisco and Los Angeles. You can take advantage of an excursion fare if you fly from San Francisco. For reservations and information in Mazatlán, call these numbers: AeroMéxico, 1-3096; Mexicana, 1-3414.

By Ferryboat

There is a ferry (27) which connects Mazatlán with La Paz, Baja California Sur, leaving at about 5 or 6 p.m. daily except Sunday; for more information, call 678/1-7020. A seat in the salon with the peasants for the 16-hour voyage costs 150 pesos, while a private cabin will be about 600 pesos. Prices to ship a car start at 900 pesos.

2. San Blas and Tepic

The road from the highway to the coast at San Blas, Nayarit (pop. 35,000), is better than you'd expect. It takes about one hour to drive and winds through ever-lusher tropical country, finally emerging into the sleepy town on the Pacific. Although there are better hotels in Tepic, our advice would be to stay here overnight as San Blas is more interesting. In fact, if you can manage to get here by noon, it makes a delightful break to rest on the beach, drink coconut milk and have a plate of fish at one of the beach shacks that pass for restaurants.

Many of the Pacific beach towns have been pretty well developed and consequently the prices for food and accommodations are high. San Blas is the exception. You will still find the tourists but thus far the developers have not taken over, so you'll be able to find hotels and restaurants at very reasonable prices. By the way, San Blas is famous for its biting gnats. The government sprays periodically which seems to help a bit, but bug repellent is necessary.

Note: The peak season for San Blas, as well as for the other Pacific Coast resorts, is Christmas, from mid-December through February, and Easter, end of March through April. Advance reservations are recommended. Off-season, the hotel rates are quite flexible so you can almost always bargain for a cheaper rate.

SAN BLAS ORIENTATION: As you rumble into the village of San Blas, you'll come to the main square. At the far end is the old church, and a new one abuilding next to it. Next to this is the town's bus station.

The main street into and through town is Avenida Juarez. After passing the square on your right, the first street to the left is Calle Battalion, an important thoroughfare which passes a bakery, the Estrella de Oro bus ticket office, the tourism office, a medical clinic; farther on, the street passes several hotels and trailer parks before coming to the beach.

WHERE TO STAY IN SAN BLAS: San Blas's selection of hotels is not a particularly good one. The tropical heat and relative lack of customers during the summer months encourage owners to sit back and "let things go" at the hotel, although this condition is somewhat alleviated in winter. If the list presented below seems to be too inclusive, it's only because I don't want you to get to San Blas and have no place to stay. The town is attractive. Soon, let's hope more of the hotels will be, too.

Hotels

San Blas's newest and tidiest hostelry is the **Motel Posada del Rey** (tel. 321/5-0123), Calle Campeche 10. A few blocks from the main square, the Posada has a dozen rooms arranged around a tiny courtyard taken up entirely by a nice little swimming pool. Rooms have private baths and ceiling fans, and rent for 440 pesos single, 580 pesos double. Nice!

The **Posada Casa Morales** (tel. 321/5-0023), on the beach and walking distance from town, is one of the newer hotels in San Blas. To get there, walk or drive to the end of Juarez, past the old Flamingo Hotel, and turn left. Follow this unpaved road for about three blocks and look for a sign pointing off to the right to the Casa Morales. The complex of bungalows, pool, and garden is on the ocean; some rooms have an ocean view, others look onto the pool and garden. All rates *include* breakfast and dinner during the winter season: singles are 880 pesos; doubles, 1100 to 1250 pesos. Summer rates are without meals: singles are 660 pesos; doubles, 880 pesos. Parking is included.

Across the street from the Casa Morales is the equally nice **Motel Las Brisas,** (tel. 321/5-0112), also with a garden and pool, and 36 new units, but here the rates are even higher than at the Casa Morales. The rooms, with table fans, are modern, bright and airy. Parking is available next to the rooms. They also have a small garden restaurant where you can get breakfast.

Apartments

San Blas is not a big enough town in which to find "apartments"—most of the villagers still live in houses made of sticks. But there are two of the establishments here which Mexicans call "suites," what I'd call housekeeping rooms, efficiencies, or self-catering flats.

The **Suites San Blas** (tel. 321/5-0047), Apdo. Postal 12, is a big new building off Calle Battalion, with "suites" renting for 990 pesos single, 1225 pesos double. Each suite has a ceiling fan, kitchenette, and private bath. In addition, the complex has a swimming pool, disco, and dining room.

The **Bungalows El Alteño** (tel. 321/5-0065), on Battalion next to the restaurant of the same name and in front of the Suites San Blas, offer very plain rental accommodations in the beachcomber class at a beachcomber's price: 525 pesos for a room for two, plus use of the kitchen.

Camping

Should you have camping gear, you'll want to know that San Blas has two trailer parks: **Los Cocos,** on Battalion near the beach, and **El Dorado,** across the street from El Alteño. Los Cocos has a wonderful luxury: an automatic laundry which advertises "Wash and dry in two hours!"

EATING IN SAN BLAS: Eating is not only good but cheap in San Blas. There are quite a number of newer restaurants but I will stick by my favorites. The two best budget restaurants in town are on Juarez, just off the plaza. You can't go wrong at either one, and in fact the fare and prices seem just about the same; perhaps the **McDonald's** is a bit cheaper. McDonalds is open every day and features delicious fried fish for 110 pesos, a fruit cocktail plate for 65 pesos, shrimp cocktail and most meat items in the 125-peso area. All meals come with fresh hot tortillas. Just down the street, on the same side, is the **Diligencias,** open 8 a.m. to 11 p.m. daily, closed Monday. They have a full breakfast for 90 pesos. The dinners are excellent: huge portions of fish and meat (125 to 175 pesos) served with frijoles and hot toasted rolls with butter.

One block down the street extending from the southeast corner of the main plaza (parallel to Battalion), the restaurant **La Isla** provides pleasurable dining outdoors. The hanging shark jawbones and fish nets set the mood for their excellent shrimp, oysters, lobster, and fish. You'll pay 250 pesos for a good dinner here. All eight tables extend from the kitchen in back where the owners diligently prepare the food.

For a light snack, homemade bread, granola, yogurt, and honey are on sale at **La Tumba de Yako**, two blocks from La Isla on Battalion. While munching, browse the store which features a variety of Mexican and Guatemalan artwork. They sell yogurt-to-go before 3:30 p.m. each day at the Tumba; the vegetarian restaurant opens at 3:30, and stays open until about 10 p.m. each evening.

For those on a starvation budget I can recommend the little shacks on the beach which serve fresh grilled fish. A fairly large fish with hot tortillas and a coco to drink will cost only 110 pesos. I have eaten at several of these little places and found them satisfactory. The best seem to be those shacks a bit off the beach, on the road leading into town. From town, take the street south from the zócalo; about half a mile down you'll smell grilling fish.

WHAT TO DO: There is nothing to do here but relax, swim, read, walk the beach, and eat fish. But such an existence! I love this little town for just these reasons. The best **beaches** are those about one mile from town; driving or walking (there's also a town bus that runs down morning and evening), take Calle Battalion from the main plaza. The road west, along Juarez, will also take you to the Pacific, but the beaches are not as nice here.

For those hunting a secluded place to swim I have a suggestion: rent a canoe and head out to the island. Beach your craft, walk to the other side, and there you are . . . *maybe* all by yourself. It's worth a try. No trees, so bring your own shade.

Almost the moment you hit San Blas, you'll be approached by a "guide" who offers "a boat ride into the jungle." This can be exciting, but it can be expensive as well, depending on how many people you're able to get together to share expenses. The rates are controlled by the Tourism Office now, and are set at about 500 pesos for a three-hour trip, this being the *price for the boatload* of one to four persons (a fifth person pays an extra 100 pesos). The guide will offer to take you to "The Plantation" during your voyage; this will cost another 100 pesos, and, in my opinion, is not worth it. Try to depart as early as possible because the first boat on the river in the morning encounters the most wildlife.

The boat winds through the beautiful freshwater jungle maze, arriving finally at a spring which is San Blas's water supply. Swimming is permitted here, so you should have your suit along—the water is luxurious and refreshing. Although I can't recommend the restaurant at the spring, I'll permit you to buy a soft drink or beer there.

The Beach at Mantachen

Three miles from the square in San Blas is Mantachen. Head out Avenida Juarez as though you were returning to the main highway, and turn right, following the signs to Mantachen. There's a little settlement here where you can have a snack or a meal, rent a boat for the jungle river cruise, etc. A half mile past the settlement is a dirt road to Las Islitas, which has a magnificent swath of sand beach. Beach-shack eateries provide sustenance, Mexican families on vacation are your company, and the beach is yours for miles and miles. Sometimes there's even transport out here from the square in San Blas.

Port of San Blas

Why San Blas? What determined that this small village should have a collection of good hotels? The fact is that San Blas was a very important port,

78 MEXICO ON $20 A DAY

like Acapulco, for New Spain's trade with the Philippines. Pirates would attempt to intercept the rich Spanish galleons headed for San Blas, and so the town had to be fortified. Ruins of the fortifications, of the old Spanish customs house, and of various foreign consulates are still visible down at the beach end of Avenida Juarez. Take a stroll down and have a look.

GETTING TO AND FROM SAN BLAS: Transportes del Noroeste de Nayarit has four buses a day between San Blas and Tepic, two a day to Guadalajara and back (morning and evening).

ON TO TEPIC: The country from San Blas to Tepic, capital of the small state of Nayarit, is lush and tropical, with many banana plantations and coconut palms. Heavy, warm rain falls almost every day in the summer.

Orientation

Highway 15, the main coastal highway, passes through Tepic as Avenida Insurgentes, but it skirts the edge of town. Motels and restaurants aimed at the tourist trade are lined up along the highway, but the real budget choices are in the center of town, about eight or nine blocks off Highway 15 / Avenida Insurgentes.

Follow the signs into the center of town and you'll pass two large squares. The first one has an impressively gaudy Palacio de Gogierno (state government building) at one end. The second one, the main square, has a hemicycle of columns at its center and a huge Gothic church at one end. One doesn't see many Gothic churches in Mexico, with all that churrigueresque stuff around.

My hotel and restaurant choices are grouped around the second, or main square, within sight of the Gothic church.

Where to Stay and Eat

Top marks for budget hotel finds I encountered on my latest visit go to the 39-room **Hotel San Jorge**, Lerdo Pte. 124 (tel. 321/2-1324). Gleaming and spotless, it offers maximum comfort for the very modest tab of 450 pesos single, 610 pesos double. There I enjoyed a palatial twin-bedded room for a fraction of what I'd have paid in Mexico City. Location is also good, 1½ blocks west of the main square. Highly recommended.

Another good hotel is the **Hotel Sierra de Alica** (tel. 321/2-0322 or 2-0324), Avenida México Norte 170, half a block south of the Gothic church and the main square. It's an older place, centrally located, big with lots of space in corridors and rooms. Plumbing fixtures are old, too, and one gets a shower, not a tub, but all is fairly well kept. Prices are 595 pesos single, 795 pesos double.

On the square itself, the **Hotel Fray Junipero** may draw your eye. A double here costs a cool 1300 pesos.

As for dining, most of the town's decent restaurants are out on the main highway in order to catch the transient crowd. Downtown you can try **Wendy's Cafeteria**, right next to the Hotel Sierra de Alica at Avenida México Nte. 170. Open virtually all the time, Wendy's has Formica tables, ceiling fans, pictures of Peter Pan characters on the walls, and a portrait of Wendy (Disney style) over the short cafeteria line. Have a big breakfast of ham and eggs, a muffin, milk, and coffee; or a lunch of enchiladas, frijoles, and soft drink; or a sandwich or burger and salad, and the bill in any case will be less than 100 pesos.

A popular and established local restaurant is **La Terraza,** Highway 15 / Avenida Insurgentes Pte. 98 (tel. 2-2521). As unpretentious as you could imagine, it looks like nothing more than a good Stateside diner on a well-traveled highway. Also furnishing an American touch is a rack filled with the latest U.S. magazines. Fare is cheap and nourishing, with four tamales and beverage for 100 pesos, and the costliest dish, filet mignon, at 300 pesos. Try one of the excellent pies—I prefer the lemon—or cakes. Ice cream addicts will like the banana split; in fact, I'll wager nonaddicts will like it too.

I do it only as a prescription against homesickness, but here it is: Tepic has a branch of the **Kentucky Fried Chicken** chain on the main highway. (If you compare prices, you'll find this rather expensive.)

3. Puerto Vallarta

Of all the Pacific seacoast resorts in Mexico, this is my favorite. The beaches are not as magnificent as those at Acapulco, not everybody speaks English as at Mazatlán, and it's not "unspoiled" as are Puerto Escondido and Puerto Angel. But Puerto Vallarta is gorgeous, with its tropical mountains tumbling right into the sea, its coves and beaches, and its Mexican town. Yes! Unlike Acapulco and Mazatlán, where the town has withered as the resort has grown, Puerto Vallarta's development—mostly on the outskirts of the original town—has lent prosperity without robbing charm.

Puerto Vallarta, Jalisco (pop. 90,000), started out as a little primitive settlement on the Bay of Banderas, far from roads, airports, electricity, prosperity, and tourism. With the making of *Night of the Iguana,* Puerto Vallarta ceased to be a well-kept secret. Elizabeth Taylor returned to the place where the movie had been shot. With the passing years and Mexico's economic development came a good highway, a jetport, prosperity, and renown.

Today, Nuevo Vallarta is the focus of charter tour activity. It's a planned resort development to the north of the old town, with golf links, high-rise hotels, yacht marina, airport, cruise ship wharf, a convention center, and all the other accoutrements of a touristic megadevelopment. But, luckily for you, the old town has remained a charming place, spanning the Río Cuale, nestled into the emerald hills. If anything, the wealth brought by the tourist boom has helped to spruce up old Puerto Vallarta and make it even more attractive.

ORIENTATION: Once in the town, everything is within walking distance. The main promenade, the **Malecon,** follows the rim of the bay from north to south, and the town stretches back into the hills for no father than about four or five blocks. Coming in from the airport, north of town, you'll pass the Holiday Inn and the Sheraton; in the town the Malecon is lined with more hotels. The area north of the Río Cuale is the older part of town—the original Puerto Vallarta, you might say. South of the Río Cuale used to be only beach, but in the last decade it has gotten as built up as the old town. Today, the best budget lodgings are to be found south of the river and inland. The several bus stations are here as well. No doubt the bus stations will all be moved to a unified terminal, a "Central Camionera" on the outskirts when Puerto Vallarta finally gets its long-awaited "Libramiento," or bypass. This will take coastal Highway 200 around behind the town, rather than right through the center of it.

Tourism Information

The **Tourism Office (16)** is at the corner of Libertad and Morelos (tel. 322/2-2555). It's near the prominent Hotel Río.

WHERE TO STAY: To facilitate your search for a suitable hotel room, I'll divide the town into areas, and start with the one boasting the best lodging bargains. When you arrive in Puerto Vallarta, you may descend from your bus in the perfect locale for finding a clean, cheery, inexpensive room.

South of the Río Cuale

The corner of Madero and Insurgentes is the center of Puerto Vallarta's bus activity, and this means that some clean, decent hotels will be nearby. The buses aren't really a nuisance either; there's not a lot of noise and hubbub because it's not that big a town.

On Francisco I. Madero: The **Hotel Lina (5)** (tel. 322/2-1661), Madero 376 between Insurgentes and Aguacate, advertises *¡¡Limpieza Absoluta!!* and that's pretty much what you find: absolute cleanliness. Aimed at the family trade, this small hotel has a tidy little courtyard (although no garden to speak of), and rooms equipped with ceiling fans and private showers for 363 pesos single, 485 pesos double.

Not far away, the **Hotel Villa del Mar (10)** (tel. 322/2-0785), Madero 440 at Jacarandas, is a simple, three-story place with big windows in the front rooms. Its 28 rooms are arranged around a tidy slot-like courtyard which manages to nurture several tall bamboo plants. Pretty tile picture panels brighten the public areas, and although the rooms are simple (naked lightbulbs, etc.) they are not what you'd call bare. The Villa del Mar is run by industrious señoras who see to its upkeep and propriety, and who charge 390 pesos single, 515 pesos double.

At Madero 473, up past Jacarandas, is the **Hotel Azteca (15)** (tel. 322/2-2750), which you'll recognize from its low brick arches, standard slot-like courtyard, and pretty garden. Twenty-eight rooms exist, and a third floor of rooms is being added. Prices are about the lowest on the street: 275 pesos single, 385 pesos double.

On Basilio Vadillo: Three blocks south of, and parallel to, Calle Madero is Calle Basilio Vadillo (or Badillo—there's no pronunciation difference in Spanish). Here you will find some more budget and moderately priced hotels (restaurants, too).

The **Hotel Posada de Roger (1)**, Basilio Vadillo 237 near the corner of Ignacio Vallarta (tel. 322/2-0836), has come up quite a ways in the world since its first inclusion in this book years ago. Once a pension, it has now become a hotel with very simple but spotless rooms at very good prices: no singles, but 150 pesos per bed in a six-bunk dorm, 495 pesos double, 595 pesos triple, and all 22 rooms have private bath. Also, there are six spacious two-bedroom apartments. The hotel keeps the same friendly *ambiente,* and guests still gather in the attractive courtyard for conversation, entertainment, and general fun.

Farther down Basilio Vadillo is the **Hotel Yazmin (2)** (tel. 322/2-0087), at no. 168. Although the Yazmin lacks the charged atmosphere of Roger's, it does have a very nice courtyard, and quite suitable rooms with baths for 385 pesos single, 485 pesos double.

By the way, if you're looking for an apartment and Roger's are full, try asking at **Apartments La Peña (22)** (tel. 322/2-1213), up on the rocks (that's what *peña* means) at Francisca Rodriguez 174. Doubles are 450 pesos, or 750 pesos for four.

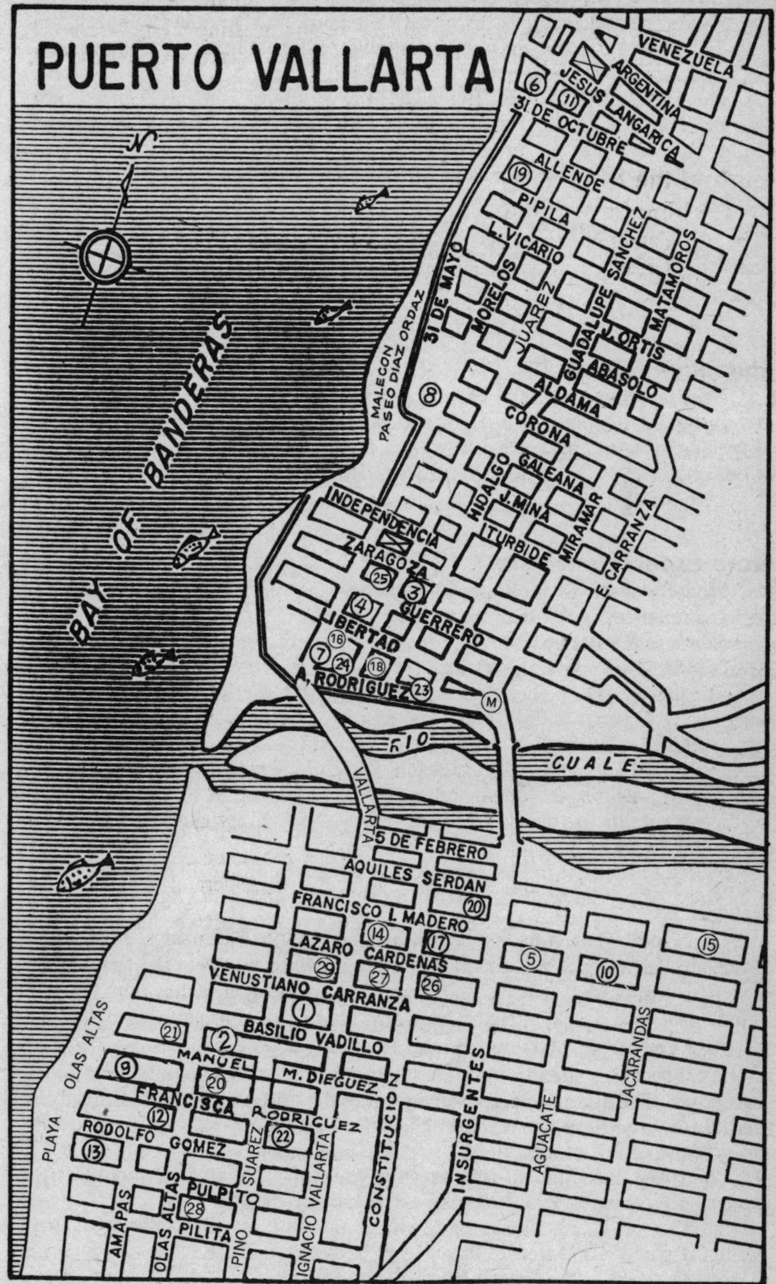
PUERTO VALLARTA
BAY OF BANDERAS
N
MALECON PASEO DIAZ ORDAZ
31 DE MAYO
MORELOS
JUAREZ
GUADALUPE SANCHEZ
MATAMOROS
VENEZUELA
ARGENTINA
JESUS LANGARICA
31 DE OCTUBRE
ALLENDE
PIPILA
L. VICARIO
J. ORTIS
ABASOLO
ALDAMA
CORONA
GALEANA
J. MINA
HIDALGO
MIRAMAR
E. CARRANZA
ITURBIDE
INDEPENDENCIA
ZARAGOZA
GUERRERO
LIBERTAD
A. RODRIGUEZ
RIO CUALE
VALLARTA
5 DE FEBRERO
AQUILES SERDAN
FRANCISCO I. MADERO
LAZARO CARDENAS
VENUSTIANO CARRANZA
BASILIO VADILLO
MANUEL M. DIEGUEZ
FRANCISCA RODRIGUEZ
RODOLFO GOMEZ
PULPITO
PILITA
PLAYA OLAS ALTAS
AMAPAS
OLAS ALTAS
PINO SUAREZ
IGNACIO VALLARTA
CONSTITUCION
INSURGENTES
AGUACATE
JACARANDAS

North of the Río Cuale

This is the real center of town, with the market (M), squares, church, and town hall. A few choices for budget lodgings still exist here, although most of the hotels are moderately priced.

The **Hotel Chulavista (4)** (tel. 322/2-0290), Juarez 263, has been modernized and renovated at least once in its present incarnation. Simple rooms with ceiling fans and bath go for 390 pesos single, 480 pesos double.

Head down Hidalgo almost to the river to find the new **Hotel Encino (18)** (tel. 322/2-0051), Hidalgo 115 between A. Rodriguez and the river. One might term this a "budget resort hotel," as it tries to be mod and stylish although the rooms are small and darkish. It seems to have been built by unskilled workmen, but it's run by better sorts who charge 389 pesos single, 534 pesos double for most of the rooms; a few cost more.

Starvation Budget

I hesitate to mention the **Hotel Central (3)** (no phone), but if you're really low on bucks this place will do. It's a cement sea of plainness, in the middle of which is a court packed with banana plants. At 140 pesos per person, it's undeniably cheap. The address is Juarez 70, right across the street from the aforementioned Hotel Chulavista.

More Expensive Hotels

Now for some hotel choices at higher prices, but with the addition of sea views, kitchenettes, or other small luxuries.

South of the River: For ocean-loving splurgers, the **Hotel Marsol (9)** (tel. 332/2-1365; Apdo. Postal 4) is located on the Playa del Sol beach. Its rooms, all with private baths (hot and cold water), rent for 770 pesos single with balcony, 1150 pesos double, and 1600 pesos for oceanfront apartments. It's a big airy place with nothing but a row of coconut palms (and a retaining wall) between its open veranda and the beach. It should be noted that they offer only rooms with breakfast included, and also that the staff tends to be grouchy. The beach restaurants are a scant 50 yards away. *Note:* Only apartments face the sea; rooms without kitchens are all in the back.

North of the River: The **Hotel Oceano (8)** (tel. 322/2-1322; Apdo. Postal 45) is located on the Malecon next to a tiny black-and-white lighthouse which is operative but actually pretty useless—a ship would have to be halfway across the Malecon to see it. The 52-room Oceano is notable for its bar (well patronized) and its location (very central). Rooms are small, with substantial wood furniture, colorful bedspreads, and stained wood shutters instead of windows, which can be adjusted to let in more or less light. Construction is of sun-bleached stucco and dark wood, and since it's right on the ocean, there's a continual soothing sound of low surf. Unfortunately, the Oceano's location at the corner of Ordaz and Morelos guarantees the unsoothing sound of traffic as well. Rates are 770 to 880 pesos single, 880 to 1100 pesos double, 1200 to 1350 pesos triple. All rooms come with ceiling fans.

With the exception of the Oceano, you don't get all you should at the moderately priced hotels. If rooms are tight, try these:

In the northern reaches of town, at no. 901 on the waterfront street variously named El Malecon, Paseo Díaz Ordaz, and Calle 31 de Mayo, corner of 31 de Octubre, is the **Nuevo Hotel Rosita (6)** (tel. 322/2-1033; Apdo. Postal 32). It is among the oldest in town, popular with Americans because of its pool and its view from the open-air bar facing the ocean. The building is huge, white, built in 1948 and recently remodeled (downstairs) à la Spanish colonial with pleasing results. The Rosita is divided into an old wing, where rooms are small, a bit weather-beaten, have frosted windows, tiny balconies, and cost 775 pesos single, 850 pesos double (12 such rooms). From there, the remaining 79 rooms are 1050 pesos single, 1275 pesos for a double. There's a pleasant restaurant on the ground floor and a bar with marvelous burled wood chairs.

Next to the Río Cuale is the **Hotel Río (7)**, Morelos 170 (tel 322/2-0366; Apdo. Postal 23), which is a sort of condensed version of the Hotel Rosita—the same white cement architecture topped with an exotic-looking sign which reads "RIO" in striped letters set askew apparently on purpose. The court is shady and lush and contains a kidney-shaped pool modeled after someone's very small kidneys. However, it's used, and guests can be seen lying precariously on its narrow, raised periphery catching rays. Rooms are several cuts above the low-cost models at the Rosita; all outside, all with bath. Rates are a little high (singles 720 pesos; doubles, 840 pesos). Large rooms with extra-spacious balconies and corner locations are more expensive.

EATING IN PUERTO VALLARTA: One of the beauties of Puerto Vallarta is its collection of small, homey restaurants aimed at the Mexican family on vacation. Moderate prices, big portions, decent service, long hours—these restaurants are a welcome alternative to the expensive and pretentious places with hyped-up tropical "atmosphere," high-decibel Muzak, and sassy waiters. I'll start our explorations of dining places south of the Río Cuale.

South of the River

We'll look first at an eatery near the hotels and bus stations on the south side, and then wander on down to the beach.

Near Hotels and Buses: The **Restaurant Gilmar (10)**, Madero 418, is a small place with brick arches, rickety wooden chairs, bright colors, and a blackboard menu. The good, simple Mexican food is whipped up by the owner-señora, who features a comida corrida for less than 100 pesos. It's nothing spectacular, just good, convenient, and low-priced.

Down Near Playa Olas Altas: On Olas Altas near the Hotel Marsol, **Las Tres Huastecas (12)** is a tried-and-true place heavily patronized by both local and foreign tourists (menus in Spanish and English). The unpretentious Formica tables are usually packed with happy diners having such high-ticket items as huachinango (red snapper) or carne asada (grilled beef) for a mere 100 pesos.

When you first look at **Los Pinguinos (20)**, on Olas Altas more or less across from Las Tres Huastecas, you'll think it's a real low-budget place. But enter the big, airy dining room (with kitchen to one side) and you'll see that thought was given to the decoration, from the painted border of flowering vines that's painted along the walls to the small flower print tablecloths and the nice paintings hung here and there. The menu has a good variety of items in all price ranges, and you can satisfy your hunger with a huge fruit salad for 100 pesos or a big Mexican combination plate at 200 pesos. Service, when I was there, was surprisingly professional.

Across the street from Los Pinguinos, in the Hotel Los Arcos, the **Restaurant Los Arcos** has a standard selection of dishes at moderate prices, and provides a more formal atmosphere than you might otherwise find on Olas Altas, a beachcombers' street.

Speaking of beachcombers, they're the reason the **Restaurant La Palapa (13)** was established many years ago. But this thatched place, right on the beach near the Hotel Marsol, has graduated at least to tourist class, and now serves sandwiches and main courses—seafood's the specialty, naturally—for slightly more than the eateries on Olas Altas. You can get by on 100 pesos for a sandwich and soft drink, 250 to 300 pesos for a more substantial three-course repast. Other, similar beachfront restaurants are nearby.

Beachcombers' Fare: About the cheapest palatable food on the beach is sold by boys who catch or buy small fish, and then cook them on a stick over a driftwood fire. You buy what amounts to a pescado-lollipop, preferably hot off the fire, for about 50 pesos, after haggling for a few seconds.

North of the River

A restaurant with excellent fresh seafood is the **Mismaloya Beach (11),** at the north end of town, 31 de Octubre no. 15. The interior is very plain but the fish is delicious; you can have, say, grilled red snapper (a huge plate garnished with french fries and vegetables), a green salad, and a soft drink for 325 pesos total. A few bits of nautical paraphernalia brighten the walls, and white tablecloths grace the tables, but this place is out of the center of activity (but near the Hotel Rosita), so prices stay low. Good service, menu in English.

Mi Tierra (23) is an open and airy lunchery at the corner of Matamoros and A. Rodriguez (no. 299), a mere half block from Puerto Vallarta's central market. This is the place for cheap eats in the more expensive part of town: a filling bowl of pozole, the traditional meat-and-hominy stew, plus a sandwich and soft drink will be less than 150 pesos. Breakfast of bacon and eggs, plus frijoles and coffee, is under 100 pesos.

For Pizza: Benito's (25), right on the corner of Zaragoza and Morelos, is a neocolonial pizza parlor with a mermaid statue in a little pool. Pizzas come in four sizes and over a dozen varieties, and the trilingual menu (Spanish, English, French) lists their prices, between 100 and 375 pesos.

More Expensive Places

For a marginally more expensive dinner, but still within our budget range, try one of these places.

For Spanish Fare: Las Cazuelas (14), Lázaro Cárdenas 263 (tel. 2-1658), is by far one of my favorite eating spots in Puerto Vallarta. Cazuela in Spanish means "earthenware cooking pot," and it is here that you can sample the savory food from such pots. It is distinctly Spanish in all ways, from the smells to the hustle and bustle. A full dinner might cost 450 to 600 pesos: appetizer (soup, guacamole), pasta dish, choice of entree, dessert, and Mexican cinnamon coffee. Open daily from 4 until 11 p.m. Call for reservations (absolutely necessary) as there are only ten tables. (*Note:* Las Cazuelas sometimes closes down in summer.)

A Chinese Restaurant: Hunting for Peking-on-the-Río Cuale? The place to look is Avenida Lázaro Cárdenas 302, corner of Constitucion, where you'll find the **Restaurant Palacio Oriental (26).** The proprietor, Carlos Chong, serves up combination dinners of five or six courses for 220 to 300 pesos. Should you order one of the à la carte delicacies such as butterfly shrimp, your bill could soar to 600 pesos or so. Chinese trinkets and decorations turn what would otherwise be a plain Mexican restaurant into a palacio oriental (well, sort of), complete with ceiling fans.

For Oysters or Beef: On Calle Libertad (no. 171) and across from the Hotel Río, is El Ostion Feliz, **The Happy Oyster,** which serves the oyster and also a host of his nautical associates. Squid, octopus, frog legs, conch, and shark are tossed right into salad makings and served up for 225 pesos; more commonly encountered dishes such as shrimp, lobster, and crab are there as well. The seafood casserole is highly recommended. Oh, yes: oysters come as a cocktail for 165 pesos, breaded or deviled for 275 pesos. The extra-specialty of the house can be commanded for extra-special occasions: it's barbecued white whale, and the minimum order is for 1000 servings.

A block away from the Happy Oyster is the **Restaurant Los Venados (24),** Calle Rodriguez 177, around the corner from the Hotel Río. Fixed up with brick arches, tablecloths, and a country-ish decor, Los Venados will serve you any of the standard Mexican repasts, including a beefsteak dinner for 200 pesos, or a big avocado salad for much less.

A Lobster Splurge: It's not difficult to guess the specialty at the **Lobster House (27)** (tel. 2-0676), Lázaro Cárdenas 254, corner of Ignacio Vallarta. Besides lobster, they serve fish, jumbo shrimp, and (much cheaper) octopus and squid. A big restaurant with many bright dining rooms, all done in quaint colonial style, the Lobster House has a lively atmosphere, and a piano player to make sure it stays that way. Expect to spend 600 pesos per person, more or less. Come between 6 and 7:30 p.m. and you can enjoy Happy Hour, with two drinks (all brands) for the price of one. Open for lunch and dinner every day.

A Culinary Circus: If you want a real extravaganza, go to **La Iguana (17)** (tel. 2-0105), a couple of blocks south of the river at Lázaro Cárdenas 311, between Constitucion and Insurgentes, where a full dinner will cost 1000 pesos, but that includes an *open bar,* and an all-you-can-eat buffet. Specialties of the house are Chinese, Mexican, and American dishes—too broad a spread, until you know that the owner-chef, Gustavo Salazar, was born to Mexican parents in Hong Kong where he later managed the American Club. La Iguana's atmosphere is as eclectic as its owner's experience. You'll cross a Mexican version of a Chinese moonridge over a wishing pool, enter a thick-walled adobe-arched pavilion, where you'll be entertained by mariachis and a Ballet Folklorico, on fiesta nights, Thursday and Sunday. It's definitely for tourist trade and rarely visited by locals.

SUNNING AND STROLLING: The beaches in Puerto Vallarta, of course, take up most people's time. They start well to the north of town, out by the airport, with **Playa de Oro,** and extend all around the bay. The most popular ones are **Playa Olas Altas,** off the street of the same name south of the Río Cuale; and **Playa Mismaloya,** in a beautiful sheltered cove a kilometer or so south of town along Highway 200.

Playa Yelapa

About the best beach around is Playa Yelapa, a two-hour trip by boat down the coast. Go to the Terminal Maritima north of town past the Holiday Inn (but before the airport), and get the 9 a.m. boat to Yelapa for 400 pesos round-trip, returning at 4:30 p.m.

Besides the beach, Yelapa has a hotel, called the **Hotel Lagunitas.** It's not fancy, and services are unpredictable, but you can spend a blissful night or two if you make reservations in advance at Mexitours (Apdo. Postal 395, Puerto Vallarta, Jalisco, México). A double room costs about 850 pesos, depending on demand. Accommodations are in little cottages-with-bath.

Cheaper accommodations at Yelapa? Ask around to see if any of the Americans living there is putting up rooms for rent; or rent a palapa hut with a dirt floor—some go for as low as $50 for a half *year.* The cheapest way of all, of course, is to sleep on the beach, but don't plan this during the rainy season! There's absolutely nothing to do at Yelapa except lie in the sun, eat, play darts, and trudge 'round the bay to a tiny Indian village of the same name.

PUERTO VALLARTA NIGHTLIFE: An interesting place to sit around, see, and be seen is the lounge of the **Hotel Oceano (8)**. A band often plays there for dancing, and there's a good deal of table-hopping by both strangers and friends. Girls from the University of Guadalajara are sometimes in Puerto Vallarta on vacation; don't think that a Mexican girl won't speak English, many of them do. Plenty of guys around too.

These days, the swinging after-dark crowds have succumbed to disco madness. The discos are very much like those at home, being high-volume, high-price, and high-times places. Expect a cover charge of about 200 pesos, and then you'll pay about 125 pesos for a Margarita, 200 pesos for whisky and a mix.

Wander down the Malecon after dark and your ears will lead you to **Carlos O'Brien's (19)**, or **Casablancas**. Here you can sit amid jungle animals dangling from the ceiling, or you can shoulder your way up to the Cuckoo's Nest.

Walk up behind the Hotel Delfin, south of the Río Cuale on Olas Altas at Francisca Rodriguez, to find **Capriccio (28)**. It's up those steep steps on what would be the continuation of Pulpito, were it not for the hill interrupting the street. Another disco to check out, especially if you're young and single, is the **City Dump (29)**, Vallarta 278, corner of Lázaro Cárdenas, open 10:30 p.m. to 4 a.m.—dark, low-key, semi-chic.

The beach doesn't go to sleep at night, for the shady palapas which provided refuge during the heat of the day provide room for bands at night. The locale and the bank can change with the phases of the moon, or even every day, but the twang of the electric guitar will draw you to the spot where the carefree and budget-minded are dancing on the beach.

SHOPPING TIPS: Puerto Vallarta's **municipal market (M)** is just north of the Río Cuale where Libertad and A. Rodriguez meet. You can pick up very inexpensive fruit, vegetables, and picnic fixings here.

Should you be in the market for those wonderfully comfy and practical sandals called *huaraches,* made of leather strips and rubber-tire soles, head for Calle Libertad between Juarez and the market. This is huarache city, with a dozen shops. Shop around, and buy a pair that fits very tightly—they stretch out almost immediately, and can become too floppy.

GETTING TO AND FROM PUERTO VALLARTA: When Elizabeth Taylor first spied Puerto Vallarta it was still a pretty remote and pristine Pacific fishing village. *Night of the Iguana* did its work, however, and a road was built. Today big jets stream in and out of the burgeoning town. This is no doubt being greeted with mixed emotions, as some mourn the increased accessibility of a once-remote resort.

By Air

Mexicana Airlines (in Guadalajara at Avenida 16 de Septiembre 495, tel. 36/13-2222; in Puerto Vallarta at Juarez 202, tel. 322/2-1808) has daily flights on jet aircraft between Puerto Vallarta and Guadalajara, Mexico City, Mazatlán, Denver, and Dallas/Fort Worth. For information regarding the flights call Mexicana's Puerto Vallarta office or the Mexico City operation at Juarez and Balderas (tel. 905/585-2666).

AeroMéxico has flights from Puerto Vallarta to Mexico City, Guadalajara, and (with one stop en route) to Chihuahua, Ciudad Juarez, and Houston. Offices are in Puerto Vallarta at Juarez 255 (tel. 322/2-0031), in Guadalajara at Avenida Corona 196 (tel. 32/25-1010), and in Mexico City at Reforma 445 (tel. 905/553-1577).

By Bus

Autotransportes del Pacifico will get you from Guadalajara to Puerto Vallarta on any of their hourly buses which run throughout the day. This is the most convenient service. They make the return run just as frequently.

Tres Estrellas de Oro will take you to Puerto Vallarta from Guadalajara six times a day (should you want to go that often). Catch the bus at the Central Camionera. Buses from Tepic run several times a day as well, but here you must wait for the bus to arrive before they sell you a seat on it—assuming there's one vacant. Time from Guadalajara is about seven hours, from Tepic about three hours.

Bus stations for most major lines—Transportes del Pacifico, Tres Estrellas de Oro, Norte de Sonora, and Estrella Blanca—are along Avenida Insurgentes between Serdan and the Río Cuale.

4. San Patricio and Barra de Navidad

Just to show that those tiny Pacific Coast villages, laid back and lovely, are still to be found, I'll take you on a tour through San Patricio and Barra de Navidad, two small villages on the beach of the Bahía de Navidad, sometimes called Melaque Bay.

The road south from Puerto Vallarta, Highway 200, joins the road from Guadalajara (Highway 80) at Barra de Navidad, and then Highway 200 heads southeast to Manzanillo. It's a three-hour ride from Puerto Vallarta to San Patricio, over five hours from Guadalajara. The distance from Barra to Manzanillo is about 30 miles.

These villages are easy of access because so much bus traffic runs between Puerto Vallarta and Manzanillo, and between Guadalajara and Manzanillo. Any bus on these routes will drop you near San Patricio. Coming from Manzanillo, Autotransportes Cihuatlán operates buses to San Patricio.

SAN PATRICIO: The most northwesterly of these communities, and the first one you'll encounter if you're coming from Puerto Vallarta, is San Patricio. On a crescent-shaped bay with curious rock outcrops at the points of the crescent, San Patricio can boast a perfect beach and an easy mood in which fishermen and beachcombers blend without difficulty. Unlike Zihuatanejo, this village hasn't been tarted up to meet jet-setters' expectations of what a Mexican fishing village should look like—this is the real thing. The paved road ends where the town begins. A few yachts bob at anchor in the harbor.

San Patricio is not exactly big enough to get lost in, but a word of orientation will help. Coming into town from the main road, you'll be on the town's main street, Avenida Lopez Mateos. You'll pass the main square and come right down to the waterfront, where there's a trailer park. The street going left (southeast) along the bay is Avenida Gómez Farías; the one going right (northwest) is Avenida de las Palmas.

The **Tourism Office** is on Avenida de las Palmas just past the Hotel Melaque, open 9 a.m. to 3 p.m. and 5 to 7 p.m. Monday through Friday, on Saturday from 9 a.m. to 1 p.m. Once you get to know San Patricio, you'll understand not to trust those hours too much.

Where to Stay

Come into town, down to the water, and turn right onto Avenida de las Palmas, and this is what you'll find:

On the left-hand side, about a block down Palmas, is the **Motel Vista Hermosa** (tel. 333/7-0002). An attractive three-story hotel built around a nice courtyard, it has little of the motel about it. Rooms are not fancy, but newish, adequate, and clean. The court is shady, with a little red-tiled gazebo in the center from which refreshments are sometimes served. Although you're right on the beach here, don't expect your room to have much of a sea view, as most rooms don't. Prices are 550 pesos single, 690 pesos double.

The **Posada de Legazpi** (tel. 333/7-0109), all the way down at the end of Avenida de las Palmas, is well worn and somewhat carelessly kept, but in a way that seems to fit the tropical climate. Rooms are clean, the beach is right out front, and the management is sympathetic. Double rooms with bath cost 700 pesos here.

Now for a look in the other direction. If you turn left onto Gómez Farías in the center of town, you'll come to the **Posada Las Gaviotas** (tel. 333/7-0129), entered from a side street called Calle Hidalgo (at no. 4). Long arches stretch from Gómez Farías all the way down to the beach, and beneath the arches are simple, cool rooms with no real sea view, but private baths. The cost is 575 pesos, single or double.

Next along the street is the attractive (for San Patricio, even chic) **Posada Pablo de Tarso** (tel. 333/7-0117), Gómez Farías 408. This two-level, 19-room place is exceptionally tidy, with brilliantly green grass and plants in the courtyard, shaded parking places, and neat, comfy rooms which rent for 770 pesos, single or double. Again, you're right on the beach here.

Where to Eat

Avenida Lopez Mateos has several little eateries here and there along its length, and these will do for light meals or snacks. For a substantial meal in pleasant surroundings, find your way to the **Restaurant Fonda Los Portales,** on Gómez Farías almost next to the Posada Las Gaviotas. A small palapa-shaded place, you can tuck into any of a dozen seafood platters here, and your entire meal will cost less than 300 pesos.

BARRA DE NAVIDAD: About three miles (five kilometers) east of San Patricio along the road to Manzanillo is Barra de Navidad, an even smaller village with equally fine beaches and an identical easy lifestyle. Also like San Patricio, Barra has been discovered, but only by a very small number of people. You'll see tanned gringos and gringas circulating on the streets leading to the beach, fishermen and townfolk going about their business.

Where to Stay and Eat

Barra is small enough that ten minutes of wandering will give you the town's entire layout. When you find Calle Morelos, make your way to no. 23 and the **Hotel Delphin** (tel. 333/7-0068), a relatively new four-story hotel surrounded by verdure. Rooms, as befits such a beach town, are very basic, cooled by sea breezes through cross-ventilation, but they're equipped with private baths. Rates are 660 pesos single, 770 pesos double.

Coming in from the highway, follow the road almost to its end at the beach and you'll see the **Hotel Tropical** (tel. 333/7-0020) on the right-hand side. This is Barra's fancy address, with well-equipped, sea-view rooms going for 880 pesos single, 1100 pesos double.

As for food, it's pretty much catch-as-catch-can in this little place. Very basic eateries will provide for your needs, or you can do what most visitors do: pick up picnic goods and make your own meals.

ONWARD TO MANZANILLO: At Barra, Highway 80 heads up into the hills of Guadalajara, but if you're bound ever southward in your tour of Mexican Pacific Coast resorts, start for Manzanillo, about 30 miles down the road. On the way you'll pass Playa de Oro and Manzanillo's airport (which is actually midway between Barra and Manzanillo), then Santiago, then the fabulous Las Hadas resort complex, then the Las Brisas district, and finally you'll pull into the city itself.

5. Manzanillo to Playa Azul

MANZANILLO: In the 17th century, Manzanillo's major role was that of a harbor for segments of the Spanish fleet, and it was from there, in 1654, that galleons set off to conquer the Philippines. Today, Manzanillo, Colima (pop. 36,000) relies on fishing and a fairly thriving resort business from Mexican tourists.

The town, which is rather less attractive than you might expect, is situated at one end of a seven-mile-long curving beach, the Playa Azul, whose northern terminus is the Santiago Peninsula. In Santiago are located some beautiful private homes as well as the best hotel in the area, the Hotel Playa de Santiago. There are two lagoons, one almost behind the city and the other behind the beach. A bus runs from town to Santiago every 20 minutes and it's a pleasant area in which to stay, if you don't mind being seven miles from downtown life and shopping.

Downtown activity centers around the plaza, which is separated from the waterfront by railroad and ship yards. The plaza sports a brilliant poinciana tree, whose red blossoms always seem to be in bloom, and a kiosk serving all kinds of delicious fruit drinks *(licuados).*

In the daytime, the major attractions are the beaches, of course. **La Audiencia Beach,** on the way to Santiago, offers the best swimming, but **San Pedrito,** shallow for a long way out, is the most popular because it is much nearer the downtown area. The major part of the Playa Azul drops off a little too steeply for safe swimming, and is not recommended for waders.

Taxis don't have meters in Manzanillo, so agree on the price in advance before you set out on any ambitious trips. Much cheaper are the local **buses** (called *camionetas*). These make a circuit back along the lagoon behind the downtown area, and out along the Bay of Manzanillo to the Santiago Peninsula. This is a lovely way to see the coast and the cost is only a few pesos.

Manzanillo is famous for its fishing—marlin, sailfish, dolphin, sea bass, and manta ray—and competitions are held in late November and late January. Many charter boats are available along the waterfront.

Arriving in Manzanillo

Manzanillo's **Central Camionera** (bus station) is located east of town just off the road to Colima. Follow Hidalgo east till you come to Galeana, and the Camionera will be off to the right.

The **airport** is quite a way northwest of town, at a place called Playa de Oro.

The **Tourism Office** is at Avenida Juarez 111, corner of 21 de Marzo, open 9 a.m. to 3 p.m. daily except Sunday.

If you need a **laundromat**, there's one at the junction of the Manzanillo–Las Brisas–Santiago roads called Lavandería Automática Gissy (that's "HEE-see"), in a little complex of shops.

Hotels in Downtown Manzanillo

The strip of coastline on which Manzanillo is located can be divided into three areas: **downtown**, with its shops, markets, and continual activity; **Las Brisas**, the motel-lined beach area immediately to the north of the city; and **Santiago**, which is virtually a suburb situated at the northern end of Playa Azul. All areas are reasonably convenient to one another by either bus or taxi. *Note:* Reservations are recommended for the Christmas and New Year holidays.

Downtown Hotels: In the downtown area, one place to stay is the **Hotel Colonial** (tel. 333/2-1080 or 2-1134), Calle México 100 and Gonzales Bocanegra, one short block inland from the center of the main square. It's a fairly involved colonial-style affair, much carved, beamed, and chandeliered. It lists its well-furnished rooms for 550 pesos single, 660 pesos double.

At the east end of the plaza is the four-story, 46-room **Hotel Miramar** (tel. 333/2-1008), Juarez 122. Although the rates—395 pesos single, 485 pesos double—are reasonable enough, one drawback is that only some of the rooms have ceiling fans. While you can get by without this convenience in breezy Las Brisas, the hotter nights downtown can be decidedly uncomfortable. Rooms are clean, if worn, and all have bath (although you may lack a toilet seat).

With prices the way they are in Manzanillo, the **Hotel Savoy** (tel. 333/2-0754) may be just the place to stay. I'll warn you at the outset that this is the sort of hotel where one screws in the light bulb to turn on the light. But that having been said, here's the good part: many of the rooms higher in the building have beautiful views of the city and the harbor, and prices are reasonable, with singles and doubles at 330 pesos. The Savoy is at Carrillo Puerto 60, at the southwest corner of the plaza.

Another choice in the downtown area is the **Hotel Manzanillo** (tel. 333/2-0183), Cuauhtémoc 139, which is seven short blocks up Avenida México from the main plaza and definitely in the low-rent district. However, the staff at the Manzanillo is extremely friendly, and the rooms are surprisingly clean, each with private bath and frosted windows looking out on canary-yellow airshafts. If you stay here, it's best to know a little Spanish. Singles cost 150 pesos; doubles, 330 pesos.

The **Hotel Flamingos** (tel. 333/2-1037), at Madero and 10 de Mayo, is one short block off the main plaza, across the street from a hospital. The ample rooms are fairly clean and bright, and rent for 355 pesos single, 445 pesos double.

Hotels at Las Brisas

Buses run out to Las Brisas from downtown. Look for "Brisas Direc" on the signboard. It's a six-mile trundle around Manzanillo Bay, ultimately curving southward. You're not all that far from town here—except that town is across the bay.

If you decide to stay in Las Brisas, your best choice is the tree-shaded, pink stucco **Hotel La Posada** (no phone), which is built around a large arch that leads to a broad, tiled patio looking out on the sea and beach. Inside are 18 rooms with natural brick walls and simple but very tasteful furnishings. The cost is 1350 pesos, single or double, breakfast included. For reservations, write to Apdo. Postal 135, Manzanillo, Colima, México.

A little farther up the beach is **Hotel Rancho Luna,** a collection of 21 attractive bungalows with kitchenettes, recently reconstructed. Of these, 16 fit six people and five accommodate four. The bungalows rent for 1320 pesos with two beds and 1700 with four beds. Parking, large pool, well-kept grounds—a good choice. For reservations write to Santiago, Apdo. Postal 180.

The eight units of the **Bungalows Jaragua** all face the beach through floor-to-ceiling glass louvers, and have clean tile floors. Outside, the building is notable for its wood louvers to deflect the sun, small swimming pool, pastel walls, and spiral staircase on the corner. Rates for a day are 990 pesos, double; for one month, 10,000 pesos.

Hotels in Santiago

Three miles north of Las Brisas is the peninsula and village of Santiago, which is home to several other hostelries. Three hotels range in price from splurge level to budget. **Hotel Playa de Santiago** (tel. 333/3-0055) is gorgeous and overpriced: singles are 850 pesos; doubles, 1050 pesos. Services include free parking, two swimming pools, restaurant, convention room, and an assortment of activities. It's located at the end of the road along Santiago Bay. You'll enjoy the playroom for children, and the spacious grounds, too.

Right next to the Hotel Playa de Santiago is the new **Hotel Marlin** (also spelled Marlyn) (tel. 333/3-0107; Apdo. Postal 288). White, breezy and open, it's right on the beach, and has a nice little swimming pool and beachfront cafe. You pay a few dollars more for rooms with a sea view: these cost 770 pesos single, 880 pesos double. If you're willing to look at the street instead, a reduction is in order.

You'll notice the old **Hotel Anita** (tel. 333/3-0161) next to the Marlin. Although it's the oldest and most well-worn of the lot here, some rooms are still suitable, especially for 525 pesos, single or double.

Eating in Manzanillo

The dining room of the **Hotel Colonial,** Calle México 100, at the corner of Bocanegra, offers a 175-peso lunch (comida) which is excellent and usually includes some sort of fish appetizer as well as a choice of fish entree. À la carte entrees range from 200 to 300 pesos in the evening.

The **Chantilly,** at the corner of Juarez and Madero, across from the plaza, has a large international menu with good cheap food. Hamburgers range from 35 to 60 pesos; fried fish plates are twice as much. They also have safe-to-eat ice cream. Club sandwiches, carne asada a la Tampiqueña, vegetable salads—the menu is wonderfully eclectic, and the place is dependably good.

On the southwest corner of the main plaza is the **Hamburguesa,** Juarez 23, a modern and even vaguely stylish place (for Manzanillo) where you can get a hamburger and soft drink for less than 85 pesos.

Mi Tierra is another clean place to chow down at low prices. It's on Avenida México at no. 289, corner of Cuauhtémoc. Open to the street, plain and simple, Mi Tierra has several set-price breakfasts (those wonderful money-savers) for 40 to 140 pesos; the standard two-eggs-and-bacon version costs a mere 60 pesos. Fried chicken is not much more, and various Mexican delights are similarly moderate in price.

The **Restaurant Savoy,** in the hotel of the same name at the southwest corner of the plaza, is as unpretentious as the hotel, which is to say pretty darn unpretentious. But it does have white tablecloths (well, not precisely white), full breakfasts for 80 pesos, and lunches or suppers for less than double that amount.

Eating at Las Brisas

El Sombrero, owned by Carmen and Otto Meyer, is one of the cheeriest restaurants in all of Mexico. The setting is simple but attractive, being in a palapa (thatched "hut"), and the food is Mexican and delicious (nothing outrageously spicy): three enchiladas will cost you 54 pesos, quesadillas (the cheese-filled wheat tortillas) are 48 pesos, or the filling hominy-and-meat stew called pozole is 48 pesos. El Sombrero is open only in the evenings from 7 p.m. to 11 p.m. It's right near the end of the bus line—turn down the street by Ralph's Super, following signs to the Hospital Naval.

Las Hadas

Brainchild of the South American entrepreneur Antenor Patino, Las Hadas is a self-contained little jet-set Eden with its own hotel and condominiums, three restaurants, four bars, two pools, a marina, a golf course, and lots of posh shops. Having done a somewhat languid business for years, Las Hadas got a boost when it figured prominently in the movie *10,* Bo Derek's sensational first picture. Whether the boost will be long-lasting, turning Las Hadas and Manzanillo into another Acapulco, remains to be seen. But you can have a look around this fascinating resort-cum-movie set; go out Highway 80 to Santiago Bay, turn left at the golf course (follow the signs to "Club Las Hadas"), and then left again at the sign to El Tesoro. Buses ("Las Hadas") run out from town.

Getting to and from Manzanillo

A good list of choices by all three means:

By Bus: You rarely go wrong riding a bus run by Tres Estrellas de Oro or one of the other big lines such as Transportes Norte de Sonora or Transportes del Pacifico. They all run daily buses to Manzanillo from Guadalajara and Mexico City. Other lines operating to Manzanillo out of Guadalajara include Flecha Amarilla, Autobuses de la Piedad, and Transportes Unidos de la Costa, although a reader advises us that the last-mentioned line makes no rest stops in the six-hour drive, and several of its drivers fancy themselves the Latin incarnation of Emerson Fittipaldi. If in doubt, you can always go . . .

By Train: A train leaves Guadalajara's main station every morning and heads toward the Pacific, stopping at Colima (see Chapter IV), to Manzanillo.

By Plane: AeroMéxico has daily flights from Guadalajara and Mexico City to Manzanillo, and also three flights a week to and from Los Angeles. The

Manzanillo office of the airline is in the Centro Comercial "Carrillo Puerto" (tel. 333/2-1267 or 2-1711).

HEADING SOUTHEAST: Highway 200, the coastal road, runs into some rough spots southeast of Manzanillo. It's a l-o-n-g detour up into the mountains on Highway 110 via Colima and Uruapan, then down to the coast again on Highway 37, to get to Plaza Azul. You can negotiate the rough coastal road, however. Here are some tips.

Ask about conditions on the road in Tecoman, and if the rainy season hasn't washed out any bridges, you might be able to make it. If bridges are out, you can ford the creekbeds if the rains haven't flooded the creeks. The rough stretch is about 220 miles long and there's *no gas* the entire length, so you'll want to buy a plastic jerry-can in a market and fill it with gas just in case. Another hint: Look for other people who might be taking that road, people hauling trailers onward to Acapulco, for instance, and team up with them. A caravan is the safest, easiest, and most pleasant way to do an unpleasant thing.

Things get better after Caleta de Campos, and in no time you'll be pulling into the Pacific hideaway of Playa Azul.

PLAYA AZUL: Playa Azul (pop. 6000) is Michoacan's entry into the offbeat tropical paradise derby. Facing open ocean rather than a bay, the town lies on a coastal plain dominated by row after row of magnificent coconut palms. The highway from Uruapan is good, but it's literally one curve after another for its entire 147-mile length to the coast. At some point in the future Playa Azul will very possibly experience a tourist boom, but until then it figures to remain off the "gran turismo" circuit. There are no phones, bus service is irregular, and you have to take pot luck on cabs that originate from sitios (cab stands) in neighboring towns.

But I don't want to depict Playa Azul as the sort of primitive place that only Albert Schweitzer could have appreciated. Although luxury accommodations have only recently come to Playa Azul, prices are high enough to make you think they've been there and building trade for decades. Who knows? What with the rage of development in Ixtapa–Zihuatanejo, the crowds may fill the hotels here soon. Note that things are pretty sleepy here in the summertime, and hotels are running at half-speed on service and facilities.

The **Hotel Playa Azul,** in the center of town, is a sympathetic three-story complex with 56 rooms equipped with either air conditioning or ceiling fans, clean and functional. Rooms have two beds each, and perpetual hot water, and cost 550 to 660 pesos single, 660 to 990 pesos double. The ocean is 500 yards away, but the *powerful undertow* makes it sort of unsafe. Swim in the hotel's pool instead.

On the paved street between the old Hotel La Loma and the Playa Azul is the **Casa de Huespedes Silva,** where rooms are small, the cement-floored bathrooms are also small, and the price is a small 300 pesos single, 350 pesos double.

The **Hotel Delfin,** half a block west of the Hotel Playa Azul, is newish, mustard-colored, filled with palms and banana plants around the pool, and reasonably priced at 440 to 550 pesos single, 550 to 770 pesos double.

The **Restaurant Marthita,** around the corner and down a side street from the Hotel Playa Azul, is the type of small-town diner which still seems comfortable in this coastal village. No beachfront prices here, and the fish is fresh: the señora even showed me her catch and asked me to choose what I liked! Price depends on your selection, but most seafood meals served here come to about 100 to 180 pesos. Lobster, the only really expensive item, is half the price here that it is in most restaurants. You can get steak here, too. The daily comida corrida costs 85 pesos.

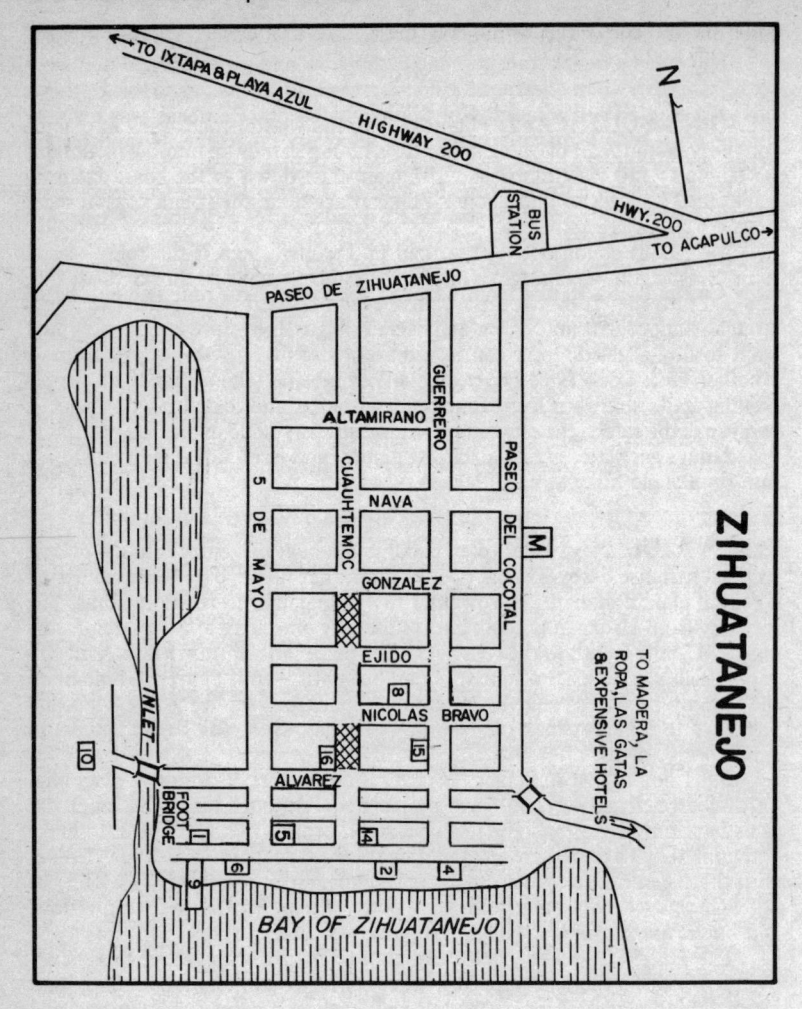

The palapa-type eateries on the beach, once to be found in every Pacific Coast town, are still thriving (as of this writing) in Playa Azul. Straw thatched roofs, dirt floors, and surrounding coconut palms create a South Seas atmosphere. Prices should be dirt-cheap, but in fact turn out to be moderate.

As for swimming, remember that the beaches here front on open surf—not on sheltered bays as in Acapulco—and therefore there is a constant, *deadly danger of undertow.* Don't go too far out. By the time you realize what's happened, it's too late.

Getting to and from Playa Azul

Those using public transport and coming by land to Playa Azul may have to pass through Ciudad Lázaro Cárdenas, a town 20 kilometers to the southeast of Playa Azul. Until a number of years ago, Lázaro Cárdenas was a sleepy fishing town with a mañana mood, but discovery has come. Now there are expensive oceanfront hotels and a steel mill belching smoke.

By Bus: Tres Estrellas runs four buses daily to Lázaro Cárdenas from Mexico City, and from there you take a local bus for a 30-minute trip or a minibus for the 15-minute trip.

By Air: Lineas Aereas del Centro (tel. 452/2-2858 in Uruapan) makes daily Cessna flights to and from Lázaro Cárdenas. Flight time is a half hour. Take a bus or minibus to Playa Azul as noted directly above.

6. Ixtapa–Zihuatanejo

As modern road and air communications expand throughout Mexico, the secluded hideaways which made the Pacific Coast an intrepid tourist's dream-come-true are being discovered en masse. Such is the fate of Zihuatanejo, in the state of Guerrero, a town which shut off its electricity at 11 p.m. only a few years ago. Now the lights are on 24 hours a day, and the primitive airstrip has been turned into a jetport welcoming daily flights from Mexico City, only 1¾ hours away by air. The draw is not Zihuatanejo itself so much as it is Ixtapa, sister development to Cancún, a planned resort catering to the charter crowd at a beautiful spot 10 kilometers northwest of Zihuatanejo.

In 1972 Zihuatanejo had a population of about 4000 souls; now it is over 16,000. Pardon me if I regret the passing of Zihuatanjeo's innocence. In my view there are plenty of super-expensive tourist complexes in Mexico—Acapulco, Manzanillo, Cancún, Cozumel—but fewer and fewer beautiful little seaside villages good for budget travelers.

The coast road from Acapulco or Playa Azul is new, good, and fairly fast. Zihuatanejo itself is absolutely beautiful. The beach curves around a small, natural bay in which fishing boats and an occasional sailboat bob at anchor, and in the town there's still a feeling of village life despite the boom.

Special Note: During the winter season from mid-December through mid-April, the rooms in Zihuatanejo are *all filled, every day.* February seems to be the worst month of all for finding rooms. If you can't get reservations and you want to chance it, get to town as early in the day as possible and find a room, any room. Then, with more time, you can search for the room that suits you best.

If there are simply no rooms vacant, you'll have to search in high-priced Ixtapa (see below), or—worse—in the next town (Petatlán) along the road, 22 miles to the southeast.

WHERE TO STAY: Even though it is no longer a sleepy little fishing village, almost everything in Zihuatanejo is either on the main street (which runs from the highway to the beach through the center of town), or on the beach itself. The more expensive hotels and nightspots are a 20-minute walk from the main street.

The hotels and pensions near the Playa Principal (main beach) are some of the best low-budget beachfront buys left on the Pacific. The beaches themselves, as yet unladen with touristic trappings such as parachutes, horses, and motorized water toys, are a real pleasure for the plain old sunbather, swimmer, or snorkler.

My favorite is the **Hotel Raul Tres Marias (10)** (tel. 743/4-2191), all the way at the west end of town just past the boat dock and over a wooden footbridge. The hotel was here a decade ago when Zihuatanejo was at the end of a dirt road; like the village, the hotel has grown, but it retains the same friendly atmosphere of previous years. There are 18 rooms, and from here you can see the whole town. The rooms are very bare and simple but bright and clean; all have showers and rent for 440 pesos single, 550 pesos double in summer. For this you get screens, a fan, and the largest bar of complimentary soap I have ever seen in any hotel anywhere. To get there from the bus station, walk down the main street to the beach, turn right onto the last street before the beach proper, and follow it to the end. The only disadvantage of the hotel is that it's not directly on the beach.

On down the beach is the **Hotel Avila (4)** (tel. 743/4-2010), quite nice but decidedly overpriced. The 20 rooms are all fairly attractive and equipped with showers and ceiling fans, and the porch-patio opening onto the main beach is a luxury. Upstairs rooms, considered more desirable, are 660 pesos single, 770 pesos double in summer; in winter, prices are 200 pesos higher. Downstairs rooms are a bit more reasonable at 500 pesos single, 600 pesos double in summer. Bargain for the price of your room here.

Another hotel not on the ocean, but within running distance, is the **Hotel El Dorado (14)**. The El Dorado is half a block from the beach, just up from the square. Singles are the regulation 440 pesos; doubles, 550 pesos. A warning is in order here: check to see that your ceiling fan works before taking the room.

The small, plain **Hotel Flores** has one row of ten small, bare, clean rooms with private baths and ceiling fans—and prices a bit higher than they should be. Double rooms here cost 660 pesos on "first ask," but if you turn away you may just get another, lower, quotation. The pleasant couple who run the Flores are not unreasonable. You'll find the hotel back from the beach more or less on the road to the expensive hotels mentioned below.

The High-Rent District

Separated from each other only by a craggy shoreline are the two other beaches accessible by road. The next one, Playa Madera, holds several small resort hotels which are at the top limit of our housing budget. The **Hotel Irma** (tel. 743/4-2025), Apdo. Postal 4, Zihuatanejo, has 30 rooms, several of them with air conditioning, plus a swimming pool and a precipitous stairway leading down the cliffside to the beach. It's a delightful *Night of the Iguana*-type place, with an open-air restaurant overlooking the water. In the winter season, you must take breakfast and dinner with your room, and the cost is 1665 pesos single, 2325 pesos double. But in April through October you can get room alone for 990 pesos single, 1100 pesos double. May and October are the calmest months, and thus the best times to bargain for lower rates.

At the nearby **Hotel Posada Caracol** (tel. 743/4-2035), the 57 rooms are mostly air-conditioned, and other extra services (two restaurants, a small nightclub, two pools, etc.) bring the room prices to a few hundred pesos more than at the aforementioned Hotel Irma.

Slightly farther along the coast from the center of Zihuatanejo is Playa La Ropa, and two more hotels which make sense to explore during the summer slow season. The 26-room **Hotel Catalina** (tel. 743/4-2137 or 4-2032) is the smaller of the two, with less variety in its collection of rooms. For 630 pesos single, 780 pesos double, 960 pesos triple, you'll have a room with private bath "cooled by refreshing sea breezes" (i.e., without fan or air conditioner). For another 550 pesos per person you can have breakfast and dinner each day. The

Catalina's sister hotel next door is the larger (44-room) **Hotel Sotavento** (same phones as Catalina), with three categories of rooms. The best rooms are in the newer building with the best sea views; cheapest are the older, bare rooms, which at least get you a place to sleep near the beach. Summer prices here range from 400 to 880 pesos single, 500 to 990 pesos double, 600 to 1100 pesos triple. I should mention that there are only three rooms at the very lowest prices. An extra bed costs 125 pesos. For best value, get three or four people together and rent a triple (with an extra bed, if needed). Rooms at the Sotavento have fans and private baths; a few are air-conditioned.

Finally, farthest away from town to the southeast, is Playa Las Gatas. Least "touristy" of all the beaches, Las Gatas bears a collection of modest houses and beach shacks as well as the rather posh **Las Gatas Beach Club.** Consider this one only if you're coming in summer, as winter rates are about 1750 pesos per person, and a minimum stay of three days is often required. You're a longish way from town here, too, although launches ply the seas between Las Gatas and Zihuatanejo throughout the day.

On the Starvation Budget

Zihuatanejo has a few pensions which have not been hit by the lust for bucks. Among these is the **Casa Bahía (6)**, an extremely modest but homely place which takes in travelers and charges them 250 pesos single, twice that double in winter. Plumbing is basic, but so is life in Zihuatanejo, the pleasures of which make up for the lack of amenities. Little tables outside overlook the beach and the municipal fishing dock.

At the **Casa Aurora (8)**, on Nicolas Bravo, two people pay 600 pesos in summer, 750 in winter, for a small and rather airless room away from the beach (only a few minutes away, though). Some rooms are better than others—check before you buy.

Staying at Ixtapa

Strictly speaking, a place like Ixtapa has no place in a book such as this, but just so you'll know: the lowest priced hotel rents its cheapest single room for about 3000 pesos *during the summer;* doubles and winter rates are a lot higher. Ixtapa was built for the charter tour or package tour visitor, and is really enjoyable only if you buy an all-inclusive package, which will be expensive, but actually a lot cheaper than making all the separate arrangements for flight, hotel, and meals yourself. By all means, don't wander into one of the fancy hotels and ask for a room for a night or two. "Rack rates," the prices given to the casual, unprogrammed guest, are the highest rates ever charged by any hotel. Buy a package if you buy at all.

There's nothing to stop you from having a look, and there's no reason why you can't put on your best tatami-sandals and mingle with the beach crowd there—an empty lounge chair is an invitation to sit down. In fact, you shouldn't miss having a look as the situation of Ixtapa is simply magnificent.

Local buses trundle between the two towns of Zihuatanejo and Ixtapa frequently (buses leave from across the market in Zihuatanejo). As you come up over the rise from Zihuatanejo, the bay of Ixtapa is spread out before you. If you've ever had dreams of paradise, they'll probably coincide with what you see. Palms line the wide beach which fronts a sea always alive with surf. The high-rise hotels are very new, modern, and ever-increasing in number. Although plans call for a total of 16 high-rises, not all have gone up to date. You'll ride along past the hotels, through well-kept grounds and a golf course, and if you get the feeling you're outclassed, remember this: all beaches in Mexico are public property, open to everyone.

WHERE TO EAT: The days are gone when Zihuatenejo offered only beach-shack seafood stands or bus station greasy spoons. Besides the hotel restaurants, there are a number of attractive places to dine. **La Bocana (2)**, close to where the main street hits the beach, is a more expensive restaurant serving red snapper for 285 pesos, half a chicken for the same, beef entrees for 225 pesos, snails for the same. You dine inside the beachfront restaurant or on the open patio, with the romance of native recorded music in the background, and at some seasons, unfortunately, the hum of lazy afternoon flies. When I last ate here, a light lunch for two consisting of one ceviche, a big salad (which was shared), a plate of red snapper, three beers and one coffee, tax and tip included, came to 750 pesos.

A step down in price, but still on the beach, is the **Canaima (6)**. The view is through airy wrought-iron or bamboo "walls" to the beach, and you get full benefit of the breeze. The snapper here is excellent, and a meal of snapper filet, oyster cocktail, beer, coffee, and dessert will cost 550 pesos. By the way, you must enter the Canaima from near the beach; if you enter from the street, that's a totally different restaurant, called the Taboga.

The **Kapi-Cofi (16)**, once highly recommended in this book, is not the bright and shiny place it was a few years ago. Still, the blessed cool from the air conditioner packs 'em in during the hot months, and the omelets, sandwiches, hamburgers, and full breakfasts are reasonably priced from 40 to 65 pesos; a daily set-price lunch goes for 99 pesos.

Besides the hotel restaurants on Madera Beach, this area has one other appealing eatery. The **Kon-Tiki**, across the street from the Hotel Posada Caracol, is a fun pizza place up the hill overlooking the beach. An average price for any of the 12 types of pizzas is 350 pesos; shish kebab is less at 200 pesos; a big vegetable salad is 140 pesos. It's open 2 to 11 p.m. I have but one question: How does a pizza-and-hamburger joint in Zihuatanejo, Mexico, get the name Kon-Tiki?

More Elegant Dining

Zihuatanejo has fortunately retained the village flavor and still managed to attract a few unobtrusive high-budget restaurants. **La Mesa del Capitan (15)**, Nicolas Bravo 18, is simply furnished with dark wooden chairs and tables. The extensive menu includes such entrees as shrimp, natural or sweet-and-sour, for 350 pesos; fish for 210 to 300 pesos, T-bone steak for 325 pesos. All meat orders come with a delicious baked potato with lots of tasty cheese. La Mesa serves from 2 p.m. until midnight.

La Tortuga ("The Tortoise") **(5)** is about the most expensive independent (i.e., non-hotel) restaurant in town. It's very atmospheric, however, and the mellow lights, soft music, and neo-rustic decor appeal greatly to day-trippers from much-more-expensive Ixtapa. You have the choice of ordering your red snapper as a filet or as a whole fish, or shrimp any of half a dozen ways, or steak, or pork chops. If you choose with care, a full meal here might cost about 750 pesos for two. If you both order shrimp (except the cheaper cocktail), and have a bottle of wine, your entire bill can climb as high as 1600 pesos. La Tortuga is a block in from the beach, northwest of Cuauhtémoc.

With the burgeoning of Ixtapa, Zihuatanejo has seen even more expensive restaurants open up. Mariano's, Don Juan, etc., all will serve you decent meals in pleasant surroundings, but for about 600 to 750 pesos per person. They can get these prices because (1) their clients are mostly from Ixtapa, (2) they're all on short but expensive vacations.

Cheap Eats

As always in Mexican towns, there's one place where the food is always basic but tasty, and the prices are dependably low: the **central market.** Located on **Paseo del Cocotal (M)**, Zihuatanejo's market has been nicely fixed up in recent years (at least, over what it was before). Local señoras always set up rough-and-ready cookshops to serve the villagers who come to market daily. The food is best at lunchtime, as most marketing is finished by early afternoon. A big bowl of pozole (meat-and-hominy stew), grilled chicken, or tacos is sure to be filling, and a dollar is about all you'll have to spend.

For another inexpensive snack location, walk down to **Calle Ejido** between Cuauhtémoc and Guerrero, where rows of little taco shops line the street. Their savory concoctions satisfy tourist and local alike, for about 16 pesos apiece. Also here is the **Expendio de Pan "El Buen Gusto,"** a bakery sales shop, and a juguería (juice stand)—in short, all you need for a low-budget feast.

BEACHES: Besides the tranquil town beach, there are three other main beaches. The town is protected from the main surge of the Pacific, but the **Madera** beach (below the Madera Hotel) and **La Ropa** beach (below the Catalina Hotel) are both open to the surf. La Ropa is the largest and most beautiful beach on the bay, and buses run to it, leaving from near the market (M).

Along a rocky seaside path that leads from La Ropa is **Las Gatas,** which is unusually beautiful and secluded. You might plan a splurge-type lunch here, as there are several open-air restaurants specializing in red snapper, clams, oysters, and lobster.

For those not up to the walk around the bay, charter boats are available to take you to Las Gatas and pick you up later in the day. For fares, see the price list posted at the **Embarcadero (9).** Theoretically, you can specify at what hour you wish to be picked up, but just remember that Mexicans are not noted for watching the clock very closely.

There is a fourth beach on the bay, about a third of a mile to the north, and accessible either by boat or footpath. Nestled between stone cliffs, and only about 100 yards wide, it is composed entirely of large stone blocks blocking the mouth of a (usually dry) river.

Bigger boats are available at the town pier for more adventurous expeditions: for instance, you can combine deep-sea fishing with a visit to the near-deserted ocean beaches which extend for miles along the coast from Zihuatanejo. As a final note, you might want to explore the small islands to the north, accessible only by boat, and noted for two small secluded beaches which make them a favorite day excursion.

The most popular is **Ixtapa Island,** about ten miles from the mainland. Here are golden sand beaches and brilliant blue water joined to an unfenced wildlife "park" filled with exotic birds and animals. The one restaurant there is expensive, but good. The excursion launch going to Ixtapa Island from Zihuatanejo is expensive, too. It stays all day, returning to the Embarcadero by 5 p.m. You might want to go to the Ixtapa Resort area or Playa Quieta and scout around for launches leaving from there for Ixtapa Island—sometimes they do, and they cost less.

Another of the main islands, **Morro de los Pericos,** is known for the great variety of birds which nest on rocky points jutting out into the blue Pacific. You'll have to rent a boat for this one, as outlined above.

ZIHUATANEJO MISCELLANY: The **market (M)** still serves as the place to go for basic food and clothing items, although a few shops now sell stuff in some ways more suitable to the tourist.

Of the nightlife places, **Los Alpes** has a lively jukebox, fluorescent lighting, and the patronage of local young bloods—cover charge is 100 pesos, and no booze is served. **Chololo** is a disco with a thatched roof and, occasionally, a live band. It's on the beach in front of the Hotel Irma, open 8 p.m. to 3 a.m., with a 200-peso cover charge.

The drive-in theater has come to Zihuatanejo—well, in a way. The only difference in the theater here is that you walk in rather than drive in, and you sit outside on a bench to watch the movie which is flashed onto the wall of a nearby building, painted white for the purpose. Gather up 30 pesos on Saturday night and enjoy a Mexican film here.

The **Tourism Office (1)** is on the beach, Paseo del Pescador, near the municipal pier, open from 9 a.m. to 2 p.m. and 4 to 6 p.m., on Saturday from 9 a.m. to 1 p.m.; closed Sunday. Sr. Hernandez Abaunza here is most helpful.

GETTING TO ZIHUATANEJO: Buses from Acapulco, Lázaro Cárdenas / Playa Azul, and Uruapan; planes from Mexico City.

By Bus

Three Estrella de Oro buses run daily from Acapulco, two express and one first-class (normal) service. Flecha Roja has buses every hour on the hour. See below under "Getting to Acapulco" for more details.

When you leave Zihuatanejo, you can choose from three departures per day to Acapulco by Estrella de Oro; six departures daily to Lázaro Cárdenas and Uruapan by Tres Estrellas and Autobuses del Occidente. Flecha Roja buses to Acapulco leave each half hour from 4 a.m. to 10 p.m., plus a bus at 11 p.m. and one at midnight. Flecha Roja is by far the less desirable line.

By Air

AeroMéxico has four daily flights from Mexico City to Ixtapa–Zihuatanejo, from early in the morning to late in the evening. Mexicana has one morning and one early-evening flight from the capital to Zihuatanejo. Offices are in these locations: Calle Juan N. Alvarez 34 (tel. 743/4-2018); Centro Comercial "La Puerta," (tel. 743/4-2929); Cinco de Mayo 14 (tel. 743/3-0853).

Mexicana has the same number of daily flights. In Zihuatanejo, they're at Vicente Guerrero and Nicolás Bravo (tel. 743/4-2208).

7. Acapulco

The truly astounding thing about Acapulco (pop. 600,000) is not its perennial romantic reputation—or even its jet-set status—but its variety. To a local businessman, staunch member of the Lions Club, Acapulco is probably as thrilling as Dubuque. To the "beautiful people," Acapulco is an exciting playground. To the aware traveler, Acapulco is not only a bustling commercial center and jet-set haven but one of those fascinating multiracial localities on the order of Trinidad and Rio. In most of Mexico, the prevailing ethnic mix is Spanish-Indian; in Acapulco it's Afro-Spanish-Indian. And this adds an extra dimension to Acapulco's charm.

A word about **climate**. Although it's fashionable to talk about six dry months and six wet months here, this is an oversimplification. June—when the rains begin—is extremely wet, but July and August considerably less so. In that interim you have what amounts to a "little dry season." The rains increase in September and October, ending at the beginning of *la seca* (the dry season) in November.

While the city is untypically Mexican, it's futile to indulge in comparisons with other places, e.g., the French Riviera, the Florida Gold Coast, or whatever. You'll encounter, as you survey local housing, expensive exquisite taste, expensive atrocious taste, drab suburbia, and some of the foulest slums this side of Rio's "favelas." The accent is ever on variety.

Even more than other places in Mexico, Acapulco is what you make of it; and what you make of it depends, to some degree, on how much you spend. Compared to a place like Mexico City, Acapulco's hotels and restaurants charge more and give less: such is the lure of resorts and romance.

I should warn you about street names and numbers in this city: the jumbled maze of streets and alleys which lace the city's hilltops and hillsides are badly marked, if they're marked at all, and street numbers are also hard to find. I've done my best to tell you how to find your way around, but you'll have to ask repeatedly to get to any destination except the most obvious ones.

GETTING TO ACAPULCO: This is an easy task because Acapulco is well served by public transportation. What follows is a brief listing of the major means of conveyance.

By Bus

Remember that buses from Mexico City to Acapulco leave from the Terminal Central de Autobuses del Sur (Metro Taxqueña) and *not* from the giant Central del Norte. The trip to Acapulco takes about seven hours.

Estrella de Oro (tel. 905/549-8520) has almost hourly buses from Mexico City to Acapulco, but you should definitely reserve your seat a few days in advance. (See Chapter VI, "Arriving in Mexico City," for information on making reservations.) Deluxe service costs a bit more than express service; the difference is a larger bus of equal comfort. As the difference in cost is not much, I'd suggest you pick your bus by departure time (that most convenient for you) and ignore the deluxe or express part of it. All the buses are air-conditioned and have toilets. I might note that the road to Mexico City is pretty windy and makes for a tedious journey.

Lineas Unidas del Sur / Flecha Roja also runs frequent buses to Acapulco from the Central del Sur, but their equipment is not generally up to the same standards as that of Estrella de Oro.

By Air

Acapulco has a *very* busy airport, and there are direct flights between this city and Los Angeles (daily), Atlanta (Eastern Airlines, two per weekend), Chicago (six a day), Dallas/Fort Worth (four a day), New York (two a day), and Guadalajara (daily). All these flights offer special low excursion rates. Operators are AeroMéxico, Mexicana, American Airlines, and Western Airlines. There are a dozen flights daily to Mexico City, mostly by AeroMéxico, a few by Mexicana.

ARRIVING IN ACAPULCO: This city has one of the most confusing layouts in Mexico, and it's growing so fast even the natives can't keep up with it.

By Bus

Coming by bus from Taxco or Mexico City, you ride past the new development called Renaissance City, through the seamier parts of town to the north of the hills ringing the bay, but then rise to a pass in these hills for a glorious change from squalor to magnificence. The bus then descends the hills to the station: in the case of Lineas Unidas del Sur / Flecha Roja, the bus station is in the market area only about six blocks from the zócalo; the Estrella de Oro bus station, however, is at Avenida Cuauhtémoc 1490. Cuauhtémoc is the major artery inland from and roughly parallel to the Costera Aleman. A taxi from the bus station of the Estrella de Oro line to the zócalo will cost about 120 pesos; to any of the larger hotels, about the same amount. Local buses pass the terminal in both directions, and are a very inexpensive way of getting to your hotel.

Important Note: Acapulco's master development plan calls for construction of a brand-new bus station for intercity buses near Renaissance City (Ciudad Renacimiento) on the north side of the hills. It may be completed by the time you read this. At the new station, switch to a city bus for the ride downtown, or take a cab.

By Air

Acapulco's airport is a good distance out of town, over the hills lying to the east of the bay. After you leave the plane, head for the baggage area, but don't just hang around waiting for your bags. Instead, step out the exit door to the curb, where you'll find a desk manned by personnel from the Transportaciones de Pasajeros company (tel. 748/2-6700). Buy your ticket and reserve your seat into town while the rest of the planeload is standing around waiting for the baggage to arrive. The exact price of your ticket will depend on where your hotel is—they operate on a zone system—but it should be around 300 pesos, *round-trip*. For your return to the airport at the end of your stay, call the number listed above at least a day (24 hours) in advance of your departure, and make a reservation for a seat back to the airport. The bus, minibus, or car (depending on demand) will pick you up about 90 minutes (domestic flights) or 120 minutes (flights to other countries) before your flight's departure time, and whisk you back to the airport.

GETTING AROUND: Acapulco, the town and its resorts, now stretches for four miles all around the bay, and so walking to see it all is not practical unless you're an Olympic type. Taxis charge 80 pesos for a ride within the city, more if you go farther out, or about 350 pesos per hour. Before you get a cab, ask to see the list of prices *(lista de precios)* in the dispatcher's booth at the cab stand (sitio) to be sure you're paying the legally authorized fare. Report any trouble or overcharges to the Department of Tourism on Hornos beach (tel. 748/2-2170).

For transport in town you'll find the city buses best, and cheapest. Best place near the zócalo to catch buses is beside Sanborn's, two blocks east. "Caleta Directo" buses will take you to Caleta and Caletilla beaches along the Costera Aleman; some buses return along the same route, others ("Caleta Flamingos") go around the southwest side of the peninsula to return to the zócalo. As for the beaches of Hornos, Condesa, and the restaurants and night-

ACAPULCO 103

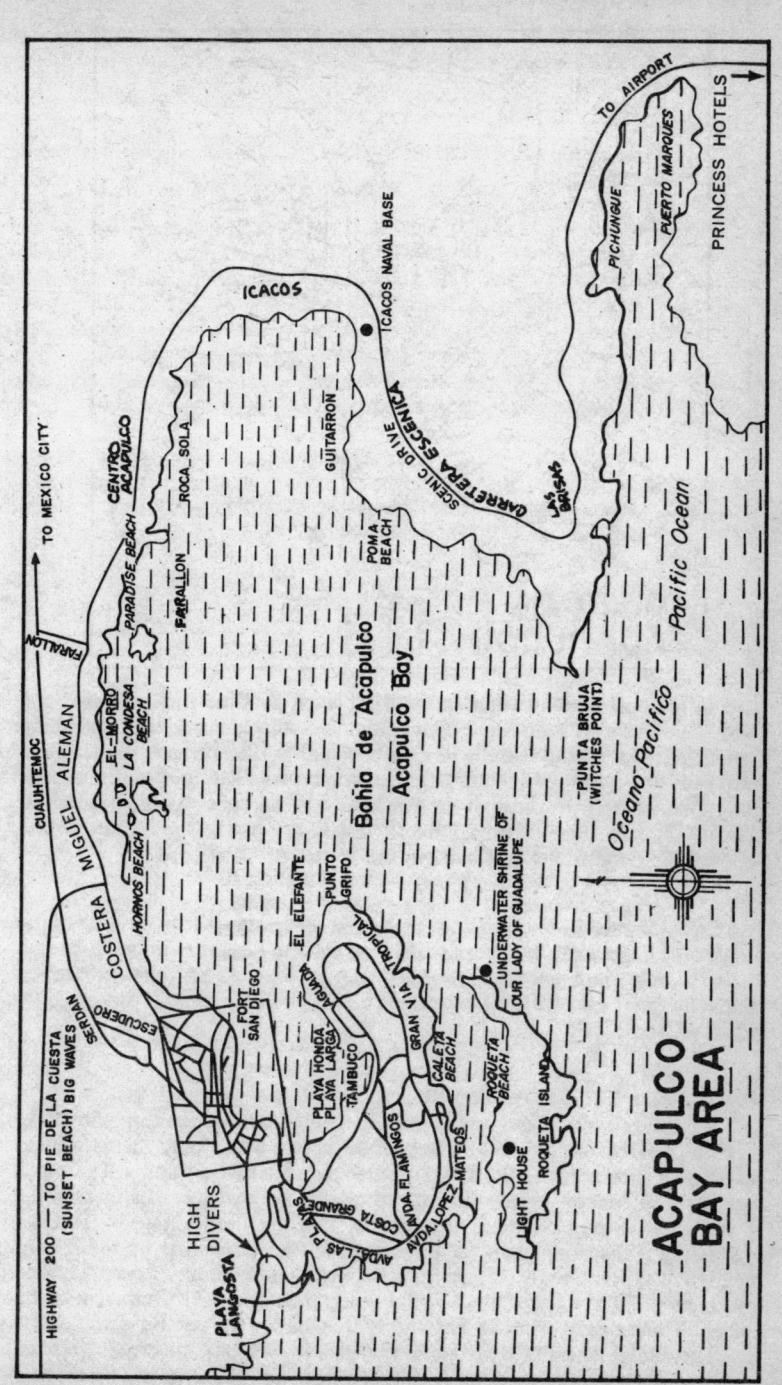

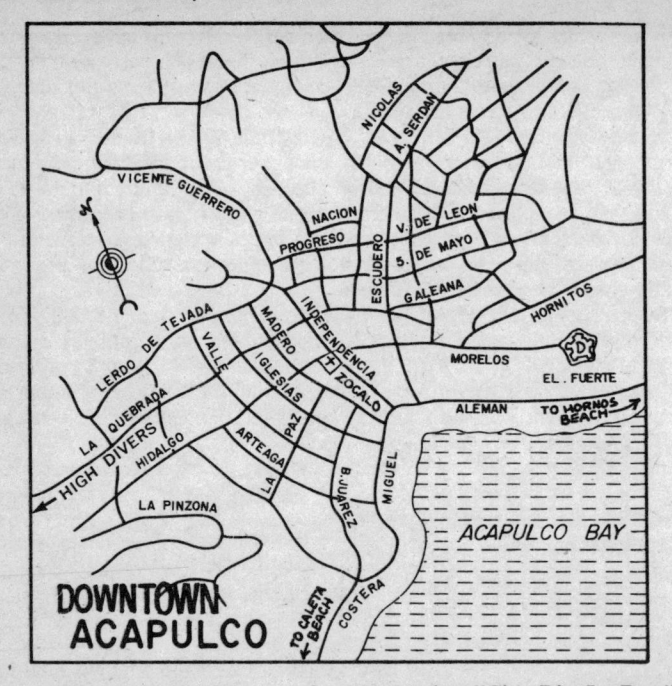

spots in the posh hotel district to the east, catch a "Cine Rio–La Base" bus beside Sanborn's. It'll go along Cuauhtémoc, a block inland and *not* along Costera Aleman, to the Estrella de Oro terminal; it then turns at the terminal and heads down to the beach at the Ritz hotel, turns left, and continues east along Costera Aleman through the Diana Circle, and out past El Presidente. "Zócalo Directo" and "Caleta Directo" buses follow the same route in the opposite direction to get you back to the zócalo or Caleta area.

WHERE TO STAY: With the exception of a few places, the hotels east of the zócalo are all fantastically expensive. For hotels near beaches within our budget range the hills south and west of the zócalo, near Caleta and Caletilla beaches, offer some good values. But the cheapest places of all are right downtown only blocks off the zócalo.

Downtown—On La Quebrada

West of the zócalo and up the hillside to where the famous high divers do their thing stretches a warren of busy little streets where only the occasional resort-wear shop reminds one that Acapulco lives mainly on visitors. The hotels are simple and cheap—much the same standard, but generally cleaner than the cheap hotels in most other Mexican towns. The one disadvantage to the Quebrada area is that four times each evening big tour buses roar up the hill for the high divers' act, some leaving their engines running until it's over. The last dive is at 11:30 p.m., so it's not really quiet until midnight. But even so, La Quebrada and neighboring La Paz and Juarez harbor the best buys in the city.

The **Hotel Angelita,** Quebrada 37 (tel. 748/3-5734), advertises *limpieza absoluta,* or absolute cleanliness, and that's what you'll find in this bright new place. White rooms are adjoined by blue tiled baths, all rooms have ceiling fans, and the sympathetic patron charges 300 pesos single, 600 pesos double, 250 pesos per person for triples and quadruples. If you stay any length of time you get a 10% reduction. Recommended.

The **Casa Amparo** (tel. 748/2-2172), Quebrada 69, is a friendly place with lots of greenery and three tiers of rooms, the upper group of which have views of the bay. Service tends to be a bit slow, although pleasant enough; what was once the dining room has now been converted to a row of rather claustrophobic guest rooms, which you'd do well to avoid. Prices are good, though, at 700 pesos in summer, 900 pesos in winter, for a double room. Bargain prices for room and one or two meals are offered.

You'll recognize the **Hotel Mariscal,** Quebrada 35 (tel. 748/2-0015), at the bottom of the hill where La Quebrada joins Hidalgo, by its mustard-colored porch and wrought-iron chairs. The 17 rooms here are airy and cool, with comfortable box springs and private baths, although the fluorescent lights and old furniture leave a little something to be desired. Rooms are 300 pesos per person in summer, 450 pesos each in winter.

At the top of the hill on La Quebrada, only a few steps from the high divers, is the **Hotel El Faro** (tel. 748/2-1365), which has had top ratings in past editions of this book but which has slipped some of late. The pleasant couple who run the hotel are invariably friendly, but not all the rooms are worth the price. Best solution is to inspect a room carefully before you rent it. Be sure to see one of the junior suites, which for a few pesos more give you a lot more room, a view on the square, even a terrace. Room prices are 450 pesos single, 550 pesos double, 800 pesos for two in a junior suite.

Finally, a choice for the person who likes this area and who has found all of the above hotels full: the **Hotel Asturias** (tel. 748/3-6548), Quebrada 45, will do in a pinch. The rooms are in ranks on an inner court, with an open dining area at one end. Bright wallpaper, fans, and aging private baths are in each room, and a small swimming pool fills the courtyard. The price is 345 pesos per person.

Downtown—The La Paz Area

La Paz is one of the streets that runs back into the zócalo, and it, too, is a good area for budget hotels. I like best a small hotel called the **Casa Anita,** Azueta 12, corner of La Paz (tel. 748/2-5046), a friendly, homey place with ferns growing out of boxes on all the window sills. Fourteen of the 27 rooms have hot water, all have private baths. Price per person is 250 to 350 pesos, depending on the time of year.

Second place goes to the new **Hotel California,** La Paz 12 (tel. 748/2-2893), where the rooms, built around an open paved patio, all have nice white drapes and sleek Formica furniture (private baths, hot water). Singles here, without meals, cost 300 to 400 pesos, doubles run 400 to 550 pesos, 100 pesos more for air conditioning. You'll find the zócalo and the city bus stops only one block away.

A fine, centrally located budget buy is the **Hotel Colimense,** Iglesias 11 (tel. 748/2-2890). All eight rooms are on the second floor and overlook a shaded courtyard supporting such homey features as swings and rocking chairs. Rooms are clean and well screened with ceiling fans to cut the heat. Rates are 250 to 325 pesos per person.

An older hotel which has been completely—but completely—redone is the **Hotel Mission** (tel. 748/2-3643), Felipe Valle 12. A dusty and none-too-handsome courtyard has been turned into a wonderland of colonial-style tiles, furniture, arches, all centered on an enormous and magnificent mango tree. In the rooms, the tiled washbasin is outside the toilet/shower area, a thoughful addition. White brick walls, ceiling fans (no air conditioning), and screens are in all rooms, as is constant hot water (so they say). The price is 500 to 700 pesos single, 750 to 950 pesos double, high for this area, but not for the style of the hotel.

Other budget hotel owners could take lessons from the owners of the **Hotel Silva,** Juarez 24 (no phone). The rooms, though spartan, are quite clean, equipped with private showers and ceiling fans (but no window screens, alas). Each room has two or three single beds, and rooms are priced at 300 pesos single, 500 pesos double, 650 pesos triple.

Southwest along Costera Aleman

If you stand in the zócalo and face the water, to your right the waterfront boulevard called Costera Miguel Aleman will take you to the next budget hotel areas. This peninsula hooks to the south and east, and hotels dot the slopes of its several hills. You can get to the bottom of any hill easily—any bus along Costera Aleman will take you there—but then you must hoof it to the top, or take a cab. But the distances are not really that great, and you get the extra bonus of good views of the bay from the ones higher up. Taxis from the zócalo or anywhere downtown cost a dollar or two to any of these hotels. Take a taxi up with your bags when you arrive; walk after that.

Heading west along the Costera from the zócalo, the first of my choices you'll come to is the **Hotel de los Reyes,** Costera Aleman 217 (tel. 748/2-2176), where each of the 33 rooms has a private bath with hot water, a ceiling fan, telephone, good cross-ventilation, and nice wooden furniture. Rates are 310 pesos per person. The Reyes is on the beach side of the road.

Near Playa Langosta

Not much farther along the Costera Aleman will be a turn to the right across the isthmus of the peninsula (a distance of 100 yards) to a small beach called the Playa Langosta, at the head of a pretty little inlet. Facing the playa is the **Hotel Mozimba** (tel. 748/2-2785), an attractive, family-type place with 41 rooms, plenty of hot water, and excellent meals. This is the kind of hotel that people return to every year, so there's always a crowd that knows one another. Rates are 880 pesos single, 990 pesos double, 1100 pesos triple, plus 150 pesos for air conditioning, without meals. In season they tend to run on American Plan (you must buy your meals there), but in the off-season of May to December 10% discounts are in order.

A Motel near Caleta and Caletilla

Whether or not you drive to Acapulco, you should consider staying at the **Motel La Jolla** (tel. 748/2-5862; in Mexico City, call 905/566-2377), Costera Aleman and Avenida Lopez Mateos, where a bright and modern double room costs only 945 pesos off-season, 1135 pesos in season. This L-shaped, two-story motel surrounds a swimming pool bordered with coconut palms, and although there is no view of the sea whatsoever, there is a flying-saucer-shaped restaurant serving sandwiches and hamburgers for 100 to 130 pesos, other entrees for more. You are quite near the beach here, although you can't see it.

Near Caletilla Beach

The beaches of Caleta and Caletilla are side by side, so access to one is access to the other. Several hotels offer good accommodations within walking distance of the water—no need to catch a bus along Costera Aleman as there was for the above choices.

The layout of streets in the peninsula is confusing, and the disorganization in street names and numbers is enough to drive one to tears: a street will be named Avenida Lopez Mateos, but so will the street meeting it at a 90-degree angle; some streets have two names, while others have none; many buildings sport two street numbers, and the like, so here are explicit directions to my hotel choices in this area. Fronting on Caletilla beach is a semicircular array of little restaurants, and behind this semicircle and across the street is a large, tree-lined parking lot for the Jai Alai Fronton, a peeling yellowish building at the far end of the parking lot. As you face the parking lot (your back to the water), a street runs along the left side of the lot up the hill. This is supposedly Avenida Lopez Mateos (also called Avenida Flamingoes) and along it, on the left-hand side of the street, are several good hotels only a few minutes' walk from the beach.

Three or four persons traveling together might want to consider the cheerful **Hotel Montemar** (tel. 748/2-4776), across from the Fronton Jai Alai at Lopez Mateos 970, built in 1968 and run by the pleasant Sra. Gertrudis Alcocer. The hotel is built on the hillside, has a terrace garden and a convent in the background. There are nine rooms altogether, one air-conditioned and eight with fans, the latter going for 350 to 500 pesos per person. Parking, pool, and kitchen privileges with agua purificada. For the air-conditioned room it's a bit more.

The new **Hotel San Antonio** (tel. 748/2-1358), to the left of the Jai Alai Fronton on Lopez Mateos, is actually an older hotel that's been completely rebuilt (1980). Now equipped with air conditioning and a swimming pool (still under construction as of this writing), rooms are rented for 575 pesos per person in summer, 625 pesos per person in winter. The San Antonio is the newest and poshest of the budget hotels in the area.

The 26-room **Motel Caribe,** Lopez Mateos 10, at Ensenada (tel. 748/2-1550), with music going constantly in the lobby, has rooms arranged around an open garden. Dark stained doors and slatted windows open off the rooms to terraces: private on one side, public walkways on the other. All rooms have private baths with hot and cold water. Rates are 400 to 650 pesos per person; the higher winter price includes a continental breakfast.

The little **Posada Caletilla** (tel. 748/2-3427), up the hill a bit farther at Lopez Mateos 3, is a private house with ten rooms which rent for 200 to 400 pesos per person, single or double. All rooms have private baths, but are otherwise quite plainly equipped. The proprietors are very friendly, the atmosphere is tranquil, and you're not all that far up the hill, really.

Now in a slightly different location is an exceptionally good place to stay: facing the Hotel de la Playa between Caleta and Caletilla beaches, take the street to your left up the hill. About 1½ blocks up the hill you'll find the sinuous facade of the **Hotel Belmar** (tel. 748/2-1525 or 2-1526), an older hotel well kept up and very pleasant. Two small pools and shady patios fill the grassy lawn in front of the hotel. The four-story hotel was built in the '50s, with air conditioning added later. The cool, breezy rooms cost 440 pesos single, 550 pesos double in summer; 550 pesos single, 660 pesos double in winter. For 400 pesos more per person you can have breakfast and dinner each day.

Back toward the center of town on the Costera, across the street from the Motel Las Palmas, is the **Casa de Huespedes Walton** (tel. 748/2-0452), Costera Aleman 223. This congenial little pension set back from the busy street is run by a bevy of happy señoras who want everything to go right: signs in the courtyard admonish people, "For the love of God, park correctly and obey the lines!" and "Don't ruin tourism with loud horns and mufflers!" Rooms at the Casa Walton rent with breakfast and dinner at the reasonable price of 450 pesos per person in summer, 550 pesos per person in winter. The small but pleasant Playa Langosta (or Angosta) is only five minutes' walk from your door.

A Splurge Hotel at Caleta

Were I to arrive in Acapulco with pockets full of cash, rather than blowing it in the Empire State Buildings arrayed along the eastern beaches I'd head for the **Hotel Boca Chica** (tel. 748/2-6014), overlooking Caletilla beach at the end of the Costera Aleman. The five-story hotel fits into the hillside fairly unobtrusively. Lawns, terraces, the pool, the bar and restaurant are on different levels. The hotel's location on the headland of the beach allows for 180-degree panoramic views. All the air-conditioned rooms have little verandas, fine marble-and-tile baths, lots of windows, and room to unfold in. The hotel can also provide facilities for waterskiing, sailing, scuba diving, deep-sea fishing, surfing, golf, and tennis. During the winter you must take breakfast and dinner in the hotel, and the cost is a hefty 2250 pesos single, 2850 pesos double. But during the rest of the year (May 1 to December 15) prices are about 18% lower, and you needn't include the meals in the price.

If you like all this so far, be advised that the Boca Chica has a toll-free reservations number in the U.S.A.: 800/223-5695; in New York City, call 212/730-8100; in Mexico City, call 905/533-5159.

Hotels East of Town, on Hornos Beach

Strictly speaking, once you go east of the zócalo along Costera Aleman, out toward the luxury high-rise hotels, you're out of our budget district, but several hotels in this area offer rates which don't do great violence to my $20-a-Day rule in the off-season months from May through October.

The **Hotel De Gante** (tel. 748/2-5961); in Mexico City, 905/535-2446), Costera Aleman 265, at Playa Suave, is one of the older "new" hotels in Acapulco, but decoration and facilities are kept well up to date, as can be seen by the great amount of gleaming marble in the lobby. Rooms are all light and modern, with good beds and bright orange-flowered drapes, plus tiled bathrooms. Those on the front have little balconies and views of the bay; the second-floor restaurant has a bay view, too. Price for a single room is 1100 to 1800 pesos, for a double it's 1350 to 2000 pesos, the higher prices being the in-season (winter) ones.

Although you may not have the bucks to stay at the Ritz, you may be able to swing a few nights at the **Auto Hotel Ritz** (tel. 748/2-1922), just off Costera Aleman inland half a block from its high-rise namesake on Avenida Magellanes. There are over 100 rooms here, in an L-shape around a swimming pool itself surrounded by trees and green arbors and set with tables which constitute the hotel's restaurant, called El Jardín. Elevators take you up to the comfortable, almost luxurious modern motel rooms which feature flower boxes on the little balconies (a few of which have sea views—ask for them on the seventh floor). Prices are 1600 to 2800 pesos single, 2000 to 3400 pesos double, the higher prices being for the winter season, when two meals daily are included.

Also in this area, a few blocks back from the beach up on the hillside, is the new and shiny **Hotel Villa Rica** (tel. 748/4-8040), Avenida Universidad at the corner of Avenida Dr. Chavez / Reyes Catolicos. Front rooms have balconies with grand bay views; all rooms are spacious, tasteful, modern, and air-conditioned. Good, firm beds, a few parking spaces inside the gates, and a quiet location are extras, but the biggest extra of all is the beautiful swimming pool. Prices are a bit high, but the hotel is new and very nice (although service lacks a good bit of savoir faire): singles are 1000 to 1850 pesos off-season, 1350 to 2050 pesos in season; doubles are 1450 to 2150 pesos off-season, 1850 to 2800 pesos in season. If they're not full or if you're staying for a few days, bargain for a reduction.

The small **Hotel Jacqueline** (tel. 748/2-6018), just across the Costera Aleman from the Paraiso-Marriott, has only nine rooms, and you must check one out before you check in. All are arranged around a lush little plot of grass and shrubs, and if the room is acceptable to you, you'll pay 600 to 900 pesos single, 800 to 1100 pesos double, with the higher rates applying in winter, and with reductions for longer stays.

WHERE TO EAT: Some of the budget hotels recommended above will insist that you take your meals in the hotel during high season in the winter (this is euphemistically called the American Plan—forced purchase), but many have no restaurant. Here are my choices of places to eat.

In the Downtown (Zócalo) Area

Alas, the restaurants in the zócalo proper which found favor in this book in previous years are now all too expensive (for what you get), or too devil-may-care about the service to get my recommendation. The place to go now is Calle Juarez, the street running west off the zócalo beside the local incarnation of Denny's restaurant chain. Down Juarez, at no. 19, is the **Picalagua,** one of the nicest restaurants in the area. Iron grillwork separates the tables from the street, and other tables are set back in a tropical garden full of chattering birds. A lamp hangs over every table, and soft Latin music wafts from above. The specialty is seafood, ranging from crayfish and lobster to such exotica as baby shark. Most entrees are around 125 to 260 pesos, and include turtle, mussels marinara, octopus Veracruzano, or steamed clams. The Picalagua is open daily 8 a.m. to 10:30 p.m. A good breakfast of eggs, bread, coffee, papaya, and frijoles is a mere 80 pesos here.

Also on Juarez, at no. 5, is the **San Carlos,** with a western motif—lots of brick and wood—and food served in pleasant surroundings at chuckwagon prices: charcoal-broiled meats for 90 to 160 pesos, fish for about the same. A comida corrida costs only 115 pesos. The San Carlos is only a few steps from the zócalo.

Mariscos Pipo is a diminutive place that specializes in seafood, and while not dirt cheap gives good value for money. An order of ceviche, which comes with lemon and lots of Saltine crackers, plus a beer, makes a light lunch for 100 pesos. Tuna, octopus, snails, and other delectables come in various combination plates for 150 to 235 pesos. Red snapper is a bit expensive, but almendrado (fish baked with cheese and almonds) is only 185 pesos. Tables stand in an airy, vine-draped room off the sidewalk five short blocks from the zócalo. Walk along Costera Aleman west toward Caleta, past the market stalls and down a passageway by the Farmacía Santa Lucia; or walk along Juarez and at the fork in the road, bear left. Legal address of the Pipo (as though any of these streets were marked!) is Almirante Breton 3. Menu in English. Pipo is open every day from 10 a.m. to 6 p.m.

Very similar to Pipo, but cheaper and a bit closer to the zócalo at the corner of Juarez and Almirante Breton, is **El Amigo Miguel,** a large inside dining room very plainly furnished. Usually it's filled to brimming with seafood lovers taking advantage of the fish at low prices.

Mariscos Milla, at the corner of Azueta and Carranza, might fool you at first into thinking prices are high here. Although the decor is upbeat and pleasant, this doesn't seem to affect the low prices. The kitchen is occupied by a platoon of hard-working señoras who will serve you ceviche (fish cocktail) for a mere 45 pesos. A delicious meal of fish filet and a beer need cost only 165 pesos. Mariscos Milla is open seven days a week from 7 a.m. to 8 p.m. You'll recognize it—an airy corner restaurant—across the street from the Hotel Sacramento, and not far from the Casa Anita.

Sanborn's, a block or two off the zócalo east along Costera Aleman, and **Denny's,** right on the zócalo (on the west side), offer American-style food and popular Mexican plates at rather high prices, but in clean and comfortable surroundings (air-conditioned!). Prices are about the same in both. If they're offering a daily special plate when you're there, order it—that's the best value-for-money, at about 220 pesos. Everything is modern and quite sanitary. Breakfast is about 180 pesos for hotcakes, an egg, juice, and coffee—and you get free seconds on coffee.

On the opposite (east) side of the zócalo from these plates is the **Terraza Las Flores,** entered via Calle Juarez across from Denny's. The menus here are in English, Spanish, and German; the friendly and engaging owner speaks Spanish and English, his son speaks Spanish and German. Glance at the blackboard, which will bear the name and price of the daily special, always a good bargain: chicken soup, "Milanesa Viena" (alias wienerschnitzel), potatoes, salad, dessert, and coffee for 185 pesos, for instance. Otherwise, à la carte dinners will cost about 220 to 280 pesos complete if you have meat or fish, a good deal less if you have something like enchiladas. You always seem to find a few exotic (for Acapulco) dishes such as pork and cabbage offered. The Terraza has about two dozen tables on two levels, lots of potted plants, and is open from 11 a.m. to 11 p.m. every day.

Rock-Bottom Prices

Restaurant Carmon's at Juarez 8 is certainly low on the price scale. You don't get so much atmosphere here, for the Carmon is pretty plain, but you don't pay for it either. The comida corrida is only 80 pesos for five courses, and the noise from the TV which thrums to itself in a corner costs nothing extra.

Acapulco's lowest prices of all are concentrated along the street named **Azueta,** near La Paz. Comidas corridas at the humble eateries along the way average 60 to 95 pesos. Follow Juarez until it meets the Costera Aleman, and tiny hole-in-the-wall cookstands will serve you a four-course lunch for as little as 55 pesos. The food will be very simple, but filling.

Caleta–Caletilla Beach Area

The area around Caleta and Caletilla beaches used to be rather down-at-the-heels, but not long ago the municipal authorities pumped lots of money into public facilities here. Now the beaches have nice shady palapas and beach chairs, clean sand, and fine palm trees. Three neo-native buildings were built to house "vestidores, regarderas" (changing rooms, showers, and lockers) and restaurants. Little dining places line the outer periphery of the buildings, and the kitchen work is done at the center (peek around to the kitchen to see boys cutting up fish for the pot).

The best way to find a good meal here is to wander along the rows of restaurants, looking for busy spots where people are eating (and not just sipping drinks). Pore over menus, which will either be displayed or handed to you with a smile, on request. Although the restaurants may tend to look all the same, you'll be surprised at the difference in prices. Filete de pescado (fish filet) might be 125 pesos at one place, and 175 pesos at another; beer can cost anywhere from 22 to 34 pesos.

If you stroll a short distance from the beach in the direction of the Hotel Boca Chica, you'll see the airy raised "patio" which is **Bertha and Bob's** restaurant. The comida corrida is quite cheap here, due in part to the fact that the restaurant is back from the beach a ways. But the view is fine, and 200 pesos is hardly a lot to pay for a full lunch.

Starvation Budget (Caleta–Caletilla)

To get a good, but inexpensive, meal you'll have to leave the beach and go back along the Costera Aleman to the Pemex station (crossroads with Avenida Americas—there's a pseudo Burger King across from the gas station). Now, behind the Pemex station and across the street from the Club de Yates under a low thatched roof and hidden by much vegetation and verdure is the **Restaurant Mitla,** a comely if humble establishment run by several hefty señoras who serve up a full comida corrida for 85 pesos, or a plate of bistek for 75 pesos. Nothing fancy—the garden terraces are artfully hedged by rows of beer bottles to support the soil—still it's a pleasant, open-air place. Jukebox, cheap cold beer, good smells, tasty food, low price. Go there from 7 a.m. to 11 p.m. every day.

Hornos–Condesa Beach Areas

Don't expect to find much that's inexpensive out here on the high-class beach area where atmosphere and snob appeal are sold (at a high price) along with the food. Here are my suggestions:

A Yucatecan restaurant, even on the Pacific coast, is never out of place when it comes to good food, and **Antojitos Mayab** is the place to sample local Yucatán dishes such as suckling pig (cochinita), roasted chicken (pollo pibil), and other regional specialties. Daily special plates cost about 150 to 190 pesos here, and the food is a welcome change from tacos and enchiladas. The Mayab is on the land side of Costera Aleman near Hornos beach, at the traffic light before the tunnel under Papagayo Park—look for the sign and the thatched roof with tables and chairs set out on a patio in front.

Even farther along the Costera, across from La Torre de Acapulco at the corner of Lomas del Mar (there's a Denny's here), is **La Tortuga,** a small restaurant with tables outdoors, a friendly Mexican family in attendance, a young clientele, and a cheery atmosphere. Beer and tacos are the most popular items served, but they have sandwiches and fancier items for 100 to 150 pesos.

For Pastries and Coffee

The **Pastelería Viena,** just east of the Diana Glorieta on Costera Aleman's inland side, is a tiny Central European haven bedecked with posters of the Tirol and cooled to Alpine freshness by a big air conditioner. In the window and in the pastry cases are various baked delights good at any time of day, although the Viena does serve regular breakfasts (140 pesos for the standard eggs, juice, toast, and coffee). Luncheon plates are a hot-weather treat: the special plate (175 pesos) holds ham, cheese, egg salad, cole slaw, and little tuna sandwiches. For a light lunch, sandwiches are about half that price. The Viena is open 8:30 a.m. to 11:30 p.m., Monday through Saturday, 9 a.m. to 10:30 p.m. on Sunday

Restaurant with a View

Los Rancheros (tel. 4-1908), on the "Carretera Escenica" in Guitarrón (the road to Las Brisas and Puerto Marques), has good food and service at reasonable prices. A western cowboy decor of red tile roofs, fences, lassos, and "Wanted" posters surrounds you as you dine on northern Mexican specialties. An immense Mexican combination plate costs 500 pesos. Tortilla soup, *codorniz* (quail, barbecued with potatoes, beans, and salad), barbecued beef with salad, and chile relleno (stuffed pepper), are some of the other delicious choices, or you can dine simply on a pot of beans with onion, epazote, and hot pepper. You'd do well to stay away from fish here. Drinks are served, too. Cold beer? It will refrigerate your interior. And now for the extra: If Los Rancheros were in the dusty hills near Fresnillo it would still be worth going to, but instead it's perched on the hillside overlooking the entire Bay of Acapulco, with its lights glistening like phosphorescent jewels at night. Plan to spend about 400 to 650 pesos per person here. Los Rancheros is open from 2 to 11 p.m. daily, and it's a bit hard to get to (that must be why it has stayed so good): take a bus to La Base, and then a short taxi ride, or a bus to Puerto Marques, and hop off at the restaurant.

The Big Splurge

Although it's probably an oversimplification to say that if you've seen one Carlos Anderson restaurant you've seen them all, I couldn't help being struck by the similarity between **Carlos 'n Charlie's**, Costera, opposite Las Torres Gemelas, and Harry's Bar in Cuernavaca. Same revolutionary posters, same sassy waiters, same ponderous humor in the menu listings ("splash" for seafood, "moo" for beef)... well, you get the idea. But food is good and the place is always packed, which is a good indication that people like what they get for the price they pay. A full meal with a meat main course will cost 350 to 650 pesos, seafood the same. Come early and get a seat on the terrace overlooking the sidewalk. While there may be many similarities among Anderson's restaurants, they also have in common the fact that virtually everyone comes away having had a good meal and a good time.

THE BEACHES: Here's the rundown, from west to east around the bay. **Playa Langosta** (or **Angosta**) is a small, sheltered cove just around the bend from La Quebrada, often deserted, and worth a try anytime. On the peninsula south of the downtown area are **Caleta** and **Caletilla** beaches, each in its own cove. In recent years Caleta and Caletilla have been favored by budget-wise Mexican families, as these are the beaches closest to the city's collection of inexpensive hotels. In the old days, these beaches were what Acapulco was all about.

Nowadays, the beaches and the resort development stretch the entire four-mile length of the bay's shore. Going east from the zócalo, you pass **Terraplen, Clavelito, Carabali,** and **Hornos.** Past the Parque Altamirano (also called Papagayo Park) is **Paraiso,** then you continue along the Costera Aleman and pass the Diana Circle (with a statue/fountain of the goddess) to get to **Condesa** beach, and later **Icacos** beach, the naval base ("La Base"), and **Guitarrón.** After Guitarrón the road climbs the hillside to the fabulous hotel called **Las Brisas,** where many of the bungalow-type rooms have their own swimming pools (there are 200 pools in all!) and cost 7250 pesos per day with a shared pool, 11,250 pesos per day for a double room with private pool in winter. Past Las Brisas, the road continues on to **Puerto Marques,** miles and miles from the zócalo, and in a way, spiritually removed from the rest of Acapulco. The fabulous Acapulco and Pierre Marques Princess Hotels dominate the landscape.

The bay of Puerto Marques is an attractive area in which to bathe. The water is calm, the bay is sheltered, and waterskiing is available.

Past the bay, there's an open beach called **Revolcadero,** and a fascinating jungle lagoon. Take a bus to Puerto Marques and then a canoe through the lagoon to Revolcadero. An alternative method is to take the daily boat between Caleta beach and Puerto Marques. Departure is at 11 a.m.—return in the late afternoon. Should you be driving to Revolcadero, you'll be charged for parking at the beach.

There are other beaches, but they're less practical without a car. One, **La Pie de la Cuesta,** about eight miles west of town (buses leave town every five or ten minutes) is a popular spot from which to watch the sunset—they're big on sunsets in Acapulco—and every sundown the beach is jumping with hammock-swinging sunset aficionados sipping gin-filled coconuts and watching the waves break along the shore. Beware that boys will try to collect money from you to sit under the thatched palapas on the public beach—you needn't pay it.

If you drive, continue right out along the peninsula, passing the lagoon on your right, until you have almost reached the small air base at the tip. All the way along, you'll be invited to drive into different sections of beach by various private entrepreneurs, mostly small boys.

Parasailing

If you've never tried this, you're in for a fantastic thrill. The operators strap you into a parachute harness which is attached by a tow rope to a fast motorboat. A few seconds later your feet leave the beach as the specially designed parachute lifts you up toward the rooftops of the giant hotels. Soon you're above them, floating, soaring, with the entire bay and the mountains in view, and although you don't stay up for more than a few minutes, it seems like about a half hour. It looks like a daredevil act, but the operators put people aloft dozens of times each day, with nary a mishap. How they manage to have you land right where they want you, into the arms of the waiting "landing men," is a sight in itself. The thrill is yours for 550 pesos, with an enlarged color portrait (optional) delivered to your hotel the next day for an additional fee. Most of the parachute rides operate on Condesa beach.

OTHER THINGS TO DO: During the day, it's pleasant to take a walk (early, before it gets too hot) around the zócalo area. Pop into the cathedral, whose big, blue, bulbous spires make it look more like a Russian Orthodox church; and then turn east along the side street going off at right angles. It has no marker, but it's the Calle Carranza and its arcade includes newsstands, shops selling swimsuits, and such-like attractions.

You can see the whole bay from the deck of a yacht, the *Fiesta,* which leaves from the pier of Bono Batani, on the waterfront just west of the zócalo. There are two basic cruises: 4:30 p.m. is castoff time for the regular afternoon cruise (400 pesos); and the moonlight cruise with dancing (550 pesos) leaves at 10:30 p.m. The two other motor yachts, the *Sea Cloud* (4:30 and 10:30 p.m.) and the *Bonanza* (4:30 p.m.) make similar trips daily.

Just across Acapulco Bay, the small island of **La Roqueta** is accessible by ferry from Caletilla Beach. On Roqueta itself, there's nothing to do but lie on the beach, but if you can spare the energy, take the paved path up through the woods to the lighthouse. The walk through the woods from the beach takes about 20 minutes.

Another fabulous view of Acapulco is had by taking a taxi or by driving (no buses) up the hill directly behind the cathedral in the zócalo, following the signs leading to La Mira. The road is good and several people are building magnificent homes up there. In any case, the view is well worth the drive.

Scuba-diving equipment can be rented on the Caleta beach, but William English of Plainville, Connecticut, warns that everyone should check their gauge before they go down as a "friend of mine nearly drowned using one of their tanks that only had enough air in it for half an hour."

Want to see how the upper 10% lives? There's no better place than Acapulco. Take a bus out past the Diana Circle and check out any of the high-rise palaces lining the beach. In fact, in sunglasses, bathing trunks, and a sport shirt, or a bikini and smock or beach jacket, carrying an English-language newspaper or a current bestseller, who's to know you aren't staying there? Somehow it's delicious to sit in the beach chairs and sip a drink, observing the local fauna, or even to try out the pool. Think: even the most observant of lackeys can't keep straight the faces of the people who inhabit his 400 rooms, and who come and go day by day.

ACAPULCO NIGHTLIFE: Up on La Quebrada each night at 8:15, 9:15, 10:30, and 11:30 p.m. the **high diver** performs. From a spotlit ledge just below the Mirador's terraces the solitary diver plunges into the roaring surf 130 feet below after praying at a small shrine nearby. To the applause of the crowd that has gathered, he then climbs up the rocks and accepts congratulations and gifts of money from onlookers.

Sitting in the **zócalo,** which is closed to vehicular traffic and refurbished with lots of benches and trees, is a very pleasant pastime and costs nothing. As you're sitting there, all kinds of pitchmen will approach you: men with barrel organs, women offering rebozos, mariachis, small boys selling gum or puppets or matches, beggars, and so on.

The Clubs

I might almost venture to say that Acapulco is more famous for its nightclubs than it is for its beaches. The problem is that the clubs open and close with revolving-door regularity, making it very difficult for me to make specific recommendations that will be accurate when you arrive. Some general tips will help: every club seems to have a cover charge of 300 to 400 pesos, drinks can cost anywhere from 135 to 275 pesos, and remember that a 10% tax, and perhaps a service charge of the same magnitude, will be added to your bill. At this rate, margaritas can approach the lofty reaches of 250 pesos apiece—be careful.

Clubs seem to have their preferred clientele. **Disco 9**, for instance, is gay, while **Armando's Le Club** (next to his Taj Mahal at Costera Aleman 2330) is for the well-heeled and successful out for a bit of painting the town red. The most infuriatingly exclusive spot when I was last in town was **Baby-O**, a disco across from Armando's Le Club, open from 10 p.m. to 4 a.m., where you can not only dance but also tingle in a Jacuzzi. At **The Gallery**, the attraction is "Les Femmes," a group of talented entertainers who—surprise!—aren't women at all. Carlos Anderson's entry into the Acapulco club sweepstakes is a disco called **Carlos's Chili 'n' Dance Hall 'n' Bar 'n' Grill**, open 10 p.m. on, informal and spirited as are the restaurants, with a cover charge slightly lower than most. New place for those with buckets of cash and tremendous wardrobes is **UBQ**, Costera Aleman 115—be dressed in your best when you go, and take one of those buckets along. **Plus 1**, Costera Aleman 182, is less formal but equally expensive.

The high-rise hotels each have their own bars, supper clubs, and nightclubs with floor shows. At least once a week many of these feature a "Noche Mexicana" with Ballet Folklorico-type entertainment. Also a good bet are the informal lobby or poolside cocktail bars, often with live entertainment. The **Condesa del Mar** is a good place to enjoy a margarita and several of the city's better Latin music combos.

The Centro Acapulco

Acapulco has its own spectacular culture and convention center, called the Centro Acapulco, on the eastern reaches of the bay between Condesa and Icacos beaches. Done with fine and extravagant Mexican taste, the Centro has rolling lawns dotted with a copy of an Olmec head, another of the Quetzalcoatl of Teotihuacán, etc.; you enter up a grand promenade with a central row of pools and high-spouting fountains. Within the gleaming modern building are all the services and diversions one could want: a mariachi bar, a piano bar, a disco, a movie theater, a legitimate theater, a café, a nightclub, several restaurants, and outdoor performance areas. Should you want to buy a stamp, make a phone call, dress a wound, buy a dress, or tape a TV show, all you need is right here. During the day you can stroll around the grounds for free; at night you pay about $1 for admission to the floodlit grounds. After that, you're free to stroll around as you wish. If, however, you *sit* at one of the café tables to watch a performance, you must order something to eat or drink, and the minimum is several hundred pesos per person.

Programs with the center's current offerings are given away around town, at hotel desks and the like, or call 4-7050 for latest word.

MISCELLANY: Shops are generally open to 8 p.m.... **Banks** are open from 9 a.m. to 1 p.m. weekdays (closed all day Saturday and Sunday). Telephone numbers for the **Department of Tourism** (Miguel Aleman and Río do Camaron, on the beach about midway between the zócalo and the beginning of the high-rise hotel district) are 748/2-2170 and 2-2246. They're open Monday through Friday from 9 a.m. to 8 p.m., Saturday and Sunday from 10 a.m. to 5 p.m.... **What to watch for:** Panhandlers, who come in many hues. Some operate in the bus station and will offer to assist you in telephoning the hotel of your choice to ask if there is a room, then no matter what answer they get at the other end will tell you there is no space and then suggest "their" hotel. The Department of Tourism suggests: (1) That you ask the rate and ask to see the schedule of rates given each hotel manager, set by the Department of

Tourism; (2) That you don't take a guide; (3) That you refuse to let anyone call your hotel for you; (4) That you report any taxi driver who refuses to take you to the hotel of your choice—yes, it has happened!

8. Puerto Escondido and Puerto Angel

Last of Mexico's fabulous resort towns are two fairly secluded little seaside villages in the wild and mountainous state of Oaxaca. Both are still small and relatively undiscovered—relative to, say, Zihuatanejo or Puerto Vallarta. But although Puerto Escondido means "Hidden Port," this and its sister town a short ride away cannot remain hidden much longer.

PUERTO ESCONDIDO: There are two villages here, actually. On the inland side of the coastal highway is the Mexican village, with pottery and produce markets, plus lots of little ma-and-pa eateries and general town life. The other village is the tourist strip on the seashore side of the highway. As you walk from west to east on the main thoroughfare, unpaved **Avenida Perez Gasga,** you'll see fruit stands on either side of the street, a few restaurants and beach hotels to your right, and some shops and houses to your left. Ahead of you, on a range of low hills overlooking the bay, is a cluster of army barracks. Beyond that, nothing . . . nothing except palm groves and a stretch of the most glorious beach you've ever seen. This is particularly true if you're facing east. The bay is irregular in shape; its western promontory consists of a tiny beach followed by rocks jutting into the sea. By way of contrast, the eastern peninsula is about a mile long with low green hills descending to meet a long stretch of bone-white sand.

Getting to and from Puerto Escondido

One of the reasons this idyllic spot remained hidden was inaccessibility. As of this writing, access is easy if you're coming by air from Oaxaca, or by road from Acapulco. But should you plan to come by road from Oaxaca, you're in for a long, bumpy ride.

By Road: It's 230 miles from Acapulco to Puerto Escondido by Highway 200, a fairly good and fast road. Whether you go by bus or car you will undergo frequent army inspections (they're looking for drugs and firearms). It's a good idea to keep your eyes open and to inspect along with the soldiers. Most are intent on doing their duty; a few have sticky fingers, and these have no right to take advantage of you. They know it, and if you let them know that you know it, you'll be treated with nothing but deference and respect.

Coming from Oaxaca, Autobuses La Solteca make the fairly arduous trip to Puerto Escondido three times a day in second-class equipment. The trip takes from 7 to 12 hours, although it is less than 150 miles. A few stretches are paved, but a good two-thirds of it is not paved, and is dusty and rutty in the dry season, muddy and rutty—and even perhaps washed out—in the rainy season.

By Air: Aerovias Oaxaqueñas S.A. will fly you between Oaxaca and Puerto Escondido in a 28-passenger DC-3 on the one daily morning flight for 1000 pesos one way. Ticket agencies are at Viajes Micsa (tel. 951/6-2700), Dr. Valdivieso 2 (near the northeast corner of the Plaza Principal) in Oaxaca; and at the Hotel Rincon del Pacifico in Puerto Escondido. A taxi into town from the airport costs (or should cost) less than 100 pesos.

READER'S TOURING TIP: "If you're driving from Acapulco to Puerto Escondido, you can break your trip at **Ometepec**, which is near the state line 126 miles east of Acapulco. The **Hotel Riviera Lopez** has clean rooms, hot showers, and secure parking for about 800 pesos double" (G. C. Kehmeiër, Denver, Colo.).

Where to Stay and Eat

Best bet is the 12-room **Hotel Loren**, (tel. 958/2-0057), located at the western outskirts of town. With three floors (the top one a sun roof offering the best view in town), the hotel looks bigger than it is. Rooms are stark but clean, and although they may betray a slight mustiness, that is the fate of all rooms in salt-breeze resorts—you'll be hard put to find a room without it. Rates are the best part of all: 450 pesos single, 525 pesos double, with a sometime seasonal rise in winter.

The **Hotel Rincon del Pacifico** (tel. 958/2-0056), on Avenida Perez Gasga in the center of town, has two floors of rooms built in a U-shape around a patch of sand shaded by a few tremendous palms and fronting right on the Pacific. The sea breeze cools all of the glass-fronted modern rooms, and jalousies allow the breeze to come straight through. They advertise that they have constant hot water in the tiled baths. Like other hotels in town, it costs a bit much for what you get, but there's no doubt it's a good place to stay. Singles are 385 to 475 pesos; doubles are 585 to 660 pesos. The hotel has a restaurant on the beach level, open from 7 a.m. to 10 p.m. daily, and it even serves a comida corrida for 155 pesos (soup, rice, filet of fish, and coffee). Breakfast here would cost 115 pesos for ham, eggs, toast, and coffee.

Up on the hill, on the road into town at the west, is the **Hotel Nayar** (tel. 958/2-0113), where 24 rooms are built into two floors around a central court. Here you have a modern place with good beds, good cross-ventilation, table-top fans, tile baths, and some fabulous views, but for some reason little niceties like toilet seats are sometimes missing. Why? The price justifies better: singles, 400 pesos; doubles, 620 pesos. Try to look at a few rooms, pick the best one, and perhaps bargain a little over the price.

Of the little waterfront fish restaurants, I think **La Posada** is pretty good. Here they furnish you with a menu in English, and the waiters even speak a bit themselves. Some of the outdoor tables are completely outside, others are under a thatched roof; there's a jukebox (not too loud when I was there), and a bar carved out of one solid piece of wood with matching seats. Among the local folk La Posada is famed for cold beer and the town's long-distance phone booth, but you might be more interested in the fish entrees, most of which sell for about 190 pesos. A passable ceviche (pickled fish cocktail) is only 85 pesos, shrimp cocktail a bit more. Meats, in general, are cheaper than seafood.

Standing down on the beach in the center of town, across the water and off to your left you will see the exotic thatched roofs of **Restaurant Zihuaraya**. A plain and rustic beachfront eatery, the Zihuaraya offers little choice, but the food is excellent: fish, rice, soup, and beer will come to about 240 pesos, with friendly service. Note that the Zihuaraya is not open all the time.

The Viva chain of modern, air-conditioned, pool-equipped hotels owns the **Hotel Viva** (tel. 958/2-0133), a modern hostelry in Puerto Escondido, which is a mile north of town, on the beach. You can make reservations from Mexico City (at Minnesota 6; tel. 905/687-1366), but when you do you'll discover that prices are about 2200 pesos single, 2800 pesos double.

READER'S HOTEL SELECTION: "We found the **Hotel Roca Mar** located a half block from the beach on Avenida Perez Gasga. They have 15 double rooms, no singles, 24-hour hot water, and electric fans. All rooms rent for 350 pesos. We were very pleased with the cleanliness, the service, and the friendly people who own and operate this hotel. And there were no mosquitos!" (Rebecca K. Enger, Paso Robles, Calif.).

READER'S RESTAURANT SELECTION: "In the village across the highway there's an arcade-like square consisting of little family restaurants. The food is better and more varied than in many of the places on Avenida Perez Gasga. But you *must* ask prices before you order, otherwise they may charge you something exorbitant. In general, people in the village are much more friendly than on Avenida Perez" (Joan Strasser, San Francisco, Calif.).

What to Do

The Avenida Perez Gasga has now sprouted a row of tourist shops selling straw hats and Puerto Escondido T-shirts, and a busy branch of the Oaxaca state Tourism Office bent on even greater development of the area. Soon, no doubt, Avenida Perez Gasga will even be paved, but for the time being a stroll along this street reveals 99% of the town's daily life to you. After that, there are the beaches, which speak for themselves and need no introduction—you'll see. Laziness here is a state of mind, sipping a cool bottle of something refreshing, feeling the sea breeze, watching the pelicans soar and wheel and then come down to race across the surface of the water. Anyone who wandered into Acapulco a half century ago might have found a similar scene and a similar ambience. The thing to do while you're in Puerto Escondido is to catch it before it's gone forever. Then, of course, there's the surfing. . . .

Puerto Angelito: Take a launch from the beach below Avenida Perez Gasga, and you'll end up at Puerto Angelito, a small cove popular with Mexican families (no surf, safe for kids) and snorkelers. If you're up for a walk, it's less than half an hour.

PUERTO ANGEL: Fifty miles southeast of Puerto Escondido along Highway 200 is the tiny fishing port of Puerto Angel, known to a handful of vacationers who come here regularly, mostly from Mexico City. A small, beautiful bay and several inlets provide rough-and-ready swimming (watch out for the undertow if the beach you choose is washed by open surf), and the village's position at the end of every road assures a sleepy tranquil atmosphere.

Every now and then a naval boat will pull in for a visit at the small naval station, and the village bestirs itself a bit. Otherwise, it's fishing as usual.

Although Puerto Angel only has a few hundred meters of paved streets, mostly along the waterfront, there are two suitable hotels. One right downtown on a small cliff rents its clean, motel-style rooms for 500 pesos single, 660 pesos double, and you may get a view if you choose your room right. The restaurant has a panoramic view.

The other place to stay is close to luxurious, with prices to match. The **Hotel Angel del Mar** stands atop a promontory with panoramic views of the town, the surrounding region, and the sea. Rooms have tiled showers, marble washbasins, two large beds, and fantastic views. There is also, for your delectation, a restaurant, bar, and swimming pool, not to mention cobbled paths and drives. Prices are quite high for our book: 900 pesos single, 1150 pesos double; bungalows with kitchen are 2450 pesos double.

Getting to and from Puerto Angel

The situation here is much like that of Puerto Escondido, mentioned above. The bus trip, although over a different highway, is only a bit less arduous from Oaxaca. As of this writing there is plane service only to Puerto Escondido.

Chapter IV

GUADALAJARA AND NEARBY CITIES

1. Guadalajara
2. Lake Chapala
3. Colima
4. Uruapan
5. Patzcuaro
6. Morelia

VIRTUALLY EVERYONE WHO has heard anything about Mexico has heard the sonorous name of her second-largest city, Guadalajara, and the fame of this great metropolis is well deserved. But several nearby cities, including two state capitals, come as surprises to the visitor who stays in Guadalajara and who later sets out for Manzanillo or Playa Azul on the Pacific Coast, or for Mexico City. The region encompassed by the states of Jalisco, Colima, and Michoacan is one rich in local crafts, local culture, and local delicacies, not to mention splendid scenery, beautiful lakes and mountains—including one recently active volcano. Everything centers on the "City of Roses," so I'll start our explorations there.

1. Guadalajara

Guadalajara (alt. 5209 feet; pop. 2,500,000), capital of the state of Jalisco, has a long and brilliant history. Given its charter as *muy leal y muy noble ciudad* ("most loyal and noble city") in 1539 by none other than Emperor Charles V, it has held a prominent place in Mexican events ever since that time. Charles, who ran most of Europe and a lot of the world at the time, certainly knew what he was doing.

As though to emphasize the great things that were expected of it, Guadalajara's Spanish builders gave the city not one but *four* beautiful plazas in its center. Today the city's leaders are giving it a fifth, the enormous Plaza Tapatía, an ambitious swath of urban redevelopment stretching for what seems a mile through the urban landscape. Scattered with trees and monuments, sprinkled with fountains, the new super-plaza links the city's major colonial buildings, opens new perspectives for viewing them, and joins the past with the great new buildings of the present. It's an ambitious project, very Mexican in its grand scope, and that's as it should be: many people consider this the most "Mexican" of cities.

By the way, *tapatío* (or *tapatía*) is a word you'll come across often in this city. No one is certain quite where it originated, but tapatío means "Guadalajaran"—a thing, a person, even an idea. The way a *charro* (Mexican cowboy) gives his all, or the way a mariachi sings his heart out. That's tapatío!

GETTING TO AND FROM GUADALAJARA: No trouble getting to or from this big city. Go to the Central Camionera and you can book a seat on a bus to virtually any point in North America and parts of Central America. Several airlines have direct flights to and from foreign countries. Trains go to the Pacific coast, Mexico City, and the U.S. border. Here are some tips.

By Bus

All of the big lines operating in this area run very frequent buses to this transportation hub. Omnibus de México has connections with U.S. companies at the border; Tres Estrellas de Oro, Transportes Norte de Sonora, and Estrella Blanca run buses both up the coast to the border and inland to the capital. Buses to Aguascalientes, Guanajuato, Puerto Vallarta, Querétaro, Patzcuaro, Morelia, etc., are all available from the Central Camionera. Remember to buy your ticket in advance (a day in advance should be enough). By the way, the trip Mexico City–Guadalajara takes about eight hours.

By Rail

The National Railways run three trains a day in each direction between the capital and Guadalajara, one in the morning early, and two in the evening suitable for sleeping-car travel. Take the later evening train which leaves about 9 p.m., for it's an express and gets you to Mexico City in slightly over 12 hours rather than the 13½ of the earlier evening train. There are also trains to Colima and Manzanillo (one morning train a day), six hours to Colima, eight to Manzanillo; and of course the two daily trains between the U.S. border and Guadalajara, one of which is the famous *El Costeno*. These are run by the Pacific Railways with connections to the National Railways. They operate morning and noon from Guadalajara, morning and evening from Nogales (connections from Mexicali), and run via Hermosillo, Ciudad Obregon, Mazatlán, and Tepic. Time from Guadalajara to the border is about 36 hours.

By Air

International service direct to Guadalajara includes a daily flight to and from Houston, and seven flights a day to and from Los Angeles. To travel between Guadalajara and Mexico City (a 50-minute flight) you can choose from any of 17 daily flights; there are also flights to these cities: Monterrey (two daily), Mazatlán (one a day), Puerto Vallarta (three or four a day), Manzanillo (one daily), Acapulco (one daily). AeroMéxico operates the bulk of these flights; Mexicana runs most of the rest. Both operate to and from Los Angeles. Any airline office or travel bureau can give you current flight times and fares.

Money-savers: Look into the excursion fares on flights between Guadalajara and Acapulco or Los Angeles.

ORIENTATION: Guadalajara is not a difficult city in which to find your way around. But it certainly is big, so some hints on arrival might be of use to you.

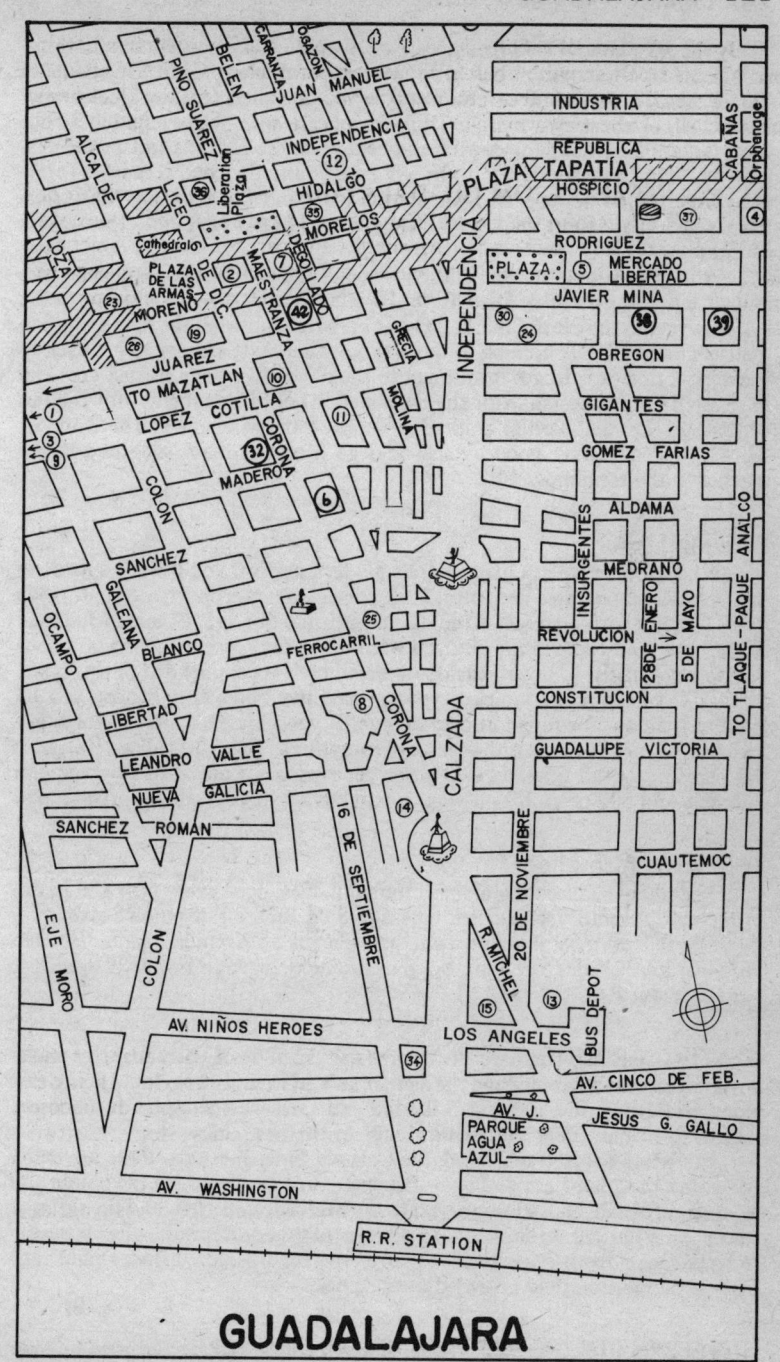

GUADALAJARA

Arriving by Bus or Train

Should you arrive by bus in Guadalajara's modern Central Camionera (bus terminal), you'll find several respectable hotel choices a few blocks away (see below). The easiest way to get downtown is to walk the several blocks out the bus station's front door down Calle Estadio to the Calzada Independencia. Any bus traveling from left to right will take you to the central market (Mercado Libertad), San Juan de Dios church (30), and the Plaza de Mariachis, from which it's a short walk to the Degollado Theater (35) and other points of interest.

From the railroad station, at the south end of Calzada Independencia, take a no. 2 bus ("San Juan de Dios–Retiro Directo") from directly in front of the station to get to the central market. Other buses tend to wind through suburban quarters before finally coming to the downtown area. It's easier to get back to the depots than it is to get from them to the downtown section. Just take any bus which has "Estación" (for the train station) or "Camionera" (for the bus station) on the signboard or painted in white on the windshield. The Ruta 61, 62, 63, or 2 buses are good choices and go from the main squares and the market to the terminals.

Arriving by Air

When you arrive at Guadalajara's modern airport, you'll walk outside to find minibuses operated by Auto Transportaciones Aeropuerto (tel. 11-5469 and 11-1855), with offices at Avenida Federalismo Sur 915, Colonia Moderna. They'll ask you where in the city you want to go; say *centro* or *zona uno* (Zone 1) if you're headed to any of the downtown hotels recommended in this book. In fact, if you've already picked your prospective hotel, they'll drop you off right at the door for no additional charge. If you haven't chosen a hotel, say *catedral,* as the cathedral is the center of everything. The cost is about 100 pesos per person in a full minibus, 200 pesos per person for only two or three in a minibus, and 300 pesos if you want a minibus all to yourself—a private taxi.

Tourism Information

The state of Jalisco maintains a tourism office, open every now and again, in the ex-Convento del Carmen, on Calle 8 de Julio off Avenida Juarez.

The federal government's Tourism Office is at Avenida Juarez 638 (tel. 36/14-0156). Hours are 9 a.m. to 3 p.m. Monday through Friday, 9 a.m. to 1 p.m. on Saturday.

GETTING AROUND: Two bus routes will fill 90% of your intracity transportation needs. Buses bearing the sign "Par Vial" run a circle route going east along Hidalgo to the Mercado Libertad and then west along Hidalgo to the Glorieta Minerva, near the western edge of the city.

For north-south travel along the Calzada Independencia, there are many buses, but the "San Juan de Dios—Estación" bus goes between the points you want: San Juan de Dios church, next to the Mercado Libertad, and the railroad station past Parque Agua Azul. This bus is best because most other buses on Independencia have longer routes (out to the suburbs, for instance) and thus tend to be more heavily crowded at all times.

HOTELS IN GUADALAJARA: Guadalajara does not have the great number of budget hotels to be found in Mexico City. In fact, the number of recommendable hotels here seems small in relation to the city's size and tourist flow. But the room situation does not seem to be particularly tight. I'll look at some moderately priced hotels downtown at first, and then suggest where to go if you want to upgrade or downgrade your accommodations.

Downtown Hotels

For an older hotel with a touch of class (and thus greater impact on the budget), try the **Hotel Morales (6)**, Corona 243 at Sanchez (tel. 36/13-2962). Massive stone arches and a huge brass chandelier complement one another in the rather dark lobby. Dark wooden doors and chairs and the black wrought-iron rails contrast elegantly with the beige absence of color on the upper floors where some of the rooms open onto an interior walkway. Each of the very small bathrooms holds a welcome extra: a tub-and-shower combination rather than just a shower alone. Prices for single rooms on the interior side are 485 pesos, or 595 pesos for an exterior single; doubles are 660 pesos interior, 770 pesos exterior.

The newish **Hotel Universo (11)**, Lopez Cotilla 161 (tel. 36/13-2815), can boast of a private garage and clean double rooms costing 990 to 1100 pesos (singles are 880 to 990 pesos). Added comforts are exceptionally nice bathrooms, piped-in music (which can be piped back out with the turn of a switch), a telephone in each room, a parking lot, and carpeted hallways.

The **Hotel Frances (7)** (tel. 36/13-6293), Maestranza 35, is on a very quiet side street right off the Plaza Libertad and near the Degollado Theater. The lobby on the ground level has crystal chandeliers, and a wonderful marble statue in a pool. The guest rooms on the second and third levels all have new private baths, telephones, good beds, and comfy furnishings for 1200 pesos double. Newly refurbished, tidy, and even a bit stylish, and exceptionally well located—that's the Frances.

The modern **Hotel Continental (8)** (tel. 36/14-1117), Avenida Corona 450 at Libertad, is halfway between downtown and the bus station. For its modernity, the Continental is surprisingly well-worn, but prices reflect the loss of its gleam: singles are 660 pesos; doubles, 820 pesos; triples, 990 pesos.

Sharing some aspects with the Continental is the **Hotel Nueva Galicia (14)** (tel. 36/14-8780), Avenida Corona 610. It's a tall, wedge-shaped building which has seen its glory days pass and is now sensible rather than snazzy. The rooms are priced at 525 pesos single, 660 pesos double. The restaurant is even better known and better patronized than the hotel; its afternoon lunch is a big event in the neighborhood.

Near the Bus Station

There is scant advantage to staying near Guadalajara's new bus station unless you're planning to leave from it early, or from the railroad station nearby—and then only if you're the kind of sleeper who snoozes blissfully through hurricanes. The mighty behemoths of the highway prowl and growl around the terminal all night, and at dawn invariably the jukebox in some all-night café coughs out Mexican rock 'n' roll. The only advantages are that you'll save the taxi fare from the hotel to station, providing you can carry your bags, and you'll be able to sleep the 10 or 15 minutes longer than it would otherwise have taken to get to the station. However, if you're dead at the end of a long day on the bus and too tired to go anywhere but to the closest quiet bed, go straight to the **Hotel Praga (13)**, 28 de Enero 733A (tel. 36/17-3760), a block from the bus station, to the right as you walk down the station steps.

124 MEXICO ON $20 A DAY

It's a fairly large (70 rooms), blue-tiled building with pine siding paneling the lower part of a large, bright lobby. The lunch counter in the lobby is the dominant feature of the decor, plus the semicircular reception desk. Rooms are clean, simple, often dark, lit by fluorescent ceiling lights; they cost 585 pesos single, 695 pesos for a double, more for a twin-bedded room.

If you have no luck at the Praga, you might try the **Hotel Canada (15)**, Estadio 77 (tel. 36/17-4004)—not to be confused with the new Gran Hotel Canada (which faces the bus station and is slightly more expensive). All rooms at the Canada have private baths and cost 440 pesos single, 550 pesos double. The place is nondescript, but clean.

The newest and most deluxe of hotels in the bus station area is the **Hotel Flamingos Guadalajara (15)** (tel. 36/18-0003), Calzada Independencia Sur 725, at the corner of Balderas. It's an eight-minute walk from the bus station, out the front doors, down Los Angeles, and right. Modern and almost posh, with air conditioning, it looks as though it must be expensive, but it's not: singles are 480 pesos; doubles, 580 to 670 pesos.

Starvation-Budget Lodgings

Like the moderately priced hotels, Guadalajara's low-budget line-up is a mixed bag. Here are the tried-and-true places.

An excellent choice for those wishing to stay close to the Mercado is the **Hotel Ana-Isabel (38)**, Calle Javier Mina 164 (tel. 36/17-7920), just across from La Libertad market. The lobby is one flight up and overlooks the bustling buying and selling. Because the rooms open onto the interior, street noise is not a problem. With cheerful staff, newly painted walls, and nice blue bathrooms, this is an excellent choice: singles are 360 to 420 pesos; doubles with two double beds, 480 pesos. They offer free parking, too.

A block down the street on Javier Mina, at no. 230, is the **Hotel México 70 (39)** (tel. 36/17-9978). Tunnel-dark halls lead to 86 average-size rooms with clean baths. Rooms facing the street have small balconies, but watch out for the street noise. One person pays 360 pesos, two pay 480 pesos for two double beds.

Don't worry about your broken Spanish as the friendly and patient staff at the **Posada de la Plata (9)**, Lopez Cotilla 619 (tel. 36/14-9146), will make you feel right at home. All rooms come with tiled bathrooms. Relax at one of the many tables in the quiet courtyard, surrounded by potted plants. Singles run 300 to 350 pesos; doubles, 450 pesos.

If the Posada de la Plata is full-up, wander down the street and take a look at the **Posada España** (tel. 36/13-5377), Lopez Cotilla 594, corner of 8 de Julio. The rooms here are well-used, but clean and extremely inexpensive.

The Big Splurge

Stepping up a notch is easy in Guadalajara, and a few of the city's higher priced hotels offer good value for money.

The new and modern 500-room **Hotel Aranzazu (25)** (tel. 36/13-3232), Avenida Revolución 110, near the meeting-point of Corona and Degollado, not only has a fine location, but a long list of luxuries as well, including color televisions in the rooms, air conditioning, two swimming pools (one for kids). Prices for all this, and for the hotel's high sheen, are not bad: 1300 pesos single, 1650 pesos double.

The 175-room **Hotel Calinda Roma (42)** (tel. 36/14-8650), Avenida Juarez 170 at Degollado, is hooked into the Quality Inn system, so you can call their toll-free numbers for reservations. An older but well-refurbished downtown hotel, the Roma is semi-posh and quite comfy, with a rooftop swimming pool and patio bar, private parking lot, television sets (and even some refrigerators) in the rooms. The location is excellent, and the prices aren't bad: 1550 pesos single, 1775 pesos double.

One of this city's most popular upper-bracket hotels with foreigners is the **Hotel de Mendoza (12)** (tel. 36/13-4646), Carranza 16, corner of Hidalgo, only steps from Liberation Plaza and the Degollado Theater. Gringos and gringas seem to enjoy the colonial atmosphere, the beautifully restored building, and the modern conveniences, not to mention the prime location. Rooms come with TVs, big beds (or two big beds), air conditioning; they have a pool and a garage. You pay 1375 pesos single, 1750 pesos double, for any of the 100-odd rooms.

Motels

Most of the best motels are on the two highways—to Mexico City and to Mazatlán—that funnel into the Glorieta Minerva. Biggest bargain is the newly remodeled **Campo Bello Motel,** Avenida Lopez Mateos 1599 (tel. 36/21-5622), which has more than its share of grace and good looks. Twenty-nine rooms and apartments are grouped around a central court-parking lot, paved with large stones and bordered with old arches heavy with blossoming shrubs and vines. The exterior is tiled with intricate brown and blue patterns and the rooms are spacious, each with private bath. Price for a room, single or double, is 685 pesos. The apartments with kitchen, large dining and sitting area, bedroom, and bathroom go for 885 pesos. Those planning a longer stay in Guadalajara should look into the special monthly rates, which have discounts averaging 30%. You don't have to take your car in and out of the city to stay at the Campo Bello, just take a "Chapalita-Cotilla" bus from midtown out to the motel.

Good English is spoken at the **Motel Chapalita,** Lopez Mateos 1617 Sur (tel. 36/21-0607), which is modern and flashy and also has a pool in the central court. Rooms are well furnished but prices are a little high: 880 pesos for singles, 920 pesos for doubles. The motel's first-class restaurant is on the ground floor.

The road from Mazatlán is lined with motels too, all advertising pretty competitive rates. On Vallarta, the selection resembles a budget-motel grouping at home, only here the rates are a lot less.

READERS' HOTEL SELECTIONS: "I chose the **Motel del Bosque** (tel. 36/21-4650), Lopez Mateos Sur 265, right off the Glorieta Minerva. It is ideal for those who don't want to stay amid the noise and dirt of a large city's downtown. The motel is walking distance from the Tequila Sauza plant (tours), and many small cafés and restaurants. Prices are quite reasonable: 550 pesos for a single room, or 630 pesos for two persons. The motel has a "country club" type garden and swimming pool; one should request an interior room facing the pool" (Shelley Harris, San Francisco, Calif.). . . . "We stayed at the **Suites Bernini,** at the corner of Vallarta and Union. We had a large bedroom with lots of closet and drawer space, tiled bath with large shower, and kitchen with eating nook. It is carpeted and boasts excellent views from floor-to-ceiling windows on two sides. The typical Mexican lack of attention to maintenance shows, but the maid service is good and the place is clean. It's at Avenida Vallarta 1885 (tel. 36/16-6736), and we paid 720 pesos per day" (Jean and Bruce Wallenberg, Santa Barbara, Calif.). . . . "A reasonable place to stay is the **Hotel Mexicali,** Calzada Independencia Sur 767; straight out the bus station one long block, then turn right and you're almost there. The people were very friendly and the price great: 300 pesos with bath, 250 pesos without—for two!" (Mara Levene, Mendocino, Calif.).

EATING IN GUADALAJARA: For a really authentic Mexican meal, which is a risky thing to promise given the variety of styles in Mexican cooking, go to **El Farol (23)**, Pedro Moreno 466, at Galeana, partly open to the street. Just inside the door, after you've elbowed your way past waiters and women flapping out tortillas, you'll pass a table loaded with beautiful fruit gelatin desserts (try gelatina de frutas—as a salad). Each table is equipped with bowls of pickled carrots and lime rinds to nibble on while you wait—first for the waiter, then for the menu, then for the food, then for the check, then for the change. You can save at least ten minutes by knowing in advance what to order: tacos (four for 80 pesos) or tamales. But save some room for the cheese pie for which the restaurant is famous. Pleasantly, and perhaps uniquely, El Farol is open very late—I've passed at 2 a.m. and seen the place full of people happily munching tacos.

A very fine place to dine in the central business and shopping district is the **Cafe Madrid (19)**, Juarez 264, a couple of doors from the corner of Juarez and Corona. The café is always full, any time of the day, and waiters in white jackets and black ties move quickly from table to kitchen and back again. For a light and inexpensive lunch, I order the generous fruit cocktail (60 pesos), and a sandwich (65 pesos) which comes with a slice of tomato, some "safe" lettuce, and fried potatoes (when you order, ask for the potatoes—they seem to cost no extra). The set-price lunch (comida corrida) costs 160 pesos. When the front section of the restaurant is crowded, there's still usually some room way in the back, next to the big mural.

It's no trouble to find inexpensive restaurants for breakfast, but one of the cheapest ever is at the **Restaurant El Cid (9)**, on the corner of Ocampo at Lopez Cotilla 451. This is a typical little Guadalajara eatery which thrives on business brought by its cheap "small plate" comida priced at 88 pesos. Other entrees are higher, with a half chicken going for 150 pesos.

Thinking of late-night places, the city market is traditionally the place for all-night eats. Down by Guadalajara's Mercado Libertad and Plaza de Mariachis, it's **Mi Ranchito (24)**, Obregon 21 (Obregon is the street which runs east off Independencia starting at the huge Cine Alameda). It's open "dia y noche," and serves pickled pig's feet for 135 pesos in a red vinyl and Formica dining room. Other entrees include enchiladas for 85 to 95 pesos.

For a snack or light supper, try one of the many *loncherías* along Juarez (open for "lonch" or supper). About the nicest I found is the **Lonchería La Playita (19)**, Juarez 242, where you get a receipt from the cashier, then present it to the waitress/cook for perhaps a sliced pork sandwich (torta de pierna), garnished with onions, tomatoes, and a single, easily retrievable hot pepper (45 pesos). Beers are 38 pesos, soft drinks less. Point to what you want—the waitress will catch on and assemble it on the spot.

One block from the Tourism Office on Juarez at no. 590 is **Balcones Mi Tierra**. It appears to have been fashioned after La Copa de Leche, lacking only the high prices and tuxedo-clad waiters of the latter establishment. The five-course comida, served on the balcony or downstairs, is 100 pesos, tea or coffee included. The menu keeps the budget-minded customer happy by offering nothing over 200 pesos: filet mignon with mushrooms is 190 pesos, fish is 115 pesos, and the two daily set-price lunches go for 140 and 200 pesos.

By the way, if you're looking for something a bit fancier in this area, look at the **Restaurant Agora**, in the ex-Convento del Carmen.

For Chinese Food

Guadalajara has several Chinese restaurants, but the most convenient one is the **Palacio Chino (10),** Corona 145 at Lopez Cotilla. One large, modern room looking onto the street, the Palacio Chino is no lunch counter, but a full-fledged restaurant. As in most Chinese places, the thing to do here is to order one of the set-price meals. Number two, for instance, provides small portions of wonton soup, a fried shrimp, two spare ribs, fried rice, good pork chop suey, dessert, and tea for 150 pesos. Other set-price meals go from 115 to 210 pesos. Open every day for lunch and dinner.

Splurge Restaurants

Perhaps the most famous and long-lived restaurant in Guadalajara is **La Copa de Leche (26),** Juarez 414. A sidewalk café, plus upstairs and downstairs dining rooms, give La Copa lots of space in which to serve a varied, eclectic menu filled with Mexican, American, and continental specialties. Just for coffee and cake you might pay 150 pesos; a full-course dinner will run as high as 500 or 600 pesos. Open daily.

Those willing to travel from downtown for a good meal should catch a no. 50 bus to Avenida Lopez Mateos, and then walk south to the intersection of Lopez Mateos and Avenida México. At this point you'll find the **Don Quijote.** The salad bar is terrific, with beautiful cauliflower, spinach, beets, carrots, lettuce, etc.—when in season. For 120 pesos, you can fill up at the salad bar as many times as you wish (all vegetables have been treated with purified water). You can save money by ordering the humble taco, and you get four stuffed with beef, pork, or chicken for 140 pesos. Otherwise, there's prime rib for 425 pesos, sirloin steak for slightly less. The food and service make the Don Quijote well worth the price.

For lunch, especially on a hot day, whiz up the elevator to the rooftop **Restaurant Terrazza Romana** of the Hotel Roma, at Juarez 170. Here you dine at poolside on the set-price lunch for about 355 pesos, from soup through dessert. Otherwise, one can dine from the bottom of the à la carte menu for about the same, all in: pork chops with a pineapple glaze, for instance, cost 250 pesos. Beer, wine, and liquor are served.

If you're planning to visit Tlaquepaque in the morning, save lunch for the **Restaurant Los Cazadores,** Golfo de Mexico 606, the last of the great patio restaurants. It will be an expensive lunch—figure 1000 pesos per person—but well worth it. The grounds are extensive, with several arcades and rooms to dine in if it rains; otherwise you dine on the shady patio. Service and food are very good, and the easy ambience is even better. Patrons start drifting in about 1:30, and the place is full by 3. The large mariachi group is one of the best I've heard, and plays for free. The only fly in the soup (so to speak) is that one or two of the waiters are not above slight overcharges, charging for an item you didn't ask for or kindly bringing appetizers you didn't remember ordering. They all speak English, so make sure they know what you want and *don't* want. Also, booze can be outrageously expensive and cocktail prices are not on the menu. Ask the price before you order!

Now that you've been forewarned, don't miss the chance to dine at Los Cazadores. To get to the Tlaquepaque branch, leave *el parian* (the square in the village) via Independencia (which is one way). At the end of this street, turn left onto Revolución, and drive back toward Guadalajara nine-tenths of a mile. At the traffic circle, go down the street to the right of the Pemex station for two blocks. Cazadores is on the right; drive into the parking lot.

Starvation Budget Restaurants

La Fuente (Trino's) (11), on the corner of Lopez Cotilla and Maestranza, offers one of the best six-course comidas corridas I've seen for 95 pesos (I might add that with this last revision I found more and more restaurants are no longer offering the comidas). Try La Fuente: the food and service are good, the prices right. La Fuente is open every day except Sunday from 8 a.m. to 10 p.m.

READERS' RESTAURANT SELECTIONS: "The second floor at the **Mercado Libertad** is packed with mini restaurants serving authentic if generally undistinguished Mexican foods. Stews are cooked in huge clay bowls placed directly on the fire. You can get cabrito (roast kid) here. Most dishes are 60 to 85 pesos, plus a few pesos more for a stack of fresh, hot tortillas" (Norriss, Edith, and Elizabeth Hetherington, Berkeley, Calif.). . . . "I stayed at the new Fiesta Americana, and discovered **El Abajeno**, right on the circle where the Fiesta is, at the intersection of Lopez Mateos and Vallarta. It was typically Mexican, a steak dinner plus beer for 250 pesos, a roving band of mariachis, just delightful, highly recommended" (Fred H. Hoon, Williamsville, N.Y.).

WHAT TO SEE: Downtown Guadalajara is becoming a district ever more congenial to pedestrians. Streets are being closed to through traffic, other streets are set aside for a few buses only, still others are left only to strollers. It's simply wonderful for the sightseer.

The Spaniards started it all 4½ centuries ago when they laid out the city with a cluster of four plazas. The **Plaza de Armas,** with its ornate central bandstand, is perhaps the favorite of *Tapatíos* and *Tapatías* (not to mention *tapatititos*). Shopping arcades line two sides, the cathedral forms another, and the ornate **Palacio de Gobierno (2),** built in 1774, fills the last. You'll want to duck into the palacio's courtyard to view Clemente Orozco's enormous mural of Hidalgo, and various scenes portraying the Mexican fight for liberty (1937). Orozco, who lived in Guadalajara, is the city's favorite artist—more on him later.

South of the Plaza de Armas is the charming **Plaza de la Universidad,** with its huge fountain (a children's favorite) and its outdoor café (an adults' favorite). The café has food and beverages, is moderately priced, and is usually full of weary shoppers resting their limbs.

The immense **cathedral,** on the north side of the Plaza de Armas, begun in 1558 and finished 60 years later, is impressive and eclectic in style. Inside, over the doorway in the sacristy, is a painting thought to be by Bartolomé Murillo (1617–1682). In front of the cathedral is the second of the four plazas,

---

KEY TO MAP OF GREATER GUADALAJARA: 1.—Minerva Fountain; 2.—Arches; 3.—Ninos Heroes Monument; 4.—Juarez Square; 5.—House of Art & Crafts, and Agua Azul Park; 6.—House of Culture; 7.—Bus Depot; 8.—Technological Stadium; 9.—Baseball Park; 10.—Cock Fight Arena; 11.—Revolution Square; 12.—Cathedral; 13.—Government Palace; 14.—Liberation Square; 15.—Museum; 16.—Post Office; 17.—Degollado Theater; 18.—Bullring; 19.—Libertad Municipal Market; 20.—Cabanas Orphanage; 21.—Alcalde Park; 22.—Public City's High School; 23.—Morelos Park; 24.—Football Stadium; 25.—New Cemetery; 26.—Estación F.F.C.C. (train station).

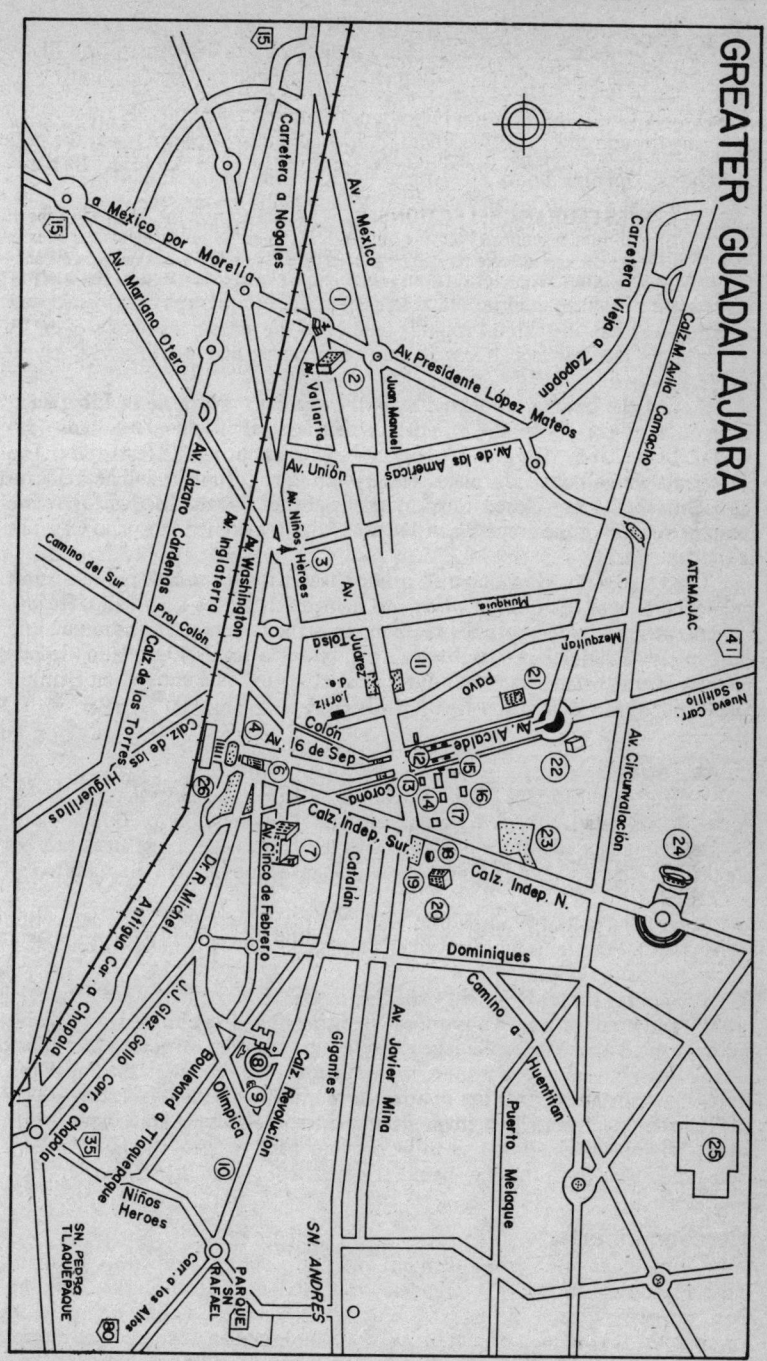

GREATER GUADALAJARA

called **Plaza de los Laureles.** One look tells you why.

On the opposite side of the cathedral from the Plaza de Armas is the **Plaza de los Martires,** with a circle of columns to commemorate Guadalajarans who fought and died for their country. East of the plaza is the museum.

The **Museo Regional de Guadalajara (Regional Museum) (36)** is open daily except Monday; admission is 10 pesos Tuesday through Saturday, 5 pesos on Sunday. Opening hours are 10 a.m. to 5:30 p.m. (4 on Sunday).

Arranged around an airy courtyard, the exhibit rooms are stocked with paintings from Mexico's long history: 17th- and 18th-century religious works, folk paintings, and works by the modern masters Orozco, Rivera, Quiroga, Vizcarra, and Figueroa. Several rooms (nos. 6 and 7) are devoted to the history of the state of Jalisco, and others hold displays of ethnography and European painting. At least one exhibit room is held open for temporary shows of crafts or works by local artists. It's well done, this place, and worth a visit by all means.

East of the cathedral, behind it, is the spacious **Plaza de la Liberación** (Liberation Plaza), with the wonderful neoclassical **Teatro Degollado (35)** (Degollado—that's "deh-goh-YAH-doh"—Theater) at its far (east) end. The two streets which bound the plaza, Hidalgo on the left (north) and Morelos on the right (south) are closed to most traffic. Look down Morelos for a fine perspective view of the great **Plaza Tapatía,** with the domed Hospicio Cabañas at the far end.

The Degollado, Guadalajara's prime theater for legitimate plays, operas, and concerts, was built in the 1850s and named for Santos Degollado. He was a local patriot who supported Juarez in the struggle against Maximilian and the French (Guadalajara was Juarez's capital for a time). Degollado, despite his fervent support of the great Juarez, lost every fight he entered on Benito's behalf. So what? He's still a hero in this city!

Plaza Tapatía

Walk down Morelos from the theater. Behind the Degollado is a new mural in bas relief, with a fountain, entitled *The Founding of Guadalajara.* Farther along is a sculpture of a tree with lions, then two huge slabs bearing the texts of Charles V's proclamations which gave Guadalajara the right to call itself a city.

Soon the concourse opens into a fine big plaza, complete with dedication stone (1982). Fountains are everywhere, and giant department stores and office blocks frame the plaza.

It's not far to the **Hospicio Cabañas,** or Cabañas Orphanage (4), founded in 1829 and used for just that purpose—housing homeless children—until only a decade or so ago. The orphanage is a huge and complex structure with many inner courts, but what you want to see is the main building with the fine dome. Here, the walls and ceiling are covered in murals by Clemente Orozco (1883–1949), brooding, frightening, magnificent paintings which will take your breath away. Wide benches allow you to lie on your back to view the murals. Now called the Instituto Cultural Cabañas, it's open from 9 a.m. to 4 p.m. every day.

Mercado Libertad

Coming out of Cabañas, turn left and find a stairway down to the mammoth Mercado Libertad (5), Guadalajara's modern central market building. One can easily wander in this great blur of color, smells, sights, and activities for an hour. If you need a quiet break, duck into the San Juan de Dios church (30). The interior's baroque, having been built in the 1700s.

Plaza de los Mariachis

Right beside San Juan de Dios is the Plaza de los Mariachis, actually a short street lined with restaurants and cafés. During daylight hours, small bands of mariachis will be loafing around here and there, sipping a cool one. But at night the place is packed with them, bashing away at their guitars and singing their hearts out for love and/or money. It's a sight you must not miss.

Parque Agua Azul

The Parque Agua Azul (near the bus station at the south end of Calzada Independencia) is filled with plants, trees, shrubbery, statues, fountains, etc. This is the perfect refuge from the bustling city. Pay the tiny admission fee, wander in, and visit the zoo (you may be lucky enough to see the hippopotamus getting his daily bath—with a firehose—or the lions their monster lunch). For kids there's "El Chuku Chuku," a rubber-tire mini-train which circulates through the grounds. "Los Espejos Magicos" is the house of mirrors. Lots more to explore and discover.

Also within the park is the **Instituto de las Artesanías de Jalisco**, the state-run crafts market, with a good selection.

Near the entrance to the park is the **flower market**. It's not difficult, after a glimpse here, to see why Guadalajara is sometimes called the City of Roses. A tremendous bouquet of three or four dozen roses sells for only a few dollars. Half a block north is the modern building of the **Experimental Theater of Jalisco**, which is well worth the admission charge, even for those who don't speak Spanish.

The state-run **Casa de la Cultura (34)** is near the entrance to the park, across from the flower market. Besides a permanent deep-relief mural they have exhibitions of contemporary art.

Rodeos and Bullfights

Also in the region of Agua Azul, actually to the east of it, is the **Aceves Galindo Lienzo**, or rodeo ring, where you can see a **charreada,** or Mexican rodeo, each Sunday during the summer at noon. Riding, roping and rope tricks, and a traditional grand promenade are all part of the action at the charreada.

Bullfights are held during the winter months at Guadalajara's **El Progreso Bullring (37)**, especially on Sunday. The ring is located between Hospicio and D. Rodriguez on the east side of Calzada Independencia, a few blocks east of the big market and San Juan de Dios church. It's almost next door to the famous Orphanage.

Orozco Museum

Clemente Orozco's Guadalajara studio (3) was turned into a museum after the artist's death, and it makes for a fascinating hour's visit. Take a Par Vial bus, or no. 40, "Plaza del Sol," on Avenida Juarez all the way to the Glorieta Minerva (1), the large traffic circle with statue and fountain on the main highway north. See the arches? The studio is at Calle Aurelio Aceves 27, just beside the arches, open Tuesday through Saturday from 10 a.m. to 2 p.m. and 3:30 to 5 p.m., on Sunday to 2 p.m., for 5 pesos admission. A modern cement building, it contains many examples of the artist's violent but bewitching work: magnificent character studies, portraits of the artist's family, and a room devoted entirely to sketches of the 1910 revolution (Orozco was 27 years old in 1910). By the way, Orozco died in 1949, in Mexico City.

Side Trip to the Tequila Plant

Now that you're out here, you might want to take a tour of the Tequila Sauza bottling plant, just a bit farther (walking distance) along Avenida Vallarta (no. 3213, on the left) on the way out of town. They're open weekdays during business hours, and if you're there between noon and 1:30 p.m. you can join in the "Happy Hour," with fantastic creamy tequila drinks. By the way, this is just a bottling plant. The distillery is—where else?—in the town of Tequila, off Highway 15 about 40 kilometers (25 miles) east of Guadalajara.

Tlaquepaque and Tonalá

The suburbs of Tlaquepaque and Tonalá are of special interest to pottery aficionados, for here is where some of Mexico's best is made. You should consider a day trip to these towns. For details, see below under "Shopping in Guadalajara."

NIGHTTIME ACTIVITIES: Center of cultural activities in the evening is the **Degollado Theater (35)** in the Plaza de la Liberacion, where concerts by the State Symphony Orchestra and visiting groups, opera performances, recitals, and ballet folklorica performances by the university's Grupo Folklorico (every Sunday) take place. Tickets to most events cost from 25 to 100 pesos, the second balcony seats being just about right. Note that the theater is not air-conditioned.

Nearby in the **Plaza de las Armas,** the Jalisco State Band puts on free concerts every Sunday evening starting about 6 p.m. during the summer.

Don't forget the **Plaza de los Mariachis (3),** down by San Juan de Dios and the Libertad Market, junction of Calzada Independencia and Juarez/Javier Mina. Every evening the colorfully clad mariachis of the city, in various tuneful keys and states of inebriation, hold forth for money (if they can get it) or for free. You can have a meal here, or a snack, or a soft drink, or just stand around spending nothing but time, and no one will bother you, except perhaps the itinerant vendors who abound in such places. Do this for sure one evening; it's fun and it's free.

Ever been to a cockfight? The local "pit" is the **Plaza de Gallos "La Tapatía,"** on the way to Tlaquepaque (take a Tlaquepaque bus from along Calzada Independencia). Profits from the blood-sport go to charity, oddly enough; matches are held every Sunday, Monday, and Tuesday evening. Be there by about 7 p.m.

Most of the downtown music-and-dance scene takes place in hotel clubs. The **Sheraton** (tel. 14-7272), Avenida 16 de Septiembre and Niños Héroes, is typical. The Bar Chinaco has a trio playing music nightly until midnight; 80-peso cover charge, no minimum. The disco here is called Delirium. There's a rooftop supper club, too, La Rondalla on the 20th floor, with shows at 11 p.m. and 1 a.m.

SHOPPING IN GUADALAJARA: Besides the mammoth **Mercado Libertad (5),** described above, in which you can find almost anything, Guadalajara now boasts the largest modern shopping center in Latin America. It's the **Plaza del Sol** megacomplex, sprawling over 120,000 square yards in an area at the junction of Avenidas Lopez Mateos and Mariano Otero, outside the center of town. Here you can buy anything from a taco to a Volkswagen; you can also cash a check, make a plane reservation, or buy a lottery ticket. There are even hotels and restaurants for weary shoppers! Take the no. 40 bus from Calzada Independencia near the Libertad Market.

Right by the junction of Juarez and 16 de Septiembre is a branch of the worldwide chain of Woolworth's. There's a convenient pedestrian passageway which runs under Juarez where there are many stalls selling candied fruits, leather belts and other goods. A better place to purchase leather goods, however, is down on **Pedro Moreno,** a street which runs parallel to Juarez.

Tlaquepaque and Tonalá

Apart from the regular around-the-streets shopping downtown, Guadalajara holds a special treat for shoppers—an excursion to the neighboring suburb of **Tlaquepaque** (pronounced TLA-kee-PAH-kee). You'll find buses labeled "Tlaquepaque" constantly along the Calzada Independencia. It's a two-mile ride. To drive, go south on Calzada Independencia (toward the Agua Azul Park) and turn left onto the Avenida Revolución. This main thoroughfare goes all the way to Tlaquepaque. You'll get to a traffic circle by a Pemex station. Revolución continues along the left side of this station. Nine-tenths of a mile from the circle, just as the tree-lined median in the road comes to an end, turn right onto the street which will take you to *el parian,* the main plaza in Tlaquepaque.

Tlaquepaque is famous for two things: its sidewalk cafés with innumerable mariachis (Sunday evenings, you can sit and hear about six different groups around you); and its pottery and glass "factories." The latter are an absorbing sight. In a score of private houses are rooms off the patio devoted to racks and racks of glazed and unglazed bowls, jars, figurines, glass and pottery animals, bathtubs big and old enough for Roman emperors to have bathed in, tiles, jugs, and miniature figures of priests, soldiers, brides, and bulls. The street on which to find all these factories is Independencia. Stop in at the **Regional Ceramics Museum** (hours are 10 a.m. to 4 p.m.; closed Monday) at Independencia 237. There is no entrance fee and the display of ceramics is worth the visit. Don't miss the figurines in clay of Mexican presidents from Díaz to Echeverria, a delightful cross between caricature and statuary.

Across the street from the museum is the glass factory. In a room at the rear of the patio, a dozen scurrying men and boys heat glass bottles and jars on the end of hollow, steel poles. Then, blowing furiously, they'll chase across the room, narrowly missing spectators and fellow workers alike as they swing the red-hot glass within an inch of a man who sits placidly rolling an elaborate jug out of another chunk of the cooling glass. Nonchalantly, the old man will leave his own task long enough to clip off the end of the boy's vase at the exact moment at which it comes within reach of his hand. Then he drops the clippers and returns once more to his own task as the urchin charges back across the room to reheat the vase in the furnace.

Tlaquepaque has become "refined" in the past years, and prices have risen considerably, making shopping there a dubious bargain. If you see something you can't resist, be *sure* to bargain for it. Perhaps due to the deluge of American tourists, prices are artificially high—sometimes even by American standards—and cash withdrawn from your wallet at the proper psychological moment or a mock exit from the store will normally bring them down to a proper level. If you purchase something, take it with you, or else you might find yourself having paid for shipping and then receiving a notice after you return home, informing you that $10 is owed in innumerable fees and shipping charges.

Final hint: Get to Tlaquepaque in the morning or evening, for the shops close between 2 and 4 p.m.

By the way, the village of **Tonalá**, three miles farther along the road, is no longer the "poor man's Tlaquepaque." The tourist traffic has finally arrived, and the town really differs from Tlaquepaque only in that it's harder to get to. There is, however, an interesting factory in which you can see the artisans painting delicate designs on their pottery. Park in the zócalo (or disembark from any no. 6 bus), and at least three boys will offer to take you there.

2. Lake Chapala

Mexico's largest lake has long been popular with foreign vacationers. The climate is perfect, the scenery gorgeous; several charming or quaint little towns border the lake; and the big city is only 26 miles away.

There's not a lot to see or do here unless you stay a while, renting a house or apartment. If you do stay, anything can happen. D. H. Lawrence ended up writing *The Plumed Serpent* during his stay in Ajijic. Those of us who are less ambitious might be satisfied to make some new friends among Ajijic's expatriate community, swim in the lake, and dine on pescado blanco, the whitefish from Chapala's waters.

Three towns—Chapala, Ajijic, and Jocotepec—border the lake and draw tourists. Each has a different ambience.

GETTING TO CHAPALA: Buses run several times a day from Guadalajara's Central Camionera (bus station) on the 45-minute run to the town of Chapala. If you're lucky enough to have a car, you'll be able to enjoy the lake and its towns more fully. Here's how to drive there:

Although you can get to Lake Chapala via Highway 15/80, be advised that most heavy truck traffic also uses this route to the south. If you're driving, I'd suggest you leave Guadalajara via Avenida Gonzalez Gallo, which intersects with Calzada Independencia just before Playa Azul Park. Going south on Independencia, you turn left onto Gallo and follow it all the way out of town past the airport, where it becomes Highway 44, the main road to Chapala. The 42-kilometer drive is through peaceful farming country, and you don't really get a view of the lake until you're almost in Chapala.

CHAPALA: With a wide but dusty main street (Avenida Madero) leading down to the lakeshore, Chapala, Jalisco, is the district's business and administrative center as well as its oldest resort. Not that there's much business, or even resort activity. Much of the town's prosperity comes from wealthy retirees who live on the outskirts and come into Chapala to change money, buy groceries, check the stock ticker, etc. It can be a pretty sleepy place. If laid-back is what you like, you'll like Chapala.

The **Tourist Information Office** (tel. 376/5-2279) is at 227 Hidalgo, on the same street as the Restaurant Viuda. They speak English, and have maps and brochures. On the other side of the street from the tourist office, at Hidalgo 202, is Libros y Revistas, a shop which carries English-language newspapers, magazines, and books.

Where to Stay and Eat

For transients, the best budget hotel in town is the **Nido,** right in the center of town a half block from the water, Madero 202 (tel. 376/5-2116). On the premises you'll find bar, pool, and a well-tended garden. The 30 rooms are spacious, with those facing the street even larger than the interior rooms. Rates for rooms alone: 370 pesos single, 460 pesos double.

The restaurant in the Nido is also very popular. Many of the retired people living in Chapala eat all three meals here and highly recommend the fare. For the casual visitor, the comida corrida is 175 pesos, and will constitute the main meal of the day.

Just up Madero at no. 412 is the **Superior,** a more modest establishment very popular with locals, both *gringo* and *indigeno*. Known for its soups, the Superior serves an excellent caldo miche (a savory fish chowder) for 60 pesos. With a tuna salad plate, your lunch will cost 150 pesos.

Still on Madero at 421 is the **Cafe Paris,** a small, bright-orange plastic table and chair place. Prices are competitive with the neighbors: have a sandwich for 40 to 64 pesos, or go elegant and dine on whitefish for 170 pesos. A good breakfast of ham and eggs, toast, and coffee, served 8 a.m. to midnight, is only 85 pesos.

La Viuda, around the corner from the wonderfully garish city hall at Hidalgo 217B, is Chapala's class act: wall-to-wall carpeting, baby-grand piano, cool and dark interior. The specialty in the evening is steak, but in the afternoon you can enjoy a good comida corrida here for only 165 pesos.

La Viuda has two attractions: the restaurant, and an adjoining delicatessen/meat market where one can buy yogurt, cheese, and meats. Many other picnic supplies, including liquor, are for sale. The **Linda Rosas bakery,** across the street and down a few steps, should help to complete your picnic preparations.

Of the numerous lakeside restaurants, the most attractive and popular is the **Beer Garden Restaurant,** where fish tacos cost 100 pesos (sandwiches are around 65 pesos, and pescado blanco [white fish] is 175 pesos). This place is generally crammed with old and young who are chatting, listening to music, or just watching the people. It's a good place day or night to catch the local activity, or to take in the superb lake view. During peak season, **El Tubo,** a disco upstairs, offers weekend dancing. By the way, the Hotel Nido restaurant and El Mirador share the same kitchen.

Located several kilometers outside of Chapala on Hidalgo (which becomes the lake drive) is the handsome 20-room **Chula Vista Hotel** (tel. 376/5-2213), with singles at 650 pesos and doubles at 750 pesos. You have to have a car to enjoy this place; without one, you're isolated. The hotel is not right on the lake, by the way, but across the highway a short distance from the shore.

AJIJIC: Past the Chula Vista Hotel, the road continues past luxurious houses and open country to Ajijic, Jalisco. As you reach this town, the highway becomes a wide, tree-lined boulevard through an obviously wealthy residential district called La Floresta. One of Ajijic's best places to stay is here, to the left, down by the lake (watch for signs); the others are in the town proper, a place of narrow, cobbled streets, a small church and square, and sunny dispositions.

Where to Stay and Eat

The aforementioned lodging in the luxury district is the **Villa Formoso** (tel. 376/5-2369), at Paseo de las Olas and Boulevard Camino Real, owned and operated by Reg and Mickey Church (Apdo. Postal 193, Ajijic, Jalisco, México). Although accommodations and service are American style, the grounds capture the essence of Mexican charm and Jalisco architecture. The studio and bedroom apartments, both with complete kitchen facilities, and the bedrooms, are all in an enclosed, 200-year-old mango grove. Other facilities include a swimming pool, a hydro-massage pool, meeting and exercise rooms, and a laundry room. Prices are in U.S. dollars: rooms are $30 to $38 double, studio apartments are $425 per month, two-bedroom apartments are $550 per month.

The best hotel right in town is the **Posada Ajijic** (tel. 376/5-2553), on Calle 16 de Septiembre. It is a posh collection of Mexican-style bungalows set in tropical gardens rampant with coffee bushes, poinsettias, and banana trees around a turquoise pool. Rates are 345 pesos single, 485 pesos double—not at all outlandish. Service, liquor, and food here are magnificent, and the whole place rather reminds one of the expensive summer houses city people go to and pretend to be roughing it. Whether you stay or not, you'll enjoy a stroll around the grounds or the conversation in the lounge. By the way, the bulletin board at the Posada has all sorts of news about rentals, sales of furniture and appliances, lessons, rides and riders, etc.

The **Motel Las Casitas,** located just outside of town on the main highway at Carretera Pte. 20 (no phone), has singles at 440 pesos and doubles at 550 pesos. You just can't go wrong here, considering these are truly *casitas* ("little houses") with separate kitchen, large dining and sitting room, bath, and bedroom. The 11 apartments aren't located in the classy lake section, but they are clean, the grounds and teardrop-shaped pool are well kept, and parking is no problem. Weekly and monthly rates are available.

Very near the aforementioned hotel is the **Posada Las Calandrias** (tcl. 376/5-2819), on the main highway, a brick, two-story building surrounding a nice pool, bougainvillea everywhere, and, on the cars, license plates from everywhere: Rhode Island, Montana, British Columbia. The very comfy rooms-with-bath cost 825 pesos, single or double.

As for dining, the **Posada Ajijic** is your best bet, featuring a comida corrida at lunchtime every day for 175 pesos (a bit more on Sunday). Brunch on Sunday is from 11 a.m. to 2 p.m., a set-price repast with wine.

What to Do

Ajijic is a quiet place, the main occupations being drinking, reading, and loafing, and the main inhabitants (apart from local fishermen) being aging divorcees and good, bad, and indifferent writers and painters, with, recently, a sprinkling of retirees. Social life centers around the cantina at the Posada Ajijic, where a band (of sorts) plays for dancing on weekends. Recently, an **anthropological museum** opened with numerous pre-Columbian ceramic pieces. It's open every day from 10 a.m. to 6 p.m.; admission is 5 pesos. It's located on the lake drive outside of town.

In the same building complex is a small shop displaying and selling regional craft items made by students who are busily at work upstairs above the shop in a school for artisans.

In the evening (except Monday) you can drop in at **El Tapanco Bar and Disco,** on Calle 16 de Septiembre in the same block as the Posada Ajijic, on the other side of the street. They always have conversation and libations, sometimes food and music. Open at 4 p.m.

JOCOTEPEC: This pretty town a few kilometers west of Ajijic has less of a tourist trade, despite its large arts-and-crafts, bar-and-restaurant establishment called the **Casa de Las Naranjitos.**

Just east of Jocotepec is the pretty motor inn called the **Posada del Pescador** (tel. 28; Apdo. Postal 67). The 14 colonial-style bungalows are scattered around the pool in surroundings which would be great for a flower garden, although one has yet to be developed. Each separate apartment has kitchenette, dining area, fireplace, bedroom, and bath. The bungalows go for 675 pesos, single or double.

3. Colima

Due south of Guadalajara lies the state of Colima. Although one of Mexico's smallest, it has an incredible range of climate and topography. Northern Colima is pine and lumber country, containing half of the 13,000-foot Volcan de Colima, the northern portion of which lies in Jalisco. This is Mexico's second-highest active volcano, which last erupted in 1941. Yet less than 100 linear miles south of these bleak uplands is a palm-fringed tropic littoral that could pass for the shores of Bali.

Many Americans, who think Colima begins and ends with the popular port of Manzanillo, are missing a bet by overlooking the state's attractive capital. This city, also named Colima, is a balmy metropolis of 80,000 that dates back to 1523. Its founder was the conquistador Gonzalo de Sandoval, youngest member of Cortes's general staff.

While Colima lies virtually at the foot of the volcano, its 1640-foot altitude makes for a climate that far more resembles Manzanillo's than that of the immediately adjacent mountain area.

Only 165 miles from Guadalajara, Colima can be reached by a picturesque road that skirts the volcano. Also visible on this trip is an even higher mountain, the 14,000-foot Nevado de Colima, which, in spite of its name, lies entirely in the state of Jalisco. Leaving Guadalajara, you take Route 80 until you reach Acatlán. Then turn left off Route 54, passing through Sayula and Ciudad Guzman until you reach Route 110. There you turn right and after a few miles right again. You're now on a state road that takes you to Colima on the route closest to the volcano. On the way you'll go through Atentique, a highland community where lumber is king.

HOTELS IN COLIMA: Colima's best budget hotel is on the zócalo, also known as the Jardín Libertad. It's the **Hotel Casino**, Portal Morelos 11 (tel. 331/2-1406), a beautiful building with classic white facade and open arches. Singles are 520 pesos, doubles go for 585 pesos one bed, for 635 pesos in two beds. All 55 rooms have ceiling fans and overlook either the zócalo or the interior patio. The Casino's main visual attraction is a large semi-open lounge separated from the street only by grillwork. The hotel also boasts an interior patio with a fountain. Both patio and lounge are generously endowed with potted plants.

Not nearly as nice is the **Hotel Ceballos**, on the eastern side of the Jardín at Portal Medellin 16 (tel. 331/2-1354); singles are 330 to 480 pesos, doubles cost 525 to 595 pesos, top price going for the hotel's three air-conditioned rooms. Frankly, although it looks great from the outside, they've done a lot of squeezing to make more rooms, and the interior has lost its courtyard as well as its charm.

RESTAURANTS IN COLIMA: The leading restaurant downtown is **Las Naranjas** ("The Orange Trees"). From the zócalo you walk down Madero (which is left of the cathedral) and take the first street on your left. Your destination, no. 32, is a handsomely decorated place with orange and white linens, light-blue walls, and orange fruit designs hand-painted on the chairs. There's a patio in the rear, blessedly cool on those hot summer days; excellent carne asada for 160 pesos, plus an assortment of tacos for 20 pesos. The comida costs 175 pesos—a bit of elegant dining for a low price.

Just one block from the zócalo (main square), near the corner of Hidalgo and Medellin, is the **Restaurant Boca de Pascuales,** a hole-in-the-wall diner serving breakfast, lunch, and dinner at bargain-basement prices.

WHAT TO DO: An absolute must activity here is a visit to the city's extraordinary **antique car museum,** the best in Mexico and certainly one of the most impressive anywhere. The entrance is at Belisario Dominguez 80, six blocks south of the zócalo, one block past Jardín Nunez, Colima's largest park. A 15-peso entrance fee entitles you to visit three lots that house 350 immaculately restored cars ranging in model year from 1912 to 1941. If, as legend states, all good Americans go to Paris when they die, it would appear that all good Pierce-Arrows go to Colima.

ONWARD FROM COLIMA: From Colima, it's almost 140 miles to the junction of Highway 15, which goes west to Lake Chapala, a resort lake popular with gringoes (see Section 2 in this chapter). Going on to Mexico City, though, you head east, toward Zamora, Uruapan, Patzcuaro, and Morelia.

All the countryside around this region, and onward right into Morelia, is lush and beautiful. It's a major agricultural area and many cattle and sheep graze in fields beside the road.

Continuing south on Route 15, the next major town is **Zamora,** Michoacan (alt. 5275 feet; pop. 85,822), an agricultural center where an overnight stop can be made. The **Hotel Mendoza,** Avenida Morelos Sur 190 (tel. 351/2-1540), is a fairly new building decorated with a heavy colonial touch, whose cool lobby has lots of dark-stained woodwork and a delightful patio with fountain in a manicured grass square. Rooms are on the small side, very clean, with substantial furniture and private baths. The cost is 440 pesos for singles, 550 pesos for doubles. Downstairs, there's a colonial-type restaurant with blue ceiling, heavy black beams, and a 160-peso comida corrida which is an endless procession of food, seven full courses plus coffee.

The **Hotel Fenix** (tel. 351/2-0266) is the biggest in town, with a large new addition. There are two entrances now: the old at Corregidora 54, the new at Madero 401 as you enter town. It is difficult to describe; suffice it to say that the place sprawls, makes ample use of stained glass, and is dominated by a tower (resembling a minaret . . . sort of), which houses the stairs and is encrusted with a series of yellow galleries and pillars. The accommodations range from 1920s-style rooms without bath for 220 pesos single, 360 pesos double, to the newer section surrounding a kidney-shaped pool. Here the rooms—tucked away behind wooden doors—are simple and clean, with private bath. These rooms are more expensive, of course. Also restaurant, bar, two pools, steambath, and nightclub.

4. Uruapan

Uruapan, Michoacan (alt. 5500 feet; pop. 150,000), has long been famous for the lacquered boxes and trays turned out in the region, and in 1943 became even better known when Paricutin, a brand-new volcano, suddenly erupted in the middle of a cornfield, pouring lava over two nearby villages and forcing thousands from their homes. The volcano, active only a short time, is now extinct and can be seen from a long way away.

Although this town in itself has little to offer in the way of dazzling tourist sights, there are a few side trips which are quite worthwhile. Because of its dearth of tourist attractions, hotels and restaurants in Uruapan tend to be reasonably priced. In fact, it's not madly unreasonable to spend the night in Uruapan and then take a day trip to more touristy (and admittedly more attractive) Patzcuaro, less than an hour's ride away.

ORIENTATION: Once you find your way to Uruapan's long main square, about 20 blocks from the bus station, you're all set. The "square" is actually a very long rectangle running east-west. The churches are on the north side, the Hotel Victoria, etc., on the south. The market is behind the churches, and in short, everything you need is within a block or two of the square.

WHERE TO STAY AND EAT: One of the nicest hotels in town is 1½ blocks southwest of the plaza on E. Carranza, at no. 15. The **Hotel Villa de Flores** (tel. 452/2-1650) is not fancy, just clean and neat and highly recommended by those who visit here frequently. The 29 good-size rooms open on the typical patio or court full of huge potted plants. Rates are 440 pesos single, 525 pesos double. The restaurant in the back is also highly recommended, particularly for its regional dishes, which usually include corn fixed in some unusual way. For something different, try the bunuelos for 50 pesos, or tamales con atole for 70 pesos.

The most advertised hotel in town, but not quite worth all the trumping, is the **Hotel Victoria** (tel. 452/2-1500), Cupatitzio 11, a block southeast of the main plaza. Five-storied, modern, and equipped with bar and restaurant, the Victoria charges a steep 820 pesos for singles, 990 pesos for doubles. It's undistinguished, but the top floor has a nice terrace with a pretty view of Uruapan and surrounding countryside.

Perhaps the city's newest and most modern hotel is the **Nuevo Hotel Alameda** (tel. 452/3-4100), Avenida 5 de Febrero no. 11, a half block south from the east end of the square. Telephones, TV sets, parking lot, slick and tidy bathrooms—all the niceties are here, and are yours for 625 pesos single, 795 pesos double.

The **Hotel Mirador** (tel. 452/2-0473), at the southwest end of the plaza, is some 50 years old and looks it. The lobby is decked out with random tubes of fluorescent lighting hanging from mustard-colored beams and, upstairs, there's wood instead of the usual stone and tile. Some of the rooms are rather big and all have private baths—of sorts—and some even have steps up to the windows. The rooms without windows at all should be avoided; some of the others will do, and even lay claim to a certain charm. After, say, 30 hours on a bus, the Mirador will do. Singles are cheap at 185 pesos, doubles equally so for 325 pesos.

The **Restaurant Las Palmas** is one short block north of the west end of the square, in a low building at the end of the block. You'll see an arts-and-crafts shop next door. Bright-orange furniture, pleasant señora, moderate prices: a lunch of soup, carne asada, dessert and coffee need cost only 350 pesos, and if you prefer antojitos (the traditional Mexican dishes such as tacos, enchiladas, quesadillas, etc.) you can dine for much less.

Those interested in meatless dining will find it quite enjoyable at the **Restaurante Vegetariano**, Avenida Independencia 16. This bright and cheery place has a comida which includes fruit or green salad, thick vegetable soup, entree, dessert, whole-wheat bread, and a licuado de fruta to drink. À la carte items range from guacamole to soybean beefsteak. Nothing on the menu costs over 125 pesos. A small health-food store occupies the front of the building. To find it, go to the west end of the square, turn right (north), then left (west)—that's Independencia, and the restaurant is along on the right.

A restaurant which attracts young and old as an evening meeting place is the **Emperador Restaurant,** Matamoros 18, right on the square (south side). The very polite waiters here wear white jackets and black bow ties, and bring you beef prepared in a variety of ways (filet mignon, at 250 pesos, is tops). Less fancy tacos, chilaquiles, and club sandwiches, however, are substantially lower in price. Coffee drinkers—and the place is full of them after dark—can indulge their habit for hours at 40 pesos per cup. Stronger drinks are served upstairs at a bar called **La Naranja.**

Holanda Helados, an ice cream parlor, is at Cupatitzio 28, down the same side street as the Hotel Victoria. Single scoops are 25 pesos, and they say they have 50 different flavors (who could ever eat even a single-dip cone of each— total cost, 1250 pesos—to prove there were duplications?).

READER'S HOTEL SELECTION: "There is a cheap, clean, quiet, and extremely cheerful hotel near the Casa de los Estudiantes and the Museo. It's the **Hotel Misolar,** Calle Juan Delgado 10. A double is 300 pesos a night. The style is traditonal Mexican, with a sunny indoor patio; some rooms have mountain views" (Marlene Engel, New York, N.Y.).

WHAT TO DO: Although I wouldn't make a special trip to Uruapan to go to the market, it's worth a look when you're in town. Look behind the cathedral on Vasco de Quiroga to find the products of Michoacan, including the famous lacquered trays, dishes, and boxes.

All markets are attended by shoppers who get hungry, and the rows of food counters here are particularly clean and appealing, bearing heavy loads of the wherewithal to make such regional specialties as huchepos (green corn with sauce), atole de grano or atole blanco (a liquid refreshment), or churipo con corundas (chicken, dried beef, pork, and vegetables in a soup). Little eateries in the market area specialize in these dishes, and a ten-minute rest on one of the three stools (they hardly ever have more) with a bowl of food and a view of the market is a real slice of Uruapan.

Uruapan also has a small museum, a reason for local pride. La Huatapera was set up for citizens, obviously, and not for tourists, and thus has a charm born of authenticity. Attached to the cathedral, La Huatapera was once (1565–1965) a hospital—one of the first in Latin America. Exhibits are mostly of regional ceramic work and dinnerware. Hours are 9:30 a.m. to 1:30 p.m. and 3:30 to 5:30 p.m. Tuesday through Saturday, 9:30 a.m. to 12:30 p.m. on Sunday, closed Monday; no charge for admission.

SIDE TRIPS TO THE VOLCANO AND NATIONAL PARK: Get up early, go down to the Central de Autobuses (city buses will take you there), and hop a bus to Angahuan, a small Tarascan village about 34 kilometers from Uruapan. Once there, you will be besieged by guides/hustlers ready to take you, for a price (about 500 pesos) to the half-buried village of Paricutin, or for about three times that price to the very crater of the volcano. Actually, you don't need a guide or a steed to get to the buried church in Paricutin; the walk takes only a little over a half hour. You may want to rent a horse and guide to get to the summit, though, as this can be perilous, and the journey can take six to seven hours. Plan an entire day for the trip from Uruapan, the ride to the summit, the return, and the trip back to Uruapan.

A less exacting side trip is that to the Parque Nacional Eduardo Ruíz, a botanical delight only eight blocks west of the main plaza (a La Quinta bus, which stops in front of the telegraph office on the main square, will even run you down to the park). You may want to "hire" one of the juvenile guides who will offer their services—just to keep the rest at bay. Then you're free to wander in a semitropical paradise of jungle paths, deep ravines, rushing water, and almost-spectacular waterfalls.

The waterfall at Tzararacua, 10 kilometers from the main plaza (catch the bus of that name in the main plaza) is the most impressive of all. The Río Cupatitzio originates as a bubbling spring in the National Park, and then runs down to cascade toward the Pacific and form these falls. A trip to Tzararacua and to the National Park can be made in a day, even in an afternoon.

5. Patzcuaro

Patzcuaro, Michoacan (alt. 7250 feet; pop. 40,000), has always been of interest to Mexican history buffs because this attractive town featured in the careers of the two most diametrically opposed figures of colonial times. One was Nuño de Guzman, the infamous conquistador whose lust for riches led him to terrorize the local Tarascan population and burn their chief alive because he wouldn't—or couldn't—disclose the location of gold deposits. The other, a humane bishop named Vasco de Quiroga, was sent to the region to undo the havoc wreaked by Guzman after the latter had been arrested by the Spanish authorities. So extensive was Don Vasco's work of reconstruction that his memory is revered in Patzcuaro to this day. Streets and hotels are named after him; his statue stands in the main plaza.

The town is also known for its lake, one of the world's highest, where fishermen catch delicious whitefish with nets of such delicate texture and wide-winged shape that they have been compared to butterflies. Although the lake is over a mile from town, buses make the run regularly from the market plaza.

Patzcuaro is an old colonial town with many nice buildings and two lovely plazas. The climate is pleasant most of the year and, being near a lake, the surroundings are lush. As Mexican towns go, Patzcuaro is pretty, clean, and quiet.

WHERE TO STAY: A small railroad station (daily trains to and from Mexico City) is near the lake. The nearest hotel to the station is the **Posada de Don Vasco Hotel and Motel (1)** (tel. 454/2-0227 or 2-0262), which has recently been taken over by Best Western. Unless you're in the mood for a big splurge; don't stay here: it's elegant—sprawling colonial-style architecture, crystal chandeliers, antique telephones, velvet drapes, bowling alleys, pool, etc.—but out of our price range, as the cheapest single goes for 900 pesos, the cheapest double for 1125 pesos.

On the elegant main plaza—not be confused with the smaller market plaza—is the **Posada San Rafael (3)** (tel. 454/2-0770), which is an excellent copy of a colonial inn. Very new and very nice, the San Rafael has 60 modern rooms with Holiday Inn-type baths and traditional furnishings grouped around a handsome wood colonnade, the type we're told "they don't build anymore." Pets are welcome, kids under 12 stay free in the same room as their parents,

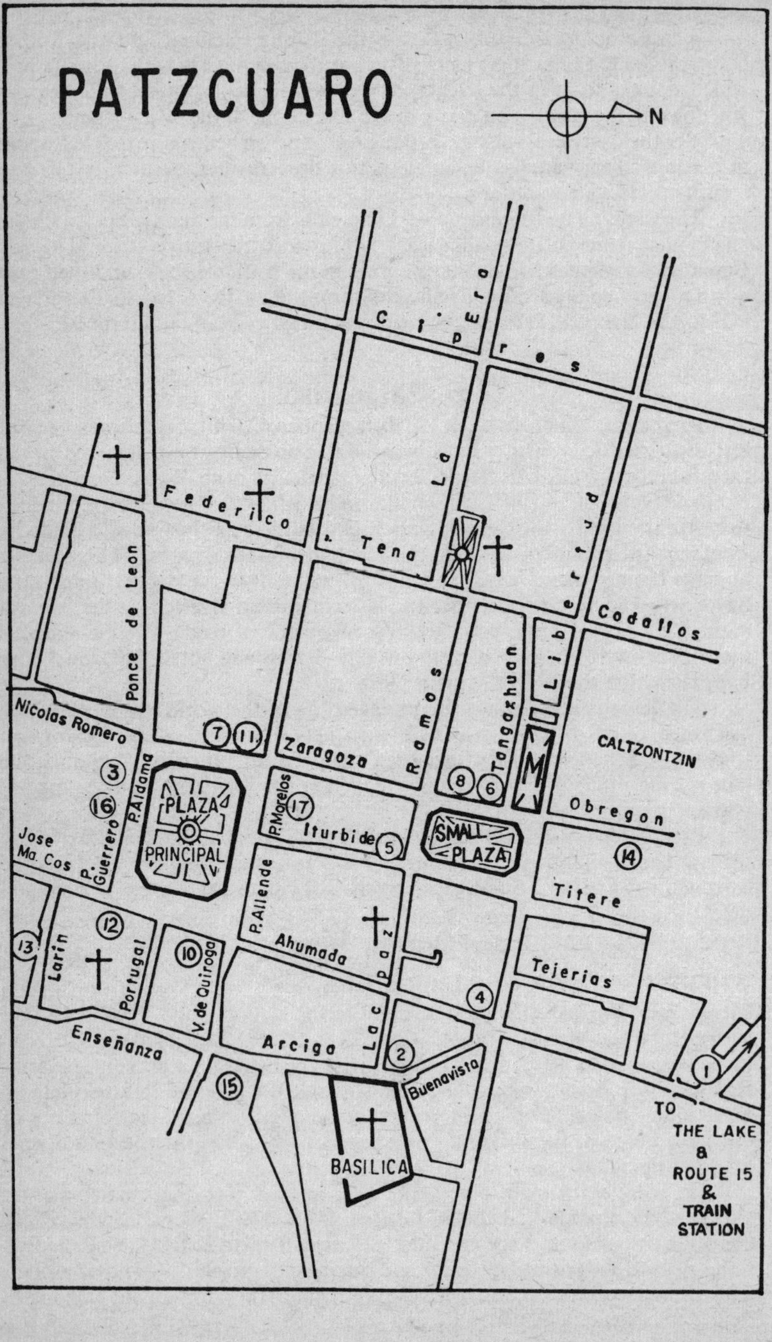
PATZCUARO
N
Cipres
La Libertad
Federico Tena
Codallos
Ponce de Leon
Nicolas Romero
Zaragoza
Ramos
Tangaxhuan
CALTZONTZIN
Obregon
P. Aldama
PLAZA PRINCIPAL
P. Morelos
Iturbide
SMALL PLAZA
Jose Ma. Cos
P. Guerrero
P. Allende
Titere
Larin
Portugal
V. de Quiroga
Ahumada
La Paz
Tejerias
Enseñanza
Arciga
Buenavista
BASILICA
TO THE LAKE & ROUTE 15 & TRAIN STATION
1
2
3
4
5
6
7
8
10
11
12
13
14
15
16
17

plus lots of garage space, and superb whitefish in the hotel restaurant. Rates are not outlandish: singles are 382 pesos; twin-bedded rooms, 495 pesos.

Moving down the price scale slightly is the 17-room **Hotel Valmen (4)**, Avenida Lloreda 34 (tel. 454/2-1161), which is likely to be the first hotel you'll see as you ride into the downtown section. The facade is old-fashioned and subdued, but accommodations are modern and extremely comfortable, and located above a colorful pink and yellow glass-roofed court. It's an excellent value for 250 pesos single, 350 pesos double, 450 pesos triple.

Also inexpensive, and on the busy market plaza, is the commercial-looking **Gran Hotel (5)** (tel. 454/2-0443), Bocanegra 6. The 30 rooms are clean, decorated in circa-1950 low-cost modern. Not much style, but bright at least, and functional: singles are 388 pesos; doubles run 498 pesos with one or two beds. The restaurant is pretty good as well, with a 150-peso comida served daily.

Back on the main plaza, another highly recommendable hotel is the **Mansion Iturbide (17)**. Spacious rooms with wooden floors and huge pieces of solid-looking colonial furniture combine to create an aura of simple elegance. The baths are large, nicely tiled, and are even equipped with shower curtains. Rooms surround a small, simple patio which also serves as a dining area. Singles are 440 pesos, and doubles are 595 pesos; add 100 pesos for an extra person.

Also on the main plaza is the 30-room **Hotel Los Escudos (11)** (tel. 454/2-0138), Portal Hidalgo 73, a cozy colonial-style hostelry with a grillwork balcony overlooking a slanting tiled patio, whitewashed walls, and a beamed ceiling. It's bright, open, and very nice, with singles for 396 pesos, doubles for 538 pesos; some rooms have fireplaces here.

Starvation Budget Hotels

Hotel Posada de la Rosa (8) (tel. 454/2-0811), a second-floor establishment on the market plaza, is very small and very cheerful. Bright flowers in wooden boxes line the open-air patio; rooms are clean and do not have bathrooms, but go for 220 pesos single, 330 pesos double. The common bathrooms are rather large, and also clean. There are some rooms with shower, by the way, for a bit more.

The **Hotel Pito Perez (7)**, Portal Hidalgo 76, is housed in a crumbling old mansion on the main square, and offers rooms without bath for 225 pesos (single or double); rooms with "bath" have a toilet, and a shower aimed into it, and cost 325 pesos (single or double).

Motels and Trailer Parks

Those of you traveling by car might want to know about the **Motel Patzcuaro**, Avenida de las Americas (tel. 454/2-0767), just 100 yards down the road from the Posada de Don Vasco. It's a relatively new place with only eight rooms, a small swimming pool, and two tennis courts. The management describes the accommodations as "clean, attractive, and rustic," and they all have private baths and fireplaces. The cost? Singles are 455 pesos, doubles (one bed) are 585 pesos, with two beds it's slightly more. Furnished houses—price negotiable—are also rented here. Buses will take you into town from the motel every 15 minutes.

Campers with tent or trailer can stay on the lake at **El Pozo Trailer Park**, where spaces rent for 125 pesos. Clean facilities, cement pads, lots of grass, and pleasant management.

WHERE TO EAT: One of the best comidas I've ever had was served at the **Restaurant Los Escudos (11)**, adjacent to the hotel of the same name. I ordered the Tarascan soup, vegetable plate, and whitefish, and the entire meal was superb, right through dessert—worth every centavo of the 230 pesos I paid. Whatever you have, start off with the Tarascan soup—it's the best!

The restaurant **El Patio (16)**, on the plaza at Plaza Vasco de Quiroga 19, offers live dinner music in addition to good, inexpensive meals. Hot bread and butter are served with meals ranging from enchiladas at 55 pesos to whitefish or filet for 100 to 160 pesos. The five-course comida at 125 pesos is delicious and plentiful.

For those with their own transportation and a splurge in mind, the **Hostería de San Felipe**, on the Avenida de las Americas, is recommended by locals who often hold receptions and group dinners there. The menu is highly rarified: the whitefish costs 225 pesos a plate, and other entrees are slightly cheaper. The hotel here, by the way, is only a moderate splurge, with singles for 770 pesos, doubles for 990 pesos.

Down by the Lake

Numerous restaurants line the road to the docks on the lake, and this is the traditional place to dine on the famous whitefish.

You can have lunch or dinner at the **Restaurant Los Redes**, Avenida Lázaro Cárdenas 6, about 500 feet from the lakeshore. For 300 pesos I recently had a meal of soup, rice, a whole whitefish, salad, and coffee. If you get there in time for the set-price lunch, you save money.

Near the railroad tracks on the road to the lake is **El Gordo**, housed in a long, narrow building. Besides whitefish, El Gordo is good for breakfast (opens at 8 a.m.), and inexpensive meals the rest of the day. For just whitefish, salad, and a soft drink you'll pay 195 pesos here.

The cheapest way to enjoy the lake's prime product is to wander right down to the wharf (embarcadero). At little stands right next to it, señoras fry up the delicious fish before your eyes. For a rough-and-ready plate including fish, garnishes, and a soft drink, the price will be less than 140 pesos.

ACTIVITIES IN PATZCUARO: Patzcuaro is a beautiful town and well worth leisurely strolls about its ancient, unchanged streets and plazas. The **market plaza** is particularly interesting and it is here, among the myriad stalls and vendors, that you can buy the varied pottery, rebozos, and serapes of the region. Market days are Sunday, Tuesday, Thursday, and Friday, the last being the day for the all-Indian market. Just a few blocks away is the splendid main plaza, a vast tree-shaded expanse of manicured lawns and elaborate stone fountains bordered by shops, hotels, and the former mansions of rich merchants. The town is much like Colonial Williamsburg from the standpoint of authenticity, and it enjoys a similar monument status. No new buildings interfere with the time-worn harmony of the colonial roofline.

One of the oldest buildings in Patzcuaro is the **House of the Giant (10)**, on the east side of the main plaza at 40 Portal de Matamoros, so called for the 12-foot-high painted statue which supports one of the arches around the patio. This residence was built in 1663 by a Spanish count and certainly represents the colonial taste of that period: carved stone panels, thick columns, and open courtyards.

The **basilica**, which is located east of the small plaza on top of a small hill, was built in the 16th century at the instigation of Don Vasco, then bishop. It opened for services in 1554, but unfortunately Don Vasco never lived to see it completed. The cathedral has been through many catastrophes, from earthquakes to the civil war of the mid-19th century (Juarists against the imperialists who followed Maximilian). There has been some reconstruction. Of note is the Virgin on the main altar, which is made of "corn-stalk pulp and a mucilage obtained from a prized orchid of the region." She is a very sacred figure to the Indians of this area, and on the eighth of each month they come from the villages to pay homage to her, particularly for her miraculous healing power.

One block to the south of the basilica is the **Museum of Popular and Regional Arts (15).** It's yet another beautiful colonial building (1540), originally Don Vasco's College of San Nicolás. The rooms with regional crafts and costumes are located off the central courtyard.

There are many old churches in Patzcuaro but the one which I found most interesting is the **Temple of the Compañía de Jesus (12),** near the museum. This church was Don Vasco's cathedral before the basilica was built. After the basilica was finished, it was given to the Jesuits, but the building was neglected after the Jesuits were expelled from Mexico in 1667. The buildings to the south of the church were once part of the complex containing hospital, soup kitchen, and living quarters for religious scholars.

Last but not least is the **House of the Eleven Patios (13),** located between José Maria Cos and Enseñanza. This edifice is one of the most outstanding architectural achievements of the colonial period. It was formerly a convent of the Catherine nuns, but now the **Tourism Office** and art-craft galleries are located in the building. Supposedly open 9 a.m. to 2 p.m. and 4 to 8 p.m., they are not overly conscientious about observing the hours. Another office (same hours) is in the main plaza. The **post office (14)** is located half a block north of the small plaza, on the right-hand side of the street.

No trip to Patzcuaro is complete without a trip on the lake, preferably across to the isolated island village of **Janitzio,** on which a hilltop statue of Morelos dominates all the surrounding countryside. The village church is the scene of an annual ceremony called the Day of the Dead, held at midnight on November 1, when villagers climb to the churchyard carrying lighted candles in memory of all their dead relatives.

While there are no fewer than 13 categories of trips to Janitzio, ranging from the special price for island residents only to the price for a special trip to Janitzio and other islands, best bet is the **colectivo, i.e.,** round-trip group fare. A complete price list is posted at the pier (follow signs saying "Embarcadero").

An ancient dance originated by the Tarascans to ridicule the Spaniards during the Conquest can be seen in its almost original form today. The Dancers of the Viejitos perform at the Hotel Posada de Don Vasco every Wednesday and Saturday at 9:00 p.m.

Side Trips

For a good view of the town and the lake, head for **El Estribo,** a lookout two miles from town (leave the main square on Calle Ponce de León, and follow signs.) It's a fine place for a picnic, and in good weather the walk will take you less than 45 minutes.

Take a short jaunt to Tzintzuntzan, ten miles from Patzcuaro on the road to Quiroga, known for its straw mobiles, baskets, and figures. In earlier centuries Tzintzuntzan was the capital of a Tarascan empire which controlled over a hundred other towns and villages. Pyramids upon pyramids still remind the casual visitor of a glorious, if also rather bloody, past. The old market is now

146 MEXICO ON $20 A DAY

housed in a new neocolonial building—a lot snazzier with prices to match. Also in town is a nice lake that has a footpath along it should you need a reprieve from shopping.

Santa Clara del Cobre (Villa Escalante), famous for its copper products, can be reached by a bus caught in front of the Church of San Francisco, or at the far corner of the Plaza San Agustín. Although the copper mines which existed during pre-Conquest times seem to have been forever lost, local craftsmen still make copper vessels by the age-old methods, each piece being pounded out by hand from pieces of scrap pipe, radiators, and bits of electrical wire.

GETTING TO AND FROM PATZCUARO AND URUAPAN: Being slightly off the main highway, most transportation is via **Morelia.**

By Bus

Autotransportes La Piedad Cabadas and Autobuses de la Piedad operate first-class buses from Patzcuaro to Morelia or Guadalajara, two buses daily to each destination. If you're headed for Guadalajara and you miss the direct bus, it's best to backtrack to Morelia and get a direct Guadalajara bus from there.

By Train

Three trains run daily in each direction between Uruapan and Mexico City, calling at Patzcuaro and Morelia. The third train's schedule requires that you spend the night in Acambaro, so it's not really worth considering. The station in Patzcuaro is down near the lake just off the main highway, and is connected with the town by municipal bus service.

BACK ON THE HIGHWAY: Once back on the main highway, there is a 27-mile run through lovely country to Morelia. Red-roofed houses cluster together on the softly sloping hillsides and from time to time the ubiquitous burro, heavily laden with firewood, can be seen followed closely by another laden with two small boys. Many of the men around here carry or wear serapes made of straw to protect them cheaply and efficiently from the heavy rain which makes the countryside so green.

6. Morelia

Morelia (alt. 6368 feet; pop. 220,000), the capital of the wildly beautiful state of Michoacan, is a lovely colonial city. Over the years it has earned a reputation as one of Mexico's more cultural cities, serving as an intellectual and artistic center for the region. As with much of Mexico, there is layer upon layer of fascinating history here. The area was inhabited first by Indians, notably the Tarascans. Founded by the Spanish in 1541, the city was originally named Valladolid, but the name was later changed in honor of the revolutionary hero José Morelos, who once lived here. The Morelos house (Morelos 323) is ostensibly a museum housing relics of the old hero—his bed, clerical robe, several portraits of him and his parents, and the table upon which the first Mexican independence documents were signed.

Many of the original colonial buildings remain in Morelia, adding that touch of ancient Mexican/Spanish elegance. In an attempt to preserve the architectural harmony, the city government has decreed that all new major construction be in the colonial style. Thus, parts of the city remind one of those reconstructions of Merrie Old English towns that Hollywood prepares so authentically for the movies about Robin Hood. The main movie theater itself, in fact, continues this motif with its oaken doors and chandeliers.

WHERE TO STAY: Next door to this theater, in the main plaza, the Plaza de los Martires (there are two such plazas, separated by the cathedral) is one of the nicest hotels in town, the **Virrey de Mendoza**, Portal Matamoros 16 (tel. 451/2-0633), which is way out of our price range (1400 pesos single, 1800 pesos double) but worth taking a look at. A lovely old colonial mansion built on the grand scale, the two-story lobby, somehow monastic with its stone arches, is dominated by a life-size portrait of one of the Mendoza forebears gazing down from the wall above the fireplace. The rooms have beautiful, highly waxed hardwood floors, Mexican "Oriental" rugs, carved colonial furniture, monogrammed bedthrows and towels, and old-fashioned telephones that would drive antique dealers to fits of avarice. The hotel's restaurant, once a marvelous baronial dining hall, has been converted into four luxury suites for the very well-heeled. The courtyard, which doubles as the lobby, is now also the restaurant, Sic Transit Splendor.

One block from the main plaza on Zaragoza at Ocampo is the **Posada de la Soledad** (tel. 451/2-1888), even more beautiful than the Virrey de Mendoza. Again, the rates are out of our price range (singles are 990 pesos; doubles, 1450 pesos), but worth looking at, especially if you need a little help to get into the colonial mood in Morelia. The unspoiled courtyard actually emanates an aura of tranquillity: stone arches heavy with vines, and a stone fountain, dominate the courtyard without overpowering it.

The **Hotel Catedral** (tel. 451/3-0783 or 3-0467), Zaragoza 37, a few steps north of the main plaza, is still fairly posh but more in our price range. Rooms here are quite comfortable, and grouped around an interior court three stories high. The old-style rooms have been redone during the last few years, and now rent for 820 pesos single, 1050 pesos double.

Moving down the price scale, the **Hotel Casino**, Portal Hidalgo 229 (tel. 451/2-0287), is housed in a fine old building laced with good touches—beams, chandeliers, columns—but tied together with rather unfortunate modernization (the central court has been filled in with a glass-brick ceiling between the first and second floors). Aesthetics aside, the Casino has an excellent location practically across the street from the Mendoza, and 50 cheerful, immaculate rooms-with-bath costing 575 pesos single, 770 pesos double. Downstairs is a large restaurant and bar, and upstairs is an enclosed court bordered by classical railings which look suspiciously like plywood cutouts.

If you are arriving by bus, you may be interested in the **Hotel Concordia**, just around the corner (left out the bus station door, then left again) from the station at Valentín Gómez Farías 328 (tel. 451/2-3052). The Hotel Concordia was recommended by several readers and on checking it I found it to be an excellent choice: modern, spacious rooms with bath; friendly staff; a quiet situation. The rates are 440 pesos single, 545 pesos double.

A hotel just one-half block from the bus depot on V. Gómez Farías at E. Rúiz is the **Hotel Plaza** (tel. 451/2-3095). The 33 rooms are small and exceptionally clean and tidy. Rates are agreeably low, at 465 pesos for a single, 575 pesos for a double. The restaurant downstairs has the same name, but is actually under separate management; prices are moderate, though.

Hotel San Jorge is on a corner of Madero Pte., at no. 719 (tel. 451/2-4610). Rooms are small and almost devoid of furniture, but clean and nice enough, and the most important piece of furniture—the bed—is of good quality and firm. The private baths are surprisingly large and well kept. Prices are 320 pesos single, 380 pesos double with one bed, 435 pesos double with two beds.

WHERE TO EAT: The restaurants in Morelia which are not associated with the fancy hotels are all well within our budget range. Food is, well, only fair, but then so are the prices. Here they are, not listed in any particular order.

Sandor's Restaurant, Madero Ote. 422C, is a clean open-fronted café-cum-luncheonette with red tablecloths and French chansons playing in the background that's good for a light lunch of chicken tacos with salad, fried chicken, hamburger, salad, and fried potatoes for only about 60 to 125 pesos. It's cheap and clean and cheerful and good. To find it, walk east past the cathedral out of the main square on Madero, and after about six uneven blocks you'll see it on the right—a street called Serapio Rendon is opposite it.

Across from the magnificent cathedral at Portal de la Nevería 103 is **El Paraiso de Morelia.** This place is always crowded with college students, business people, and those waiting in line to use the phone. (Note that for a small fee someone will place a call for you while you wait.) Pescado blanco here is 120 pesos, beefsteak is slightly less; the daily set-price breakfast is 85 pesos, and that includes a beverage. With each meal comes a basket overflowing with bread, pastries, rolls, and tempting cookies. I ate quite a variety of these for a mere 10 pesos, and I still have no idea how the waiter settled on that small amount.

Morelia's dependable comida corrida restaurant is **El Tracadero,** Hidalgo 63 (Hidalgo runs south from the middle of the main plaza), about half a block from the square on the left-hand side. One high-ceilinged room here is festooned with bullfight posters and other such memorabilia, and filled with chunky pseudo-colonial tables and chairs. Service is slow but friendly—shall I say leisurely?—but the food is good and the price right. I recently had a delicious five-course lunch for 145 pesos, and I could have ordered a huge Mexican plate for even a bit less. Open for dinner, too.

For espresso coffee, head to the **Cafe Catedral** on the main plaza, the best place to restore your constitution.

Across from the square and cathedral and on the same side of the street as the Hotel Casino is an entire block filled with sidewalk cafés. All of them seem to enjoy about the same degree of popularity, all are pretty crowded, and prices are competitive. A breakfast of fruit, eggs, toast, and coffee is less than 100 pesos. A comida lunch is 95 pesos almost anywhere along the block. These daytime cafés become Morelia's nightlife after dark: then the coffee is hot, the beer cold, the setting peaceful, and the college crowd lively, even exuberant.

Near the bus station and in the same building as the Hotel Plaza is the **Hotel Plaza Restaurant.** This eatery is run by an American who came to Morelia years ago and decided to stay. The comida in this plain, clean diner is 90 pesos; a banana split is 60 pesos, and comes topped with fresh strawberries in season. Open from 7 a.m. to 11 p.m.

A WALK AROUND TOWN: Besides being a way-station on the road to Mexico City, Morelia has a personality and charm all its own. Those planning to spend a day or two here can see what there is to see with a few well-planned walking and city bus tours.

Heading eastward toward the cathedral from the Hotel Virrey de Mendoza, walk up Madero past the plaza, call in at the **cathedral,** and then continue along Madero. The cathedral took 104 years to build (1640–1744) and has two impressive spires which can be climbed (the doors are locked but the man with the key is usually hanging around at midday). The interior of the church is awesome, particularly if you are fortunate enough to be there when the resident organist is playing or practicing.

The **Government Palace,** across the street (Madero) from the cathedral, is worth a brief examination. Most interesting here are the grand murals depicting the history of the state of Michoacan and of Mexico. Some of them were done by a well-known local artist named Alfredo Zalce.

A "must" stop for regional arts fans is the **Palacio del Artesano.** Here, crafts are displayed in an old colonial structure attached to the Church of San Francisco, on the Plaza de San Francisco, one block south of Madero on Fray de San Miguel. To get there, walk east on Madero and then turn south onto Vasco de Quiroga for a block. The church is on the east side of the square; admission is free and visitors are welcome Monday through Saturday from 10 a.m. to 8 p.m., on Sunday from 10 a.m. to 2:30 p.m. The three large rooms hold lacquerware from Patzcuaro and Uruapan: delicately flowered trays inlaid with gold, plus several types of trays done in *embutido,* the original process of inlay which involves treating the completed trays with a preparation of colored earth, axle oil, and linseed oil to create a waterproof finish. Also you'll see beautiful deep-green, brown, and black glazed pottery from San José de Gracia and Patambam; items with cross-stitch embroidery from Taracuato; lovely hand-worked pine furniture, and smaller portable items such as boxes and breadboards from Cuanejo; close woven hats from the Isla de Jaracuaro; lots of copperware, and even more. Everything on display is for sale at reasonable prices.

Across the street from the Plaza de San Francisco is the market. South to Avenida Lázaro Cárdenas will take you near the huge Mercado Independencia, actually not all that interesting except on Sunday, the big market day.

In the other direction from the cathedral, going west on Madero, is the "campus" of the **College of San Nicolas de Hidalgo,** a beautiful colonial university which lays claim to the somewhat frayed title of "Oldest in the Western Hemisphere." Founded in Patzcuaro in 1540, it was moved to Valladolid (i.e., Morelia) in 1580 and incorporated into the University of Michoacan in 1957.

The **Tourism Office** is in the same area, in the Palacio Clavijero, staffed by a friendly enough crew. English is spoken and there is a charge for maps and leaflets.

A little farther along, a block off Madero on Farías, is the delightful mercado de dulces, a jumble of shops laden with *cubitos de ate* (candied fruit wedges), jelly candies, honey, goats milk, strawberry jam, and chongos (a combination of milk, sugar, cinnamon and honey).

A BUS RIDE THROUGH TOWN: Begin at the zócalo on Madero and board a bus marked "Directo" for the trip east, and soon you'll see the results of the city hall order to build in colonial style: banks, office buildings, even Woolworth's, are all in that style.

Six blocks from the zócalo on the left is the massively impressive **Palacio Federal,** which houses the post and telegraph offices: impressive to think that this huge pile is your instrument for mailing postcards.

Leave the bus at the corner of Madero and Avenida Acueducto and walk along the Bosque Cuauhtémoc, which holds the **Museum of Contemporary Art.** Across the street is the three-mile-long aqueduct, constructed in 1785.

Turn right on Calzada Ventura Puente and board a bus labeled "Alberca," which will take you south to the Paseo de La Camelina, and then west (right). The city's **Planetarium** is at this intersection, with shows nightly at 6:30 p.m.; admission is 45 pesos. The bus will continue west to the Parque Juarez, which has a nice little zoo complete with elephants and tigers for only a few pesos admission.

Outside the park, board the bus marked "Santa Maria" for the ride north to the zócalo along Calzada Juarez and on Abasolo. This last leg of the tour presents an enjoyable view of the narrow streets in the residential quarters of the city's interior. On the corner of Abasolo and Allende is the **Museo Michoacano,** the place to go for an introduction to local history.

The bus will take you right to the zócalo. Fares are so low that you can ride along this route, hopping off at every interesting prospect, and still end up paying a good deal less than a dollar for the entire trip.

GETTING TO AND FROM MORELIA: Those arriving by bus in Morelia will want to break their journey with a night in a hotel before continuing on to Mexico City. For train information, see above under "Getting to Patzcuaro."

BACK ON THE HIGHWAY: From Morelia to Mexico City is a comfortable day's ride of a little less than 200 miles. You wind up and down through lush mountain country with some breathtaking vistas before leveling off on the plateau. It'll take you about four hours to get to Toluca (see Chapter XI) and another hour to get to the center of Mexico City. The route takes you right down the capital's main drag, the Paseo de la Reforma, which winds through lush and wealthy residential districts before entering Chapultepec Park and the center of town.

Before going on to the capital, however, I'd advise a detour north to one of the most beautiful areas in all Mexico—the northern reaches of the Valley of Mexico, dotted with several magnificent colonial silver cities.

Chapter V

THE COLONIAL SILVER CITIES

1. Zacatecas
2. Aguascalientes
3. San Luis Potosí
4. Guanajuato
5. San Miguel de Allende
6. Querétaro

BETWEEN THE MOUNTAIN RANGES of the Sierra Madre lies the heartland of Mexico, a high plateau sculpted by rains and rivers over the eons and now a maze of highlands, lakes, and valleys. This is Anáhuac, the center of ancient Mexican civilization, today called the Valley of Mexico.

When the Conquistadores had subdued Tenochtitlán (Mexico City) in the early 1500s, they sent their armies and colonists into the other parts of the Valley of Mexico in search of mineral wealth. They found it: lead, tin, zinc, iron, and antimony were found in abundance, and also gold. But what made the fortunes of the early Spanish governors, and of the cities of the northern valley, was silver. So rich were the mines here that the silver cities of the northern Valley of Mexico became incredibly wealthy, and stayed that way for centuries.

Today these cities, more than any others, are Mexico's colonial showpieces, with architectural beauty rivaled by none. Guanajuato is almost a fairytale town, San Luis Potosí exudes wealth and civic pride from its grand government buildings, cathedral, churches, and monasteries. Each city has a lot to offer and a visitor who has not made the rounds of the silver cities hasn't seen colonial Mexico.

No matter how you're traveling in Mexico, the silver cities are easily accessible despite their locations, nestled in mountain valleys. Coming overland from El Paso, Zacatecas is the first real colonial city you'll encounter; from Monterrey and Saltillo Highway 57 goes straight to San Luis Potosí; from Guadalajara it's only a few hours' drive to Aguascalientes. Mexico City is linked to Queretaro by a fast, limited-access toll highway, and from Querétaro one can drive to any other of the silver cities in a few hours' time. Bus service is fast, frequent, and comfortable.

1. Zacatecas

Zacatecas (alt. 8200 feet; pop. 120,000), capital of the state of the same name, was already an old town when the Spaniards arrived in 1548. A city made rich by silver mines, it has picturesque, cobbled streets ascending the hillsides, a plaza watched over by a white marble angel atop a column, and a real dearth of tourists.

The facade of the wildly churrigueresque cathedral is the first sight which visitors want to see—you might say they're going for baroque—but the less obvious Convento de Guadalupe, a short way from town, and the ruins at La Quemada are also good for a look. You can see it all from the hilltops which dominate the town, most notably the Cerro de la Bufa.

During your time in Zacatecas, be aware of two things: first, that it's very hilly here, and you'll be doing a lot of climbing. Second, that you're at more than 8000 feet altitude in this town, so you'll become winded very quickly going up those hills.

WHERE TO STAY: You needn't walk far from the bus station to get a room in Zacatecas. Despite its colonial heritage, there are very modern hotels as well as older, more romantic places to choose from.

The **Hotel Calinda** (tel. 492/2-3311), a Quality Inn hotel, on Boulevard Lopez Mateos (Highway 45) very near the bus station ("Central Camionera"), is a hot and dusty bus traveler's dream come true. Although prices are a bit high (950 pesos single, 1150 pesos double), that sum buys you the use of a modern lobby loaded with light blue marble, a covered swimming pool on the roof, and all the air conditioning you can take. Decor in the rooms is nice without being overdone, and all are new and comfortable. As rooms on the street side may be a bit noisy, ask to see a room on the other side as well. To find the Calinda as you leave the bus station, just look left.

The busiest corner in town is the intersection of Avenidas Juarez and Hidalgo, next to the telegraph office. A few steps from this corner are two popular hotel choices. The **Hotel Condesa** (tel. 492/2-1160), Avenida Juarez 5, has a handsome stone exterior and an old-fashioned lobby equipped with newish furniture and a constant handful of TV addicts. The rooms are quite acceptable and cost 485 pesos single, 550 to 630 pesos double. Across the street, the **Posada de los Condes** (tel. 492/2-1412), at Juarez 18, offers a slightly more modern interior and charges a bit more for its rooms-with-bath: 535 pesos single, 660 pesos double.

Nearer to the cathedral and the very center of town are several good hotels. The **Hotel Reina Cristina** (tel. 492/2-1130), Jardín Hidalgo 703, is right on the main square (the Jardín Hidalgo, no less). Its tenuous perch on the line between luxury and economy is best seen in the high-ceilinged lobby: the chandeliers are of crystal, but they are in need of a dusting. Prices are definitely budget, however, as single rooms go for 440 pesos, doubles for 565 pesos, both with bath. Subterranean parking is available.

Perched high above town is the **Motel del Bosque** (tel. 492/2-0745), Avenida Días Ordaz (also called El Periferico), with 42 rooms in various positions which give them various views of the city below. You should definitely ask to see several rooms, and be specific in your request for a room with a view, for that is the del Bosque's great advantage over downtown places. When you've chosen one, you'll find that a modern *quarto con bano* will cost about 660 pesos single, 880 pesos double. The little restaurant is best ignored, but the view from the bluff behind it is exceptionally good. By the way, you need only a bit of the mountain goat in you to walk up and down the hillside between town and the hotel.

WHERE TO EAT: All the aforementioned hotels have their own restaurants. The one at the **Hotel Condesa** is popular with travelers despite its spartan decoration. Prices are okay: egg dishes and most *antojitos* (appetizers) are 55 to 75 pesos, and meat plates are 125 to 240 pesos.

One of Zacatecas's most popular and colorful restaurants is **Los Sarapes**, well disguised at Hidalgo 119, a half block from the corner of Hidalgo and Juarez on the left-hand side as you go toward the cathedral. True to its name, sarapes bring brilliant color to the walls of the darkish dining rooms lit by colored glass globes. The five-course comida corrida is the best bargain here, served from about 1 to 4 p.m. and costing 100 pesos. Otherwise, you can have bistek or chicken plates for 105 pesos or so, and many other dishes for about the same. Los Sarapes is open daily from 11 a.m. to 1 a.m.

The latest "in" place in Zacatecas seems to be the **Restaurant La Mina**, Juarez 15, just a few doors down from the Condesa. Broad stone arches, white walls, red tile floor, fluorescent lights—very Mexican mountain town. It's not elegant or refined, but the food's hearty. Have a plate of bistek de res con papas and a bottle of beer, and your bill will be 165 pesos.

The Plaza de la Independencia is the park just down from the Hotel Condesa. Between this plaza and the bus station is a winding little street simply lined with taco shops, snack stands, and hole-in-the-wall eateries just fine for a quick or light bite at a ridiculously low price. Stroll down and see what appeals to you.

WHAT TO DO: Zacatecas is a fine place to take a day off for sightseeing, should you be barreling southward from the U.S. border. A walk around town reveals, first of all, the cathedral with its fantastically ornate facade which has earned it the name of "Parthenon of Mexican Baroque" (whatever that means). It took 22 years to build (1730–1752). Take a close look at the zigzag carving along the lower surfaces, the huge stone pillars inside, and the quaint motif of ears of corn on the ceiling.

The **Jardín Hidalgo**, the town's main square, is where you'll find the state and city government buildings. In the city hall is a modern mural (1970) by Antonio Rodriguez.

Walking down Avenida Hidalgo toward the south you'll pass the **Teatro Calderón** (inaugurated in 1891), a fine and stately building now in great need of some fixing up.

Continue on Hidalgo, across Juarez, and mount the hill to **Cerro de Alica park** (the street changes names up the hill and becomes Avenida Gral. Jesus Gonzalez Ortega). The equestrian statue (1898) is of none other than General Gonzalez Ortega himself, hero of the Battle of Calpulalpan. Behind it is a gazebo with marvelous acoustics, and a green and shady park for a picnic.

At the far end of the park is the **Museo F. Goitía**, a former governor's palace built in 1945. Having been occupied by three governors, each for a four-year term, it was converted into a high school, and then a very fine museum. Exhibits on the ground floor are the work of Francisco Goitía (1882–1960); upstairs are changing exhibits featuring other modern Mexican artists. You can visit the museum without paying a thing, Tuesday through Sunday, 9 a.m. to 2 p.m. and 4 to 8 p.m.

Still heading south, the famous **Aqueduct of Zacatecas** looms over the street. The wealth of this mining city at the turn of the 18th-19th century allowed it to undertake such impressive public works. Water passed along the aqueduct to a large cistern downtown.

It's hard to miss Zacatecas's **market** as it's right downtown very near the cathedral. As Mexican markets go it's a fairly good one, and that means fabulous by most other standards. The hundreds of colors and the thousand little vignettes of Mexican daily life could fascinate an "outsider" for days.

To take it all in at once, climb (slowly, please! remember the altitude!) up to the Motel del Bosque on the Cerro Grillo hill, and take the cable car across the valley to the **Cerro de la Bufa.** When the sun is low in the sky, turning the sandstone town to a golden wonder, and the lights begin to twinkle on, it'll all seem magical. Watch your time, though, as the teleferico (cable car) is in operation only Tuesday through Sunday, 12:30 to 7:30 p.m. The cost for a ride is 50 pesos. Before you make that long climb, look: Are the cars actually running? Beware of breakdowns!

Of Zacatecas's churches, many are notable: San Agustín dates from 1613, when construction was started, although dedication had to wait until 1782; San Francisco was the church of a convent, begun in 1567; the Templo de Jesús was built between 1887 and 1913. But the most famous religious edifice besides the cathedral is about four miles east of Zacatecas on Highways 45/49. In the town of Guadalupe, look for a red-brick church and steeple, and turn right just past it onto Calle Independencia. A few blocks down this street is the **Convento de Guadalupe.** It's open daily from 10 a.m. to 5 p.m.; entry to the museum costs 10 pesos. You enter through a small park or courtyard with stone mosaics—look up at the different domes and doorways of the convent. The museum building is to your right. Inside the convent proper, every wall seems to be covered in paintings. Remember as you tour that these cloistered premises were reserved for the men of the cloth, and that normal folk were not meant to see the paintings. Less were they meant to see the sumptuous "cells" in which the monks—or, rather, students and teachers, as this was a sort of college—spent their spare time. The chapel to the left of the main building (as you face the convent from the front court/park) is called the Capilla de Napoles. You will note with a gasp that it must have taken a king's ransom in gold to decorate it. By the way, you can get the guard to show you the chapel either from the organ loft or from the ground floor—give him a tip for opening the doors and turning on the lights.

Those without cars can get a bus to the town of Guadalupe from Zacatecas's main bus station, the Central Camionera, leaving about every five minutes or so, and costing a few pesos. A taxi to Guadalupe and back will run about 65 pesos.

ZACATECAS MISCELLANY: The **Casa Jaquez,** Avenida Hidalgo 202, is a convenient supermarket and wine shop; it's four blocks from the cathedral, heading south. The **post office (Correos)** is *not* in the building with the Telegrafos at the corner of Juarez and Hidalgo, but rather on the side street called Allende. Zacatecas has its **National Fair** from mid-May to early June each year. Cockfights, bullfights, band concerts, and general hoopla prevail; particularly famous toreadores are laid on, and bullfight tickets go for 100 pesos and up; buses leave for the gigantic Plaza de Toros (and also for the nearby cockpit) from in front of the Central Camionera on days when fights are held. Zacatecas is famous, among craftsmen, for its sarapes, its carvings in stone and wood, and its leatherwork.

GETTING TO AND FROM ZACATECAS: The Central Camionera is about four or five blocks from the center of town, depending on how you measure the distance.

As Zacatecas is on the main highways between Ciudad Juarez / Mexico City and Monterrey / Guadalajara, buses buzz in and out of town all during the day and night, and there is hardly ever a problem finding a seat to any destination. Make your arrangements at least a few hours in advance, just to be sure.

From Zacatecas to her sister city of Aguascalientes, it is barely a two-hour ride. Those going to Guadalajara on Highway 54 will get a chance to stop at the ruins of Chicomoztoc, also called **La Quemada**.

LA QUEMADA RUINS: Thirty-four miles south of Zacatecas on Highway 54 is the archeological site of a 12th-century Indian culture developed by the Nahuatlacas tribe. The pyramids here resemble somewhat the ones at Mitla and Monte Alban, much farther to the south. The largest pyramid, called the Temple, has been restored and offers you your first glimpse of this fascinating aspect of Mexico's past. The rest of the site is not very well preserved, but the 11 pillars built of granite stones serve to give you an idea of the grandiose palace which once stood here. Stone-paved avenues and terraces crowded with foundations of houses mark the Ciudadela, atop which is an observatory from which the Nahuatlacas studied the movements of stars and planets and—who knows?—tracked the course of early extraterrestrial visitors. You can visit the ruins from sunup to sundown daily, for 10 pesos per person. Get the bus to La Quemada from the Callejón de Tampico, several blocks east of the Central Camionera.

2. Aguascalientes

Aguascalientes (alt. 6000 feet; pop. 300,000) means "hot waters," so it isn't hard to figure out that the city has hot springs. Underneath the town there's a maze of tunnels believed to have been excavated by some ancient peoples who left no explanation of their feats; the tunnels are not open to the public.

Today Aguascalientes is known for its copper mining as well as for its embroidery and knitwear. Most of the town women are involved in this craft and those who aren't are humming away on their sewing machines. In the streets beside and behind the cathedral and the Plaza Principal, you'll note several stores selling the products of this industry.

As this city has grown, it has lost some of its colonial charm. The residents no doubt revel in the modernity which progress has brought, but the tourist in search of colonial treasures will find them between newer and less interesting buildings. Aguascalientes is still a nice place to visit, but only as a stop in passing, really.

In recent years, the Mexican government has shown a tendency to move its tourism offices well beyond the reach of tourists, and the one in this city is no exception. It's located at Avenida Circunvalación Sur and Avenida Mahatma Gandhi (tel. 491/6-0123). Look for the "Edificio Piscis," first floor above street level.

WHERE TO STAY: The number-one budget choice in town is the 31-room **Hotel San José (2)**, Hidalgo 207 (tel. 491/5-5130), the outside of which is pretty plain; inside, however, it's quite nice. Accommodations are small, well scrubbed, acceptable, and fairly cheerful. All have private baths and are a good buy for 375 pesos single, 500 pesos double, 575 pesos triple. Parking costs extra.

Going up the scale, there's the old **Hotel Imperial (3)**, 5 de Mayo 106 (tel. 491/6-1664), housed in a once-imposing stone building on the Plaza Principal across the street from the cathedral. The Imperial "lobby" is a tiny little entranceway at the side of the building, the original lobby having been converted into a Bancomer branch. Guest rooms are big, and the outside ones are cheerful and especially bright; in fact, the whole place is cheerful. The price is 515 pesos single, 660 pesos double.

For a few pesos less you can stay at the other end of the plaza in the middle-aged **Hotel Senorial (4)**, Colón 104 (tel. 491/5-1473), whose immaculate plastic lobby leads to 32 clean and simple rooms. The older part of the hotel is the most deluxe, with Louis XIV-influenced plywood furniture which is worth seeing; otherwise the rooms aren't too distinguished. Singles are 350 pesos; doubles, 475 pesos.

The **Hotel Río Grande (5)**, José Maria Chavez 101 (tel. 491/6-1251), is a little further up the price scale. Located on the main plaza, the Río Grande has a large contemporary lobby that's exceptionally nice for such a small town, and clean, well-furnished singles for 585 pesos, doubles for 695 pesos.

The elegant **Hotel Francia (6)**, Avenida Madero and Plaza Principal, has a synthetic tile floor that looks absolutely like marble and a huge blow-up print of Aguascalientes's Plaza Principal as it looked a century ago. Its huge, modern rooms are very well appointed; but the cheaper rooms are the ones within our range at 660 to 830 pesos single, 880 to 1100 pesos double. Parking costs extra. The clientele at the Francia tends to be well-groomed business types with the occasional wealthy farmer in sleek cowboy hat.

WHERE TO EAT: To sample the variety of Aguascalientes's regional fare, try the **Restaurante Cascada (8)**, on the Plaza Principal. Most local delicacies are yours for about 75 to 90 pesos per plateful; meat dishes are about twice that price. You'll dine with local people here—but many of them will be staring at the popular TV set.

Nicest place in town to eat is the **Restaurant Mitla (10)**, Madero 220, which is spotlessly clean and has such good service that the waiter brings you a plate of rolls, butter, and cheese (cheese at a slight charge) the moment you sit down. Lots of selection in edibles: kidneys and onions, chicken dishes, and excellent chilaquiles (chunks of pork and corn tortillas covered with a hot sauce and sprinkled with cheese) for 135 to 175 pesos.

On the Plaza Principal, a sign above the tiny **Restaurant San Francisco (11)** proclaims "the best ice cream in town," which is hard to dispute unless you plan to become the world's only expert on ice cream concoctions in Aguascalientes. You can have a "banana spleet" for 65 pesos, other ice cream for 20 to 55 pesos, and a fairly wide selection of hot dishes.

Finally, the Hotel Río Grande's restaurant, **Las Bugambilias (5)**, is popular as a businessmen's lunch hangout; the comida is 195 pesos.

WHAT TO DO: You might find it relaxing just to walk along the Avenida Carranza to the attractive **Jardín de San Marcos**, a lovely enclosed park where the only sounds are those of hundreds of birds in the treetops and the shouts and laughter of children playing around the bandstand.

The only other sight of the quiet town is the **State Palace (1)** on the Plaza Principal. As you enter you'll be stopped short by the astonishing perspective

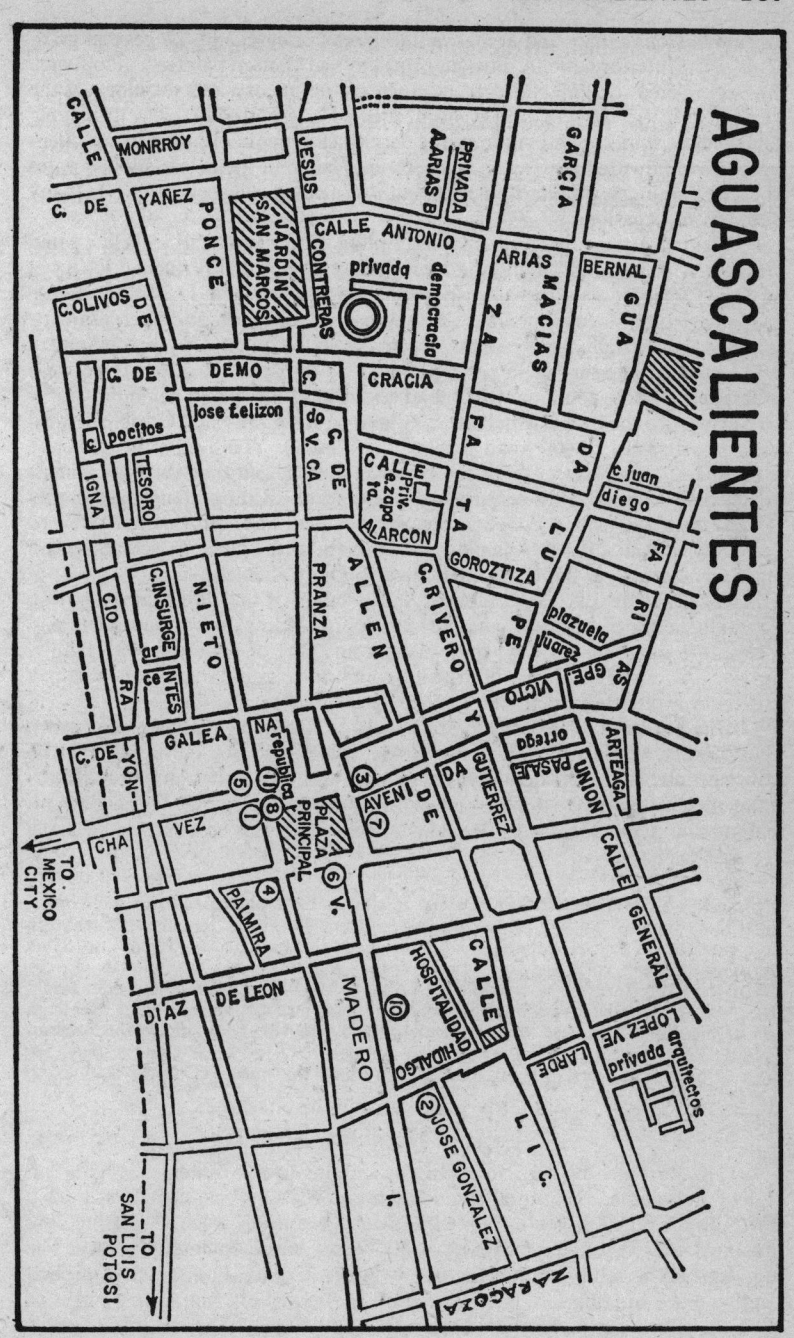

AGUASCALIENTES

of carved stone pillars and arches, a sweeping staircase, and the general grandeur of the interior patio. A glorious mural by the Chilean painter Ualdo Ibarra was completed in 1957 and depicts much of the history and sociology of the region. Industry mingles with pastoral scenes, long-haired maidens displaying embroidery, miners climbing from the depths, cannons booming, and succulent grapes overflowing their vases. The ceramic plaque in the palace's lobby notes that the building was erected in 1665, but it has obviously been redone on many subsequent occasions.

Visiting Aguascalientes without sampling its thermal facilities is like going to Blarney Castle and leaving the Blarney Stone unbussed. Principal local spa is **Ojo Caliente** on the eastern outskirts of town (tel. 491/5-4721), whose waters are highly recommended for rheumatism, arthritis, and liver ailments. The spa is open daily from 7 a.m. to 7 p.m., from 7 a.m. to 4:30 p.m. on Sunday and holidays. The sum of 35 pesos permits you to dip in the general pool, and a smaller "family pool" is available at the rate of 350 pesos per hour.

To get to the baths, which are a mile or so from the Plaza Principal, head east on Highway 70 (the road to San Luis Potosí). You'll pass the Mercado Reforma at a traffic circle near the railroad station, and then the road widens to become a broad 19th-century-style boulevard. Riding along past evenly spaced trees and ornate globed lampposts, benches, and statues, the boulevard suddenly ends in a Pepsi-Cola plant; to the right of the plant, smack at the end of the boulevard, is the unmarked entry to Ojo Caliente.

Ojo Caliente, like the boulevard, is a product of the 19th century, with a fountain in the little court and lots of doors leading to various pools and dressing rooms. By the way, the price for any sort of pool—general, family, private—doesn't include use of dressing room, towels, and soap. You must pay for them as you use them.

The last week in April, a **fiesta** is held to honor the town's patron saint, San Marcos, and craft exhibits, fireworks, rodeos, and bullfights entertain the townspeople. Bulls, incidentally, are bred in the area, and you can make arrangements to visit two well-known breeding ranches, the **Hacienda Chichimeco** and the **Hacienda Penuelas**. Proprietors can be contacted via the Tourist Office.

READER'S SIGHTSEEING TIP: "Be sure to stop at **Encarnacion de Díaz,** a charming little town 16 miles south of Aguascalientes on Route 45. The plaza consists of fantastic tree prunings. There is Columbus with his three ships (the *Nina, Pinta,* and *Santa Maria*); there are kings and queens with ermine robes; zebras; lions; all pruned from cedar trees. To show my appreciation, I called to the old man on a stepladder busily trimming. He ignored me completely, silently snipping away. A Mexican came over from across the street. 'He's deaf, can't hear a word you say.' Upon questioning the Mexican informed me José Cervantes, the only man taking care of this outstanding display, has been at his job 40 years. A true artist . . . don't miss this must!" (Dorothy Schmieder, St. Louis, Mo.).

3. San Luis Potosí

The most picturesque and prosperous mining towns of Mexico include San Luis Potosí among their number, and once you visit this bustling city (alt. 6200 feet; pop. 380,000) you'll see why. Rich, beautiful colonial architecture abounds, accented by the city's long (400 years) and momentous history. The San Luis of the name is Louis, the saintly king of France; Potosí is the Quechua Indian word for richness, borrowed from the incredibly rich Potosí mines of Bolivia, which San Luis's mines were thought to rival. The colonial city was founded in 1583 by Fray Magdalena and Captain Caldera on the site of the Chichimec Indian town of Tanga-Manga—Indians had been living in a town on this spot for three centuries before the Spaniards arrived. The Spaniards came in search of silver and found it, mostly at a small town called San Pedro some 25 miles from San Luis Potosí. But the mineral springs at San Luis made it a better place to settle than San Pedro, so this became the center of the mining region.

Along with the prospectors came the friars in search of converts: the Franciscans were the first, followed by the Jesuits and the Carmelites. San Luis owes much of its architectural heritage to the vigor—and lavish expenditure—of these groups.

Later, during the Mexican Revolution, the "Plan of San Luis" was proclaimed here. The city has in fact been twice the capital of Mexico—in 1863 and 1867—when Benito Juarez led the fight against European intervention, governing the country from the Palacio de Gobierno (on the Plaza de Armas). From this palace he pronounced the death sentence on Maximilian and his two generals.

Today San Luis Potosí lives on industry rather than silver. Everything from automobiles to mezcal is produced in the factories ringing the city, but happily the colonial center has been preserved intact. It's the capital city of the state of San Luis Potosí, as well.

ORIENTATION: San Luis is today a big city, but transportation and accommodation present no great problems, as most of what you'll want to see is in the downtown section which holds a good selection of older hotels in a range of prices. Meals are also easy to come by, from snacks to elegant dinners.

The city's **Central Camionera** is a short distance from town, near the grand Benito Juarez Monument. As you exit from either the first- or second-class parts of the bus terminal you'll see bus stops for city buses which will run you to the **Jardín Hidalgo** (the main square, also called the Plaza de Armas, or just the Zócalo).

From the railroad station you can walk—providing your bags are not super-heavy—to most of the hotel selections listed below, the lower priced choices being by and large not more than two or three blocks from the station door.

For information, a map showing the whole town, or answers to questions, the **Tourism Office (1)** (tel. 481/2-3143) in the Palacio de Gobierno on the Jardín Hidalgo is definitely the place to go. The staff here, perhaps the most accommodating in all Mexico, is knowledgeable and ready to help. At least one person there will speak English.

WHERE TO STAY: The area south of the Jardín Hidalgo is a grid of narrow streets lined with graceful and for the most part unmodernized old mansions. These low, elaborate, and ancient homes are built in the Spanish style and each contains a lush central garden courtyard. It's well worth a stroll down here to peek through the delicate iron traceries that cover the windows, and if you're lucky you can catch glimpses of cool, aristocratic rooms lined with gilt and velvet, looking as they have for almost a century.

The modern **Hotel Maria Cristina (3)** (tel. 481/2-9408), Juan Sarabia 110, is one of San Luis Potosí's most substantial downtown hostelries, with the deluxe touches some love to have, although others would rather not pay for them. If you like the comforts, you'll find them here: a rooftop restaurant and swimming pool, and elevators to take you there, lots of carpeting and lots of telephones. Higher priced rooms even come with TV. Singles cost 675 to 850

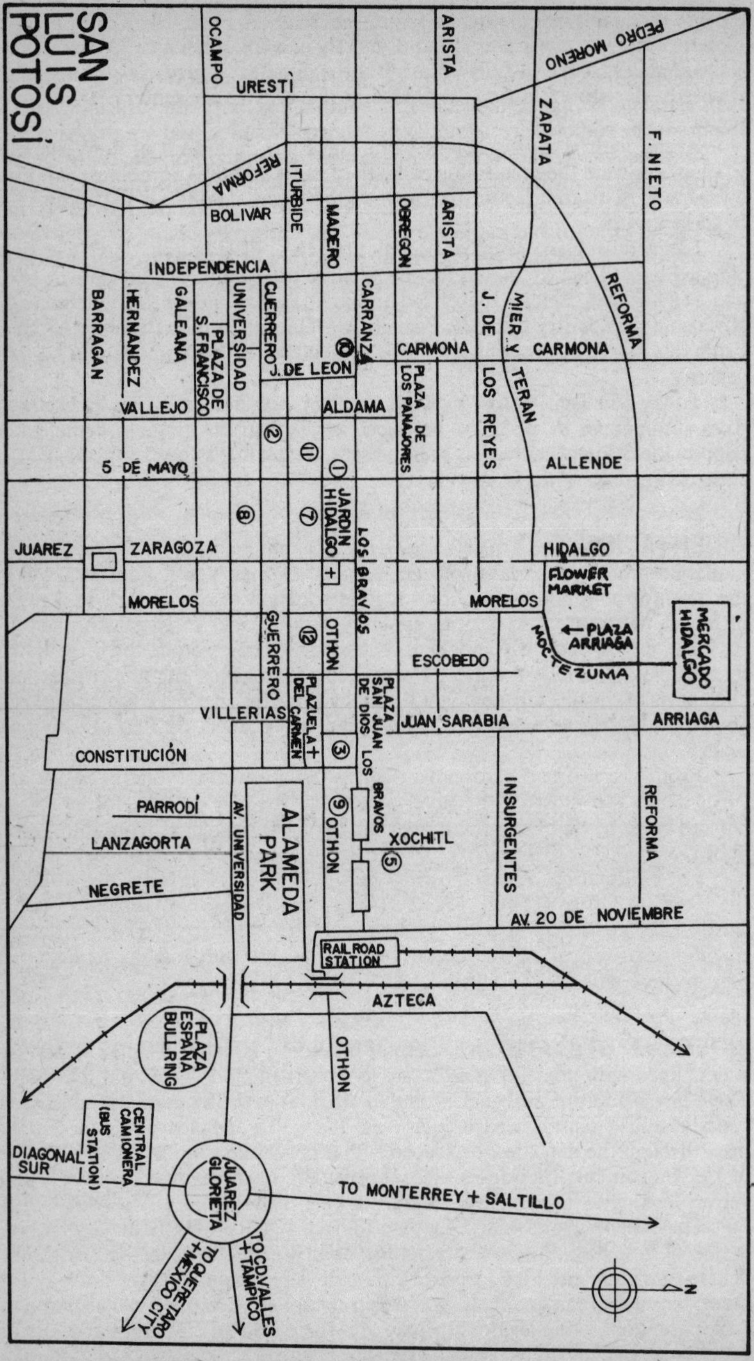
SAN LUIS POTOSÍ
OCAMPO
URESTÌ
ARISTA
PEDRO MORENO
ZAPATA
F. NIETO
REFORMA
ITURBIDE
MADERO
OBREGON
ARISTA
BOLIVAR
INDEPENDENCIA
BARRAGAN
HERNANDEZ
GALEANA
PLAZA DE S. FRANCISCO
UNIVERSIDAD
GUERRERO
CARRANZA
CARMONA
PLAZA DE LOS PANAJORES
J. DE LOS REYES
MIER Y TERAN
CARMONA
REFORMA
J. DE LEON
VALLEJO
ALDAMA
5 DE MAYO
ALLENDE
JARDIN HIDALGO
LOS BRAVOS
JUAREZ
ZARAGOZA
HIDALGO
FLOWER MARKET
MORELOS
MORELOS
PLAZA ARRIAGA
MERCADO HIDALGO
MOCTEZUMA
GUERRERO
OTHON
ESCOBEDO
PLAZUELA DEL CARMEN
PLAZA SAN JUAN DE DIOS
VILLERIAS
JUAN SARABIA
ARRIAGA
CONSTITUCIÓN
LOS BRAVOS
INSURGENTES
REFORMA
PARRODÍ
ALAMEDA PARK
OTHON
XOCHITL
LANZAGORTA
AV. UNIVERSIDAD
NEGRETE
AV. 20 DE NOVIEMBRE
RAILROAD STATION
AZTECA
PLAZA ESPAÑA BULLRING
OTHON
CENTRAL CAMIONERA (BUS STATION)
DIAGONAL SUR
JUAREZ GLORIETA
TO MONTERREY + SALTILLO
TO QUERETARO + MEXICO CITY
TO CD. VALLES + TAMPICO
N

pesos, doubles are 775 to 995 pesos. Be sure to take a look at the classic little parlor, complete with marble fireplace, just off the incongruously modern lobby.

Next door to the Maria Cristina is the **Hotel Napoles (3)** (tel. 481/2-8418), Juan Sarabia 120, in somewhat stiff competition with the Maria Cristina. Rooms at the Napoles are, again, quite modern and nice, and are priced at 575 to 795 pesos single, 660 to 985 pesos double, depending on the luxuries you require. Most of the rooms, alas, are at the high end of this range.

The **Hotel de Gante (1)** (tel. 481/2-1492), yet another modern hotel, has a very good location and moderate prices. The entrance is Calle 5 de Mayo no. 140, but in fact the building is right at the corner of 5 de Mayo and Madero, on the Plaza de Armas. Although its exterior appearance is very modern, the rooms are a bit older, having seen long use. You'll find you may get a crystal chandelier in exchange for putting up with a little chipped paint. An interior room costs 440 pesos single, 660 pesos double; one overlooking the plaza will be 100 pesos more.

Should you want to put up in such a style yourself, try the **Hotel Filher (8)** (tel. 481/2-1562), at the corner of Zaragoza and Universidad. The courtyard has been glassed over, but the hotel still whispers elegance and charm. Street parking in front of the hotel is reserved for guests. Rooms cost 650 to 800 pesos single, 750 to 1000 pesos double. Here you're three short blocks from the main square.

Many of San Luis Potosí's budget hotels are as much colonial monuments as the grand edifices on the Jardín Hidalgo. Such a place is the **Hotel Progreso (2)** (tel. 481/2-0366), at Aldama 415, between Iturbide and Guerrero, only two blocks south of the Jardín Hidalgo. Like many other hotels in the city, it's an old mansion converted to a hotel. The lofty court (now the lobby) is filled with heavy colonial wood furniture, and two voluptuous but woebegone caryatids support the arch at the bottom of the grand staircase leading to the rooms. All with baths, the rooms are an odd lot, old-fashioned but passable in a pinch. Singles are 330 pesos; doubles, 385 to 440 pesos. The desk clerk can help you with parking. This is not the nicest or most refined of the mansions-turned-hotels, but it is certainly one of the most curious ones, and is the best for the money.

Right near the Hotel Jardín is the modern and only slightly weatherbeaten **Hotel Anahuac (5)** (tel. 481/2-6504), at Calle Xochitl 140. As there are few street numbers on this street, look for the second big (four-story) white building on the right-hand side of the street as you walk down Xochitl from Calle de los Bravos. You'll spot the Anáhuac's cavernous, bare lobby. Rooms are equally without frills, but clean and suitable, renting for 355 pesos single, 465 pesos double. The hotel has its own big parking lot. The area around the Jardín and the Anáhuac is only a few steps from the railroad station. Once it was pretty rundown, but urban renewal has swept away the crumbling buildings and replaced them with parks, public buildings, and a mammoth public parking garage.

Finally, if you prefer older buildings with the wistful air of better days, try the small **Hotel Plaza (7)**, Jardín Hidalgo 22 (tel. 481/2-4631), conveniently located on the south side of the main plaza. The Plaza's 30 rooms are dark and old-fashioned (except for the few facing the plaza), but are scrupulously clean, each with private bath. Rates are 310 pesos single, 390 pesos double.

WHERE TO EAT: Right at the northeast corner of the Jardín Hidalgo, corner of Los Bravos and Hidalgo, is the **Tanga-Manga**. New, modern, and shiny-bright, its colorful booths and imitation brick contrast with the weighty solidity of the surrounding architecture. The prices make it popular with young Potosiños: for under 200 pesos, it's easy to have a full meal. The more modest your entree, the less the price for the entire meal. Scan the menu by the entrance before you walk in and sit down.

The **Restaurant-Cafe Tokio (9)**, facing the Alameda at Othon 415, is not far from the railroad station. Indeed, it looks sort of like a station inside: bright and bare, always busy with waiters and customers scurrying. It's open 24 hours a day and serves sandwiches to filet mignon. A good bargain is the enchiladas potosiñas plate: five enchiladas topped with chopped onions, cheese, generous dollops of refried beans, and guacamole. With rolls and a beverage, you'll pay only 125 pesos. The Tokio has been dependably good for decades.

A good place for a light lunch or snack is the **Cafe Versalles (11)**, a bright and comfy modern place just off the Jardín Hidalgo at Madero 145 between Aldama and 5 de Mayo. Breakfast huevos rancheros here cost only 60 pesos, coffee is 28 pesos, and pastries are 36 pesos. The Versalles is patronized by business-suited types in the morning and late afternoon, by mod young people in the evening.

La Parroquia (10), at the corner of Carranza and Díaz de León, is one of several café/restaurant/ice cream parlors patronized by the business set. When the cinema next door lets out, the café tables fill up for conversation, seeing and being seen, people-watching—the food is definitely less important than the social life. It's fun, and the menus offer everything from steaks to banana splits. Walk up here for dessert after dinner to take in the nightlife.

A Starvation Budget Restaurant

Where can you get a full comida corrida for 90 pesos in San Luis? Right on the Jardín Hidalgo, of all places, at the above-mentioned **Hotel Plaza (7)**. Served after 1 p.m. in the courtyard restaurant, the comida does indeed seem to be the hotel's reason for existence these days, and is enjoyed by many more people than the number that stay at the hotel.

READERS' RESTAURANT SELECTIONS: "For the budget-minded, **Las Tortugas del Charco Verde,** located on the corner of Obregon and Hidalgo, offers a wide selection of tortas in various combinations (egg, ham, pork, avocado, sausage). Prices range from 16 to 35 pesos. The atmosphere is friendly and informal. Quality products are utilized in the preparation and the place is always very clean" (Curt Bennett, Salt Lake City, Utah). . . . "**La Cigarra,** in the 900-block of Carranza (a ten-minute walk in the direction of Parque Tequis) is one of the best restaurants for the price in all Mexico. A plate of tacos de pollo includes four tacos, french fries, beans, and salad for less than 100 pesos; pozole (one bowl is a full meal) costs about the same. Everything's delicious and economical" (Dorothy A. Rissel, Bloomington, Ind.).

WHAT TO SEE: The place to begin a walk around town is the **Jardín Hidalgo.** The plaza itself dates from the mid-1700s—before that it was a bullring. After the plaza was laid out, the **Palacio de Gobierno** was begun. What you see today of this building has been much repaired, restored, and added to through the centuries—the back and the south facade were redone as recently as 1973. The front of the building retains much of the original 18th-century decoration, at least on the lower floors.

Across the plaza from the Government Palace is the **cathedral.** The original building had only one bell tower, so another one—the one on the left—was built in 1910 to match, although today the newer tower looks to be the older. The **palace** on the north side of the cathedral was built in 1850 by the Count of Monterrey and was loaded with great wealth—paintings and sculpture—little of which has survived the plaza's stormy history. When the count died in 1890 the palace was taken over by the bishop, and later in 1921 by the city government. Since that year it's been San Luis's City Hall.

By the way, the bandstand in the center of the plaza was built in 1947 (although in colonial style), using the pink stone famous to the region. You'll see the stone throughout San Luis. The band plays here Thursday and Sunday evenings, for free.

From the Jardín Hidalgo, stroll along the **Calle Hidalgo,** heading north out of the plaza. This street's reserved for pedestrians, and it's a treat to walk from the Jardín almost all the way to the city's Central Market.

The Plazuela del Carmen and the Alameda

Southeast of the Jardín Hidalgo is one of the city's most famous and pretty squares, the Plazuela del Carmen, named for the **Templo del Carmen** church. From the Jardín, walk east along Madero-Othon to Escobedo and the plazuela. The entire area you see was once part of the lush grounds of the Carmelite monastery, built in the 17th century. The church survives from that time, and is perhaps the Potosiños' favorite place of worship, but the convent has been destroyed. In 1857 the government confiscated the convent building and used it as a jail for a time before it was destroyed. The **Teatro de la Paz** now stands on the site, having been built there in 1889. The square is a fine place to take a rest by one of the fountains before heading on a few more blocks east to get to the Alameda, the city's largest park. This is the coolest park as well, because of the shade trees; walk all the way to the center and you barely notice the traffic on the busy streets surrounding the Alameda.

Other Plazas

San Luis Potosí has a lot more plazas than the two most famous ones mentioned above. The **Plaza de San Francisco** (also called the Plaza de Guerrero) is south of the Palacio de Gobierno along Aldama, between Universidad and Galeana. The square takes its name from the huge monastery of the Franciscan order at the south side of the plaza. The church on the west side is dated 1799, and next to the church is the interesting **Museo Regional de Arte Popular,** housed in a turn-of-the-century (20th century!) building, renovated to hold the museum in 1953. You can visit the museum weekdays from 10 a.m. to 2 p.m. and 5 to 8 p.m., on Saturday from 10 a.m. to 1 p.m., and on Sunday from 10 a.m. to 2:30 p.m., to see the exhibits in glassed-in rooms around the open court. The displays run the gamut of Potosiño crafts: ceramics, inlaid wood, paper-mâché "sculpture," the local designs in rebozos, and so forth. Right now the price is right—the museum's free.

Another square with a church to visit is the **Plaza de los Panadores,** at the intersection of Obregon and Aldama (northwest of the Jardín Hidalgo). You'll want to take a peek through the baroque doorway of the **Loreto Chapel,** dating from the 16th century, and the neighboring headquarters of the **Compania de Jesus**—the Jesuit order. In the chapel is a magnificent golden sunburst over the altar, a reminder of past glories.

Markets

It's about ten blocks along the pedestrian Calle Hidalgo from the Jardín Hidalgo to the city's new Mercado Hidalgo, a mammoth building devoted mostly to food but also carrying some baskets, rebozos, and straw furniture.

While here, be sure to try some *queso de tuna,* a specialty of the region. Although called a "cheese," in fact it's a sweet paste—something like dried figs or dates with a molasses or burnt-sugar taste—made from the prickly pear cactus fruit. It's delicious, and costs about 35 pesos for a 100-gram (quarter-pound) cellophane-wrapped bar.

But the walk along Calle Hidalgo is itself an introduction to the city's commercial life. Hardware stores, craftsmen's shops, groceries, and taverns all crowd the street—and have you ever seen so many shoe stores in your life? How on earth do they all survive?

Off to the right (as you walk along Hidalgo from the Jardín Hidalgo) is a large and well-worn building which is San Luis Potosí's flower market, a joyous riot of colors and scents anytime of day.

GETTING TO AND FROM SAN LUIS POTOSÍ: Being a state capital, and right in the geographical center of Mexico, San Luis Potosí is well served by a large number of bus lines. It's an easy day's bus ride (eight hours) from Monterrey or Saltillo, only three hours from Zacatecas or Aguascalientes. There are several daily buses to Guanajuato and San Miguel de Allende, and many to Mexico City via Querétaro. Get tickets in advance at the Central Camionera.

Trains run from Monterrey and Saltillo to San Luis. The same train continues on to Mexico City. There is a morning train from the capital's Buenavista Station to San Luis. These are the "Rapidos"; slower trains, including a night train from the capital with sleeping cars, also run daily. It's best to have a first-class reserved seat, so check in at the station the day before you plan to leave.

4. Guanajuato

Guanajuato (alt. 6724 feet; pop. 80,000) could be described as 15 plazas in search of a city. At first sight, it's a hopelessly confusing place with one plaza after another opening off the Avenida Juarez, which is what the main highway becomes once it has entered the town. The confusion in part stems from the subterranean highway running south through town which has no signs and practically no exits; once you're on it, you stay on it until you emerge at the other end of town. It's also easy to drive calmly down a ramp onto the subterranean and discover three quarters of a mile later that you're going the opposite direction from the rest of the traffic.

Guanajuato is an unusually attractive town with an inexplicable air of isolation about it. It was built in 1559 around the Río Guanajuato, and the narrow winding streets of today reflect the meanderings of the past. The river itself was diverted from the town after the last flood in 1905, leaving an excellent bed for the subterranean highway. Most of the stonework and arches you'll see were already there in the 17th century. All that was needed was stone pavement and street lights.

Guanajuato has a rich history, being one of the most important colonial cities (along with Queretaro and Zacatecas) in the 16th, 17th, and 18th centuries. Here was mined over a third of all the silver in the world; and, like the gold rush towns in the U.S., it bloomed overnight with elaborate churches and mansions, many in the Moorish style. Today, Guanajuato seems like an old Spanish city that has been dumped lock, stock, and barrel onto a Mexican hillside.

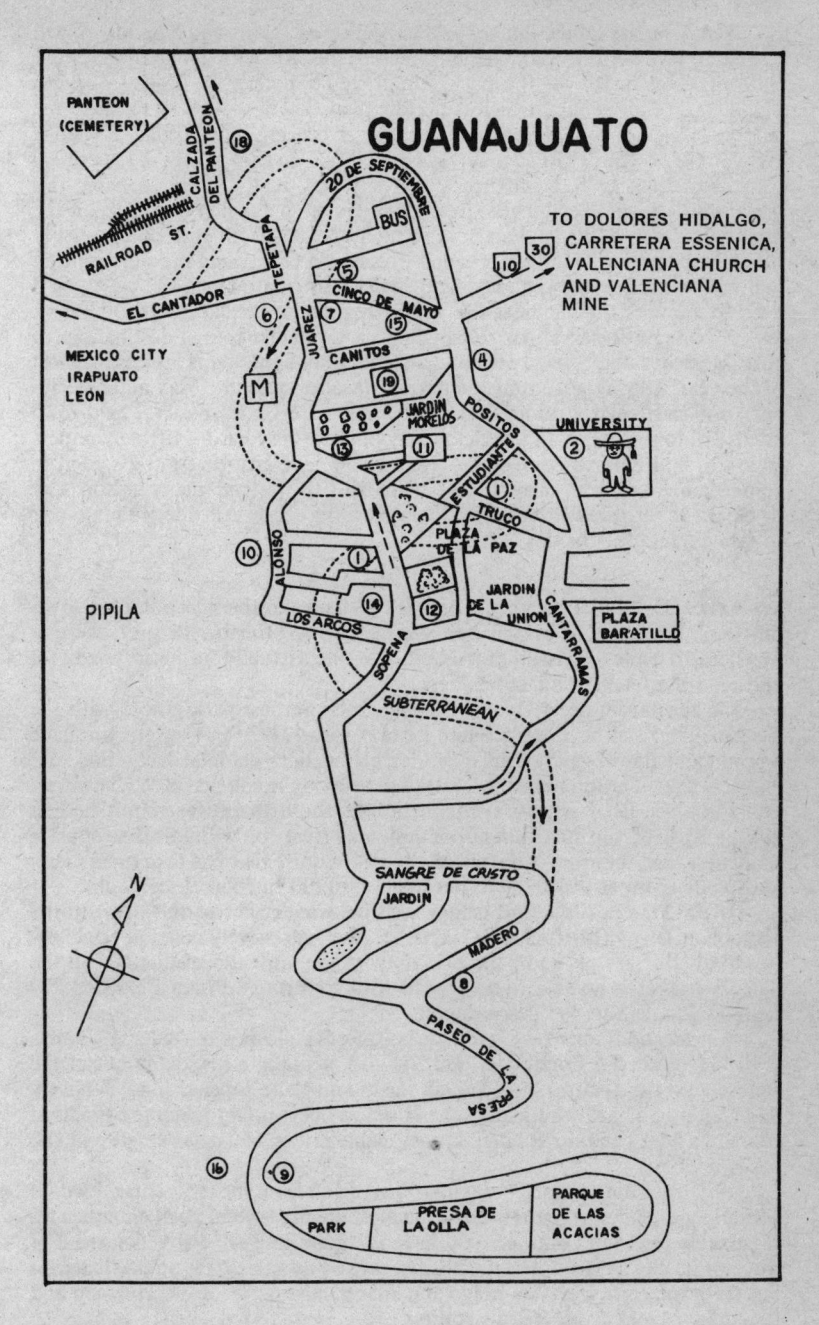

GUANAJUATO

The **Tourism Office (5)**, at the intersection of Juarez and 5 de Mayo, will be glad to give you a free and detailed map of the city, with a map of the entire state of Guanajuato on the back. On it you'll notice the legend *Conozca Guanajuato Caminando,* which is no idle plea. There is no way to make the narrow streets of this ancient city capable of bearing more traffic, and so if people "Get to Know Guanajuato on Foot" it will do a lot to relieve the critical traffic situation. In fact walking is the only way really to get to know this labyrinthine town. For longer stretches of travel in the city, just hop on the main bus, marked "Presa–Estación," which operates from one end of town at the railroad station to the other end at Presa de la Olla, using the subterranean highway when going south (subterranean bus stops are along the way; you'll need to know of the one near the Teatro Juarez, off the Jardín de la Union).

A Note on Reservations: Guanajuato is a popular tourist destination for both Mexicans and foreign visitors, and the room situation is a bit tight most of the year. During government workers' vacation periods (May and December), and particularly during the International Cervantes Festival held from late April to mid-May, and in October, rooms are very hard—virtually impossible—to find unless reserved, and even if you have a reservation it's good to come claim your room early in the day. During the festival, many visitors stay in places as far away as Querétaro and San Miguel de Allende, coming over to Guanajuato for the day.

WHERE TO STAY: There has been little change in the selection of in-town hotels of Guanajuato for the past decade or so, probably because there is nowhere to build. The sumptuous places—one virtually an entire medieval castle—are a bit high for our budget.

On the Jardín de la Union, Guanajuato's prettiest park graced with the Teatro Juarez, is the **Posada Sante Fe (12)** (tel. 473/2-0084). Here you have a bright and almost gaudy display of tiles, chandeliers, colonial decoration, and classical urns. The immense tiled murals get you in the colonial mood, however, and the place itself is very sympathetic. As the demand for rooms here is constantly high, the men at the front desk may treat you with less than effusive politeness, and they may—if it's really busy—require that you take three meals with your room at 990 to 1275 pesos single, 1100 to 1550 pesos double.

If the Posada's full, and it may well be, wander across the street to the **Hotel San Diego (14)** (tel. 473/2-1300), a less aggressively colonial establishment but still very pleasant, and priced about the same except that here at the San Diego there's no need to take meals with your room. Prices are 480 to 770 pesos single, 595 to 895 pesos double.

A newer addition to the Jardín de la Union's collection of "colonial" hotels is the **Hosteria del Frayle** (tel. 473/2-1179), actually a few doors out of the square, past the Teatro Juarez and up the hill on Calle Sopena, at no. 3. Nicely done, although hardly authentic, the Hosteria offers pretty much the standard room of a Mexican tourist hotel, at reasonable prices: 660 pesos single and 880 pesos double.

If you are not opposed to taking a bus to and from the city center, I would recommend your staying outside of town. There are several good choices with reasonable rates, and out here you have the quiet tree-lined streets instead of the city bustle. These hotels are easily reached by taking the Presa–Estación bus from the corner of 5 de Mayo and Juarez, just north of the Mercado and less than a block from the bus station.

The best choice out of town is the **Motel de Las Embajadoras (8)**, Paseo Madero 44 (tel. 473/2-0081). It's very quiet, the rooms small but clean and going for 440 to 550 pesos single, 660 to 880 pesos double. The nicest thing, however, is the surrounding grounds. The only daytime sounds are birds chirping, a radio playing, and chairs being scraped across the floors as maids clean the pretty little rooms. There's a patio at the rear, with tables, chairs, and a hammock, and climbing geraniums complete the tranquil scene. A nice little restaurant takes care of meals.

Farther uptown in this direction, and conveniently located at the end of the bus line, is one more place. It is the **Villa Goerne (9)**, Paseo de la Presa 158 (tel. 473/2-0279), a quiet Victorian house (former residence of Maximilian's grand chamberlain) set back from the road in a garden. The core of the house has been hollowed out and replaced with modern rooms. Out back is a terraced hillside garden with plenty of steps and a large cement trough which they insist on calling a swimming pool. The old rooms are delightful with crystal chandeliers, beams, antique armoires, and lots of mirrors; the new rooms are nice but ordinary. Rates aren't particularly cheap: 475 to 550 pesos single, 550 to 820 pesos double.

Just a block from the bus station is the recently redone **Hotel El Insurgente (6)** (tel. 473/2-2294), Juarez 226. All the nice old stone doorways have been left intact, and the little lobby fixed up with attractive wood and stone. The rooms-with-bath here are quite small, and could be claustrophobic—look before you buy. Those with windows onto the busy street don't have this problem, but do have the problem of noise; better take a small but quiet one on the glassed-in central court, on the third or fourth floors. Right now the 70 rooms are priced at 455 pesos single, 580 pesos double, but when renovation is fully complete the TVs, elevator from the mezzanine, and steam baths will raise them somewhat.

Those looking for a European-style pension should seek out the **Casa Kloster (10)** (tel. 473/2-0088), Calle de Alonso 32, across the street from Telefonos de México. This 15-room *casa de huespedes* has a large central courtyard brilliant with birds and flowers, around which are ranged the very plain, but clean, bathless rooms. Showers are available for a small fee, but no meals are served. You pay 190 pesos per person per night.

Two more hotels worth a look if everything else is full are on Highways 110/30, the road to Dolores Hidalgo, the Valenciana Mine, just two blocks from the Tourism Office. The **Hotel Mineral de Rayas** (tel. 473/2-1967), Alhondiga 7 y Callejon del Apartado, is a labyrinthine building which you enter through a ground-floor restaurant. Ascending to the second floor, the reception desk is at the end of a long corridor. Rooms are plain, done in black and white or in solid colors, and the large number of rooms (46 in all) come in various price ranges from 400 to 450 pesos single, 500 to 550 pesos double; some rooms have three and four beds, good for families and friends traveling together. The Mineral de Rayas takes groups and may be filled with a busload when you visit. Nearby, the **Hotel Alhondiga** (tel. 473/2-0525), Insurgencia 49, is a similar hotel with 33 rooms right off the Plaza Alhondiga, not far from the bus station or the market. Front rooms are the nicest, but also, remember, the noisiest. A single person pays 375 pesos, two persons pay 510 pesos in a room with private bath.

WHERE TO EAT: Look for the apple sign of **La Manzana (11)**, Plazuela San Fernando 27—it's everything good about the American hamburger (big 'n sloppy) and mug of beer (cold 'n frosted). It's a small place with stone walls and arches, owned by an American and his wife who have been living in Mexico for 11 years. Comfortable atmosphere, and you can't help but feel at home when the good American sounds roll off the recorder. Hamburgers begin at 54 pesos, with seven or eight varieties and additions which cost several pesos more. They also offer a luncheon special for 65 pesos which includes soup, hamburger, and drink (only offered 1 to 4 p.m.).

Even cheaper burgers are yours at **La Hamburguesa Feliz,** Sopena 10, right near Teatro Juarez. A single burger costs a mere 40 pesos; a jumbo, 55 pesos. With french fries and a drink, your supper should cost less than 100 pesos. There are good, cheap, set-price breakfasts, too. Self-service, no tipping.

Las Palomas, Calle de la Campaña 19, is right next to the post office (Correos). Newish and modern, this split-level place will serve you a full lunch for 115 pesos, a big Mexican combination plate for a good deal less, and antojitos such as chilaquiles for 75 pesos.

One of Guanajuato's newer and snazzier little restaurants is the **Rincon de la Plata** (tel. 2-0881), on Juarez at Alonso. They don't serve a comida corrida here—everything's à la carte—but the food and service and decor (Tiffany lamps, wine racks on the wall, etc.) are a cut above many other places. Portions tend to be huge. A full meal based on enchiladas might cost 190 pesos; one based on meat, chicken, or fish, 400 pesos.

The best inexpensive lunch in town is the 125-peso one served at the peaceful **Cafe El Retiro,** opposite the Oficina Federal de Hacienda, just past the Teatro Juarez at Sopena 12. The meal consists of soup, rice with cheese, steak or pork, pastry, coffee. With its vases of flowers on the sideboard, cafeteria-modern furniture, El Retiro seems more like somebody's living room than a restaurant, and the service is just as informally friendly.

Also on the Jardín de la Union, just across from the Teatro Juarez, is **Casa Valadez (12),** a combination restaurant-soda-fountain-film-shop that has reasonable prices. Lunch is 120 pesos, but isn't served until after 2 p.m. The Valadez stays open fairly late.

The **Restaurant La Union,** on the corner of the Jardín across from the Santa Fe, is a nothing-special eatery that's popular with students because of its cheap prices. They offer a comida for 110 pesos, chicken for 75 pesos, and tortilla dishes for half that.

If this is still too high for your budget, I have just the place for you: the **University Cafeteria** offers an excellent set lunch from noon to 4 p.m. for 50 pesos (55 pesos with a drink) which includes soup, pasta, meat, frijoles, salad, and dessert. Although it is supposedly only for students, I've never been questioned so I doubt you'll have any problem—it's certainly the best bargain in town. To get to the cafeteria, take the middle entrance to the university on the ground level off Calle Positos. Turn right immediately after you enter, and go downstairs to the small but nice cafeteria.

Young sophisticates and students with a little cash patronize **Pizza Piazza (11)** which is—surprise!—a colonial pizza parlor right in the Plazuela San Fernando. Comfy niche-booths and roughish furniture provide a sympathetic ambience for romantic encounters or easy camaraderie: this is one of the best places in town to meet young Mexicans of both sexes. I have no idea how the colonial viceroys of Mexico liked their pizza, but here you can get it small, medium, or large for 95 to 250 pesos. The large pizza can feed five or six people. Beer and sangría are also served, either in the dining room or at the tables under the tree in the plazuela. They serve up lots of spaghetti, too. Open from noon to midnight every day.

Starvation Budget Restaurants

How you can do better than the aforementioned university cafeteria I don't know, but if the university's not in session when you're there, head for the little row of eateries (7) facing the parking lot in front of the Hotel El Insurgente. From the hotel all the way to the market, on the opposite side of the plaza/parking lot from these two buildings, are half a dozen very inexpensive home-style cookshops offering four-course set lunches at 70 to 85 pesos, or sandwiches and daily special plates for even less. **El Cedro** is typical, and perhaps the best.

AROUND THE TOWN: Walking around the city, it's almost hard to believe that the outside world knows of its existence, and certainly Guanajuatans themselves don't want it to change (the **Church of San Diego [1]** stands as it did in 1633). An exception to this is the magnificent **university (2)** founded in 1732, but whose entrance was rebuilt in 1945 in a stately manner which makes the building dominate the whole town. The university (Diego Rivera was a graduate), which is just behind the Plaza de la Paz, is open every day and nobody objects to visitors looking around. There's a cafeteria (open 8 a.m. to 10 p.m.) on the ground floor, also an excellent Spanish bookstore. While you're around this part of town, the **post office (3)** is just to your left, at the end of the block as you come out of the university. And the **birthplace of painter Diego Rivera (4)** is to your right, at Calle Positos 47. The crumbling house has been refurbished and made into a museum; on the wall is a plaque commemorating *"el pintor magnifico."* That Rivera was an "unperson" in his hometown for so long is not happenstance or coincidence. Guanajuato, strongly clerical and conservative, sympathized with the rebels during the Catholic counterrevolution of 1926-1929; later the town was an important base for the neofascist Sinarquista movement. Given this atmosphere, it is easy to understand the unpopularity of the city's most illustrious native son, an avowed Marxist whose most famous mural proclaims that "God does not exist." The museum is open from 10 a.m. to 2 p.m. and 4 to 6 p.m. Monday to Saturday. Entrance is 5 pesos, 5 more for camera. The house has been completely redone and, unfortunately, it is more like a museum than a home. Upstairs there's a fine collection of Rivera's early paintings. Diego began painting when he was 12 years old, and moved to Paris where he became a Marxist during World War I. You can see the cubist influence in his painting of this period. There are sketches of some of his earlier murals, the ones which made his reputation, but most of his works on display are paintings from 1902 to 1956. On the third floor is a small auditorium where lectures and conferences are held.

The Cervantes Festival

Partly because of the university and, in part, because of long traditions, Guanajuato is a fairly cultural place. Every year, in the spring, the state of Guanajuato sponsors the International Cervantes Festival, which offers two weeks of performing arts from all over the world. Recently they had marionettes from Czechoslovakia, the Elliot Feld dance company from New York, the Cuban National Ballet, and a host of Mexican artists. The shows are held at various places—the **Plazuela San Roque** and two attractive theaters: the **Teatro Principal (13)**, just off the Jardín de la Union (where aside from the Cervantes Festival you can hear a good piano recital for 20 pesos), and the magnificently ornate **Teatro Juarez (14)**, across the same plaza, which, with its columns, friezes, and velvet-draped interior, is a relic of the past century when a theater represented all that was elegant. The foundations for the theater were laid in 1873, but they soon ran out of money so construction was stopped until 1893 when Porfirio Díaz supplied the wherewithal to finish it. You can browse through this beautiful building for 5 pesos, daily from 9 a.m. to 2 p.m. and 4 to 7 p.m.

Pipila

High above the town, with a great view overlooking the Jardín de la Union, is the city's monument to José Barajas, also known as Pipila, a brave young miner who, on the orders of Hidalgo, set fire to the strategically situated grain warehouse, the Alhondiga de Granaditas, in which the Royalists were hiding during the War of Independence. Hidalgo, a young priest who had appealed for Mexico's independence from Spain, on September 16, 1810, led an army which captured Guanajuato. In this bloody battle 600 inhabitants and 2000 Indians were killed, but the revolution was on its way. Guanajuato became the rebel capital, but its history was short. For ten months later, the revolutionary leader, Hidalgo, was captured, shot in Chihuahua, and his decapitated head sent to Guanajuato to be exhibited.

The climb up to Pipila can be made via automobile or bus ("Pipila"), but I highly recommend that you try it on foot. Walk up Calle Sopena from the Jardín de la Union, and turn to the right up the Callejon del Calvario. A sign on the wall reads: "Al Pipila." (No, his name wasn't "Al.") A rugged winding pathway (wear flat shoes) wends past little homes and gardens perched precariously on the hillside. In one garden you'll see cows; in another, giant cacti. It's a tiring trip, but well worth it.

From the statue at the top (you can climb inside the statue, too, if you wish), the lovely city unfolds below. Churches appear everywhere, bronze figures atop the Teatro Juarez appear to be gesturing to the crowd in the Jardín, and it is easy to see how well the massive university, despite its newness, integrates perfectly with the landscape. There's a little park, nicely landscaped, beside the statue. Kids play ball, families picnic, and the atmosphere (and view) is delightful.

The Alhondiga

The **Alhondiga de Granaditas (15),** the doors of which Pipila burned, was a prison from 1864 to 1949, and before that it was the granary. Here the heads of Hidalgo, Allende, Aldama, and Jimenez hung from 1811 to 1821, to remind the populace of what happens to revolutionaries. On the four corners of the building the name-plaques below the cornice commemorate the four heroes of this stormy period.

The Alhondiga is now a museum, and one of the best in Mexico. It is open Tuesday to Sunday from 9 a.m. to 2 p.m. and 4 to 6 p.m.; closed Monday. Admission is 5 pesos for adults, 2 pesos for students, 1 peso for children, and 5 pesos for a camera. There are two levels to the museum, with rooms off the courtyard. The lower level (on which you enter) has rooms of regional crafts and several rooms of the prehispanic art collection of Chavez Morado, the artist responsible for the murals on both stairwells. There is also a long corridor which contains bronze masks of the revolutionary heroes as well as an eternal flame in their honor. Upstairs is a Bellas Artes section with shows (both temporary and permanent) of national and international artists. Following are several rooms showing the history of the state of Guanajuato and its dozen mines, the first one begun in 1557 on orders of Charles V. There are some interesting lithographs showing the city as it was in the 18th and 19th centuries, as well as 20th-century photographs. You'll also see numerous pre-Columbian relics: pots, decorative seals and stamps, terracotta figurines, and stone implements.

The Markets

The **Mercado Hidalgo (M)**, housed in a building that resembles a Victorian railroad station (built 1909), has a cavernous lower level and an upper balcony which encircles the whole building. It is stacked with every conceivable kind of pottery and ceramic ware, even including ones imported from Japan. From this balcony you can look down onto one of the neatest layouts in Mexico: symmetrical rows of stalls and counters providing splashes of orange, green, red, brown, or black in tones of the fruits and vegetables with which they are covered. Very few people sprawl around on the floor or in the aisles, unlike most markets, but whether this is due to the local ordinance or an untypical sense of orderliness, I can't say. The market is open every day, from morning to evening.

One item worth trying, in the market or elsewhere, is the brightly colored candy called *charramusca*. It's sort of a poor imitation of England's peppermint rock. Among the most popular charramuscas, by the way, are those in the shape of mummies. They're up to a foot long, wrapped in colored cellophane, have raisins for eyes, and are stuffed with coconut.

Right beside the Mercado Hidalgo is the **Mercado Gavira,** which is a very different sort of place. Modern, soiled, and bustling with cookshops à la Marrakesh, this is a good place for the fearless to try native cuisine. If your stomach is beyond insult, launch into a serving of birria, barbacoa (barbecue), pozole (stew), menudo (tripe). Choose kettles that are boiling and you should do alright. As for prices, observe the sign which says (in Spanish): "Avoid disappointments, ask to see the price list!"

The Mummies

At the northwest end of town is the Calzada del Panteon, which leads up to the municipal cemetery. It's a steep climb on foot, but the bus labeled "Presa–Estación" runs along Juarez and this will take you to the foot of the cobbled hill. Guanajuato's cab drivers, for this trip, will invariably tend to charge what the traffic will bear.

When you reach your destination, the cemetery, you'll find there's a cavern with a long hallway along which the mummies are displayed in glass showcases. It seems that the dryness in certain sections of the Panteon is such that decomposition is virtually halted. Due to the lack of space in the cemetery, people are buried for only five years and if at the end of that time there are no relatives to continue paying for the grave, the bodies are exhumed to make room for more. At this juncture, the authorities look at the corpses and if they have become mummified, they are displayed in the underground chamber; if not, they are burnt. Don't ask whether gravesites that are proven mummifiers cost more, because I don't know. The mummies, or *momias* as they are called, are not wrapped Egyptian style, but are just standing in glass cases, grinning, choking, or staring. It's impossible to resist the temptation to go up and look at them—everybody does—and this is the only graveyard I've ever seen with souvenir stands next to the main gate. There are even special hours to see the mummies: 9 a.m. to 6 p.m. every day. Entrance fee is 10 pesos; cameras, the same.

More Cheerful Destinations

Guanajuato is a strangely colorful town with all kinds of enchanting sights to be seen in the side streets and tiny plazas. Try to see the **Plazuela del Baratillo,** just off the Jardín de la Union. A beautiful fountain (a gift from Emperor Maximilian) is its pride and joy and you'll always find people sitting around peacefully, some in the shade and others in the sun, for late in the afternoon the plazuela is almost exactly divided between *sol* and *sombra.* **Plazuela San Fernando (11)** is larger and has a stone platform where very often there will be local Mexican dances with the younger generation decked out in bright costumes.

The **Church of La Compañia de Jesus,** next door to the university, was built in 1747 by the Jesuit order and was the biggest of their churches at that time. It is distinctly churrigueresque on the outside but the interior, which was restored in the 19th century, is not. This church was built as part of the Jesuit university, founded in 1732 on orders of Philip V, on the site of the present university, the last of 23 universities built by the Jesuit order in Mexico.

If you want to go on a suburban outing, why not hop the Presa-Estación bus to the **Parque de la Acacias** and the **Presa de la Olla,** the artificial lake? There are several parks, lots of trees: a good place for a lazy afternoon.

While in the neighborhood, you might note the **Government Palace (16)** on Paseo de la Presa, with its pink stone front and green tiled interior. The neighborhood around here is residential and will give you another glimpse of Guanajuato, away from the bustle of the plazas.

Last but not least are the **silver mines** in the surrounding mountains. The most famous is **La Valenciana,** said to have produced a fifth of the silver circulating in the world from 1558 to 1810. It can be reached by taking Route 30, the Dolores Hidalgo road, three miles northeast of town (buses are "J. Perones-Marfil" with "Valenciana" in soap on the windshield). The mine was closed about 40 years ago, but a caretaker is there to show you the eight-sided vertical shaft (1650 feet deep) and the once-grandiose courtyard. While you're there, visit the magnificent church built in 1765 by the first Count of Valencia. It is one of the most beautiful of the colonial churches in churrigueresque style—a true masterpiece. Also nearby, in **Marfil,** are restored mansion-haciendas of wealthy colonial mine owners.

Entremeses

The word *entremeses* means, literally, "intermissions," and it's the term given to short sketches that were written to be presented between performances. In Guanajuato, it means a very special entertainment: an evening under the stars in a medieval-style courtyard, the **Plazuela de San Roque (19),** with about 90 minutes of acting and action by students and faculty of the University of Guanajuato. The entremeses are presented on weekend nights (with the exception of those weekends which fall on a fiesta) and are some of the best theater you'll ever see. Tickets (which must be bought in advance) can be bought at the Teatro Juarez. The Tourist Office (tel. 473/2-0086) can give you a list of dates for which the performances are scheduled.

Let me emphasize again that these are no ordinary amateur theatricals. If you are in the vicinity, or conceivably can arrange to be in the vicinity of Guanajuato, when a performance is scheduled—drop everything and buy, beg, borrow, or steal a ticket. You'll never regret it. The fact, also, that the show takes place in a real courtyard with galloping horses, water thrown from windows, church bells ringing, gusts of wind blowing out the candles, and people in authentic period costumes looking not too out of place in 20th-century Guanajuato, makes it all the more impressive. Don't miss it.

Guided Tours

Perhaps your best bet for obtaining information or for seeing Guanajuato is to go to **Transportes Turisticos de Guanajuato,** next door to the church of San Diego (1). They offer free information in English as well as an excellent tour of the city which includes the Panteon, the Valencia mines, and Pipila, all of which are otherwise hard to reach. The cost is 195 pesos; there are three tours (3½ hours long) daily, morning, noonish, and afternoon. They have bilingual guides. Passengers are picked up at various hotels, so check to see at what time and where you can catch the minibus. This is one of the best tours offered in all of Mexico.

NIGHTLIFE: A bit posh, with an older, sedate crowd, are the bars at the **Hotel San Diego** and the **Hosteria del Frayle.** Even posher is the **Cantarranas Bar** at the Hotel Real de Minas, on the road to Mexico City. There is a beautiful view of the city from here and the lounge has a piano player who entertains on weekends. You can get there by cab from the city.

GETTING TO GUANAJUATO: It's not hard to get to Guanajuato, despite its mountain location.

By Bus

Flecha Amarilla lines serves Guanajuato with 6 buses daily to San Luis Potosí, 6 to Aguascalientes, 15 a day to Mexico City (but some of these are locals—be sure you get an express), 10 buses a day to San Miguel de Allende, and 15 to Querétaro. There are 17 buses to Guadalajara.

Omnibus de México also serves the town with three buses a day between here and Guadalajara, three to Querétaro, two to Dolores Hidalgo and San Miguel de Allende.

Other lines serving the town include Estrella Blanca, Transportes Chihuahuenses, Transportes la Piedad, Tres Estrellas de Oro, La Altena, and Autobuses de Occidente.

By Rail

It is possible to reach Guanajuato by rail via the spur from Irapuato and Silao, but there is only one train per day in each direction along the spur, leaving Irapuato at 6:30 a.m. The return train from Guanajuato leaves at 8:20 a.m., making it easier to *leave* the town by train than to enter it. Don't try to reach Guanajuato by rail from, say, Mexico City unless you're willing to sit in the Irapuato station for three hours in the middle of the night waiting for your connection.

DOLORES HIDALGO: For the most scenic route onward to Mexico City, continue on the road to Dolores Hidalgo, then stop in San Miguel de Allende. Dolores Hidalgo (pop. 80,000) has little to offer. It is famous because it's where the local priest, Miguel Hidalgo, first made his proclamation for the independence of Mexico, the "Cry of Dolores," on September 16, 1810. The church on the main plaza was the site of the proclamation and Hidalgo's house, at

Morelos 1 (one block from the bus station), is now a museum filled with flags, photos, and documents. Since the drive from San Miguel to Guanajuato takes only about two hours, an overnight stop isn't really necessary. If you just want refreshments, stop in at the town's cleanest restaurant, the **Restaurant Jardín**, which is located right on the plaza. The Jardín has three comidas, priced at 85, 105, and 135 pesos. Soup and a sandwich, called a "lonch commercial," is 70 pesos.

5. San Miguel de Allende

San Miguel de Allende (alt. 6134 feet; pop. 16,000) may well be the prettiest town in Mexico and, like Taxco, has been declared a national monument, which means that even Frank Lloyd Wright would have had to go through plenty of red tape before he'd be allowed to build so much as a hot-dog stand. The town has not become as spoiled by tourists as has Taxco, possibly because the five- or six-hour trip puts it just out of range of one-day trippers. But it's hardly out of range of American artists, real or would-be, who flock to the little town in droves, creating an artsy-craftsy society of their own superimposed upon that of the local Mexicans, who are mostly minding their own business.

San Miguel has cobbled streets reminiscent of Cornwall or Nantucket, and the best known view of the town, where the highway enters it from the south, has been featured in innumerable movies and picture postcards. As mentioned, a sizable colony of American artists and writers has established itself here, although the major portion of this group tends to turn over about twice a year. Apart from the financially successful, which includes those who have retired here to live relatively well on incomes ranging upward of $500 per month, the town's American colony is always composed of teachers, painters, writers, and others who have saved up enough to buy themselves six months in the sun.

You'll awake early in San Miguel. On the stroke of eight, and often before, the bells of a score of churches will simultaneously begin clanging like a score of hammers on a score of different-shaped anvils and soon the booming of the **parroquia** (cathedral) will superimpose itself as the others begin to fade away. If you're lucky, you'll arrive at the time of a festival (San Miguel loves festivals; the main one is on September 29), when throngs of ragged boys in homemade masks will precede and follow a makeshift band (with violins!) through the narrow streets, past French Park, where the women can be seen each morning scrubbing their clothes in a communal trough, and into the grounds of the 18th-century church. The crowds will ebb and flow around makeshift rings of the sort in which cattle are judged, to watch two masked and hooded boys attempt to remove each other's hats with the aid of long whips. Men will be selling candy and sliced pineapples, babies will be peeping from the shelter of their mother's rebozos, and when darkness falls all will turn their eyes heavenwards to watch exploding firecrackers fill the sky.

If you can, try to get a look around at least one of the houses in which resident Americans are living. Shabby and almost universally drab from the outside, they open inside onto pretty, cool, flower-filled patios with french doors, lily ponds, and breathtaking views.

Virtually everything in San Miguel is quite lovely, but there aren't many particular landmarks around town worth seeking out. The best fun is just to wander up and down the cobbled streets, peeping into doorways and haggling in the stores. The town's biggest draw, apart from the excellent scenery and climate, is the **Instituto Allende (1)**, an accredited arts and crafts school in what was once a large convent. The Instituto has a predominantly American

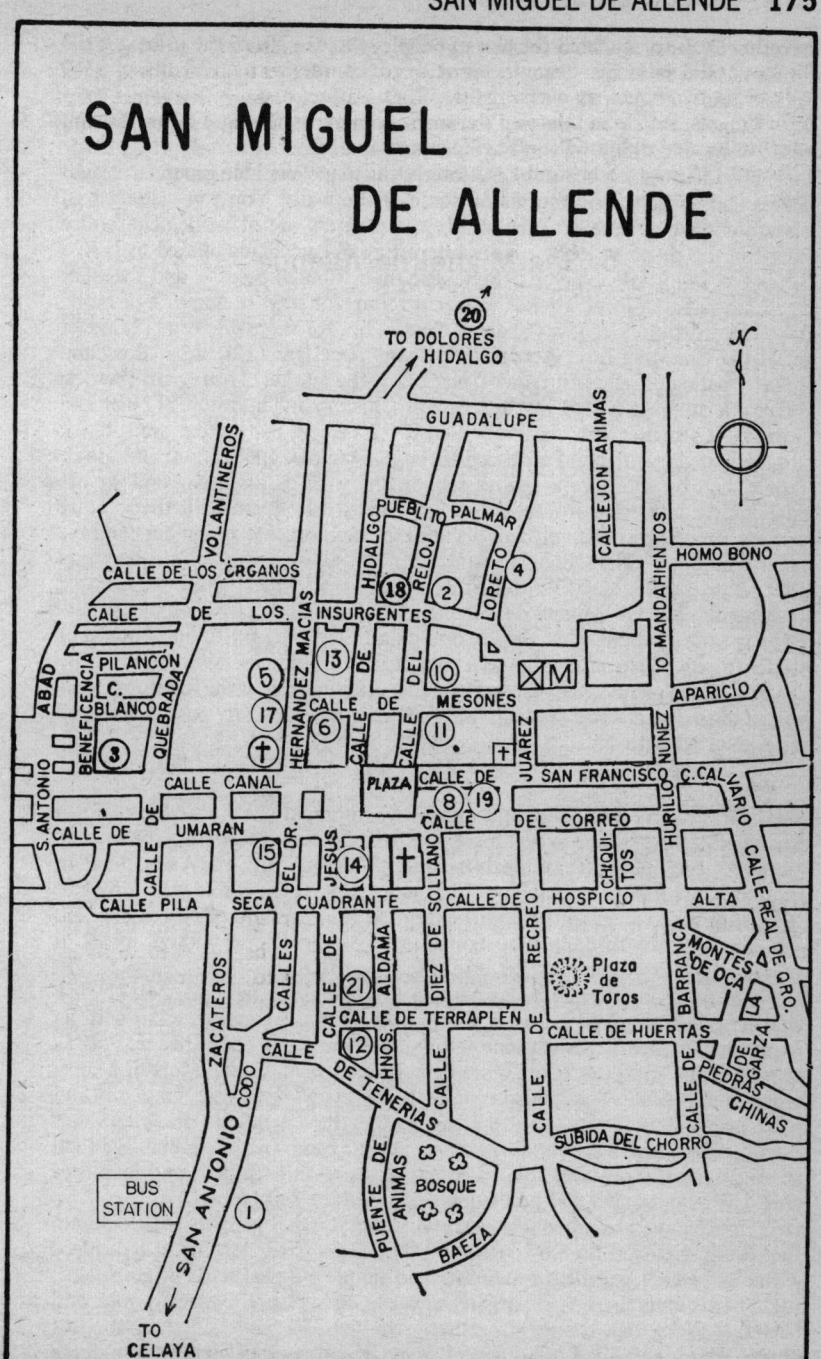

SAN MIGUEL DE ALLENDE

enrollment, most of which consists of people who can afford the price of $100 a month (plus fees) for a complete program of courses with no credits, or $350 for an academic quarter with credits.

Rumor has reached me that the Instituto may be closing. I hope this isn't true. Write and check, if you have plans to attend.

The Instituto is a beautiful and interesting place, with big grounds, elegant patios and gardens, and murals on some of the walls. You can wander past classrooms where weavers, sculptors, and painters are at work. The notice board in the entrance lobby carries interesting offers ("Ride offered to L.A."; "Paperbacks for sale, Shayne to Schopenhauer, from 20 pesos"), and the office maintains a list of local families who rent rooms for stays of a month or more.

The Instituto also gives Spanish classes, but for these you're really better off at the charming little **Academia Hispano Americana (2)**, situated around a pretty patio on Calle Insurgentes, just below the market. The registrar writes: "This is a language school, teaching Spanish, history and literature of Spain and Mexico. It's small, with classes limited to 12 people; instructors are rotated; grammar is presented and absorbed through example, application, and usage, rather than by rule. It's a serious school, the work is intensive, and we are particularly interested in students who plan to use Spanish in their future careers, people who sincerely feel the need to communicate and understand the other Americas." The school has winter, spring, summer, and fall sessions, and a brochure is available by writing to Registrar, Academia Hispano Americana, Insurgentes 21, San Miguel de Allende, Gto., México. These people are extremely serious about what they're doing and they even try to find homes for students with Mexican families as a part of their total immersion program. By the way, if you come to San Miguel to study either here or at the Instituto, come with a tourist visa, *not* a student visa, the latter having vastly complicated red tape involved with it.

WHERE TO STAY: There are ample accommodations for visitors in San Miguel, but the problem is that most hotelkeepers insist on renting rooms only on the American Plan (three meals included). Theoretically, the American Plan rates are only for "in season," but in practice almost the whole year turns out to be considered in season, with the exception of the month of November, and sometimes March through June. Some hotels do rent rooms without meals all year, and for convenience's sake, I'll list these first.

The 34-room **Posada de las Monjas (3)**, Canal 37 (tell. 465/2-0171), is a charming little inn and a former convent of pink stone construction with its name emblazoned in relief stone letters over the front door. Inside, it is as quaint as you'd expect: bold colors, heavy wood furniture and lots of beams, arches and the like. The rooms are quite pleasant and done with simplicity and good taste—double rooms are the best as they have windows and views, but even the tiny singles are good. Best buys are the rooms with a double bed (350 pesos single, 550 pesos double). The big rooms with twin beds and fireplaces cost 450 pesos single, 660 pesos double; suites are 880 pesos.

Tucked away amid cobbled lanes and well-tended gardens is the **Quinta Loreto (4)**, Callejón Loreto 13 (tel. 465/2-0042), a fairly new motel-type place with a large pool, excellent restaurant, and simple but pleasantly bright rooms. Lunch or dinner here is a bargain, and the owners are extremely nice and friendly. Thirty-one rooms altogether, rent for 330 pesos single, 440 pesos double. *Warning:* The Loreto is very popular and is often booked up months in advance.

The 25-room **Hotel Sautto (5)** (tel. 465/2-0052), at Hernandez Macias 59, has a very large courtyard and grounds, lemon and lime trees, a fountain, and sweet-smelling flowers everywhere. The hotel itself is an old colonial mansion somewhat fixed up, with single rooms with bath renting for 330 pesos, doubles with bath for 440 pesos. Meals are served in the modest restaurant.

The **Hotel Meson de San Antonio (6)** (tel. 465/2-0580), at Mesones 80, near the intersection with Hernandez Macias, has 14 rooms arranged around two nice clean courtyards and an entrance graced by mustard-yellow tiles. Cast-iron garden furniture adds romance. Because rooms look onto the courtyards, they're a bit dark, and although plain, are still quite acceptable. With bath, rooms go for $11 to $18 per person, three meals included. In the dining room are little circular tables with white cloths at which you consume breakfast, lunch, or dinner.

The **Mansion del Bosque (12)** (tel. 465/2-0277; Apdo. Postal 206), Aldama 65 near the park *(bosque)*, is one of several places to stay in San Miguel which are run by *norteamericanos*. Ruth and George Hyba have 24 rooms in their rambling lodging complex, each one is unique and has its own particular charm. Colors are bold but harmonious, rooms tend to be large, and all double rooms have tub-and-shower combinations. During the heavy winter season (January through March) one must rent by the month and take two meals at a cost of $20 to $26 per person per day; off-season rates are $14 per person, $15 to $18 with two meals. Charming, cheerful, quiet, and well-tended—that's the Mansion del Bosque.

For a long stay in San Miguel (more than a month), it's advisable to check at the **Institute** or the **Academia** for their list of apartments or rooms to rent at rates from 3500 pesos a month. The apartments are equipped with kitchens and bedding, some with maid service.

READERS' HOTEL SELECTION: "The **Parador San Sebastián**, Calle de Mesones 7 (tel. 465/2-0707), has huge, clean rooms with shower (one double bed and one single) for 385 pesos" (Petrien Uniken Venema and Anton van Enst, Utrecht, Holland).

WHERE TO EAT: Because of its large foreign colony, and popularity with Mexicans as a tourist destination, San Miguel has an interesting assortment of restaurants—but it changes frequently. New places open all the time, while eateries only a few years old close down overnight. Part of the reason for the bad survival rate can be ascribed to the town's hostelries, many of which require that guests purchase meals with their rooms. But you won't starve in San Miguel.

A good, attractive, all-round suitable restaurant close to the main plaza is **El Patio (8)**, at Calle del Correo 10. Come here for lunch or dinner (till midnight). The daily set-price lunch costs only 220 pesos, and it's substantial. For a light supper there are choices such as avocado and tuna salad, or a varied Mexican plate (190 pesos). Drinks are served, and you can relax in one of the old leather seats in the corridor and sip one before you enter the plant-filled court to dine.

Biggest bargain for eating? That's **Quinta Loreto (4)**, Callejon Loreto 13; go down the very cobbled street and turn right through a gate and then left into an expansive garden on the right. Tucked away at the back is a swimming pool, and adjoining the pool is a terraced café which serves some of the best home cooking in Mexico. The comida corrida is 155 pesos and excellent. The dining room tends to be a bit noisy.

If your palate is at all adventurous, you should stroll by **El Meson de las Bugambilias (10)**, Mesones 53 at the corner of Reloj, to see what's being offered. Last time I visited, the 175-peso comida corrida began with pineapple soaked in kirsch, and then went on to steak tartare and other delectables for the main course. Dining tables are arrayed in the cool, darkish courtyard of a great old house, well away from street noise.

Pan y Vino (11), at Calle del Reloj 7, serves much more than its name ("bread and wine") would suggest. This is the place to go for crêpes, for instance, and they come stuffed with avocado, mushrooms, cheese, etc., for 115 pesos. The menu gets richer, too, offering chicken, pork chops, and even lasagne for 75 pesos more. The bread comes with your meal, and the wine is yours for about a dollar a glass. The restaurant is upstairs, two shady rooms with dark-wood chairs and tables, red-and-white checkered tablecloths, plants, and several oil paintings. Open from 2 p.m. to midnight each day, Pan y Vino is a good choice for lunch, dinner, or a late-night supper.

The decor at **El Carrusel (7)** is whimsical, to say the least. As you enter the restaurant on Calle Canal half a block west of the plaza and across from the Casa Maxwell, you'll plunge into a small courtyard filled with café tables topped by colorful umbrellas. You don't get to dine on a merry-go-round, but nonetheless a carnival air is unmistakable. The fare is light and upbeat: chili, lima-bean-and-ham soup, and various sorts of burgers priced from 68 to 96 pesos. Lunch and dinner are the meals served.

Casual, cheap, and hip—that sums up the atmosphere at **Mama Mia (15)**, Umaran 8, and the cuisine is as light and spirited as the clientele—lots of salads compounded of familiar and exotic fruits and vegetables, Mexican quesadillas, coffee and pastries. Although the menu is limited to such things, the conversation and interaction range freely in this comfy spot. Service is slow, but while you're waiting for your quesadillas and mineral water (100 pesos, all in), you meet the most wonderful people. Open daily from 11 a.m. to 1 a.m., there's jazz nightly except Monday and Tuesday.

Some Splurges

The **Villa Jacaranda (21)** (tel. 2-1015 or 2-0811), Aldama 53, is San Miguel's poshest: dinner is served each evening by appointment only; the restaurant closes at 10 p.m. You can have lunch from noon on, however. Plan to spend about 500 to 750 pesos for a fine, full-course meal including soups and, say, filet mignon, stuffed shrimp, or chicken Cordon Bleu. You'll enjoy it: the soft music, twittering birds, ivy, vines, exotic flowers, and the elegance of the restaurant's decor all make it so. Remember to call for those dinner reservations, though.

At **Señor Plato (14)** (tel. 2-0626), Calle de Jesus 7, you enter a fine old courtyard with a graceful gazebo at its center. All around are white-clothed tables and dark-blue director's chairs. Yellow and red carnations brighten each table, and soft jazz wafts in from somewhere. Brick walls and arches, myriads of plants, provide visual interest. Elegant and comfortable at the same time, Señor Plata caters to American appetites with barbecued spare ribs, prime rib au jus, or shrimp stuffed with cheese. The many Mexican dishes are priced much lower, however—just over half these prices. A meal for two, with wine, will come to something like 800 pesos if you order neither the cheapest nor the most expensive items on the menu. Señor Plato is open from 1 p.m. to midnight every day but Monday. Look for the sign "Bazaar 7" when you're walking along Calle de Jesus.

WHAT TO DO: San Miguel, being an artsy tourist town, is full of shops and galleries. The biggest and best of the shops is **Casa Maxwell,** which has recently expanded to take up the entire block between Canal 14 and Umaran. It's a beautiful house and garden with every imaginable craft displayed, some high-priced, others fairly reasonable. It's well worth a look around; open 9 a.m. to 2 p.m. and 4 to 7 p.m.; closed Sunday. These hours, by the way, are standard for San Miguel, as all shops and galleries close between 2 and 4.

The best of the art galleries is the **Gallery San Miguel,** Plaza Principal 14. It is run by a charming Mexican woman, fluent in English, who is a well-known art dealer and exhibits the work of local residents, both Mexican and American. The salons hold a wide variety of art, most at fairly high prices. Open 9 a.m. to 2 p.m. and 4 to 7 p.m.; closed Sunday.

Next door to the Gallery San Miguel is the **Tourism Office,** San Francisco 23 in the Oficinas del Gobierno. They have brochures and a map of the city as well as a helpful staff (same hours as the gallery).

The **Centro Cultural Ignacio Ramírez (17)** is a center for instruction in arts such as drawing, jewelry making, guitar, batik, etc. Housed in the beautiful old Convent of the Conception, built in 1775, it contains a courtyard of lush trees, fountain, and murals, as well as numerous rooms on two levels housing art exhibits and classrooms. The major attractions here are several murals by Siqueiros as well as memorabilia of the artist, all very interesting, plus a student gallery and cafeteria, frequent films, and you get to enjoy the grounds as well. The center is located at Hernandez Macias 75 near the corner of Canal; open all day every day for free. They have a bulletin board listing concerts and lectures given at this institute, and elsewhere in the city.

If you're in town on a Sunday, you might be interested in a **tour** through some of the colonial houses in San Miguel. The tour starts at noon, leaving from the Instituto Allende or Posada San Francisco. The **Biblioteca (18),** Insurgentes 25, is a useful place to know about as it is the gathering point for the American community. It has a good selection of books, some to rent and some to buy. Here too is a courtyard with tables where you can relax and read a book or magazine (open 10 a.m. to 2 p.m. and 4 to 7 p.m. daily; closed Sunday).

The town's movie theater, the **Aldama,** is on San Francisco, in the block between the Jardín and the San Francisco church. The **Post Office and Telegraph (19)** are at Calle Correo 18 (closed 1 to 4 p.m. daily and all day Sunday).

There are several **hot springs** just outside San Miguel on the road northward to Dolores Hidalgo, about five miles out of town. The **Hotel Balneario Taboada** is out of the range for this book, but it does have a delightful hot springs swimming pool which you can use for 100 pesos. There are buses that leave from Calle San Francisco several times a day (the schedules change frequently so check with the Tourism Office for times).

A Side Trip

About the most pleasant three-hour excursion you can make from San Miguel is to **Atotonilco el Grande,** an Indian town which contains a wonderful 16th-century oratorio, (the church of an Augustinian monastery). The frescoes are very imaginative and animated, and although they've been ravaged by time, restoration is under way.

The trip itself is an introduction to Mexican country life: hop a bus on Calle Llamas ("Oratorio"), and you'll trundle out of San Miguel on the road to Taboada. Past Taboada you'll take a left at signs reading "Manantiales de la Gruta" and "La Flor del Cortijo." The road passes two large mansions which are now spas, then an aqueduct and a little narrow bridge. It's all super-picturesque, and in no time you're in the small town square of Atotonilco with the Oratorio in front of you.

NIGHTLIFE: I approach the subject of San Miguel's nightlife with trepidation, as clubs and discos here tend to spring up and to die with great rapidity. Still, here are some tips:

The disco called **El Ring**, 25 Hidalgo, in a lovely old building on the right side of the street as you come from the main plaza (Jardín), has a very elaborate layout including strobe lights and other visual hallucinogens (but visual *only*). Cover is 150 pesos; composition of the crowd changes according to the seasons, depending on who's in town for the Spanish courses.

The **Club Tiovivo**, in the Restaurant El Carrusel, opens at 1 p.m., and caters mostly to a local clientele with various floor shows and entertainments. Cover here is the same 150 pesos.

MISCELLANEOUS: Ms. Key of Boulder, Colorado, found the best **laundromat** (open 8 a.m. to 2 p.m. and 4 to 6 p.m.) in all of Mexico in San Miguel, located at Canal 37, three blocks from the main zócalo, across the street from the Posada de las Monjas.

GETTING TO AND FROM SAN MIGUEL: You can drive easily to San Miguel, or you can take a train or bus. For the train, catch the *Aztec Eagle* from Mexico City or Nuevo Laredo, or points en route. It arrives in San Miguel in the afternoon. Bus service, however, is the most frequent service to this beautiful town. The bus station in San Miguel is right across the street from the Instituto Allende (1).

By Bus

Tres Estrellas de Oro has one bus a day to and from Mexico City via Querétaro, a four-hour trip, and two buses a day between San Miguel and Guanajuato.

Autotransportes Corsarios de Bajío also has several buses between San Miguel and Mexico City and Guanajuato.

Omnibus de México has two buses a day to and from Mexico City, and also one bus a day to and from Guadalajara (via Guanajuato).

Flecha Amarilla has the greatest number of buses daily to and from Mexico City: 17 trips in all, counting all the buses in both directions, but the equipment is not quite up to Tres Estrellas's standards.

To get from Guadalajara to San Miguel, take a bus from the central bus terminal to Guadalajara to the town of Celaya; in Celaya catch a Turismo Allende bus for the last hour of the trip. Turismo Allende operates buses between San Miguel and Celaya every hour from 7 a.m. to 9 p.m.

6. Querétaro

After San Miguel de Allende, you'll come upon Querétaro (alt. 5873 feet; pop. 250,000), a state capital and a prosperous city with a fantastic history. It was here that Mexico's fight for independence was instigated by Hidalgo in 1810; here that, with the treaty of Guadalupe, Hidalgo sealed the peace of the Mexican War; here that the Emperor Maximilian was executed in 1866; and finally, here that the present Mexican constitution was drafted in 1916.

GETTING TO AND FROM QUERÉTARO: As Querétaro is on the main toll road between Mexico City and points north and east, transportation is a snap. During daylight hours, and in some cases afterward, lots of buses roll in and out of the Central Camionera by the Alameda on the three-hour trip from the capital. You can also get to the capital by train from Querétaro, leaving slightly before noon or in the early evening. Trains in the opposite direction (Mexico City to Querétaro) are best caught early in the morning at about 7 and 8 a.m. The trip takes between 3½ and 5 hours, depending on the train. Rumor has it that the government is planning to establish a fast electric-train rail link between Mexico City and Querétaro. Ask and see how it's coming along.

From the central bus station near Querétaro's lovely Alameda Park you can catch a "Burocrata" city bus to take you the few blocks to the main square *(plaza principal)*. The bus comes through the front parking lot of the Central de Autobuses about every ten minutes. Those in a real hurry can take a cab.

STAYING IN QUERÉTARO: The **Gran Hotel,** Madero Ote. 6 (tel. 463/2-0124), on the main square, has an elegant streetfront and a roofline decorated with four stone urns in various stages of decomposition. Inside there's a vast lobby with leather chairs and marble-topped tables. Prices for rooms are 330 pesos single, 550 pesos double. But all rooms are large, if sparsely furnished, and all have private baths. The Gran seems considerably bigger than 66 rooms, and modern corridors lead off in every direction. In the downstairs dining room, brightened by striped walls, menu choices are limited and rather expensive.

The **Hotel San Agustín** (tel. 463/2-1195), Pino Suarez 12, is plain and bare, but the 35 rooms are clean if simple, and prices are reasonable: 330 pesos single, 380 pesos for two persons in one bed, 480 pesos for two in twin beds.

About a block farther down the street is the **Hotel Hidalgo,** Madero Ote. 11 (tel. 463/2-0081), with a central patio, paved and arched with heavy stones, that doubles as a parking lot. Accommodations aren't exactly luxurious but are quite clean. Tiny bathless singles cost 85 pesos, doubles run 95 to 125 pesos; rooms with bath cost 220 pesos single, 325 pesos double. The Hidalgo's restaurant, toward the back of its patio, is a bit gloomy, but menu prices are reasonable.

A modern hotel providing Querétaro with accommodations near the bus station is the **Hotel Impala** (tel. 463/2-0344), next to the Alameda park at Colón 1, corner of Zaragoza and Corregidora. The 100 rooms here are all nice and clean, with blue-tiled baths, and even (in some rooms) TV. Beds can be a bit spongy or rocky, so pick your room by the bed and by the noise factor: quietest rooms are those which look into the Alameda, or which open onto an airshaft. Prices are reasonable: singles cost 350 to 450 pesos; doubles are 500 to 660 pesos.

EATING IN QUERÉTARO: In addition to the above-mentioned hotel restaurants, all of which stay open all day every day, several pleasant eating places are on or near Querétaro's main plaza.

La Flor de Querétaro, Juarez Norte 5, a few doors down from the Hotel Plaza, is one of the best budget choices in town. Its tablecloths are spotless, the wood-paneled walls are adorned with old scenic photos, and a TV set, always tuned to the bullfight on Sunday, occupies an unobtrusive corner. A large selection of food is offered here, including soups at 40 to 65 pesos, meats at 100 to 175 pesos, sandwiches at 35 to 60 pesos, and eggs for a few pesos more. The comida corrida is 145 pesos. Open daily 9 a.m. to midnight.

On the other side of the plaza, you'll find the **Salon del Valle,** on Calle 16 de Septiembre at no. 18. On Sunday particularly, the place is filled with lively young couples. Soup to dessert, you might pay 210 pesos. Open daily, 8 a.m. to midnight.

A block from the main square along Corregidora is the **Cafeteria La Mariposa,** Angela Peralta 7. It's a good place for light lunches such as enchiladas and a fruit salad (100 pesos), or pastries, ice cream, coffee. Right next door is a wickedly tempting sweet shop featuring such irresistibles as candied figs, peaches, bananas, and papaya. You can order these in the restaurant, as the two enterprises are under the same management.

The **Ostioneria Tampico** is Querétaro's answer to a seafood craving. Just off the main square at Corregidora Norte 3, you can chow down on ceviche, fried fish, salad, and soft drink for 185 pesos. Plain, darkish, with a lunch counter and some Formica tables, it's simple, busy, and handy.

Gretchen Gibson of Albuquerque, New Mexico, discovered the **Cafeteria La Calabaza,** Avenida 16 de Septiembre Pte. no. 8, a bright and modern place serving a set-price lunch for 145 pesos. For that price one gets fruit cocktail, soup, rice, "ropa vieja" ("old clothes!"—a savory stewed meat dish), dessert, and coffee. La Calabaza is half a block off the main square, on the right, set back from the street, open seven days a week from 8 a.m. to 10 p.m.

The Big Splurge

Querétaro's most elegant restaurant is a lively place a block from the main square, on the small square at the intersection of Calle de Juan Caballero y Ogio and Calle Angela Peralta. It's called **Josefas Restaurant and Bar,** and has that distinctly Carlos Anderson air about it: a sign by the door announces that the restaurant has been there "Since 1330." Like the Anderson restaurants in Mexico City, Mazatlán, Acapulco, Cuernavaca, etc., etc., the menu features a mixed grill entitled "Moo-Oink-Pio" for 285 pesos, but you can have cheaper main courses, like chicken, for about 250 pesos. Table settings are well done in blue and white, with fresh flowers and gleaming wine glasses. Josefas is closed Tuesday, but open for lunch and dinner every other day of the week.

QUERÉTARO SIGHTS: Walking up the pedestrian way off the main plaza, with its pleasant little Jardín Obregon, you'll soon reach the **Plaza de la Independencia,** graced by manicured, umbrella-shaped trees and pretty fountains. And leading off almost any street, you'll find well-tended little plazas and various cobblestone streets reserved for pedestrians.

To the south of the main plaza, walking along **Calle Juarez,** you'll find the **Plaza de la Constitucion,** which used to house the town's market on its raised central square. Nowadays, it's a pastel pink piazza boasting a large statue of Venustiano Carranza, who gazes up the polished stones bordering the square and bearing the names of the states of Mexico. A few blocks farther, Juarez meets Avenida Reforma—lined with red-brick, colonial-style homes.

Querétaro is the proper place to send off that long-postponed card to the folks back home because doing so brings you a bonus: the town's **post office** is housed in a former bishop's palace which must be seen to be believed. To find it, walk west out of the main square along Madero for one block to Calle Allende; turn left on Allende and the **Correos** is down the block on the left-hand side, next to the church.

Follow Reforma two blocks west, and you'll hit Calle Guerrero. Four more long blocks south down Guerrero will bring you to Fernando de Tapia and the town's **market**. The market isn't as interesting as it used to be—once the Plaza de la Constitucion offered odd-shaped balustrades on which birdcages could be hung—but there's still enough color and noise to intrigue you. Among other things, you can buy very cheap cloth for shirts, skirts, blouses, and dresses if you know a tailor who'll make it up cheaply (three meters for a shirt).

The hills around Querétaro are rich in semiprecious stones, and in town, you'll find several little **lapidary shops,** specializing in setting the stones into jewelry boxes, and other objets d'art.

Other places of interest in Querétaro include the **cathedral,** or **Temple of San Francisco,** on Calle Madero with its Moorish-style tiled cupola, and various sculptures and pictures inside; and the **Hill of Bells (Cerro de las Campañas)** outside of town, topped by a titanic statue of Juarez. Just below the statue is the site of the execution of Maximilian, ruler of the short-lived Empire of Mexico. In 1901 the Austrian government built an Expiatory Chapel on the side of the hill. The caretaker (who is rarely around to let you in) takes pleasure from showing you the three small columns in front of the altar, and telling you that the stones mark the exact spot where Maximilian and his generals Miramon and Mejia stood before the firing squad. (Maximilian was in the middle, but he ended by giving that place of honor to Miramon.) The caretaker will also inform you that Maximilian gave each member of the firing squad a gold coin so that they would aim at his chest instead of his head. They complied.

Definitely worth seeing is the **Regional Museum** at Corregidora 3, a few steps west of the main square (open every day except Monday from 10 a.m. to 5 p.m., to 4 p.m. on Sunday). The building was built as the Grand Convent (monastery, that is) of Saint Francis of Assisi, and is the oldest such building in the city—the order for its construction was given in 1540. In 1861 it was used as a fortress by the Imperialists who backed Maximilian. The structure is one of those palatial edifices which the "humble" friars favored, replete with arches and Corinthian columns. The first room as you enter holds fascinating memorabilia. Here, several Mexican paintings are informatively compared with European works of the same time; various classical paintings are presented together with modern ones, accompanied by well-written (in Spanish) texts pointing out similarities in form, theme, color, and so forth. Unfortunately, most visitors skip this room and gape at the much duller colonial paintings and furniture in other rooms. In a far wing of the museum is the Sala de Historia, which contains numerous items of (perhaps morbid) interest, including Maximilian's coffin, and countless period photographs. Admission: 5 pesos.

Around the corner from the museum at Avenida Independencia 58 (half a block up the hill from the Plaza de la Constitucion) is the interesting **Artesanías** shop which holds a good selection of local lapidary creations as well as conventional jewelry and folk art objects.

Querétaro has more colonial monuments, among them the **Palacio Municipal,** where Dona Josefa Ortiz de Dominguez (the mayor's wife who advised Hidalgo to start the revolution) lived; ask the guard, who stands at the doorway on the Plaza de la Independencia, to show you the Dona's rooms *(quartos)*—a tip is customary. The **Neptune Fountain** on Calle Allende just off Madero; the **Convent of Santa Rosa de Viterbo,** built in the 18th century by Mexico's greatest religious architect, Eduardo Tresguerras; and other old churches are all worth a look.

A SIDE TRIP TO TEQUISQUIAPAN: Seventy-five kilometers from Querétaro, a short distance off the toll road to Mexico City, is the resort town of Tequisquiapan, Querétaro. From a little farming town in the rich Bajío ("lowlands") region, Tequisquiapan has grown to become a favorite weekend getaway destination for residents of the great metropolis only two hours' drive away.

Besides farming, "Tequis" was famous for its crafts, and for some hot springs, and a few big hotels capitalize on the waters today. As the flow of visitors increased, Tequis underwent a good deal of "charm enhancement," whereby dusty streets were replaced with fanciful paving blocks, the native market was moved to the outskirts, and boutiques sprung up in its place.

Despite this clever fakery, Tequis is still a pretty place. The best time to visit is when you can indulge in the region's two choicest products: wine and cheese. Every year at the end of May and beginning of June these two bounties come together and set off the town's **Fería Nacional del Queso y el Vino**—a grand wine and cheese festival. Day and night the festivities rage as sports matches, rodeos, cockfights, even exhibits of children's paintings keep one and all on the go. Wine- and cheese-tasting parties are provided—many of them free of charge—by the big dairies and wineries, and so the gaiety is full-blown and long-lived. If you're in or around Querétaro during the festival, go catch some of its color and fun. Buses run to "Tequis" frequently from Querétaro's Central Camionera, with a lot of extra buses laid on during the wine and cheese festival.

The **Hotel San Alberto** is new and charges $30 for two with three meals. This is comparatively expensive, but the rooms are spacious, the water hot, the dinners good, and the dozen or so colonial-style rooms wrap around a nice pool and spot of lawn. The manager, Ms. Castellanos, speaks reasonably good English. **Posada Tequisquiapan** is older and a little cheaper and has a natural pool.

A SIDE TRIP TO TULA: The ancient Toltec capital of Tula is one of Mexico's most awe-inspiring archeological sites, well worthy of a visit. It's 20 kilometers north from the Querétaro–Mexico City toll road, Highway 57D, on State Highway 126. The bus from Querétaro's Central Camionera will go through Tepeji del Río, where you may have to change to another bus for Tula. Look below in Chapter XI for full details of this "City of Atlantean Men."

Chapter VI

MEXICO CITY: BASIC ORIENTATION

1. Arriving in Mexico City
2. Public Transportation
3. Organized Tours
4. Tourism Information

MEXICO CITY GLITTERS with all the fascination and excitement of a world capital. It's a vital, romantic place of monuments, palaces, parks, broad boulevards, tall buildings, and smart boutiques. It's the fountainhead of government, from which all orders flow, and in every way the center of Mexican life. It's not even "Mexico City" but simply "Mexico" in the lexicon of every Mexican who talks about it.

The region of Mexico City (alt. 7240 feet; pop. 16,000,000) has held the most important place in the country's history since the rise of Teotihuacán in 300 B.C. Later, in A.D. 1300 the Aztecs built their great capital of Tenochtitlán on an island in the middle of Lake Texcoco following a prophecy that they should build where they saw a "sign": an eagle perched on a cactus with a serpent in its beak. Lake Texcoco, now shrunken in size, used to fill the entire valley right to the base of Chapultepec ("Grasshopper Hill" in the Aztec language), and the island was reached from the shore by broad causeways built by Aztec engineers. Nothing remains of this magnificent city of 300,000 inhabitants. What we know of Tenochtitlán is from the 16th-century chronicles of the Spanish conquerors, especially of Bernal Díaz del Castillo who saw "the great towers and temples and buildings rising from the water—it was like the enchantments."

After the Aztec defeat, the Spanish made the city their capital, and in the centuries that followed the lake was filled in and the city limits were greatly extended. Maximilian of Habsburg did much to beautify the city and make it the capital of an empire during his short and stormy tenure. He remodeled Chapultepec Palace, built by a Spanish viceroy in 1783, and established the grand boulevard now named the Paseo de la Reforma.

You can see many signs of Mexico City's varied history: the pyramids of Teotihuacán are a short ride from downtown; Xochimilco, a reminder of the Aztec Floating Gardens in Lake Texcoco, is close by; the Zócalo with its cathedral and National Palace is Spain's standard contribution to colonial town planning. And the Mexican Republic has made the city what it is today.

In more ways than these the city is still a creature of its history. In fact, it's literally *sinking* into it, for the soft lake bottom gives easily under the weight of such formidable structures as the marble palace of the Bellas Artes or the skyscraping Latin American Tower. But it gives only an inch a year, so you needn't worry—take your time in visiting one of the most fascinating capital cities in the world.

1. Arriving in Mexico City

Tackling a strange city of some 16,000,000 people is enough to give the most experienced traveler nightmares, but fortunately Mexico City is quite well organized for the arriving traveler. Try to arrive during daylight hours, but if you can't, don't worry. You won't have to spend the night in some terminal. The following information will help you glide through, and will also help you when you depart from the metropolis, no matter in what direction.

ARRIVING BY BUS: Mexico City has a bus terminal for each of the four points of the compass: north, east, south, and west. You can't necessarily tell which terminal serves which area of the country by looking at a map, however. Below you'll find descriptions of the terminals and the exact destinations they serve. For a handy list of bus rider's terms and translations, see Chapter XVI, under "Buses."

Terminal Norte	**T.A.P. Oriente**	**Terminal Sur**	**Terminal Poniente**
Aguascalientes	Amecameca	Acapulco	Toluca
Chapala, Lake	Cancún	Cuernavaca	
Chihuahua	Campeche	Ixtapa	
Colima	Chetumal	Taxco	
Durango	Cozumel	Zihuatanejo	
Guadalajara	Ixta-Popo Park		
Guanajuato	Jalapa		
Guaymas	Merida		
Hermosillo	Oaxaca		
Los Mochis	Pachuca		
Manzanillo	Palenque		
Monterrey	Puebla		
Morelia	San Cristóbal		
Patzcuaro	de las Casas		
Puerto Vallarta	Tehuacan		
Querétaro	Tuxpan, Ver.		
Saltillo	Tuxtla Gutierrez		
San Juan	Veracruz		
Teotihuacán	Villahermosa		
San Miguel			
de Allende			
Teotihuacán			
Torreon			
Tula			
Zacatecas			

Terminal Central de Autobuses del Norte

Called by shorter names such as "Camiones Norte," "Terminal Norte," or "Central del Norte," or even just "C.N.," this is Mexico's largest bus station,

MEXICO CITY: ORIENTATION 187

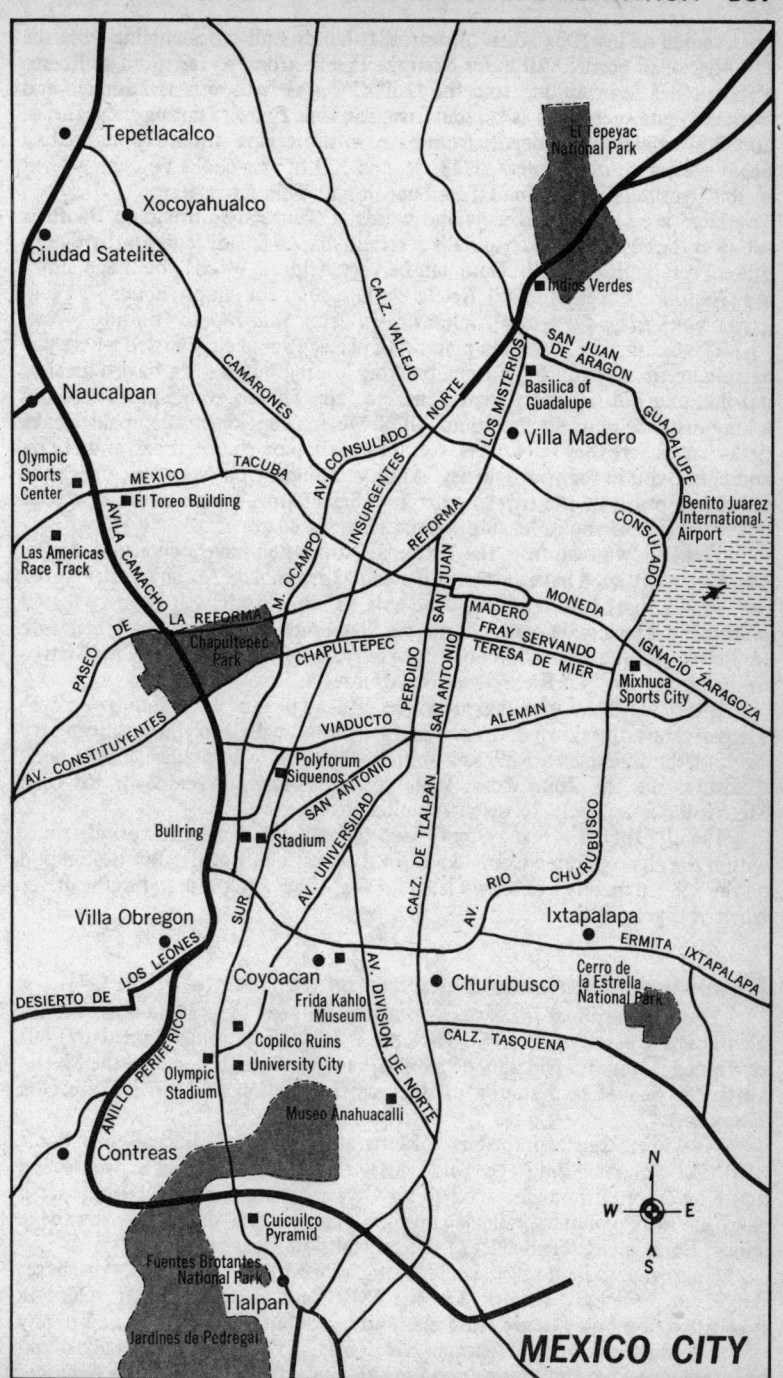

on Avenida de los 100 ("Cien") Metros. It handles all buses coming from the U.S.–Mexican border. All buses from the Pacific Coast as far south as Puerto Vallarta and Manzanillo, from the Gulf Coast as far south as Tampico and Veracruz, and such cities as Guadalajara, San Luis Potosí, Durango, Zacatecas, and Colima arrive and depart from here: in short, this is the terminal for all buses dealt with in Chapters II, IV, V, and XII of this book. You can get out to the Pyramids of San Juan Teotihuacán and Tula from here.

Here are some useful facts and words: a **Tourism Information Booth** is set up at the center of the terminal's crescent-shaped facade, and nearby there's a hotel reservations booth. Both can be very helpful. Words you'll encounter are: *Taquilla* (ticket window), *Recibo de Equipajes,* or simply *Equipajes* (baggage claim), *Llegadas* (gates), *Sanitarios* (toilets), *Sala Espera* (waiting room).

The Central del Norte is a mammoth place, a small city in itself where you can change money (during normal banking hours), buy a shirt, have a meal or a drink, take out insurance, rent a car, etc., etc. There's even a post office and a long-distance phone installation. All of Mexico's major bus companies have desks here where they sell tickets, give information on routes, times, and prices, and check you in for your journey. After you alight from your bus, check the times and prices of the trip to your next destination—you needn't buy your ticket yet unless you're leaving within a day or so.

To get downtown from the Terminal Norte, you have a choice of modes. The Metro will soon have a station (Estación Terminal de Autobuses del Norte, or T.A.N.) right here, and you'll be able to hop a train and connect for all points. If the terminal's station is not yet in operation when you read this, walk southeast (out the bus station door, turn left) along Avenida de los Cien Metros six blocks to the "La Raza" Metro station.

Buses will take you downtown as well. The no. 17 ("Indios Verdes–Tlalpan") bus runs down Avenida Insurgentes and will drop you within an easy stroll of the Buenavista Railroad Station, Plaza de la República, Paseo de la Reforma, and the Zona Rosa. Walk southeast along Avenida de los Cien Metros for four blocks to reach Avenida Insurgentes.

Finally, there's a taxi system based on set-price tickets to various zones within the city, operated from a kiosk in the terminal. Locate your destination on the zone map, buy a ticket (boleto) for that zone, and present it to the driver when you get there.

Terminal de Autobuses de Pasajeros de Oriente ("TAPO")

The new terminal for eastern routes has a very long name but a conveniently short acronym: TAPO. Take a no. 20 ("Hipodromo–Pantitlán") bus east along Alvarado, Hidalgo, or Donceles to get there. If you take the Metro, go to the San Lázaro station on the eastern portion of Line 1 (Direccion Zaragoza).

As you emerge from the bus or Metro station, the translucent green dome of TAPO will catch your eye. Underneath the dome you might expect to find anything from an immense toad to an Olympic swimming pool, but instead there are ticket counters, toilets, a post office, a cafeteria, bookstalls, and snack shops. Enter along "Tunel 1" to the central dome.

Companies which sell tickets here include Autobuses Unidos, Autobuses de Oriente, Fletes y Pasajes, Estrella Roja, and Cristóbal Colón. Once in possession of a ticket, a growling mammoth machine will whiz you off to any of those points covered in Chapters XII, XIII, XIV, and XV of this book, and also to Amecameca and Ixta-Popo Park (Chapter XI), and Pachuca (Chapter

II). Looking for a bus to Oaxaca, Yucatán, or Guatemala? This is the place to look.

Terminal Central de Autobuses del Sur

Mexico City's southern bus terminal is the Terminal Central de Autobuses del Sur, right next to the Taxqueña Metro stop, last stop on that line. The Central del Sur handles buses to Cuernavaca, Taxco, Acapulco, Zihuatanejo, and intermediate points. Easiest way to get to or from the Central del Sur is on the Metro, all the way to Taxqueña (or Tasqueña, as it's also spelled). If you prefer the bus, catch a no. 29 "La Villa–Carrasco" or a no. 29-A "La Villa–Tlalpan" heading south along Bolívar, or a no. 31 or 33 "La Villa–Xochimilco" bus along the street named Correo Mayor, behind the National Palace.

By the way, the same taxi ticket system as at the Central del Norte applies when you travel from the Central del Sur into the city. Buy your ticket in the terminal before you exit.

If you take the Metro to the Central del Sur, when the train pulls into the Taxqueña station leave the car, head straight through the turnstiles and out the door. Walking in a straight line from the train door will bring you to the Central del Sur. I mention this because the Taxqueña station is plastered with "Central de Autobuses" signs which lead you to a row of slots for *city* buses and not to the Central del Sur. Ignore these signs.

Terminal Poniente de Autobuses

The western bus terminal is conveniently located right next to the Observatorio Metro station, which you can reach by Expresso Reforma buses (see below) as well. Smallest of the terminals, the Terminal Poniente's main reason for being is the route between Mexico City and Toluca, but some other cities to the west and northwest are served as well.

Buying Bus Tickets Downtown

It used to be easy to get bus tickets in the center of Mexico City, but no more. Greyhound (tel. 905/591-0338) has an office at Paseo de la Reforma 27, and they'll sell you tickets on their buses and Mexican connecting lines. Autobuses de Oriente ("A.D.O.") will save you a trip to the Terminal Norte by selling you a ticket in their office at Avenida Buena Vista 5, three blocks south of Buena Vista Railroad Station and three blocks north of the Monument to the Revolution (Metro: Revolución). Cities served by the ticket windows are Aguascalientes, Chihuahua, Guadalajara, Ciudad Juarez, Mazatlán, Monterrey, Saltillo, San Luis Potosí, Tuxpan, and Zacatecas.

ARRIVING BY TRAIN: The Buena Vista railroad station is called officially the **Terminal de Ferrocarriles Nacionales de México.** You can get away with **Estación Buena Vista.** Walk out the right-hand set of front doors in the terminal, and get your bearings on the front steps. You're facing south. That big boulevard on the right is Avenida Insurgentes, the city's main north-south axis. You can catch a no. 17 "Indios Verdes–Tlalpan" bus south along Insurgentes to get to the Plaza de la República, Paseo de la Reforma, and the Zona Rosa; catch one north to get to the Terminal Norte (main bus station). Straight ahead of you about 12 blocks away, the dome of the Monument to Revolution floats on the skyline from its site in the Plaza de la República. To the left of it, the spire of the Latin American Tower juts skyward from the intersection of Avenida Juarez and Avenida Lázaro Cárdenas.

Bus no. 22 "Cuatro Caminos–Economia" runs east along Mosqueta (the street in front of the station), and you can catch this bus to the intersection with Avenida Lázaro Cárdenas, then transfer to a trolleybus (no. 27 "Reclusorio Norte–Ciudad Jardín") heading south into the center of town, but these buses are often jam-packed. You may feel better taking a taxi to your chosen hotel.

ARRIVING BY PLANE: The fastest way to get downtown from the airport is to take a **cab** right from the terminal, but this can cost as much as 600 pesos. You can cut this price in half if you walk toward the "Aeropuerto" Metro station and catch a cab on the street. Many of the cabs prowling the airport area have those sinister black cloth bags covering their meters, a signal that this is a "Touristic" taxi—the driver can charge whatever the traffic will bear. Find a cab with the meter uncovered for the best deal, or read on for inexpensive alternatives:

Special red VW minibuses bearing the initials **S.E.T.T.A.** fill up outside the air terminal and trundle passengers to downtown hotels for a fraction of the taxi rate. Tickets are sold in a special booth; the price depends on how far you're traveling, based on a system of zones. Tell them your destination, and they'll tell you what to pay; it's usually about 100 pesos.

Even cheaper? You can go by city bus for a small fraction of the S.E.T.-T.A. fare if you're willing to walk for 15 minutes and change buses at least once. Go out the air terminal doors and turn left, heading for the Holiday Inn. You'll pass a six-story parking garage on your right, and come to a busy highway, with the Holiday Inn on the other side of the highway. Turn left, and down a block is a pedestrian bridge over the highway. See that Pemex gas station near the bridge? The street beside it is "Norte 33," or "Norte Treinta y Tres." A five-minute walk down this street, on the right at Calle Oriente 184, is the starting point for no. 18 buses. The no. 18 winds through neighborhoods for a while, then shoots west down Eje 1 Norte (Avenida Rayón), a major east-west artery. You'll want to transfer to a southbound bus somewhere along this artery. The trip will take 30 minutes to an hour.

For the Zócalo, get off at Calle Carmen and take a no. 31 bus ("La Villa–Xochimilco"), which runs south to the east of the Zócalo.

For the Zócalo, get off at Allende and take a no. 29 or 29-A bus ("La Villa–Carrasco" or "La Villa–Tlalpan"), which runs south along Allende and Bolívar, west of the Zócalo.

For Avenida Lázaro Cárdenas (Eje Central), get off at Lázaro Cárdenas and take a no. 27 bus ("Reclusorio Norte–Cd. Jardín") or trolleybus south.

For the Plaza de la República, Sullivan Park, and the Zona Rosa, get off at Avenida Insurgentes and catch a no. 17 ("Indios Verdes–Tlalpan") bus south along Insurgentes.

You can also take the Metro (subway) from the airport to downtown. Soon there will be a station right at the Terminal Aerea (airport passenger terminal), and you'll be able to board a fast train, transfer at Consulado or La Raza, and be downtown for a very low price in a very short time. Right now you must walk to the Puerto Aereo station, about a mile from the terminal, in order to pick up the Metro.

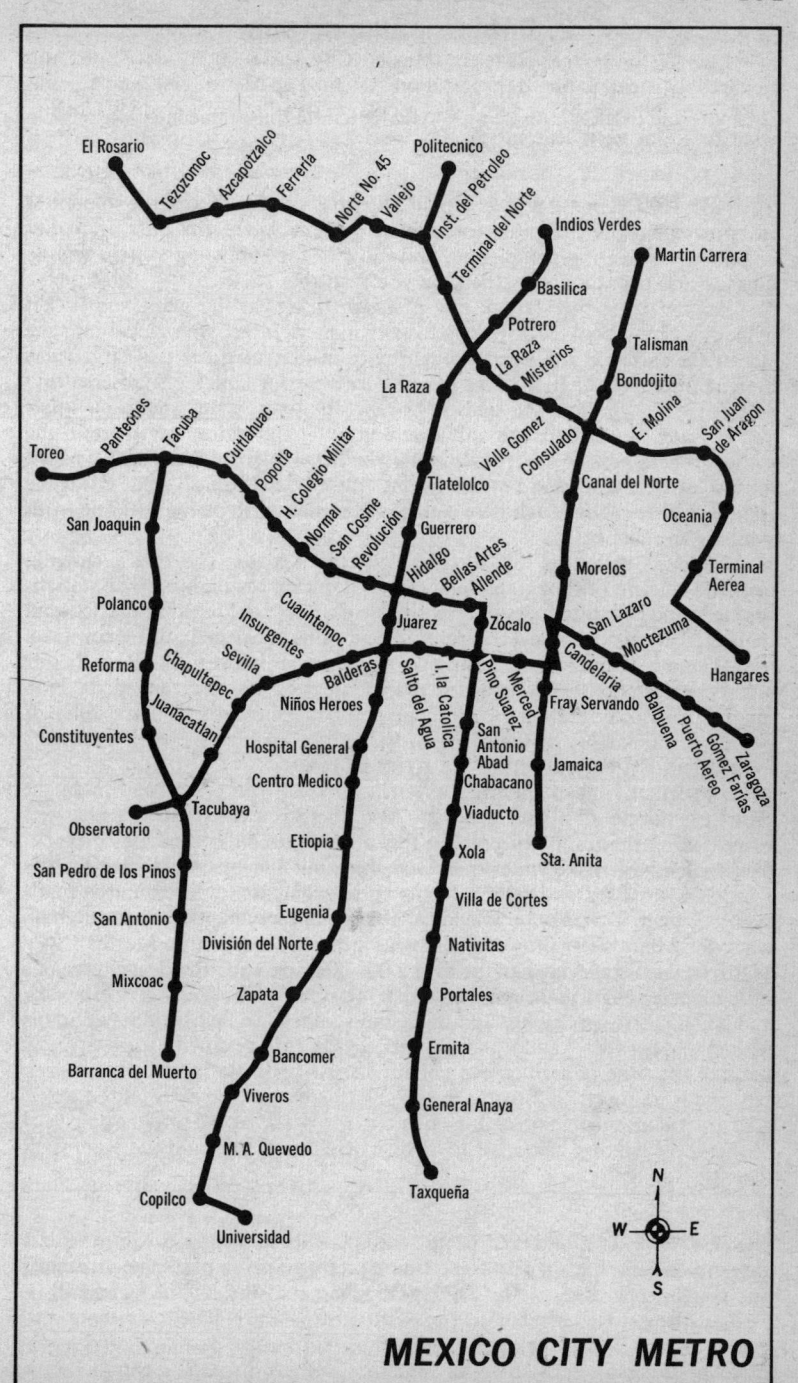

MEXICO CITY: TRANSPORTATION 191

MEXICO CITY METRO

2. Public Transportation

Luckily for budget travelers, Mexico City has a highly developed and remarkably cheap public transportation system. The Metro, first- and second-class buses, jitney cabs *(peseros)*, and regular taxis will take you anywhere you want to go for very little money.

THE METRO: The subway system in Mexico City offers one of the smoothest rides for about the cheapest cost anywhere in the world. Six lines are either completed or nearing completion, and most of the sprawling system will be finished and operational by the time you read this.

As you enter the station, buy a *boleto* (ticket) at the glass *caja* (ticket office), or buy a booklet of tickets to save money. Insert your ticket into the slot at the turnstile and pass through; once inside you'll see two large signs designating the destination of the line (for example, for Line 1, it's Observatorio and Zaragoza). Follow the signs in the direction you want, and *know where you're going*, since there are only a few maps of the routes anywhere in the station. There are, however, two signs you'll see everywhere: *Salida*, which means "exit"; and *Andenes*, which means "railway platforms." Once inside the train, you'll see above each door a map of the station stops for that line, with symbols and names.

Transfer of lines is indicated by *Correspondencias*. The ride is smooth, fast, and efficient (although hot and crowded during rush hours). The stations are clean and beautifully designed with lots of stone, tiles, piped-in music—and the added attraction of several archeological ruins unearthed during construction. There is also a subterranean passage that goes between the Pino Suarez and Zócalo stations so you can avoid the crowds and the rain along Pino Suarez. The Zócalo station has dioramas and large photographs of the different periods in the history of the Mexican Valley, and at Pino Suarez there is the foundation of a pyramid from the Aztec empire.

Important Notes: The Metro system runs between 6 a.m. and midnight *only;* it is not an all-night operation. Also, there is a rule that *no baggage* is permitted on the trains. In practice this means that bulky suitcases or backpacks sometimes make you *persona non grata,* but a large shoulderbag such as I use is not classed as luggage; nor is an attaché case, or even a case that's slightly bigger. You may be able to get away with carrying more in the evening when the Metro's less crowded. The reason for the rule is that Mexico City's Metro on an average day handles over 2,000,000 riders and that leaves precious little room for bags! You should note that metro travel is usually very crowded, and consequently pretty hot and muggy in summer. In fact, you may find (as I have) that between 4 and 7 p.m. on weekdays the Metro downtown is virtually unusable because of sardine-can conditions. At some stations there are even separate lanes roped off for women and children because the press of the crowd is so great someone might get hurt. Buses, peseros, and taxis are all heavily used during these hours. The trick is to leave yourself some time and energy to walk during these hours.

BUSES: Moving millions of people through this sprawling urban mass is a gargantuan task, but the city fathers do a pretty good job of it. The municipal bus system, operated by the DDF (Departamento del Distrito Federal, or Federal District Department), is run on an enormous grid plan. Odd-numbered buses run roughly north-south, even-numbered buses go east-west, and a special express service runs along the main routes downtown. You can pick up a

Spanish-language tabloid guide to the bus system in the DDF building on the south side of the Zócalo. I'll provide you with most of the routes and numbers you'll need, however.

The buses themselves are modern but they age very rapidly. They tend to be crowded or very crowded. The fare is very inexpensive. Downtown bus stops bear signs with route descriptions.

One of the most important bus routes is the **Expresso Reforma,** which runs between the Zócalo and the Auditorio (National Auditorium in Chapultepec Park) or the Observatorio Metro station. The route is via Avenida Madero or Cinco (5) de Mayo, Avenida Juarez, Paseo de la Reforma; maps of the route are posted at each bus stop.

Another important route is no. 17, **"Indios Verdes–Tlalpan,"** which runs along Avenida Insurgentes connecting the northern bus terminal (Terminal Norte), Buena Vista Railroad Station, Reforma, the Zona Rosa, and—far to the south—San Angel and University City.

Watch for Pickpockets!

Mexico City is unique in many ways, but in one matter it resembles any big city anywhere: pickpockets. Crowded subway cars and buses provide the perfect workplace for petty thieves, as do thronged outdoor markets and bullfights, or indoor theaters. The "touch" can range from lightfingered wallet lifting or purse opening to a fairly rough shoving by two or three petty thieves. Watch out for them anyplace tourists go in numbers: on the Metro, in Expresso Reforma buses, in crowded hotel elevators, at the Ballet Folklorico.

Luckily, violent muggings are pretty infrequent in Mexico City. But if you find yourself up against a handful of these guys in a crowded spot, the best thing to do is to raise a fuss—no matter whether you do it in Spanish or in English. Just a few shouts of "Robo! Robo!" ("Robbery!") or "Robador!" ("Thief!"), or anything loud, should convince the thieves that it'd be best for them to disappear.

TAXIS: Mexico City is pretty easy to get around by Metro and bus, and these methods bring you few hassles. Taxis are another matter, but there are times when nothing else will do. Cabs operate under several distinct sets of rules, one of them being highway robbery. The others are as follows: the Volkswagen beetle cabs are your best bet for low cost and good service; the larger American makes are more expensive. Avoid by all means the cabs sitting at stands before snazzy hotels with black bags over their meters. They get what the traffic will bear, and you must bargain for a price. In other cabs the meters run, and these meters are of two types. The "D" (for distance traveled) meter will show a figure, and you will pay about twice this figure. The "DT" (for distance and time) type meter gives you the flat figure you pay. With inflation rampant, the actual fare may be figured from a chart based on meter readings. Decals within the cab give tables to help you figure. Both meters end up with about the same fare for similar trips—unless you ask the cab to wait while you run in somewhere, of course. Late at night there is a 10% surcharge on the fare shown by the meter. Cabs from a *sitio* (cab stand) often charge a peso or two above the meter fare. If you call a cab by phone, the meter will be started when the cab begins the trip to your hotel and *not* when you get in.

PESEROS (COLLECTIVOS): Also called *taxis de rutas fijas* ("taxis with fixed routes"), these are sedans or minibuses, usually white, which run along major arteries. They pick up and discharge passengers along the route, charge fares according to distance (it usually works out to two or three times the bus fare), and provide more comfort and speed than the bus. Routes are displayed on cards in the windshield; often a Metro station will be the destination. One of the must useful routes for tourists is Ruta 2, which runs from the Zócalo along Avenida Juarez, along Reforma to Chapultepec, and back again.

Note that some of the minibuses on this route have automatic sliding doors—you don't have to shut them, a motor does.

As the driver approaches a stop, he'll put his hand out the window and hold up one or more figures. This is the number of passengers he's willing to take on (vacant seats are difficult to see if you're outside the car).

CAR RENTALS: For information on renting a car, see Chapter XVI under "Car Rentals."

3. Organized Tours

I've already mentioned that Mexico City is a great place for looking around on your own, and in general, this is the cheapest way to see whatever you like. However, if your time is limited, you may wish to acclimate yourself quickly by taking a tour or two.

The most popular tours are: the four-hour city tour which includes such sites as the National Cathedral, the National Palace, and Chapultepec Park and Castle; the four-to six-hour tour of the Shrine of Guadelupe and the nearby pyramids in the Teotihuacán archeological zone; and the Sunday tour that begins with the Ballet Folklorico, moves on to the floating gardens of Xochimilco, and may or may not incorporate lunch and the afternoon bullfights. Almost as popular are the one-day and overnight tours to Cuernavaca and Taxco. There are also several popular nightclub tours.

In the past this book has listed a variety of agencies and their tour itineraries, but recently I've had so many letters from readers who got "taken" on tours that I cannot in good conscience recommend anybody. Service is erratic, at best mediocre. There are exceptions, the particular guide or driver devoted to his work and considerate of his customers, but I know of no company where this is the rule. The best plan is to find someone who has recently taken a tour and liked it (your hotel or a popular restaurant or café is the place to ask).

4. Tourism Information

The **Secretaria de Turismo,** Avenida Presidente Masaryk 172, north of Chapultepec Park in the district known as Polanco, is a bit out of the way. But any telephone will serve to get you information if you dial 250-0123. They'll speak English.

MEXICO CITY: TOURS/INFORMATION

Downtown near the intersection of Avenida Juarez and Paseo de la Reforma, at Juarez 92, is an **information desk** of sorts. It's in the lobby of the Migración (Immigration) building.

The **Chamber of Commerce** maintains an information office which can provide you with a detailed map of the city (or country) at least, and answer some of your questions at best. It's conveniently located at Reforma 42—look for the Camara Nacional de Comercio de la Ciudad de México, open from 9 a.m. to 2 p.m. and 4 to 7 p.m. Monday through Thursday, to 6 p.m. on Friday; closed Saturday and Sunday.

And now you're ready to get down to the serious business of finding a good, reasonably priced place to stay in the world's largest city.

Chapter VII

MEXICO CITY: ROOMS ON A BUDGET

1. Getting the Most for Your Money
2. Choosing a Hotel Location
3. Hotels in the Zona Rosa
4. Hotels Near the Jardín del Arte
5. Hotels Near the Revolución Monument
6. Hotels Near Alameda Central
7. Hotels Near the Zócalo
8. Hotels Near Bus, Train, and Air Terminals
9. Apartment Hotels

IT COSTS LESS to stay in Mexico City than in most European capitals, or in almost any U.S. city of any size. The city is truly a bargain when you consider that for $15 to $20 you can find a double room in a fairly central hotel complete with bathroom, decent furnishings, often with extras such as air conditioning, television set, or a balcony. Many hotels have their own garages where guests can park for free. Most of the new construction in the last decade has been of more luxurious hotels with central air conditioning, elevators, restaurants, and the like; these are usually at the top of our budget. Cheaper hotels tend to be the older ones, well kept up but built in less affluent times without all the extras that tend to inflate prices. Here first are some tips on how to save money in the hotel you select from my recommendations.

1. Getting the Most for Your Money

First, remember that Mexican hotels have an assortment of rooms, and that those with a view of the street may be more expensive (and noisier!) than those with windows opening onto an airshaft. Second, rooms are usually furnished with one single bed, one double bed, or two twin beds; the best buy is for two people to take the double bed—twins are almost always more expensive. To get the double bed ask for *una cama matrimonial*. Third, although all rates are supposedly controlled by the Mexican government, these rates are the *maximum* allowable, and in many cases a desk clerk will quote you a lower price if business is slack or if you suggest a slight reduction. By the way, the room rates are required to be posted in plain view near the reception desk and as a rule they generally are, places like Acapulco being the exceptions. Ask the clerk to show you the *Tarifa,* and get to recognize the official form it's on to help you locate it in other hotels. Fourth, *test the beds* if you intend to stay any length of time. Price often has nothing to do with the comfort of the beds. Why pay good money for something that's going to give you a backache? Often the cheaper hotels will have beds bought at different times, so one room may have a bad bed but another one a good bed. Remember also that the 10% IVA tax will be added to your bill. When you register, remember to ask if it's been included in the rate quoted to you, or will be added later.

2. Choosing a Hotel Location

My recommendations below are grouped around major landmarks in Mexico City, places which are well known by every city-dweller and easily identifiable by first-time visitors. To find your chosen hotel area, or to get a bus going in that direction, all you need do is collar any passerby and ask, "Donde esta . . ." (DOHN-deh ess-TAH) and then the name of the place: "El Monumento a la Revolución," "El Zócalo," "La Zona Rosa," etc. You'll know your way home in no time at all. Our maps, showing these areas, will be a great help, too.

Here's a summary of the major areas. The **Zona Rosa** is Mexico City's Mayfair, Faubourg St-Honoré, or Gramercy Park: the status address. The chic boutiques, fancy restaurants and cafés, and expensive hotels are here. My hotel choices, in and near the Zona Rosa, are thus at the top of our daily budget.

The **Jardín del Arte (Sullivan Park)** is a wedge-shaped park extending west from the intersection of Paseo de la Reforma and Avenida Insurgentes. It has a wonderful range of hotels, old and new, colonial and modern, flashy and humble. Many are on quiet streets, some have views of the park, all are close to the Zona Rosa and to transportation.

The **Revolución Monument (Monumento a la Revolución)** is in the large Plaza de la República, at the very western end of Avenida Juarez. Here you're centrally located, about equidistant from the Zona Rosa and the Zócalo, and you're near major transportation routes, but most of the hotel streets are quiet.

The **Alameda Central,** right next to the Palacio de las Bellas Artes, is closer to the downtown shopping district, a bit farther from the Zona Rosa. Transportation is still good. Most of the hotels are well-used modern structures on streets to the south of the Alameda.

The **Zócalo** is the heart of historic Mexico City, surrounded by colonial buildings and Aztec ruins. It's also the heart of the downtown shopping district, with interesting small stores to the west, and the gigantic Mercado Merced to the east.

For those arriving tired, or late at night, there is a section describing lodging possibilities near the major termini.

Finally, I list and describe some of Mexico City's apartment hotels, establishments (mostly in or near the Zona Rosa) where you can rent a fully furnished studio or one-bedroom apartment with kitchen by the week or month, at rates similar to or lower than those in a hotel. If you're traveling with a small group or a family, if you're staying for a week or more, apartment hotels may be the way to save money.

3. Hotels in the Zona Rosa

It's very difficult to find a hotel within our budget range in the posh Zona Rosa, but there are undoubtedly some readers who will want to throw budget and caution to the wind when they hit this glamorous city. For these fortunate

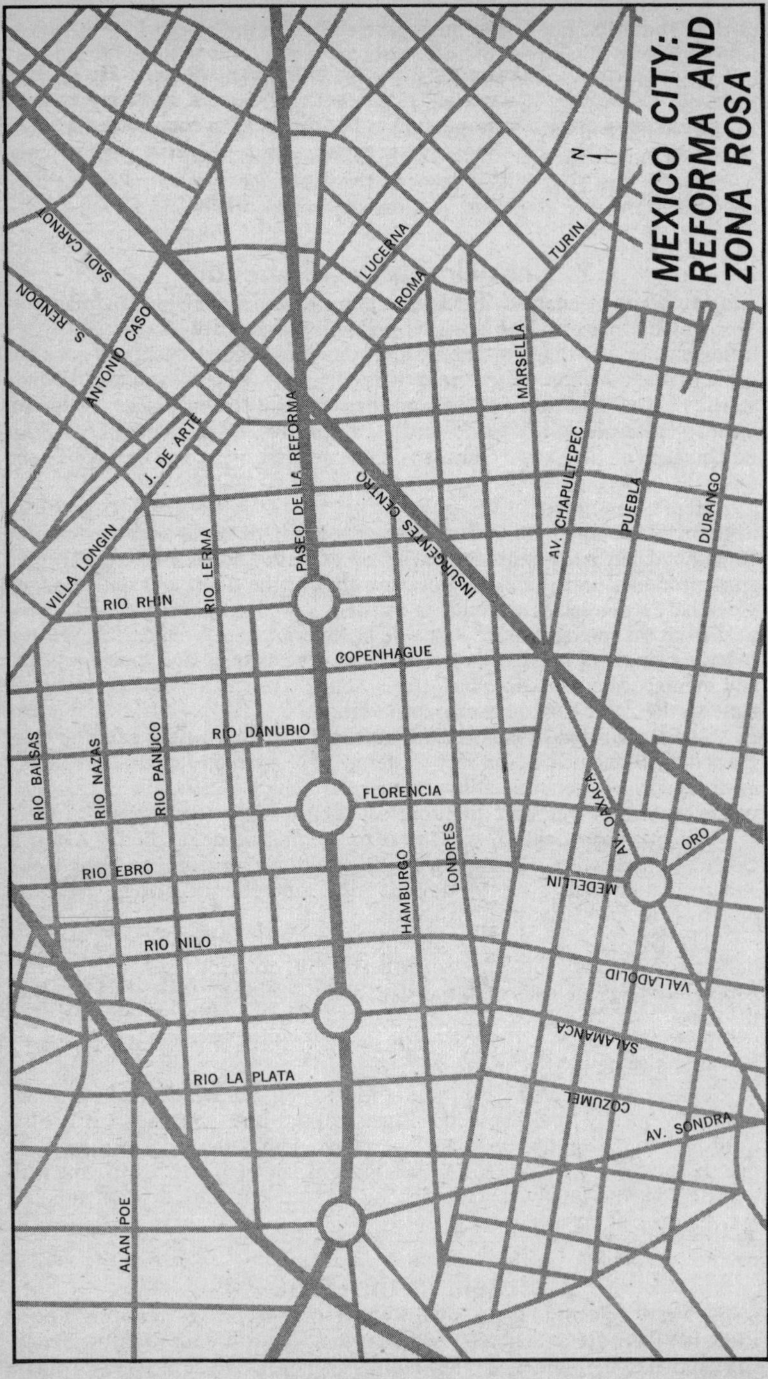
MEXICO CITY: REFORMA AND ZONA ROSA
N
TURIN
LUCERNA
ROMA
SADI CARNOT
S. RENDON
ANTONIO CASO
MARSELLA
J. DE ARTE
PASEO DE LA REFORMA
INSURGENTES CENTRO
AV. CHAPULTEPEC
PUEBLA
DURANGO
VILLA LONGIN
RIO RHIN
RIO LERMA
COPENHAGUE
RIO DANUBIO
RIO BALSAS
RIO NAZAS
RIO PANUCO
FLORENCIA
AV. OAXACA
ORO
RIO EBRO
HAMBURGO
LONDRES
MEDELLIN
RIO NILO
VALLADOLID
SALAMANCA
RIO LA PLATA
COZUMEL
AV. SONORA
ALAN POE

travelers, I suggest the following hostelries within and on the fringes of the Zona Rosa.

The dowager of Mexico City's tourist hotels, the 378-room **Hotel Geneve** (tel. 905/525-1500), Londres 130 at the corner of Genova, had a reputation for condescending service some years ago. But recently it's come under new management and now bears the exhausting name of Hotel Geneve Calinda Quality Inn, and the service is much improved. Although the hotel has undergone extensive facelifting recently, its rather grand lobby ringed by fancy shops, dotted with richly carved furniture, and decorated with dark-hued Spanish paintings still whispers opulence. You'll love "El Jardín," the incredibly long glass-topped and plant-filled cocktail lounge, affectionately referred to as "The Jungle" by the Geneve's staff. Rooms here come in three price ranges, depending on newness, size, and comforts, but base prices are 2100 pesos for singles; doubles are 2280 pesos; an extra person pays 375 pesos; kids 16 and under stay free. You can even reserve a room toll free in the U.S. by calling 800/228-5151; in Maryland, 800/492-2930; in Canada, call 800/268-8990 (except Toronto: dial 416/485-2600). As everywhere, watch out for street noise when you select your room.

The **Hotel Montejo** (tel. 905/511-9840), Reforma 240 at the corner of Niza, is in a building said to have been built by Don Francisco de Montejo, one of Cortes's officers and the founder of the city of Merida. For all that antiquity the building is comfortably up-to-date in construction, although decoration harks back to Mexico's romantic colonial era. In the lobby is an engaging statue of St. Francis, and there's even a fascinating colonial shoeshine chair (why not? Didn't Montejo need his boots polished?). The rooms tend to be small but cozy, with small and very clean tiled baths. The rooms with a view of the Reforma cost 910 to 1022 pesos single, 1190 to 1246 pesos double; those in the back of the hotel are cheaper. On the top (fifth) floor of the Montejo is a restaurant-bar called Cancún, with an indoor dining area with glass walls, and several outdoor tables with thatch "umbrellas." The Montejo is a small, quiet, personal hotel at a prime location in the Pink Zone.

On the Fringes of the Zona Rosa

Several hotels are a short walk from the Zona Rosa, and give you the convenience of being almost right there. The **Hotel Viena** (tel. 905/566-0700), Marsella 28 between Dinamarca and Berlin, is actually an older hotel but you wouldn't know it from its sleek, modern exterior. The 60 rooms are all well kept, although a bit older than the facade would indicate; some have bathrooms with tubs and twin beds, and cost 1250 pesos double. The cheaper rooms have one double bed and cost 1200 pesos double. Blown-up color photos of forest scenes and Alpine views abound. There's a parking lot beneath the hotel, and a little Swiss-style restaurant at sidewalk level. The rooms at the Viena may be the quietest in the downtown area.

Across Reforma from the Zona Rosa is the **Hotel Bristol** (tel. 905/533-6060), on the little Plaza Necaxa which is at the intersection of Panuco and Sena. Although many of its rooms are filled with sedate tour groups or long-term residents, the eight-story structure usually has rooms to spare for 1680 pesos double. Although bright and modern, shiny and clean, the Bristol is a fairly somnolent place. A branch of the Denny's chain restaurants is in the ground-floor level of the hotel.

The **Casa Gonzalez** (tel. 905/514-3302), Río Sena 69 near the corner of Río Lerma, is a congenial hostelry made up of two mansions which have been converted to hold several dozen guest rooms, each one unique. The houses, with little grassy patios out back and a huge shady tree, make an extremely pleasant and quiet oasis in the middle of the city. Meals (optional) are taken in a dining room bright with stain glass. All the rooms have private baths (some with tubs). The owner, Sr. Jorge E. Ortiz Gonzalez, speaks flawless and effortless English, and always seems to be smiling. Prices are 420 to 490 pesos for a single or 700 to 840 pesos for a double room. Breakfast costs 140 pesos; lunch is 280 pesos; dinner is 210 pesos. There's limited parking in the driveway. The Casa Gonzalez is highly recommended, especially for young women traveling alone.

4. Hotels Near the Jardín del Arte

The Jardín del Arte, also called Jardín Sullivan or Sullivan Park, extends westward from the intersection of Reforma and Insurgentes. A broad open plaza is actually the roof of a subterranean parking garage. At the end of the plaza is a grand monument to motherhood, and behind that a green park filled with artists displaying their wares on Sunday afternoons. The streets off the park, especially Calle Río Lerma, have numerous hotels—a real assortment.

The **Hotel Mallorca,** Serapio Rendon 119 (tel. 905/566-4833), charges a bit more than I'd like to pay, but it's modern and even luxurious, with wall-to-wall carpeting almost everywhere, Muzak, air conditioning, a parking garage, coffeeshop, bar, and restaurant. Every room has its own TV (good for Spanish practice). If two get a *matrimonial* (double bed) the cost is 980 pesos; twin beds cost a high 1260 pesos; singles, a high 840 pesos.

Should the Hotel Mallorca be full, you can go across the street to the **Hotel Sevilla,** a similar hotel, at Sullivan and Serapio Rendon (no. 126) (tel. 905/566-1866), with rooms and prices very similar to those at the Mallorca. Here your room will have a telephone, television, FM radio, purified water; the hotel sits atop its own parking garage, and has a central air-conditioning system. There's a restaurant and bar, which will provide room service, too.

Too much? The 17-room **Hotel Maria Angelo's,** Lerma 11 at Río Marne (tel. 905/546-6705) is everything the Mallorca's not. An older place with rooms of all sizes and shapes, it's recently undergone some renovation, although many of the bathrooms remain unredeemed. The tiny lobby adjoins a small reading lounge to which departing guests sometimes contribute (you'll find English magazines, Spanish paperbacks). There is also a cheery (and cheap) café and restaurant entered from the street or lobby, which offers a full lunch for only 100 pesos, and stays open from 9 a.m. to 9 p.m. There's no elevator, and only one telephone per floor, but each room has a private bath with a tub, freshly painted walls, and windows so wide that the sun streams in each morning. Single rooms cost 720 pesos, doubles are 860 pesos, and some rooms are large enough to accommodate three or four persons (an extra bed is 200 pesos per night). In addition, there are eight suites. The suites are quite large and have their own terraces—a fine extra.

The **Hotel Doral** (tel. 905/592-2866), Sullivan 9, just off the intersection of Insurgentes and Reforma, is a good example of the sort of medium-priced hotels beginning to be seen throughout Mexico City. A high-riser of almost 20 stories, it overlooks the plaza (with a public parking lot beneath) at this major intersection, and from its swimming pool, sundeck, and bar on the roof one can see most of the city. Rooms are close to the standard motel or medium-priced hotel in the U.S. or Canada, with fine bathrooms. The location couldn't be better. The price isn't bad: 896 pesos single, 980 pesos double.

At the **Hotel Stella Maris** (tel. 905/566-6088), Sullivan 69, the starfish motif is carried to the lengths of having a brass effigy of this sea creature attached to each room key. Other than this, though, there's little nautical about the place except the small rooftop swimming pool. The rooms in this new building are sort of small and some are a bit dark, but part of this is due to the agreeable subdued colors. TV, radio, bathrooms with separate washbasin cubicle, bottles of pure water in each room, and (from front rooms) views of Sullivan Park and its Sunday art exhibitions are the extras. Prices are not low, but you get your money's worth, for sure: single rooms cost 882 pesos, and doubles are 1008 pesos; junior suites are 1050 to 1260 pesos. The hotel's restaurant serves a good set-price lunch for only 132 pesos. This is a fine, modern hotel, not all that far from Reforma.

The small triangle formed by Insurgentes Centro, Antonio Caso, and Reforma has other good hotel choices, most more expensive than the Hotel Maria Angelo's but much more deluxe. The 40-room **Hotel Uxmal,** Madrid 13 (tel. 905/566-7044), is a small place with a cafeteria, elevator, central air conditioning, free parking lot, and tiny balconies overlooking the street from some of the rooms. The hotel boasts a purified water tap in each room, and, of course, tile bathrooms equipped with showers. Most rooms have TV. Rates are 630 to 770 pesos single, 770 to 910 pesos double. Try the Uxmal, for the hotel is well run, the staff friendly.

The Uxmal's sister hotel (same ownership) is the rather swankier **Hotel Mayaland,** half a block away at Antonio Caso 23 (tel. 905/566-6066). The 91 rooms here all have purified water taps, huge closets (with lots of hangers!), and lots and lots of extras: parking lot under the hotel, air conditioning, elevators, beauty salon, restaurant, travel agent, sauna (for a fee). Prices reflect this opulence: rooms cost 840 to 980 pesos single, 1050 to 1190 pesos double.

Another good choice, very much like the two preceding hotels, although not so friendly, is the **Hotel Regente** (tel. 905/566-8933), at Paris 9, between Madrid and the three-way intersection of Antonio Caso, Insurgentes, and Paris. Over 100 rooms plus a garage fill this modern building. Bold-patterned bedspreads and flowered drapes, plus wall-to-wall carpeting, make the rooms lively and comfortable. Bathrooms with showers are pretty small but new and quite adequate. A restaurant and travel agent desk are at your disposal in the lobby. Here one person pays 700 to 840 pesos, two pay 840 to 980 pesos. Again, the location and transportation possibilities are excellent.

5. Hotels Near the Revolución Monument

From the intersection of Avenida Juarez and Paseo de la Reforma, the western extension of Avenida Juarez (actually named Calle Ignacio Ramírez) leads to the large Plaza de la República. The plaza was chosen by Porfirio Díaz as the site of a Chamber of Deputies, and the mammoth dome was under construction when the Mexican Revolution (1910) interrupted Díaz's plans, not to mention Díaz himself. After the dictator fled the country, the building was restructured as a monument and two heroes of the revolution, Venustiano Carranza and Francisco Madero, were buried in its pillars.

The Monument to the Revolution is an odd, stolid, massive structure which I find peculiarly fascinating, and very art deco. The monument is illuminated at night; even during the day its somber dome is visible from many points in the city.

This is a fairly quiet area, near the major arteries and a Metro station (Revolución). You're about the same distance from the Zona Rosa as from the Zócalo, and next door to the Jardín del Arte and the Alameda—an excellent area.

For what you get, rooms at the modern **Hotel Principado** (tel. 905/592-2211) are a surprising bargain. The good-looking, tall new hotel is just off the

MEXICO CITY REVOLUCION AND ALAMEDA

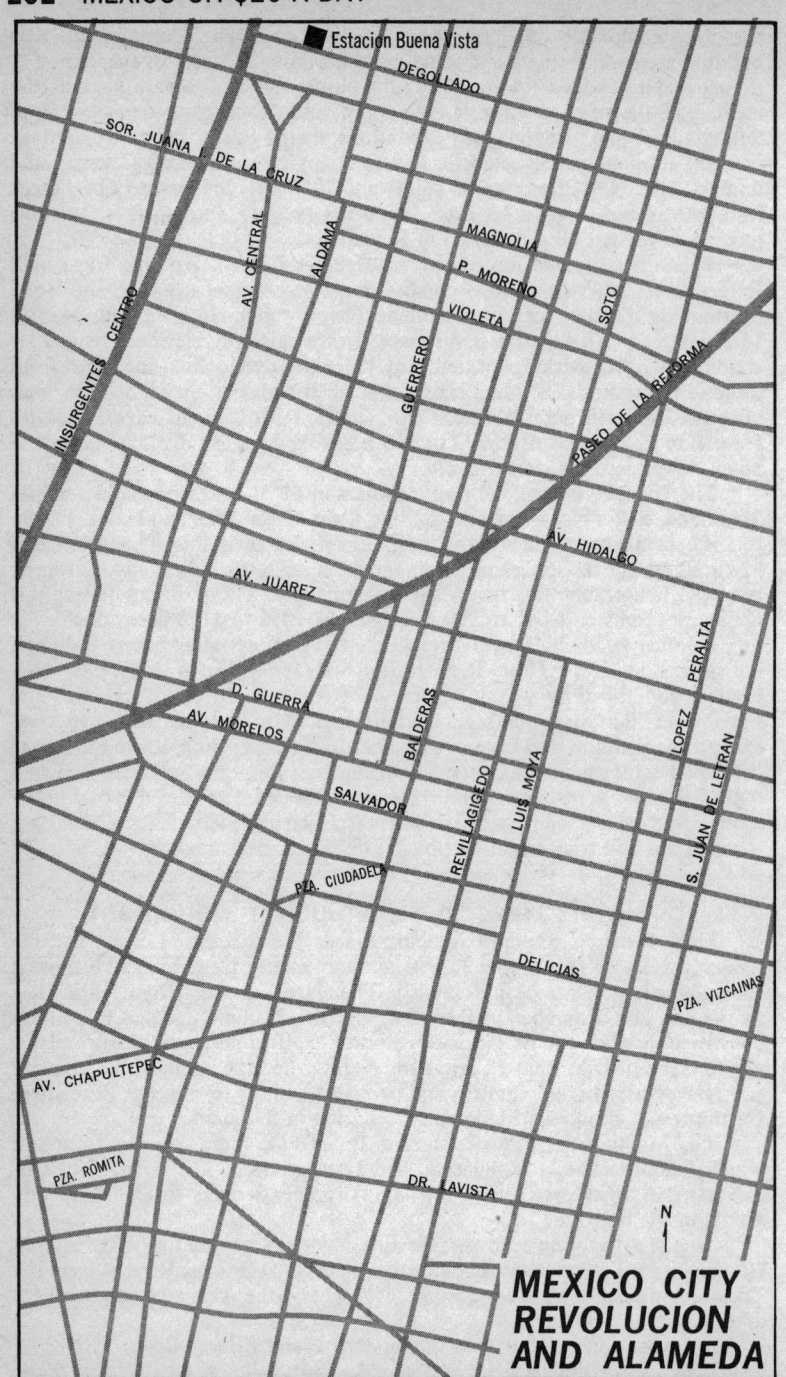

Plaza de la República at José Maria Iglesias 55. Many rooms have fine views of the plaza and the monument; all have TVs, clean tile baths or showers, air conditioning, and lounge chairs. A decent little restaurant is off the lobby, and a parking lot is underneath. For this comfort, the price is just 910 pesos single, 1025 pesos double, 1200 pesos triple—excellent value.

Considering its appointments, the five-story **Hotel Jena** (pronounced "hena"), Jesus Teran 12 at Puente de Alvarado (tel. 905/566-0277), is a good medium-priced choice. From the swanky exterior, you might think it beyond our means, but not so. The 60 rooms, nicely furnished with "hotel Formica," each with large mirror, telephone, and glistening tile bath, cost 700 to 1050 pesos single, 840 to 1260 pesos double, the higher double price being for a huge room with a couch, rather like a junior suite. The hotel has a restaurant and free parking, and some of the rooms have television.

On par with the Jena but slightly less expensive, the **Hotel New York**, Edison 45 (tel. 905/566-9700), is a large four-story building, a cubist's dream of mosaic tile, grass-green paneling, and glass. The 45 rooms are equipped with telephones and tile baths, carpeting, Formica furniture, wood paneling on one wall, and hanging glass lamps—very pleasant. Prices: 775 pesos single, 900 pesos double. The small restaurant off the lobby solves the breakfast problem with hotcakes, eggs, and coffee for 100 pesos. It's open every day from 7 a.m. to 10 p.m. Parking in the hotel's locked garage is free.

The 100-room **Hotel Frimont,** Jesus Teran 35 (tel. 905/546-2580), stands up well when compared to the Jena and the New York. Singles here rent for 630 pesos, doubles for 770 to 840 pesos, triples for 1050 pesos, four-to-a-room for 1190 pesos, all with telephones and private baths. But it is a pleasant hotel boasting a slick marble lobby, 72 nicely decorated rooms, free parking, and a medium-priced restaurant just off the lobby (open daily from 7 a.m. to 1 a.m., featuring a 110-peso lunch from 1 p.m. to 5 p.m.).

The **Hotel Edison** (tel. 905/566-0933), Edison 106, a block from the Revolución Monument at the corner of Iglesias, is a real find. In the midst of the city's noise and bustle, its odd construction around a narrow court with grass and trees gives a sense of sanctuary. Some rooms are built in tiers overlooking the court, and even larger ones are hidden away down hallways. These latter rooms tend to be dark, but big and comfortable with huge kingsize beds, and cost 560 pesos single, 660 pesos double; of the other rooms, a few singles go for 440 pesos; most are a bit higher; other doubles go for 770 pesos, with a few extra-luxurious rooms costing more. Blond wood and light colors, piped music, and sunlight make this a cheerful place. Services include bathrooms with separate washbasin areas, and some even have bidets, plus tub-shower combinations. The location is fairly quiet and near downtown.

Another hotel choice convenient to the Monument to the Revolution is the **Hotel Arizona** (tel. 905/546-2855), Gómez Farías 20 at Insurgentes. For prices of 630 pesos single, 728 pesos double, you get very clean rooms with tile showers, black-and-white TV sets, telephones, air conditioning, and a large covered parking garage right next door. Color TVs are yours at a small additional charge. Try not to get a room that looks onto busy Insurgentes. The Arizona is only half a block from the Monument.

Going to the top of the price scale, the **Hotel Palace** (tel. 905/566-2400), at Ignacio Ramírez 7, just off the Plaza de la Revolución, was one of Mexico's outstanding luxury hotels only a few decades ago. Today it retains its comfort, its good location, its experienced staff, and over 200 well-kept, bright, and modern rooms. The bustle of a large hotel surrounds you here, with tobacco kiosk and travel desk in the lobby, bag-bearing bellboys scurrying here and there, and the occasional busload of tourists. Of the rooms, about half are priced at 840 pesos single, 980 pesos double; the rest are about 100 pesos higher in price.

At the low end of the price scale, to be used if you simply can't afford (or can't find a room in) the hotels recommended above, are several other places. The **Hotel Paraíso,** Ignacio Mariscal 99 (between Arizpe and Arriaga; tel. 905/566-8077), advertises *"mas comfort a menos costo"* and its 40 rooms do deliver exactly this with bright colors in the rooms, good tiled bathrooms, all very solid and comfortable if a slight bit frayed at the edges. The facade is rather discouraging and looks like anything but the gateway to Paradise, but don't let it put you off. Rates are 580 pesos single, 640 pesos double in one bed, 680 pesos double in two beds. The street is a relatively quiet one.

Similar to the Paraíso, and half a block off Arriaga, is the **Gran Hotel Texas,** Ignacio Mariscal 129 (tel. 905/546-4626). Free parking in the hotel's locked lot is the bonus here, as is the relative quiet of the street. The hotel is kept quite clean, and the staff is friendly. Singles cost 575 pesos; doubles are 625 pesos in one bed and 675 pesos in twin beds.

6. Hotels Near Alameda Central

The Alameda Central is Mexico City's downtown park, always filled with strollers, lovers, newspaper-readers, loafers, children playing in the fountains, and vendors hawking everything from dried pumpkin seeds to serapes. It's a pleasant place, right next to the marble Palacio de las Bellas Artes (Fine Arts Palace) and only a block from the skyscraping Latin American Tower.

Most of my recommended hotels here are actually on the streets to the south of the Alameda. Hotels with views of the park itself tend to be out of our price range.

The streets south of the Alameda harbor a cross-section of downtown life: little eateries and juice bars, shops selling pumps, sinks, car parts, blenders, electrical gear, homeopathic remedies, you name it. Not particularly beautiful, the area still manages to be sympathetic as a real slice of life. Its hotels are mostly of the modern type, well used and decently priced. Some specialize in tour groups because of the central location.

On the street with the unpronounceable name of Revillagigedo, the **Hotel Guadalupe** (tel. 905/518-5240), at no. 36, has colonial touches such as lamps on chains and prints of an equestrian Bolívar. The staff is young and mostly English-speaking, and is used to handling tour groups (which the hotel does frequently). Prices are a bit high at 770 to 880 pesos single, 880 to 1100 pesos double. The restaurant features a 200-peso lunch; garage parking is free.

Also on Revillagigedo, at no. 35, is the **Hotel Fleming** (tel. 905/510-4530), a building of 100 rooms from which I've had good reports which were borne out by my inspection. Although well used, the heavy service has still left the rooms quite presentable, and the bathrooms are larger than most. Elevators take you to the upper floors. Singles at the Fleming cost 585 pesos; doubles are 610 pesos in a double bed, 690 pesos in twin beds. A blindingly colorful coffeeshop-restaurant is located next to the lobby, and offers a set-price lunch daily.

Last choice on Revillagigedo is the **Hotel Monte Real,** Revillagigedo 23 (tel. 905/518-1149), where the attractions are a good location, good beds, TV in the rooms, a rooftop terrace-cum-solarium, and a hotel garage. Prices are a bit high, though (it's the TV sets): singles are 705 pesos; doubles, 895 pesos.

The **Hotel El Romano** (tel. 905/510-8800), at Humboldt 55, at the corner of Guerra/Articulo 123, is more up-to-date than many others in this area, with over 150 rooms going for moderate prices: 1150 pesos single, 1250 pesos double.

The private baths here are often made of a dramatic black stone, although the rooms are kept light by bright-colored spreads, walls, and curtains. Ten of the rooms—are you ready?—have circular beds. The roof terrace or patio has grass, a tiny swimming pool, and a tremendous view, plus a rather elegant palapa-topped restaurant.

The **Hotel Ambassador** (tel. 905/518-0110), Humboldt 38, specializes in tour groups, but if rooms are tight you might try here as groups often have cancellations which leave a few rooms unexpectedly available. Rooms are clean and modern, and the hotel has just had extensive renovation. Prices are 1000 pesos single, 1200 pesos double, with bath and piped-in music; a travel desk, garage, and multilingual staff complete the picture.

STARVATION BUDGET HOTELS: At the **Hotel del Valle,** Independencia 35 (tel. 905/585-2399), over half of the rooms cost only 550 pesos single, 660 pesos double. The hotel has a little lobby, an elevator, a mixture of Formica and wooden furniture, slightly worn rugs, and telephones in the rooms as well as tile baths. Here you are just a block off Juarez.

Although the **Hotel Conde** (tel. 905/585-2388) is five blocks off Juarez and equally far from Reforma, it offers the best rooms for the best price in this area. The hotel's entrance is at Pescaditos 15, but the building is on the corner of Revillagigedo, and would be numbered about Revillagigedo 56. It's fairly new with clean bathrooms, a small marbled lobby, wall-to-wall carpet, TV, and FM in the rooms, free garage parking. Rates are 500 pesos single, 705 pesos double.

FOR WOMEN ONLY: The **Associación Cristiana Femenina** (tel. 905/585-0655) translates as the **YWCA,** and the association's headquarters at Humboldt 62, a mere block off Avenida Juarez, holds very clean and respectable rooms for women costing $15 (U.S.) per day, with private bath. A budget-priced restaurant is in the same building.

7. Hotels Near the Zócalo

The center of the city's shopping and banking district is a great place to stay for many reasons, but most of all for location. Here you are a short walk from the Alameda Central, Bellas Artes, Latin American Tower, the art and craft stores, and the Zócalo. Transportation by bus, Metro, and *pesero* to other parts of the city is easy and inexpensive. Hotels tend to be older ones with little of the glitter and flash of the more expensive places in the aforementioned areas, but this makes them even better bargains as prices are kept low. Many of the hotels east of Avenida Lázaro Cárdenas have their own garages and restaurants, and other good restaurants are scattered throughout the district. Staying here will permit you to stretch your budget dollars and stay a longer time in Mexico City.

I'll describe first of all the moderately priced hostelries west and south of the Zócalo, then a few tips for the Big Splurge: staying right on the Zócalo. Finally, I'll look at the lodging possibilities north and east of Mexico City's main square.

HOTELS WEST AND SOUTH OF THE ZOCALO: Bronze statuettes cradling cut-glass lamps set the tone at the entrance of the **Hotel Gillow,** Isabel la Católica 17 at the corner of Cinco de Mayo (tel. 905/518-1440). It's a

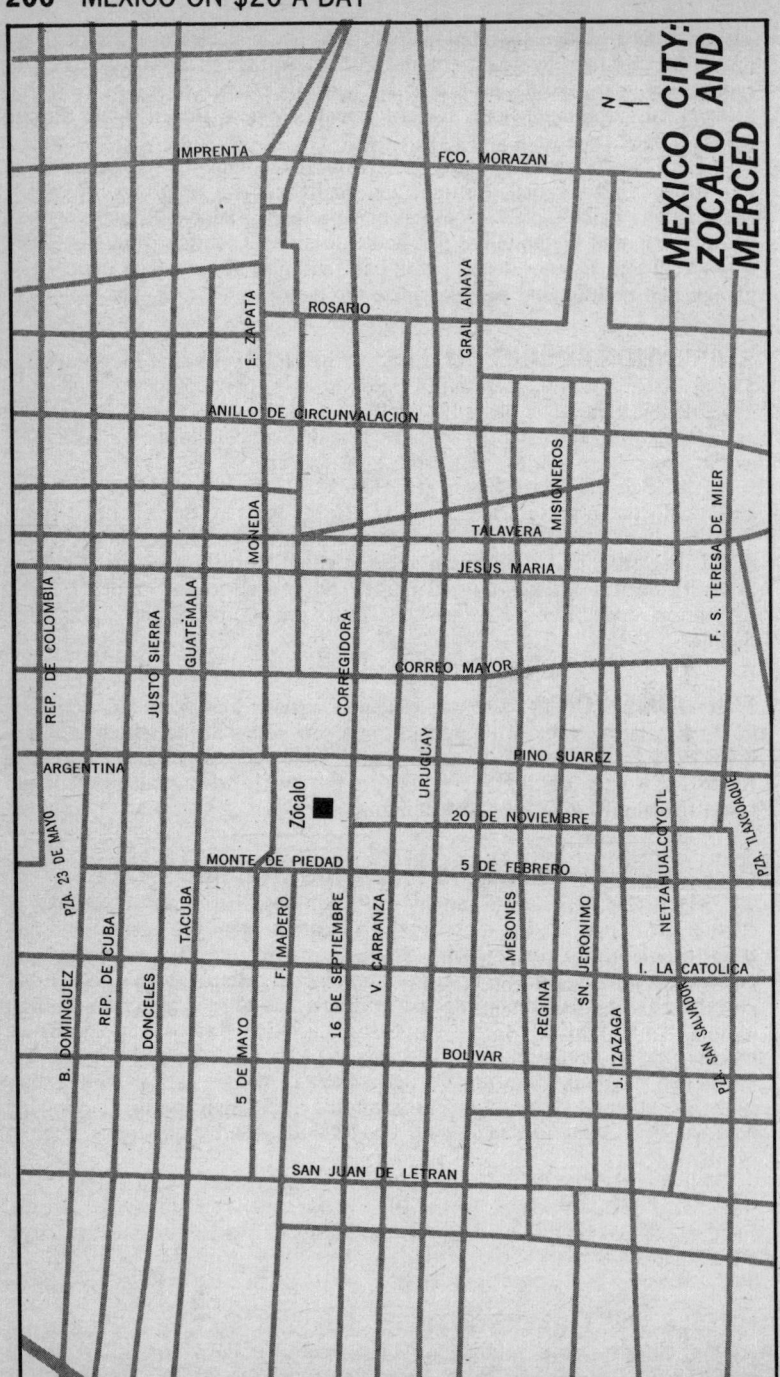

MEXICO CITY: ZOCALO AND MERCED

dignified old establishment built during an era when space was not at a premium: nearly every room boasts a small entrance hall. Tall french doors open onto tiny balconies from the exterior rooms. All 115 rooms are comfortably furnished in a modern style with carpeting, boldly patterned bedspreads, newish furniture, and telephones, and a good many of the bathrooms are equipped with tubs. They even follow the curious custom of putting a white paper band bearing the words "Sterilized for your Protection" across toilet and washbasin. Rooms come in several sizes and prices, from 600 to 750 pesos single, 820 to 920 pesos double, which puts the Gillow right at the top of our budget range. The restaurant, handy for breakfast eggs and coffee, also serves a six-course comida corrida featuring such delectables as oyster cocktail, enchiladas suizas, and paella a la Valenciana for a reasonable 250 pesos, plus tax and tip.

Farther south along the same street (and therefore not quite so convenient) you'll come upon the four-story **Hotel Isabel,** Isabel la Católica 63 at Calle El Salvador (tel. 905/518-1213), an older place with a mix of Mexican and foreign clientele. In the lobby, a somber painting of Queen Isabel gazes out over the vast lobby while guests gaze at the TV set on the mantelpiece just below the queen. (You can rent a set for your room for an extra charge.) Comforts include an elevator, a good restaurant and bar, and all-day room service. Each of the 72 rooms is old-fashioned and spacious, with dark wood or painted furniture, carpeting, telephone, and tiled bath. Larger rooms have tubs as well as showers, little tiled entrance halls, and frosted-glass doors opening onto wrought-iron balconies. No garage, sad to say. Rates are 525 pesos single, 680 pesos double, with bath. You can wangle yourself a reduction if they're not full.

The four-story **Hotel Concordia,** Uruguay 13 just off Avenida Lázaro Cárdenas (tel. 905/510-4100), is only two blocks from the Latin American Tower, the Bellas Artes, and the Alameda—a very convenient location. The multipillared lobby is at the end of a corridor. The 55 rooms are old but decently kept, all have baths, some have tubs as well as showers. The hotel boasts that it is *"totalmente alfombrado"* ("completely carpeted"). Besides the ubiquitous carpeting, there is an elevator and a garage for guests with cars. Rates at the Concordia are 425 pesos single, 495 to 550 pesos double, the latter double-room price being for twin beds.

Next choice is the **Hotel El Salvador,** República del Salvador 16 (tel. 905/585-1933), a five-story hotel of 91 rooms just half a block off Lázaro Cárdenas. Look for a glass front broken by marble balconies. Inside, up a few marble steps, the monastically bare lobby is a world of red carpeting, low Danish furniture, and wood paneling. The rooms, all sunny, are suffused in a pleasantly soothing monochromatic tan color scheme—TV sets, Formica furnishings, tan bed throws, drapes, and carpeting. Naturally there are telephones, hot and cold bathrooms. Rates are 500 pesos single, 700 pesos double. Breakfast in the hotel's adjoining restaurant costs 100 pesos for fruit, eggs, toast, and coffee. The special lunch costs 200 pesos. Free parking in the hotel's subterranean garage. Recommended.

STARVATION BUDGET HOTELS: Just two blocks south of the Zócalo stands the **Hotel Roble** (tel. 905/518-1000), at the Avenida Uruguay 109, near the corner of Pino Suarez. It's not a place for sybaritic sorts and its accommodations could best be described as functional, but the odd-shaped rooms all have private showers and TV sets, and even manage to be cheerful. The hotel has an elevator, and the area nearby has lots of restaurants and several parking garages. The 40 rooms are well priced at 460 pesos single, 560 to 680 pesos double.

If the Roble is full, the desk clerk will direct you to a sister hotel (same management), the **Hotel Principal** (tel. 905/585-2166), Bolívar 29 between Madero and 16 de Septiembre, which has 100 rooms, all with baths and telephones, priced *lower* than those at the Roble.

Between Bolívar and Isabel la Católica, and parallel to these streets, is a short street named Motolinía. At Motolinía 40, near the corner with 16 de Septiembre, is the **Hotel Lafayette** (tel. 905/521-9640), an older building kept up-to-date through renovation and patronized mostly by Mexican travelers. Not much English is spoken here, but with patience the staff will figure out your wants. You're right in the center of shopping here, on a pedestrians-only street. Rooms cost 440 pesos single, 525 pesos double.

One of the funniest looking hotels in all of Mexico is the **Hotel Monte Carlo,** Uruguay 69 (tel. 905/585-1222), where you drive through the front doors and the lobby to reach the garage. An old place with an interior courtyard, red iron stair railings, and a curved marble stairway, it sports an English-speaking manager who will be delighted to explain its history to you. Theoretically, the Monte Carlo was built about 1772 as an Augustinian monastery, and afterward was the residence of D. H. Lawrence for a time. The 35 rooms with bath are quite large, crammed with carved antique pieces and equipped with telephones; some have little balconies. The 25 rooms without bath—they're small, perhaps built as cells or prayer rooms—have hot running water, and are furnished with whatever odd bits and pieces will fit in. Prices at the Monte Carlo are 325 pesos single, 375 pesos double for a room without bath; 450 pesos single, 525 pesos double for a room with bath. The manager won't take reservations over the phone—you have to show up in person to claim a room.

Ignore the unattractive facade of the **Hotel Capitol,** Uruguay 12 (tel. 905/518-1750), one of the larger places in the old area, with 93 rooms ranged on four elevated tiers around a central glass-roofed lobby where you can sit and let the noontime sunlight beam down on you. All rooms have immaculate shower-baths, telephones, and are reasonably light and airy, although their walls and aging furniture show some signs of neglect. Rates are 360 pesos single, 500 pesos double, 100 pesos extra for an additional bed. You can park nearby in a commercial lot.

If the Hotel Capitol is just too dark and plain for you, walk across the street to the **Hotel Concordia,** which is much better for just a bit more money.

The **Hotel Ontario** (tel. 905/518-5460) is a plainish and modest place, although the entryway and lobby seem to heighten the tone somewhat. You have a choice of rooms and suites here, priced at 400 pesos for a double bed (one or two persons), and 480 pesos for twin beds. The location isn't bad, at the corner of 5 de Febrero and Uruguay.

THE BIG SPLURGE—STAYING RIGHT ON THE ZÓCALO: If you're feeling flush, a modest outlay above and beyond our $20-a-day budget will get you a room overlooking the Zócalo at the **Hotel Majestic** (tel. 905/521-8600), Avenida Madero 73. A hotel of the Hostales de México group, the Majestic has 85 rooms which look onto Mexico City's main square, the Avenida Madero, or the hotel's own inner court. The attractiveness of the hotel starts with its lobby, a place of stone arches, brilliant tiles, and warm colors, plus a pleasantly gurgling little stone fountain at the far end. On the second floor is the courtyard, with a floor of glass blocks (actually the ceiling of the lobby) set with sofas, tables, and chairs, and decorated with pots of vines and hanging plants all the way up to the glass roof six stories above. Nice touches of art and color are everywhere: each room doorway has a border of blue-and-white tiles to lighten the darkness of the heavy, colonial-style doors. Inside the rooms, however, colonialism is left behind in favor of pastel colors, simple and attractive decors, and newly redone tile bathrooms with tubs. On the lower floors facing the Avenida Madero noise from the street may be a problem, but on the upper floors and in the rooms which front on the Zócalo you needn't worry.

The finishing touch to the Majestic's luxury offering is a rooftop café-restaurant in which you can choose a table shaded by a bright yellow umbrella for breakfast or just a drink or a cup of tea.

For all this comfort and class, the prices are surprisingly moderate: single rooms cost 1300 pesos; double rooms are 1500 pesos.

Although Mexico City can boast of many tremendous, splendid hotels, I can't imagine that any has more grandeur than the **Gran Hotel Ciudad de México** (tel. 905/510-4040), 16 de Septiembre no. 82, just a few steps off the Zócalo. It is, very simply, palatial! You enter a rather unprepossessing doorway only to find yourself underneath a brilliantly glistening crystal chandelier. You ascend a short flight of stairs to the lobby, four stories high, ringed with fancy metalwork balustrades at the story levels, and crowned by a simply magnificent stained-glass canopy. At either end of the lobby are semi-elliptical "birdcage" elevators which glide quietly up and down. Lighting in the lobby is provided by brass-and-crystal lamps, each with ten milk-glass globes. Two Tiffany birdcages are filled with (stuffed!) songbirds, and the chirping is electronically simulated. Take a seat on one of the circular sofas to take it all in.

The rooms are similarly elegant, with white walls enlivened by gilded trim (not real gilt, though), comfortable furnishings, large bathrooms, and lots of headroom. The hotel was completely restored and redone in 1968, and was reopened by none other than the president of the Republic, Sr. Gustavo Díaz Ordaz. Cheap? Not exactly. Reasonable? Where else can you stay in a palace for 1960 pesos single, 2100 pesos double, 2240 pesos triple (deluxe rooms cost 440 to 880 pesos more). Nowhere else will you get so much art nouveau for so little money. Even if you can't stay here, have a look, or buy a drink in the bar off the lobby.

HOTELS NORTH AND EAST OF THE ZÓCALO: Although not quite so convenient as my other accommodations areas, this one can be said to harbor the best of the bargains—hotels that would cost sometimes twice as much if they were located in a classier neighborhood. This is by no means a classy neighborhood, but no one can say it's not interesting: hardware stores, record shops, used bookstores, and pharmacies specializing in herbal and homeopathic remedies abound. There are enough tiny *taquerías* to feed the entire *Ejercito Nacional* (Mexican army) at one sitting, and enough streetlife to keep a squad of urban sociologists busy for years. Ignore the chipping paint and crumbling plaster here—everybody else does—and concentrate on the surprising bargains to be had in the way of accommodations and parking.

Urban renewal is slowly coming to this section, and besides new government offices going up you will see work crews restoring ancient churches, monasteries, and houses affected by sinkage. Calle de la Moneda is now a nice pedestrians-only street. The lake bottom upon which Mexico City was built is particularly soft here, and so huge old facades, steeples, and bell-towers lean and lurch at crazy angles. Somehow it reminds one of Venice (which has a similar problem with sinkage) and adds to the area's interest.

One block north of Tacuba is Calle Donceles, a street noted for its gunsmith shops. Here, set back from the street by a passageway lined with stores, is the six-story **Hotel Catedral,** Donceles 95 (tel. 905/518-5232), very popular with Mexico's middle class. Behind the big cool lobby is the hotel's restaurant-bar, bustling with white-jacketed waiters and featuring a special luncheon at 210 pesos. The 140 rooms are extremely well kept, all equipped with telephones and private baths, some of which have tubs. Rates are 550 pesos single, 693 to 800 pesos double. Bonuses here are a parking garage next door, exceptionally high housekeeping standards, and rooms on the upper floors with views of the great rockpile which is Mexico City's cathedral.

Another fantastic bargain is the **Hotel Antillas**, Belisario Dominguez 34 (tel. 905/526-5674), with rooms priced at 595 pesos single, 560 to 735 pesos double. The Antillas is rather old-world, a five-story study in burnished red lava block with huge plate-glass windows hung with rust drapes. Inside, the lobby is lit by black wrought-iron chandeliers. It has a lot of charm. The 70 rooms, all with telephones and private baths, are extraordinarily large and very clean, with lots of new paint and new furniture. Parking is free, making it an excellent choice if you have a car. Without, it's a short walk to a main transportation artery.

The Antillas is a top choice of Mexican families, and is one of the best hotels—for the price—anywhere in the city. Prices are low because the area is dingy—but urban renewal has already begun.

The **Hotel Moneda**, Moneda 8 (tel. 905/522-4927), is east of the Zócalo, and opposite the old quarters of the National Museum; to reach it walk all the way across the Zócalo from Madero, past the National Cathedral, and look to your left for Calle Moneda. The hotel has no large sign, just its name carved in the gray stone above the brass-studded front door. The lobby, built completely of pale polished stone, resembles a well-tended museum sans relics, but all 40 rooms are furnished with bed, chair, wardrobe, and telephone, and each has a private hot- and cold-water bath. Next door, the Restaurant Moneda provides cheap, ample breakfast, plus snacks and numerous entrees costing under 75 pesos. Rates at the Moneda are officially 440 pesos single, 580 pesos double, but you will almost certainly be quoted a price 25% lower if business is slow. You're in good company here: city police and military police headquarters are almost next door, and shops catering to these services are all around.

8. Hotels Near Bus, Train, and Air Terminals

It might just happen that you'll arrive in this dauntingly large city late at night, or very tired, or both. In this case, you might want to go directly to the nearest suitable hotel, stay a night or two, and then find a better or more conveniently located place to stay. Well, here are the good places near the bustling terminals.

HOTELS NEAR THE AIRPORT: Mexico City's Benito Juarez International Airport is big, new, shiny-clean, and well run, but it's no place to spend the night. You can turn left out the terminal doors and walk a block to the local **Holiday Inn Mexico City–Airport** (tel. 905/762-4088), Boulevard Puerto Aereo 502. Do this only if you want to blow half a week's budget on one night's lodging, however, as the Holiday Inn charges about $60 single, $75 double for a room.

Instead, find your way to the **Hotel Riazor** (tel. 905/657-4470), Viaducto Miguel Aleman 297, about ten minutes by taxi from the airport (ask around for the best rate). This new 175-room hotel charges 1500 pesos for a double room complete with king-size bed, TV, telephone, tiled shower, bidet, and—if you get a room on the upper floors—a view of the city. I'm grateful to Bill Newsom of San Diego, California, for tracking down this one.

A HOTEL NEAR BUENA VISTA RAILROAD STATION: An excellent value, that's the fairly new **Hotel La Riviera,** Calle Aldama 9 at Orozco y Berra (tel. 905/566-3611), half a block from Puente de Alvarado and only three blocks south of Buena Vista station. It offers a good many features of larger and more expensive establishments: air conditioning and heating, music in every room, and free parking. Look for a pink tile facade; inside, the lobby glistens with marble and one wall is given over to a mosaic mural of the Mediterranean coast. The hallways are laid with red carpets, as are the rooms, which are furnished in "motel Formica." Everything is light and airy. The hotel's restaurant—the only hotel that has one for blocks around, incidentally—serves combination breakfasts for 85 pesos, a special lunch for 170 pesos, and is open from 7 a.m. to 11 p.m. every day. Rates are 460 to 580 pesos single, 560 to 680 pesos double.

A HOTEL NEAR THE TERMINAL NORTE: Say you've just arrived in the bus terminal after a trip of 1000 miles and you emerge from your bus in almost a liquid state, unable to face the prospect of searching for a hotel. Good news: The **Hotel Brasilia** (tel. 905/587-8577) provides luxurious refuge for travelers only 2½ blocks from the terminal. The ultramodern V-shaped hotel is at Avenida de los Cien Metros 4823—go out the doors of the terminal, turn left, and walk the short distance. The hotel sign is visible from the terminal and assures you of the proper direction. Up the flashy black-and-white marble steps is a haven of piped-in FM music (three channels), air conditioning, polite service, hot baths, and a well-stocked bar and restaurant. You may even have color TV in your room. Prices for the 200 rooms and suites vary with sleeping accommodations, and start at 1000 pesos single, 1100 pesos double (for two people in a double bed). You may even consider spending two nights here if you're just passing through Mexico City, but for any longer stays you should move downtown.

9. Apartment Hotels

Years ago Mexico City could boast of several apartment hotels, a type of establishment just now catching on up north. Apartment hotels have the best of both worlds: the privacy, space, and cooking facilities of an apartment, and the convenience and services of a hotel.

Apartment hotels, often called *"suites"* (soo-WEE-tess) are found in several city districts, but mostly in and near the Zona Rosa. Who stays here? Families, businessmen, and consultants on extended stays; people waiting to find houses or permanent apartments; tourists staying for a week or more. Some apartment hotels rent by the day, but preferential rates really come into play with stays of a week or more.

The **Hotel Suites Michelangelo** (tel. 905/566-9877), Río Amazonas 78 (between Calle Río Lerma and Paseo de la Reforma), has 40 suites with one or two bedrooms, living room, dining area, television, private telephone line, kitchenette with refrigerator, bathroom, and closet. The area, just north of the Zona Rosa and near the British and American embassies, is quiet and residential. By the week, rates are about 1500 pesos per day for two persons; the rate drops 5% if you stay two weeks, and much more if you stay a month. Two people can pay as little as 1000 pesos per day for a month's stay, depending on the size of the apartment. You can rent by the day if you wish, too.

The **Suites Imperiales Niza,** (tel. 905/511-9540), Calle Niza 73, right in the Zona Rosa, is quite deluxe. A high-rise with balconies on each room, the decor stresses dark wood paneling and a "formal" feel of luxury. Complete apartments for two people cost about 2300 pesos per day (by the day), or 1900 pesos per day (by the month).

Remember that the IVA tax of 10% will be added to these room prices.

FINDING A REAL APARTMENT: What if you're planning a truly lengthy stay, of several months? The first place to look is in the classified ads section of *The News.* This will give you an idea of the choice neighborhoods and the going rates. To save money, you might then dust off your Spanish and look at the similar sections in the Spanish-language dailies. As landlords advertising in *The News* will obviously be catering to foreigners, their rents may well be higher than the norm.

Another good idea is to make the rounds of the bulletin boards at the various language schools, cultural centers, and other places where foreigners congregate. Sublet and rental notices often find permanent places on such bulletin boards.

Chapter VIII

MEXICO CITY: MEALS ON A BUDGET

1. About Mexican Restaurants
2. In and Near the Zona Rosa
3. Near Jardín del Arte / Revolución
4. Near the Alameda and Bellas Artes
5. In the Zócalo Area

EVERYBODY EATS OUT in Mexico, from the wealthy executive to the peasant. Consequently you can find restaurants of every type, size, and price range scattered across the city. There are so many restaurants here, most of them good, that to cover all of them would be impossible. I get numerous letters each year from readers who have discovered another great restaurant, and indeed they have and so can you. Therefore, what I have tried to do in this section is give you a list of some of the tried-and-true establishments, on side streets and behind café curtains; I have sifted through a myriad of restaurants and have listed those that will give you the best food for the best price within the appropriate class: medium-priced, splurge, budget, and specialty.

I have not included here the various American-type chains such as Burger Boy, Pizza Hut, Vip's, Denny's, Woolworth's, and Tastee-Freez, as they have standard and familiar fare which, although good to cure a bout of homesickness, tends to be a good deal more expensive than Mexican food for what you get.

1. About Mexican Restaurants

Mexico City is a diner's delight, but to enjoy it fully, and at the best possible price, one must know about Mexican restaurants and dining habits.

The best bet for breakfast is a place which offers set-price meals: 150 pesos for bacon and eggs, juice, toast, and coffee, for example. Breakfast can be very expensive if you end up ordering your hotcakes, or eggs, or cereal à la carte.

THE COMIDA CORRIDA: Remember that Mexicans have their biggest meal of the day in the afternoon between 1 and 4 p.m., and that many restaurants offer a set-price lunch called a *comida corrida*, or *cubierto*, at a price much, much lower than the four or five courses would cost if priced à la carte. Take advantage of the comida corrida for it's the biggest money-saver in

Mexico, and then have a light supper in the evening. Be sure to get to the restaurant between about 1 and 4, or they won't serve you at the special price.

Comidas corridas can range in price anywhere from 100 to 500 pesos, but by no means are all 100-peso comidas (or, for that matter, 500-peso comidas) the same. For the ultimate in high-level dining and low-level spending, you've got to compare menus. A 300-peso comida which starts with oyster stew and goes on to sauteed trout and carne asada, finishing up with fettucine Alfredo and pêche Melba with coffee, is an indisputable bargain. But a meal for the same price which lists chicken broth, enchiladas, rice, pudding, and a soft drink is clearly a rip-off. Read carefully.

TAXES AND TIPPING: Mexico's 10% IVA tax, levied on everything from diapers to dirigibles, will be tacked onto your restaurant bill as well. I haven't included the tax in the prices quoted below unless specifically noted. You'll have to add a tip to the total, too. Want a rule of thumb? Select your main course, double its price, and—excluding wine and drinks—you've got a pretty fair estimate of the total bill you'll pay.

In the more expensive restaurants, particularly in the Zona Rosa, you'll be able to pay with a major credit card. Bonus: The charge won't show up on your bill at home for a month or more.

For tipping suggestions, see Chapter XVI under "Tipping."

2. In and Near the Zona Rosa

The select area known as the Zona Rosa is clearly defined: bounded by Insurgentes, Chapultepec, and the Reforma. Within this compound there are more charming restaurants than almost anywhere else in the world. You can find any type of food or ambience from the café set to the taco stand. As someone once remarked about the Zona Rosa, it reminds everyone of somewhere back home.

First prize for good food at good prices with good atmosphere goes to the **Nuevo Restaurante 7½**, located at 45 Niza, near Hamburgo. The restaurant is on the second floor and is always packed with hungry people. They offer a 140-peso comida, five courses and lots of food. If you're not in the mood for a big meal you might try enchiladas, tacos, or sandwiches which range between 50 and 120 pesos. They also serve breakfast from 8 a.m. onward. Here's a good bet for eating cheaply in the otherwise expensive Zona Rosa.

Close by is another popular place with a very reasonable menu; it's **La Carretta Rosa**, Hamburgo 96—you'll recognize it by the painting of the wagon over the pink door and two large wagon wheels which flank the tiled entrance. This is a down-home place patronized by Mexicans homesick for real country cooking: menudo (tripe soup), pozole (meat-and-hominy stew), chicharrón (pork crackling), and tacos of grilled or roasted meat. Specialty plates abound, mostly featuring northern cuisine. You can spend as little as 100 pesos or as much as 300 pesos, but the average bill is 150 to 225 pesos. Jukebox, fluorescent lights, hefty señoras—you might as well be in some small Sonoran ranching town.

Back to the café scene: There are two more very good choices, but the prices are a bit higher than the previously mentioned restaurants. At the corner of Hamburgo and Genova there's **Kineret**, where you can scarcely find room to sit down, especially at the outdoor tables. It's a delicatessen with an extensive menu including such items as borscht, chopped liver pate, herring, and blintzes. After 1 p.m. they offer dinner platters which range from 100 to 350 pesos. The liver-and-onions dinner, for instance, includes a choice of appetizer (the pâté is very nice), soup, dessert, and coffee.

Find your way to the passage at Londres 104, just off Geneva. Here you'll see outdoor cafés, art galleries, craft shops, and cappuccino drinkers. This is the heart of the Zona Rosa, and the home of the **Restaurant Toulouse Lautrec**, an outdoor café and restaurant. During the day many of Mexico's young artists and writers drop in here for a cappuccino, but the weekday lunch specials (200 pesos) are fine bargains—watermelon juice or vegetable soup; either breaded pork chops, green tomato enchiladas, or a ham omelet; frijoles (refried beans); custard, and coffee. À la carte items include a very fine—and huge—Mexican combination plate for 275 pesos. And it's a colorful place—red-checkered tableclothes over old-fashioned ice cream parlor tables with wire chairs. Open 9 a.m. to 1 a.m. They serve drinks (75 to 140 pesos), and have live entertainment in the evenings.

The specialty at **La Crepa Suiza** (tel. 511-3734), Florencia 33 between Hamburgo and Londres, is crêpes, of course, but that's not all. Diners crowd the few tables set out in the courtyard off Florencia, and the cozy indoor dining room, for a plentiful luncheon buffet costing 250 pesos served from 1 to 5 p.m. After that, you must order à la carte: dinner crêpes with various delicious stuffings cost 90 to 125 pesos, dessert crêpes are half that price. For more filling fare, you can't miss with the fondue bourguinonne: succulent morsels of beef which you can cook yourself in a pot of hot oil, and then dip into any of six different sauces. With garlic bread, the fondue is 520 pesos for two people. La Crepa Suiza is open for breakfast daily, as well.

Mexico's trade with Japan is burgeoning, as is the number of Japanese businessmen who visit the city. This has led to a healthy, and very welcome, growth in the number of restaurants serving Japanese cuisine. My favorite is the **Restaurant Tokyo** (tel. 525-3775), at Hamburgo 134, corner of Amberes, on the second floor. Be sure to glance at the "models" of sample meals set out in the glass cabinet by the entryway. Upstairs, the mood is soothing, with quiet Japanese Muzak and a spare but comely decor. You may not believe how friendly the staff is. Start with a "Princess Kiku," a refined rocket fuel made of sake and cherry liqueur, the sweetness fo the liqueur being cut by the sake's salt-bitterness. Sukiyaki, shabu shabu (vegetables in beef broth, cooked at your table), tempura, and sashimi (raw fish) are all offered. For best value, order one of the set meals (210 to 390 pesos). Even the cheapest is a treat. Open every day from 12:30 p.m. to midnight, Sunday from 2 to 10 p.m.

Another restaurant in the tried-and-true category is the **Restaurant Viena**, Amberes 4, just off Reforma. Amberes is a fashionable street with lots of interior-decorator and art shops, and for all this class the Viena is an unassuming little place with café tables and wood paneling. Recently the Viena has come under new management, and the menu now includes a few hard-to-find Jewish items such as matzoh-ball soup. But Viennese specialties such as stuffed cabbage and wienerschnitzel (200 pesos each) are still the mainstays. Menu in English. The Viena is open from 12:30 to 11 p.m. daily, 1 to 11 p.m. on Sunday.

Cafe Konditori, Genova 61, near Londres, is a lovely Danish coffeeshop that also serves light meals and breakfast (open 7 a.m. to midnight daily). There are outdoor tables here, and the front room is glassed in and looks out on the street. They have a good onion soup for 72 pesos. Sandwiches range from 80 to 105 pesos. Their pastries are excellent. Cappuccino is 24 pesos. This is quite an "in" spot so it will probably be busy any time you go. Breakfasts, by the way, cost 99, 135, and 175 pesos, the last being composed of two eggs, ham or bacon, fruit, a pot of coffee, bread and butter, and jam.

Shirley's, famous for its very pleasant and successful main location on Reforma, has a branch in the Pink Zone at Londres 102, open 7:30 a.m. to 11:30 p.m. daily, Friday and Saturday nights till 1 a.m. Vaguely western in decor following that at the main restaurant, diners sit in red booths or captain's chairs as they pore over the long menu of appetizers, soups, salads, sandwiches, Mexican specialties, meats, fish, side orders, and desserts. A Mexican combination plate is a filling and delicious meal in itself for 245 pesos; beef and vegetable pie is 195 pesos. Although it appears very American, Shirley's is patronized most heavily by Mexicans who know good food and service, and who want it at a reasonable prices. Note that here in the Pink Zone you can order wine with your dinner.

The **Meson del Perro Andaluz,** Copenhague 28, very near the Hotel Aristos, has two levels inside, a few outdoor tables (always crowded in the evenings), and a very loyal clientele. Although prices in the evening are fairly high, with such delicious things as duck in olive sauce *(pato a la aceituna)* and similar items going for 285 to 365 pesos, the luncheon specials (180 to 290 pesos) make it especially attractive for a midday meal. Try the tuna and avocado salad or a bowl of the hearty minestrone soup. Note that entrees come ungarnished (without vegetables or salad). They have wine, both Mexican and imported, but you'll pay a high 365 pesos for a half bottle. The Meson del Perro Andaluz is open from 1 p.m. to 1 a.m. daily; arrive early in the evening if you want a seat at one of the café tables out front.

FOR PIZZA: Pizza Real, Genova 28, at the corner of Estrasburgo, boasts that it serves 50 different varieties of pizza, priced at 24 to 78 pesos the piece, 130 to 416 pesos the medium-size pie, and 170 to 545 pesos the giant *real* ("king-size") pie which can serve eight people. They even serve a selection of five comidas corridas featuring soup, fruit salad, pizza, dessert, and coffee, or, in the more expensive comidas, an Italian entree such as ravioli. Although it is billed as a pizza joint, Pizza Real is half pizza parlor, half Italian restaurant, with wide black-and-white stripes on the brick walls, yellow tablecloths, and a pizza-cutting counter by the front door. It's open from 8 a.m. to 11:30 p.m. Monday through Saturday, 1 to 11:30 p.m. on Sunday.

FOR AFTERNOON TEA: The Zona Rosa would have to have some fine places for afternoon tea as they serve it on the continent, and the finest I've found yet is **Auseba,** Hamburgo 159-B at Florencia, which serves pastries and candies along with its tea and coffee. The glass cases hold the most delicious-looking display of cookies, meringues, bonbons, cakes, pies, puddings, and *tortas* I've ever seen in the city. Paintings decorate one wall, fancy candy boxes another, and the little circular tables with white cloths all have modern black plastic chairs—eclectic, but comfortable. Pastries cost about 65 pesos, coffee or tea is about half that much; you can get away with spending only 95 pesos (for coffee and croissants) or you can spend 160 pesos (for a rich pastry and Viennese coffee). Auseba is open daily for breakfast, and stays open until about 10:30 p.m. On Sunday, the hours are 11 a.m. to 10:30 p.m.

Very near Auseba, right on the corner of Florencia and Hamburgo, is the **Duca d'Este,** another *salon de the* with a rich decor, and prices to match.

STARVATION BUDGET: If all you want is a quick cheap snack, go to **Tacos Beatriz,** Londres 148. The Beatriz chain, founded in 1910, is to tacos what McDonald's is to you-know-what. The tacos range from 18 to 28 pesos each, and a filling, tasty guisado (stew) goes for 75 pesos. This lonchería is always busy, and people line up for tacos which the señoras still make by hand. Closed Sunday.

SPLURGE AND SPECIALTY RESTAURANTS: At least half our friends in Mexico swear that **Chalet Suizo,** Niza 37, between Hamburgo and Londres (tel. 511-7529), is the most dependable restaurant around. The decor is Swiss, of course, with checked tablecloths, enormous wooden horns, and Alpine landscapes; the service is very good. The menu features hearty French onion soup for 90 pesos and a wide range of interesting entrees, some of which are changed daily, for 135 to 275 pesos; among these are sausages with sauerkraut, smoked pork chops, baby veal tongue, sauerbraten, and excellent fondue. Wine is served, a half bottle of local wine costing 200 pesos. Open from about 12:30 p.m. to midnight daily. Menu in English.

If you crave a Yorkshire pudding, the place to go is the **Picadilly Pub** (tel. 514-1515), Copenhague 23, between Reforma and Hamburgo. Roast beef and Yorkshire pudding sell for 325 pesos—a bit steep, but you're paying for the snazz. Far swanker than the average English public house, it boasts such features as hunting prints, soft leather banquettes, an inner dining area called the Henry VIII Room, and a proprietor in a tuxedo. House specialties include Irish stew, and beefsteak-and-oyster pie, both priced at 235 pesos, and both excellent. On the lower end of things is the Welsh rarebit for 170 pesos.

The **Fonda El Refugio** (tel. 528-5823), Liverpool 166, near the corner of Liverpool and Amberes, is a very special place to dine *a la Mexicana*. Although small, it's unusually congenial with natural blond wood floors, a large fireplace decorated with gleaming copper pots and pans, and rows and rows of culinary awards and citations behind the desk. It manages the almost impossible task of being elegant and informal at the same time. Service is careful, efficient, and extremely polite, and the menu is one which runs the gamut of Mexican cuisine. You can run part-way by having a sopa de verduras (vegetable soup), then perhaps arroz con platanos (rice with fried bananas), or perhaps tamales de elote con pollo; for a main course, you can try the chalupas poblanas (tortillas topped with chicken, onions, cheese, lettuce, and green chile sauce), or perhaps enchiladas con mole poblano, topped with the rich, thick, spicy chocolate sauce of Puebla. Desserts are the authentic traditional ones, like sweet marzipan figurines and "camotes" (delicate cylinders of a flavorful sweet potato paste). Wine, liquor, and beer are served, and if you go all-out and order whatever you like, plus a half bottle of wine, the check should come to something like 500 to 700 pesos per person. You can dine for not much more than half that, though, if you like. The Fonda El Refugio is very popular, especially on a Saturday night, so get there early—remember, it's small.

For dining in the French manner, you can save some money and aggravation by seeking out **La Belle Époque** (tel. 525-8435), at Río Sena 45 near the corner of Nazas, on the north side of Reforma. Clearly, the decor here follows the name and so you'll see lots of turn-of-the-century plush and gilt, old photographs and tintypes, posters, and artifacts. Besides the several comfy interior dining rooms (once parlors in a converted house), La Belle Époque has a beautiful garden dining area in the rear, with a tremendous birdcage, vines and flowers, and awnings to protect diners from Mexico City's unpredictable afternoon showers. The chef is a veritable Frenchman (don't laugh, few are!) who knows what good onion soup is—it comes loaded with cheese for 120 pesos. The daily special at lunch costs between 220 and 340 pesos, and could be anything from a delectable red snapper through tournedos béarnaise to conejo (rabbit) done with a special touch. An exceptional treat here, because the chef worked for some years in North Africa, is a fine couscous (served Thursday and Sunday only). French wines can be had, but they're expensive at about 520 to 975 pesos the bottle; better to stick with the very good selection of Mexican wines for around 350 pesos. La Belle Époque is open 1 p.m. to midnight daily except Saturday; lunchtime is busiest because of the embassy crowd, and dinnertime is more relaxed and quiet. Highly recommended.

Luau (tel. 525-7474), Niza 38, is a Chinese-Polynesian restaurant in the heart of the Zona Rosa and its prices reflect it. But the food is excellent and sometimes nothing else will taste as good as sweet-and-sour pork spare ribs or wonton soup. Combination dinners cost anywhere from 215 to 450 pesos. It's an attractive restaurant with a goldfish pond, rock garden with a waterfall, and other amusements. Open noon to midnight.

La Gondola, Genova 21, has a posh atmosphere of stained-glass windows, beamed ceiling, thick carpets, and a maître d' in tuxedo who cooks the spaghetti in a chafing dish at your table. A popular place for lunch with well-heeled businessmen and Mexico City's elegant women who shop in the area, yet the prices aren't staggering. Most Italian meat entrees—chicken tetrazzini, breaded veal cutlet—run 210 to 235 pesos. For a light lunch I can recommend their hearty minestrone soup (72 pesos) and a Caesar salad (90 pesos). Open 1 p.m. to midnight daily.

NORTH OF REFORMA: The area north of Reforma and south of Melchor Ocampo is mostly residential, so there is not a great number of restaurants. Among the few, the best for your money is the **Restaurant Rhin**, Río Rhin 49 at Río Panuco, one of those terrific little neighborhood restaurants every travel writer dreams of discovering. The Rhin is a modern place. The tables are dressed in red, the waiters are in natty black and white uniforms. I always try to order the 100-peso comida, but one look at the menu and I invariably weaken in favor of the Rhin's enchiladas Suizas, a little triumph of tortillas in a creamy sauce stuffed with Swiss cheese for 70 pesos. Needless to say, they're soothing to pepper-pricked tummies, besides being delightfully tasty. There are plenty of other Mexican plates—lots of tacos, etc.—as well as such comforts as soup, hotcakes, and french toast for about 65 pesos. Open 8:30 a.m. to 9:30 p.m.

On the same street, tucked away in the area of the British Embassy, is the little **Cafeteria Marianne**, Río Rhin 63, a few blocks north of the Reforma-Insurgentes intersection (tel. 528-7289), where the atmosphere is European-coffeehouse and the specialty is pastries and cappuccino, but they also serve an excellent three-course lunch for 90 pesos. Open 9 a.m. to 9 p.m. daily.

Las Fuentes (tel. 525-0629), at Tiber and Panuco, two blocks north of the Angel Monument, is another branch of the "Restaurant Vegetariano y Dietetico." This is the most modern and luxurious of the three, filling the ground floor of a hotel building. More expensive than the other two, it's still well worth the money you pay for what you get. The daily set-price lunch costs 285 pesos, but huge portions are the rule, and for that price you may enjoy lentil soup, carrot- and potato-filled tacos with apple salad, a side order of peas or beans, then coffee or tea and whole-wheat-and-honey cookies. Las Fuentes is open daily from 8:30 a.m. to 11:30 p.m., till 10:30 p.m. on Sunday. Highly recommended.

A Pastelería-Deli

North of Reforma, at the corner of Río Lerma and Río Sena, is a handy pastryshop-deli, just the thing for do-it-yourself breakfasts and snacks. The **Del**

Angel has one of the best assortments of rolls, danishes, cookies, cold meats, and drinks I've encountered in the capital. Prices are a bit higher than at pastelerías in less wealthy sections, but you can still make a paper bag heavy with goodies here and pay less than 100 pesos. By the way, the full name of this place has got to establish some sort of record for length. According to the sign, it's the "Dulcería, Pastelería, Bizcochería, Salchichonería, Abarrotes Vinos y Licores Gastronómica Del Angel"!

Cheap Eats

Cheap eats in Mexico usually means tacos, and at **El Caminero Tacos al Carbon** you'll find three cooks very busily chopping and filling to make a dozen different types. A plate of three tacos costs 66 pesos; a beer, only 30 pesos. The counters are usually crowded with hungry taco munchers who come for the good food, low prices, and clean, attractive atmosphere. El Caminero is north of Reforma, at Calle Río Lerma 138, near the intersection with Río Po.

3. Near Jardín del Arte / Revolución

The Pink Zone siphons off the carriage trade from surrounding areas, and what's left are mostly little eateries good for breakfast or incredibly inexpensive comidas corridas. Out on Reforma are a few classier places, including the dependably satisfying Shirley's—but more of that later. First, for some cheap lunches.

NEAR THE JARDÍN: The **Restaurant America**, on Villalongin facing Sullivan Park, half a block in from Insurgentes, serves a 150-peso comida that's worth every centavo and more. The small room (eight tables only) is almost always close to full with diners-who-know. Our test meal started with delicious mushroom soup, went on to "espaguetti ala francesa" (spaghetti with a sauce of cheese and butter), a choice of three main-course dishes—beef, pork, or chicken—ice cream or good pastry, and coffee or tea. Such a feast is served daily between 1 and 5:15 p.m.

If you're staying in this area, or find yourself near the intersection of Reforma and Insurgentes, walk west along Villalongin (which skirts the southern edge of Sullivan Park), turn left and walk through the little plaza bearing a bust of Giuseppe Verdi, and you'll come to the Calle Río Lerma. A half block southwest on Lerma, on the right-hand side, is the **Restaurant Nucleo**, Río Lerma 5 at the corner of Río Marne, a small and simple restaurant worth a walk because of its two daily comidas corridas, one costing 70 pesos; the other, 90 pesos. For the lower price you might get a cream soup, rice, charcoal-grilled beef, frijoles, and dessert; for the higher price you get a wider selection of main courses and slightly larger portions. The Nucleo is very popular with young office workers, and is sometimes crowded, but seats seem to come available quickly, and sharing tables with strangers is the custom here. The restaurant is open for breakfast and supper as well, but it's closed Sunday. By the way, two other, similar eateries with similar prices are within a half block of the Nucleo, one of these being the café-restaurant in the Hotel Maria Angelo's.

Giorgio's Cafe y Arte, Villalongin at Río Marne, is well located to catch the crowds from Sunday's open-air art show in Sullivan Park. Totally modern in decor, Giorgio's serves up very old-fashioned pastry treats and freshly brewed coffee. Breakfast is served from 8 to 11:30 a.m. daily; after that, select a caloric atom bomb from one of the pastry cases and, with coffee, you'll pay

100 to 180 pesos. Good! They serve pizzas, salads, and beer along with the baklava.

A Good Little Japanese Place

Daruma, a Japanese restaurant not far from the intersection of Insurgentes and Reforma at Río Tamesis 6 (where Tamesis meets Finlay and Villalongin), is a bit hard to find but worth the effort. Informal as can be, the boys cook behind the sashimi bar while mom tots up the bills and makes change. The lunch counter and small tables are of heavy natural wood, however, and like the rest of the simple furnishings impart a good deal of dignity to the proceedings. The food is good, and even if you're not familiar with Japanese cuisine, here you can safely order what your neighbor's having and come out alright. The specialty of the house is tori-katsu, boned chicken breast stuffed with vegetables and with noodles. Sashimi is more expensive, but prices are not outrageous: about 112 to 210 pesos per order. You can dine at Daruma from 1 p.m. to midnight every day but Saturday.

NEAR REVOLUCIÓN MONUMENT: Even cheaper, and convenient to the hotels on and near Calle Edison, is the **Cafe Rosales,** Rosales 13 between Edison and Mariscal/Badillo, just off Reforma. Crema de elote (bean soup), barbecued spare ribs, frijoles refritos, dessert, and coffee make up a normal 90-peso comida corrida, which you consume while sitting in a cozy booth. Stop in at the Rosales for lunch on your way back to your hotel from sightseeing in the Alameda–Zócalo area. Closed Sunday.

It is hard to beat the America and the Rosales, but I think the **Covadonga** can come a close third. Located near the Plaza de la República at Edison 57, on the corner of Alcazar, it offers friendly service as well as a very good comida for 145 pesos. They're open for breakfast as early as 7 a.m.: a full breakfast is about 150 pesos.

A bit of alpine Europe is yours just off the Plaza de la República at the **Cafeteria Monique,** Vallarta 7. An Austrian ambience, a lofty ceiling with lots of light, a glass case full of cookies and cakes, and various sorts of coffee make this a good spot for an afternoon refresher. You can buy the cookies by the kilo if you're starving, but just a few, plus a cup of brew, will come to 60 pesos or so.

Taco Row

Antonio Caso, a street running east and west between Insurgentes and Vallarta, is loaded with little *fogatas,* or hole-in-the-wall eateries where you can pick up a cheap breakfast or a luncheon snack of tacos or tortas. **El Taco de Oro,** at Antonio Caso 30, is run by an efficient señora and several young fellows who keep their customers happy with a 58-peso breakfast of two eggs, a choice of ham, sausage or bacon, a bizcocho (croissant-type roll), and coffee. For lunch or supper they sell positively huge tacos (two is all you'll need) made with meat, tomato, onion, lettuce, and *hot* chiles for 45 pesos (ask for yours *sin chiles,* without peppers), a smaller version of the same for a bit less. Tortas are similar concoctions made with bolillos (bread rolls). The Torta Especial comes with the works (avocado included). Closed Sunday.

ALONG REFORMA: Right on Reforma, northeast of the Insurgentes intersection, are two cafeteria-type restaurants, both noted for their good food and comfortable atmosphere. First of these is **Shirley's,** on the east side of the street at Reforma 108 (open 7:30 a.m. to 11:30 p.m. daily, Saturday till 1 a.m.). Shirley's is the epitome of efficiency, from the navy-blazer'd maître d' to the light-blue-uniformed waiters and waitresses; everything runs smoothly, and the atmosphere is one of order and friendliness—a good bet for anyone who's homesick. In fact, from first (a glass of water brought automatically) to last (the check says "Please Pay the Cashier") Shirley's shows its American heritage. You can start the day with waffles or the house special, English muffins with cheese and ham; for lunch try a hamburger—any of these dishes will cost about 100 pesos. Air-conditioned, open early and late, open Sunday—a very pleasant place!

On your way to a day's sightseeing, you might want to drop in at **La Calesa,** Reforma 36 near the intersection with Antonio Caso, for a spot of breakfast. The huevos motulenos, for instance, consists of two tortillas topped by two eggs covered with ham, cheese, peas, frijoles; and fried bananas. This costs 95 pesos, but most other items are somewhat less. A simply enormous glass of fresh-squeezed fruit juice costs 40 pesos. The daily comida corrida is a budget-pleasing 155 pesos, and with it comes the view of the action on busy Reforma, seen through plate-glass windows. La Calesa's open Monday through Friday from 8 a.m. to 9 p.m., on Saturday to 5 p.m.; closed Sunday.

4. Near the Alameda and Bellas Artes

The center of the downtown area is a particularly good place to look for a good, inexpensive comida corrida. The rich concentration of banks and businesses means lots and lots of hungry office workers must be served. Competition for the trade is stiff.

Along the south side of the Alameda, on the bank streets between Bucareli and Lázaro Cárdenas, are numerous restaurants, some old and well established, others new and modern. For a pleasant, relaxing comida corrida in the moderate price range I can recommend these special places.

THE BEST ALL-AROUND PLACES: Perhaps the best all-around restaurant in this area is also the most convenient. It's the **Restaurant Rhin,** Juarez 36-C, facing the Bellas Artes. From the street all one sees is the sign, a tiny doorway, a crowd of munchers, and a lunch counter. But read the comida menus (there are always two) posted at the doorway, go down the passage to the warren of dining rooms, and you'll find good food, moderate prices, careful service, and long hours (it's open till late, even on Sunday). Start with caldo Tlalpeño, a stew of chicken broth and meat, vegetables, and chiles; then have carne asada a la Tampiqueña (tender strips of grilled beef with a half-dozen garnishes) and a beer for 350 pesos. The comidas are much cheaper, usually 150 and 200 pesos.

One of the best long-standing restaurants is **Sorrento,** in the arcade of the Banco de Industria y Comercio building which runs between Azueta and Balderas, just south of Juarez near the southwest corner of the Alameda. There's a large sign on Azueta so you shouldn't have any trouble finding it. This is a businessmen's eating house, complete with comfortable red leather chairs and white-jacketed waiters. The place is always busy but the service remains excellent nonetheless. They offer a very good comida (all those businessmen, remember) for 200 pesos with a selection of appetizer, soup (the cream of asparagus is especially good), an entree which comes with vegetable and pasta, dessert, and coffee. They also have à la carte items with some Italian specials like lasagne (very tasty) and cannelloni for 125 to 200 pesos.

One of the lowest priced and most filling comidas corridas in town is served daily at **Los Faroles,** Luis Moya 41, one block from Independencia. It's a big, busy place littered with tables and chairs, with several chefs toiling away at a central grill and kitchen. Tacos are the forte, and the comida may well include a few of these. The price for the set lunch is 115 pesos.

One of the most teeming restaurants during comida-time (1 to 4 p.m.) is the **Restaurant Danubio,** Uruguay 3 at Lázaro Cárdenas, which has a huge 220-peso lunch that is practically an institution. The restaurant itself is big and old-fashioned, its high ceiling carved and hung with wrought-iron lanterns. There's nearly always a marimba playing at the doorway during the lunch hours, but shoulder your way through the crowd and find a table. A typical comida consists of a shrimp or oyster cocktail, maybe Valencia soup or tomato consommé, boiled lentils, a choice of a hot or cold fish dish, a choice of three entrees, custard or fruit, and coffee or tea. The à la carte menu is extensive, but you get better service during the busy time if you stick to the comida corrida. They serve cocktails, wine, and beer. There is also a room upstairs to accommodate the lunchtime overflow, although many in the overflow don't know it, so you may find more breathing space aloft. Open 1 p.m. to midnight daily.

Note: The house specialty is langostinos (baby crawfish) and well worth the splurge!

OTHER GOOD PLACES: The above are my favorites, having a special flavor of Mexico City not found everywhere. Now I'll describe a few more finds which, while they don't have the special feeling of the aforementioned establishments, still give you good, inexpensive, food in clean, although perhaps mundane, surroundings.

A very busy café which serves the office community all day long is **Mi Pebeta Cafeteria,** Humbolt 62, just north of Guerra in the YWCA building. I like this place every time I go back; it's nothing fancy but the red and white checkered tablecloths give a bit of a European flair. The service is friendly and the food is good. The comida costs 95 pesos and includes soup, main course, refried beans, dessert, and coffee. Most à la carte items range between 60 and 85 pesos. The cheese omelet is good. Also open for breakfast. Closed Thursday.

The **Restaurant Guajalote,** a half block south of Juarez on Dolores (no number), which is just one street west of Lopez, has an ordinary atmosphere—just a number of booths and tables covered with tablecloths. On the right is a food bar and the smells are certainly tempting. The 130-peso comida includes juice, soup, rice, main dish, dessert, and coffee; most Mexican plates are fairly expensive, but breakfasts are cheap. No English menu. Long hours: from 8 a.m. to 2 a.m. daily.

Heading down Calle Revillagigedo, you'll pass two good restaurants. The first, **Hi-Lo Restaurant,** Revillagigedo 40-B, just below Articulo, is owned by an American couple who by this time are a long-established señor y señora. An attractive place, with a big front opening (no door), it's exceptionally clean and tidy and specializes in American-type food with a Mexican touch. The set lunch costs 125 pesos, and is likely to consist of fruit cocktail, spinach or chicken soup, rice, choice of roast beef, pork chops, fish, liver, or veal (lots of choices), plus dessert and coffee. Set meals served after 1 p.m. À la carte entrees are available all day. Open 8 a.m. to 6 p.m., closed Sunday.

MEXICO CITY: RESTAURANTS

STARVATION BUDGET: All over Mexico are phenomenally cheap working-class eateries that could almost be classified as soup kitchens. They're called *taquerías* or *fogatas* ("cookfires") and are much patronized by families who find it cheaper to eat here than to cook at home. Sometimes they're dives, so it's best to look them over carefully and test them gingerly. Also note that no English will be spoken, so know your Spanish menu.

The **Lonchería "Los 2 Pericos"** located at Donceles 2, just two blocks north of the Bellas Artes and near the corner of Avenida Lázaro Cárdenas, is a restaurant with two parts. The fruitería sells every imaginable sort of fruit (22 varieties). Licuados made from the fruit cost 13 to 26 pesos, depending on the size: the vaso (glass) is small; copa (goblet) is the large size. Try the guanabana, with a taste somewhere between that of a pear and a lichee-fruit. The other part of the place serves tacos and tostados made of grilled or roasted meat, onions, and other nice things. There's a huge wooden bowl of pickled carrots, peppers, and chiles, and all in all it's a mouthwatering sight. But watch what you order, for some of their tacos are not for the squeamish: cabeza (head), ubre (udder), tripe, lengua (tongue), and various other organs are all offered. There are more conventional stuffings as well, including Milanesa (veal), cecina (dried beef), and salchicha (sausage). Prices vary according to the filling, but are generally 13 to 36 pesos for tacos or tostadas. It's a bargain, and the beautiful wall tiles give you more than your pesos-worth of taco enjoyment: the place stays open all day.

SPECIALTY RESTAURANTS: For something out of the ordinary, this is a rich area as well. Herewith, my recommendations for dining places when you crave something a little different.

For Seafood

If you can't get down to Acapulco but you still want to wet your whistle with some of the sumptuous fish found in the Pacific, head for the **Restaurant Nuevo Acapulco,** Lopez 9, a half block south of Juarez. They have a handsome display of fresh fish on the counter, a crocodile hanging on the wall in front of you, and a turtle on your right. Although neither of the latter two is served, there is a wide range of soups in the 100-peso range (125 pesos for oyster stew with 24 oysters), and fish entrees are 170 to 225 pesos. The highest price on the menu is for lobster. Their camarones (shrimp) are fresh and flavorful, and they make an excellent camarones-and-cheese casserole. Although the food here is excellent, the prices have more than doubled over the past few years, and all sorts of seafood have become luxury items. The restaurant has three rooms which are kept busy and full (mostly with businessmen and others who can pay a bit more). If you're dying for good fish, by all means go to the Acapulco, but note that it's not all that inexpensive.

For Chinese Fare

There is a small Chinese section in Mexico City located on Dolores between Independencia and Articulo 123. The best of the restaurants here is the **Shanghai,** a few doors up from Articulo at Dolores 30. Numerous salons open off the entrance and during the lunch hour they are almost always full. The food here is good but the prices are high for what you get—but then, if you're in the mood for Chinese food nothing else will usually do. They offer a series of combination plates for one to four persons ranging from 235 to 540 pesos per person. The last time I ate there I got two 280-peso lunches which included a quite good noodle soup, spare ribs (costilla al horno), fried shrimp (only two, unfortunately), fried rice, beef chow mein, and of course a full pot of good Chinese tea. The à la carte items are high at 160 pesos for egg foo yung with chicken, even more for the chop sueys. Open from noon to midnight.

Another nice little Chinese restaurant, outside Chinatown and nearer the Alameda, is **Howah,** at Humboldt 23, just *north* of Juarez: tidy glass-and-aluminum facade, simple but neat interior, efficient service, and a set-price Chinese comida corrida for 225 pesos.

An Architectural Landmark

From the Bellas Artes, walk to Avenida Madero and the **Sanborn House of Tiles** ("Casa de Azulejos"). This gorgeous antique building was once the palace of the Counts of the Valley of Orizaba, but now houses a branch of the Sanborn's restaurant-and-variety store chain. Dining tables are set in an elaborate courtyard complete with carved stone pillars, tiles, and peacock frescoes. It's a lovely place for a rest and a cup of coffee with some apple pie à la mode, but even this modest snack is relatively expensive here. Coffee (a little pot) is 24 pesos; eggs with bacon are 110 pesos. If you dine, order a daily special, which gives you the best value (125, 145, and 210 pesos).

A Vegetarian Place

I can't say enough good things about the food at the **Restaurante Vegeteriano y Dietetico,** Madero 56 not far from the Zócalo. There's no sign on the sidewalk, so look for a stairway marked **Panella,** or the menu posted outside on the entrance, walk one flight up, and you'll enter the restaurant. The decor is nothing special but the food is fantastic, and they have a piano player who plunks out Oldies-but-Goodies while you feast on the 130-peso comida (or one with gigantic portions for just slightly more). As the name implies, they serve no meat, but you can easily have your fill starting with a huge salad (watercress, tomato, radishes, grated carrot, and beets), followed by superb cream of tomato soup, a choice of two entrees (berengena empanizada, or breaded eggplant; ensalada trigo, or bulghur salad), a delicious cake made of whole wheat and honey, served with coffee or tea. This place is good—you must try it yourself to appreciate it. Menu in Spanish only; open every day except Sunday from noon to 6 p.m. There's another Vegeteriano at Filomata 17, between 5 de Mayo and Madero, five blocks west of the Zócalo.

Hot Chocolate and Churros

Those interested only in a snack at lunchtime should head for **El Moro,** Avenida Lázaro Cárdenas 42, at Uruguay. A man in the window turns out fresh doughnut-type treats called churros or estillos, which he then smothers in sugar and serves piping hot. The churros are offered in combination with hot chocolate (the best and richest chocolate I've ever tasted): 45 to 48 pesos for the delectable hot chocolate and a plate of four churros, or 30 pesos for the plate of churros plus coffee and milk. Try it—an authentic *churrería* is a bit of true Mexico City daily life.

Best Coffee in Town

One of the oldest establishments in town is the **Cafe La Habana,** on the corner of Morelos and Bucareli. The cavernous interior reverberates with the sound of clinking glasses and tinkling silver as businessmen and local folk have breakfast and enjoy the best coffee in town. In the front as you enter is a coffee-roasting machine which is whirling to ensure that the coffee is the freshest. I always bring home bags of their coffee to the delight of my friends.

5. In the Zócalo Area

Here's my roundup of restaurants and cafés in and near the Zócalo, an area extending westward almost to Avenida Lázaro Cárdenas.

The **Cafe La Blanca** on 5 de Mayo between Motolinía and Católica is a large cafeteria-style place with two levels. There is no decor to speak of but the fare is good as is attested by the teeming business that they do from 7 a.m. to midnight, every day of the week. They serve only à la carte items but with daily specials: huachinango (red snapper) or jumbo shrimp for about 175 pesos, meat dishes for 80 to 200 pesos, sandwiches and salads for 70 to 125 pesos. You cannot go wrong eating here.

The **Cafe de Tacuba,** on Tacuba at no. 28 very near the Metro station, looks as though it's been here on this street in Mexico City since the city began—or, at least for a hundred years or so. The wainscoting in the two long dining rooms is of orange, white, blue faíence; the lamps are of brass, dark and brooding oil paintings share wall space with a large mural of several nuns working in a kitchen (maybe it was here from the time of Cortez, at least?). The waitresses wear white uniforms with matching caps, and they're on duty every day from 8 a.m. to midnight. Soups here cost 50 to 65 pesos, with the top price going to cream of asparagus with biscuits; grilled chicken and most meat dishes are 140 to 200 pesos, but such things as enchiladas and chilaquiles con crema are cheaper. Rather than the customary comida corrida, the Cafe de Tacuba offers a selection of daily lunch plates, served with soup, costing 300 to 380 pesos. The best is the last, however, as a tempting selection of what certainly look to be homemade cakes and pastries wait in a glass case near the front of the restaurant. Wine, beer, and liquor are served. You won't believe it, but the Tacuba dates from 1912.

Some of the cheapest and best Mexican food in the city is yours at **El Rincon Mexicano,** Uruguay 27 between Avenida Lázaro Cárdenas and Bolívar. Plain, but clean and bright with a nice tiled grill, El Rincon offers a menu on which few items are priced above 55 pesos. The daily comida corrida is somewhat spartan, but an indisputable bargain for only 70 or 95 pesos: chicken consommé or cream of asparagus soup, rice or spaghetti, grilled bananas or chicharrón (that's pork crackling), and a choice of nine main courses. Something is sure to be right on, from Virginia ham to chicken casserole, from pork chops with chiles to three different types of enchiladas. Dessert and coffee are included in the ridiculously low price.

Are you up for a walk? If you go five blocks south of Madero on Isabel la Católica to no. 72, between El Salvador and Mesones, your reward will be a fine lunch or dinner at the **Restaurante Rebeca.** A big place with colorful red-and-white cloths on the tables, the Rebeca specializes in good food, big portions, and lots of variety. At lunchtime the 180-peso comida gives you a choice of several appetizers, two kinds of soup, six different main courses, and four desserts—almost as though you were ordering from an expensive à la carte list. Relax and enjoy it.

FOR BREAKFAST: The least expensive breakfast is the breakfast you make yourself by picking up rolls and pastries from the **Panificadora Novedades,**

Bolívar 78. It opens at 7 a.m., in plenty of time for you to drop by, pick up the goodies, and find a congenial café.

STARVATION BUDGET: For those after an adventure while keeping to a tight budget I have an ideal spot: the **Comedor Familiar,** located at Carranza 105 just off Pino Suarez. To get to the restaurant walk through the leather shop arcade, turn right, go through a double door, climb a flight of stairs, walk past the busy kitchen, and wait for a seat (this place gets a lot of business). There are three rooms packed with Mexicans (not a single foreigner) after 1 p.m. waiting for their 75-peso comida which includes soup, rice, main course, frijoles, pastry, and coffee. You can't beat it!

For the smaller, cheaper *taquerías* (taco shops), go to Uruguay between Bolívar and Avenida Lázaro Cárdenas. The street is lined with places offering 65- to 95-peso comidas, with the general fare being soup, pasta, main course, frijoles, dessert, and coffee. The cleanest of the lot appears to be at Uruguay 25, and I can attest to the quality of the señora's homemade tortillas.

TWO SPECIAL PLACES: Walk northeast of the Zócalo, through dingy streets, to find **Las Cazuelas,** Columbia 69 (just down from Carmen), housed in a beautiful 18th-century tiled mansion. The dreariness of the street disappears as you enter Las Cazuelas, for you are surrounded by beautiful wall tiles, hand-painted chairs, and a lively group of mariachis. The kitchen, which is immediately visible when you enter, is lined with large earthen pots and casseroles, and thus the name *las cazuelas*. This place is always swinging (especially on a Sunday when the whole family is out for a good time) and it's no wonder, considering the prices they charge: 170 to 265 pesos for most items, which are distinctly Mexican, like costilla de res (grilled beef ribs), cabrito al horno (roast kid), chicharrón (pork crackling) with guacamole. There is no English menu here and the waiters do not speak English, so you'll have to know your Spanish menu. A full meal, with drinks, for two people will be between 500 and 700 pesos, including tip. Highly recommended! Open daily noon to midnight, but the best time to come is late afternoon between 2 and 6.

A bit higher in class and price is the **Hostería de Santo Domingo,** said to be the oldest restaurant in the city still in operation (established 1860). It is located at Dominguez 72 just east of Rep. de Chile. The place has been redecorated lately so a lot of the antiquity is gone, replaced by bright walls, a few plants, and 20th-century murals. The à la carte prices are low—many entrees between 90 and 190 pesos—and the food's excellent. Try, for example, the stuffed peppers with cheese, pork loin, or the unusual bread soup. Note that the Santo Domingo is best for lunch—it's dead in the evening.

A DELICATESSEN: The Mexican equivalent of a deli is a shop that sells *productos ultramarinos* (imported goods). Although it's not a deli as we know it, **La Villa de Madrid** (tel. 512-3782), Uruguay 36 at the corner of Bolívar, still has a tempting assortment of hard-to-find goodies in its sidewalk windows, with more inside. (Don't confuse the deli entrance with the nearby grubby cantina of the same name.) Imported liquor—everything from Schlitz to Dom Perignon—cookies, crackers, nuts, cheese, and cold meats are sold daily, 9 a.m. to 9 p.m.; closed Sunday.

To fill out your picnic basket, cross Bolívar and right there is the **Rostic- ería Italiana,** where a freshly roasted chicken will set you back only 300 pesos.

READERS' RESTAURANT SELECTIONS—ZÓCALO AREA: "We found a clean bakery and eating establishment right around the corner from the Hotel Monte Carlo at 5 de Febrero no. 25, corner of Uruguay. It's the **Cafeteria Madrid,** and it has very inexpensive croissants, several kinds of juices, and dishes such as huevos rancheros and chiles rellenos for about 50 or 60 pesos. The owner speaks English and is very friendly; open 7:30 a.m. to 9:30 p.m." (Stan Peyton, no address given). . . . "A new place I went for breakfast is the **Cafeteria Restaurant Sienra's.** It has good coffee, good food, and good prices. It is right below the Zócalo on 20 de Noviembre near Uruguay" (Marc Killinger, Philadelphia, Pa.). . . . "Near the Zócalo we recommend a plain but busy place, the **Cafe Fornos,** that has a long menu, fast service, and medium-low prices. It's on the east side of Bolívar between Cinco de Mayo and Madero" (Rev. Edgar and Mrs. Phyllis Peara, Wilmette, Ill.).

"The **Restaurant Borda,** Madero 27 (tel. 512-2797), which you enter around the corner on Bolívar, has the best comida in this 'city of palaces'—appetizer, broth or soup, main course, salad, basket of various breads, coffee, and dessert for about 190 pesos. It has a very old-fashioned, sedate, quiet atmosphere, with older men as the attentive waiters and established bourgeois and professors as the clients" (Sergio D. Elizondo and Szilvia Nagy Vajda, Las Cruces, N.M.).

Chapter IX

MEXICO CITY: DAYTIME ACTIVITIES

                              1. **A Walk Around Town**
                  2. **Museums in the Downtown Area**
                                3. **Outdoor Markets**
                            4. **Arts and Crafts Shops**
               5. **Chapultepec Park and Its Museums**
                  6. **Attractions on the Outskirts**
               7. **The Bullfights and Horse Races**

NOW THAT YOU'RE comfortably installed in one of the world's most exciting cities, and you have absorbed enough of the preceding chapters to be able to find your way around, you'll be eager to begin delving into the life of Mexico City. This chapter will concentrate on the inexpensive activities available to you, or at least the more inexpensive ways to do those things that inevitably cost money—like going to the horse races.

You'll find that in Mexico even such routine activities as walking in the park are fraught with unexpected and delightful surprises, and even an ordinary stroll around any of the city's markets will offer you the opportunity to admire dozens of exotic items unavailable in the markets at home.

A final point: In the summer, always take along a raincoat when you venture out in the afternoon. The rain comes at between 2 and 4 p.m. every day, so predictably that you can almost set your watch by it. In winter carry a jacket or sweater: stone-built museums are cold inside, and when the sun goes down, the outside air gets chilly. We'll start in the most economical way possible, on a do-it-yourself tour, on foot.

1. A Walk Around Town

Much of what you'll want to see and do in Mexico City will be found along two main arteries, **Reforma** and **Juarez**, good points of reference for anything downtown.

The **Paseo de la Reforma** (Reforma for short) heads northeast from Chapultepec Park, past the fashionable shopping, restaurant, and hotel district known as the Zona Rosa ("Pink Zone"). The **Independence Monument**, a gilded angel high on a pillar above a traffic circle in Reforma, is sometimes used as a symbol for this romantic city. Just about everyone calls it the Angel

Monument, or simply the Angel, and it's a good point of reference itself, being about a third of the way up Reforma to Avenida Juarez. Two-thirds of the way along Reforma is the intersection with **Insurgentes**, the major north-south artery. Past Insurgentes a ways is the intersection with **Avenida Juarez**, the other main artery you need to know. At this intersection is the art deco **National Lottery Building**, another landmark. To the west a block is the Monument to the Revolution, an art deco behemoth which looks as though it should be sheltering an Eternal Flame, but isn't. To the east from the intersection of Reforma and Juarez is yet another National Lottery Building, this one modern glass-and-steel rather than the original art deco tower. Here, at the beginning of Avenida Juarez, is where you begin your walk.

Heading east along Juarez, you'll pass on your right what *used* to be the offices of the Secretariat of Tourism. There is still an information booth of sorts in the lobby, and the offices of *Gobernación* (Interior) and *Migración* (the Immigration Service) are still here. You will have to deal with them if you have Tourist Card troubles. (The new Tourism offices are fairly inaccessible, located out in the Polanco section.)

Soon on your left you'll come upon the **Alameda Central**, a beautiful park good at all times of the day for a quiet stroll to collect your thoughts. The large white marble semicircle of columns fronting on Juarez is the **Juarez Monument**. The poor Zapotec Indian boy from Oaxaca who became a lawyer, and then president of the Republic, and then vanquisher of Maximilian and the Napoleonic force sits grandly here, virtually enthroned, as angels crown him with a laurel wreath. While you're right here, take the time to cross the street and take a turn through the Hotel Del Prado's lobby.

Main reason for the last-mentioned is the Del Prado's famous mural *A Sunday Dream at the Alameda Park*, 50 feet long and 13 feet high, painted by Diego Rivera in 1947. The mural, if you can figure it out, shows all the personalities who have gone through the park since Hernan Cortes.

This section of Avenida Juarez is also a prime area for crafts shops, details of which are given below in Section 4. While you're right here, you may want to refer to that section and drop in to some of these fascinating stores.

THE BELLAS ARTES: At the east end of the Alameda is the Palacio de las Bellas Artes (that's "BEY-ahs ARR-tess"), the supreme achievement of art deco lyricism, which, aside from being the concert hall, also houses permanent and traveling art shows. You can visit the galleries free of charge Tuesday to Sunday from 11 a.m. to 7 p.m. There are galleries on both the first and second levels which exhibit temporary shows. I have seen a number of exhibits here, all of them excellent: a delightful Rumanian art show; works by a Mexican-Hungarian, Gunther Gerzso, whose use of texture and contrasting colors creates a particular intensity of depth in his paintings; Carlos Merida's Braque-like cubism . . . and the list goes on. If you like galleries then by all means stop by to see what is being exhibited; it will certainly give you an opportunity to see art which is rarely shown in the U.S.

On the third level are the famous murals by Rivera, Orozco, and Siqueiros; they simply surpass your wildest imagination, so by all means go to see them. So much emotion and human struggle has been painted into the work! Don't miss Rivera's mural *Man in Control of his Universe*, which is a copy of the one commissioned for Rockefeller Center in New York in 1933 and later painted over because of its leftist views. There are four rooms off the corridor which contain some excellent paintings by Mexican artists from the late 19th century to the present.

There is a monthly listing of art activities in *La Semana de Bellas Artes*, which can be obtained free at the Bellas Artes. All cultural events of the Museum of Modern Art, the National Auditorium, Teatro del Bosque, San Carlos Museum, and the Bellas Artes are listed in this bulletin.

Note: Another major north-south street passes along the east side of the Bellas-Artes: now called the Avenida Lázaro Cárdenas (since 1980), for many years its name was Avenida San Juan de Letran. On some maps you'll no doubt still see this name used.

Another sort of street-name confusion you'll encounter in Mexico City, and indeed throughout all Mexico, is that streets change names after only a few blocks, or there will be no street signs whatever. It's also fairly common to find two or even more street numbers on the same building, the result of successive reorganizations. (In Cuernavaca I once found a building with *five* different numbers ranging from 3 to 547!)

LA TORRE LATINOAMERICANA (Latin American Tower): A true bird's-eye view of the city is to be had from the Observation Deck of the Torre Latinoamericana, the Latin American Tower, soaring above the intersection of Juarez and Cárdenas.

Buy a ticket for the deck (open 10 a.m. to midnight every day) at the booth as you approach the elevators—admission fee is 50 pesos; tokens for the telescope up top are on sale here, too. You then take an elevator to the 37th floor, cross the hall, and take another elevator to the 42nd floor. A man will ask for your ticket as you get off.

The view is magnificent. Mountains surround the capital on all sides, but those to the north are the nearest, and Avenida Lázaro Cárdenas seems to head for them straight as an arrow. To the north just below is the marble pile of the Bellas Artes, and west of it, the green patch of the Alameda. Due west is the Monument to the Revolution, just beyond the intersection of Juarez and Reforma. You can't see Reforma too well because it's hidden by the buildings which line it, but the green swath of Chapultepec Park and its palace on the hilltop are easy to spot. To the east is the Zócalo, dominated by the cathedral. To the south is an area densely packed with homes, factories, and tall apartment buildings.

Climb the spiral staircase two flights—if it's open—and you're on the open roof. You can climb even higher—assuming you don't suffer from acrophobia—round and round for 129 steps in a spiral tower, until you are alone in a circular framework of steel 500 feet above the ground, the wind whistling through your hair. Now you've seen it all!

In the **Muralto** bar, a floor below the observation deck, you can contemplate the panorama at your leisure over a soft drink, beer, or margarita (100 pesos) without paying the admission charge. In fact, if you'd rather take a quick look then spend money for a long look, head for the Muralto (without buying that admission ticket), walk around for a glance at the view, ask to see a menu, and then "decide you're not that hungry" and take the elevator back down. No one will mind.

THE HOUSE OF TILES ("Casa de Azulejos"): Just past the Bellas Artes and the Latin American Tower, Avenida Juarez runs into (and becomes) the Avenida Madero, a one-way street going all the way to the city's main plaza. As you proceed down Madero from the intersection with Avenida Lázaro Cárdenas, you can't fail to notice the mammoth Banco de México buildings (main building and Guardiola Annex) to your left, and behind these giants a small and wizened oldtimer decked out in gorgeous blue-and-white tiles. This building is one of Mexico City's most precious colonial gems, and was built at the very end of the 1500s for the Counts of the Valley of Orizaba. The tiles are a fine example of Puebla's craftsmen's work, and the making of faïence is still one of Puebla's outstanding crafts. Today the House of Tiles is used as a branch of the Sanborn's restaurant-newsstand-gift shop chain. You can stroll through to admire the interior (and it's air-conditioned!) or sit and have a refreshing drink or a cup of something hot.

ITURBIDE PALACE: After your brief respite at Sanborn's House of Tiles, exit onto Madero again and walk the short distance to no. 17, a beautiful ornate stone palace with huge hand-carved wooden doors and a wildly baroque 40-foot-high carved stone archway. The mansion was built in the 1780s for a wealthy Mexican family, but was ceded in 1821 to Don Agustin de Iturbide, who later became the self-proclaimed Agustin I, Emperor of Mexico (1822–1823). His reign lasted only a matter of months, for although he was a partisan of Mexican independence, his political outlook was basically royalist and conservative, and the future of Mexico lay in the liberal social reforms advocated by the great revolutionaries Hidalgo and Morelos.

Financiera Banamex, present owner of the building, undertook restoration of the palace in 1972 and the result is beautiful, if a bit stark. Enter to a courtyard with three tiers of balconies; the ground floor is a banking office, the upper floors have executive offices. Period paintings and statues grace walls and corners, and the second-floor chapel has been beautifully restored. Banamex has had a brief guide to the building printed up, and this leaflet, like your self-guided tour of the palace, is free of charge. Come in and have a look anytime Monday through Friday from 9 a.m. to 5 p.m. Closed holidays.

THE ZÓCALO: Six more blocks along Madero and you'll come to the Zócalo (Metro: Zócalo), a spacious plaza bounded on all sides by the darkened stone of 17th-century buildings.

There's a wonderful view of the Zócalo from the seventh-floor restaurant, partly open-air, of the **Hotel Majestic,** which is on the corner of the Zócalo and Madero. You can start your trip with breakfast here, or pay a late visit to the bar which adjoins the restaurant, a bit expensive but worth the splurge. From this vantage point, the people strolling casually in the vast expanse of square below look as though they have been choreographed by some omnipotent chess player, as indeed they may have been.

The odd Indian word "zócalo" actually means "pedestal," or "plinth." A grand monument to Mexico's independence was planned, and the pedestal built, but the project was never completed. The pedestal became a landmark for visiting out-of-towners, and pretty soon everyone was calling the square after the pedestal, even though the pedestal was later removed. Its official name is Plaza de la Constitución. In imitation, the main square in any other Mexican town is often called "el zócalo," whether it ever bore a pedestal or not!

The Zócalo is being closed to vehicular traffic as Mexico City's pedestrian plans reach fulfillment. Soon, most of the streets around the square will be for people only, not cars, and you'll be able to stroll at leisure through what used to be the very center—the *tianguis* (market) and *teocalli* (sacred center)—of ancient Tenochtitlán. The paving in the square is being given a stone mosaic which shows a portion of the Mendocino Codex, an Aztec "picture-text" of the founding of Tenochtitlán.

The National Cathedral

Take a look inside the cathedral, begun in 1573 and finished in 1667. If you wander quietly around past the innumerable small chapels, you'll almost certainly come across a guide who is busily demonstrating some of the cathedral's more outstanding features: the tomb of Agustin Iturbide perhaps, placed here in 1838, or the fact that the holy water fonts ring like metal when tapped with a coin. Like all good big churches it has catacombs underneath (which you can visit); unlike some churches it is immense, brilliant almost to blinding, overpowering.

Next to the cathedral and communicating with it is **El Sagrario,** another tour de force of Spanish baroque built in the mid-1700s.

In your look around the cathedral and the Sagrario, be sure to note the sinkage of the great building into the soft lake bottom beneath. The base of the facade is far from being level and straight, and when one considers the weight of the immense towers, the sinkage is no surprise.

Around to the east side of the cathedral is a quaint reminder of medieval trade life. Here is where carpenters, plasterers, plumbers, painters, and electricians gather who have no shops of their own—modern journeymen. Each has his tool box and may display the tools of his trade along with pictures of his work, paint color charts, and various other attractions.

Big things are about to happen to the area off the cathedral's northeast corner. Several years ago the ruins of an immense Aztec temple were discovered near the corner of Calle Rep. de Guatemala and Avenida Rep. de Argentina. Excavations are well under way, and plans call for an open-air museum and theater. The surrounding district, one of the oldest in the city, has suffered long neglect, but a project inaugurated in 1980 should restore much of its colonial charm. Designated a Historical Zone, the district is eligible for urban renewal funds. The first product of the plan is the beautifully restored mansion at the corner of Donceles and Rep. de Chile. Built as the home of Don Manuel de Heras y Soto in the 18th century, it is now the Mexico City Historical Center. Take a look in through the gates. Don Manuel, by the way, was one of the notables who signed Mexico's Act of National Independence.

The **Pyramid of Huitzilopochtli** which has been uncovered in the archeological zone on the northeast corner of the Zócalo can be seen on Saturday mornings (from 10 a.m. to noon), free. Entering the site at the corner of Guatemala and El Seminario, you can see foundations of the great pyramid as well as a number of stone serpent heads which once formed the edifice of the magnificent Temple of Quetzalcoatl. These are just a few of the monuments left from the Aztec capital of Tenochitlán. Most of the remnants from this past empire have been moved to the Anthropological Museum or the National Museum of the Cultures, but a large moon stone equal in size to the famous Aztec Calendar has been left on site because it is cracked. There are no guides to show you around but they do hand out a small brochure about the excavations (in Spanish only, though).

The National Palace

On the east side of the Zócalo stands the impressive National Palace, begun in 1692, the last addition completed late in the 19th century. A complex of countless rooms, reached by wide stone stairways and adorned with carved brass balconies opening onto a series of courtyards, the National Palace is where the president works from 8 a.m. to 2:30 p.m. (regular hours for government employees in Mexico). Enter by the central door any day from 8 a.m. to 6 p.m. The guards will let you by if you ask.

Continue across the courtyard to the biggest attraction here, for Mexicans and tourists alike, the enormous murals painted over a 25-year period by Diego Rivera. All the murals are labeled, and some are quite easy to understand. There is, for instance, *The Legend of Quetzalcoatl,* depicting the famous legend of the flying serpent bringing a white man with a blond beard to the country; when Cortes arrived, many of the Aztecs remembered this legend, and believed the newcomer to be Quetzalcoatl. Another mural tells of the *American Intervention,* during the War of 1847, when American invaders marched into Mexico City. It was on this occasion that the military cadets of Chapultepec Castle (then a military school) fought bravely to the last man; the final six wrapped themselves in Mexican flags and leaped from the windows to avoid surrendering. (You'll see a monument to the boy heroes later, in Chapultepec Park.) The pride and joy of palace murals is one called the *Great City of Tenochtitlán,* a pictorial study of the original settlement in the Valley of Mexico. The city takes up only a small part of the mural, and the remainder is filled with what appears to be four million extras left over from a Cecil B. De Mille epic. In fact, no matter what their themes, most of the murals incorporate a piece of ancient Mexican history, usually featuring Cortes and a cast of thousands.

On Saturday and Sunday nights from dusk to 11:30 p.m., and throughout the month of September (Mexico's independence month), the palace and other buildings around the Zócalo are beautifully lit. The **Municipal Palace,** seat of government for the Federal District, is the structure on the south side of the Zócalo, with roads heading down the middle and on both sides of it.

NATIONAL PAWN SHOP (Nacional Monte de Piedad): Who ever heard of touring a pawn shop? In Mexico City it's done all the time, for the Nacional Monte de Piedad, across the street (Monte de Piedad) from the west side of the cathedral, is a huge and rather imposing building which turns out to be a department store for used items—the world's largest and most elegant Good Will/Morgan Memorial thrift store. Electric power tools, jewelry, antique furniture, heavy machine tools, sofa beds, and a bewildering array of other things from trash to treasure are all on display. Buying is not required, but taking a look is recommended.

Tired after the walk? I have just the place to recoup. For sunshine and a view of the Zócalo, it's the rooftop café-restaurant of the aforementioned **Hotel Majestic.** But if you don't mind being inside, make your way past the jewelry shops on the west side of the Zócalo to the southwest corner of the square and the beginning of Avenida 16 de Septiembre. A few steps west on this street (back in the direction of the Alameda, more or less) will bring you to no. 82 and the entrance of the **Gran Hotel Ciudad de México.** Full particulars are given in the hotel chapter. The lavishly old-fashioned lobby, topped with its breathtaking stained-glass canopy, is served by a bar off in one corner, and a restaurant off in another. Both are sort of expensive, but a drink in the bar, although a rather steep 100 pesos, is a real pleasure. Beer or a soft drink will be cheaper; you should get a bowl of peanuts, *gratuito.* Even if you don't want to stop, and even if you don't plan to stay here, you should have a look at the magnificent lobby. By the way, the reason the birds in their splendid cages aren't flitting here and there is because they're stuffed. The bird calls you hear are electronic simulations!

If you're of the hearty breed whose feet are made of Teflon and whose stomach is content with a handful of pumpkin seeds, you can continue your walk by visiting the museums in this area (mentioned below), or by heading down Pino Suarez to the colorful markets of the city. For most people, though, a good inexpensive restaurant serving the traditional comida corrida (from, usually, 1 to 4 p.m.) is what's called for. Refer to the restaurant chapter and make your selection.

2. Museums in the Downtown Area

THE JUAREZ MUSEUM: A comparatively little-discovered (by tourists) museum in the Zócalo area (Metro: Zócalo) is the one dedicated to Benito Juarez, and situated in the National Palace. When facing the palace, take the farthest left of the three entrances, walk across the courtyard to the statue of Benito Juarez, and then up the stairs to the left. The Juarez Museum consists of the well-preserved home of the former president of Mexico, and is usually bustling with school children studying the handwritten letters and papers that are carefully kept in glass cases around the room. In other cases are tablecloths, silverware, medals, shirts, watches, a briefcase, and symbolic keys to the city—all personal effects of the much-loved former president.

There's a beautiful library here (same hours as the museum), with lots of wood paneling, desks, history books arranged around the walls, and the wonderfully musty smell of mellow leather and aging paper that's indigenous to all respectable libraries. Anyone may study the books.

The last room at the rear is Juarez's bedroom, which gives one the eerie feeling that the former president might walk in at any moment; his dressing gown is laid out on the four-poster bed, and a chamber pot peeks from beneath the coverlet. Authenticity to the *n*th degree.

The museum is open from 10 a.m. to 7 p.m. Monday through Friday, from 10 a.m. to 3 p.m. on Saturday and Sunday. Admission is free after signing the registry books.

NATIONAL MUSEUM OF THE CULTURES: The pedestrian street just to the left of the National Palace, on the east side of the Zócalo, is Moneda. The museum is in the middle of the block at no. 13. It is not tremendously exciting, but does give an idea of what was going on outside Mexico while the Aztecs were building their pyramids. It displays art from North America, Japan, Peru, Greece, and Italy. They also have temporary exhibits here, as well as a bulletin board of current cultural events in the city. Open every day except Sunday from 9:30 a.m. to 6 p.m.; admission costs 5 pesos.

RIVERA MURALS: From the northeast corner of the Zócalo, Calle República de Argentina heads north. If you head north too, you'll soon cross Calle Gonzalez Obregon, and on your left will be the headquarters of the Secretaría de Educación Publica. The building is open during normal working hours (9 a.m. to 2 p.m.), and the attraction is its courtyards. The walls are decorated with a great series of over 200 murals by Diego Rivera, Mexico's outstanding artist in this medium. Other artists did a panel here and there, but it's the Riveras that are superb. The building itself dates from the 1930s.

On your way back to the Zócalo, take a peek at the murals in the Escuela Nacional Preparatoria, a block south of the Secretaría, at the corner of Argentina and Donceles. Here the murals are by the three Mexican greats, Rivera, Orozco, and Siqueiros.

MUSEUM OF THE CITY OF MEXICO: The easternmost of the three roads leading from the south end of the Zócalo is Pino Suarez. Three blocks south on this road, just before the corner of Calle El Salvador and Pino Suarez, pop through a stone doorway and you'll find yourself in the courtyard of a mansion built in 1528, and known originally as the House of the Counts of Santiago de Calimaya. Back in 1964 this classic old building, with its massive stone staircase and crumbling walls, was converted into the Museum of the City of Mexico (Metro: Pino Suarez or Zócalo—equal distance).

This museum is underrated, and should be visited by any newcomer to Mexico who wants to get the historical and prehistorical outlines of a fascinating culture. It deals solely with the Mexico Valley. The first arrival of man in the valley was in 8000 B.C.; he is portrayed as a nomad and hunter of the anthropological period called "Paleolithic Superior." There are some fine maps and pictographic presentations of the initial settlements, outlines of the social organization as it developed, and a huge mockup of Tenochtitlán, the city of the Aztecs. The conquest and destruction of Tenochtitlán by the Spaniards is fantastically portrayed with a mural of Capdevila that appears to have been painted in fire.

After a brief inspection of the elegant old carriage in the courtyard and the little room behind it devoted to the history of transportation in Mexico City, ascend the broad stairs and turn right. The second-floor exhibits begin with a potpourri of beautiful religious paintings, then continue the story of the city's history. Portrayals and notes on the "founding fathers," a fine picture of the Plaza of Mexico, and a series of figures clad in period costumes bring you up to the 1857 revolution. Among the tributes to Juarez and photos of the Villa/Zapata insurrection, there's a marvelously fierce and slightly cross-eyed painting of "the agrarian martyr," Emiliano Zapata, with so much artillery strapped to his chest that he could have won a good-size battle single-handed. (He probably did!)

Calmer, but no less interesting, are the photos and sketches of Mexico City in the present and the future. And on the third floor, you'll find the sun-drenched studio of Mexican impressionist Joaquin Clausell (1866–1935). The walls are completely covered with his fragmentary works, and two easel paintings still stand.

The Museum of the City of Mexico is open from 9:30 a.m. to 7:30 p.m. Tuesday through Sunday; closed Monday; admission is free. Every Thursday evening at 7 p.m. there is a scheduled lecture at the museum.

PINACOTECA VIRREYNAL DE SAN DIEGO: As mentioned in Section 1 above, the Palacio de Bellas Artes is an art gallery as well as a concert hall. The same administration responsible for the Bellas Artes's shows is in charge of the Pinacoteca Virreynal de San Diego, Dr. Mora no. 7, at the northwest corner of the Alameda near the Hotel de Cortes (Metro: Hidalgo). This former church is now a gallery of paintings, mostly from the 16th and 17th centuries, and mostly ecclesiastical in theme. Highlights are apparent immediately as you walk around: in the wing to the right of where the altar would have been is a room with a gorgeous blue-and-gilt ceiling with gleaming rosettes and a striking mural by Federico Cantu (1959), one of the few modern works. Upstairs in a cloister are many small paintings by Hipolito de Rioja (who worked in the second half of the 17th century), by Baltazar de Echave Ibia (1610–1640), and others. By the way, the tremendous painting on the cloister wall called *Glorificación de la Inmaculada*, by Francisco Antonio Vallejo (1756–1783) can be viewed better from upstairs—the lighting is better.

The Pinacoteca is open Tuesday through Sunday from 10 a.m. to 5 p.m.; entry is free.

MUSEO DE SAN CARLOS: The San Carlos Academy is Mexico's foremost school for artists, and most of the country's great painters—Diego Rivera among them—count it as their Alma Mater. Connected with the academy is the San Carlos Museum, Alvarado at Arizpe, a few blocks west of the Alameda. The converted mansion which now houses the museum is very fine indeed, having been built in the early 1800s by architect Manuel Tolsa for the Marques de Buena Vista.

In the mansion's elliptical court you'll first come to displays of 19th-century Mexican statuary and busts by Manuel Vilar and his pupils, and off to one side is a pretty garden court shaded by rubber trees.

The various rooms on the first and second floors hold some of Mexico's best paintings, by both Mexican and European artists. In Sala IV, for instance, you can view *Christ in Limbo* by Mostaert (ca. 1534–1598), and also two paintings by Lucas Cranach the Elder: *Adam and Eve,* and *Federico de Sajonia*. Upstairs treats include *La Coqueta y el Jovenzuelo* by Fragonard and a portrait of Sir William Stanhope attributed to Sir Joshua Reynolds.

Admission to the Museum of San Carlos is free as of this writing, and it's open from 10 a.m. to 5 p.m. Tuesday through Sunday.

OPEN-AIR ART EXHIBITS: Every Sunday from 9 a.m. to 3 p.m. there's an open-air art exhibit in the **Jardín del Arte (Sullivan Park)**, near the intersection of Insurgentes and Reforma. Come to buy, or just to look, or just to stroll through the pretty greenery flashing with the electric colors which emanate from the paintings done in questionable taste. Lots of the paintings are fine, though. There's a similar exhibit in the suburb of San Angel on Saturday—see below under "Attractions on the Outskirts."

3. Outdoor Markets

From the Zócalo, head down Pino Suarez, which is loaded with little *tiendas* selling everything from belt buckles to shoestrings, until you reach the broad divided boulevard which is Fray Servando Teresa de Mier. Beginning here and for about six blocks east along Servando, through side streets and alleys, is an exciting maze of vendors and craftsmen.

Bargaining: Before entering this labyrinth, here's a word about buying, or specifically, bargaining. First and foremost, *never start bargaining unless you intend to buy.* Once you've looked around the shop or shops (at leisure and never showing too much enthusiasm over any one object, especially the one you're thinking of purchasing), ask the price. After he's answered, you might respond with *"es muy caro"* (it's very expensive), or better yet with no response at all. The owner will probably lower his price or ask you, *"¿Cuanto quiere pagar?"* (How much do you want to pay?). Don't answer at this point, just keep looking around, asking prices of things you're interested in. Once you have an idea of his prices and have decided the price you're willing to pay, then you can begin to bargain.

There are two approaches I've used—the first is probably the best: I set a price I want to pay for the goods (never wanting it so much that I can't leave without buying it). I look around a bit more (perhaps there's something else, and it's always easier to bargain a "two-for-one" price), then I state my price *"a la mas, veinte pesos"* (at the most, 20 pesos). Simple: No bargaining, just state the price you want to pay. This approach, of course, is good only if you're a fair judge of quality and know the going prices around town. Obviously, if he asks 400 pesos for a hand-embroidered shirt and you tell him 50 pesos, then all you've accomplished is an insult!

The second approach is to halve the quoted price (depending on the product) and work on up to a compromise: He asks 100 pesos, you say 50, and you end up at 75—plus or minus 5 depending on who's the more adept at bargaining.

MERCED MARKET: Having had this brief lesson in haggling, try your skill at the Merced Market, the biggest in the city (Metro: Merced). Continue down Fray Servando about six blocks and take a left on the Avenida Anillo de Circunvalación. The market is three or four blocks up this street.

The Merced Market consists of several modern buildings. The first is mainly for fruits and vegetables; the others contain just about everything you would find if a department store joined forces with a five and dime—a good place to go looking for almost anything.

The area to the north of the market is a tangled confusion of trucks and stores, in which cascades of oranges spill gloriously down onto sidewalks. At the corner of Circunvalación and Calle Gómez Pedraza, a crowd has gathered to watch a street entertainer do his tricks. His rolled-up handkerchief lies on the ground and, as he beckons it toward him, in a cracked voice, interruptions come from a small figure in a battered fedora hat. The crowd roars, as much at the incongruity of the urchin's painted cheeks, oversize black mustache, and baggy pants, as at anything he says. Finally, feigning uncontrolled indignation, the entertainer seizes his straight "man" by the tie and drags him around the circle. But the boy (who can't be older than seven) has slipped out of the noose, which hangs limply from the entertainer's hand, and continues blithely on his way. A shower of coins testifies to the crowd's appreciation.

These street entertainers, the equivalent of Europe's age-old buskers, can be found everywhere in the capital. Many of them are strolling musicians or mariachis, but sometimes they are youthful crosswalk teams with amazing mass appeal. It isn't necessary to speak Spanish to appreciate the down-to-earth humor of, say, a pair who can sometimes be found doing a "Knock, knock, who's there?" routine at the head of the Calle Talavera, which goes into the Plaza Merced.

To return to the Zócalo or anywhere else within the city, take the Metro from the Merced station, which is just outside the enclosed market. You can change at Pino Suarez (first stop) to take you to the Zócalo.

LAGUNILLA MARKET: A few blocks north of the Plaza de Garibaldi (Metro: Allende) is another market well worth visiting. The Lagunilla Market, whose two enclosed sections, separated by a short street, Calle Juan Alvarez, have different specialties, is noted for clothes, rebozos, and blankets to the north, and tools, pottery, and household goods, such as attractive copper hanging lamps, to the south. This is also the area for old and rare books, many at a ridiculously low cost, if you're willing to hunt and bargain. Most, however, are in Spanish.

THIEVES' MARKET: On Sunday mornings, you might enjoy a visit to the famous Thieves' Market, next to the Lagunilla Market on the corner of Allende and Libertad. To get there take the Metro to the Guerrero station and walk east on Mosqueta which intersects Reforma; just past the intersection is the market. Or, you can take a bus up (north on) Avenida Lázaro Cárdenas—almost any bus will do. Sunday mornings, the area is filled with stalls and sidewalk blankets piled with goods of every description. Principally, there are antiques, brass candlesticks, and weighing scales, but you'll also see such prosaic items as sunglasses and old magazines, furniture and jewelry, coins, extinct banknotes, and buttons. It's a place where bargaining is expected. f you want to buy anything, offer half the price asked and be prepared to forget the whole thing if the vendor won't lower his price. Best time to arrive is about 11 a.m. Watch carefully for pickpockets.

THE BAZAR SÁBADO: The Bazar Sábado in San Angel, a suburb a few miles south of the city, is held on Saturday, as its name indicates. If you like outdoor markets, you'll like this one. Plan to spend all of Saturday touring the attractions on the southern outskirts of the city, guided by Section 6, "Attractions on the Outskirts," below.

DEPARTMENT STORES: Woolworth's (Insurgentes Sur 376 and Reforma 99); **Sears Roebuck** (San Luis Potosí 214); **La Ciudad de México** (5 de Mayo and Zócalo); **Sanborn's** (Madero 4, Reforma 45), **Niza** (at Hamburgo, Reforma 333, Juarez 70, Salamanca 74, Insurgentes at Aguascalientes). And on the 20 de Noviembre, in the block south of the Zócalo, is **Palacio de Hierro,** recently under new management and catering to the very posh set. **Paris Londres,** 16 de Septiembre (near the Zócalo) is a high-quality store.

4. Arts and Crafts Shops

Mexico is famous the world over for the quality and variety of its arts and crafts. Today it often costs only a little more money to buy these things in the capital than at the source, if one knows a good shop. Several government-run shops and a few excellent privately run shops have exceptionally good collections of Mexico's arts and crafts. As fascinating as a fine art gallery, these shops deserve a visit whether you intend to buy or not.

ARTES POPULARES SHOPS: If the teeming Merced Market is a bit too fast for your blood pressure, don't fret, because the city is loaded with Artes Populares (handicrafts) shops. Two of the nicest shops with the most varied assortment of gifts are those run by the government, and the *prices are fixed* so you can avoid haggling. The **Exposicion Nacional de Arte Popular** (Metro: Hidalgo or Juarez), located at Juarez 89, has simply everything! There are two floors of papier-mâché figurines, woven goods, earthenware, colorfully painted candelabras, hand-carved wooden masks, straw goods, beads, bangles, and glass.

When you're finished here, walk down a few blocks to the **National Museum of Popular Industrial Arts,** located across the street from the Benito Juarez statue in Alameda Park at Juarez 44. They have similar Mexican crafts from all over, and because the prices are fixed you can get an idea of quality vs. cost for later use in market bargaining. Even if you don't buy anything you should visit the shop, as it displays an enormous selection of crafts. Both government shops are open every day except Sunday, 10 a.m. to 6 p.m.

The first store described above, the Exposicion Nacional, and also the attractive store at Juarez 70 (in the Hotel Del Prado), plus the store at Juarez 92, are all operated by the quasi-governmental body known as FONART (Fondo Nacional para el Fomento de las Artesanias). FONART helps village craftsmen with problems of quality control and marketing.

VICTOR'S ARTES POPULARES MEXICANAS: This is a shop for serious buyers and art collectors. The Fosado family has been in the folk art business for 50 years and is a reputable authority. The store is located near the Alameda at Madero 10, second floor, Room 305 (Metro: Juarez). They buy most of their crafts from the Indian villages near and far, and supply various exhibits with native craftworks.

SAN JUAN BASKET MARKET (Mercado de Curiosidades): This is a large, rather modern building set back off a plaza on the corner of Ayuntamiento and Dolores (Metro: Salto del Agua). It's comprised of a number of stalls on two levels selling everything from leather to tiles. They have some lovely silver jewelry and, as in most non-fixed-price stores, the asking price is high but the bargained result is often very reasonable.

ARTESANOS de la CIUDADELA: A fairly new market (Metro: Balderas), large, clean, and with numerous little streets, it rambles on forever just off Balderas and Ayuntamiento in the Plaza de la Ciudadela. The merchandise is of good quality, well displayed, and bartering is a must. I think this is probably the best place for buying anything you want is here. The shops don't really get going until 11 or 12 so it's best to save your shopping in this area until the afternoon. Open until 8 p.m. You might want to come for lunch before shopping; if so I can highly recommend the restaurant in the market called **Fonda Lupita,** just off the small plaza from the Balderas and Ayuntamiento entrance. It has Spanish decor, and it's immaculately clean. A very handsome white-haired lady keeps the place shipshape and also prepares the very tasty food. A set lunch costs only 65 pesos.

CENTRAL CRAFTS MARKET: Not far from Buena Vista Railroad Station (Estación Buena Vista) is the Central Crafts Market, a commercial concern with a lot of floor space and an uninspired collection of crafts at rather high prices. If you want to take a look, get a no. 17 bus going north on Insurgentes to the railroad station. Get off and walk in front of the station—you'll be heading east. The first real north-south street you will come to is Calle Aldama, and the Central Crafts Market is at Aldama 187, just a few steps away. Or you can hop a no. 4 bus going west on Juarez, and it'll drop you right at the market.

Note: The Central Crafts Market employs undercover agents who prowl the length of Avenida Juarez and other tourist-frequented areas to tout the excellence of the market's wares. Offering "free tourist information" or "free guide service," they are friendly and helpful, but their goal is to persuade you to visit the market.

Note about Chapultepec Park Map

Chapultepec Park, which covers about three square miles, is divided into three areas: (1) Chapultepec Castle (Museum of Modern Art, Historical Museum); (2) Anthropological Museum (National Auditorium and Galería, Zoo); (3) New Bosque (Technological Museum, Natural History Museum, Amusement Park). The map is meant solely as a graphic representation of these areas. *It is not drawn to scale.* The immensity of the park plus barriers such as fences and the Periferico Highway make it more time-consuming to get around on foot than one might suppose from first glance at the map.

---

5. Chapultepec Park and Its Museums

One of the biggest city parks in the world, Chapultepec Park is more than a playground: it's a whole way of life. Every day of the week the number of holidaying Mexican families that it can accommodate must be seen to be believed. They swarm over the grass, picnic under the century-old trees, stroll around the *lago* (lake) or crowd into rowboats, buy colorful balloons, trinkets, and eats from the numerous vendors, and file through the beautiful 18th-century castle that tops the 200-foot hill. It's here that you can really begin to understand the diversity and enormity of the population of Mexico City.

If you want to see this wonderful conglomeration of people at play amid nature, then head for Chapultepec by collectivo or Expresso Reforma bus heading west on Reforma. The park opens daily at 9 a.m. and closes promptly at 6 p.m. It used to be that you could have a nice outing here (picnic with wine and cheese, etc.), but the park over the years has become so well used by people that with this use has come the accumulation of litter. Regardless of the signs pleading for *"limpieza"* the litter still goes to the ground. I'm sorry to say that the park has become more a place to practice sociology than sociability. The following sites are all within Chapultepec Park. A map (not drawn to scale) is included to help you find your way.

CHAPULTEPEC CASTLE: As you come down Reforma, at the foot of Chapultepec hill you'll notice six marble shafts carved as stylized torches placed in a semicircle around a small plaza. This is the Monument to the Boy Heroes (Niños Héroes)—the six cadets who jumped to their death rather than surrender to the U.S. Marines who attacked the castle during the war with Mexico in 1847. You can walk up the hill from here by following the right fork at the small castle-like gatehouse (now a house of mirrors) or take the elevator (free) which is on the left a short way up the hill (usually a very long line on Sunday). Better to take the minibus to the top which runs daily from 9 a.m. to 4:45 p.m. Catch it at the foot of the hill where the road begins its ascent.

Although on the site of Chapultepec Castle there had been a fortress since the days of the Aztecs, the present palace was not built until the 1780s. At the time of the previously mentioned U.S. invasion, it was in use as a military college, which is how it came about that Mexican army youths, including the unlucky sextet, were defending it.

The castle offers a beautiful view of Mexico which, from the balconies, appears to be covered solid with trees. It's reported that in the days of the French occupation during the 1860s, Carlotta could sit up in bed and watch

MEXICO CITY: SIGHTS 241

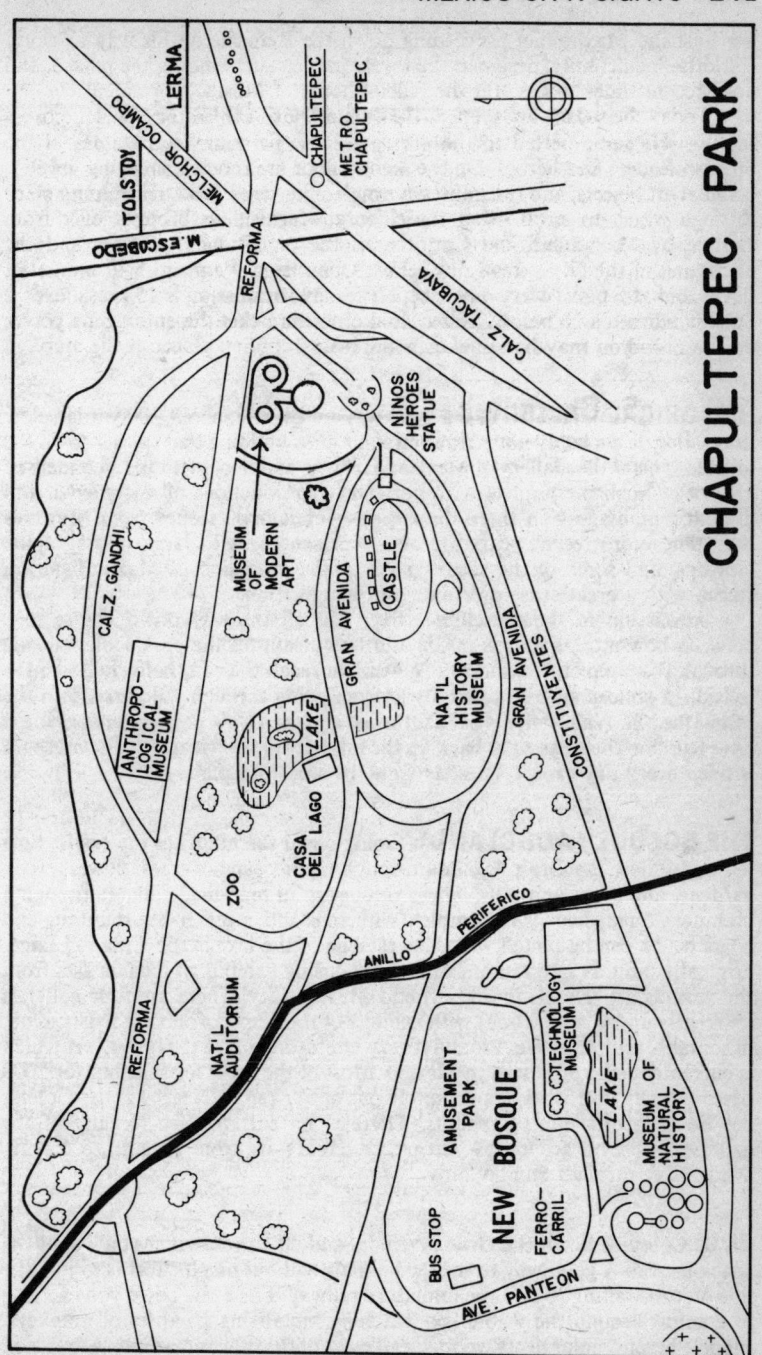

her husband Maximilian proceeding down the Reforma on his way to work. Carlotta, incidentally, designed the lovely garden surrounding the palace, and until recent times it was still the official home of Mexico's president.

Today the palace houses the **Museum of National History,** which covers the post-Hispanic period to the present—large paintings and statues of the Spanish leaders and heroes. On the second floor are rooms displaying jewelry, colonial art objects, and the impressive malachite vases. It's an intriguing place through which to stroll, from the elaborate furnishings brought over from Europe by Maximilian and Carlotta, to the patios and fountains and the panorama of the city spread out below. Open from 9 a.m. to 5:40 p.m. (last ticket sold at 5 p.m.) every day except Tuesday. Admission is 15 pesos, except Sunday when it's 10 pesos. (Note: Hold onto the ticket the entire time you're on the hill—you may be asked to show it.)

HISTORICAL GALLERY: On your way up the hill, about 200 yards below the castle you probably noticed the circular glass building that spirals down the hillside. This is the Gallery of Mexican History, and in content it's a condensed history of Mexico complete with portraits, reproductions of documents, and dramatic montages—in three dimensions—of famous scenes from Mexico's past. The more recent years are also represented, with large photographic blowups, and some of the scenes, such as the execution of Maximilian, are staged with a great sense of drama and imagination.

Admission to the museum is free, and all the way down you're torn between how attractive it is inside and how beautiful the park looks outside through the big picture windows. When you reach the exit, halfway down the hillside, a policeman tries to stop you from going through the park down the rest of the hill. Wait until his back is turned and then walk past; otherwise you'll have to climb the steps right back up the hill to come down again. The museum is open every day except Tuesday from 10 a.m. to 5 p.m.

THE BOSQUE (WOODLAND): Going down the hill from the castle, turn left and follow the Gran Avenida through a landscape of trees, flowers, rock gardens, fountains, and hills. There is a beautiful man-made lake (although a bit mucky on my last visit), complete with an island, a geyser-like fountain, and boats which can be rented. On the west side of the lake is the **Casa del Lago,** originally built as a restaurant and now housing exhibits of local artists from the various art schools in and around Mexico City. There are four galleries (currently under restoration) with exhibits of the works of sundry artists in oil, lithograph, sculpture, etc. I found it very interesting to see the type of art which is currently being produced in Mexico. Most of the art is for sale, but for 2000 pesos (and up) per work it's definitely out of our range. Nearby is the Galería del Bosque with similar exhibits. There is no entrance fee for any of the galleries, so stroll around as you please. Hours are from 11 a.m. to 5 p.m., Wednesday through Sunday only.

ZOO: Continue down the Gran Avenida, and off to your right you'll spot the spacious zoo. A good way to see the animals without much effort is to join the line of kids waiting to ride the miniature railway. For a few pesos you can ride in comfort around the whole zoo, catching tantalizing glimpses of monkeys, hippos, herons, polar bears, zebras, and most of the other creatures. Admission to the zoo is free.

AMUSEMENT PARK: This, complete with roller coaster (named the "Montana Rusa," or Russian Mountain) and ferris wheel, is in **New Chapultepec Park**—the area at the far western end. Continue in a southwesterly direction from the zoo and you'll come to the Periferico Highway (about half a mile or a 20-minute walk); the Amusement Park is just on the other side. If you are coming straight from downtown, you can take bus 30 along Servando Teresa de Mier, Río de la Loza, and Avenida Chapultepec to Avenida Constituyentes. Alight at the Natural History Museum, and it's a 15-minute walk to the concessions (for walking directions, see under "Technological Museum," below).

Admission is 10 pesos; children under 3, free. The gates are open Wednesday and Thursday from 11 a.m. to 6:30 p.m., on Saturday and Sunday from 10:30 a.m. to 7 p.m. The two large buildings to the right of the Amusement Park are the Technological Museum, open everyday except Monday, 9 a.m. to 5 p.m. (See below.)

THE MUSEUMS: The nicest things about Chapultepec Park are its timelessness and spaciousness; it is big enough to accommodate almost anything that can be designed for it. Within this complex have been built five varied, beautiful, and exciting museums. They combine a superb sense of proportion with an equally good sense of design.

National Museum of Anthropology

By general consent, the finest museum of its kind in the world is Mexico's National Museum of Anthropology, which was built by architect Pedro Ramírez Vasquez and a team of worthy helpers in 1964. If Sr. Ramírez never did another thing, he'd still deserve the fame of centuries.

An Expresso Reforma "Auditorio" bus up Reforma will drop you right outside the museum, which is situated off the broad boulevard about half a mile past the Diana statue, opposite Chapultepec Park Zoo. Line 1 of the Metro will take you to just outside the park; walk through the park, past the Museum of Modern Art, along Reforma, and you're there in 15 minutes. The museum is open Tuesday through Saturday from 9 a.m. to 7 p.m., on Sunday from 10 a.m. until 6 p.m., closed all day Monday. Admission on Sunday is only 10 pesos, 15 pesos all other days.

The museum, breathtaking in its splendor, with a massive patio half-sheltered by a tremendous stone umbrella, will take at least two or three hours to look around even if you are a dedicated museum rusher.

There are three sections, to all intents and purposes. First of all is the entrance hall to the museum proper. Here you'll find a check room, and a sign which states that you *must* check coats, umbrellas, all cameras and camera bags, and any handbag that is at all large. You simply cannot take your camera into the exhibition rooms with you. The museum shop, off the entry hall, has a nice collection of souvenirs and an excellent collection of guidebooks, large and small, to cultural, culinary, and archeological attractions in Mexico.

Inside the museum proper is an open courtyard with beautifully designed spacious rooms running around three sides at two levels. The ground-floor rooms are theoretically the most significant, and they are the most popular among studious visitors, devoted as they are to history and prehistoric days all the way up to the most recently explored archeological sites. These rooms include dioramas of the way Mexico City looked when the Spaniards first arrived, and reproductions of part of a pyramid at Teotihuacán. The Aztec calendar stone "wheel" takes a proud place here.

Save some of your time and energy, though, for the livelier and more readily understandable upstairs rooms. They're devoted to the way people throughout Mexico live today, complete with straw-covered huts, tape recordings of songs and dances, and lifelike models of village activities.

There is a lovely restaurant in the museum, but the food tends to be expensive for what you get. I'd recommend either bringing something with you to munch or going across the street to the little eateries in the park. The museum deserves at least a full day of viewing and you'll need to take a break.

READER'S RESTAURANT SELECTION: "In the area of the Anthropological Museum and Chapultepec Castle is the Plaza de los Leones, and a block away at Reforma 489 is the delightful **Restaurant Flaminia**. The comida corrida costs 145 pesos, and the size of portions, atmosphere and location make it well worth the price" (Helen Moloney, Garden City, N.Y.).

Museum of Modern Art

The Museum of Modern Art is actually two buildings, set together in a statue-dotted section of grassy park, with two entrances: one on Reforma, the other across from—sort of behind—the Niños Héroes monument. The museum's interior is the perfect vehicle for showing works of art, simple with its handsome parquet floors, marble and stone walls, wood slatted ceiling, and circular windows (always covered by heavy drapes, presumably so the pictures don't get bleached by the sun).

The museum is open daily except Monday from 11 a.m. to 7 p.m., for an admission of 15 pesos (10 with a student card). You get to it just through the entrance to Chapultepec Park at the western end of Reforma.

The museum section at the Reforma entrance has four salons, two on each level, around a central dome of incredible acoustic properties. The salons are attractive in their spaciousness, and give you the nice feeling that you're the only person in the museum. Exhibits in salons I, II, and III are temporary, and have featured both Mexican and foreign artists including greats such as Magritte, Delvaux, Antonia Guerrero, Bissier, and Nay. Last time I visited there was also a fine show of Latin American photographs.

Salon IV houses a permanent collection of contemporary art, which seems to get even better each year. Most of the works are by Latin American artists and I—very critical when it comes to modern art—find most of them very palatable, and a few exceptional, such as Juan O'Gorman, Moro Hideo, and others.

In the circular rooms across the garden, near the Niños Héroes entrance to the museum, are more temporary exhibits. Note that the permanent collection of works by Mexican artists which used to be here has been moved to the Museo de Arte Carrillo Gil, in San Angel (see Section 6 of this chapter for details). This exceptionally fine collection encompasses works by Rivera, Kahlo, O'Gorman, Siquieros, Tamayo, Merida, Orozco, Gerszo, Romero, and others, and deserves a visit by all devotees of modern Mexican painting.

Museum of Natural History

An outstanding part of **New Chapultepec Park,** mentioned above, is the series of ten interconnecting domes which comprises the Museum of Natural History. From a distance the museum looks like a set of "topes" or brightly colored inverted bowls surrounded by foliage and flowers.

You can get there by bus 30 (see above, "Amusement Park"). Although it takes longer and costs more, you can also take the Metro to "Chapultepec" and get the no. 30 bus there.

Inside the museum, you'll see stuffed and preserved animals and birds, tableaux of different environments such as desert, seashore, tropical forest, and arctic tundra with the appropriate wildlife. Other domes contain exhibits relating to geology, astronomy, biology, the origin of life, and such displays as a relief map of the world's mountains and an illuminated map of Mexico showing the origin of various minerals.

The museum, fascinating for anyone with the slightest curiosity about nature and totally absorbing for youngsters, is open from 10 a.m. to 5 p.m. daily except Monday. There is no admission fee. Note: The large display cases of arctic bears and moose have pushbutton lighting (on the left)—a good idea in our age of conservation.

Just outside the museum and to the left is the **Ferrocarril,** a rubber-wheeled train, on which for a few pesos you can ride around this area. From here you can take the 15-minute walk to the Amusement Park or the Technological Museum, or if returning to the downtown area catch any of the no. 30 buses outside the museum.

Technological Museum

This museum is located in the western end of Chapultepec Park between the Amusement Park and Avenida Constituyentes. The best way to get there is to follow the directions to the Museum of Natural History given in the preceding section; from there it is only a 15-minute walk through very pleasant surroundings, as follows: take a northeasterly direction, past the Ferrocarril station on your left and then the lake on your right. When you come to a fork, bear left (downhill) to the large fountain and domed building on the left. Turn left at this rather weird fountain, then right through a series of fountains with circular snake reliefs. The Amusement Park and Technological Museum are a short distance straight ahead.

The museum is open from 9 a.m. to 5 p.m. daily, closed Monday. Entrance is free. The polyhedral dome outside is the **Planetarium,** which has scheduled shows at 10 a.m., noon, and 2 p.m. daily.

The museum is educational, to say the least. It is always filled with students madly taking notes on scientific developments through the ages. Inside and outside there are trains and planes, mockup factories, experiments of Morse and Edison, and various energy exhibits. When you're thoroughly exhausted head for the basement, wherein a cafeteria for food or refrescas.

Galería del Auditorio

There is a newly opened galería for art exhibits on the second and third floor in the National Auditorium, across from the El Presidente hotel. It is free and open from 9 a.m. to 5 p.m. Tuesday through Sunday. The exhibits change three or four times a year with works by local and internationally acclaimed artists. In 1980 they sponsored a weaving exhibit with some absolutely extraordinary display of cloths from Mexico and Central America. To get to the galería, you enter on the ground level of the National auditorium just off Reforma.

READERS' SIGHTSEEING TIPS: "On Belisario Domingues near Aquiles Serdan (this is the continuation of Avenida Lázaro Cárdenas) is a museum dedicated to **Los Niños Héroes.** The museum is very simple but effective with portraits of each of the young men who died in the Mexican-American war. Interesting to history buffs" (Frances Collins, San Francisco, Calif.). . . . "For the foot-sore and weary who have tramped through Chapultepec Castle, there is a perfect place for rest and recuperation. At the bottom of the hill from the Historical Gallery, turn left and follow the road as it circles the bottom of the cliff counterclockwise. After about a quarter of a mile on your right is an elaborate fountain splashing into a pool, and on your left a sort of stone amphitheater. Walk around behind the left side of the amphitheater and you'll find yourself in the **"Audiorama,"** an open space with comfortable plastic chairs surrounded by a rose garden and topiary, where high-fidelity speakers play classical music from all four sides to delight the people sitting in the chairs. It's free" (C. N. Stockton, St. Paul, Minn.).

6. Attractions on the Outskirts

Now that you've seen some of Mexico City's best downtown attractions, you might want to take an adventure farther afield. We'll look now at sights and activities in the southern and northern reaches of the city which you can explore in a day or less. I've grouped these sites together into "Southern" and "Northern" headings so that you can most efficiently plan your excursions, and avoid backtracking.

Speaking of planning, you should make your trip to San Angel on Saturday if possible, as that's the day for the famous Bazar Sábado ("Saturday Bazaar"). On Saturday, Coyoacán has a small market as well. For many other sights—the Polyforum, University City, Plaza de las Tres Culturas—the day of the week doesn't matter. As for Xochimilco, it's busiest on Sunday, which is good if you like colorful crowds and activity, but bad if you hate crowded buses and haggling over prices. Don't go south on Monday, as most museums are closed then.

HEADING SOUTH: It might be best to plan two days for southern Mexico City. On a Saturday, catch a pesero ("San Angel") or bus no. 17 ("Indios Verdes–Tlalpan") south along Insurgentes near the Zona Rosa. It will take you past the Polyforum Cultural Siqueiros to San Angel and its Bazar Sábado. After you've visited these places, hop the same bus south to University City, Pedregal, and the Cuicuilco Pyramid. The bus trip takes almost an hour, straight through.

In a short while the Metro should be completed to the "Universidad" station, which will give you a fast way to get back into town.

Heading south along Insurgentes, your first stop is at the mind-boggling edifice called the Polyforum.

The Polyforum Cultural Siqueiros

Although this gleaming new arts center is much lauded by promoters, there's no way I can hide my lack of enthusiasm—it's a modern monstrosity with overpowering murals, low claustrophobic ceilings, and poor acoustics that echo the slightest sound. However, it does contain the world's largest mural (90,655 square feet) by a very well-known muralist, David Alfaro Siqueiros.

The polyforum is open from 10 a.m. to 9 p.m. every day and costs 40 pesos if you want to see the overambitious sculptured murals, *The March of Humanity on Earth* and *Toward the Cosmos,* by Siqueiros. They also stage a Sound and Light show here every evening at 6 in English.

Most of the Polyforum is devoted to art: on the floor that you enter is a small exhibition of visiting artists; on the two floors below are handicrafts from Mexico which you can purchase, although the prices are a bit high: the first level down has some art objects in glass display cases, while the floor below is basically the basement and things are just here and there in a wide open space.

After boggling your mind at the Polyforum, get back on Insurgentes and escape south in another pesero or bus, to San Angel.

In San Angel

In the suburb of San Angel there are several famous colonial houses and the convent of the Carmelites. If you go on Saturday, you can combine your museum tour with a visit to San Angel's Bazar Sábado—see Section 3 of this chapter for details.

A pesero will terminate at the intersection of Insurgentes and Avenida La Paz; as for the bus, ask to get off at La Paz. There's a pretty park here, to the east, and on the west side of Insurgentes is a Sanborn's store and restaurant, good for a quick, moderately priced lunch. (My favorite is the fruit-and-sherbet salad plate, with a soft drink, for 150 pesos, all in.)

Walk west, up the hill on La Paz, and in a block you'll come to Avenida de la Revolución. To the left (south) is the dark colonial stone bulk of the Museo Colonial del Carmen. To the right, a few blocks north, is the Museo de Arte Carrillo Gil. And straight ahead across Revolución is the shady Plaza del Carmen.

The **Museo Colonial del Carmen** is a former Carmelite convent, now filled with religious paintings, other ancient artifacts, and a batch of mummified nuns in glass cases in the cellar! The museum, a maze of interlocking halls, corridors, stairways, chapels, and pretty flower-filled patios, is very pleasant to look around and is open from 10 a.m. to 5 p.m. every day except Monday, for a few pesos admission.

San Angel's outstanding contribution to Mexican painting is the **Museo de Arte Alvar y Carmen T. Carrillo Gil,** sometimes called the Museo de la Esquina ("Museum on the Corner") as it is at a major intersection on the Avenida de la Revolución, at no. 1608. This modern gallery's collection of exhibit rooms include those dedicated to the works of Jose Clemente Orozco (1883–1942), Diego Rivera (1886–1957), David Alfaro Siqueiros (1896–1974), and rooms with works by a variety of Mexican painters. It's open 11 a.m. to 7 p.m. daily except Monday, for a few pesos admission.

Having filled yourself with Mexican culture, both colonial and modern, head up the hill through the Plaza del Carmen on Calle Dr. Calvez. Soon you'll come to the beautiful **Plaza San Jacinto,** filled with artists and their paintings on Saturday. Many of the old buildings surrounding the Plaza San Jacinto have fine courtyards where crafts are sold. The Centro Cultural Isidro Fábela, at no. 15, deserves special mention.

Many famous personalities of show business, government, and social life maintain homes in San Angel, but the most famous house now belongs to the nation, to which it was recently donated by Isidro Fábela, an international jurist, statesman, and art collector. His house, the **Casa del Risco** ("House of Broken Porcelain"), was built during the 17th century and furnished in magnificent colonial style with ornate doors, fireplaces, coats-of-arms, statues, portraits, chairs, chests, and, as the pièce de résistance, a fantastically decorated fountain which sits against one wall of the open patio. You'll have to see this fountain to believe it, for the decorative tiling consists of broken and unbroken pieces of porcelain that once comprised half a dozen banquet-size sets of porcelain. The Casa del Risco is open 10 a.m. to 6 p.m. every day except Monday, and entrance is free.

Two doors away from the Casa del Risco is the famous **Bazar Sábado,** in another colonial building. Be sure to take a turn through the building, whether or not you intend to buy. The crafts, the crowds, and the building itself are all wonderfully colorful.

Leaving the bazaar, spend some time in the plaza examining paintings. Some are excellent, others are quite good, and still others are, well, rather unfortunate. Prices are open to haggling.

Up the hill a few more steps from the Plaza San Jacinto is another, smaller plaza crowded with sellers of crafts, art objects, souvenirs, and tourist junk. The square is shady and interesting, festooned with printed and woven wall hangings.

After your shopping, are you up for a stroll? Continue uphill past the aforementioned little plaza on Calle Juarez. Soon you'll see a big old house— now a school—on your right at an intersection. Turn left, then left again, and you'll find your way to the gorgeous little **Plaza de los Archangelos.** Filled with bougainvillea (and often with adolescents in love), the plaza is a peaceful, flower-filled refuge away from the market bustle. The houses all around have high walls, exotic gardens, enormous gateways, and breathtaking price tags. When you're ready, retrace your steps; if you take that other road out down the hill you'll walk farther, and in traffic, to get back to the plaza.

Ready for lunch? The **Sanborn's** on Insurgentes (mentioned above) is a good, inexpensive bet. You can also have the buffet in the courtyard of the Bazar Sábado (about 500 pesos, all in). Or you can dine in a marvelous colonial setting at the **San Angel Inn** (tel. 548-6746), at the corner of Palmas and Altavista. To get to the inn, walk up Calle Juarez out of the Plaza San Jacinto, past the little plaza, and turn right on Calle Reyna (or Reina). At the end of Calle Reyna, turn left onto Avenida Altavista. The inn is four blocks up—you can see it in the distance where the road curves.

The inn's courtyard is, well, like heaven I guess. Lush, green, peaceful, tasteful, a quiet refuge absolutely essential for anyone touring Mexico City. You can order a drink to be brought to one of the small, low tables here, or you can dine. The luncheon *menu turistico,* with tax, tip, and beverage all in, will run you 750 pesos or so.

All done in San Angel? Catch a no. 56 bus ("Alcantarilla–Col. Agrarista") at the San Angel Inn, or along Altavista, to get to Coyoacán or the Anahuacalli (see below). For University City, get back to Insurgentes and catch anything, pesero or bus, with "Ciudad Universitaria," or simply "C.U.," in the window.

University City

This is the site of the world's most flamboyant college campus and, indeed, of one of the world's most flamboyant architectural groupings. Appropriately enough, it is located about 11 miles south along Insurgentes.

University City (it houses Mexico's National Autonomous University) was planned to be the last and grandest achievement of the regime of former president Miguel Aleman. The original university is said to date back to 1551, which would make it the oldest university in the Western Hemisphere.

It's an astonishing place and well worth going out to see for its gigantic and brilliantly colored mosaics and murals. The most outstanding of these, by Juan O'Gorman, covers all four sides and ten complete stories of the library building. Fittingly, the mosaic wall depicts the history of Mexican culture and covers a space in which 2½ million books can be stored. The two lower stories are glass-enclosed and are used as the library's reading rooms.

The administration building, closest to the road, is mostly travertine onyx but also has an immense outer mural. This was executed by David Alfaro Siqueiros and depicts Mexican students returning the fruits of their labors to the nation. Diego Rivera's famous contribution is a sculpture-painting which adorns the world's largest stadium (capacity: 102,000) across the highway. The stadium was used for a number of events in the 1968 Olympics.

Nobody will object if you wander at random around the campus, which accommodates 300,000 enrollment. There is a cafeteria on the ground floor of the humanities building and this, especially in summer, is well patronized by American students attending classes. All the university cafeterias are open to the public, and charge very reasonable prices.

Upstairs in the humanities building, you will find various notice boards. They merit a few moments' study, as their signs sometimes offer low-priced excursions or rides back to the States on a cost-sharing basis.

The university will soon boast its own Metro station, at the end of the Indios Verdes line. If it's not open when you go, plan to catch a no. 17, 19, or 19-A bus north, back to Reforma. Are you interested in seeing another pyramid? Then catch a no. 17 bus heading south on Insurgentes, and just after it crosses the Anillo Periferico Sur, hop off. You're only a 15-minute walk from the Museo y Ruinas de Cuicuilco.

The pyramid, open to visitors at all hours, represents some of the earliest civilization in the Valley of Mexico. Built in the pre-Classical period, around 1800 B.C., it was completely covered by a volcanic eruption (in 300 A.D.), surviving only because it was protected by a strong outer wall.

The Pedregal

Near University City is Mexico's most luxurious housing development, the **Jardines del Pedregal de San Angel**. The word *pedregal* means lava, and that's precisely what this enormous area, stretching well beyond the university, consists of. In the Jardines del Pedregal, the only restriction placed upon homeowners is that they have enough money to buy at least 2000 square meters of land and hire an architect to design their home. The result is that all the houses are exceptionally lavish, with swimming pools scooped out of the rock, split levels with indoor gardens, solid glass walls, and, in one case, an all-glass sunroom on a narrow stilt above the house—like an airport's observation tower.

The pedregal, or lava, all came from the now-extinct volcano Xitle, whose eruption covered the above-mentioned Cuicuilco Pyramid. Only in recent times has the pedregal been regarded as anything but a nuisance; at one time, many of its caves hid bandits. Today, all kinds of odd plants and shrubs grow from its nooks and crevices, and if you are interested in botany, you'll want to take a good look around. The main street is the north-south Avenida Paseo del Pedregal.

Two in Coyoacán

There are two interesting museums in the suburb of Coyoacán, south of the city near San Angel. If you have an extra morning I would strongly recommend a visit to the House and Museum of Trotsky and the Museo Frida Kahlo, the latter the former home of muralist Diego Rivera and his painter wife, whose name the house bears.

Coyoacán is a pretty, and wealthy, suburb with many old houses and cobbled streets. At the center are two large, graceful plazas, the Plaza Hidalgo and Jardín Centenario, and the Church of San Juan Bautista (1583). Once the capital of the Tepanec kingdom, Coyoacán was later conquered by the Aztecs, then by Cortes. The great conquistador had a palace here for a while.

The Metro will soon reach to the "Bancomer" station, within walking distance of Coyoacán's museums. As of this writing, however, you'll have to depend on buses 23 and 23-A ("Iztacala–Coyoacán") to get you from the center to this suburb. Catch the no. 23 going south on Bucareli, or the no. 23-A on Miguel Schultz, Antonio Caso, Río Rhin, or Niza.

Coming from San Angel, catch a no. 56 bus ("Alcantarilla–Col. Agrarista") heading east along the Camino al Desierto de los Leones or Avenida Altavista, near the San Angel Inn. When the bus gets to the corner of Avenida México and Xicoténcatl in Coyoacán, descend. Or, simpler, take a cab for the 15-minute ride.

Museo Frida Kahlo: The museum is about six blocks north of the plazas. There is a sign pointing east off Calle Centenario to the museum; follow this one block east to Allende. The house is on the corner of Allende and Londres—you can't miss it, for it's painted a brilliant blue with red trim.

Frida was born here on July 7, 1910, and occupied the house with Rivera from 1929 to 1954. The house is basically as she left it, and as you wander through the rooms you will get an overwhelming feeling for the life that they led. Their mementoes are in every room, from the kitchen, where the names Diego and Frida are written on the walls, to the studio upstairs, where a wheelchair sits next to the easel with a partially completed painting surrounded by paint brushes, palettes, books, photographs, and other paraphernalia of the couple's art-centered lives.

The bookshelves are filled with books in many languages, nestled against a few of Rivera's files bearing such inscriptions as "Protest Rockefeller Vandalism," "Amigos Diego Personales," and "Varios Interesantes y Curiosos." Frida's paintings hang in every room, some of them dominated by the exposed human organs and dripping blood that apparently obsessed her in the final surgery-filled years of her life.

Frida was a collector of pre-Columbian art, so many of the rooms contain jewelry and terracotta figurines from Teotihuacán and Tlatelolco. She even went to the extreme of having a mockup of a temple built in the garden where she could exhibit her numerous pots and statues. On the back side of the temple are several skulls from Chichén-Itzá.

You will no doubt be spurred on to learn more about the lives of this remarkable couple. I can recommend the book written by Bertram D. Wolfe entitled *Diego Rivera: His Life and Times.*

House and Museum of Trotsky: This most interesting place is located two blocks north and 2½ blocks east of the Frida Kahlo house, at Viena 45 between Gómez Farías and Morelos. You will recognize the house by the brick watchtowers on top of the high stone walls. There is a thick steel door which more than likely will not be open, but will be opened for you by the caretaker from 10 a.m. to 2 p.m. and 3 to 5:30 p.m., Tuesday through Friday, 10:30 a.m. to 4 p.m. on weekends; closed Monday.

During Lenin's last days, when he was confined to bed, Stalin and Trotsky fought a silent battle for control of the Communist Party in the Soviet Union. Stalin won, and Trotsky fled in terror for his life. He settled here on the outskirts of Mexico City (this area was mostly fields then) to continue his work and writing on political topics and communist ideology. His ideas clashed with those of Stalin in many respects, and Stalin, wanting no opposition or dissension in world communist ranks, set out to have Trotsky assassinated. A first attempt failed but it served to give warning to Trotsky and his household, and from then on the house became a veritable fortress, with riflemen's watchtowers on the corners of the walls, steel doors (Trotsky's bedroom was entered only by thick steel doors), and round-the-clock guards, several of whom were Americans who sympathized with Trotsky's philosophies. Finally a man thought to have been paid, cajoled, or blackmailed by Stalin directly or indirectly was able to get himself admitted to the house by posing as a friend of Trotsky's and of his political views. On March 20, 1940, he put a mountaineer's axe into the philosopher's head. He was, of course, caught by the guards; Trotsky died of his wounds shortly after.

If you saw the film *The Death of Trotsky* with Richard Burton, you already have a good idea of what the house looks like, for although the movie was not made here, the set which was used was a very good replica of the house and gardens. You can visit Natalia's (Trotsky's wife's) study, the communal dining room, Trotsky's study (with worksheets, newspaper clippings, books, and cylindrical wax dictating records still spread around), and his fortress-like bedroom. Some of the walls still have the bullet holes left during the first attempt on his life. Trotsky's tomb, designed by Juan O'Gorman, is in the garden of the house.

Once you've seen Coyoacán, find your way to Calle Centenario or Avenida México–Coyoacán, and catch the no. 23 or 23-A bus north to get back to the center. If you're heading west to San Angel, catch a no. 56 on Calle Cuauhtémoc; going east to the Anahuacalli, catch a no. 56 on Calle Xicoténcatl, then transfer to a no. 25 ("Zacatenco–Tlalpan") or no. 59 ("El Rosario–Xochimilco") going south on the avenue called División del Norte.

Diego Rivera Museum (The Anahuacalli)

Probably the most unusual museum in the city is that designed by Diego Rivera before his death in 1957 and devoted to his works as well as an extensive collection of pre-Columbian art. Called the Anahuacalli Museum and constructed of pedregal (lava rock with which the area abounds), it is similar in style to Mayan and Aztec architecture. The name Anáhuac was the old name for the ancient Valley of Mexico.

The museum, admission free, is open daily from 10 a.m. to 6 p.m. (closed Monday), and is situated on the southern outskirts of the city in the suburb of **San Pablo Tepetlapan**, at Calle Tecuila 150, off Calle del Museo. Take the Metro (Line 2) to the Taxqueña terminal. From the terminal, catch a SARO bus no. 136 ("Tasqueña–Peña Pobre") west, and it'll take you right past the museum.

Another way to get there is bus no. 25 ("Zacatenco–Tlalpan") south along Balderas, or no. 59 ("El Rosario–Xochimilco") south along Avenida Vasconcelos, Nuevo León, and Avenida Divisón del Norte. Hop off at the Calle del Museo stop.

The museum is a ten-minute walk west along Calle del Museo from Avenida División del Norte. Signs point the way. If you see the no. 136 bus coming, you might as well hop aboard.

In front of the museum is a reproduction of a Toltec ball court, and the entrance to the museum itself is via a coffin-shaped door. Light filters in through translucent onyx slabs and is supplemented by lights inside niches and wall cases containing the exhibits. Rivera was a great collector of pre-Columbian artifacts and the museum includes literally hundreds of them, stashed on the shelves, tucked away in corners, and peeking from behind glass cases.

Upstairs, a replica of Rivera's studio has been constructed, and there you'll find the original sketches for some of his murals and two in-progress canvases. His first sketch (of a train) was done at the age of three, and there's a photo of it, plus a color photograph of him at work later in life in a pair of baggy pants and a blue denim jacket. Rivera (1886–1957) studied in Europe for 15 years, and spent much of his life as a devoted Marxist. Yet he came through political scrapes and personal tragedies with no apparent diminution of creative energy, and a plaque in the museum proclaims him "A man of genius who is among the greatest painters of all time."

Xochimilco

As you might guess from its name, Xochimilco (pronounced "so-chee-MEEL-co") is a survival from the civilization of the Aztecs. They built gardens on rafts called *chinampas,* then set them afloat on a series of canals. Now, of course, the gardens are gone, but flower-bedecked boats still run to and fro.

Sad to say, Xochimilco is not in the best of shape today. Aside from the fact that it's become badly commercialized (from the moment you arrive, you'll be pestered by people trying to sell you something or persuade you to take one boat over another), the canals themselves are a bit polluted. On Sunday, the place is jammed with foreign tourists and Mexican families with babies and picnic hampers; on weekdays, it's nearly deserted.

To reach Xochimilco, take the Metro to Taxqueña and then a bus. The buses (31, 33, 35, 37, 39, 59) run all the way across the city from north to south to end up at Xochimilco, but they take longer than the Metro. Of the buses coming from the center, the most convenient are nos. 31 and 33 ("La Villa–Xochimilco"), which you catch going south on Correo Mayor and Pino Suarez near the Zócalo; or no. 59, which you catch near Chapultepec on Avenida Vasconcelos, Avenida Nuevo León, and Avenida División del Norte.

When you get to the town of Xochimilco, you'll find a busy market in operation, specializing in garish, brightly decorated pottery. Turn along Madero and follow signs that say "Los Embarcaderos." If you can resist the blandishment of the inevitable salesmen and shills, you will eventually arrive at the riverbank.

The boats are priced according to their size and the number of people they can hold, plus your skill as a bargainer. The going rate for a medium-size boat which can hold five or six persons is about 350 pesos per hour. If you have a group of four or five people, a picnic lunch, and a few six-packs of beer or soft drinks, the ride can be a pleasure. For single people or even couples, the minimum rental fee is a bit much, and Xochimilco is definitely the sort of place which is best enjoyed in a small group.

HEADING NORTH: Within the northern city limits are two more interesting locations, and another is just a short ride outside. You can take the Metro to the Plaza de las Tres Culturas (Tlatelolco station), and then continue up the same line to the Basilica de Guadalupe (Basilica station). Finally, the terminus at Indios Verdes is the place to catch a bus for the short ride to Tepotzotlán.

Plaza de las Tres Culturas

A few miles north of the Alameda, in **Tlatelolco,** stands this monument to the long and varied history of Mexico: all three cultures—Aztec, Spanish, and contemporary—are architecturally represented here.

During the Aztec Empire, Tlatelolco was on the northern edge of Lake Texcoco and for a long time it maintained its autonomy, independent of the Aztecs. In May of 1521, it was to Tlatelolco that Cuauhtémoc and his army withdrew when Cortes marched for the second time on the great city of Tenochtitlán. Cuauhtémoc would not surrender and after a three-month siege, with thousands of his army dead from starvation or wounds, he was finally captured. Reduced to a wretched state of captivity, he grabbed Cortes's dagger and fell upon it. The Plaza de las Tres Culturas is where this heroic siege took place, and a plaque commemorates it.

Afterward, Tlatelolco was officially abandoned, and it remained so until 1960 when the government began a redevelopment program to clean up the slum area which had grown during the years of neglect. Tlatelolco today is a suburb of housing projects, and not a very attractive one at that, but these tall building complexes represent the "contemporary" aspect.

The beautiful Spanish church which stands in the plaza, albeit at a slight angle as a result of sinking into the lake bed, is the famous **Cathedral of Santiago Tlatelolco.** Built in the 16th century entirely of volcanic stone, it echoes Aztec construction, which was made from the same stone. Inside, most of the frescoes have been badly damaged over the years; the interior has been tastefully restored, preserving little patches of fresco in stark white plaster walls, with a few deep-blue stained-glass windows and an unadorned stone altar.

To get to the plaza, take the Metro (Line 3) to Tlatelolco, leave the terminal by the exit to Manuel Gonzalez, and turn right on this street. Walk two blocks to Avenida Lázaro Cárdenas and turn right again. The plaza is about half a block south, on the left, just past the Clinico Hospital. The walk takes less than 15 minutes.

Basilica of Guadalupe

The Basilica of Our Lady of Guadalupe is on the site of the spot where a poor Indian named Juan Diego is reputed to have seen a vision, on December 9, 1531, of a beautiful lady in a blue mantle. The local bishop was reticent to confirm that Juan had indeed seen the Virgin Mary, and so he asked the peasant for some evidence. Juan saw the vision a second time, and it became miraculously emblazoned on the poor peasant's cloak. The bishop immediately ordered the building of a church on the spot, and upon its completion the image was hung in the place of honor, framed in gold. Since that time millions upon millions of the devout and the curious have come to this spot to view the miraculous image which experts, it is said, are at a loss to explain. The bluemantled Virgin of Guadalupe is the patron saint of Mexico.

So heavy was the flow of visitors—many of whom approached for hundreds of yards on their knees—that the old church became insufficient to handle it, and an audacious new basilica is being built, designed by the same architect who did the breathtaking National Museum of Anthropology. It won't be completed for many years, in the tradition of great religious edifices the world around, but it's in service already and you can visit and admire this all-new monument to the humble peasant's miraculous experience. The problem of handling the flow of traffic past the portrait of the Virgin has been dealt with by modern means: a moving walkway provides a brief look at the image, and keeps small groups from monopolizing the ground immediately in front of it.

At the top of the hill, behind the basilica, is a cemetery and also several gift shops specializing in rather tasteless trinkets encased in seashells and other irrelevancies. The steps up this hill are lined with flowers, shrubs, and waterfalls, and the climb, although tiring, is worthwhile for the view from the top.

Should you be lucky enough to visit Mexico City on December 12, you can witness the grand festival in honor of the Virgin of Guadalupe. The square in front of the basilica fills up with the pious and the party-minded as prayers, dances, and a carnival atmosphere attract thousands of the devout.

Easiest way to reach the basilica is to take the Metro (Line 3) to the "Basilica" station.

If you are driving, a trip to the basilica can be fitted conveniently into a day's outing to the pyramids, farther north. Drive northward up Insurgentes, past the Buena Vista Railroad Station on your right and the pyramid-shaped Monumento a la Raza, and then, about six miles from the Juarez, turn off to the right beside the Lindavista Cine sign (in the suburb of Lindavista) and head down Avenue Montevideo about half a mile to Guadalupe Plaza.

Tepotzotlán

Interested in baroque architecture? Want a close-up view of small-town Mexican daily life. Set aside a morning or afternoon for an excursion to the colonial town of Tepotzotlán, 24 miles north of Mexico City. Tepotzotlán's fine **church** (1682) is among the finest examples of churrigueresque (Mexican baroque) architecture, and the museum attached to it has a rich collection of paintings (including a Tintoretto), church ceremonial objects, vestments, pottery, and carving. Plan your visit for any day Wednesday through Sunday; the church is closed on Monday, and the museum is closed on Tuesday.

You can make the trip in a morning or an afternoon by taking the Metro to the Indios Verdes terminus station, and then catching a bus to Tepotzotlán. If you drive, go west on Paseo de la Reforma, and shortly after you pass the Auditorio Municipal (on your left) in Chapultepec Park, turn right (north) onto the Anillo Periferico. This soon becomes the Avenida Manuel Avila Camacho, which in turn becomes Highway 57D, the toll road to Querétaro. About 35 kilometers (22½ miles) out of the city, look for the turn to Tepotzotlán, which is about 2 kilometers west of the highway.

Whether you come by bus or car, you'll soon end up in the town's main square, where you'll spot the church's extravagantly elaborate facade at once. This is considered one of the three finest examples of churrrigueresque decoration, the other two being the Santa Prisca in Taxco, and La Valenciana in Guanajuato.

The grand extravagance of the facade is echoed inside the church, which is richly decorated with carved altarpieces and paintings. When your senses start to reel from the power and weight of it all, stroll outside, turn right, and enjoy the shady park standing in front of the museum.

The **National Viceroy's Museum** was once the Novitiate of the Company of Jesus (1585). Besides the dozens of rooms with displays of colonial treasures, be sure to inspect the Domestic Chapel, dating from about the same time as the neighboring church.

After you've seen Tepotzotlán's colonial monuments, you might want to have a look at the market, or simply wander the cobbled streets for a while. The bus back to Mexico City passes right through the main square. Those with cars might want to continue on (north) along Highway 57D, the Querétaro toll road, to the ruined Toltec city of Tula (see Chapter XI).

7. The Bullfights and Horse Races

The capital's **Plaza México** is the biggest bullring in the world. It seats 64,000 people and on Sunday during the professional season (usually December through April, but no fixed dates) most of them are taken. On other Sundays through the year, the arena is given over to the beginners or *novilleros;* most of them are as bad as the beginners in any other sport. Six fights make up a *corrida,* which begins precisely at 4 p.m. and is one of the few things in Mexico that's always on time.

There are several ways to reach the Plaza México, which is situated two or three miles south along Insurgentes. Any big hotel or tour agency will be happy to book you onto a tour with limousine, guide, and reserved seat, but this can cost anything from 750 pesos and up—and that's real luxury living. Alternatively, you can take a pesero; the meager number of peseros that normally roam Insurgentes is supplemented by Sunday afternoon taxis headed for the plaza, and they'll often pick up extra passengers going their way. Or you can catch the buses marked "Plaza México" which travel down Insurgentes on Sunday afternoon. Finally, you can catch a no. 17 bus along Insurgentes.

Roughly 25 minutes after you start out, the bus will pass the bullring on the right. At the point at which you should alight, the ring is hidden by buildings, so you'll have to watch for a gray, modern apartment building to your right, its exterior more windows than walls. (This is Insurgentes 949, and its owners are so proud of it that, as in many cases of modern buildings in Mexico, they have listed the architect's name, Francisco Artigas, above the entrance.)

Most of the people on the bus will alight here, so you'll know you're at the bullring, which is just around the corner ahead. On the way you'll see dozens of men and women squatting on blankets selling nuts, hats, and all kinds of whatnots. Look for a woman or muchacha selling chewing gum and waving small "programs." If you buy the chewing gum, she'll give you (free) the one-page sheet which lists the names of the day's toreros.

Unless you want to pay more, take your place in the line at one of the windows marked *"Sol General."* It will be in the sun and it will be high up. But the sun isn't too strong (it sets soon, anyway), and you won't see many other tourists that way. Try to avoid the seats numbered 1-100; for some reason, the roughnecks prefer to gather in this section. Seats in *la sombra* (shade) are more expensive, of course.

Usually, there are six separate bulls to be killed (two by each matador) in a corrida, but I'd suggest that you leave just before the last bull gets his—to avoid the crowds. Outside, around two sides of the bullring is a scene of frantic activity. Hundreds of tiny stalls have masses of food frying, cold beer stacked high, and radios blaring with a commentary on the action inside the ring.

A DAY AT THE RACES: Mexico City's racetrack, the **Hipodromo de las Americas,** is as extraordinarily beautiful as many of its other tourist-popular spots. Approached by way of a tree-lined boulevard and containing a small lake on which an occasional swan or heron basks, it has stands built on the hillside for a good view of the track.

The track operates on Tuesday (in winter only), Thursday, Saturday, and Sunday for 11 months of the year; it is closed only for part of September and October. Take a pesero marked "Hipodromo" along Reforma, which takes you through Chapultepec to the Anillo Periferico (also called Avenida Manuel Avila Camacho). The track is just off this main artery, near the intersection with Calzada Legaria.

Once at the track, you may enter through a special (free) tourist gate. The normal price of admission is through purchase of a program. If you don't get a program, you won't have much idea what's going on, so you'd better buy one at the gate. Two or more people may enter on one program, but each must pay the program's tax. Inside, head for the stands and grab a seat. If you're willing to spend the extra loot, you can climb one level higher and sit at a table where the view is excellent and a minimum amount must be consumed in either food or drink. Racing begins at 2:15 p.m.

Betting: You can bet either to win *(primera)*, to place *(segunda)*, or to show *(tercera)*. All windows have signs in both English and Spanish. On certain races, marked on the program with bold letters—"SELECCIÓN 1-2" —you can win a substantial sum by picking the horses that will come in first and second and placing a bet on your selections. In some races, there is an alternative way of betting called the *quiniela*. This operates on a similar principle, except that your choices for first and second can come in second and first.

To get back to the center, take any bus or pesero marked "Zócalo."

Chapter X

MEXICO CITY: BUDGET NIGHTTIME ACTIVITIES

**1. Nightlife in the Zona Rosa
2. Mariachis, Music, and Margaritas
3. Movies and Theaters
4. The Ballet Folklorico
5. Jai Alai
6. The National Lottery Drawing**

MEXICO CITY POSITIVELY SHINES with the glimmer of a billion lamps as night comes on. A torrent of headlamps floods rapidly along the Paseo de la Reforma in each direction of traffic, whizzing in circles around the Angel Monument which itself is dazzlingly illuminated by powerful floodlamps. At the foot of the monument lies the Zona Rosa, the city's brightest nighttime quarter.

Survey all this from the top of a tall hotel, or from the Latin American Tower, and it is certainly a captivating sight. Launch out into this glimmering sea for an evening's amusement and you can easily—*easily*—end up thousands of pesos poorer. If your entertainments are of the contrived type (say, a supper club at a fancy hotel, with drinks and a show, cover charges, minimums, service charges, tips) you can enjoy them here at a price that compares favorably with any other major city, but which is still a lot of money. On the other hand, if you're willing to let *la vida Mexicana* put on its own fascinating show for you, the bill will be no more than a few dollars, or even nothing at all.

People-watching, café-sitting, music, even a dozen mariachi bands all playing at once, can be yours for next to nothing. To start, let's go straight to the heart of the city's nocturnal brouhaha, the famous Pink Zone.

1. Nightlife in the Zona Rosa

Although the Zona Rosa has a well-deserved reputation as Mexico City's high-priced playground, it is also true that the Zona Rosa by night in summer is an unending carnival of people and places, lights and sights. You can enjoy yourself here for zero-dollars-and-zero-cents by window-shopping, people-watching, and generally taking it all in. Or you can spend a few pesos and have dessert and a cup of coffee, or perhaps a drink, and watch the ebb and flow of traffic. It's worth saving up some extra money to have at least one dinner here (see the restaurant chapter for detailed suggestions). Whichever way you decide to take in the Pink Zone, you'll be glad you came to see this slice of life (taken from the upper crust, of course). Here are some prime locales for Pink Zone promenades:

The streets named for Genova, Copenhague, and Oslo have been turned into pedestrian-only streets (save for the occasional car zipping in to the Aristos hotel), and sidewalk café-restaurants have sprung up making Copenhague one of Mexico City's most delightful "in" places. Tables are usually packed unless you come early. Some establishments are selected by the cognoscenti as "in," and chairs are then at a premium; while other places do a slower business and have tables more readily available. On Oslo the attraction is the several coffeehouses with coffee, pastries, and fortune-tellers. Try, for instance, the **Elite Cafe Turco,** at no. 3, where coffee and pastry is about 75 pesos, plus a reading of the Tarot deck just-for-you. The low, mod decor here draws mostly people in love and people who are looking to fall in love. At Oslo 10 is a tiny student beer hangout called **La Cavita,** where the guests make their own music for entertainment and the barman is zealous in the refilling of your mug.

Another such crossroads for live entertainment is in the arcade located at Londres 104, just off Genova. Half a dozen restaurants here (Alfredo's, La Trucha Vagabunda, Toulouse-Lautrec, Le Bistrot, La Cabaña) also serve as cafés, and Toulouse-Lautrec has live entertainment most evenings. Come for a margarita (100 pesos), a shrimp cocktail, or a full meal—by sitting in the outdoor section of one restaurant, you get to enjoy what's going on in neighboring places as well.

2. Mariachis, Music, and Margaritas

MARIACHIS: At some time or other, everybody—Mexicans and turistas alike—goes to see and hear the mariachi players. The mariachis are strolling musicians who wear distinctive costumes, which make them look like cowboys dressed up for a special occasion. Their costume—tight spangled trousers, fancy jackets, and big floppy bow ties—dates back to the French occupation of Mexico in the mid-19th century, as, indeed, does their name. Mariachi is the Mexican mispronunciation of the French word for marriage, which is where they were often on call for music.

In Mexico City, the mariachis make their headquarters around the **Plaza de Garibaldi** which is a ten-minute stroll north of the Palacio de Bellas Artes up Avenida Lázaro Cárdenas, at Avenida Rep. de Honduras. You pass dozens of little stores selling cheap rings, a fun-fair, and a couple of burlesque houses.

In the Plaza de Garibaldi itself, mariachi players swarm all over. Wherever there's a corner, guitars are stacked together like rifles in an army training camp. To the east of the square, some of the mariachis sit eating at counters. If you're hungry, try a bowl of pozole—a popular thick soup of hominy and meat. For music, see what there is of it in the square itself (hottest about 9 or 10 o'clock in the evening, especially on Sunday). Young musicians strut proudly in their flashy outfits, on the lookout for señoritas to impress. They play when they feel like it, or when there seems to be a good chance to gather in some tips, or when someone orders a song—the going rate seems to be around 250 pesos per song.

After all that singing, a man's got to wet his whistle, and so the plaza is surrounded with places for drinking and singing. Most famous of these is the **Tenampa,** once an all-male preserve but now open to men and women (no children, though), tourist and local alike. Across the plaza is the **Tlaquepaque,** a rather fancy restaurant where you can dine to strolling mariachis. But perhaps the most adventurous spot for newcomers to Mexico City is the **Pulquería Hermana Hortensia,** near the northeast corner of the plaza at the corner of Amargura and Rep. de Honduras. Unlike most pulque bars, La Hermana Hortensia is a *pulquería familiar* (a "family" bar, i.e., you can bring your wife—but not your kids). Pulque (that's "POOL-keh") is a thick and flavorsome drink made by fermenting the juice of a maguey ("century") plant. Discovered by the ancient Toltecs and shared with the Aztecs, pulque was a sacred drink forbidden to the common people for centuries. One of the effects of the Spanish Conquest was to liberate pulque for the masses. Was this good or bad? Ask your neighbor in La Hermana Hortensia as you quaff the thick brew. Pulque packs a whallop, by the way, although it's not nearly so strong as those other maguey-based drinks, tequila and mezcal. By the way, the pulque here can be ordered with nuts blended in for a different flavor.

In any of the eating and drinking establishments around the plaza you can enjoy the mariachi music that swirls through the air. But remember—if you give a bandleader the high sign, you're the one who pays the price for the song, just like outside in the square.

Don't get the idea that you'll see only your countrymen in the Plaza Garibaldi, for it is indeed a Mexican phenomenon. As evening falls, lots of people from the neighborhood come to stroll or sit, catching some of the music or trying their hand at one of the stands where they can bust a balloon with a dart to win a prize.

The **Plaza Insurgentes,** built above the Metro station of the same name, is another lively spot in the evening. The plaza, sunken below street level, is always full of young mods, mariachis, and rock groups. Cafés ring the plaza, and you can sit in one and enjoy a beer (50 pesos) or a drink (100 pesos) and watch the action. Day or night, this is a fun place to be, as business people, secretaries, and students hurry here and there. Music issues from the cafés to the outdoor tables; sometimes it's live rock, sometimes records. The beer costs money, but the show's for free.

Devotees of the best in mariachi music will want to spend the money for an evening at the upstairs (mezzanine) lounge called La Fería de la Musica in the **Hotel Alameda,** on Avenida Juarez at Calle García Lorca, by the old-fashioned diligence (stagecoach). The show here is an almost continuous succession of mariachi numbers, by bands of highest quality. There's a 200-peso per-person cover charge, and drinks cost 140 to 200 pesos apiece. You certainly get your money's worth in music.

MUSIC: The plushest circumstances under which I've ever listened to a pianist were at the **Hotel Maria Isabel,** Reforma 325, near the Angel. A split-level fountain tips you off as to the quality of this hotel even before you enter. Once inside, you'll sink ankle-deep into lush red or blue carpets, admire hunks of Mayan architecture spotlighted in corridors, and eventually find your way to an elegant, second-floor cocktail bar. Drinks here cost about 100 to 200 pesos each, and for this you'll hear some marvelous arrangements from whichever "musica romantica" group happens to be featured—usually dreamy Latin stuff.

For contrast and high decibels, try **Le Rendezvous** at Madero 29, across from the Ritz Hotel several blocks west of Zócalo. From about 7 p.m. until midnight the place has jazz and rock groups which change hourly. There is a 50-peso cover. Drinks run about 100 pesos, Cokes are a bit less. A popular place—I've returned on several occasions always to find a jolly atmosphere.

MARGARITAS: I make it a point, every time I come to Mexico City, to have at least one margarita (usually my first) in the **Muralto** bar of the Latin-American Tower on Avenida Lázaro Cárdenas at Juarez. The observation deck costs something just to get in, but you get the same view from the Muralto with your drink at no extra charge. And what a view! Cynics will say you could be anywhere: Top of the Hub in Boston, Top of the Mark in San Francisco, or any other skyscraper. But to me the feeling of gazing down at the Bellas Artes and the Alameda, Paseo de la Reforma out to Chapultepec and the Monument to the Revolution, is always a unique thrill. The late-afternoon thunderstorms are a sound-and-light show of great power, for from the Muralto you can follow the path of every lightning bolt to earth. You can dine here, too, but equally good food at lower prices is to be had elsewhere. I note with some chagrin that margarita quality has been dropping although the price has been increasing—it's now over 100 pesos. But the view is still the best in town.

The ubiquitous **cantinas** are more or less off limits for the average American tourist, especially women (they're usually not allowed inside). It is in the cantinas that you see the liveliest side of the Mexican male; it can be bawdy as the men "let loose" after a few tequilas. The **Bar Negresco,** on the corner of Balderas and Victoria (Morelos), is one such cantina, and even though it hangs out the "women welcome" sign the liveliness of the gatherings has not been refined. It's a grand ol' place, and dates back a long time. In fact, it was in the 1940s that an American correspondent, Alma Reed, entered the cantina and broke the sex barrier. The drinks here are 70, 80, and 90 pesos, and if you arrive in late afternoon you'll be treated to a free plate of entremeses (hors d'oeuvres).

For Men Only

To my knowledge, no Mexican legislator has yet proposed a Mexican Equal Rights Amendment, and even if one passed it is doubtful that things would change at **La Opera Bar,** a staunchly masculine drinking and dining establishment at 5 de Mayo no. 14, corner of Filomeno Mata, a block from the Bellas Artes if you're heading toward the Zócalo. Men may enter and enjoy the gilded baroque ceilings, the dark wood booths with patches of bevelled mirror and exquisite small oil paintings of pastoral scenes, or sidle up to the heavy carved wooden bar for some tequila and lime. La Opera is the Mexican's equivalent of a Londoner's club, and men in shirtsleeves or dark suits will be playing dominoes or cards, drinking beer (50 pesos) or *copas* (hard liquor of whatever sort, 75 to 125 pesos), and perhaps having supper from the selective menu. La Opera Bar is open every day, but it closes early (9 p.m.) on Saturday night. Women should at least take a look, as much of the interior can be seen from the sidewalk.

3. Movies and Theaters

MOVIES: You'll find many current first-run hits playing in Mexico City, usually in the original-language version with Spanish subtitles, and usually under the same title (although the title will be translated into Spanish). Thus, if you see *Cazadores del Arca Perdida,* you'll know they're running *Raiders of the Lost Ark.*

The best place to check for what's currently being shown is in the entertainment section of Mexico City's English-language paper, *The News.* Note that various cinema clubs, and the National Museum of Anthropology, also screen films from time to time.

Tickets cost about 60 to 80 pesos, even at the fancy movie houses along Reforma. At the gigantic Cine Diana there's a bonus: an enormous mural stretching the entire length of one wall, which is almost worth the price of admission alone.

THEATERS: Mexico City's Theater district is near the Plaza de la República, centered on Calle Antonio Caso. Bright marquees advertise the plays or vaudeville shows currently running, and box offices sell reserved-seat tickets in advance. It's all in Spanish, of course, but still very entertaining. As ticket prices are low, you have little to lose by trying an evening at the theater. Check the entertainment listings in the daily Spanish-language newspapers for current theater offerings.

The English-language community in Mexico City sponsors plays and shows in English from time to time, and *The News* will always carry details.

The **National Auditorium** in Chapultepec Park, fronting onto Reforma, is usually the biggest bargain in town. International ballet, opera, and theater companies play here at prices as low as 20 pesos per seat. Often they are the same companies that played at the elegant Bellas Artes theater with a 215-peso minimum. The newspapers list performances at both, but it's worth walking past the National Auditorium once in a while to see what forthcoming events they are announcing. By the way, at the National Auditorium, the ushers frequently run out of programs and are too lazy to get more. Keep asking; eventually they'll bring you one.

BOLETRÓNICO: This is the name of Mexico City's electronic ticket system, similar to the Ticketron outlets known in the U.S. Bullfight tickets, those for the Ballet Folklorico, and for other attractions are all on sale in the booths of this municipally run system; the booths are scattered around the city, and your hotel clerk will know which one is most convenient for you.

4. The Ballet Folklorico

A combination of religious ceremony, can-can, pantomime, low comedy, and sheer beauty of color, design, and choreography—that's the **Ballet Folklorico de México.** There are two companies—three, if you count the one usually on tour—and their performances are given at the Palacio de las Bellas Artes (tel. 585-4888, ext. 29).

Performances are on Sunday at 9:30 a.m. and 9 p.m. and on Wednesday at 9 p.m.; you cannot buy your tickets before Monday for the Wednesday performance, or Thursday for Sunday. The box office is open 10:30 a.m. to 1 p.m. and 4 to 7 p.m.; tickets range from galleria seats at 215 pesos (on the third floor) to 450 pesos for second-floor and 500 pesos for first-floor seats. The show is popular and tickets are bought up rapidly (especially by tour companies) so if you want a seat go early, or book seats through a tour agency (at twice the cost). The box office is on the ground floor of the Bellas Artes, main entrance.

A typical program will include Aztec ritual dances, agricultural dances from Jalisco, a fiesta in Veracruz, a Christmas celebration—all welded together with mariachis, marimba players, singers, and dancers.

As many other events are held in the Bellas Artes—visits by foreign opera companies, for instance—there are times when the Ballet Folklorico is moved. Usually, it reappears in the National Auditorium in Chapultepec Park. Check at the Bellas Artes box office; if it's at the "Auditorio," catch an Expresso Reforma bus for "Auditorio" from the Juarez Monument on Avenida Juarez. *Note:* The theater tends to be very cold so you may want to bring a sweater.

An alternative to the Ballet Folklorico de México is the Ballet Folclorico Nacional Aztlán, in the Teatro de la Ciudad at Donceles 36. Performances here are as good as the better-known ones in the Bellas Artes, but tickets are a lot cheaper and much easier to get hold of. Shows are at 9:30 on Sunday mornings and 8:30 on Tuesday evenings.

5. Jai Alai

Jai alai (pronounced "hi-lie") must be the fastest game in the world, and is exciting to watch even without prior knowledge of how it is played. Games take place most Tuesday, Wednesday, Thursday, Saturday, and Sunday nights throughout the year in the Fronton México, on the Plaza de la República, which is the plaza dominated by the Monument to the Revolution. The plaza is a few blocks along Juarez west of Reforma. Any bus going west along Juarez will take you to the Juarez–Reforma intersection, and it's a short walk from there, or you can take the Metro to the Revolución station, and walk three blocks down Arriaga (south) to the plaza. Actually, many of my recommended hotels are so close to the fronton that you can walk there easily. It doesn't much matter what time you arrive. The box office opens at 6:30, and there are several games on each night's card.

As you walk into the fronton, the ticket office is to your left; pay 20 pesos at the "Admission General" window, then walk the length of the big lobby to a stack of small brown programs on a cigarette counter to your left. Take one, they're free. And then take a seat—the game will probably already be under way.

Jai alai players wear small baskets on their right arms, with which they catch and sling a fantastically resilient ball against the wall to the right of where you're sitting. In the best games, four players, two with blue armbands and two with red ones, are competing with each other in a fashion similar to tennis, but even more similar to squash. The member of one team throws the ball against the wall, and the other team has to return it. The whole thing is done at an incredible speed, and how they manage to see, much less catch, a ball traveling at about 80 miles per hour is just bloody marvelous.

The most fun, of course, is in the betting; you'd be amazed at how much more exciting a game seems to you when you have money riding on the result. Wait until the program announces a game of 30 points *(partido a treinta tantos)* and watch the bookies. These colorful gentlemen, who all wear white jackets and bright-red berets, carry little pads of betting slips edged in red *(rojo)* or blue *(azul),* and when the game begins, they'll be offering only a slight edge on one team or another—say 95 pesos to 100. When the scoring starts, however, the odds will change. If you're as good a mathematician as most jai alai aficionados, you'll be able to bet with impunity on both sides at different points of the game—and still finish up ahead.

6. The National Lottery Drawing

Any Monday, Wednesday, or Friday, walk in the front door of the older National Lottery Building, where Juarez meets Reforma, go straight up the steps, and take a seat in the small auditorium that faces you. Sharp at 8 p.m. a dozen pages, clad in maroon uniforms, enter to begin the ceremony of picking small wooden balls from two revolving cages. One cage contains 50,000 balls (or more, depending on the number of tickets issued for the lottery), the other contains balls relating to the number of prizes with the total of each prize on it. As each ball is picked and dropped into cages, the pages keep up a sing-song patter of the winning numbers. The big-money winners are posted on a board at the end of the stage. The whole ceremony is broadcast, and the winning numbers are also printed in the papers next morning and listed at all the stands where lottery tickets are sold. Attendance at the lottery takes on a whole different element of suspense if you are clutching a 50-peso ticket in your hand as the numbers are called.

Chapter XI

ONE-DAY TRIPS FROM THE CAPITAL

1. Pyramids of San Juan Teotihuacán
2. Tula
3. Toluca
4. The Volcanoes
5. Cuernavaca
6. Taxco

JUST AS PARIS has its Versailles and Rome its Villa d'Este, so Mexico City is surrounded by suburban areas that are every bit as fascinating as the city itself—and all of them can be reached by a bus ride that is ridiculously cheap. Each of the places described in this chapter can be visited within a couple-of-hours journey, making each of them suitable for one-day trips that can be followed by an evening back in town (although for Taxco you may want to make an exception and stay overnight).

First stop is the most exciting trip on the outskirts of the capital: the breathtaking, ancient pyramids of Teotihuacán. Later I take you farther afield, southwest from University City over the mountains to Cuernavaca; and thence to silver city of Taxco, on the road to Acapulco.

1. Pyramids of San Juan Teotihuacán

The pyramids of San Juan Teotihuacán were built about 300 B.C., the time when the Classical Greeks were building their great monuments on the other side of the world. Teotihuacán was the dominant city during the Classic Period, with its magnificent pyramids, palaces, and houses covering eight square miles. At its zenith around A.D. 500 there were 125,000 inhabitants, more than in contemporary Rome. But little is known about the city's inhabitants or about why they abandoned the place in A.D. 700. Today what remains are the rough stone structures of the three pyramids and sacrificial altars, and some of the grand houses. This is one of Mexico's most remarkable ruins, and you shouldn't miss it.

You may want to pack a lunch to take to the ruins. Restaurants exist, but they are expensive, or disappointing, or a long walk from the ruins, or all of the above. If you forget your box lunch, don't panic. Drinks and snacks are sold by vendors, so you needn't starve. For further recommendations on meals at Teotihuacán, see below.

PYRAMIDS OF SAN JUAN TEOTIHUACÁN

GETTING THERE BY CAR: Driving to San Juan Teotihuacán on the toll Highways 85D and 132D will take about an hour. Head north on Insurgentes to get out of the city. There are two roads to the pyramids; one passes through picturesque villages and the like, but is excruciatingly slow, due to the surfeit of trucks and buses; the other is the toll road, which is a little duller but considerably faster. However, if you're in the mood for a leisurely drive, you might as well take the old two-lane road, slow as it is. And now I'll mention a few of the sights you'll pass.

About 15 miles from town, the village of **San Cristóbal Ecatepec** looms off to the left. Note, also on the left, an old wall centuries ago to keep what was then a lake from flooding the area. When the road forks a mile or so farther north, take the road to the right.

Three miles farther along this road, is the ancient **Convent of San Augustine Acolman** (1539–1560). Only a few years ago the monastery was in ruins, the only sounds being the ticking of a modern clock, the faint braying of sheep from the fields outside, and the chatter of birds building nests on the roof. Now, however, the monastery and church are restored (probably done for Mexico's Olympics).

The next mile or so is as typically rural a slice of Mexico as can be found. Goats and horses graze beside the road outside gardens fenced in by giant cactus; bales of hay can be seen stacked high on a thatched farmhouse roof; women scrub their clothes in a small brook, spreading them out on the ground or on the trees and shrubs to dry.

GETTING THERE BY BUS: Don't let *anyone* tell you that it's difficult to get to the pyramids by bus, and that you should take a tour or a cab! It's simple, relatively fast, and very inexpensive to go by bus. Two different lines serve the route between Mexico City and San Juan Teotihuacán.

Buses leave every half hour (6 a.m. to 8 p.m.) every day of the week from the Terminal Central de Autobuses del Norte. Cost for a one-way ticket is 36 pesos, and the trip takes one hour. To get to the Terminal Norte, take bus 17, "Indios Verdes–Tlalpan," going north on Insurgentes. Or take the Metro to "La Raza" or "Terminal A. Norte."

When you reach the Terminal Norte, look for the Autobuses Teotihuacán desk, located at the far west end. Try to go early in the morning and give yourself plenty of time to wander around the ruins, for there is a lot to see. While you're waiting for your bus, strike up a conversation with other readers of this book who may be waiting there as well (if they've avoided the shills and misinformants who railroad tourists into tours and cabs, they're most likely readers like yourself). You may be surprised by how much your Mexican experiences coincide. When you've compared notes, write me a letter—I love getting feedback. Your letter, with its suggestions, experiences, complaints, and praise will help literally thousands of other readers have better trips south of the border. But to get back to the pyramids. . . .

Another way to get to the pyramids by bus is to walk from the Zócalo north on Rep. de Argentina, then right on Justo Sierra. Walk five blocks on Sierra (which changes its name to Mixcalco and then to Alarcon) and cross Avenida Vidal Alcocer. Buses ("Pyramides") leave from the "Garage Teotihuacán," on the right-hand side of Mixcalco, just before Calle Bravo, about every 15 minutes for the hour-long trip to Teotihuacán. The fare is 32 pesos. For the return journey, catch the same bus at the main gate to the museum or take a bus at the traffic circle near the pyramids entrance closest to the museum. The Mexico-Metro bus will drop you off at the Indios Verdes Metro station, from whence it is a short ride to any other point in the city.

SEEING THE PYRAMIDS: During your visit to the pyramids and temples of Teotihuacán, please keep in mind these important points:

—You will be doing a great deal of walking, and perhaps some climbing. It is a full mile from the Pyramid of the Moon to the Unidad Cultural (Museum) and Ciudadela; and there are 248 steep steps up to the top of the Pyramid of the Sun.

—Because the site is so vast, I'll describe it in sections. Whichever entrance you use to the site, locate the section nearest you and visit it first. Backtracking takes too much time and energy.

—Remember always that you're at an altitude of more than 7000 feet, and you will tire more easily than usual. Take it slowly. Also, the sun and heat can get you. Protect yourself.

—In the summer rainy season, it rains almost every afternoon. Plan to be in the museum or a restaurant when the showers come at 2 or 3 o'clock.

Admission

Teotihuacán is open every day of the week from 9 a.m. to 5 p.m. to 5 p.m. (you must be off the site by 6); admission is 20 pesos, and there's a 15-peso parking fee if you have a car. On Sunday and holidays you pay less for admission, but the same for the car.

The Layout

The grand buildings of Teotihuacán were laid out on a cosmic plan. The front wall of the Pyramid of the Sun is exactly square to (facing) the point on the horizon where the sun sets on the day it reaches its zenith. So if a line were drawn from the pyramid to the sun at noon on the day when the sun reaches its highest point (i.e., it seems to be directly overhead), and another line were drawn from the pyramid to the sun when the sun reaches the horizon later that same day, then the pyramid would be exactly square to these lines. The rest of the ceremonial buildings were laid out at right angles to the Pyramid of the Sun.

The main thoroughfare, called by archeologists the Avenue of the Dead, runs roughly north-south. The Pyramid of the Moon is at the northern end, and the Unidad Cultural (Museum) and Ciudadela are on the southern part of the thoroughfare. Actually, the great street was several miles long in its heyday, but only a mile or so has been uncovered and restored.

The Pyramid of the Sun is on the east side of the Avenue of the Dead.

Pyramid of the Sun

As pyramids go, this one is Number Three. The Great Pyramid of Cholula, on the Mexico City–Puebla road, is the largest structure ever built by man. Today it's so ruined that it appears as a muddy hill with a church built on top. Second largest is the Pyramid of Cheops on the outskirts of Cairo. In third place is Teotihuacán's Pyramid of the Sun, which is almost—at 730 feet per side—as large as Cheops at the base. But at 210 feet high, the Sun pyramid is only about half as high as its Egyptian rival. No matter. It's still the biggest restored pyramid in the Western Hemisphere, and an awesome sight.

PYRAMIDS OF SAN JUAN TEOTIHUACÁN

Although the Pyramid of the Sun was not built as a great king's tomb, it does have secret tunnels and chambers beneath it. A natural grotto was enlarged and restructured into a four-room chamber which was used for some occult purpose—no one knows what. The tunnels are not open to the public.

The first structure of the pyramid was probably built a century before Christ, and the temple which used to crown the pyramid was finished about 400 years later (A.D. 300) By the time the pyramid was discovered and restoration was begun (early in our century), the temple had completely disappeared, and the pyramid was just a mass of rubble covered with bushes and trees.

If you're game, trudge up the 248 steps to the top. The view is marvelous, if the smog's not too thick.

Avenue of the Dead

As you stroll north along the Avenue of the Dead toward the Pyramid of the Moon, look on the right for a bit of wall sheltered by a modern corrugated roof. Beneath the shelter, the wall still bears a painting of a jaguar. From this fragment, build a picture of the breathtaking spectacle which must have met the eye when all the paintings along the avenue were intact.

The Avenue of the Dead got its strange and forbidding name from the Aztecs, who mistook the little temples which line both sides of the avenue for tombs of kings or priests.

Pyramid of the Moon

The Pyramid of the Moon faces an interesting plaza at the northern end of the avenue. The plaza is surrounded by little temples, and by the Palace of Quetzal-Mariposa (or Quetzal-Butterfly), on the left (west) side. You get about the same range of view from the top of the Pyramid of the Moon as you do from its larger neighbor, because the moon pyramid is built on higher ground. So if the prospect of dragging yourself up the sun pyramid was just too much, you can go up the 150-foot-high moon pyramid with less effort. There's a bonus, too: the magnificent perspective straight down the Avenue of the Dead.

Palace of Quetzal-Mariposa

The Palace of Quetzal-Mariposa lay in ruins until the 1960s, when restoration work began. Today it echoes wonderfully with its former glory, as figures of Quetzal-Mariposa (a mythical exotic bird-butterfly) appear painted on walls or carved in the pillars of the inner court.

Behind the Palace of Quetzal-Mariposa is the **Palace of the Jaguars**, complete with murals showing a lively jaguar musical combo, and some frescoes.

Ciudadela and Unidad Cultural

Along the southern reaches of the Avenue of the Dead, a 15-minute stroll from the Pyramid of the Moon, are two more important Teotihuacán sights.

The **Unidad Cultural** is the only modern building of any size on the grounds of Teotihuacán. It houses an entrance to the grounds, rows of little shops, a restaurant, a book and souvenir shop, and the **museum**, which is worth a look.

First thing you'll notice as you wander into the museum is an enormous statue (a copy, actually) of the goddess Chalchiuhtlicue. She stands in a small pool, which is appropriate as she was the goddess of water. Behind, around, and above her are various exhibits outlining the culture of Teotihuacán, as well as some artifacts found during excavations on the site. Useful in planning the rest of your visit is a scale model of the city of Teotihuacán.

Across the Avenue of the Dead from the Unidad Cultural is the **Ciudadela,** or Citadel, so named by the Spaniards. Actually, this immense sunken square was not a fortress at all, although the impressive walls make it look like one. It was the grand setting for a temple to Quetzalcoatl, the famed "plumed serpent" who appears so often in Mexican folklore. Once you've admired the great scale of the Ciudadela, go down the steps into the massive court and head for the ruined temple, in the middle.

The **Temple of Quetzalcoatl** was covered over by an even larger structure, a pyramid. As you walk toward the center of the Ciudadela's court, you'll be approaching the pyramid. Walk around to the right of it, and soon you'll see the reconstructed temple close behind the pyramid. There's a narrow passage between the two structures, and traffic is supposed to be one-way—which is why I directed you to the right.

It wasn't unusual for early temples to be covered over by later ones in Mexico and Central America. Rather, it was a very common practice. The Pyramid of the Sun may even have been built up in this way. As for the Temple of Quetzalcoatl, you'll notice at once the fine big carved serpents' heads jutting out from aureoles of feathers carved in the stone walls. Other feathered serpents are carved in relief low on the walls. The temple provides a vivid example of pre-Columbian public decoration. The decoration at Chichén-Itzá, Uxmal, and Tikal is certainly more elaborate, but these sites are thousands of miles from Mexico City. Luckily, you can still get a good idea of the glory of Mexico's ancient cities from this temple. Don't miss it.

Where to Have Lunch

If you heeded my earlier advice to bring a box lunch, you can take a break wherever you like: in the shade of a tree or a palace, or atop a pyramid. Vendors sell soft drinks and various snacks, wandering with their wares throughout the ruins.

Outside the Unidad Cultural there are often primitive cookshops set up by local señoras, and you can sit at a rustic table under a shady tree and partake of whatever rough-and-ready fare is being served up. People prone to stomach grumbles had better head for a bona-fide restaurant, however.

There is a restaurant in the Unidad Cultural, but more suitable places exist along the road which rings the archeological site. **La Gruta,** for instance, is a ten-minute walk east of the Pyramid of the Sun (go out the gate behind the pyramid and follow the signs). Open from 10 a.m. to 9 p.m. every day, La Gruta is just that—a huge, delightfully cool natural grotto filled with table and chairs, natty waiters, and the sound of clinking glasses. Soft drinks and beer are served till 3 p.m., and then the full bar opens. As for food, the set-price lunch of five courses will cost you about 300 pesos all in, although you can have lunch for about half that price if you order a hamburger and soft drink. La Gruta is exactly three-tenths of a mile from the Pyramid of the Sun, but after the blazing heat, the delicious coolness makes you think you're at the center of the earth.

Behind the Pyramid of the Moon, to the north, is the modest **Restaurant Tepantitla,** where your lunch will be a bit cheaper than at La Gruta, but without the delightful coolness. Next door to the Tepantitla are the fairly uninteresting ruins of Tepantitla. **El Chinanco,** on the ring road between the entrances at Pyramid of the Sun and Pyramid of the Moon, is a similar place.

Yet another classy place is **Pyramides Charlie's,** which has all the marks of a Carlos Anderson restaurant (you'll meet with others in various Mexican cities). Expect to pay 400 to 500 pesos for a good, full lunch here. Pyramides Charlie's is on the ring road between the two highways to Mexico City, the "México Libre" (Highway 132) and "México Cuota" (Highway 132D). It's not all that far from the Unidad Cultural.

SOUND AND LIGHT SHOW: The Mexican Tourist Office has organized a spectacle of sound and light nightly October to May, except Monday, in English at 7 p.m. and in Spanish at 8:15 p.m. For 100 pesos you can relive some of the Aztec legends; it's splendidly engineered, very impressive, and features the National Symphony Orchestra and the voices of such notables as Charlton Heston (The Sun), Vincent Price (a Narrator), Ricardo Montalban (Tecuciztecatl), Agnes Moorehead (Black Ant), and numerous others. **Note:** Warm clothing is a must with that cold night wind howling around the pyramids! Phone 521-5602 for reservations. There is a bus which leaves from the Plaza de la República (by the Revolution Monument), but *only* for the 8:15 show (in Spanish). They have not found it worthwhile to provide a bus for the English performance.

2. Tula

In A.D. 900 or thereabouts, Teotihuacán was overrun by a people called the Chichimecs. Many Teotihuacanos, or Toltecs, fled northward to found the city of Tula, which flourished from 900 to 1156. In that year the Chichimecs caught up with their former enemies the Toltecs again, and wiped out Tula. But the one-time Toltec capital's impressive pyramids, giant statues, and curious three-legged pottery survived to be uncovered by modern archeologists.

The city's remains are memorably beautiful, although its history is a sad story. The peace-loving king of the Toltecs, Quetzalcoatl (the "feathered serpent" in later lore) sought to purge his people of such things as human sacrifice and to direct their efforts to peaceful agriculture. The warlike party in Tula disagreed with the king's aims, and forced him and a band of his followers to flee the city in about 987. They wandered as far as the Yucatán and Chichén-Itzá, spreading Toltec culture along the way and giving birth to the legend of Quetzalcoatl (see the "Brief History" in Chapter I).

The Chichimecs seized Tula in 1156, but in 1200 a drought drove them out. They were succeeded by the Aztecs by 1325, and by the Spaniards in 1519, but Tula never regained its former glory.

Most striking of the city's remains are the 15-foot-high "Atlantean men," gigantic basalt figures mounted atop the Temple of Tlahuizcalpantecuhtli (that Toltec mouthful means "Morning Star"). At one time, they supported the roof of the temple. The city's ball court, said to be the earliest ball court built on the continent, has been restored beautifully. To the west of the temple is the Burnt Palace (Quemado) where you'll be able to see several painted reliefs and a statue of Chac Mool, the reclining figure with head turned to one side. Between the temple and the ball court is a large wall with fantastic reliefs of the feathered serpent, skulls, eagles, and jaguars.

There's a small museum at the site containing a few Toltec artifacts as well as some Aztec pottery. The most interesting items here are the two stone figures once thought to be standard holders. The ruins and museum are open daily from 8 a.m. to 6 p.m.; admission costs 15 pesos.

GETTING TO TULA: Tula is about 50 miles due north of Mexico City along Highways 57D (a toll road) and 126. If you take the bus, you'll be obliged to walk out from town (about 15 minutes), or take a cab.

You won't find any food or drink at the ruins, not even soft drinks, so you might want to have a bite or a sip in town before you hike out. The **Cafe "El Cisne"** on Tula's tidy main street, can fill your light lunch wishes admirably and cheaply. Assuming you won't eat heavily before walking to the ruins, you'll end up paying about 90 pesos for the daily set-price lunch, a bit more if you order à la carte.

By Bus

Buses leave every quarter hour from Mexico City's Terminal Central de Autobuses del Norte, reached by a no. 17 city bus ("Indios Verdes") going north along Insurgentes or by Metro to "La Raza" or "Terminal A. Norte." When you enter the giant bus station, turn left and walk down to the far end to the Tula ticket counter, marked "Autotransportes del Valle del Mezquital." The trip takes about an hour and 20 minutes, and you should ask to get off the bus before it gets to the center of town. Cross the railroad tracks and the junction of Highways 22 and 87, and, going along 87, follow signs as mentioned above. The walk will take about 15 minutes.

By Car

Driving north on the fast toll road (57D), there are no less than three turnoffs for Tula, at km. 58 ("Petrolera–Tula"), km. 69 "Tepeji del Río–Tula"), and km. 84 ("Jilotepec–Tula"). Take the first, most southerly one at km. 58 to avoid a toll.

When you reach the modern town of Tula, ask for directions to the Zona Arqueologica (there may be scattered signs), or follow signs to—get this—Tlahuelilpan. The ruins are about a mile from the center of town. Watch out for a sharp left turn just past a Pemex housing development.

3. Toluca

At 8760 feet, Toluca is the highest city in Mexico, and the hour-long trip there from Mexico City offers spectacular scenic views. Pine trees and icy-looking blue lakes dot the landscape, and only an occasional cactus plant or brightly colored painting, drying in the sun, will remind you that you're in Mexico. Toluca isn't a particularly exciting city, but it has an immense market you'll want to visit on a Friday, as early as possible in the day before the tour buses roll in.

It's easy to get to the market by bus from Mexico City. Take the Metro to the Observatorio station, and look for the Terminal Poniente bus station. Enter the terminal, turn left, and look for the Toluca counter. Buses ("Toluca Directo") depart every 20 minutes on the hour-long trip.

Don't expect a small, backward Indian town at the other end of the bus trip. Toluca (pop. 150,000) is the capital of the state of México, and has been an important town since the Aztec times. You enter town along a beautiful parkway.

The gigantic **Mercado Juarez,** at the edge of town on the highway to Mexico City has both market buildings and open-air grounds. Shops in the buildings are open all week, but it's on Friday that the people from surrounding villages come and crowd the plaza. The bus from Mexico City pulls into a terminal right across the street from the Mercado Juarez. You'll recognize the market by the pair of slender concrete slabs which tower above it to serve as a landmark.

Because of the natives' bargaining powers, a peaceful walk around the market is not an easy matter. Every time you pause to admire such unfamiliar sights as a boxful of chattering chickens, a two-foot-high pile of assorted shoelaces, or an array of framed saints' pictures, some man or young boy will accost you with cries of *"Serapes, rebozos, Señor, very cheap."* And sooner or later the heat and crowdedness of the market will begin to get you down; you will barely raise your head as the man with the pig under his arm or the woman with a turkey sticking its head from the back of her shawl brushes past.

Some sights will make you pause—a marimba band banging away cheerfully between the stalls, and a little, open-fronted bakery where chains of tortillas can be seen pouring off a conveyor belt into a basket.

Finding a place for lunch is never a problem in such a huge market, but if none of the little market eateries appeals to you, there is an alternative. Search the skyline for the red-and-yellow star sign that identifies the local branch of **VIP'S** (pronounced "beeps"), a clean, bright, and cheery American-style restaurant.

4. The Volcanoes

One of the nicest picnic spots in all of Mexico is the **Ixta-Popo National Park**, whose raison d'être are the volcanoes of **Popocatepetl** and **Ixtacchihuatl**. These snow-capped peaks are usually associated with the city of Puebla, a three-hour trip from Mexico City, but it is by no means necessary to go all the way to Puebla to see them.

Take Metro Line 1 east, in the direction of Zaragoza, to the San Lázaro stop. As you come to the surface, you'll see the green-domed TAPO ("Terminal de Autobuses de Pasajeros de Oriente"), Mexico City's eastern bus terminal. Walk along "Tunel 1," the corridor to the central domed area, and look for "Lineas Unidas–Cristóbal Colón" buses to Amecameca and Popo Park. Buses leave every half hour, every day, on the two-hour trip.

The bus will take the Puebla road (Route 190) out of Mexico City, turning off to the right (Route 115) at the village of Chalco. A few miles farther on is Amecameca (pop. 22,000) from where the best view of the volcanoes can be obtained. Situated at a height of 7500 feet, Amecameca is a fresh, clear town, with a big square and a 200-year-old parish church. Behind it are the two lovely mountains, neither of which has erupted in this century.

About the best hotel in Amecameca is the very plain but clean **Hotel San Carlos**, right on the main square to the right of the church, at Plaza de la Constitución 10 (tel. 597/8-0344). A room with one double bed costs 300 pesos; with twin beds, 350 pesos. All rooms have baths and hot water. The San Carlos's restaurant serves light meals.

Getting to Ixta-Popo National Park from Amecameca takes some doing. You can hitchhike, or try to catch one of the rickety old village buses which leaves from the main square—look for the *camioneta azul* (blue minibus) marked "San Pedro–Los Volcanes." Otherwise, to get to the mountain lodge at Tlamacas you'll have to hire a taxi for about 650 pesos one way. Check at the Hotel San Carlos for other passengers, and perhaps you'll be able to split the cost. Make a deal with the taxi driver to come pick you up at a later time as there's no telephone at the lodge; or you can take a chance and try to thumb a ride down the mountain, which is often easily done.

THE LODGE: The **Albergue Vicente Guerrero**, at Tlamacas (alt. 12,800 feet, or 3900 meters), Parque Nacional Ixta-Popo, was opened in 1978. It's beautiful: an ultramodern mountain lodge done in native stone and natural wood, complete with bunkrooms, showers, a cafeteria, and a restaurant. If you want to stay the night, especially on a weekend, it's best to call or drop by the Mexico City office of the lodge for a reservation: the address is Avenida Lázaro Cárdenas 661 (tel. 590-7694). A bunk with sheets, blankets, and pillow costs 200 pesos.

Outside the Albergue is the snow-covered summit of Popocatepetl, 17,887 feet (5452 meters) at the rim. In the morning the clouds may drift away for an hour, yielding an incomparable closeup view. Across the valley, Popo's sister volcano, Ixtacchihuatl, may be exposed as well. When you see them gleaming in the morning sun, surrounded by the chilly morning air, you'll remember the moment for a lifetime.

THE TRAILS: Please take me in dead seriousness when I say that Popocatepetl is no mountain for rookie climbers, or for any expert climber who's not in top shape. At the lodge trailhead, the air is so thin that even walking makes a normal, healthy person dizzy—and the air's considerably thinner at 17,887 feet! And it's *cold* up here, even in the sweltering heat of summer. But if you're an expert climber, pack your down sleeping bag, crampons, and what-not, and check in at the rescue hut next to the lodge. You'll have to pass an equipment check, and sign your name in the hikers' register, before you set out. Maps of the various trails to the summit, showing the several huts and selters, are on view in the rescue hut. The trek to the summit takes from 9 to 12 hours, depending on what shape you're in and which trail you choose. You must camp at the summit that night, and return the next day.

When you return to the lodge, if all the bunks are taken, no one will mind if you pitch your hiking tent in the pine grove just below the lodge.

5. Cuernavaca

Cuernavaca (alt. 5058 feet; pop. 360,000), capital of the state of Morelos, has been popular as a resort for people from Mexico City ever since Emperor Maximilian built a retreat here over a century ago. Mexicans say the town has a climate of "eternal spring," and on weekends the city is crowded with day-trippers from surrounding cities, especially from the capital. On weekends the roads between Mexico City and Cuernavaca are jammed, and so are restaurants and hotels in this city. Cuernavaca has a large American colony, consisting mostly of well-to-do retired people, plus students attending one of the myriad language and cultural institutes which crowd the city. Despite its reputation as an educational fount, Cuernavaca has in recent years lost much of the colonial charm it once had. The downtown area is not nearly so attractive as similar sections of cities such as San Luis Potosí, Veracruz, or even Puebla, and burgeoning industry—notably the CIVAC complex on the outskirts—has created pollution problems and tarnished Cuernavaca's image as a haven for clean air and the simple life of plain living and high thinking.

Popularity with well-to-do visitors from Mexico City and North America has caused havoc with the town's restaurant prices and with some hotel prices, so you must be careful where you eat and where you sleep, if you want to stay within our budget here.

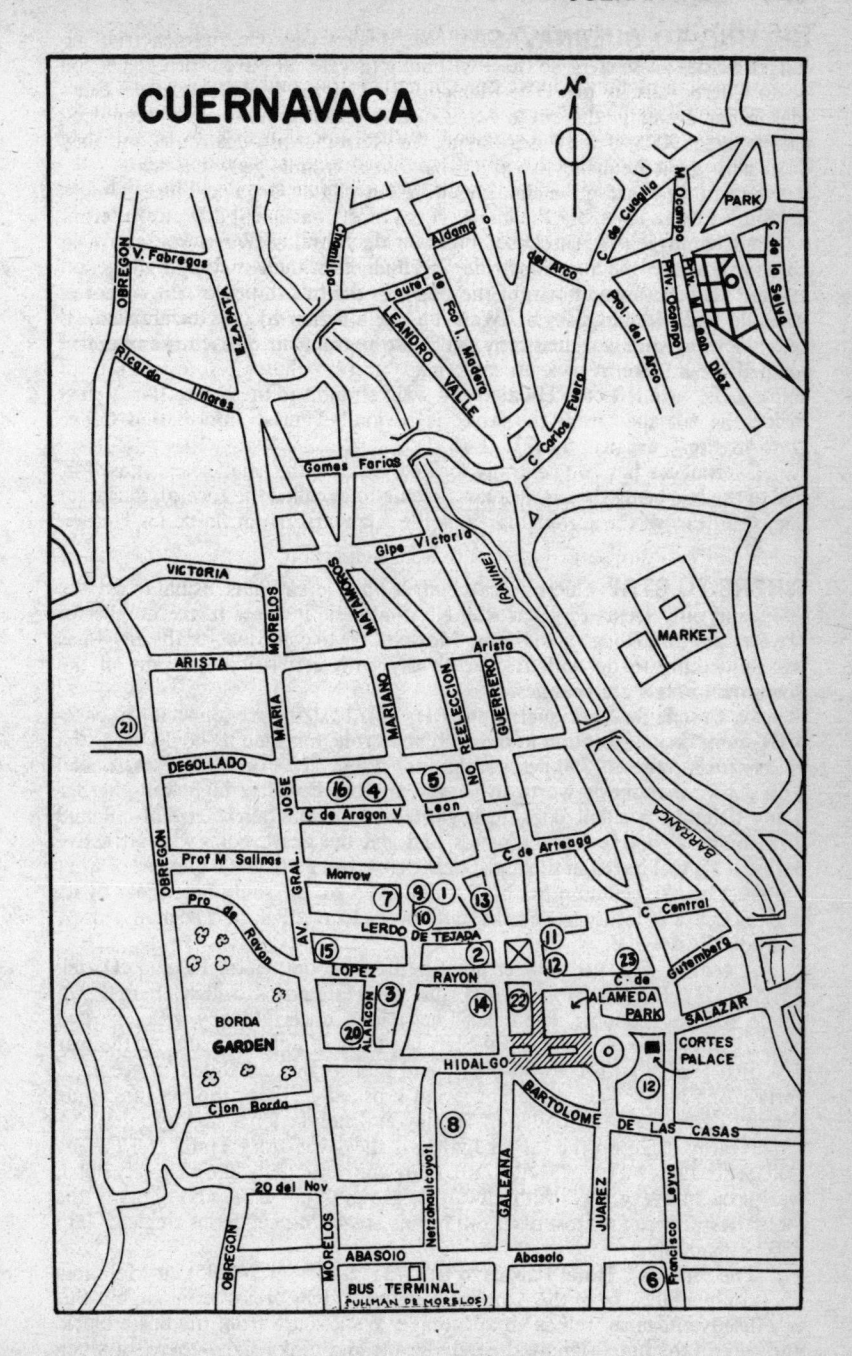

CUERNAVACA

GETTING TO CUERNAVACA: The Mexico City–Cuernavaca train no longer carries passengers, so those without a private car have little choice: you go to Cuernavaca by bus. The Mexico City **Central de Autobuses del Sur**'s reason for being is the route Mexico City–Cuernavaca–Taxco–Acapulco–Zihuatanejo: 90% of the buses leaving that terminal ply this route, and they do it with great frequency, so you'll have little trouble getting a bus.

Several lines serve the city, including Estrella de Oro and Lineas Unidas del Sur / Flecha Roja, but the line with the most convenient downtown terminal in Cuernavaca is Autobuses Pullman de Morelos. When you arrive in Cuernavaca after the hour-long ride, you'll alight at the last stop (don't get off at the "La Selva" stop north of the city!), in the bus station at the corner of Abasolo and Netzahualcoyotl. Walk up the hill (north) on Netzahualcoyotl two blocks to Hidalgo, then turn right onto that street to reach the center of town. If you'd like to pick up some maps and brochures before you set out sightseeing, turn left onto Hidalgo and walk straight to the Jardín Borda. Just inside the entrance from the street is a small **Tourist Information Office** (Information Turistica; tel. 731/2-1815).

Cuernavaca has two centrally located squares, the smaller and more formal of the two being the Jardín Juarez (sometimes called the zócalo); the larger one, southeast of the Jardín Juarez, is the Alameda, or Jardín de los Héroes.

WHERE TO STAY: Cuernavaca's budget hotel situation is dismal to say the least, and only seems to get worse. No doubt the increase in the number of private cars—allowing visitors from Mexico City to come just for the day—has had something to do with it. I can't say with conviction that any of the downtown hotels are beauties.

La Posada de Xochiquetzal (6) (tel. 731/2-0220), pronounced "so-chee-KET-zahl," is an exception to the drab hotel rule, but then it should be, as the charge for a room is 1250 pesos single, and 1500, 1700, or 1900 pesos double. You get your money's worth in beauty, for the Posada's high walls harbor many delights: a small pool, lush gardens with fountains, tasteful colonial furnishings, a good restaurant, patios, and spacious guest rooms with attractive baths. It's a real haven in the midst of the city, and gives you a glimpse of what life must be like behind other high walls. Even so, the sooty buses roar by its door at Leyva 201, just two blocks south of the Cortes Palace. The mail address is Apdo. Postal 203.

A centrally located budget hotel is the 16-room **Hotel Palacio (1)** (tel. 731/2-0553), Dwight Morrow 204, just off Matamoros, which charges 725 single, 955 pesos double. The Palacio has a long, cheerful lobby with a glassed conservatory-type roof that always lets in plenty of light and sun. At the rear is a tiled garden with colorful plants and foliage, and inhabited by scores of early-rising birds. The restaurant is not especially cheap; the big lunchtime comida costs 275 pesos daily, on Sunday and holidays it's slightly more.

Nearby, right on the Jardín Juarez, is the seven-story **Hotel Del Parque (2)**, Jardín Juarez 2 (tel. 731/2-4750), more conventionally like a big-city hotel, well used in every way, with elevators, ground-floor café, and slippery tile lobby. Rates here for most of the 40 rooms are 440 to 660 pesos single, 500 to 880 pesos double.

The rambling **Hotel Papagayo** (tel. 731/2-4694 or 2-4695), at Motolinía 13, is only a block from the Autobuses Pullman de Morelos terminal, but this is a disadvantage as well as an advantage. Walk south from the bus a block, and there's the hotel (ignore the ugly facade and dinky sign—there's a much nicer entryway at the address given above). The Papagayo's scores of rooms must be picked over to find a good, quiet one (remember those buses passing outside), but once you've located a good room, you can enjoy the bonus: a big swimming pool. Prices are moderate: 550 pesos single, 880 pesos double for a room with shower, breakfast included.

On the street with the unpronounceable name of Netzahualcoyotl is the **Hotel** (or Hostería) **San Marcos (8)** (tel. 731/2-4960), at no. 117, not far from the intersection with Hidalgo. Rooms here, too, are well worn, but a bonus is the quiet location and the small swimming pool. Singles cost 525 pesos, double beds are 790 pesos, and doubles with two beds are 940 pesos.

The 22-room **Hotel Iberia (3)**, Rayón 9 (tel. 731/2-6040), positively sparkles with cleanliness, and you'll see why when you arrive: the blue-aproned women who run the hotel are forever polishing and scrubbing the fine tiled floors or bright tiled walls. Flowers hang or stand in pots around the small courtyard (parking here is free), and one or two canaries chirp-gaily. Prices for this haven now stand at 585 pesos single, 795 pesos for two in one bed, 975 pesos for two in twin beds.

Cuernavaca's budget center is the street called Aragon y León, between Morelos and Matamoros several blocks from the center of town. Along this street are a number of low-priced lodging choices and some of the most inexpensive restaurants in town. Best place to stay on this street, for the price, is the **Casa Marilu (4)**, Aragon y León 12 (tel. 731/2-1057), with 25 plain but clean and suitable rooms for 220 pesos single and 330 pesos double without bath, 330 pesos single and 440 pesos double with bath. How long these prices can hold I can't say, but even if inflation forces them up a bit the Marilu will still be the best bargain in the city.

Another little *casa de huespedes* along Aragon y León is the small **Hotel America (4)**, at 16 (or no. 111—it has two numbers!) which doesn't have the spit-and-polish of the Marilu, yet costs slightly more: 360 pesos for a big bed, whether occupied by one person or two, and 475 pesos for two people in two beds.

Several blocks north of the Jardín Juarez is the 35-room **Hotel Penalba (5)**, Matamoros at Degollado (tel. 731/2-4166), which looks vaguely Florentine with its brick tower and turrets. The pseudo-Italian gives way to tropical lushness when you enter the courtyard filled with jungle plants and flowers. Usually a few animals are to be seen in cages around the court, anything from a duck to a ticu. The restaurant is snazzier than the hotel, charging 195 to 225 pesos for its set lunch. The rooms, by contrast, cost 500 pesos single, 600 pesos double, although they are not luxurious.

READER'S HOTEL SELECTION: "I would like to recommend the **Hotel Maria Christina**, Obregon 329 (tel. 731/2-6198 or 2-6500). It has lovely grounds with a swimming pool, parking, and a nice dining room with good meals at reasonable prices. I paid 440 pesos for a single" (Doris Higgins, Cuernavaca, Mexico).

WHERE TO EAT: Because of the huge influx of visitors from out of town, Cuernavaca is well equipped with places to dine. Here are my favorites, starting with an elegant patio restaurant and ending with a little ma-and-pa eatery.

Cuernavaca can boast of many extremely elegant garden restaurants, but often times these places will have such a steady stream of local, regular customers that they become virtual private clubs. Service to "nonmembers" from out of town suffers accordingly. But everyone is treated equally, and treated well, at **Lancers (7)** (tel. 2-0132), Calle Dwight Morrow 13, near the corner with Comonfort. The restaurant and bar are ranged around a central garden plot of emerald grass and well-kept verdure far (it seems) from the bus-choked streets nearby. Service is polished and pleasant, and prices are in the moderate-to-high range. Although steaks are the specialty, seafood and chicken are served as well. Start with sopa Lancers, made with garlic bread and cheese, and pass on to filet mignon cooked any way you like. Finish with pastry or a fancy dessert, and coffee, and the bill for one will be about 900 pesos, tax and tip included. Add 150 pesos per drink or 575 pesos for a bottle of wine. Lancers is open from 1 p.m. to 1 a.m. seven days a week.

Very different in cuisine, atmosphere, and price is the **Restaurant Vienes (10)**, at Lerdo de Tejada 4 near Comonfort. Open from 11 a.m. to 10 p.m., the Vienes tries hard for a Central European ambience, although it has the convenience of an English-speaking manager. You can order an excellent quiche with vegetable and salad, or the chef's special: a "Farmer's Plate" consisting of pork ribs, roast veal, frankfurters, sauerkraut, and potatoes. Menu items range from 145 to 275 pesos. Closed Tuesday.

Next door to Las Plazas, across from the Jardín Juarez, is the similarly named **Viena Cafeteria (11)**, Guerrero 104, where the specialty—besides people-watching—is excellent pastry, coffee, and ice cream. The cappuccino here is reputedly the best in town. Ice cream or pastry will put you out about 50 to 95 pesos, but for slightly more you can have a hot or cold luncheon plate (100 to 200 pesos) which is a full meal in itself.

A few doors down from the Viena Cafeteria is **La Parroquía (12)**, off the Jardín Juarez, at Guerrero 102. They have an open-air restaurant as well as a few outdoor café tables. This place does a teeming business, partly because of its great location right off the jardín and partly because they have fairly reasonable prices for Cuernavaca. Four quesadillas con pollo (with chicken) go for 85 pesos, or you can just sip a beer for 40 pesos.

Rosticería Cuernavaca (13), Matamoros 100, on Jardín Juarez is a cheerful place, with green checked tablecloths. As it's open from 8 a.m. to midnight daily, you can have breakfast here. Try an omelet a la francesa for 75 pesos. Add juice and cafe con leche for 165 pesos total. Later on, chicken or ham enchiladas cost 65 pesos. This place is always busy.

The **India Bonita Restaurant (9)**, Dwight Morrow 9 is a cheery place with painted cane chairs and bright-colored tablecloths. The menu is a blackboard on the wall which lists a number of Mexican plates like enchiladas with vegetables and salad, or chicken mole with potatoes, all in the range of 150 to 250 pesos. Open daily except Monday.

Mama's Carleone Pizzaría—and boy, can she ever make a good pizza. This is a family operation located at Salazar 3, east of Alameda park down a set of stairs to the left of the Cortes Palace. There is an outdoor garden in the back with tables set among the flower pots and big ferns and reeds. Upstairs is a small room with wooden benches, very cozy although, a little hot from the oven downstairs which is pushing out pizzas: small, medium, and large for 100 to 225 pesos. I liked this place a lot.

Budget Restaurants

There are two restaurants right next to each other at no. 2 Galeana, corner of Rayón: **La Cueva** and **El Portal (14)**. I put them together because there seems to be stiff competition between them with each one vying daily to offer the lower prices.

Both are clean with friendly service and good food. They both offer four-course comidas between 100 and 150 pesos which include soup, rice, fish or meat filet, dessert, and coffee. They also have à la carte items which range from 75 to 200 pesos. The comida menus are written on blackboards in front of the restaurant so your best bet is to check to see which menu and which price agrees with you.

Going down the price scale a bit there are several hole-in-the-wall eateries which offer 50-peso comidas, consisting of four courses, which are not as fancy as you'll get elsewhere (for a higher price) but substantial. There are two such on Aragon y León between Morelos and Matamoros: **Mary** and **San Miguel (16)**, which served soup, omelet, frijoles, and salad the last time I was there for a mere 75 pesos.

WHAT TO DO: First sight to see here is the ancient **Cortes Palace**, just off the Alameda to the south across the traffic circle. Begun by Hernan Cortes in 1530, it was finished by the conquistador's son Martín, and later served as the legislative headquarters for the state of Morelos. It now houses the **Museo de Cuauhnahuac** (that's the original Aztec name for the town), open from 10:30 a.m. to 6 p.m. weekdays except Thursday, and 11:30 a.m. to 7 p.m. on Saturday and Sunday. Besides the historical exhibits, you should be sure to see the chamber where the state legislature met until only recently, presided over by a huge painting of Morelos. Also on the second floor, on an open loggia, are murals by Diego Rivera presented to the city by Dwight Morrow, former U.S. ambassador to Mexico. One panel is of Morelos, whimsically painted with Rivera's face, leering at Zapata directly opposite. Other panels are of Cortes extracting gold from the Indians, of the Spaniards crossing the barranca on their arrival in Cuernavaca, using a bent tree for a bridge, and of the Aztecs in tiger and eagle masks doing battle with the armored Spaniards.

Cuernavaca offers excellent sport for the shopper. You'll have no problem finding things to buy. The main **market** is just to the right of Calle Guerrero, across the barranca (ravine). You'll find the best prices here, but bargaining is necessary.

For a group of shops in a beautiful setting, visit the **Artesañías Galería de Arte**, corner of Comonfort and Hidalgo. At the entrance to this "estate" is a lovely pool with huge ferns that are enjoying the water dripping from above into the pool. The coolness and sound of the water is just an indication of the quiet, soothing atmosphere inside. This was originally built as a private residence, and as you look around you will appreciate how truly sumptuous these places were. Don't miss the sunken garden in the back complete with several pools, palms, large trees, and gardens. The shops are elegant, the wares expensive but of the finest quality. The items are really collectors pieces with fabulous masks, statues, furniture, painting, copper, and silver jewelry. The shopkeepers are relaxed and friendly so by all means feel free to browse around. It's open every day from 10:30 a.m. to 7 p.m.

A large **shopping center**, complete with food stores, is located at the corner of Morelos and Motolinía. Open every day until 8 p.m.

The **Jardín Borda** (Borda Gardens) at Avenidas Morelos and Hidalgo, used to be the summer retreat of one-time Emperor Maximilian and Empress Carlotta. The place was built by one José de la Borda, a Taxco silver magnate (see the next section in this chapter), in the mid-1700s, and later taken over by the Habsburg couple. In recent times it had become pretty rundown, but now it's been fixed up and a pretty high admission charge has been tacked onto what, in its unredeemed state, was a free place to wander. Handicraft and art shops in the rooms off the entry court can be visited for free, but to get into the small preserve of the gardens proper costs 15 pesos per person, 8 pesos for students.

Since Borda started the trend, and Maximilian promoted it, many other well-to-do outsiders have moved to Cuernavaca in search of the perfect climate and a lavish garden. Cuernavaca thus became a "city of gardens," but virtually all of these are hidden away from the casual visitor behind high walls. What you're liable to see most of downtown is buses and people, although the two central parks have been nicely fixed up in recent years, and a few streets closed to vehicular traffic.

For a glimpse of what the "other" Cuernavaca is like, stroll down Morelos south of 20 de Noviembre, down the hill from the Jardín Borda. Ignore the thundering buses if you can, and peek through gates and doorways, and over walls, to get some idea of why the late Shah of Iran chose this town as his first home-away-from-home. Many estates on the outskirts are even more sumptuous—but even more inaccessible.

INCIDENTAL INTELLIGENCE: Now down to some serious business. There are a number of language schools in Cuernavaca which offer scheduled or private instruction as well as summer sessions at the university with college credits. For information on schools, schedules and fees, drop in at the Tourist Office in the Jardín Borda.

The National Institute of Fine Arts (21), Degollado and Obregon, houses some interesting murals and paintings by Mexican painters. This is also a school of art and there are several rooms exhibiting some of the student art.

The **post office** is on the south end of the **Palacio de Gobierno (22),** which is just to the west of the Alameda Park.

CUERNAVACA NIGHTLIFE: After spending the day shopping and touring the city, it might be a good idea to return to your hotel and rest up for the evening's activities. This town has a number of cafés right off the Jardín Juarez where people gather to sip coffee or drinks till the wee hours of the morning. The best of the cafés are **La Parroquía** and the **Cafeteria Viena,** previously mentioned in the restaurant section. There are band concerts in the zócalo (Jardín Juarez) on Thursday and Sunday evenings.

Another addition to the Carlos Anderson chain (Shrimp Bucket in Mazatlán, Carlos 'n Charlie's in Acapulco), is **Harry's Bar (23),** Gutenberg 3 (tel. 2-7679). Their with-it atmosphere includes stereo, long-haired waiters, and Mexican revolutionary posters. Open Tuesday to Thursday from 6 p.m. to 1 a.m., Friday and Saturday from 1:30 p.m. to 1:30 a.m., on Sunday from 1:30 p.m. to midnight.

EXCURSIONS FROM CUERNAVACA: If you have enough time, you should try to make some side trips around Cuernavaca. To the north you'll find pine trees and an alpine setting; to the east, lush hills and valleys. On the road north to Mexico City you will climb several thousand feet within a half hour into some gorgeous mountain air. If you have a car you can go for a brisk morning hike (it's cold up there) or a lazy afternoon picnic lunch.

Tepoztlán

Take a bus from the Flecha Roja bus station (see below), leaving every 20 minutes or so, for the 12-mile ride to Tepoztlán. This Tlahuica Indian village predates the Conquest, and still holds the ruins of a temple, plus a Dominican monastery (1580) and the thatched huts of the residents. It's a slice of village life only minutes from the big city.

Xochicalco Ruins

About 26 kilometers (16 miles) south of Cuernavaca along Highway 95 (the "Libre"—no-toll—road to Taxco) is the town of Alpuyeca; 15 kilometers (9½ miles) northeast of Alpuyeca are the ruins of Xochicalco, the "House of Flowers." High on a mountaintop, Xochicalco boasts a magnificent situation, and an interesting complex of buildings dating from the 600s through the 900s A.D. Most interesting is the **Temple of the Feathered Serpents**, with beautiful bas reliefs. There's also a ballcourt, some underground passages, and other temples. Xochicalco is of interest to archeologists because it seems to have been the point at which the Teotihuacán, Toltec, Zapotec, and Maya cultures met and interacted. You can visit the ruins from 8 a.m. to 5 p.m. daily, but you'll need a car to get there.

Cacahuamilpa Caves

The Grutas de Cacahuamilpa lie some 74 kilometers (46 miles) southwest of Cuernavaca, 8 kilometers (5 miles) north of the Taxco road, Highway 95. Come at 11 a.m., 1 p.m., or 3 p.m., and you can join the group tour of these mammoth caverns, said to stretch some 43 miles within the earth (don't worry —you don't get to see the entire 43 miles!). If you have a car and are driving to Taxco, this makes a nice detour.

By the way, this road (Highway 55) which goes to the caves is also the road to Toluca, which is 127 kilometers (79 miles) north from Highway 95. On the way, 45 kilometers (28 miles) from Highway 95, is the pretty spa town of **Ixtapan de la Sal**, with a dozen hotels specializing in the cure: bathing in the natural mineral waters of the area.

ONWARD (AND BACKWARD) FROM CUERNAVACA: Those returning to Mexico City from Cuernavaca need only make their way back to the terminal of Autobuses Pullman de Morelos. But to catch a bus onward to Taxco or Acapulco, head for the terminal of Autobuses Estrella de Oro (first class; tel. 2-3035) at Morelos 900; or Autobuses Unidas del Sur / Flecha Roja (tel. 2-0066) at Morelos 503.

6. Taxco

Taxco (pronounced TAHS-ko; alt. 5850 feet; pop. 70,000), famous for its silver, sits on a hill among hills, and almost everywhere you walk in the city there are fantastic views. The famous church of **Santa Prisca**, with its twin spires, recently repainted and repaired, was built by a French miner, José de la Borda, who made a packet in the 18th century. It is illuminated at night.

Taxco's renowned silver mines, first worked in the time of Cortes four centuries ago, were revived, for all practical purposes, by an American, William Spratling, about 50 years ago. Today, its fame rests more on the 180 silver shops, most of them little one-man factories, which line the cobbled streets all the way up into the hills. It is no place to come for bargains, with some silver prices actually higher than in Mexico City because of the magnitude of the tourist trade. In some cases, though, the bracelets and other items are heavier and this accounts for the difference in price.

You can get the idea of what Taxco's like by spending an afternoon there, but there's much more to this picturesque town than just the zócalo and the shops surrounding it. You'll have to stay overnight if you want more time to climb up and down its steep streets, discovering little plazas and fine churches. The main part of town stretches up the hillside from the main highway, and although it's a steep walk it's not a particularly long one. But you don't have to walk: vehicles make the circuit through the town, up the hill and down, picking up and dropping passengers along the route. There are *burritos,* yellow VW minibuses which run the route, and small city buses as well. Both these vehicles run from about 7 a.m. until 9 p.m.

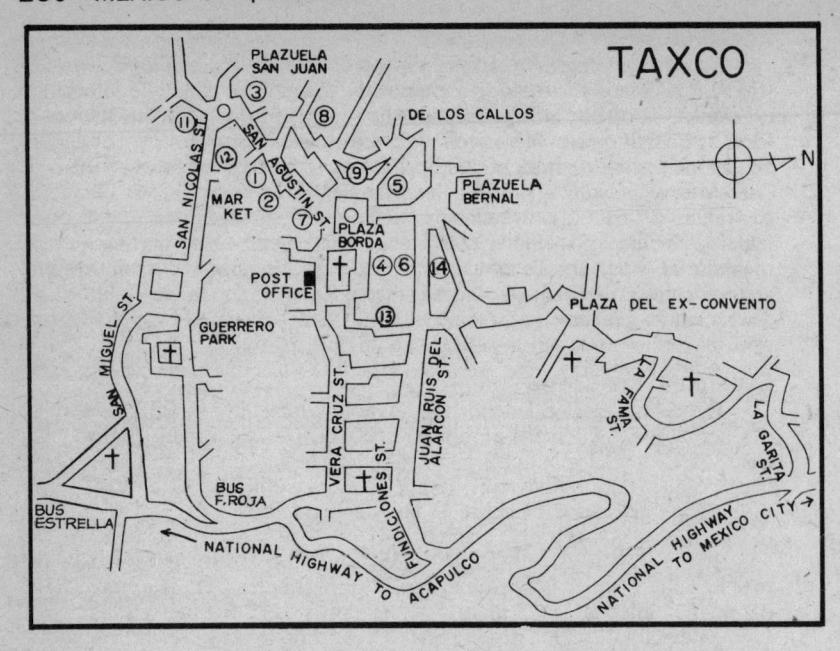

Beware of self-appointed guides, who will undoubtedly approach you in the zócalo and offer their services—they get a cut (up to 25%) of all you buy in the shops they take you to. Should you want a guide, however, ask to see his Departamento de Turismo credentials. Call 732/2-0579 or go to the Department of Tourism office on the highway at the north end of town to engage a licensed guide (at about 200 to 300 pesos per hour).

GETTING TO TAXCO: The drive from Mexico City takes about 3½ hours, with a toll road at each side of Cuernavaca, the halfway point. Fill up with gas at Cuernavaca.

By Bus

Estrella de Oro, Calz. de Tlalpan 2205, at the Central de Autobuses del Sur in Mexico City (Metro: Taxqueña; tel. 549-8520), has five buses a day to Taxco, both first class and deluxe. Lineas Unidas del Sur / Flecha Roja also has several buses a day from the Central de Autobuses del Sur, but is a second choice to Estrella de Oro. From Cuernavaca you can catch an Estrella de Oro bus as it passes through, if there are seats. It is also possible to stop in Taxco on your way back from Acapulco or Zihuatanejo; two buses per day will drop you in Taxco.

WHERE TO STAY: Compared to Cuernavaca, Taxco is an overnight-stop visitor's dream: charming and picturesque, not noisy or polluted, with a respectable selection of well-kept and delightful budget hotels. The prices aren't even that bad, although they do tend to "bulge" in the heavy summer season and at holiday times. Here are my favorite places to stay:

On a quiet side street just down the hill from the zócalo are two charming hotels at very reasonable rates. The **Posada de Los Castillo (6)** (tel. 732/2-1396), at Juan Ruíz de Alarcon 7, is a beautiful colonial mansion completely restored in 1980. Boasting lots and lots of plants (some even in planters in the bathrooms!), its "new colonial" rooms surround a courtyard on four levels—like a 17th-century Hyatt Regency, let's say. All 15 rooms are small, but equipped with private baths, some with tubs. One person pays 435 to 558 pesos, two pay 576 to 678 pesos, whether in one bed or two.

Right across the street from Los Castillo is its more luxurious and expensive sister hotel, the **Hotel Los Arcos (14)** (tel. 732/2-1836), Juan Ruíz de Alarcon 12. Larger and more sumptuously fitted out, Los Arcos is in fact a converted monastery (1620), and the monks never had it this good: swimming pool (small but nice), a courtyard restaurant-bar, and a maze of little courts and passages hiding 28 very comfortable rooms-with-bath. Prices are 630 pesos single, 770 double, 910 pesos triple. Whichever of these two hotels you pick, you'll be immersed in colonial charm, blissful quiet, and you'll still be only a five-minute walk from the zócalo.

The **Hotel Melendez (1)**, Cuauhtémoc 6 (tel. 732/2-0006), has 42 rooms with baths, all renting at 370 pesos single, 510 to 595 pesos double. It's a nice hotel just off the zócalo, and its airy bedrooms have blue-tiled walls and ornate glass and metalwork doors on the bathrooms. Several have terrific views. The hotel's restaurant has fairly reasonable prices—a complete dinner for 195 pesos, or a breakfast of fruit, soft boiled eggs, coffee, and toast for about 150 pesos.

The **Hotel Jardín (4)**, Celso Munoz 2 (tel. 732/2-0027), on the north side of Santa Prisca church just off the main square, is also a fine choice. The hotel is marked only by a small sign above the door, and resembles very much a European pension. It's surprisingly peaceful inside, with a fine view of the mountains from the flower-filled balcony patio. Clean, large rooms rent for 195 pesos per person, each of the seven rooms having a private bathroom.

The **Hotel Agua Escondida (5)**, Spratling 4 (tel. 732/2-0726 or 2-0736), on one corner of the zócalo, is an exceptionally clean and well-tended establishment. Prices are 280 to 390 pesos single, 490 pesos double; rooms have extra touches such as vases of fresh flowers and bottles of mineral water at each bedside. An extra bed costs 90 pesos in either section.

Big Splurge Hotels

One of the older and nicer hotels in town is the **Hotel Santa Prisca (11)** (tel. 732/2-0080), in the Plazuela de San Juan. There are 59 cozy comfortable rooms with couch, tile floors, wood beams, and a colonial atmosphere. There are two lush patios with fountains, and a lovely dining room done in mustard and blue. They offer the American Plan (three meals) with singles for 948 pesos, doubles for 1595 pesos; the Modified American Plan (two meals) and rooms without meals are, of course, cheaper by far. An excellent choice for those wishing a splurge.

WHERE TO EAT: Taxco gets a lot of people down from the capital for the day, or passing through on their way to Acapulco, and so there are a lot of restaurants to fill the demand for lunch. But the demand is so great that prices are high for what you get. If you have a big breakfast and pack a lunch you'll save money. Otherwise, the cheapest meals near the zócalo are these: in the building called El Patio de las Artesañías you'll find a small pizza parlor called the **Pizzaría Dama.** Walk through the courtyard and to the left. The small outdoor tables enjoy a fine Taxco view, plus lots of peace and quiet. The medium-sized pizza will feed two people, if you're not terribly hungry, for 160 to 225 pesos. A *grande* (large) will feed two hungry souls for 210 to 260 pesos. Beer and soft drinks are served. For a soft drink that's not cloyingly sweet, order *manzanita,* a carbonated apple soda pop.

Down along the main highway, near the bus stations, are several **loncherías** where a torta or lamb chop will run 50 and 125 pesos, respectively, but the highway is noisy, the eateries are not very congenial, and you'd do better to stay near the zócalo, all things considered.

Still, lunch can be part of the fun at Taxco, and if you look on it as entertainment as well as nutriment you may be able to rationalize the 250 to 350 pesos you'll spend on a comida corrida at one of the places listed below. You can get a sandwich in most of these restaurants, but as it will cost about 100 pesos, it's not really value-for-money. Get the comida corrida.

Perhaps the best comida bargain these days is the 195-peso lunch at the **Hotel Melendez (1),** served in an attractive tiled dining room overlooking the town and the valley. You pour the soup from the tureen yourself (no need to skimp!). There follows rice-and-vegetables, a meat-and-vegetable plate, melon or pudding, and coffee or tea. For Taxco, you get your money's worth here.

The **Restaurant Arnoldo's (9)** overlooks the main square (it's directly across the square from the Santa Prisca church, but you enter by a little side street which runs around back of the restaurant), and offers a 180-peso comida as well as à la carte items like a hamburger, roast chicken, or a pork chop for 100 to 140 pesos. The señora who runs it is interested in pleasing her customers and will make sure everything is up to expectations.

You'll find atmosphere at **Restaurant de la Rosa (5),** Calle Bailar, around the corner from the Hotel Agua Escondida, just a half block off the zócalo, where there are open arches, flagstone floors and stone walls, hand-carved wooden tables with colorful covers and napkins, all lit by wrought-iron lamps. The best time to be here is on Sunday afternoon when there's music from 1:30 to 4. The 190-peso comida is available daily, and may consist of, for instance, a choice of mushroom or asparagus soup, broiled filet mignon, T-bone steak, broiled pork chops, or a Mexican plate, lemon cream pie or peaches in cream, coffee or tea. Breakfast costs 98 pesos. Open 8 a.m. to 11 p.m. daily.

On the attractive Plazuela de San Juan (the one with the fountain) you'll spot the **Restaurante Ethel.** A family-run place, it's kept clean and tidy, with cloths on the tables and a hometown atmosphere. The hearty daily comida corrida consists of soup or pasta, meat (perhaps a small steak), dessert, and coffee for 170 pesos, tax and tip included. And if that modest amount seems like too much, you should check out the **Restaurante Santa Fe,** just down the street from the Ethel, and even less expensive.

The busiest restaurant in town the last time I visited was the **Cielito Lindo,** on the main plaza at the corner near where the Calle San Agustín begins. The tables clad in white were packed on this weekend afternoon, and plates of food were disappearing as fast as the waiters could bring them. For an à la carte feast of soup, roast chicken with two vegetables, pineapple pie, and coffee, tax, and tip, expect to pay 350 pesos.

READER'S RESTAURANT SELECTION: "We 'discovered' a terrific restaurant on the road between Mexico City and Acapulco, just six kilometers south of the city of Iguala on the east side of Highway 95. The **El Amigo Miguel** has food that is delicious, very very Mexican, and relatively inexpensive. We had a serving of rabbit and iguana, a portion of rice with an egg on top, a bowl of farm-fresh sour cream, a ripe avocado, a locally produced ranch cheese, a bowl of beans, lots of hot corn tortillas with hot sauce, and mineral waters. The total bill was a pleasant surprise. What most favorably impressed me was the extremely high level of warmth and hospitality on the part of the owner, and other employees" (Craig R. Reubens, San Pablo, Calif.).

DAYTIME ACTIVITIES: In a word—shopping! When you're tired of that, perhaps you'd like a snoop through some colonial houses. **Casa de las Lágrimas** (House of Tears), also known as Casa Figueroa, above the zócalo, has been turned into a private art gallery and charges 5 pesos for a look around. Next door, incidentally, is the local art school.

Or you might sneak in for a look at Juan O'Gorman's mural beside the swimming pool at the **Hotel Posada de la Mision** (on the highway; go via burrito).

Taxco has a fine little museum, called the **Museo Guillermo Spratling (13)**, almost directly behind the Santa Prisca church (open every day but Monday from 10 a.m. to 2 p.m. and 3 to 6 p.m. for an admission charge of 10 pesos). Don't write it off. The building and displays are of the high quality that's normal in Mexico. The entrance floor and the one above display a good collection of pre-Columbian statues and implements in clay, stone, and jade. A quote in Spanish by Gordon Willey sets the mood for this pre-Columbian exhibit: "Man speaks to man through art and emotional effect that does not change with the passing of centuries." The lower floor has a display on the history of Taxco. Documents, clippings, letters, engravings, and photographs give you an idea what it was like a century or two ago in this mountain mining town: miners' implements, helmets, lanterns, and such add a touch of realism to the display. Look for the samples of silver ore, Taxco's raison d'être. A plaque (in Spanish) explains that most of the collection and the funds for the museum came from William Spratling, an American born in 1900 who studied architecture in the U.S., later settled in Taxco, and organized the first workshops to turn out high-quality silver jewelry. From this first effort in 1931 the town's reputation as a center of artistic silver work grew to what it is today. In a real sense, Spratling "put Taxco on the map." He died in 1967 in a car accident.

After your visit to the museum, stroll along Ruíz de Alarcon street right near the museum, looking for the richly decorated facade of the **Von Humboldt house**. The renowned German scientist and explorer Baron Alexander von Humboldt (1769–1859) visited Taxco and stayed in this beautiful house in 1803. Besides the beauty of the house, and the lingering fame of its illustrious guest, you're here to see the **Exposición Nacional de Platería**. A collection of fine craft items, particularly silver work, fills the main hall. Everything you see is for sale.

After shopping, a walk around town, and a visit to the museum, drag yourself back to the zócalo and up the flight of cobbled steps lined with geraniums to **Paco's Bar (9)** overlooking the zócalo. Drinks are anywhere from 30 pesos (soft drinks), through beer at 40 to 55 pesos and rum or tequila at 75 pesos, to more sophisticated concoctions. The celebrated "Berta," originated across the square in another bar (see below under "Nightlife"), is only 55 pesos here. In the summer a trio plays at Paco's from 5 to 9 p.m.

The Flower Festival

In 1978, Taxco's city fathers held the first annual **Festival de la Flor en Taxco** at the end of May and beginning of June. This gala event packed the city's hotels and restaurants, and there wasn't a parking spot to be had for miles. The president of the Republic himself opened the festival, which included art exhibits, concerts and performances, discussions, and conferences. The date of the festival's principal activity, May 30, was the bicentennial of the death of Taxco's first silver king, José de la Borda (he died in 1778), and the festival will no doubt center on this date in years to come. At festival time, have an ironclad hotel reservation, or plan to come just for the day.

TAXCO NIGHTLIFE: Taxco's nighttime action is centered in the luxury hotels which have sprung up to catch the influx of well-heeled tourists. The **Holiday Inn** (tel. 732/2-1300), **Posada de la Mision** (tel. 732/2-0063), and **Hotel de la Borda** (tel. 732/2-0025) all have their clubs and nighttime shows. You'll need a taxi to get to any one of these, and then there will be the inevitable cover charge. With two drinks apiece, an entire evening for a couple can cost about 750 to 1000 pesos.

Completely different in tone is **Berta's (7)**, right next to Santa Prisca church. Open since the early '30s by a lady named Berta who made her fame on a drink of the same name (tequila, soda, lime, and sugar syrup), Berta's is traditionally the gathering place of the local gentry. Spurs and old swords decorate the walls, a saddle is casually slung over the banister of the stairs leading to the second-floor room where tin masks leer from the walls. A Berta costs 60 pesos, rum the same, scotch is 130 pesos, and beer costs 45 to 60 pesos. Open 9 a.m. to around midnight.

Chapter XII

TO THE GULF

1. Orizaba and Cordoba
2. Jalapa
3. Veracruz
4. Tuxpan and Tajin
5. Lake Catemaco

THE BOOM IN TRAVEL to the Yucatán has benefited the towns of the Gulf Coast, somewhat neglected in earlier years by the hordes rushing to Acapulco. Veracruz, chief among these, does not make its living from tourism —it's Mexico's biggest and most active port, and always has been—but it welcomes tourists (especially Mexican tourists on weekends) and has a great deal to offer. If you've come by land from the north to Mexico City you'll probably consider continuing on to the Yucatán, in which case you can make a convenient and rewarding stop in Veracruz. The toll road, although expensive, is advisable, for the old mountain road that twists and turns is neither as safe nor as fast. The bus will take the toll road, passing through the towns of Puebla (see Chapter XIII), Orizaba, and Cordoba along the way. From Veracruz it is possible to drive or take a bus to the nearby lake resort of Catemaco, and from there to the Isthmus of Tehuantepec. Jalapa, capital city of the state of Veracruz, can make an interesting detour if you're not in a blind rush to get to the coast.

1. Orizaba and Cordoba

ORIZABA: Famous as a manufacturing city, Orizaba, Veracruz (alt. 4000 feet; pop. 100,000), sits at the foot of Mexico's highest mountain, Citlaltépetl, or Pico de Orizaba (18,275 feet), and has a pleasant, cool climate which does little to encourage consumption of its most well-known product: various brands of Moctezuma beer. Maximilian and Carlotta had a hacienda on the outskirts of the town (now ruined and hardly worth seeing), but the major architectural attraction these days is the fanciful **Palacio Municipal.** The style might be called Victorian gingerbread house, but the construction is all steel. Fabricated in Belgium during the 1800s, it was later taken apart, shipped across the Atlantic, and bolted together here in Orizaba.

The drive from Mexico City to Veracruz can easily be done in a day, but should you find it necessary to stop in Orizaba, the **Hotel Aries** (tel. 272/5-3699), at Oriente 6 no. 265, will put you up in style. Restaurant, bar, and swimming pool are all at your service, rooms are modern—even stylish, almost

—and feature wall-to-wall carpets, telephones, and spanking-clean bathrooms. One person pays 990 pesos, two people sharing the same bed pay 1100 pesos, two people in two beds pay 1200 pesos. The hotel is only about two blocks up the street from the A.D.O. bus station.

Almost across the street from the Aries is the older and less expensive **Grand Hotel de France** (tel. 272/5-2311), at Oriente 6 no. 186 (corner of Sur 5). The France, although well-worn, is still quite respectable: the town's tourist office is in the same building. It seems as though no two rooms are alike, and you would do well to inspect several before choosing one. Singles are 550 pesos, and doubles are 660 pesos.

CORDOBA: This is a bustling city (alt. 3000 feet; pop. 123,000), with a huge market district, an imposing cathedral with a famous set of bells, and a pretty main square complete with Muzak (everything from Hawaiian guitars to Scott Joplin). Cordoba, Veracruz, is a center for Mexico's coffee industry, and several brands proudly claim origin in the hills surrounding the town.

If you stay here, try the **Hotel Virreynal** (tel. 272/2-2377), Avenida 1 and Calle 5, at the side of the cathedral off the main square. The facade is baroque, the lobby brilliant with tiles, but the three floors of rooms are fairly modern and comfortable—providing you don't get a room on the front where the traffic noise and the famous churchbells can disturb your sleep. Prices are very reasonable: 480 pesos single, 580 pesos double, with an 80- to 110-peso charge for parking in the hotel garage (price depends on length of your car).

The Virreynal has a restaurant, attractive in an old-fashioned way with wood furniture and white tablecloths. Seafood cocktails cost about 115 pesos, most entrees are about 200 to 275 pesos, soups and salads cost 55 pesos.

Prime activity for the traveler laying over a night in Cordoba is people-watching, coffee- or cocktail-drinking, and dining on the main square. The **Hotel Zevallos,** fronted by an arcade along one side of the square, is famous for having seen the signing of Mexico's Pact of Cordoba (1821), which granted independence from Spain. Today the Portal Zevallos (the arcade proper) is lined with café-restaurants, each having a different character: there is the one for gilded youth, the one for ma and pa out to dinner, the one for an all-male cast of domino-players, etc. The **Restaurant & Cafe Parroquía,** Avenida 1 and Calle 1, in the Portal Zevallos, is a general mix of people and offers a varied menu. The end of the arcade is a good vantage point for ogling the other cafés and the square while having a sandwich (60 pesos), a chicken dish (100 to 170 pesos), a plate of *antojitos* (various appetizers, 75 to 150 pesos), or even filete a la Tampiqueña (250 pesos). Beer, wine, and cocktails are served. You can also get an early breakfast at the Parroquía. Huevos rancheros, tortillas, and coffee will cost about 115 pesos.

2. Jalapa

Capital of the state of Veracruz, Jalapa (or Xalapa; alt. 4500 feet; pop. 200,000) is an interesting town to explore for a day. Although modern, the city is riddled with old and narrow streets that wind downhill, apparently to nowhere in particular.

The center of town is midway down the mountainside. The cathedral (1773), Palacio de Gobierno, and the pretty, formal Parque Juarez are here, perched on a terrace beyond which the town continues its downward tumble. The view from the park, of the red tile roofs, orange trees, and the Cofre de

Perote volcano in the far distance, is the finest memory you'll take with you from Jalapa.

Arriving by A.D.O. bus, you'll be about ten minutes' walk from the center of town. Turn left out the bus station door, and walk down the slope on the road named Enriquez, which will bring you to the park. By A.U. bus, you'll arrive a bit farther up the hillside. Walk downhill on Avenida de la Revolución (the street in front of the bus station) to reach the Palacio de Gobierno.

WHERE TO STAY AND EAT: The town's all-purpose favorite is the modern **Hotel Maria Victoria** (tel. 281/7-5600), right behind the Palacio de Gobierno down the hill, on Calle Zaragoza. The rooms, though modern, have seen hard usage, but all come with air conditioners, tiled baths, television sets, and often with two double beds. Ask for a room on the far side away from the street; this cuts the noise level, and also gives you a fine view of the Cofre de Perote mountain. Restaurant, bar, gift shop, swimming pool—the Maria Victoria has everything, all well-used, although prices are not low. Being so close to the center of state power, it finds many business and government travelers willing to pay 950 pesos single, 1100 to 1350 pesos double, all in.

Perhaps in years to come the brand-new **Hotel Xelapa** (tel. 281/7-1700), Victoria and Bustamante, a gleaming white fortress perched on a hill overlooking the A.D.O. bus station, will corner the carriage trade, forcing the Maria Victoria to bring prices down.

A lower-priced alternative is the older **Hotel México** (tel. 281/7-5030), Dr. Lucio 4, just across the street diagonally from the cathedral. Rooms are grouped around the central courtyard (which serves as parking lot) on three floors, and some peek through frosted glass onto the plaza out front. Accommodations are a little plain, but the prices aren't fancy either: 660 pesos double, complete.

As for dining, the town favorite, good for all occasions, is the **Cafeteria Terraza Jardín,** on Enriquez—that's the street which runs in front of the cathedral and Palacio. Right across from the Parque Juarez, the Jardín has three huge tiers of indoor seating, plain tables and chairs, no decor to speak of. Despite its name and the self-service line on the top tier, the Jardín is a waiter-service restaurant serving full breakfasts, lunches, and dinners. Just a sandwich and a drink? You can get away spending 90 pesos or less. Something more substantial? I can recommend the carne asada con chilaquiles (a strip of broiled beef served with sliced tortillas and onions in a spicy tomato sauce). With a bottle of beer, you'll pay 160 pesos for such a tuck-in. You can order more expensive items, but you shouldn't.

At Enriquez 31 is the old Hotel Regis, and beside it a little alley called the Calle Antonio Maria de Rivera. One block up this street on the right, at no. 16, is the **Restaurante El Diamante,** a clean, attractive, and modern place with prices roughly half those of the more centrally located Cafeteria Terraza Jardín. Other restaurants on this street invite experimentation, as well.

READER'S RESTAURANT SELECTIONS: "**El Che**, serving intermediate-priced Argentine food, specializes in beef Argentine style. Most dishes are priced under 500 pesos, and quality is excellent. It's at Murillo Vidal 11 (tel. 7-7646). Also, **La Pergola** offers outdoor tables and gigantic servings of lobster for about 600 pesos a person. The best food runs in the 750- to 1000-peso range, though. Look for it in Lomas del Estadio, near the stadium (tel. 7-4714). Finally, the **Restaurant La Palama,** Pino Suarez 67 (tel. 7-2429), has the best seafood in town" (Jack G. Mudry, Xalapa, Veracruz).

WHAT TO DO: Take a look at the murals by José Chávez Morado in the Palacio de Gobierno, and also a glance in the massive cathedral. Walk through the streets and admire the bougainvillea, fruit trees, and flowers. Jalapa is halfway between the mountains and the tropics, so they have coffee plantations and sultry breezes at the same time.

The **Agora**, a hang-out for artists, students, and other cosmopolitan types, is just off the main park. Books, records, films, conversation, concerts—look here first. Afterward check out the **Teatro del Estado**, at Manuel Avila Camacho and Ignacio de la Llave. This is Jalapa's official cultural center, always with something going on.

Many people come to Jalapa just to visit the **Veracruz State Museum**, on the road to Mexico City, in a university complex on the left (southwest) side. The museum has the distinction of owning one of the few gigantic Olmec heads ever found. The head, and other pieces of sculpture, are in a park surrounding the museum, while the interior rooms hold some 25,000 pieces of Huastec, Totonac, and Olmec art. You can visit from 9 a.m. to 6 p.m. every day.

From Jalapa, the road winding down to the coast takes about 1½ hours to negotiate as far as Veracruz, 110 kilometers (68 miles) away. The weather gets hotter and the air gets thicker and muggier with each foot you descend.

3. Veracruz

From Cordoba or Jalapa, Veracruz is less than a two-hour ride. Veracruz (that's "bay-rah-CROOS"; pop. 450,000) is Mexico's principal port and has been since Hernan Cortes landed there on Good Friday in 1519. His name for the town he founded was Villa Rica de la Vera Cruz (the Rich Town of the True Cross). The Spaniards used to ship most of their gold and silver out of the port, so it became a popular calling point for pirates, who periodically would shut up the townfolk in the parish church, or abandon them on an island in the bay, while they methodically ransacked the town. The citizens took two major precautions: they built a high wall around the old town (around the **Plaza de Armas**) and they constructed a massive fort, **San Juan de Ulua (15)**, on what was then an island in the harbor but is now connected to the mainland by a curving pier. Neither precaution was entirely effective; the port was pillaged by pirates in 1654 and 1712, invaded by the French in 1832 and 1861, and by the Americans in 1847 and 1914.

Veracruz, a raucous, swinging port town, has an intriguing combination of European and African influences, and an impressive shoreline. Near the sea, the **Bank of Mexico (16)** building, all glass, steel, and gray stone, does double-duty as a lighthouse (Faro).

Important Note: Veracruz has become a favorite weekending spot for tourists from the capital city. Every Friday afternoon and evening, buses, trains (especially the sleepers), and planes fill up in Mexico City and empty out in Veracruz. The flood back up into the mountains is reversed on Sunday. In addition, ponderous Customs procedures in this, Mexico's largest port, demand that importers and exporters come to the city often, and they fill hotel rooms. Arrive as early in the week, and as early in the day, as possible. You will find a room in any case, but unless you arrive early, it may not be the room you want.

ORIENTATION: The **Tourism Office** (tel. 293/2-1613) is right downtown in the main square, the Plaza de Armas, in the Palacio Municipal (Town Hall), on the east side of the square, open Monday thru Saturday 9 a.m. to 1 p.m.

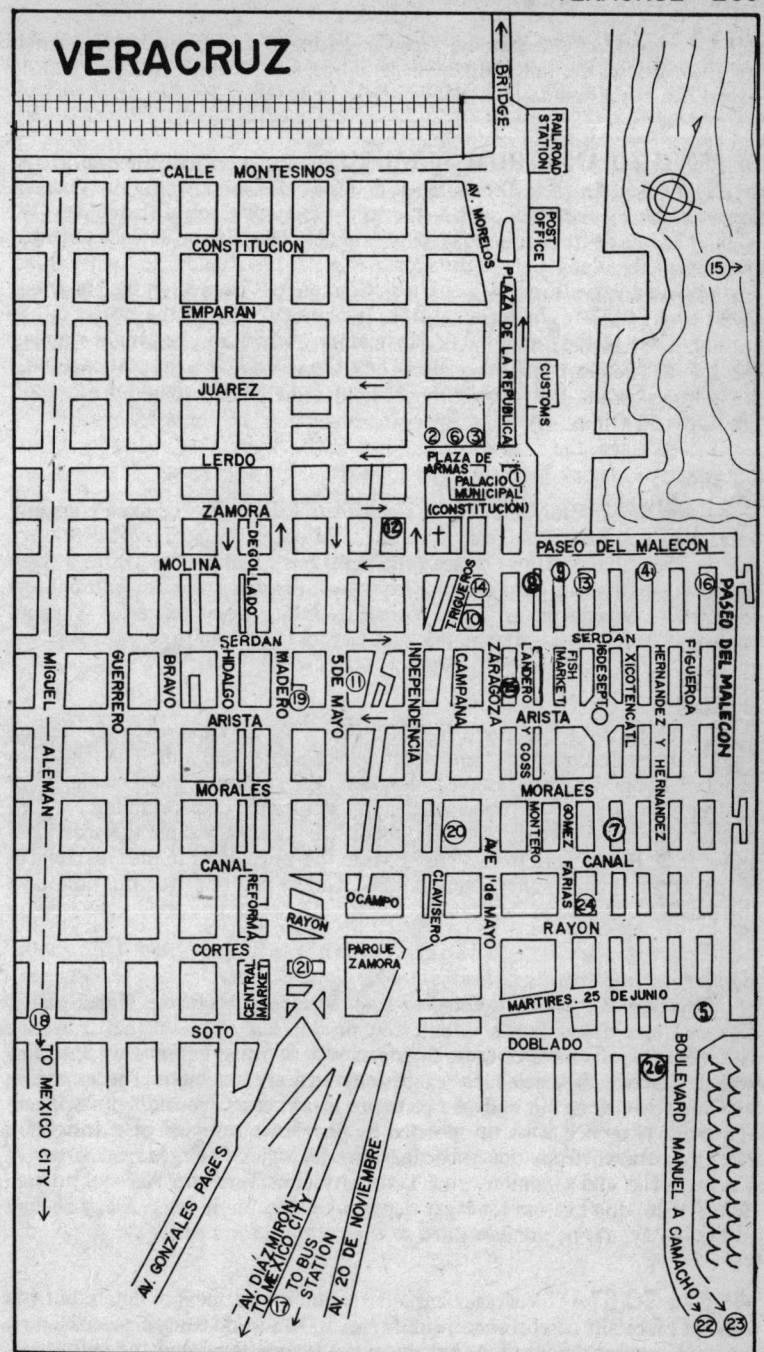

VERACRUZ

and 4 to 8 p.m.; closed Sunday. Tips for getting to and from the bus station are given below; the railroad station is only a few blocks from the Plaza de Armas, on the Plaza de la República right near the water (see map).

GETTING TO AND FROM VERACRUZ: Most northern Mexican cities, the capital itself, Oaxaca, Tehuantepec, and the cities and towns of the Yucatán are accessible by direct bus from Veracruz. Veracruz's **Central Camionera (17)** is about 15 blocks from downtown on Avenida S. Díaz Mirón at Calle Orizaba. Buses running along Díaz Mirón pass the Parque Zamora and then head downtown on various routes. Look for "Camionera" painted on the bus windshield to get back to the terminal from downtown. Two of the easiest to use are the "Díaz Mirón" and "20 de Noviembre," which can be caught running along Avenida 5 de Mayo. These buses pass the second-class bus station as well as the first-class Central Camionera. The railroad station is right downtown on the Plaza de la República.

By Bus

From the Central Camionera (also called A.D.O. for the main company operating here) buses head from Veracruz to Mexico City (scores of buses every day, a seven-hour trip) to Oaxaca (one night bus), and Merida (three a day). As the bus station is a good distance from downtown, try to make your onward reservations when you arrive in Veracruz. Other buses leave for Tuxpan, Brownsville, Reynosa, Matamoras, and Cardel (for Zamora).

By Rail

Three trains a day leave from Mexico City to Veracruz, two evening (night) trains and one day train which leaves about 7:30 a.m. The trip takes about 12 hours. You can reserve a sleeper on the evening trains. One day train runs in each direction between Puebla and Veracruz. Trains running between Mexico City and Veracruz tend to be good, although not without the occasional annoyance. But onward from Veracruz into the Yucatán or to the Guatemalan border, train quality suffers considerably. Unless you're a true rail buff, take the bus.

By Air

You can fly between Veracruz and Mexico City (three flights daily), Oaxaca (one daily flight), Monterrey or Merida (three flights a week). AeroMéxico runs most of these flights as well as three flights a week to Los Angeles on which special low excursion rates are available. The airport is indicated by **(18)** on our map. A taxi to the airport costs about 275 pesos. There is a minibus service of sorts, operated by people working out of a dress shop two doors down from the Mexicana Airlines office (5 de Mayo, corner of Serdan). The green minibuses of Transportación Terrestre Aeropuerto (tel. 293/2-3520) don't go out for every departing flight, but if you're lucky enough to get one, you'll pay only a third of the cab fare for a seat.

WHERE TO STAY: Veracruz has a fairly good assortment of hotels, but you must be especially careful of noise in this town—auto and truck noise to be sure, but also *marimba* noise, for this is a gay, raucous town and the enthusiasts among the musicians keep it up until the early morning hours.

As a rule of thumb, you should plan to pay for air conditioning if you stay on or very near the Plaza de Armas. Hotels six or seven blocks away from the plaza are quieter, and you probably won't have to keep your windows closed as you would have to on the square.

Newest of Veracruz's moderately priced hotels is the **Hotel Baluarte (7)** (tel. 293/6-0844), at Canal 265, corner of 16 de Septiembre. Five stories high, modern, and very attractive, it has a location which helps to make it my first choice, for it's right on the square dominated by the romantic Baluarte de Santiago, now a museum. It's very quiet here, and although you're five blocks from downtown, the walk is a pleasant and brief one. The 60 rooms all have individual air conditioners, and each machine is thoughtfully equipped with a plastic tube so that condensation doesn't drip onto sidewalk passersby. Guests can use the hotel's own garage, and a small restaurant off the lobby is good for breakfast or a light meal if you don't feel like going out. Singles go for 495 pesos, doubles for 578 pesos, and are well worth it.

One of the more centrally located hotels in town is the four-story **Hotel Oriente (1)**, Miguel Lerdo 6, at the south end of the Plaza de la República (tel. 293/2-0100). The Oriente's lobby is rather bare, furnished only with a few plants and low seats, and the rooms are quite noisy, but the manager is a kindly gentleman and the 57 rooms are clean if well-worn and contain telephones, private showers, ceiling fans, and terraces. Rates are 425 pesos single, 495 pesos double, plus 75 pesos more for air conditioning.

Still in the same area is the **Hotel Prendes (2)**, Independencia 88 at Lerdo (tel. 293/2-0153), whose three floors of recently renovated plush guest rooms are garnished with wood balconies and wood-louvered french doors. There's a little tiled lobby with several iron chandeliers and a stained-glass railroad mural above the desk. Rooms are very well kept and comfortable, spacious, and most outside rooms have balconies. Rooms cost 880 pesos single and 1050 pesos double.

Newest addition to the collection of hotels located on the Plaza de Armas is the **Hotel Concha Dorada (3)** (tel. 293/6-1400), officially located at Lerdo de Tejada 77, almost next door to the Hotel Colonial and Hotel Ruíz. The tiny reception desk might make one think this is a starvation-budget hotel, but in fact the smallish rooms, although somewhat dark, have some of the better touches: tile bathrooms, radio, telephone, air conditioning, and all-new furniture. Prices are in line with the modernization, and are a bit high (but consider the location): 475 pesos single with fan, 525 to 575 pesos single with air conditioning; 585 pesos double with fan, 632 to 720 double with air conditioning. The small inner rooms, while a bit claustrophobic, are bound to be quiet.

The **Hotel Colonial (6)**, right on the Plaza de la Constitución (tel. 293/2-0193), has two sections, the older with ceiling fans and the newer with air conditioning. All the expensive hotel services are here, including private, covered parking for guests. You pay 655 pesos single, 775 pesos double for one of the older rooms (still very nice, mind you), 855 to 985 double for the air-conditioned rooms. This is a pleasant place to stay.

Prices are slightly less in the imposing **Gran Hotel Diligencias,** (facing the Plaza de Armas), but in my opinion the Hotel Colonial offers the best value-for-money.

The **Hotel Emporio (16)** (tel. 293/2-0020 or 2-7520), out on the Malecon near the Banco de México tower, is a huge, older place, functional but well kept, with a second-story swimming pool and sundeck. The Emporio's decoration and ambience call to mind Veracruz in the '50s, when this must have been the elegant place to stay. Nowadays you can enjoy the good location, the sea view, air conditioning, and pool for 1160 pesos double, less on weekdays. Singles pay 990 pesos.

The Big Splurge

Feel like spending some money? The brand-new **Hotel Puerto Bello Centro (9)** (tel. 293/8-0088 or 8-0332), 458 Malecon, is a dramatic modern tower with posh, air-conditioned rooms and a gleaming swimming pool, plus private parking for guests (which costs extra). A big double room here goes for 2300 pesos. On weekends, they probably get it, too.

On the Starvation Budget

It's probably only a matter of time before the musty old **Hotel Imperial** (tel. 293/2-0173), on the north side of the Plaza de Armas, is gutted, renovated, and catapulted out of our price range. But at present you can get a double room here for 660 pesos, and if you get one of the rooms overlooking the square—which are better kept—it might just be worth it.

Two blocks south of the Plaza de Armas is the street named after Aquiles Serdan. Two inexpensive hotels here are worth a look if the weather is not too hot. The **Hotel Amparo** (tel. 293/2-2738), Serdan 478-482 near the corner with Zaragoza, has a tiled facade, a tiled lobby, and a stone-lined corridor leading to an inner court. All this stonework won't keep you cooler—you'll need the windows open here if it's hot, and the street noise can be fierce. Take a room in the back of the building. They cost 280 pesos single, 360 pesos double.

Across the street from the Amparo is the **Hotel Mallorca** (tel. 293/2-3189), Serdan 481, also with a tiled facade, and simple rooms-with-bath at prices very similar to those at the Amparo. The Mallorca does have a few rooms with air conditioning, too, which rent for 520 pesos double.

Near the Beach

Right at the northern (beginning) end of the Boulevard Manuel Avila Camacho is the **Hotel Villa Rica (26)** (tel. 293/2-0782), at no. 7. Mexican families and young people on vacation choose this neat-and-tidy little place as a favorite because it's near the beach and not all that far from downtown, either. Rooms are simple and clean with tiled showers, and one has the choice of a fan or of air conditioning; prices are 728 pesos single, 888 pesos double; and if you take a room at the rear of the hotel you have an air conditioner (rooms in the front have ceiling fans and a sea view).

The **Hotel Villa del Mar (23)** (tel. 293/2-0227), farther south and east along Boulevard Camacho, is a large and rambling older place with modernized, air-conditioned rooms renting for 880 pesos double. Older, less well-kept rooms with fans only are a bit too expensive at 795 pesos double. The reason the prices are this high is obvious: the hotel has its own private little swimming pool, and the public beach is just across the busy boulevard. Take a room with air conditioning, it's the better value.

Right next door is the **Hostal de Cortes (23)** (tel. 293/2-0065), a new six-floor hotel boasting an elevator, sea views from little balconies attached to some rooms, color television sets, and servi-bars, a restaurant, bar, and swimming pool. One pays for all this posh, though, as the 113 rooms go for 1660 pesos double—a bit out of our range.

Much better in terms of price, although quite a bit older, is the **Hotel Mar y Tierra (5)** ("sea and land"; tel. 293/2-0260), right at the junction of the Malecon, Boulevard Camacho, and Avenida Figueroa near the aforementioned

Hotel Villa Rica. Brightly colored tiles gleam at you when you enter the lobby. Approaching the desk, remind yourself to ask to see several rooms on different sides of the building—sea views are excellent from here. Also, think of the sun's heat and how it will hit your windows, at what time of day. The relatively quiet rooms come with ceiling fans for 440 pesos single, 550 pesos double; with air conditioning for 660 pesos single, 770 pesos double.

Out of Town—On Mocambo Beach

The **Hotel Mocambo (22)** (tel. 293/3-1500) is quite a way out of town to the east, right on one of Veracruz's best stretches of beach. A palatial layout with rooms, halls, terraces, pools, grounds, etc., it must qualify as a splurge hotel. All 100 rooms have air conditioning, private baths, and sea views, and you can use their huge filtered pool or the beach, the Ping-Pong tables, tennis court, or other facilities. Cost is a cool 1100 pesos single, 1325 pesos double. Even if you don't decide to stay here, you might want to come out for a look and a swim. The beach is public—you needn't stay at the hotel. Note that at the Mocambo they may nickel-and-dime you, charging 20 pesos or so as a "telephone charge," whether you use the phone or not.

Next to the Bus Station

Right next door to Veracruz's Central Camionera, at Avenida Díaz Mirón 1612, is the **Hotel Central (17)** (tel. 293/3-2222). Although hardly central as its name implies, it is indeed convenient for those arriving by bus as long as you follow my caution about noise. The marbled halls of the Central lead to very worn rooms with tile showers and well-used furnishings; some rooms come with fans, for 495 pesos double, and some come with air conditioning for 565 pesos double. Air conditioning allows you to keep the louvered windows closed and thus the noise out. When choosing a room, remember the buses. This place is for emergencies only.

WHERE TO EAT: Now that the Plaza de Armas, the main square, has been turned into a pedestrian zone, the restaurants under the portals which surround it have become even more attractive, and, sadly, more expensive. But you needn't wander far from downtown to enjoy what Veracruzans love best: seafood.

You get more than a meal when you dine at **El Chato Moyo (8)**, down on the waterfront at Landero y Coss 142, corner of Insurgentes Veracruzanos. Sit outside on the Calle Prof. J. S. Montero, and you'll be treated to a view of a hundred itinerant peddlers (none of whom will give you a hard time); of at least two marimba or mariachi bands, competing for the scarce silence by trying to drown one another out. Shoeshine boys, beggars, sellers of tasteless model ships and cheap jewelry make up an endless procession. Sound like a horror? Somehow it's all great fun at the Chato Moyo. The food is quite good, the service all right for the size of the place, and the prices very competitive. Fish is ordered by size and costs 175 to 250 pesos, depending. Meat plates are 195 pesos, but you should try seafood here. Start with an oyster, shrimp, or octopus cocktail for 90 pesos. Special plates go as high as 400 pesos, but you needn't spend that much. If the Chato Moyo's crowded, you might try one of the two other similar restaurants next door.

Devotees of Spanish food will undoubtedly like **La Paella**, Zamora 138 (Plaza de Armas), where a five-course comida goes for 150 pesos. Three of the courses include such internationally known Spanish specialties as caldo gallego (a fish broth), paella valenciana, and Basque-style sea bass. The walls are festooned with bullfight posters—all Spanish, none Mexican. La Paella is right at one corner (the southeast) of the Plaza de Armas—look for its tiled, very colonial facade.

The **Hotel Prendes (2)** restaurant is still *numero uno* in the plaza area—especially where seafood is concerned. Premises are spacious, well lighted, air-conditioned, and—rare for Veracruz—free from excessive noise. Supplementing a 260-peso comida are à la carte dishes ranging from 170 to 325 pesos.

The aptly named **Restaurant El Unico (10)** may in fact be the only place where you can get such a good, filling comida corrida for a really low price anymore. For 95 pesos the señora will bring you soup, rice, a choice of meat or fish, dessert, and coffee. The comida corrida is just about all anyone orders during the afternoon, but you can also get plates of fish for 185 pesos, egg dishes for 40 to 90 pesos. The decor is nothing much, of course, but the food is very tasty indeed, and can't be beaten at the price—or higher. The restaurant is located at the corner of Aquiles Serdan (no. 493) and Trigueros (a small street parallel to and in between Zaragoza and Independencia).

You might take a look at Veracruz's newest seafood restaurant, **La Olímpica del Puerto (4)**, at Malecon 376. Big, bare, and bright, La Olímpica may take its name from the fact that it seems big as a football field. The cloth-covered tables are rarely full, nor is every dish on the endless menu ever offered all at once. But of the fish they have, you may pay 350 to 600 pesos for a full meal. When I tried it last, La Olímpica still had a way to run before it equaled, say, El Chato Moyo in quality, price, and ambience. Perhaps it will have reached its goal by the time you arrive. Open every day for lunch and dinner.

Starvation Budget—Seafood

Market areas are famous the world over for providing hearty, inexpensive fare, and because Veracruz is on the water, the market fare here includes seafood. On Landero y Coss between Arista and Zaragoza is the **Municipal Fish Market**, its street level chock-a-block with little *ostionerías* (oyster bars) and shrimp stands. Take a stool, ask the price, and order a plate of boiled shrimp, fresh oysters, octopus, or conch. The price for plate should be about 75 pesos.

A Pastry Shop or Two

You should eat a big lunch as the Mexicans do to save money, so you won't want too much for breakfast. The cheapest way to get going in the morning is to seek out a pastry shop and pick up some sweet rolls or cakes (they're incredibly cheap and good in Mexico) and then find a café, order a cup of coffee, tea, or chocolate, and you'll have a good, tasty breakfast for less than a dollar. **El Fenix (11)** is a *panadería/pastelería* (bakery and pastry shop) which has a very wide selection of Mexican rolls and pastries for prices ranging from 5 to 15 pesos. You can't miss the assortment and the smell at Avenida 5 de Mayo 170, corner of Arista. A similar establishment is the **Paris** at 5 de Mayo and Molina. By the way, neither of these places has tables where you can consume their wares on the spot. Rather, take a tray and a pair of tongs, select your pastries, and take them to the counter to be counted. Pay the total to the cashier.

A Café

One of Veracruz's most successful and popular places to while away the hours over coffee is the **Gran Café de la Parroquía (12)**, right across the street from the parish church *(Parroquía)* just off the Plaza de Armas on the Avenida Independencia. Bright and bare, it takes its character from its clients, an assortment from most facets of Veracruz's daily life. Cappuccino is 16 pesos (small) or 28 pesos (large), desserts are 20 to 28 pesos, breakfasts for 65 to 105 pesos. So popular is the Parroquía, in fact, that the management has opened up a new and shiny branch of the café **(13)** on the Paseo del Malecon out toward the Bank of Mexico building, open 6 p.m. to 1 a.m. only. Take your newspaper and try out both.

Here's an interesting bit of Parroquía lore: notice the two waiters scurrying about with big aluminum kettles? One kettle has thick black coffee, the other has hot milk. Order cafe con leche and you'll get a few fingers of coffee in the bottom of your glass. Then, pick up your spoon and bang on the glass to call the waiter with the milk—that spoon-banging is a constant chime in La Parroquía.

WHAT TO DO: Veracruz has beaches, but none of them are very good because the sand is a dirty brown color and the water tends to be shallow. There are points all along the waterfront downtown where people swim, but the nearest legitimate beach is at the **Villa del Mar (23)**, an open-air terrace and palm-lined promenade at the southern end of town. (To orient yourself, north is on your left as you look toward the gulf from town.) To get to the beach, catch a trolleycar from behind the Palacio Municipal, or take the bus marked Playa V. del Mar which travels south on 5 de Mayo. The trip takes about 15 minutes.

The better beach is the one in front of the Hotel Mocambo, mentioned above.

Take a walk around town. Veracruz has a special affinity for lighthouses (no surprise), and they are to be found everywhere. In fact, the **Bank of Mexico** building **(16)**, mentioned in the introduction to this section, is also called *El Faro Nuevo* (the new lighthouse), and indeed it is so equipped, as you'll see if you walk down that way in the evening. Other lighthouses include the Faro Juarez, on the Plaza de la República, and the one named for Venustiano Carranza, part museum and part Naval Headquarters, down past the Hotel Emporio on the way to the Bank of Mexico. The museum part, called the **Museo Historico de la Revolución "Venustiano Carranza"** is open Tuesday through Friday, 9 a.m. to 1 p.m. and 4 to 6 p.m., on Saturday 9 a.m. to 1 p.m., Sunday and holidays 9 a.m. to noon; closed Monday. Admission is free.

You can go out and look at the fort of **San Juan de Ulua (15)** either by driving across the bridge that heads north out of the Plaza de Armas between Avenidas República and Morelos and then turning right past the piers (a bus from the corner of Landero y Coss and Lerdo marked "San Juan de Ulua" also takes this route), or by taking one of the boats that run from the Malecon (pier) to the left of the big Bank of Mexico building on the waterfront. There isn't much to see in the castle, by the way, except a pleasant view of the city across the still waters of the harbor.

Another interesting trip is to the **Isla de Sacrificios**, so named because the Spaniards are said to have witnessed human sacrifices there. Boats leave from the docks in front of the Hotel Emporium, but during the winter, between October and February, boat schedules depend on the winds, which can be pretty strong and unpredictable—in other words don't plan a trip to the Isla de Sacrificios from October to February. The round-trip fare on a scheduled boat is 50 pesos per person, but often there will be no group boats and you'll have to hire a boat by the hour.

The **Fort of Santiago (24)**, located on the corner of Rayón and Gómez Farías, is open to the public Monday to Saturday from 10 a.m. to 1 p.m. and 4 to 7 p.m., on Sunday from 4 to 7 p.m., for an admission charge of 2 pesos. The fort was built in 1636 as part of the city fortifications against the pirates; this bastion is all that is left of the old city walls. It's remarkable to see the type of construction which was used in those days: solid, to say the least!

Finally, the recently restored **City Museum Building (20)**, Zaragoza 397, is 120 years old, and was built originally as an orphanage. Some years ago it was converted into a museum, and recently it was completely renovated. There is a beautiful courtyard with fountain, and about 12 rooms off the courtyard (on two levels) which house archeological relics from the Gulf Coast pre-Columbian sites. The collection is small compared to the museum in Jalapa or Villahermosa, but the displays are attractive and the setting is lovely. The Indian cultures represented here are the Olmecs (a civilization of the pre-Classic period from around the Villahermosa area); the Totonacs (the Classic civilizations of Tajin and Zempoala, north of Veracruz and south of Tuxpan); and the Huastecas.

There are several rooms displaying regional costumes and crafts. Off the courtyard, there are gardens and split-level terraces with hanging plants and flower pots, bare stone arches, and white stucco walls, all architecturally very soothing. There is a very enthusiastic fellow who has worked in the museum for 12 years, loves to speak English, and will be only too happy to show you around: ask for Luis Aguilar. The museum is open daily except Tuesday from 10 a.m. to 6 p.m.; admission is 10 pesos.

More than anything about Veracruz, you'll remember its gaiety. There is a certain carefree spirit about this bustling seaport. From noon on, you'll hear mariachi and marimba bands playing in the Plaza de Armas, and on Thursday and Sunday from 7 to 10 p.m., you can hear the band play in front of the Palacio Municipal. Up and down the Malecon and in the square, people gather to socialize, listen to the music, or sell knickknacks. It's a gay town, especially on a Sunday, which seems to be the big socializing day.

Carnival in Veracruz

If you dig swinging parties, go to Veracruz at Mardi Gras time. The carnival, which takes place in March, is one of the best in the hemisphere—friendlier than New Orleans, less frantic than Rio. You'll find the town packed with visitors from the capital, and the impassive Indians who've walked a day's journey from their villages. Even the townspeople, normally attentive to their own affairs, join the crowds in the music-filled streets. You'll see a local beauty crowned as queen and, although the government discourages the practice, you may see the Spanish equivalent of the Lord of Misrule being tied to a lamp post (a stuffed figure, of course, not a man).

There are fabulous floats (in Spanish, *carros Alegoricos*, "allegorical cars") made with the Mexican flair: bright colors, papier-mâché figures (even the Muppets showed up on a float), large flowers, and live entertainment. Groups from the neighboring villages don their peacock- and pheasant-feathered headdress in preparation for the dances which they will perform during the festivities. There are costumed Draculas and drag queens and girls in sparkling dresses parading down the streets.

Most of the activities center in the Plaza de Armas, and begin after the heat of the day, around 3 p.m., lasting well into the night, of course.

Do remember that if you plan to be in Veracruz for the carnival, reserve hotel space months in advance, for everything's jammed full at this time.

BOCA DEL RÍO AND MOCAMBO BEACH: About five miles south of Veracruz along the Gulf Coast is the beautiful beach of Mocambo; a little farther on at the mouth of the Jamapa River is the fishing village of Boca del Río. Both of these can easily be reached by taking the buses which leave every 30 minutes (on the hour and half hour) from the corner of Serdan and Zaragoza (25) near the municipal fish market. The bus stop is marked with a sign "Costa Verde" or "Boca del Río"; the trip takes 30 minutes and costs 5 pesos. Boats, snorkeling equipment, and water skis can be rented at Mocambo beach.

4. Tuxpan and Tajin

The coastal country to the northwest of Veracruz is particularly lush and beautiful, and the town of Tuxpan is very pretty in a tropical way. Along the road to Tuxpan from Veracruz one can visit the Totonac ruins at Zempoala, pass through the vanilla-growing town of Papantla, stop for a look at the marvelous Totonac city of Tajin, and whiz as fast as possible through the oil boom town of Poza Rica. Note that as of this writing, the highway (180) northwest of the town of Cardel is in terrible shape.

ZEMPOALA AND TAJIN: These are both pre-Columbian ruins of the Totonac Indians. Both cities flourished during the Classic Period (A.D. 300–900), but Tajin was burned and abandoned in the 13th century when the barbarian warriors (the Chichimecs) from the north invaded the city, while Zempoala continued to thrive and was the capital of the Totonacs at the time of the Spanish Conquest. It was, in fact, the Totonacs at Zempoala who helped Cortes and his men make the journey inland to capture the Aztec capital of Tenochtitlán.

A 16th-century Spanish scholar described the Totonacs as "fun loving with no affront of words, no ugly or unjust things . . . calm and amiable." If you look at the artwork of these people you can see the joyfulness which he described. The figurines are delightful, most of them in animated positions with large smiles across their faces.

The ruins at Zempoala are not quite as impressive as those at Tajin but still very interesting. Zempoala means "place of the twenty waters," and was so named for the many rivers which converged at the site. This area is really gorgeous with lush foliage and rich agricultural land.

Most of the buildings at Zempoala date from the 14th and 15th centuries— quite late for pre-Columbian structures. This city was, however, inhabited before the time of Christ. The great temple is interesting because it resembles the Temple of the Sun in Tenochtitlán, probably a result of Aztec influence during the 15th century. There are several other temples. One of the most unusual is the Temple of the Little Faces, which has many stuccoed faces set into the walls, along with hieroglyphs painted on the lower parts of the walls. Then there is the Temple of Quetzalcoatl and Ehecatl (the gods of the feathered serpent and the wind, respectively). Both gods are represented in the building structure: Quetzalcoatl by the rectangular portion, Ehecatl by the round structure.

Zempoala is about 25 miles north of Veracruz. Driving time is 30 minutes on Highway 180 to Cardel. The ruins of Zempoala are just north of Cardel. There are buses on the La Fuega line (second-class bus), which is located just behind the Veracruz first-class A.D.O. Terminal. The trip takes 1½ hours, and is truly a beautiful trip through tropical forests. Entrance to the ruins is 10 pesos.

The ruins at Tajin are divided into those in the old section *(Tajin viejo)* and those in the new section *(Tajin chico)*. The most impressive structure is the **Pyramid of the Niches** which is found in the old section. The pyramid is made of stone and adobe, with 365 recesses on all four sides of the building. The pyramid was once covered in painted stucco, and is today one of the most unusual pre-Columbian structures in Mesoamerica. Near this pyramid is the ball court with beautiful carved reliefs on the vertical playing sides depicting religious scenes and sacrifices.

The **Temple of the Columns** is in the new section. A stairway divides the columns, three on either side, each one decorated with reliefs of priests and warriors plus hieroglyphic dates. There are many mounds which are still uncovered; the view from on top of one of the pyramids overlooking the rich green forests, dotted with these mounds, is quite impressive. This is definitely worth a stop if you are driving the Gulf Coast Highway. From Veracruz take Route 180 to Papantla; from there take Route 127, which is a back road to Poza Rica, going through Tajin. It is not a well-publicized site and there is not much traffic. A.D.O. runs daily buses to Papantla; from there take a taxi to the ruins. The entrance fee is 10 pesos, parking is 5 pesos. A small refreshment stand serves cool drinks.

READERS' TOURING SUGGESTIONS: "We believe the best way to see El Tajin is to stay in the pretty town of **Papantla**, which is just a few miles from the ruins. We stayed at the **Hotel El Tajin** and had a very nice room for less than $15 U.S. The short trip to the ruins can be made by bus (change buses at the crossroads) operating from the bus depot one block from the square. The bus leaves you off one mile from the gate. Don't miss the *voleadores* ("fliers") who perform just inside the entrance to the ruins on weekends. It's worth the trip there just for this demonstration of courage and skill by colorfully dressed Totonac Indians" (Carol and David Hopkins, San Diego, Calif.). . . . "If you're going on to the ruins of El Tajin from Tuxpan, take a bus to **Poza Rica** (run every half hour, trip takes 1½ hours). The driver will drop you off at a place, and then you catch another bus to 'las ruinas'; they're blue and are marked 'La Margarita,' and they drop you off right outside the entrance. Later on, you can flag down a bus that goes to Papantla" (Paul Traves, England, and Nora Solis, U.S.A.).

TUXPAN: Although coming of age now, not long ago Tuxpan, Veracruz (that's TOOSH-pahn; pop. 90,000), was the best example on the Gulf Coast of an unspoiled fishing town. The fishing boats are still moored in town at the mouth of the Río Tuxpan, and a fishing festival is held in early summer, but Tuxpan is growing. One of the benefits of this growth is the presence of several very good places to stay and to dine. Why stay in Tuxpan? It's simple: for the unhurried, tropical ambience, and for the magnificent beach, about six miles from town.

Where to Stay and Eat

Avenida Juarez, Tuxpan's main downtown street, holds the prime hotels. At the **Hotel Plaza** (tel. 783/4-0738), Juarez 39, a modern air-conditioned room goes for 625 pesos single, 960 pesos double. All the conveniences are here: elevator, coordinated wood furniture and headboards, individual room thermostats, tile baths. Rooms are functional rather than fancy, but offer good accommodation. The Plaza's restaurant is one of the town's more popular places to dine, partly because it is air-conditioned. Seafood is king here, and rightly so: start your meal with an oyster cocktail, then pass on to boiled shrimp with enchiladas, or perhaps huachinango a la Veracruzana (red snapper in tomato sauce), and finish up with banana cake, and your bill should be 365 pesos. A number of photographs of Tuxpan in the 1920s and '30s spice up the restaurant's otherwise unremarkable modern decor.

The **Hotel Florida** (tel. 783/4-0222), Juarez 23, is perhaps the best budget choice as it has some rooms with fans for 575 pesos single, 650 to 800 pesos double; rooms with air conditioning cost 70 pesos more. The Florida is Tuxpan's older and well used but still sturdy and serviceable hotel. An elevator serves the several floors, and as some rooms have been remodeled more recently than others it would be good to look before you buy; another reason to look is that the Florida is one of the few hotels with river views—only a few rooms offer this.

Although it looks old-fashioned from the outside, the **Hotel Reforma** (tel. 783/4-0210), Juarez 25, is in fact Tuxpan's most modern place to stay. Actually, the building dates back some time, and the lofty inner court has been preserved and is not furnished with cast-iron tables, chairs, a little pool with a fountain, and bar service. The court is not air-conditioned but the lobby and guest rooms are. All rooms have been modernized, and cost 775 pesos single, 875 pesos double in one bed, 995 pesos double in twin beds. The Reforma has its own restaurant (open 7 a.m. to 11 p.m.), entered from either the court or the street.

READER'S HOTEL SELECTIONS: "We'd like to suggest the **Hotel Parque,** right next to the zócalo, with rooms for 275 pesos single and 400 pesos double, with fan and shower. Also, for starvation-budget people, the **Hotel Colón** is a big, tatty-looking place right by the river, very basic, probably the cheapest in town. No fan, and the showers are down the hall, but a really good view of the river. While in Tuxpan, readers should try one of the delicious fruit drinks they make at stands in the square."

Getting to the Beach

Now that you've cased the town and sniffed its tropical ambience, take a run out to the beach. Bring your bathing suit, and catch a red-and-white bus marked "La Playa" from near the first-class A.D.O. terminal, down by the bridge. The bus will drop you right on the hard-sand beach, where you'll find changing cubicles and showers. The bus comes by every now and then to buzz you back into town.

5. Lake Catemaco

Ninety-miles southeast of Veracruz over good roads is Lake Catemaco, described by many as the most beautiful body of water in Mexico. The lake region is located between the only mountains on the steaming coastal plain that reaches from Tampico to Yucatán. Both peaks are named **San Martín** and are in the neighborhood of 7000 feet; one is a volcano while the other is not. The Catemaco area is a balmy oasis in a region where the rule is muggy heat relieved only by chilly northerns. Its healthful climate has led overenthusiastic boosters to refer to Catemaco as the "Switzerland of Veracruz." Although a Switzerland it ain't, this detracts in no way from Catemaco's charms. Free from extremes of heat and cold, this is another region of the eternal spring so typical of Mexico's highlands.

At the northwestern end of the ten-mile-long lake is the town of Catemaco, Veracruz, (alt. 1000 feet; pop. 8700). As might be expected, what action there is centers on Catemaco's attractive zócalo, somewhat atypical as central plazas go.

WHERE TO STAY AND EAT: My favorite place to stay in Catemaco is the **Posada (Motel) Koniapan** (tel. 294/3-0063), right on the lakeshore at the intersection of Malecon and Revolución (as you go down the hill toward the lake from the plaza and come to the shore, turn left onto the lakefront Malecon and walk along till you come to it). Bright, and clean, the Koniapan provides a fan in each room, screens on the windows, and small but spotless tiled bathrooms. The furniture is heavy neocolonial, but not bad for all that. There's a small swimming pool in the front yard; sometimes a small restaurant next to it is open and serving. Rooms cost 480 pesos single, 680 pesos double with fan; with air conditioning, the prices are 125 pesos higher.

At the top of the budget range—but worth every peso—is the lush and expansive **Motel Playa Azul** (tel. 294/3-0001 or 3-0042; Apdo. Postal 26), east along the lakeshore from town two kilometers (1¼ miles). Take a bus marked "La Margarita" from the town square, or hire a taxi for the short ride over a dusty and rather bumpy road. At the end of it is a bit of paradise: stately palms, verdant and flower-filled gardens, a fine swimming pool overlooking the lake, a big restaurant, and modernish rooms renting for 675 pesos single, 850 pesos double with ceiling fan, 980 pesos single, 1025 pesos double with air conditioning (which you should not need). The loudest noise here is that of the birds.

Too expensive for what it is, the **Hotel Catemaco** (tel. 294/3-0203 or 3-0045), at Carranza 8, is the next choice in town. It's located right on the plaza, has a small pool out back, and features air conditioning, which accounts for its rather high prices: 800 pesos single, 1100 pesos double. It can't fill up at these Mexico City rates, so try offering a lower price and see if they'll go for it.

A good, plain, but serviceable budget choice is the **Hotel Tío Tin** (tel. 294/3-0084), right down on the water at Avenida Playa 14. Some of the older rooms here have lake views, and several beds (good for families). Showers are tiled, and there's lots of hot water (although it may take a while for it to come up). A single person pays 385 pesos, two persons pay 420 to 580 pesos; a few very modern rooms with very fine lake views go for 95 pesos more per room. Free parking in the yard.

Right above the A.D.O. bus station is the **Hotel Los Arcos** (tel. 294/3-0111), a small place with boldly colored rooms, each equipped with ceiling fan—there's good cross-ventilation, too—and motel-style walkways to the rooms which also serve as balconies for the lake view. Prices are surprisingly moderate: 375 pesos single, 575 pesos double, and that's for a room with two double beds.

Down on the shore are several restaurants, my favorite being **La Ola**. A thatched roof and fish net decorations put you in the mood, and other attractions such as a small zoo containing turtles and alligators, or concerts of *jarocho* (Veracruz-style) guitar music are sometimes offered. The set lunch or dinner at La Ola is offered whenever the custom warrants, which it usually does in summer and on holiday weekends. Otherwise, try barbecued chicken for 160 pesos or the famous whitefish (mojarra) of the lake for 200 to 285 pesos, depending on size.

La Luna, right nearby, is a similar restaurant without some of the sideshows of the Ola. Prices are virtually the same. As enthusiasm of cooks and staff wax and wane through the seasons, the best plan is to head for whichever restaurant seems the busier at the moment.

Although the lake is famed for its whitefish, gastronomy is not always of the highest quality in Catemaco. Perhaps the best all-around restaurant, good for breakfast, lunch, and dinner, is the dining room of the **Hotel Catemaco**. A view of the town's busy plaza adds to the pleasant, if simple, decor. For a light lunch of salad or a sandwich you'll pay from 100 pesos; for a full-course dinner based on anything from chicken to seafood, 250 to 500 pesos.

If the street market is in operation around the Hotel Los Arcos, little cookshops will be set up throughout. Here's the cheapest and most colorful place to sample the lake's mojarra, or any of a dozen other sorts of rough-and-ready fare. Prices are not set, and will depend on how the fishing season's going, how much money has been made that day, and how prosperous you look to be.

WHAT TO SEE AND DO: If you're sports-minded, boats are available for waterskiing or fishing. If sightseeing is your preference you can just about choose the trip to fit your budget. The cheapest way to get to Playa Azul and Playa Hermosa beaches is by bus. Look for the bus marked "La Margarita" from the town square. The same bus goes out to the Cuetzalapan River, known for its transparently clear waters, flowers, bird life, and interesting rock formations.

You can take a tour of the lake by boat, stopping at the aforementioned beaches, the river, a mineral spring called Arroyo Agrio, and another called Coyame—you may have seen its water bottled and on your dinner table. Cost for the 1¼-hour lake tour is about 1000 pesos per boatload. Talk to the boatmen down at the wharf on the Malecon.

GETTING TO AND FROM CATEMACO: There is daily first-class bus service from the A.D.O. terminal in Veracruz. You have your choice of 18 daily departures, but most of these will be going only as far as the cigar-making town of San Andres Tuxtla, 7½ miles short of Catemaco. Two or three buses a day do go directly to Catemaco from Veracruz, however, and you should try for one of these. Otherwise, go to San Andres, and catch a local bus for the last short leg, or hire a taxi (bargaining like mad).

The next leg of your journey, whether your destination be the Yucatán or San Cristóbal de las Casas and Guatemala, is along the Gulf Coast past Coatzacoalcos to Villahermosa. This is the route to the Yucatán, but from Villahermosa buses cross the mountains on Highway 195 to Tuxtla Gutierrez and San Cristóbal. There is no reason to travel via Highway 185 which traverses the Isthmus of Tehuantepec, for the isthmus is flat, unscenic, full of traffic, and hot and muggy.

READERS' HOTEL SELECTION FOR TUXTLA: "The **Hotel Castellanos** in Santiago Tuxtla is a new hotel that overlooks the town square in the center of which is a gigantic Olmec head found on the hotel grounds during construction. The hotel is a family operation set in a tropical oasis: warm in the day, cool at night. The hotel has an excellent restaurant, huge pool, gorgeous rooms in tile and cherrywood. Rooms without meals are 440 pesos single, 660 pesos double" (Pat and Dave Schouweiler, Minneapolis, Minn.).

Chapter XIII

SOUTH OVER THE MOUNTAINS

1. Puebla
2. Tehuacan
3. Oaxaca
4. Tehuantepec

SHOULD YOU HAVE the time to go deeper into the country south and east of Mexico City, one of the best ways you can spend that time is by traveling to Oaxaca. It's a ten-hour, 325-mile ride over a road that sometimes winds through the mountains cutting your speed considerably, so it's unlikely you'll try to do it in one day. The flight is only 40 minutes; the train is an overnight trip. Oaxaca, like the Yucatán, is a center of Indian culture and archeology besides being an interesting city in its own right. Sometimes you can witness Indian ceremonies in the villages surrounding Oaxaca (always you can see the Indian costumes) and it is in Oaxaca and the area around it that you find the finest heavy blankets—almost rugs—of traditional design; and only a few miles out of the city are the Zapotec ruins of Monte Alban, and a bit farther afield are the ruins of Mitla. From Oaxaca you can go southeast to the mountains of Chiapas and San Cristóbal de Las Casas, and on to Guatemala; or you can go northeast to the gulf and to the Yucatán, or back to Veracruz.

If you can take the ten-hour ride on the bus, do so. Those driving will have to spend a night along the way. Figure that you'll drive two hours to get to Puebla, and three more hours to get to Tehuacan, another possible overnight stop.

There are now two roads to Puebla from the capital: an old, winding one which you'll drive with great frustration, following strings of lumbering trucks, with no chance to pass; and a classy, new toll road which is faster. The bus usually follows the new highway.

Whichever road you choose, you'll find that the route is unusually scenic, with many distractions to keep your eyes occupied. You'll see little shrines built into the sides of the road at intervals, roadside stands with fruit elaborately piled into pyramids, and occasionally, the passengers of a decrepit, second-class bus sitting patiently while the driver crawls underneath to effect repairs. Weather permitting, you'll also see the beautiful snow-capped volcano peaks of Popocatapetl and Ixtaccihuatl, the former dormant, the latter extinct, and dozens of enormous churches. Many of these have brightly painted domes of blue or gold and look very grand. Mostly, however, they are not as impressive inside. There are said to be 365 churches on this drive—one for every day of the year.

The border between the states of México and Puebla is reached halfway at Río Frío, in wild, mountainous country that was once heavily infested with bandits. Río Frío, where the buses now make a brief stop, was a renowned bandit town, but even more so was Huejotzingo, about 65 miles out of Mexico City on the Puebla road. Huejotzingo was the headquarters of a guerrilla named Augustin Lorenzo, whose capture is still celebrated every Shrove Tuesday with a colorful, firecracker-filled carnival.

A STOP IN HUEJOTZINGO: You might find yourself able and willing to stop in this pleasant town, especially if you're driving. Huejotzingo, Puebla (alt. 7550 feet; pop. 25,000) has a fine big main square where open-air markets are held on Thursday and Saturday. Even if you don't come for market day, you can stop and enjoy a glass or two of the local sparkling (alcoholic) cider, a specialty.

For sights, Huejotzingo has a prizewinner. The **Franciscan monastery**, right across the main road from the town plaza, was built between 1529 and 1570. As you walk up the stairs from the main road and enter the monastery compound, notice the little square chapels topped by pyramidal roofs which stand at each corner of the enclosure. They're nicely decorated. The cross mounted on a pedestal in the courtyard dates from the 1500s as well.

The church, very austere on the outside, has a wonderfully lacy Gothic vault inside, and a dazzling altar in the Plateresque style. The monastery proper is next door, entered through the double-arch doorway. The monastery has a lovely chapel, a cloister for the monks, and the necessary places: kitchens, dining room, etc.

The Franciscan monastery, one of the oldest in Mexico, is open from 9 a.m. to 1 p.m. and 3 to 5 p.m. every day; you pay a few pesos for admission.

Should you be in town on market day, be sure to look over the woolen goods, especially the serapes and blankets.

If you continue along Highway 190 (not the toll highway, 190-D), you'll pass through the colonial town of **Cholula,** 9 miles (14 kilometers) from Huejotzingo and 6 miles (10 kilometers) from Puebla. The **Great Pyramid of Cholula,** perhaps the largest man-made structure in the world, is on the southern outskirts of the town. The Great Pyramid is not much to look at these days, having become merely a huge mound or small mountain with a church perched on top. But in the depths of the mound are some interesting frescos which you can visit. For details, see below in the Puebla section under "Day Trip to Cholula."

1. Puebla

Puebla (alt. 7049 feet; pop. 950,000) has retained a lot of the wealth and the architecture from the 19th century when it was the principal stopping point on the way to Veracruz, Mexico's main port. The rich and famous built themselves mansions here so they could rest overnight in style. And like San Luis Potosí and Oaxaca, the church chose Puebla as a center of its activities. A full 99 churches remain from this time, along with numerous grand monasteries, convents, and a magnificent Bishop's Palace next to the cathedral.

Today Puebla is growing at an amazing rate, and it shows: the streets teem with people walking or people selling things, everything from tacos to kitchen utensils. Cars jam the streets, and the ever-present buses, spewing fumes, trumpet and roar. In fact, the Poblanos are like peasants living in a palace who will bust up the Biedermeier to cook a chicken. The overcrowding and fumes and noise make it unpleasant to stay in this otherwise graceful and architecturally fascinating city for more than a day. The city fathers are trying to deal with the problems by closing off downtown streets to all but pedestrian traffic. But a lot remains to be done.

Not to discourage you further, but I have never—*never*—in ten years of looking, found a well-run, good value-for-money hotel in this city. Puebla has lots of hotels, but none that meets those simple criteria. Perhaps it's Puebla's industrial wealth, such as that gigantic Volkswagen plant on the main highway, cement plants, faïence works, etc., that keep the hotels full at inflated prices.

But you really should see Puebla. Get an early start from Mexico City, tour Puebla for a few hours and perhaps sample the famous Poblano cuisine at lunch, then head on to Oaxaca, or Tehuacan, or Veracruz.

The one indispensable fact, essential to finding one's way around the city, is that most streets running east and west are *avenidas,* and those running north and south are *calles.* Avenida de la Reforma divides the city north and south, with even-numbered avenues to the north and odd-numbered avenues to the south. Calle de 16 de Septiembre, which changes its name to 5 de Mayo north of Reforma, is the east-west dividing line, with even-numbered streets to the east.

WHERE TO STAY: The 70-room **Hotel Colonial (3)**, Calle 4 Sur 105 (tel. 22/42-4950), 1½ blocks from the bus station, is a decent choice. It has a good supply of character, with statue-filled alcoves, elevators, garage, roof garden, and all the appurtenances of its type. It's surprisingly reasonable, too, for what it offers: single rooms (about 19 of them) for 660 to 770 pesos; double rooms, 880 to 990 pesos. There's a good restaurant in the hotel, where lunch costs 230 pesos.

My next choice is near the upper edge of our budget. The **Gilfer Hotel (4)**, Avenida 2 Ote. 11 (tel. 22/42-9800), is all glass and marble with large potted plants in the lobby, large and quite comfy rooms for 700 pesos single, 888 pesos double. Extras include a very good location, covered garage, restaurant, bar, and a fairly well-to-do Mexican and foreign clientele. The Gilfer even has its own nightclub.

Similarly modern, although not quite so posh, is the **Hotel Senorial (5)**, (tel. 22/42-4030), Calle 4 Norte no. 602, an edifice of aluminum, glass, and shiny black stone. Here, besides 72 rooms with bathrooms, wall-to-wall carpeting, and telephones, guests can use the hotel's garage, beauty and barber shops, and even their Turkish baths. Be careful with bus noise in street-side rooms. Singles are 730 pesos and doubles are 825 pesos in one bed, a few pesos more for twin beds.

Two Expensive Neocolonial Favorites

Two of Puebla's "colonial" hostelries have shown different ways of providing modern services without losing the feeling of Old Mexico. At the **Hotel Posada San Pedro (6)** (tel. 22/46-5077), Avenida 2 Oriente 202, the solution to the problem is unabashed neocolonialism: the rough walls and dark wood here are accented by bright blues and oranges in the spreads, drapes, and carpets. A small but very beautiful swimming pool is the centerpiece for a grassy inner courtyard open to the sky; nearby is a bar which features an

PUEBLA 305

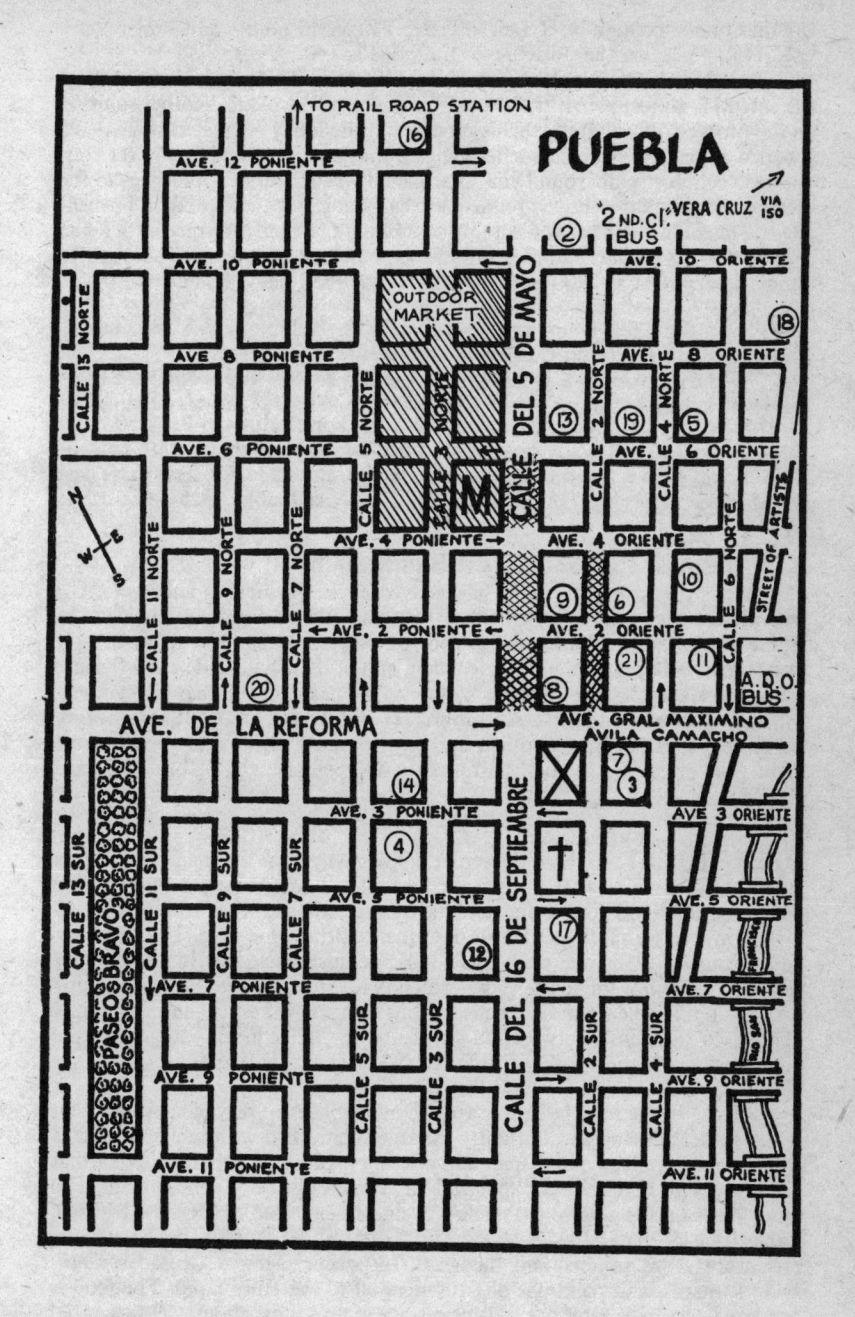

organist or combo nightly. Rooms (all have TV) on the pretty, quiet inner court cost 1450 pesos; on the noisy street the price is 1600 pesos.

The **Hotel Palacio San Leonardo (21)** (tel. 22/46-0555), Avenida 2 Oriente 211, almost across the street from the San Pedro, has another solution to the problem of antiquity-versus-modernity: the lobby is entered by massive wooden doors, a crystal chandelier hangs from the ceiling, and as you register, the 18th century is all around you. But once the bellboy takes your bags to the elevator, it's all 20th century: rooms have carpeting, TVs, and modern furnishings throughout. On the roof is a tiny swimming pool and a terrace with a fine view of the city's church domes and the surrounding mountains. There are 75 rooms, overpriced at 990 pesos single, 1100 to 1250 pesos double.

Right on the Plaza

While you're staying in Puebla, you might as well stay right next to its prettiest spot, the zócalo. The **Hotel Royalty Centro (8)** (tel. 22/42-0202 or 42-4740) is on the north side of the plaza, at Portal Hidalgo 8. A 50-room colonial hotel, the Royalty boasts tasteful old-fashioned rooms with bath or shower, and even a few rooms with little refrigerators and TV sets (these cost extra). Basic prices are 725 pesos single, 1075 pesos double, 1325 pesos triple.

Near the A.U. (Second-Class) Bus Station

Here's the scenario: you've just arrived at the Autobuses Unidos (A.U.) second-class bus station on Avenida 10 Oriente, it's late, and you just want to find a room—quick. Walk out the door onto Avenida 10 Oriente, turn right (west), and walk past Calle 2 Norte. Soon, on the right-hand side at 10 Oriente no. 6, you'll see a hardware store. Walk into the passage, and that big stairway will take you up to the **Hotel Cabrera (2)** (tel. 22/41-8897). It's no beauty anymore, but it tends to be quiet, inexpensive, fairly clean, and good for one night. The prices are the best part: 360 to 440 pesos single, 480 to 560 pesos double.

WHERE TO EAT: Right at the center of town where the two main boulevards intersect is the main square, or zócalo. Several restaurants on this main square offer good food and good value, and have the extra advantage of allowing you to dine and to watch the action in the square at the same time. The **Hostería de los Angelos (7)** is one of Puebla's most popular places for lunch. Hungry *poblanos* come not for the setting—which, while modern and nice, is nothing special—but for the set-price lunches of four courses (175 pesos) and six courses (260 pesos). Besides the two extra courses in the latter meal, you get, for the higher price, a higher quality entree such as roast beef with onions. One of the Hostería's lunches will last you the rest of the day.

All the way across the square are two more places worthy of mention. First is the **Cafe La Princesa,** a brightly lit large room filled with tables draped in colorful cloths, all spic-and-span and offering a 150-peso comida corrida that gives you a good number of appetizers and main dishes to choose from. The other place on the square is Puebla's businessmen's café, the **Cafe El Vasco.** Tables outside on the sidewalk are in the midst of activity, but inside the restaurant all is somber and medieval, the decor using a Crusades motif: swords, maces, and paintings of Crusaders off to the Holy Land. The food is good and service is attentive, but prices are high: soups, about 100 pesos; red snapper, 220 pesos; chateaubriand, 280 pesos. You can have enchiladas Suizas for only 115 pesos, but most other entrees are in the 200- to 350-peso range.

Too much? Then a few steps from the zócalo at Calle 5 de Mayo no. 4 is the **Cafe Aguirre (8)**, part of a photo shop advertised by a big yellow-and-white Kodak sign. The clientele is of all ages, the food largely snacks, sandwiches, and ice cream, with the notable exception of the daily 95-peso fixed-price lunch (150 pesos on Sunday), served from one o'clock on. Breakfasts are good—and cheap—here.

Mixed Mexican-American ambience is what you get at the local **Sanborn's (9)**, set up just like those in Mexico City with sales counters for magazines, cameras, and what-not, and a rather plush dining room in a fine colonial courtyard, with tables set out around a stone fountain—you wouldn't believe it from the store's modern facade on Avenida 2 Ote. no. 6. Enjoy the atmosphere, which is cool and quiet (a treat in Puebla). Stay away from the tenderloin tips, and order the breaded pork cutlet with chilaquiles (225 pesos) instead. Sanborn's is not particularly cheap, but prices are reasonable and it's very restful. Open daily 7:30 a.m. to 11 p.m., until midnight on Saturday.

The **Cafe Venecia (10)** is a clean, cheery, but simple place with a good variety of items for a lunch or light dinner at decent prices. For instance, a hamburger, ham sandwich, fruit cocktail, enchiladas, and chicken casserole are all priced between 35 and 85 pesos. Comidas are 95 pesos. Food is served on two levels, the second floor being a balcony or loft overlooking the first floor. The Venecia is at Avenida 2 Ote. 207, in the same building as another little place called **La Grecia**, which also has good food—the roast meat smell from the sidewalk is enough to draw you in by the nose—and good prices. The featured item is tacos con tortilla arabe, which translates as a falafel sandwich, for 28 pesos, tortas (sandwiches) for about the same. They have yogurt also.

Regional Restaurants

Want to try some Puebla-style food? I can recommend two interesting places. First is the **Restaurante Del Parian (11)**, corner of 6 Norte at Avenida 2 Ote. 415, decorated in what a Puebla city dweller must think is rustic country style: high clay pots line an old-fashioned charcoal range, tiles and carved wood abound, and the menus are on slices of plywood. Puebla cuisine is very complex, based on chile sauces articulated with dozens of other ingredients. *Pipian* sauces, made from pumpkinseed, are usually not super-spicy, *adobos* are dark wine-colored concoctions made with chiles, and can be very hot, *mole poblano* is a dark and very spicy sauce with a bitter chocolate base and a variety of other ingredients, including raisins, chile peppers, onions, and nuts. As the kitchen area is right by the door in El Parian, you might take a look at what's cooking, ask what it is, then be sure to ask, *"¿Es muy picante?"* ("Is it very spicy?") and take your pick. (No English spoken.) Prices are reasonable, with Puebla-style enchiladas at 125 pesos, chalupas (boat-shaped tortillas that are filled with a meat mixture) at 55 pesos.

Second is the **Fonda Santa Clara (4)** (tel. 42-2659), Calle 3 Pte. no. 307, a bit more formal place, although still in the "cozy little restaurant" class. Again, the cuisine is pure Puebla: pollo mole poblano, with the spicy chocolate sauce, is a standard choice for those unfamiliar with Puebla's complex cuisine. Remember, always, that the "chocolate sauce" is not sweet, but savory and spicy, even slightly bitter. It's hearty and delicious, once you've acquired the taste, but it's definitely not "chocolate-covered chicken" in the American sense. Expect to spend 400 to 550 pesos for a full meal here.

On **Calle 6 Norte**, up in the region of the A.D.O. bus station, are many more little Puebla-style eateries, all pretty cheap, and all doing their part to uphold the reputation Puebla bears as a culinary fount.

A Splurge Restaurant

El Cortijo (12), near the corner of Avenida 7 Pte. at 16 de Septiembre no. 506, is a closed patio charmingly decorated and always crowded. The atmosphere is comfortable, the food tasty, the prices not too high, ranging from 225 pesos for pork chops to a delicious jumbo shrimp at 280 pesos. The cubierto (or comida corrida) is a filling five courses for 245 pesos. This is also a good place for an evening drink.

Starvation Budget

If you want to prepare your own picnic, you'll find two roast chicken places opposite the Cine Coliseo at Calles 2 Pte. and 3 Nte.

One of the best snackbars in town is the tiny **Cafe Modelo (13)**, Avenida 6 Ote. no. 4, a small, clean, luncheonette-type establishment with two daily comidas at 95 pesos and 175 pesos (for the latter price one gets a very filling main course, such as a quarter of a chicken in mole poblano). A la carte entrees tend to the low-priced.

At the **Nevería Hermilo,** Avenida 2 Ote. and Calle 4 Nte., the sandwiches are many and varied, being made from a long hot table. The hot table fits in with the modern-cafeteria mood of the place, and the prices are pretty low: 46 pesos per sandwich, 95 pesos for the monster club sandwich. "Nevería" means "ice cream parlor," and so dessert is—you guessed it!

For Dessert

Besides the famous mole poblano chocolate sauce, Puebla is also known throughout Mexico for its *dulces* (sweets). Scattered about in the city are small shops with display windows brim-full of marzipan crafted into various shapes and designs, candied figs, guava paste, and *camotes,* which are little cylinders of a fruity, sweet potato paste wrapped in wax paper. Camotes are fairly bland and fairly expensive (40 to 90 pesos, depending on size). Beware! Both your budget and your diet could suffer irreparable damage in Puebla's sweetshops.

WHAT TO DO IN PUEBLA: Puebla is a fascinating place to explore, but unfortunately the army of polluting buses makes it quite unpleasant to walk the streets. If you are here, however, bear the smog and venture out to see some of these really marvelous colonial monuments to a period when Puebla was the residential way station between the major port of Veracruz and the seat of finance, Mexico City.

The **Bello Museum (14)**, now called the Museum of Art, is located at Avenida 3 Pte. no. 302 on the corner of Calle 2 Sur. It is open from 10 a.m. to 5 p.m. daily except Monday for 5 pesos admission. (This is the standard cost of admission to all museums in Puebla, and these are the hours when the museums are open.) This museum is rarely visited, even though the house has some of the finest 17th-, 18th-, and 19th-century art I've seen anywhere. Señor Bello made his fortune in tobacco and, having no children to leave his money to, began to collect art from all over the world. (He, himself, never traveled, but he had art dealers who did.) Later, Señor Bello, who was himself a fine artist and an accomplished organist, organized a museum, which he left to the state when he died. His taste is evident throughout the house: velvet curtains, French porcelain, beautiful hand-carved furniture, several very fine organs, and numerous paintings. A worthy museum! Be sure to visit it when you are here.

The **Casa de Alfenique (15)**, which looks like an elaborate wedding cake and in fact means "the sugar-cake house," now houses the State Regional

Museum (open 10 a.m. to 5 p.m. every day except Monday for an admission charge of 5 pesos). The 18th-century house is the most interesting part of the museum, but inside there is a small collection of pre-Hispanic artifacts and pottery as well as displays of regional crafts.

Puebla was a religious center like San Luis Potosí and Oaxaca, and today you can see several of the beautiful churches and convents left from that period. Most of the churches date back to the 17th and 18th centuries. A burgeoning antireligious movement climaxed in 1767 when most of the orders were thrown out of the country and their convents closed. The **Convent of Santa Monica,** Avenida 18 Poniente no. 103, holds a certain amount of curiosity value. When the convents were closed in 1767, this one and two others operated secretly, using entrances through private homes, which hid the convent from public view. Very few people knew this convent existed; in fact, it was not discovered until 1935! Today this convent is a museum, kept as it was found (open 10 a.m. to 5 p.m. daily, except Monday, for a few pesos admission).

The largest convent in Puebla was of the Dominican order, called **Santa Rosa (16),** located at Calle 3 Norte no. 1203. It now houses the Museum of Popular Arts and the Cocina (kitchen) de Santa Rosa. It was in this kitchen that many native Mexican dishes were first devised. Both the museum and the kitchen can be visited every day from 10 a.m. to 5 p.m. (closed Monday) for 5 pesos admission. The convent has been beautifully restored, and you can wander through two levels of rooms filled with elaborate examples of Mexican arts and crafts. This is a government-operated museum and the displays include some of the finest crafts around Oaxaca: six-foot earthenware candelabras, regional costumes, minute scenes made of straw and clay, hand-tooled leather objects, and so on. A small shop sells crafts of the area, but it is not as good as the government shops in other cities.

On the ground level of the convent, off the courtyard in the back, is the recently opened **Santa Rosa Restaurant and Bar,** where the decor is colonial. They serve lunch à la carte at moderate prices. Drinks range between 20 and 30 pesos. This is a nice quiet place to get away from the noise of Puebla.

The cathedral, which is absolutely immense, is also worth inspection, especially for its interesting paintings. Begun in 1562 on the orders of King Philip of Spain, it was finished in 1649, before Mexico City's cathedral. You can visit the cathedral every day, no charge. Just across the street from the cathedral, on the corner of Avenida 5 Oriente and Calle 16 de Septiembre is the old **Archbishop's Palace (17),** which now houses the **Casa de la Cultura** and the **Biblioteca Palafoxiana.** The entrance to the Cultural Center and the Library is about halfway down the block on Avenida 5 Ote. You enter a courtyard; the marble stairs to the right will take you up to the second floor and the Biblioteca Palafoxiana. This library, which is the oldest one in the Americas (also the most beautiful), was built in 1646 by Juan de Palafoxe y Mendoza, then archbishop and founder of the College of SS. Peter and Paul. It bespeaks the glory of this period with its elegant tiled floor, hand-carved wood walls and ceiling, inlaid tables, and gilded wooden statues. Bookcases are filled with 17th-century books and manuscripts in Spanish, Creole, French, English, etc. A lofty place!

The **Mercado Victoria (M)** is one of those Victorian railroad-station-like monsters covering an entire block between Avenidas 4 and 8 Poniente on Calle 3 Norte. The market and the entire area from Avenidas 4 to 10 Pte. and Calle 5 north to Calle 5 de Mayo (shaded area on the map) is teeming with unimaginable activity. You literally cannot walk on the sidewalks for the number of vendors on mats and knees selling vegetables and plastic trinkets—it's a maze of narrow pathways, blocked by old women in ill-fitting brightly colored clothes, who squat over piles of withered fruit. This is one of the most hectic and exciting markets you'll see in all of Mexico. **Note:** Puebla is a place to buy onyx, for most of the onyx of Mexico is shipped into Puebla where skilled craftsmen carve the stone.

While you're in the market area, stop in for a look at the **Iglesia de Santo Domingo,** on Calle 5 de Mayo between Avenidas 6 Ote. and 4 Ote. Finished in 1611, the church was part of a monastery at first. Be sure to see the Capilla del Rosario, a symphony of gilt and beautiful stone dedicated to the Virgin of the Rosary and built in 1690.

For a more systematic approach to your marketing, why not head for the **Barrio del Artistica,** Calle 8 Norte between Avenidas 2 and 6 Oriente. The Barrio (also called the "Mercado El Parian") looks for all the world like a colonial shopping mall, with neat brick shops in rows. Designed originally for artisans, the shops are run now by entrepreneurs who sell various crafts/products, much of which is standard souvenir stuff. Bargain to get a good price. While you're in this area you might take a look at the **Principal Theater (18),** which is said to be the oldest theater in the Americas. The interior has been restored and is being used for concerts (see the Tourism Office for schedules). The theater is only open when there is a scheduled event.

Another 18th-century house, now a museum, is the **Casa de Aquiles Serdan (19),** Avenida 6 Oriente no. 206, which houses the Regional Mexican Revolutionary Museum, complete with bullet holes in the front facade of the house! It has collections of arms and photos of the great turmoil of the mid-19th century: the battle between the Juarists (liberals) and those who followed the imperialists (conservatives). Since Puebla lies between the main seaport of Veracruz and the capital, it was often under bombardment by besieging armies. The records and mementos of the various battles are here.

Two forts, about two miles from the zócalo, are worth a look. A cab will take you there for 100 pesos, or you can take a "Fuerte" bus to **Fort Loreto** and **Fort Guadalupe;** admission to the first of these costs 5 pesos, to the latter it's free. The forts commemorate the defeat of the French here—2000 Mexicans against 6000 Frenchmen—on May 5, 1862, during Maximilian's attempt to dominate all of Mexico. You can buy a booklet (50 pesos and not worth it) at Fort Loreto telling the whole story. The battle's date is the origin of the street name "Cinco de Mayo," that pops up in almost every Mexican city and town.

DAY TRIP TO CHOLULA: The town of Cholula, located about six miles northwest of Puebla, is one of the most holy places in Mexico. It was here that Quetzalcoatl, the famed feathered serpent, lived in exile after he was forced to leave his city of Tula, capital of the Toltecs, in A.D. 900. Even during pre-Hispanic days pilgrims came here to pay their respects to this great leader.

The Cholulans organized some of the toughest resistance to Cortes and his men: one plot might have succeeded in wiping the Spaniards out, but Cortes found out about it, and instead some 3000 Cholulans lost their lives.

Today Cholula has, so they say, a church for every day of the year, as well as the famed University of the Americas—the only U.S.-accredited university in Mexico. The great pyramid of Cholula, left from pre-Hispanic times, is slowly being excavated and restored, but as this is not a major archeological site it's hard to find a guidebook to the area. You'd do best to hire a guide if you care to see the hidden tunnels and the famous frescoes which are deep within the pyramid. The frescoes are some of the most famous in Mexico, and date back to the Classic period. And before you leave the site, climb to the top of the pyramid for the fine view of the town's steeples and spacious plaza. Admission to the ruins of the pyramid is 10 pesos.

To get to Cholula take the red-and-white buses marked "Cholula" at the corner of Avenida 8 Pte. and Calle 5 Nte. in Puebla.

PUEBLA NIGHTLIFE: The mariachis play nightly in the Plaza de Santa Inés at Avenida 11 Poniente and Calle 3 Sur. They stroll through the crowds gathered at a number of cozy sidewalk cafés. Another square which attracts mariachis is the Plaza de los Sapos, Avenida 7 Oriente near Calle 4 Sur. To get there, walk two blocks south from the Zócalo and take a left onto 7 Oriente, toward the river. Keep your ears open and you can't miss the plaza.

PUEBLA MISCELLANY: The **Tourist Office (20)** is at Avenida 5 Oriente no. 5, at the side of the cathedral and next door to the Biblioteca Palafoxiana (tel. 46-1285). They're very friendly here, have a good map of the city, and are open from 9 a.m. to 2 p.m. and 5 to 7 p.m. Monday through Friday, from 9 a.m. to 2 p.m. on Saturday; closed Sunday. . . . The **post office** is in the Archbishop's Palace (17) beside the cathedral at the corner of Avenida 5 Ote. and Calle 16 de Septiembre (no sign!). . . . Puebla's big **market** day is Saturday. All shops, even Woolworth's, close for lunch and siesta from 1:30 to 4 p.m. . . . There's a new **game preserve** called African Safari, located southeast of town at Avenida 11 Oriente no. 2405, 15 minutes by car from downtown. They have a good collection of African animals: gazelle, antelope, lions, ostriches, and elephants, to name but a few; entrance fee is 100 pesos. . . . "Puebla has a little *tintorería* which will wash your clothes with same-day service, on 6 Norte about two blocks above 10 Oriente (go up the west side of the little park)," writes Lorraine Walters of Mississauga, Ontario.

GETTING TO AND FROM PUEBLA: Because it's so close to Mexico City, and because it's astride the main routes to Veracruz and Oaxaca, transportation to and from Puebla is a snap, both by bus and by train.

By Bus

The first-class line to take to Puebla is A.D.O. (Autobuses del Oriente). Besides many buses each day between the capital and Puebla, the A.D.O. line also runs six buses a day from Puebla to Veracruz and back, seven a day to Villahermosa, five a day to Oaxaca, and seven a day to Tehuacan. The A.D.O. terminal is downtown at the corner of Avenida Gral. Maximino Avila Camacho and Calle 6 Norte, as of this writing. It is probably only a matter of time until all bus traffic is moved to a central terminal outside the city, as has been done in most other large Mexican towns.

Another line, Autobuses Unidos, also provides convenient second-class service from Mexico City to Puebla, from Puebla to Tehuacan (nine buses a day), and to Orizaba, Cordoba, and Veracruz, at rates slightly cheaper than those of the A.D.O.; service and equipment are pretty good. The A.U. terminal is presently at the corner of Avenida 10 Oriente and Calle 4 Norte, about seven blocks from the main square.

The trip from Mexico City to Puebla takes about two hours by bus, and it's another two hours from Puebla to Tehuacan.

By Train

The fastest train from Mexico City to Puebla leaves at 5:32 p.m. from Buenavista Station, arriving in Puebla at 10:30 p.m. Bus service is much preferable. A local, slow, day tain—*not* recommended—leaves at 9:30 a.m., arriving at 6:30 p.m. There's also a night train leaving Mexico City at 9:25 p.m., arriving in Puebla at 6:10 a.m.

Puebla's railroad station is at the far northern end of Calle 7 Norte, some distance from downtown. City buses ("Estación") ply between the station and the downtown area. Catch one downtown at a sign which lists the Estación bus as stopping there.

By Car

From Puebla you have a choice of roads to Oaxaca, whether you go by bus or car. One route (Highway 190) goes south through Izucar de Matamoros, famed for black pottery (not much in evidence in the town—most of it's shipped to the big cities for sale!), and Acatlán, famous for its red animal pottery; then to Huajuapan de León, where the road becomes full of curves as it twists through the mountains to Oaxaca. Another route, taking about the same time to negotiate, runs southeast to Tehuacan, the mineral bath town, along Highway 150 which is now completed and paved all the way to Oaxaca, the Tehuacan-Oaxaca portion bearing the designation Highway 131. This road, also, is full of twists and turns, and although it's slow it does afford fine mountain vistas and curious stands of cactus. But before you wind up into the mountains, you might want to stop for lunch, or even overnight, in Mexico's most famous spa.

2. Tehuacan

Tehuacan (alt. 5409 feet; pop. 90,000), is a clean, attractive town that is popular with the wealthy and the unhealthy, its bigger hotels being pretty expensive and its mineral waters said to be good for hepatitis, kidney, and stomach ailments. Apart from drinking the waters (no charge) at **El Riego**, to the west of town, and **San Lorenzo**, off the road to Mexico City in the northwest, there isn't too much to do. Matter of fact, it isn't even necessary to go out of town because next door to the posh **Hacienda Spa Penafiel**, at the northern end of town, is a luxurious cave with tiled walls and silvered wrought-iron gates. Actually, it's not really a cave, but rather a long, downward-sloping hallway with plaster of Paris "rocks" on the ceiling. At the foot of this Dr. Caligari-type passage is a little modern patio with the waters gushing out of spigots on the wall and on the floor. There's nothing to drink from, so bring an empty bottle. No charge is made for all you can guzzle. The cave is apparently maintained by the Penafiel bottling company, whose plant adjoins it. About two blocks north, on the highway, is the post office and, adjoining it, a small tower which can sometimes be climbed to give a limited view of the tree-filled town.

ORIENTATION: Happily for visitors, several of Tehuacan's more regrettable faults have been swept away in recent years. The town's two main streets used to be named after two men with names identical except for their middle names, and so if someone sent you to the Avenida Camacho you din't know which avenue they meant: Avila Camacho or Maximino Camacho. Now the two main thoroughfares are named Reforma (north-south) and Independencia (east-west).

Also, the A.D.O. company has a new and shiny bus station for first-class traffic at Independencia 119. It serves 16 buses a day each way between Tehuacan and Puebla, 15 to Oaxaca, and three per day to and from Veracruz. The bus station has its own cafeteria, but you can walk easily to other restaurants: just head out the front door of the station, turn right, and in a few minutes you'll be at the center of town, the intersection of Independencia and Reforma.

The second-class bus station, serving Autobuses Unidos lines, has yet to be redeemed. It's at Calle 2 Oriente 311 or 509 (depending on which building number you believe), near the corner with Calle 3 Norte, 2½ blocks east of Avenida Reforma and the Templo del Carmen. Six buses run to Puebla daily, four to Veracruz. If you have the misfortune to arrive here, walk out of the terminal, turn right, and walk to Reforma and the Carmen church. Turn left to reach the center of town.

WHERE TO STAY AND EAT: The posh **Hacienda Spa Penafiel** (tel. 238/2-0190), for many years mentioned in this book as "The Impossible Dream" place to stay, has been taken over by the Dubin chain with good results. Prices now, although high, are very reasonable for what you get: a full spa hotel with baths, the spring right next door, and lovely rooms, shady trees, and verdant grounds. One person pays 880 pesos, two pay 1100 pesos; with all three meals, two pay 2400 pesos total. The hotel is on the Avenida José Garci-Crespa, the continuation of Avenida Reforma Norte (also Highway 150 north of town, going toward Puebla). If these prices stay where they are, you can't go wrong here.

The **Hotel México** (tel. 238/2-2319), right at the intersection of Reforma and Independencia, is another colonial wonder, without the same full measure of grace as the Penafiel, but very plush nonetheless. Prices, though, are a bit higher than the aforementioned hotel.

The **Casa Fagoaga**, at Reforma Nte. 213 (tel. 238/2-0220), is a cheerful little pension built around several small courtyards that catch lots of sun. The rooms, by contrast, tend to be dark, but the señora keeps them very clean, and serves up three tasty meals a day to go with each. Price is a very reasonable 275 pesos single, 525 pesos double; all eight rooms have bath.

Right next door to the Fagoaga is a functional establishment called the **Posada de Tehuacan** (tel. 238/2-0491), at Reforma Nte. 211. In this modern, kelly-green building, trimmed with black and white ceramic stripes, are plain but suitable rooms for 225 pesos single, 400 pesos double, 525 pesos triple. The restaurant on the ground floor is well within the budget range, too, with most entrees being in the 40- to 85-peso range. Service is pleasant and the food—although hardly delicate fare—is well worth the reasonable price. The señora in the kitchen will do her best to accommodate your whims and wishes.

From the intersection of Reforma and Independencia, walk east ("Oriente") on Independencia and after a block you'll reach the exceptionally pleasant Parque Juarez, shaded by grand old trees. The **Hotel Iberia**, a peeling colonial mammoth of a place just a bit past the park on the left-hand side of Independencia, might serve you as a last-gasp hotel choice. But the center of interest here is the group of restaurants surrounding the park.

Of the places to dine on the park, the most elegant and expensive is the **Restaurant Penafiel**, on the eastern side. Meat and fowl entrees here cost from 150 to 250 pesos, egg dishes about 75 pesos, and you must plan on spending at least 400 pesos for a decent full meal. But across the park on the west side are much less expensive places with intriguing names such as **El Pato Loco** ("The Crazy Duck") and **La Lonja** ("The Lodge," or "Guild"). Meal prices here are, in general, 25% to 35% lower.

WHAT TO SEE: Once you've quaffed some mineral water and strolled through the Parque Juarez, the only thing left to do is to walk up Avenida Reforma Norte to the **Templo del Carmen,** finished in 1783. Its dazzling domes are covered in polychrome faïence which you probably noticed when you came into town. Hidden in the former convent (monastery) connected to the church is the **Museo del Valle de Tehuacan,** open from 9 a.m. to 1 p.m. and 3 to 6 p.m. every day but Monday; admission costs 5 pesos.

Some frescoes remain from the time the monks were in residence, but the exhibits on the lower floor go back much farther in time. In the early 1960s, Dr. Richard MacNeish discovered that the valley of Tehuacan had been the earliest maize (corn) growing center in the world—dating from 5000 B.C. You can trace the development of sculpture in the valley, from primitive pointy-chin female figurines to beautiful obsidian knives.

ON TO OAXACA: If you've chosen to go to Tehuacan, your best bet for the next leg of the journey to Oaxaca is the new Highway 131, which takes 4½ hours to negotiate by car, slightly more by bus, as the bus stops at Teotitlán en route. Five buses a day of the A.D.O. line pass through Tehuacan on their way to Oaxaca; the route is also served by several more local lines originating in Tehuacán.

On the road to Oaxaca, you wind through beautiful mountain country, dipping down into valleys filled with mango trees and climbing hillsides crowded with more gigantic cacti than you'd think possible.

3. Oaxaca

Oaxaca (pronounced wa-HAH-kah; alt. 5070 feet; pop. 200,000) is a mountain city, and its location in a valley high in rugged mountains has determined its character. *Oaxaqueños* (pronounced wah-hah-KEHN-yos) think of their native city as someplace special and unique, set off from the rest of the world—something of the feeling island dwellers have for their turf. Industrial and commercial development is making Oaxaca a booming, busy, wealthy town with a cosmopolitan touch, but local people are careful to preserve the beauty and special feeling of the city.

Local people include descendants of the Zapotec Indians who came to this high valley about 800 years before the birth of Christ and built a beautiful city and a flourishing culture at Monte Alban, six miles from the modern town. There had been people in the valley since 8000 B.C., but these early inhabitants were very primitive. It wasn't until the pre-Classic period that cities were built, about the same time as they were in Teotihuacán. This building was the beginning of Monte Alban. There is speculation about who these early peoples were. Some authorities see a distinct resemblance in their art and calendar system to the Olmecs of the Gulf Coast. In any case, it was certainly the Zapotecs who raised the city's cultural life to a high level and built the monuments visible at the site today. But after this flowering of Zapotec culture (about A.D. 300–700), another tribe, the Mixtecs, built a rival center at Mitla, 36 miles away on the other side of what is today Oaxaca, and the two tribes struggled with one another for control of the valley until the Aztec threat united them against the common enemy. But even the two tribes united were no match for the Aztecs, and in the late 1400s and early 1500s Aztec influence predominated.

The local tribes didn't have to worry about the Aztecs for long, however, because in 1521 an even more formidable enemy appeared. After the Spanish subdued the valley they set up a military post called Antequera here; six years

OAXACA 315

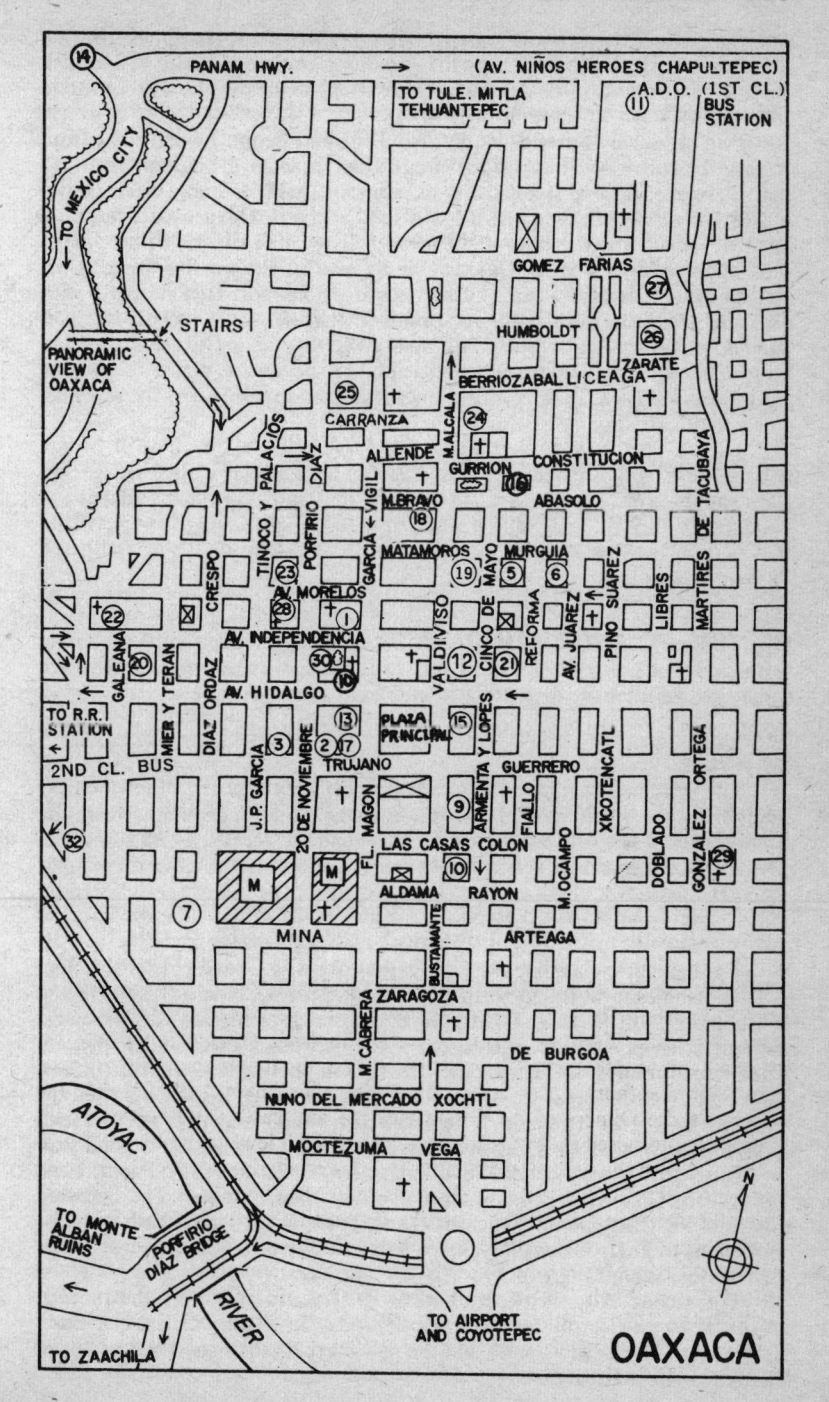

later the town of Oaxaca was founded. Hernan Cortes was later given the title of Marques del Valle de Oaxaca by the Hapsburg Emperor Charles V, and with the title came grants of land, which remained in the hands of his descendants until the Mexican Revolution in 1910.

Two of Mexico's presidents, Porfirio Díaz and Benito Juarez, came from Oaxaca. Nobody does much to remember Díaz these days, but monuments to Juarez are everywhere: statues, murals, streets named for him, even a Benito Juarez University. In fact, the city's official name is **Oaxaca de Juarez.** A Zapotec Indian who was born in the nearby village of Guelatao, Benito Juarez was "adopted" by a wealthy Oaxacan family who taught him Spanish, clothed and educated him in return for his services as a houseboy. He fell in love with the daughter of the household, and promised that he would become rich and famous and return to marry her. He managed all three, and Oaxaca adores him for it. After law school his experiences led him to become governor of the state of Oaxaca (1847–1852), later a resistance leader and president of the republic, and a national hero.

There's plenty to do and see in Oaxaca—visits to the ruins at Monte Alban, Mitla, and other smaller sites, visits to the outlying Indian villages for cloth shopping or festivals, several very good museums, convents, and colonial buildings in the city itself, and a wonderful zócalo at the city's center where the band plays every other night and sidewalk cafes provide the perfect perch for people-watching.

GETTING TO AND FROM OAXACA: Although hidden in its mountain fastness, Oaxaca is well served by bus, rail, and air transportation. Here are some tips, with advice on getting to and from each terminal.

By Bus

The first-class bus station in Oaxaca is north of the center of town on the main highway, which, as a city street, bears the name Calle Niños Héroes de Chapultepec. Taxis between the bus terminal and the zócalo cost 75 pesos, and perhaps this is your best bet, as direct city bus transportation must be caught several blocks down the street (turn left as you leave the station) at the intersection of Niños Héroes and Vasconcelos, a long walk with a suitcase. Buses, if you're game, are marked "Col. America" and "Col. Reforma."

The main first-class lines serving Oaxaca are A.D.O. and Cristóbal Colón; A.D.O. handles most traffic north and west, Cristóbal Colón serves the region south and east of Oaxaca. Twenty buses a day run to Mexico City's Central del Norte, seven a day to Puebla, ten a day between Oaxaca and Tehuacan. There are also buses to Tehuantepec (seven a day), Tuxtla Gutierrez (three a day), San Cristóbal de las Casas, a 13-hour trip (one a day), Tapachula and the Guatemalan border (two a day), Veracruz (one a day), and Villahermosa (two a day). Buy your tickets a day in advance to be sure of space and a good seat.

Buses to Puerto Escondido and Puerto Angel, Oaxaca's two Pacific coast resorts (see Chapter III), leave from the first-class terminal. The Sociedad Cooperativa "Estrella del Valle" has three buses a day which bash over the mountains to Puerto Escondido, seven a day to Puerto Angel. Leave an entire day for this exhausting trip.

For second-class buses, head west out Trujano and cross the railroad tracks. The new Central Camionera de Segunda Clase (second-class bus terminal) is near the railroad station and the new market buildings. Take an "Estación" bus along Hidalgo.

By Train

Oaxaca's main station is west of the Cerro del Fortin hill, some distance from the center of town. Taxis to the Plaza Principal cost 75 pesos, or you can take the "Estación" bus which runs along Avenida Hidalgo between the station and the plaza.

Two trains a day connect Oaxaca with Puebla, Tehuacan, and the capital, leaving at 10 a.m. (arriving at Tehuacan 5:41 p.m., and Puebla at 9:29 p.m., where you must change trains and wait for the 10:35 p.m. night train to Mexico City); and there's a night train with sleeping cars which leaves Oaxaca at 7:30 p.m, arriving Tehuacan 2:13 a.m., Puebla at 5:06 a.m., and Mexico City at 10:19 a.m. From Mexico City the schedules are as follows: depart the capital at 5:32 p.m., arrive Puebla at 10:42 p.m., arrive Tehuacan at 1:23 a.m., arrive Oaxaca at 8:15 a.m. Make your reservations for these trains as far in advance as possible.

By Air

Transportaciones Aeropuerto Oaxaca (tel. 951/6-7878) operates an airport limousine service between the center of town and the airport for 100 pesos per passenger, one way—a considerable saving over the 300-peso taxi fare. Drop by their office on the Alameda de León (in front of the cathedral), between the Hotel Monte Alban and the Correos (post office).

Flights to Puerto Escondido are run by **Aerovias Oaxaqueños.** Ask about the daily morning flight and get tickets at Viajes Micsa (tel. 951/6-2700), just off the northeast corner of the Plaza Principal at Valdivieso 2.

AeroMéxico (tel. 951/7-3765), Avenida Hidalgo 513, has nonstop flights between Oaxaca and Acapulco, Mexico City, Tapachula, and Villahermosa; other cities by connection. Mexicana Airlines has many daily nonstops between Oaxaca and the capital, plus a nonstop to Tuxtla Gutierrez. Contact them at Fiallo 102 at Avenida Independencia (tel. 951/6-8414).

ORIENTATION: Questions out of the ordinary can be taken to the **Tourism Office (1)** at the corner of Independencia and G. Vigil, very near the cathedral and just off the main square. The office is open Monday to Saturday from 9 a.m. to 3 p.m. and 5 to 7 p.m.

I feel I must tell you about one of Oaxaca's few flaws. Petty crime is on the increase everywhere, and it seems to have come to Oaxaca. Take the normal precautions and you should have no trouble: park your car in a lot overnight, don't leave anything in the car within view, don't leave your things unattended one second in bus stations, and be especially careful of very professional pickpockets in the markets and buses—they'll have a wallet out of your back pocket, or out of your handbag, or out of your knapsack, and you won't know it until the time comes to pay for dinner. Luckily, violent crime (mugging and the like) is still very rare here. In any case, the police are no help at all.

WHERE TO STAY: Oaxaca is a boom town as far as the tourism industry goes, and this means that there is often a shortage of rooms. The rooms one does find are all priced about the same, no matter what they look like (the managers can get their price because the demand is so great), and budget rooms are not too common. But the middle range of hostelries offers some decent buys, outlined herewith:

Few hotels can be said to be run superbly these days, but one of those few is Sr. Raul Rodriguez's **Hotel Plaza (2)**, Trujano 112 (tel. 951/6-2200), a half block from the zócalo. The hotel is not large (only 14 rooms and 5 junior suites), but it is maintained with meticulous care. Rooms are beautifully kept up, and the service is perfect: rooms are polished, fresh sheets spread, blankets changed and aired, all with an expert touch and a smile. But the hotel's greatest asset is Sr. Rodriguez himself, who receives and aids you with the greatest consideration, and just seems to make questions and problems vanish. Rates are reasonable: 385 to 550 pesos single, 550 to 660 pesos double (higher prices being for the junior suites), especially considering that once you bed down at the Plaza, you don't want to leave; 50 pesos extra for a continental breakfast. Considering the prices at other hotels in Oaxaca—rising fearfully these days—I can state with conviction that the Plaza is one of the few hotels where you can get more than your money's worth.

Location and colonial charm are but two of the reasons to consider staying at the **Hotel Monte Alban (10)** (tel. 951/6-2777), right on the Alameda de León, a stone's throw from the main square. The large, airy rooms in the front of the hotel are the ones closest to colonial times in their atmosphere, but the smaller interior rooms (servants' quarters?) are also fine, and a bit lower in price. All rooms have tile showers and colonial-style touches. Prices are 525 pesos single, 845 pesos double. The courtyard is topped by a glass canopy which shelters a restaurant. Here on the Alameda you're in the best of company: the cathedral, the regional headquarters of the P.R.I., and the post office are right next door.

The **Hotel Francia (3)**, at the corner of Calle 20 de Noviembre and Calle Trujano (tel. 951/6-4811), is your next choice. Rooms are full of ancient furniture, and all have bathrooms. The court around which the rooms are built has been roofed over. The Francia is not fancy, but functional and quite pleasant. Single rooms cost 435 pesos; doubles, 610 pesos. The Francia has expanded from its original hotel building to engulf adjoining buildings, and so you can avail yourself of a wide choice of rooms. Watch out for street noise when choosing your chamber.

The **Hotel Principal (5)**, Calle Cinco de Mayo 208 (tel. 951/6-2535), has no restaurant, but even the smallest of the 23 rooms is clean and attractive. Recent remodeling has done something for the lobby and the courtyard, but nothing much for the rooms or their prices. Still, it's reasonable and very popular with young travelers. Rates are 350 pesos single with bath, 400 to 575 pesos double with bath.

The **Hotel Virreyes (6)**, at the corner of Morelos and Reforma (tel. 951/6-5555), has its courtyard covered with painted glass which lets in such a mellow light that the air seems to be colored beige. The whole hotel is mellow in a way, quiet, solid, functional, from its cool blue walls to the white tablecloths on the tables in the court. Most of the 31 rooms are quite big, all have tiled bathrooms, and all are priced at 435 pesos single, 575 to 625 pesos double. Of the doubles, nine cost 575 to 600 pesos, another 16 go for 610 pesos, and the few left are 625 pesos for two.

The **Hotel Antequera (12)** (tel. 951/64020), Avenida Hidalgo 807, was excluded from this book for several years, but it now has a new administration. The hotel's location is especially good, being right off the Plaza Principal. Rooms tend to be darkish, but cool with high ceilings and fans, television sets, and modernized showers. A cafeteria fills the courtyard. The price? 465 pesos single, 575 pesos double.

The **Hotel Isabel (19)** (tel. 951/6-4053 or 6-4900), Murguía 104 between Cinco de Mayo and Alcala, has some rooms that are good and others that are unsuitable—the only way to know what you're getting is to look beforehand. If they have a good room available, you'll be happy at the price: 340 pesos single, 420 pesos double. There are 64 rooms in all, with a private shower and telephone in each.

Most reasonably priced of the hotels right near the zócalo is the 35-room **Hotel Ruíz (9)**, three doors down Calle Bustamante (no. 103; tel. 951/6-3660) from the southeast corner of the zócalo. The rooms are okay for the price, and all have showers. Look at several before you move in. Single rooms cost 300, 360, or 430 pesos; doubles are 360, 460, or 560 pesos.

Most recent entry to the list of Oaxaca's colonial hostelries is the **Posada San Pablo (21)** (tel. 951/6-4914), at De Fiallo 102, near the corner of Avenida Independencia. Completely restored now, this was in olden times the Convent of Saint Paul. Today the rooms are simple (as befits a former convent, perhaps), but very nice and certainly comfortable. All have private baths. Prices depend on the length of your stay—each day gets less expensive the longer you stay—but for just a night or two you'll pay 600 pesos per day, or 10,000 pesos per month double. The San Pablo is just around the corner from the interesting little Plazuela Reforma.

Near the Francia in location, price, and comfort of accommodations is the **Hotel Meson del Rey (3)** (tel. 951/6-0033), at Trujano 212, two blocks from the main square. The hotel's restaurant is always occupied by a few Oaxaqueños waiting for their long-distance phone calls to go through as this is the location of a convenient *caseta de larga distancia,* but they won't disturb you. The rooms are plain but comfy, with good clean bathrooms and sound-absorbent carpet on the floors. Prices are 390 pesos single, 520 pesos double.

Near the First-Class (A.D.O.) Bus Terminal

Those arriving by bus late at night could try the **Hotel Veracruz (11)**, virtually next door to the terminal at Avenida Niños Héroes de Chapultepec 1020 (tel. 951/5-0511). The Veracruz is modern and kept pretty clean; room decor is uninspired but neat and functional. Although they're allowed to charge more for the 30 rooms, the going rates are 375 pesos single, 500 to 575 pesos double. To get to the Veracruz, leave the terminal by the front door, turn left, and walk a few steps and you'll find it on the same side of the street.

Near the Second-Class Bus Terminal

The **Hotel Meson del Angel (7)** (tel. 951/6-6666) has an odd location—not in town and not out—which is good for you if you're arriving at Oaxaca's second-class bus terminal, west of downtown. It's at Mina 518, corner of Mier y Teran, a big modern building with louvered windows and *screens,* a restaurant, bar, and even a swimming pool. You pay a bit extra for the pool, but prices are still good: 380 pesos single, 595 pesos double, 790 pesos triple.

A Moderate Splurge

If the Plaza's full, and you want a touch of the posh life, you might try the **Hotel Senorial (13)**, Portal de Flores 6 (tel. 951/6-3933), right on the zócalo. It's less expensive than Oaxaca's other luxury places, but it provides several expensive services to its patrons such as a small private swimming pool, and 91 rather luxurious rooms, all with telephones, private baths, and reproductions of Diego Rivera paintings. Prices are high, though: 660 pesos single, 880 pesos double in season (mid-July to mid-September); 550 pesos single and 770 pesos double off-season. There's a roof-garden and bar.

I can't help mentioning Oaxaca's **Hotel El Presidente (16)** (tel. 951/6-0611) because it's so uncharacteristic of the establishments in this mammoth quasi-governmental chain. Rather than have a tall, modern shaft towering over this colonial city, El Presidente's directors chose (thank goodness) to convert the former four-centuries-old Convent of Santa Catalina to a hotel, and it has been recently designated a "national treasure." Two floors still adorned with some frescoes and colonial relics now hold 100 guest rooms, plus a swimming pool, laundry, souvenir shops, and all the other paraphernalia of a top-class hotel. Prices are: 1550 pesos single, 1675 pesos double, 1800 pesos triple. An extra bed costs another 250 pesos. Children 12 and under stay for free in their parents' room. Even if this is way out of our range, you would enjoy a turn through the corridors and public rooms, or perhaps a sandwich (100 to 185 pesos) in the restaurant. You'll find El Presidente at Avenida 5 de Mayo no. 300, corner of the Plazoleta Labastida.

Starvation Budget Hotels

Oaxaca's low-budget hotels are near the market and the red-light district, which is either an advantage or a disadvantage, depending on how you look at it. Adventurous but impecunious types should look them over: go to the corner of Trujano and Díaz Ordaz, and start your explorations.

WHERE TO EAT: Finding good restaurants with reasonable prices and good service is difficult in Oaxaca; dining here, in other words, is not the big attraction. Even though the afternoon hours from two to four o'clock are set aside for the comida corrida, and most shops and museums close for these hours, one must pick carefully to choose a good comida.

A special note is in order for restaurants and cafés in the arcades surrounding the main square. Sitting in one of these places, having a leisurely meal or snack and watching the action in the plaza—this is a prime attraction to Oaxaca. Consequently, prices in plaza eateries tend to be high for what you get, and service less attentive than it should be. You'll get more for your money if you go off the plaza, but you lose the bustle and excitement as well. Here, then, are my recommendations for places to dine, both on the main square and off.

Of the places to dine on the plaza, my first choice is the **Guelatao (15)**, Portal de Mercaderas 2, one of several restaurants located right next to one another in the arcade on the east side of the plaza. The Guelatao offers a daily set-price lunch for 125 pesos: soup, pasta, meat or fish, frijoles or salad, dessert, and coffee. If you don't want that much, just order a portion of lomo de cerdo (roast pork with potato salad, 160 pesos), or perhaps tamales Oaxaqueños de mole (corn dough wrapped around bits of chicken, in a dark, rich mole sauce, the whole thing wrapped in banana leaves, 55 pesos). Prices, food, and service seem better here than at the neighboring establishments. By the way, the outdoor tables at the Guelatao are distinguished from the tables of neighboring next-door restaurants only by the color of the cloth—be sure you're sitting in the right section.

On the same side of the main square is the ever-busy, booming **Bum Bum**, which serves a large assortment of licuados (liquefied fruit drinks) made with water for 22 pesos, with milk for 30 pesos, and with a beaten egg for 36 pesos. Closed Sunday.

Across the main square, on the west side, are more café-restaurants, and the "in" place here for both gringo and Oaxaqueño is the **Restaurant del Jardín (17)**. The no-frill aluminum tables are always crowded with a varied crowd sipping beer or coffee and watching the action. This is the prime place to wait out one of Oaxaca's brief but intense afternoon thundershowers, provided you get a table when the first drops come down (after that they fill up fast). To dine, they recommend that you enter their indoor room—they say the service is faster there, but I suspect they want to keep the sidewalk portion a café rather than a restaurant. The food is moderately priced: Mexican plates such as enchiladas for around 85 pesos and meat entrees for 100 to 210 pesos.

Oaxaca's best-value-for-money comida corrida may now be the one served daily at the restaurant named **Korinto**. No Greek chef here as the name might imply, just good Mexican fare such as soup, rice, "bistec," frijoles, dessert, and coffee for 135 pesos. For the same price you could order soup, a chop, and a beverage. Of the Korinto's two rooms, the pseudo-colonial is more attractive than the driveway-dinette. Look for the Korinto on Hidalgo (no. 405) between Tinoco and Díaz Ordaz. It's open seven days a week.

At the **Cafe El Sol y La Luna,** Murguia 105 near Alcala, you can indeed eat by the light of the sun and the moon as it is open for business from 1 to 5 p.m. and from 7 p.m. to midnight, Tuesday through Sunday. You'll come for the food and not the lighting when you discover what they serve: yogurt with granola and honey, avocado salads, hamburgers with salad and french fries, melted cheese plates, even a Chinese plate. Prices range from 65 to 105 pesos for the light meals, 125 to 200 pesos for the latter items. Wine and beer are served at competitive prices, and there's free guitar music on Thursday, Friday, and Saturday nights. Needless to say, the food, entertainment, and the two small rooms done in rough wood with a nice fruit bar attract a lively and good-looking crowd from Oaxaca's universities.

An Institution

The restaurant of **Dona Elpidia** is virtually an institution in Oaxaca, for Dona Elpidia has been catering to a refined and selective local clientele for more than 40 years. Walking past Miguel Cabrera 413 (Cabrera's the southern entension of Garcia Vigil; no. 413 is about six blocks south of the main square), you'd hardly think it housed a restaurant, but inside the shabby-looking door is a beautiful courtyard filled with birds and plants. Two large dogs on the roof keep watch. Five tables are set out in the arcade, and about a dozen more fill the indoor dining rooms. Last time I visited, the five-course comida corrida cost 200 pesos and included an appetizer of chicharrón (delicious deep-fried pork rind) and pork spare ribs, vegetable soup, fried fish with a garnish of warm pickled vegetables, a Swiss steak with rice, a dessert of cinnamon rice pudding, and Mexican coffee (with cinnamon). Although rumor has it that Dona Elpidia is thinking of retiring, you will be able to enjoy her cooking—some of the best in Oaxaca—until she does. Lunch only is served, from 1 to 5 p.m. daily; menu only in Spanish.

The Best of the Rest

Down the price range a bit—but with no sacrifice in quality—are several good places without flair or fanfare (no piped music, either), but with very good food at very agreeable prices. First place on this list goes to the **Cafeteria Tito's,** Garcia Vigil 110 about a half block north of the cathedral (which itself is on the north side of the main square): look for the yellow-and-black-striped awning which marks Tito's doorway. Always busy with a young student crowd happily drinking coffee or consuming one of the chickens cooked in the rotisserie next to the front door (110 pesos for a half chicken), Tito's offers mostly light meals such as sandwiches, hamburgers, and traditional dishes priced from 40 to 115 pesos. I tried the pozole, the famous rich stew of hominy with meat or chicken (95 pesos, tortilla chips included), and it was the best I've ever tasted—and very filling. You might also try the burritos with ham, cheese, and a side order of guacamole, also excellent. Tito's is a good place for breakfast: hotcakes, juice, and coffee goes for 85 pesos. The restaurant is open daily from 8 in the morning till midnight; it closes early on Sunday, at 4 p.m.

Gino's Pizza is a tiny place with three wooden benches and a large beer keg. Small, medium, or large pizzas are offered, and the general wisdom has it that a small cheese pizza (100 pesos) will feed two people, while a large ham pizza (225 pesos) will do for three. The beer costs 30 to 45 pesos. Gino's is open from 1 to 4 and from 6 to 11 p.m. daily.

The Comedor Familiar

Of the inexpensive dining places in Mexico, the *comedor familiar* ("family dining room") is the institution which usually proves to be cheapest and best. Usually a plain little place with a minimum of decor and a señora with children in attendance, comedors serve what is basically home cooking at very modest prices. One of my favorites is the **Restaurant Pisces (20)**, which offers vegetarian fare on a menu that changes daily. The comida corrida (118 pesos) gives an example of the offerings: vegetable soup, a plate of lentil stew with carrots and pineapple, frijoles, fruit salad, and tea. You'll find the Pisces at Avenida Hidalgo 119, five blocks west of the zócalo. It's open from noon to 4 and 7 to 9 p.m. every day but Sunday.

One block south of the Santo Domingo church, at the corner of Alcala and Bravo, is the **Cafe Tavos (18)**, another small eatery run by a husband-and-wife team. No set-price lunch is offered, but the menu includes interesting things such as Yucatán-inspired *tacos cochinita pibil* for around 70 pesos, hamburgers for 55 pesos, and cheese pies for 30 pesos. Breakfast will cost you about 70 to 105 pesos. You can dine here from 8 a.m. to 9 p.m. except Sunday, when they close early, at 4 p.m.

Out in search of the city's cheapest comida corrida? Walk west on **Trujano** until you come to the two-block section between 20 de Noviembre and Díaz Ordaz. These little hole-in-the-wall eateries are very basic, but very cheap, a four-course meal costing only about 75 pesos.

Pastries and Snacks

At festival time in Oaxaca, sidewalk stands are set up in the market area and near the cathedral to sell *buñuelos*, the Mexican equivalent of a poppadom, only sweet. You'll be served your buñuelo in a cracked or otherwise flawed dish or bowl, and after you're finished you smash the crockery on the sidewalk for good luck. Don't be timid! After a while, you may find yourself buying more and more buñuelos (about 25 pesos apiece) just for the fun of smashing plates.

For a more conventional snack or light breakfast, pick up your fill of pastries, cookies, sweet rolls, and breads from the large **Panificadora Bamby**, at the corner of Morelos and Garcia Vigil, two blocks north from the Plaza Principal.

The Big Splurge

I got a surprise the last time I was in Oaxaca. The price of a room at the **Hotel El Presidente (16)** (tel. 951/6-0611), Avenida 5 de Mayo no. 300, was way up, and the price of a meal was way down. If you choose carefully here, you can even have a pleasant dinner in rich surroundings. Consider this: sopa de frijol (bean soup), tasajo a la Oaxaqueña (a beef dish), pie, pastry or ice cream, a bottle of beer, with tax and tip, came to 400 pesos for one person—hardly what one would call outrageous. Let's hope prices stay this way.

The **Restaurant Catedral** (tel. 6-3285), at the corner of Garcia Vigil and Morelos, calles itself "la casa del filete" (the house of steaks), and so it is. Not a steakhouse in the American sense, with enormous cuts sizzling on a grill in plain view, the Catedral is rather a high-ceilinged, sparsely decorated restaurant specializing in beef. A common order here is the filete mignon, which comes wrapped in bacon, with potatoes, zucchini, and ham, for 200 pesos. Other items are slightly less expensive, but you should plan on spending 350 to 400 pesos for a full meal here. The daily set-price lunch costs 220 pesos on weekdays and Saturday, 275 pesos on Sunday, and offers very good value for money.

WHAT TO DO: There's plenty in Oaxaca to keep you busy: some 27 churches, lots of colonial buildings, two excellent museums, the market, and the sidewalk cafés on the Plaza Principal. Remember that Oaxaqueños observe the siesta from 2 to 4 p.m. and most shops and museums will be closed. To get a feel for this lovely city I would recommend a walking tour of the churches and monuments and then (mañana) a visit to the Regional Museum and the Rufino Tamayo Museum of pre-Hispanic art. You may want to visit the market and the various popular art shops around town: the craftwork of this state is some of the finest.

Start your tour in the Plaza Principal with a look at the **cathedral** (begun in 1544) with its 18th-century baroque facade and glittering interior of five naves and a bronze altar.

Go one block north to Independencia, turn right, and on the southeast corner of the intersection with Armenta y Lopez is the beautiful art nouveau **Teatro Macedonio de Alcala (21),** built in 1903. The theater holds 1300 persons and is still used for concerts and such, and therefore is not usually open during the day. Peek through the doors to see the marble stairway, Louis XV vestibule, and other such flourishes, and come back for an event in the evening (usually about 20 pesos)—a list of happenings is posted by the doors.

Walking west along Independencia, you pass the University of Oaxaca on your right between Calle Lopez and G. Vigil (look for the graffiti). Two streets past G. Vigil is the **Church of San Felipe,** on the corner of Tinoco y Palacio and Independencia. The church was built in 1636 and mirrors all the architectural opulence of that period: the altar and nave are covered with ornately carved and gilded wood, the walls are frescoed. Somehow, although it's ornate, there seems to be enough free wall space to keep the feeling from being overpowering.

The **Basilica de la Soledad (22),** corner of Independencia and Galeana, is probably one of the most important religious centers in Oaxaca. Here is where you'll find an effigy of the town's patron saint carved in black stone. The basilica is in fact a huge complex of buildings including a garden, convent, and a smaller theater where spectators can witness the famous Fiesta de la Soledad (see below under "Festivals"). The basilica was built in 1682–1690, and has four levels on the outside, each displaying several niches inhabited by carvings of saints. Although it's handsome on the outside, the basilica inside is overpowering with chandeliers, lunging angels, gilt ceiling, paintings, and statues. The statue of the Virgin de la Soledad (the patron saint of Oaxaca) is in the museum around the back of the church, to the right as you exit. The statue is draped in black velvet and placed in a chapel filled with white bouquets made of glass, pearl, and plastic. The museum is open from noon to 2 and 5:30 to 7 p.m. every day, admission free. Other than the display of the Virgin, the only item of interest is a three-foot-square case of innumerable miniature glass figurines (birds, angels, animals, and flowers) surrounding the Christ Child—if you like miniature glass figurines you'll love this. From the basilica you can walk east to visit the Rufino Tamayo Museum, the **House of Benito Juarez,** and the Santo Domingo Convent, or you can head south to see the oldest church in Oaxaca (San Juan de Dios) and the teeming market.

The **Rufino Tamayo Museum of Pre-Hispanic Art (23),** Avenida Morelos 503, is one of the most beautiful museums in all Mexico. It prides itself on being unique in that the artifacts are displayed "solely for the aesthetic rank of the works, their beauty, power and originality," rather than as curious geegaws left from a dead way of life. The collection was amassed over a 20-year period by the artist Rufino Tamayo, born in Oaxaca. The museum itself is very attractive —pink, blue, lavender, green, and orange rooms follow in succession, holding a wealth of sculpture from the pre-Classical period up to the Aztecs: terracotta figurines, scenes of daily life, lots of female fertility figures, Olmecan and Totonac sculpture from the Gulf Coast, Zapotec long-nosed god figures and such. Plaques in Spanish give the period, culture, and location of each find, but you find yourself ignoring this information and just admiring the works and the displays, which are works of art in themselves. The museum is open from 10 a.m. to 2 p.m. and 4 to 7 p.m., closed Tuesday. Admission is 15 pesos.

Whatever your interest or lack of it in churches, you should make a special effort to see the **Santo Domingo Church (24)** at the corner of Constitución and Cinco de Mayo. Started in the 1550s by Dominican Friars and not finished until a century later, it contains the work of all the best artists of that period. Walls and ceiling are covered with ornate plaster statues and flowers, most of them gilded, and two stained-glass panels at one end are particularly attractive. The church has recently undergone complete restoration—inside and out. Everything glistens, especially the large gilded rosary chapel to the right as you enter. Also, be sure to notice the genealogical tree of the Guzman family in the apse as you enter. Don Feliz de Guzman was the founder of the church.

Next to the Santo Domingo is the convent which now houses the **Regional Museum of Oaxaca.** The admission is 10 pesos (5 on Sunday and holidays); it's open Tuesday through Sunday from 10 a.m. to 1 p.m. and 4 to 7 p.m. The interior is an arched courtyard somewhat restored with faint traces of elaborate frescoes along the walls and ceilings. The building must have been magnificent, judging from what remains. You can still feel the pervasive peacefulness of the place: all the rooms open onto the courtyard, where the only sound is that of the fountain. On the top floor, first room to the right, are objects left from the Dominican convent. Counterclockwise, the next three rooms are dedicated to finds from Monte Alban, a nearby Zapotec city, which flourished from 800 B.C. until it was abandoned in A.D. 900; following this was the Mixtec domination in the 14th century. Unfortunately there's no guidebook to the museum, and all the plaques are in Spanish, so you'll have to rely on information picked up elsewhere. Here are a few hints: the Zapotecs had a numbering system of bars and dots, similar to that of the Olmecs and the Maya, and a collection of glyphs which, perhaps, represent a calendar; another thing to note is that most of the ceramic sculpture here has the characteristic Zapotec touches of prominent teeth, proboscises, elaborate headgear (often as an eagle or jaguar mask), and large earplugs. Many of the figures have mouths similar to the one found in Olmec sculpture—it's thought that the Olmecs influenced the early development of Monte Alban. Be sure not to miss the room holding the incredible treasures found in Tomb 7 at Monte Alban, in 1932. The tomb contained seven bodies (hence its name) and dated from A.D. 500. Whether the tomb was Zapotec or Mixtec is still being debated. The beauty of the jewelry in gold, turquoise, conch shell, amber, obsidian, and the bowls of onyx and glass—this is no subject of dispute! Some 500 pieces of jewelry and art objects were found. The lower floor holds crafts and costumes of the Oaxaca region: mannequins dressed in authentic regional dress portray facets of religious, social, and cultural life.

The **House of Benito Juarez (25)** is located one block west and one block north of the Santo Domingo convent, on Garcia Vigil, left-hand side of the street across from the church. Look for the small plaque over the door which indicates that this was the residence of the local hero from 1818 to 1820. The house and museum are only moderately interesting. (Admission is 5 pesos, 3 pesos on Sunday; open 10 a.m. to 1 p.m. and 4 to 7 p.m. every day except Monday). Four rooms around a courtyard are set up to show the style in which the great man lived. The school across the street—it looks like a fortress—was once the convent-church of **El Carmen,** run by the Carmelite order. Next to the convent-church is the nice Plazuela del Carmen Alto, a good place to rest.

The earliest church in Oaxaca, built 1525–1530, is the **San Juan de Dios,** in the market area on the corner of Aldama and 20 de Noviembre. The exterior is nothing special but the interior has an ornate altar and paintings on the ceiling by Urbano Olivera. A glass shrine to the Virgin near the entrance and one to Christ (off to the right) are especially revered by Oaxaqueños, and much visited. Because it's in the market, many of the people who visit the church are villagers who've come in to buy and sell.

MARKETS AND SHOPS: Oaxaca's market is big and busy every day, but especially on Saturday when the villagers come in droves bringing their wares. The covered market is the "M" on our map, and the shaded area around it is all open street market teeming with vendors of chiles, string, parrots, talismans, food, spices, cloth, blankets—absolutely everything! It is the most exciting and probably the best market in all of Mexico, partially because the people who come to sell are so colorful and partially because the food and crafts are so colorful.

This used to be Oaxaca's central produce market, but the center of food trading has been relocated to a new building west of downtown, across the railroad tracks and near the second-class bus station. Both places are now filled with market-day hubbub, but if generalizations can be made, I'd say that the downtown market has mostly clothing while the new market specializes in food.

If all this is too mind-boggling and you desire a more essential collection of crafts, there are a number of Casas de Artes Populares or Curiosidades, shops specializing in popular arts and crafts. The prices will be distinctly higher, but then you save haggling. Two I can recommend for their quality, prices, and attitude to customers are Victor's Artes Regionales and Yalalag de Oaxaca.

Victor's, at Porfirio Díaz 111, is housed in a 17th-century monastery and run by Sr. Ramon Fosado. Ramon goes to the villages himself in search of the best Indian art. He speaks English, and is very pleasant. **Yalalag de Oaxaca,** corner of Morelos and Alcala (no. 104), is in an old mansion, and displays a multifarious collection of black pottery, terracotta figurines, tin sculpture, jewelry, rugs, beads, necklaces, papier-mâché sculpture, and lots more. Owner Enriqua de la Lanza speaks English, as do most of her staff, and her prices seem okay. Yalalag has the widest assortment of stuff I've seen in one shop.

The **Casa Brena (26)**, across the street from the park at Pino Suarez 58, is mostly a textile shop with some pottery sold. Inside is a large courtyard with a tienda (store) off to the left, and looms in the back. You'll hear the slapping of the wooden paddles as the men tighten the shuttled thread between the warp. Walk back and look around. The boys are dying the wool in bright colors from fluorescent pink to canary yellow, the young girls spinning the thread, and the men working the looms. All in all, it's an impressive operation and I can almost guarantee you'll want to buy something. The prices here are about as low as you'll find anywhere, and the quality is the best. The "Colonia Reforma" bus will take you to the corner at Pino Suarez and San Martin. Casa Brena's looms work from 9 a.m. to 3 p.m. daily; the shop is open then, and also from 4 to 7:30 p.m. Closed Sunday.

A word about buying sarapes and blankets in Oaxaca: There is so much variance in quality and prices on both these items that I strongly recommend that you do a little research before buying. If you don't know what to look for in quality, I would recommend the friendly *patrons* in Victor's, as they are willing to tell you about the differences in materials (wool vs. synthetic), dyes (natural and chemical), and designs. You can also scout around and compare the various products in the open markets.

While you're in the neighborhood you might be interested in the **Oaxaca Lending Library (27)** at Pino Suarez 802. It was started over a decade ago by a group of American residents and they now have a good-size collection of books in English, Spanish, and French. There is a membership fee if you plan to be here any length of time; otherwise they welcome visitors, but ask them to leave a deposit which is refunded when all borrowed books are returned. The library is a quiet, relaxing place for an afternoon stop to read about Benito Juarez. The hours are 10 a.m. to 1 p.m. and 4 to 6 p.m. Monday through Friday. They also accept and appreciate any books you may want to donate.

Market days for the surrounding villages are as follows:

Tuesday: Ejutla, 65 kilometers south
Wednesday: Etla, 15 kilometers north
Thursday: Zaachila, 18 kilometers southwest
Friday: Ocotlan, 30 kilometers south
Saturday: Oaxaca itself; Tlaxiaco
Sunday: Tlacolula, 32 kilometers southeast—visit the chapel as well.

To take all this sightseeing in at a glance, those with cars can drive to the **Cerro del Fortin**, a hill to the west of town from which you can get a panoramic view of the city, especially good just before sunset. Recognize the hill by a statue of—who else?—Benito Juarez, and a stadium built to hold 15,000 spectators.

You can walk to the hill as well. Head up Díaz Ordaz/Crespo, and look for the *Escaleras del Fortin* ("Stairway to the Fortress") shortly after you cross Calle Delmonte.

Oaxaca now has a branch of the quasi-governmental **FONART** shops ("Fondo Nacional para el Fomento de las Artesañías), at the corner of M. Bravo and Garcia Vigil, open Monday through Saturday from 9 a.m. to 1:30 p.m. and from 4 to 8 p.m.; closed Sunday. Quality and selection are good here, and prices are fixed.

READERS' SIGHTSEENG TIPS: "The Tourist Office will give you a map showing the nearby villages where beautiful handicrafts are made. It's a fun excursion by car or bus through luxuriant countryside and very interesting to wander the rutted street. At **Teotitlán del Valle**, you can see rug weavers at their loom, sheep in the yards. In San

Bartolo de Coyotepec, the primera purveyor of the black pottery, Dona Rose has been a potter for more than 60 years. She and her son give frequent demonstrations on the method used to make these distinctive ceramics, which are in vast quantities at reasonable prices" (Nick West, Lafayette, Calif.). . . . "There's a new artisans' market on Zaragoza—bargain before you buy!" (Petrien Uniken Venema and Anton van Enst, Utrecht, Holland).

FESTIVALS: Oaxaca is famous for its festivals, filled with the color and exuberance of traditional life. The three most important ones are during Holy Week at Eastertime, in July, and in December. Plan ahead and get hotel reservations if you're thinking of coming to any of the festivities.

During the week preceding Palm Sunday (the Sunday before Easter), figurines made of palm leaves are made and sold on the streets by village women. On Palm Sunday itself there are colorful street processions, and on the Thursday after that, Oaxaqueños follow the Procession of the Seven Churches. Hundreds of the pious move from church to church, taking communion in each one to ensure a prosperous year. Throughout the week each church sponsors concerts, fireworks, fairs, and other entertainments. On the day before Easter the famous *guelaguetza* is danced in the Plaza de la Soledad, followed by a candlelight service in the Santo Domingo church.

In mid-July you can witness the **Fiesta Guelaguetza** (offering) of the Virgin Carmen. From this day through the following two Mondays there are fairs, exhibits, and of course the much talked-about regional dances performed in the stadium on the Cerro del Fortin each Monday. It is a marvelous spectacle of color, costumes, music, and dance. Some 350 different *huipils* and dresses can be seen during the performance as the villages of the seven regions of Oaxaca present their traditional dances. This is definitely worth seeing. Admission ranges from 100 to 250 pesos and *must* be reserved in advance (no later than May). A travel agency could handle this for you. I recommend sections 5 and 6 in Palco A for the best seating in the Cerro del Fortin Auditorium. The color of your ticket matches the color of your seat. You will be sitting in strong sunlight so wear a hat and long sleeves. On Sunday night before the Guelaguetza, the university students present an excellent program in the Plaza de la Soledad. It is called the Bani Stui Gulal. The programs begin at 8 p.m., but since the event is free you should get there no later than 5:30 if you hope to get a seat.

The December festivals begin on the 18th with the **Fiesta de la Soledad** in honor of the patron saint of Oaxaca. On that night there is a cascade of fire from a "castle" erected for the occasion in the Plaza de la Soledad. December 23rd is the **Night of the Radishes** when the Oaxaqueños build fantastic scenes and sculptures out of radishes (the most prized vegetable cultivated during the colonial period), flowers, leaves, and fruits. They are on display in the garden off the zócalo. On December 24th each Oaxacan church organizes a procession with music, floats, and crowds bearing candles. All processions meet in the zócalo to display their musical and artistic talents, each hoping to have outdone the other. New Year's Eve is celebrated with the **Petition of the Cross** where villagers from all over come to a forlorn chapel on the hill beyond Tlacolula (about 35 kilometers southeast of Oaxaca near Mitla) to light candles and express their wishes for the coming New Year. Mock bargaining, with sticks and stones to represent livestock and produce, is part of the serious game of expressing hopes for the New Year: tiny symbolic farms and fields are built and their wealth traded, enlivening hopes that the year to come will see the same prosperity, only for real.

OAXACAN NIGHTLIFE: The cheapest, and perhaps the best, evening entertainment is, of course, in the Plaza Principal, where band concerts are scheduled on Tuesday, Thursday, and Sunday, but more often than not during the summer some sort of musical group will be holding forth every night. Oaxaca's is perhaps the jolliest and most active zócalo in all Mexico, enjoyed by everyone in town from 3-year-olds to octogenarians, from those who can't afford a Chiclet to those who could ransom the whole city. Don't miss it.

The Guelaguetza, famous regional dance of Oaxaca, is performed at **La Mansion (28),** Independencia 387, on Wednesday, Friday, and Saturday evenings. Admission is 40 pesos. During the summer months, folk dances are also performed in the **Teatro Alcala** (mentioned above) and at the hotel Monte Alban. Check at the theater or at the Tourism Office for schedules.

As mentioned above, the **Teatro Macedonio de Alcala** has concerts, dance programs, and the like all year long. Schedules are posted by the front doors of the theater, located at Independencia and Armenta y Lopez. The **Casa de la Cultura (29),** corner of Colón and G. Ortega, offers exhibits, lectures, films, and various art and music classes. Anyone staying in Oaxaca for some length of time should certainly check it out.

Cine Oaxaca is on Calle Morelos two blocks south of the zócalo; **Cine Mitla** is east of the plaza on G. Vigil.

The **Cinema Ariel 2000** is new, clean, and modern; films change every two or three days, and a ticket is a very moderate 25 pesos. Look for it at the corner of Juarez and Liceaga (that's the continuation of Berriozabal, six blocks north of the Plaza Principal).

On my last visit, Oaxaca's hottest disco was the one in the **Hotel Victoria (14),** on the Cerro del Fortin northwest of the center of town. You'll need a taxi to reach it, however.

OAXACA MISCELLANY: The **Tourism Office (1)** is on the corner of Independencia and G. Vigil, a few steps from the Plaza Principal and open from 9 a.m. to 3 p.m. and 5 to 7 p.m. Monday through Saturday. . . . The main **post office (30)** or *Correos* is at the corner of Independencia and the Alameda Park. . . . There is a good Spanish-English **bookstore,** just off the southeast corner of the Plaza Principal at Guerrero 108, called Librería Universitaria. They carry mostly new books, but there is a small corner that has some used English books for sale. . . . For some reason, tourists seem to have more intestinal problems in Oaxaca than in most of the other states. Speaking of illnesses I might mention that the number of malaria cases has increased on the Pacific coast, and, in fact, it is becoming quite a problem. There are clinics which distribute free quinine tablets in Puerto Escondido, Salina Cruz, and Potchutla. The Spanish word for malaria is *paludismo*.

SIDE TRIPS FROM OAXACA: Monte Alban and Mitla are the two most important archeological sites near Oaxaca, but there are several smaller ruins that are also interesting, so I have included a word about them, too. Following this I mention a few day trips to the more interesting villages outside Oaxaca. (For Puerto Escondido, see Chapter III.) If you don't have a car, you can get to any of these places by taking a bus, the information for which will be given under the individual headings. It is also possible to hire a taxi from in front of the cathedral in the Plaza Principal in Oaxaca. The rates are fixed and printed on the board for all to see and if you get a party together (cabs will take five people), it can work out cheaply. The trip to Monte Alban, about six miles outside the city, will cost 250 pesos by cab; to Mitla, 500 pesos.

Monte Alban

Autobuses Turisticos at the Hotel Meson del Angel (7), Mina 518 at Mier y Teran, runs three daily buses to Monte Alban, leaving at 9:30 and 11:30 a.m., 12:30 and 3:45 p.m. Return service runs at noon, 2, 4:30, and 5:45 p.m. Round-trip fare is 20 pesos (you must choose a return time when you buy your ticket), and it's a 15-minute ride. Admission to the ruins is 10 pesos (3 on Sunday).

Monte Alban is a beautiful ancient city dating from 1500 B.C. to A.D. 1400, almost 3000 years of occupation. This site was first inhabited by Olmecan descendants who used this as a "city of the gods." What is left from this period are the Danzantes friezes, which are believed by Mario Perez Ramirez, in his book *El Enigma del Arte Hispanica,* to indicate the beginning of pre-Hispanic medicine. He thinks that Monte Alban at this time was used as a medical center to study pathological conditions.

The Zapotecs began to build their ceremonial center in 500 B.C. Later on, this site was used by the invading Mixtecs who came into the valley of Oaxaca from the west in the 11th century. Most of the excavated ruins represent the Zapotec culture, as the Mixtecs did little building; rather, they just occupied what was left of the abandoned city. It is thought that Monte Alban was an elite center of Zapotec merchants and artists, who were greatly influenced by contemporary cultures outside of the valley of Mexico. You can see a resemblance to Mayan art in many of the masks and sculptures. When Monte Alban was at its zenith in A.D. 300, Teotihuacán was the most influential city; you can see borrowed ideas from that site in the architecture of the Zapotecs.

The site of Monte Alban is about 40 square kilometers centered on the Great Plaza, a large grassy area which was once a mountaintop that was flattened by the Zapotecs in 600 B.C. From this plaza, aligned north-south, you can overlook the luxuriant green land of the Oaxacan valley, a gorgeous setting for any civilization. The excavations at Monte Alban have revealed some 170 tombs, numerous ceremonial altars, stelae, pyramids, and palaces.

Begin on the eastern side of the Great Plaza where the I-shaped ball court is. This ball court differs slightly from Mayan and Toltec ball courts in that there are no goal rings and the sides of the court are sloped. Also on the east side of the plaza are several altars and pyramids constructed with ocher stone that was once covered with stucco. Note the sloping walls and the wide stairs and ramps which are typical of Zapotec architecture and resemble the architecture of Teotihuacán. The building slightly out of line with the plaza (not on the north-south axis) is thought to be the observatory and was probably aligned with the heavenly bodies rather than with the points of the compass.

The south side of the plaza has a large platform which bore several stelae, most of which are now in the Museum of Anthropology in Mexico City. There is a good view of the surrounding area from the top of this platform.

The west side has more ceremonial platforms and pyramids. On top of the pyramid substructure are four columns which probably held the roof of the temple at one time.

The famous building of the Dancers (Danzantes) is on the west side of the plaza. This is the earliest structure at Monte Alban, dating back to around 800 B.C., perhaps a little later. This building is covered with large stone slabs carved into distorted, naked figures. There is speculation as to who carved these figures and what they represent. There is certainly a distinct resemblance to the

Olmec "baby faces" seen at La Venta. The distorted bodies and pained expressions of the faces perhaps imply disease. There are clear examples of figures representing childbirth, dwarfism, and infantilism. Because of the fluidity of the figures, they became known as the Danzantes, but this is only a modern label for these ancient and mysterious carvings.

The Northern Platform is a maze of temples and palaces interwoven with subterranean tunnels and sanctuaries. Wander around here, for there are numerous reliefs, glyphs, paintings, and friezes along the lintels and jams as well as the walls.

Leaving the Great Plaza, head north to the cemetery and tombs. Of the 170 tombs so far excavated the most famous is Tomb 7, to the east of the cemetery. Inside were found some 500 pieces of gold, amber, and turquoise jewelry as well as silver, alabaster, and bone art objects: a most amazing collection, which is now housed in the Regional Museum of Oaxaca.

If you have more than one day to spend at Monte Alban be sure to visit some of the tombs, for they contain some really magnificent glyphs, paintings, and stone carvings of gods, goddesses, birds, and serpents. Two of the tombs which are especially absorbing, tombs 104 and 105, are now locked and inaccessible.

A new museum, a shop selling guidebooks to the ruins, and a crafts shop now serve visitors to Monte Alban. The guidebook to this site is well worth purchasing.

Mitla, with a Stop at Santa Maria del Tule

The Fletes y Pasajes bus line (32), located in the second-class terminal, five blocks west of the Plaza Principal on Aldama, across the railroad tracks, runs buses every half hour from 6 a.m. to 6 p.m. to and from Mitla. Cost is 25 pesos one way, and the trip takes an hour and 15 minutes. En route you can visit the famous El Tule tree, eight miles outside of Oaxaca. Bring your flashlight—there are some tunnels at Mitla.

Santa Maria del Tule is a small town that appears to be filled with turkeys, children, and rug vendors. This town is famous for the immense ahuehuete tree (water cypress) in a churchyard just off the main road. Some idea of the size of this 2000-year-old tree can be gained by the fact that it takes about 33 seconds just to walk around it! Unfortunately, there is now a fence around the tree which will keep you from timing it yourself—as if a tree that has survived 2000 years needs protection! This tree is still growing today, as is evidenced by the foliage, and will likely continue to do so as long as the water level remains high. This whole region around Santa Maria del Tule was once very marshy; in fact, the word *tule* means reed.

Beside the tree is a small stall selling refreshments, postcards, Mitla rugs, and some of the famous black pottery of the region.

Beyond El Tule is agricultural country, and at siesta time you'll see whole families sitting in the shade of giant cacti resting from the day's work. Mexican farmers and their wives don't bother with babysitters; they take the kids with them into the fields.

It's 22 miles farther southeast to Mitla. The turnoff comes at a very obvious fork in the road.

The road to **Mitla,** which stretches for 2¾ miles from the highway, eventually terminates in the dusty town square. If you've come here by bus, it's only half a mile up the road to the ruins; if you want to hire a cab, there are some available in the square. You'll probably find the drivers anxious to act as guides, and that isn't a bad idea, if you can fix a suitable price in advance.

Admission to the ruins is 10 pesos; 5 on Sunday and holidays. The ruins are open every day from 9 a.m. to 5 p.m.

Mitla was contemporary with Monte Alban, being settled by the Zapotecs as early as 800 B.C. However, it never reached the excellence that Monte Alban did during the Classic period. In fact, it wasn't until after the Zapotecs had abandoned Mitla (in A.D. 900) and the Mixtec tribe from the west had arrived (in the late tenth century) that the city began to flourish. This city of the Mixtecs was still flourishing at the time of the Spanish Conquest, and many of the buildings were used through the 16th century.

Mixtec architecture is based on a quadrangle surrounded on three or four sides by patios and chambers, usually rectangular in shape. The chambers are provided with a low roof which is excellent for defense, but which makes the rooms dark and close. The buildings are constructed of stone, covered with mud, and inlaid with small stones cut in geometric patterns. It has been estimated that there are over 100,000 pieces used in the mosaics at Mitla.

There are five groups of buildings divided by the Mitla River. The most important buildings are on the east side of the ravine. The Group of Columns consisted of two quadrangles, connected at the corners with palaces fronting on the rectangles. The building to the north has a long chamber with six columns and numerous rooms decorated with geometric designs. The most common motif is the zigzag pattern, the same one seen repeatedly on the Mitla blankets. It's uncommon to find human or animal depictions in Mixtec art; in fact, there is only one surviving frieze left at Mitla, and this is found in the Group of the Church, in the north patio. Here, you'll see a series of figures painted with their name glyphs.

Mitla is not a very large site and you can easily see the most important buildings in an hour or so. You might spend the rest of your day seeing Yaagul or Tlacolula. (See below for more information.)

Outside the ruins you will be bombarded by vendors. The moment you step out of a car or taxi, every able-bodied woman and child for ten miles around comes charging over with shrill cries and a basket full of bargains. Heavily embroidered belts, small pieces of pottery, ungenuine archeological relics, cheap earrings—all may be picked up invariably for half the price at which they are originally offered. By the way, prices are lower in town than in the modern handicrafts market near the ruins.

In the town of Mitla, the University of the Americas maintains a small museum which contains some Zapotec and Mixtec relics. Admission is 1 peso. Next door to the museum is the delightful **Posada La Sorpresa,** an old hacienda with a few rooms, which rent from 200 to 440 pesos single, 500 to 750 pesos double. The restaurant serves breakfast (110 pesos), and a comida (175 pesos) daily.

Another thing you'll notice in the town of Mitla, and out on the highway going south, are "expendios de mezcal," actually "factory outlets" for little distilleries which produce the fiery cactus *aguardiente*. To be authentic, a bottle of mezcal must have a worm floating in it—presumably in a highly advanced state of alcoholic bliss. The liquor is surprisingly cheap, the bottle labels are surprisingly colorful, and the taste is astoundingly horrible. But mix a shot of mezcal with a glass of grapefruit or pomegranate juice, and you've got a cocktail that will make you forget the heat, even in Mitla (remember that worm!).

Yaagul, Dainzu, and Zaachila

Yaagul is about 20 miles southeast of Oaxaca on the road to Mitla. There is a small sign indicating the turnoff to the left (a dirt road, but fairly good). This was a fortress city on a small hill overlooking the valley. The setting is absolutely gorgeous, and although the ruins are not nearly as magnificent as Monte Alban, there is still a lot which is of interest. (Admission is 5 pesos.)

The city was divided into two sections: the fortress on the hill, and the area of palaces lower down the hill. The center of the palace complex is the plaza, surrounded by four temples. In the center is a ceremonial platform, under which is what's known as the Triple Tomb. The door of the tomb is a large stone slab decorated on both sides with beautiful hieroglyphs.

Look for the beautifully restored ball court, typical of Zapotec ball courts (which are without goal rings). North of the plaza is the incredible palace structure built for the chiefs of the city, a maze of huge rooms off six patios, decorated with painted stucco and stone mosaics. Here and there you can see ceremonial mounds and tombs decorated in the same geometric meanderings that are found in Mitla. This is one of the most interesting palace structures in Oaxaca.

The view from the fortress is worth the rather exhausting climb: it offers a whole panorama of the Oaxaca valley.

Dainzu, which is a more recently excavated site, is not terribly interesting to the layman because very little restoration has been done on the buildings. A caretaker on the premises will be happy to show you some of the more interesting points; he has a storeroom of relics unearthed during the excavation which are fascinating: massive stone carvings which resemble the Danzante carvings seen in Monte Alban. Admission is 2 pesos. The site is located on a dirt road heading southwest from the highway (190) to Tehuantepec. Sixteen miles from Oaxaca, look for the turnoff to Teotitlán. Almost directly across the road will be an unmarked dirt road which will take you to Dainzu, approximately four miles in from Highway 190.

Zaachila, at the time of the Spanish conquest, was the last surviving city of the Zapotec rulers. When Cortes marched on their city, they did not resist and instead formed an alliance with him, which outraged the Mixtecs, who invaded Zaachila shortly after. Only a few pyramids and mounds plus some very interesting tombs of the Zapotecs and Mixtecs remain. These can be visited from 9 a.m. to 1 p.m. and 2 to 6 p.m. daily; admission to the ruins is 5 pesos. Several of the tombs have been cleared of rubble, but the buried have been left as they were found. The tombs are elaborately decorated with mosaics and carved figures. You'll find the tombs and the pyramids near the church in the main plaza of the town of Zaachila. Most of the art objects found in the tombs have been moved to the Museum of Anthropology in Mexico City.

Zaachila is located 12 miles southwest of Oaxaca. You might want to plan your trip to Zaachila on a Thursday, since this is market day, and to stop in Cuilapam, a nearby village which has a 16th-century Dominican monastery.

Note: The last time I was at Zaachila, there was no one around to unlock the tombs, and so it was impossible to visit. Be advised.

Some Interesting Village Side Trips

Gueletao is a wonderful town about 65 kilometers north of Oaxaca. It's the birthplace of Benito Juarez, and there's a beautiful monument in his honor. The town is situated in the mountains, and the scenery from Oaxaca to Gueletao makes it well worth the trip.

Cuilapam is located about seven miles southwest of Oaxaca. Follow the road out of town which goes to Monte Alban, take the left fork after crossing the Atoyac River, and follow the signs to Cuilapam. Here, the Dominican friars built their second monastery in 1555. Parts of the convent and church were never completed, because of financial problems. The roof of the monastery has fallen, but the cloister remains, as does that portion of the church which was finished and later restored. The church is still used today. There are three naves with lofty arches and large stone columns plus many frescoes.

Tlacolula is 32 kilometers from Oaxaca southeast on the road to Tehuantepec. It is famous for its Dominican chapel, which is considered by many to be the most beautiful of the Dominican churches in the Americas. Note the wrought-iron gates, choir loft, and bannisters of the pulpit, plus the frescoes and paintings in relief. A few years ago a secret passage was found, leading to a room which contained valuable silver religious pieces. The silver had been hidden during the Revolution of 1916 when there was a tide of antireligious sentiment; the articles are now back in place in the church. Sunday is market day in Tlacolula.

READER'S MOTEL SELECTION IN ARRIAGA: "A very complete and comfortable motel at Arriaga, on the road from Oaxaca to Tapachula, is **El Parador**. Although it is not inexpensive, it has a swimming pool and restaurant and can be a lifesaver for those following this route" (Mrs. R. E. Maret, Calgary, Alberta, Canada).

4. Tehuantepec

From Oaxaca to Tehuantepec is a comparatively short trip of 155 miles, but a fairly arduous one if you're driving, since you'll have to negotiate dozens of S-turns and innumerable climbs and descents.

The first thing you'll notice about Tehuantepec (alt. 200 feet; pop. 102,000) is that it's hot and the women wear long trailing skirts with heavy velvet embroidered huipils. I can't figure it out! The town of Tehuantepec, itself, has very little to offer, and I wouldn't recommend that anybody stay there. Should you want to surprise your wife or girlfriend with one of those magnificent Tehuana costumes, they're sometimes obtainable in the market. Although beautiful, a full-length skirt seems the last thing one would want to wear in this humid heat.

The oil boom in Tabasco and Chiapas has had its spinoffs here in Tehuantepec, most notably out on the highway past the Pemex station on the way to Tuxtla Gutierrez. Here the formerly dowdy **Hotel Calli** (tel. 971/5-0085) has had an incredible facelift, its air-conditioned but fly-blown rooms having been superseded by a spiffy new addition à la Conrad Hilton. Part of the old hotel has been turned into a restaurant, and the new addition positively shines, keeping its air-conditioned cool. But you pay to escape Tehuantepec's mugginess: singles are 1000 pesos; doubles, 1250 pesos; triples, 1500 pesos. Outrageous for Tehuantepec? Not for the oilfield foremen, bank vice-presidents, and Pemex executives driving from the capital to the oil regions.

The alternative in town is the folksy, multicolor **Posada Donaji**, a clean if homely hostelry of 40-odd rooms facing a tiny plaza next to a Walt Disney church (you'll see what I mean). Run by a local family, the Donaji rents rooms with bath for 475 pesos double.

If the Donaji is full and the Calli too expensive, your last resort is the **Oasis Hotel**, just off the main square.

Tehuantepec's hotels and restaurants have, as you will see, little to offer, and you might be best advised to move on to your next destination if possible. It is a long haul to San Cristóbal de las Casas, or Palenque, or Veracruz if you leave from Oaxaca. Consider it, though. An alternative overnight stop can be made in Acayucan, at the northern end of Highway 185 near the Gulf Coast, if you're off to Villahermosa, Palenque, and the Yucatán. See Chapter XIV for details.

Chapter XIV

THE ISTHMUS AND CHIAPAS

1. **Acayucan**
2. **Villahermosa**
3. **Palenque**
4. **Tuxtla Gutierrez**
5. **San Cristóbal de las Casas**
6. **Tapachula**

THE ISTHMUS OF TEHUANTEPEC occupies an interesting place in Mexican history, for it was across this narrow, flat band of land that a railroad was built and operated by an American firm before the opening of the Panama Canal. Tehuantepec was to be the site of the Atlantic-Pacific canal at one time, but the choice finally fell on Panama, and once the canal was opened, all the trade which had crossed at Tehuantepec switched to the Panama route (the earliest route had been all the way around South America) and Tehuantepec fell back into the muggy torpor it had known previously.

Just east of the isthmus are the states of Tabasco (on the gulf) and Chiapas (on the Pacific). Three routes traverse this area to take you into Mesoamerica, the Maya homeland; to the north, Highway 180/186 comes from Veracruz and Lake Catemaco past Acayucan to Villahermosa, capital of the state of Tabasco, and then to the fabulous Maya ruins at Palenque before heading for the Yucatán (see Chapter XV); Highway 190 comes from Oaxaca past the town of Tehuantepec (see Chapter XIII), meets the transisthmian highway, and then climbs into the mountains (where it's cool!) to Tuxtla Gutierrez and San Cristóbal de las Casas before going down to the Guatemalan border; and Highway 200 heads southeast to Tapachula and the Guatemalan border on the Pacific Slope. Going through the isthmus straight to the Yucatán you'll want to take the first of these routes; if you plan to go to Guatemala (which I can't recommend at the moment) take the second route; if you're in a great hurry to get to Guatemala City and don't care about scenery or keeping cool, take the third route, via Tapachula.

It's a longish drive, and an even longer bus trip (about nine or ten hours) to cover the 300 miles from Veracruz to Villahermosa in a day, but I recommend doing it if you have the stamina as it's hot, muggy, and uninteresting in the low-lying isthmus. For those who want to stop over I've included some tips on the way-station town of Acayucan. Those coming by train from Veracruz will have to change at Medias Aguas for Coatzacoalcos, and in Coatzacoalcos transfer to the Ferrocarriles Unidos del Sureste line to continue on the Palenque, Campeche, and Merida. For Tapachula, you can get a direct sleeping car in Veracruz. Details below.

From Oaxaca there are seven buses a day to Tehuantepec, three buses a day to Tuxtla Gutierrez, and one bus which takes you all the way to San Cristóbal and even farther on to the Guatemalan border. The trip to Tehuantepec takes about four to five hours, to Tuxtla another four to five, and to San Cristóbal another two hours. Unless you can't stand long bus rides, I'd recommend that you take the bus straight to San Cristóbal. All these buses belong to either the Cristóbal Colón or A.D.O. lines. It's best to reserve a day in advance for all bus travel in Mexico.

Those driving can do the trip a bit faster, but not much, for most of the road is winding, although fairly good and all paved. Luckily, you can zoom through the isthmus over flat, straight roads at high speed. Plan at least ten hours if you intend to go straight from Oaxaca to San Cristóbal.

These days you can expect to be held up for a half hour or so in the bridge traffic at Coatzacoalcos, and after that, the traffic on Highway 180 to Villahermosa will be pretty heavy.

1. Acayucan

The small town of Acayucan (pronounced "ah-ka-YOO-kan"), Veracruz, at the intersection of Highways 180 and 185, is a pleasant emergency stop during a long drive. At the center of town, a small but beautiful main plaza has as its centerpiece a Spanish gazebo with Chinese overtones; the plaza abounds in shrubs and trees.

Besides being pleasant and manageable, Acayucan has another advantage: rooms are often still available here when the oil-boom towns of Coatzacoalcos and Villahermosa are brim-full of visitors, with not a hotel room to be had (this happens very frequently in summer). If you plan a stop in Acayucan, you will be able easily to make it to Palenque, Oaxaca, or Veracruz the next day.

The **Hotel Joalicia** (tel. 924/5-0877), right on the main plaza at Zaragoza 4, is used to receiving lots of one-night guests because it has served as a way station on Highway 180 since it was built a few years ago. It's Acayucan's best hotel, and can usually offer you a choice of rooms, with fans or air conditioners, at 440 pesos single and 550 pesos double with shower and fan, or 550 pesos single and 660 pesos double with shower and air conditioner. Besides the 42 rooms, the Joalicia has an elevator and a garage, and also a bright and modern little restaurant off the lobby. Many of the meat entrees cost 250 pesos and up, but other meat and chicken dishes are priced near 175 pesos. A bowl of hearty pozole with a large fruit salad is a nutritious and tasty lunch for less than 200 pesos. For postprandial coffee, an espresso machine (out here in the wilderness!) stands ready to hand. By the way, the Joalicia is right next door to the A.D.O. bus station.

Directly across the plaza from the Joalicia is the **Hotel San Miguel** (tel. 924/5-0018), at Avenida Hidalgo 8. Rooms here are plainer and less congenial than at the Joalicia, but are still suitable. Prices are about the same as the aforementioned hotel, but the bonus at the San Miguel is a small pool. Parking is available in the courtyard lot, and by the looks of it this is where well-to-do farmers park their pickups and put up for the night when they come to town. Prices, as you can see, are pre-oil-boom. The restaurant here is good, as well.

2. Villahermosa

Villahermosa (pop. 200,000), the capital of the state of Tabasco, is right at the center of Mexico's oil boom, and seems to grow in size visibly every day. From a somewhat dowdy provincial town, the oil wealth has helped transform it into a fairly attractive and obviously prosperous modern city.

The boom has brought difficulties as well, and the major one you'll encounter is a shortage of hotel rooms. This is bad enough, but the upshot of the shortage is that hotels can charge what they want for rooms, and not bother about maintenance or service, and they'll still get customers—the oilmen have to sleep somewhere. When they come in from the fields, they're ready to let loose, too. Villahermosa thus has something of a frontier town mood about it.

I'd tell you to whiz by Villahermosa, except that it's a long ride to the next stop, Palenque or San Cristóbal de las Casas, and you really shouldn't miss the fabulous Parque La Venta. Tabasco is where many of the most important Olmec relics were discovered, including the mammoth heads. Parque La Venta holds significant Olmec displays in a beautiful setting, and the beautiful new Regional Museum of Anthropology holds others from all over Mexico.

If you want like anything to avoid the considerable hassle of locating a hotel room here—any hotel room, let alone one that's cheap and decent—there is a way. Take an early bus from wherever you're coming, and when you hit Villahermosa, check the schedules for your onward journey in the bus station. Locate a bus leaving in an hour or two, buy a ticket for it, and then grab a taxi to the Parque La Venta, a short buzz up the highway from the bus station (either one). Allow at least an hour for the park. If there's time to spare, grab another cab to the Museo Regional de Anthropologia Carlos Pellicer Camara (open Tuesday through Sunday from 10 a.m. to 1 p.m. and 5 to 8 p.m.). Allow a minimum half hour here, and then race back to catch your bus. This is no way to run a vacation, but, then again, hot, muggy Villahermosa is no place to spend one.

ORIENTATION: The hotels and restaurants I recommend are located off the three main streets running north and south: Madero, Pino Suarez, and the Malecon. Highway 180 skirts the city, so a turn onto Madero or Pino Suarez will take you into the center of town. Coming in from Villahermosa's new airport, which is 6½ miles east of town, you'll cross a bridge over the Río Grijalva and turn left to reach downtown. The airport minibuses charge 88 pesos, whereas a taxi will want a hefty 400 pesos at least.

Your point of focus in town can be the **Plaza de Armas,** or main square, bounded by the streets named Zaragoza, Madero, and Juarez. The plaza is the center of the downtown district, with the Río Grijalva to its west and Highway 186 to its north. If Villahermosa can be said to have a main downtown thoroughfare, then it is **Avenida Madero,** running south from Highway 186 past the Plaza de Armas to the river, where it intersects with the riverside Malecon.

The **Central Camionera de Primera Clase** (first-class bus station, sometimes called the **A.D.O. terminal**) is on Avenida Javier Mina. To get to the Plaza de Armas, go out and turn right on Javier Mina, then go left for about six blocks to Avenida Madero. Turn right onto Madero, and the Plaza de Armas is about four blocks along.

The **Central Camionera de Segunda Clase** (second-class bus station) is on Highway 180/186 near the traffic circle bearing a statue of a fisherman. Buses marked "Mercado-C. Camionera" leave frequently from the bus station for the center of town.

The **Tourist Office** is at Zaragoza 103, at the Malecon (the riverside drive along the Río Grijalva).

WHERE TO STAY: The area around the intersections of Avenidas Juarez and Lerdo is now one of the best places to stay, for these two streets have been closed to cars and made into pedestrian malls. First choice here is the **Hotel San Miguel**, Lerdo 315 (tel. 931/2-1500), where 30 rooms have been renovated, each with tiled bathrooms and ceiling fans, and going for 770 pesos single, 990 pesos double with air conditioning. The lobby of the San Miguel is plain, but graced by one very important appliance: a super-cold water dispenser.

A collection of air-conditioned rooms is at the **Hotel Palma de Mallorca**, Madero 516 (tel. 913/2-0144), where singles are 660 pesos, and doubles run 880 pesos. For the price, you don't get what you should, but this is the problem with all hotels in this town.

The aforementioned hotels, while adequate, may not be up to what you want after a long, tiring trip, so here are the alternatives. The fanciest place right downtown is the **Hotel Olmeca**, Reforma 304 (tel. 913/2-0022), a modern establishment of glass, aluminum, and brightly colored plastic furniture equipped with virtually everything your heart could desire: elevator, air conditioning, and television and refrigerator in every room. Price for all this luxury is high at 850 pesos single, 1100 pesos double, but the hotel situation in Villahermosa is not good.

The older **Hotel Manzur**, Madero 14 (tel. 913/2-2499), has about the same prices for older but well-kept accommodations, all air-conditioned of course. Strictly speaking it's not worth the money, but in fact it depends on how tired you are.

Near the Bus Stations

Just off Highway 186, not far from the first- and second-class bus stations is the **Hotel Ritz** (tel. 913/2-1611), Avenida Madero 1013. Its three modern stories hold 40 good rooms at rather high prices: 1045 pesos single, 1350 pesos double, all centrally air-conditioned. While it's a block off the highway, the Ritz is not subject to any more noise than other Villahermosa hotels. Note, however, that this is not a choice particularly for those arriving late at night by bus—like other hotels in this city, it's almost sure to be full by early evening, at the latest.

High-Budget Motels

The Hotel Villahermosa Viva (tel. 913/2-5555), the Hotel Maya Tabasco (tel. 913/2-1111), and other luxurious establishments on Highway 180/186 will put you up if you can find no other place to stay, but it will cost you dearly: plan on spending in the range of 2250 pesos for a very posh air-conditioned double. Kees Snoek, of Ann Arbor, Michigan, writes: "In Villahermosa, I walked around for one hour, carrying my bags, sweating, looking for a vacant room. I didn't realize that reservations were essential in this town (accommodations are insufficient), and I ended up paying $40 a night at a fancy motel. Some people I met had to stay the whole night in the bus station, and others paid hundreds of pesos just to *sit* in a fancy hotel's lobby for a night."

READERS' HOTEL SELECTION: "We recommend the **Hotel Balboa** (tel. 913/2-4550 or 2-7268), at Bastor Zozaya 505: 550 pesos for a double, clean, fan and shower, only slightly less for singles. Also try the **hospedaje** along the same street. To reach them, walk past the supermarket behind the bus terminal and take the first right, then walk down five or six blocks" (Paul Traves and Nora Solis, Austin, Texas).

WHERE TO EAT: The **Restaurant Los Pepes**, (tel. 2-0154) Madero 610, near the Plaza de Armas, is probably the cleanest of Villahermosa's open cafés, and highly recommended by the townspeople. Each of the tables is covered in colorful placemats, it's fairly cool with large ceiling fans. Almost every dish here costs between 100 and 250 pesos (liver, pork chops, chicken, shrimp) and the menu is fairly extensive. One of the tastiest dishes is the filete Tampiqueño at 250 pesos, but starvation-budget devotees might stick to the turkey tamales —you get three good-size ones for 60 pesos. Open daily 7 a.m. to 1 a.m.

PARQUE MUSEO LA VENTA: This is a lovely outdoor museum park located outside Villahermosa on Route 180 (take Paseo Tabasco northeast to Highway 180, turn right, and it's less than a mile on your right, next to the Exposition Park). As you walk through on a self-guided tour you'll see Olmec relics, sculptures, mosaics, a mockup of the original La Venta, and of course the colossal Olmec heads. These heads were carved around 1000 B.C., are 6½ feet high, and weigh around 40 tons. The faces seem to be half-adult, half-infantile with that fleshy "jaguar mouth" that is characteristic of Olmecan art. Even stranger is the fact that the basalt, for carving, had to be transported from the nearest source, which was over 70 miles from La Venta! A total of 13 heads has been found: five at La Venta, six at San Lorenzo, one at Tres Zapotes, and one at Santiago Tuxtla, all cities of the Olmecs. On your tour through the park, notice the fine stone sculptures and artistic achievements of the Olmecs, who set forth the first art style in Mesoamerica. Their exquisite figurines in jade and serpentine, which can be seen in the Regional Museum of Anthropology, far excelled any other craft of this period.

La Venta, by the way, was one of three major Olmec cities during the pre-Classic period (2000 B.C. to A.D. 300). The ruins were discovered in 1938, and there in the tall grasses were the mammoth heads. Today, all that remains of the once-impressive city are some grass-covered mounds—once pyramids— some 84 miles west of Villahermosa. All of the gigantic heads have been moved from the site. You'll see three heads in Parque La Venta.

Parque Museo La Venta is open from 8:30 a.m. to 5 p.m. every day; admission is 25 pesos to nonresidents, 10 pesos to residents.

REGIONAL MUSEUM OF ANTHROPOLOGY: Tabasco's shiny new Museo Regional de Anthropologia Carlos Pellicer Camara, was opened in February 1980 to replace the older Tabasco Museum. The new museum is architecturally bold and attractive, and very well organized inside. There is more space and therefore the number of pre-Hispanic artifacts on display has greatly increased to include not only the Tabascan finds (Totonac, Zapotec, and Olmec), but the rest of the Mexican and Central American cultures as well.

The museum is beautiful, with parquet floors, wood dividers, and numerous plants. There is a very open and airy feeling about this place. Take the elevator to the top of the museum and walk down past large maps showing the Olmec and Mayan lands. Photographs and diagrams make it all easier to comprehend, but the explanatory signs are all in Spanish. Look especially for the figurines that were found in this area and for the colorful *Codex* (an early book of pictographs).

The Regional Museum is a mile south of the center of town, right along the river's west bank, open Tuesday to Sunday from 10 a.m. to 1 p.m. and 5 to 8 p.m. As of this writing the museum is free, but I expect that in the future there will be a fee.

GETTING OUT OF VILLAHERMOSA: If you're driving, you already know how you're going to get out of town. If not, you have two choices.

By Air

Mexicana (tel. 2-1169 or 2-1164), Madero 109, has six flights a day to Mexico City. AeroMéxico (tel. 2-6991 or 2-9492), Malecon 1611, has nonstop flights to Merida, Mexico City, Oaxaca, and Tuxtla Gutierrez every day.

Small regional carriers operate out of Villahermosa's old and new airports, starting up and then going bankrupt at irregular intervals. At the moment, Transporte Aereo de Tabasco (tel. 2-1645) flies from the new airport to Tuxtla Gutierrez and Tapachula every midmorning, except Sunday. Aerotúr (tel. 3-2244) flies to Ciudad del Carmen and Merida about noontime every day except Sunday.

By Bus

From the first-class bus station (see above under "Orientation"), A.D.O. and Cristóbal Colón buses depart daily for Veracruz, Mexico City, and points along that route, to Oaxaca, and to Merida via Campeche.

To Palenque, there's one first-class A.D.O. bus a day, leaving about 8 a.m. and returning about 3 p.m. Buy your reserved-seat ticket as far in advance as possible.

If you take a second-class bus, be sure to ask about arrival times. Sometimes these buses take hours and hours because of all the stops en route.

From Villahermosa to Tuxtla/San Cristóbal

Highway 195 connects the Tabascan capital of Villahermosa with Tuxtla Gutierrez, the capital of the state of Chiapas. Daily Cristóbal Colón buses ply the route from the tropical savannahs into the rugged Chiapan mountains, and the trip takes most of a day. The road is paved all the way, and although curvy and hilly, is fantastically scenic—a real treat.

An alternate route which has recently become practicable is that running between Palenque and San Cristóbal de las Casas, a road which as yet has no highway number. See below in the Palenque section for details on this jungle road.

3. Palenque

Certainly some of the most fascinating and beautiful Mayan ruins are those on the edge of the jungle at Palenque, in the state of Chiapas.

GETTING TO AND FROM PALENQUE: Highway 186 from Villahermosa passes the turnoff to Palenque, and there are daily first-class (A.D.O.) and second-class buses to take you the 90 miles from Villahermosa to the site. (Make sure you tell them *which* Palenque—the town or the ruins—you want a ticket to.) You can return to Villahermosa the same day, or stay overnight in Palenque village, or go on to Campeche and Merida by bus or train. For the bus, buy your tickets in advance. Trains leave Palenque station for Campeche and Merida daily, arriving in Campeche the next morning, and in Merida several hours later. To Coatzacoalcos, the transfer point for trains to Tehuantepec (for Oaxaca and Tapachula), and Medias Aguas (for Veracruz and Mexico City), trains leave Palenque every day. Taxis between Palenque town and the station cost 150 pesos by day, 200 pesos by night.

Important: It can take almost the whole day to get from Villahermosa to Palenque on a second-class bus. Be sure to ask about arrival times. Also note that trains operating east of the Isthmus of Tehuantepec tend to be slow, late, and badly maintained. Several readers have written to say they chartered a small plane to fly them from Villahermosa to Palenque and back in a day. This takes money.

From a Pemex station on Highway 186, a road turns right and heads for Palenque, 27 kilometers (17 miles) off the main road. First you'll come to Palenque Junction (the railroad station), then a few miles later to a fork in the road—there's an incredibly dramatic statue of a Mayan here, so you can't miss it. Left at the fork takes you a mile or so into Palenque village with its bank, restaurants, hotels, stores, and ice house. Right at the fork takes you past several motels to Palenque ruins. A municipal bus is supposed to run between the town and the ruins every hour or so, but in practice it's not very dependable. A taxi costs only about 30 pesos per person, and might just be worth it.

The first-class (A.D.O.) bus station is on the main square, more or less across the street from the Hotel Lacroix. Second-class buses have an office on Avenida Juarez near the Pemex station in town, across the street from the Hotel Avenida and not far from the Mayan statue.

WHERE TO STAY AND EAT: You must decide where you want to stay: at the fork in the road, in the village, or on the road to the ruins. Here are the possibilities, in that order.

Near the Mayan Statue

If you stand staring head-on in rapture (or horror) at the Mayan statue at the fork in the road, just off to your left will be a wooded area, a dirt road, and four lodging places. First is a camping area, the **Canada Tulipanes** (full hookups, and rather primitive showers and toilets for 160 pesos per night).

Just behind the camping area down the dirt road is the **Hotel Tulipanes** (tel. 934/5-0230), run by the same family as the camping area. The "hotel" is actually several small buildings with very simple but adequate rooms-and-baths renting for 550 pesos double. There's a ceiling fan in each room.

Back along the dirt road a bit farther is **La Selva**, a restaurant very near a shop selling replicas of Maya stonework. La Selva rents rooms in several two-unit bungalows at Tulipanes prices, but they are less desirable.

At the far end of the dirt road is the **Motel La Canada** (no phone), a group of fairly authentic Maya-style thatched-roof cottages surrounded by dense woods and thus pretty secluded. Birds sing always, and there's a wonderful sense of peace and quiet. The Morales family, owners of La Canada, are used to hosting foreigners as they provide hospitality for many archeologists' groups who come to Palenque. They have a pet boar named Petunia. In their quaint dirt-floored restaurant, you can get a tasty supper of chicken tacos or quesadillas, with a cold bottle of beer, for 170 pesos; meat entrees cost twice that amount. Near the restaurant, a two-story thatched "club" throbs to disco music. It never seems to be crowded, although it's the ideal setting for a *Night of the Iguana* romance.

Sound interesting? The Motel La Canada is my favorite place to stay in Palenque, but it's often full. Write for reservations early, if you can. Cottages cost about 750 pesos double, a few dollars less for a single.

A short distance back toward Villahermosa—only a half mile from the Maya-statue fork in the road, really—is the **Hotel Tulija** (tel. 5-0165), one of

Palenque's more modern hotels with air-conditioned rooms going for 725 pesos single, 825 pesos double, 925 pesos triple; without air conditioning, rooms are about 200 pesos cheaper. The rooms without air conditioning have ceiling fans, and in fact they're bungalows scattered in a field just up the road from the Hotel Tilija. The hotel has a restaurant and bar, and a very nice swimming pool. They take credit cards. Mailing address, by the way, is Apdo. Postal 57, Palenque, Chiapas, México.

Turning left at the fork and heading toward the village, you'll pass a Pemex station on the left, and then you'll spot the **Hotel Avenida** (tel. 934/5-0116), a good choice if you're backpacking and saving money. The hotel is right across the street from the *second-class bus station,* halfway between the village center and the Mayan statue. The rooms are very bare and well used, with cold water only, and no screens to keep the bugs out (have plenty of insect repellent). Choose a room at the back so the buses roaring up and down the street won't disturb you, and then prepare to pay 600 pesos double for it. There's a restaurant downstairs with a menu in English.

In Palenque Village

The fanciest place to stay in Palenque Village is a bright new mini-hotel called the **Hotel Casa de Pakal** (no phone), on the main street (Avenida Juarez) near the central park. Each of the rather small rooms here comes with a TV set, servi-bar, and piped-in music, plus that blessed air conditioning, for 770 pesos single, 935 pesos double.

Very near the Casa de Pakal is the slightly older **Hotel Misol-Ha** (tel. 934/5-0092), with a dozen or so small rooms still well kept. With a ceiling fan, you pay 440 pesos for two people; with air conditioning, the price is 594 pesos double.

A good choice for the starvation-budget reader is the **Hotel Lacroix** (no phone), facing the main square or park (as you come up Avenida Juarez into the center of town, turn left at the park, then right, and the hotel is down a block on the left-hand side). Darkish and simple rooms are kept cool by shady trees, fans, and breezes, and each opens onto a cool veranda overlooking lush gardens of palms and banana plants. Primitive murals decorate the place, and prices are low: 200 pesos single, 400 pesos double, 600 pesos triple. As you might imagine, the Lacroix is often full-up.

On the other side of the park from the Lacroix is Palenque's oldest hotel, the **Hotel Palenque.** It has had its ups and downs over the years; currently it seems to be up, because of the increased competition from newer hotels. Some of the Hotel Palenque's ancient rooms have been redeemed with paint, paper, and air conditioners, and the courtyard garden can be pleasant enough, but be sure you *inspect your room* before you take it—this is an "iffy" place. Rates are 385 to 485 pesos single, 570 to 816 pesos double, 690 to 995 pesos triple, with air conditioning and private shower.

Village Restaurants: Downtown Palenque's restaurants are located near the central park. The **Restaurant Maya,** on the park near the Correos (post office), is breezy and open, about the cleanest in town, and family run. A comida corrida of soup, beef with rice, flan (caramel custard), and coffee or tea costs 180 pesos here; a full breakfast of eggs, fruit juice, frijoles, bread, and coffee is 130 pesos.

Next door to the Maya is the **Restaurant Nicte-Ha,** a much less cool and clean place, but with advantages of its own: more food for less money. The dishes seem to be about the same in both places, so choose on the basis of coolness, attractiveness, and price.

Down near the village market is the **Restaurant La Barca** (walk down Juarez from the central park one block, turn right, and the restaurant is half a block up on the left). The specialty here, in landlocked Palenque, is seafood, which the chef presumably garners fresh from the market across the street. You won't find a comida corrida here, and à la carte prices are slightly higher than at the aforementioned restaurants. But a light lunch of caldo de pescado (fish stew), with a stack of fresh, hot tortillas, will be 125 pesos. Seafood platters are priced from 200 to 240 pesos.

On the Road to Palenque Ruins

Closest hotel to the ruins is actually a motel-style place named the **Hotel Las Ruinas,** Apdo. Postal 49 (that's the mailing address), operated by a friendly gentleman named Prof. Ismael Corzo. A nice swimming pool serves as the motel's centerpiece; 22 rooms are arranged around it, all modern, bathroom-equipped, and all with ceiling fans for 600 pesos single, 800 pesos double. Here you're only a half mile from the ruins.

I'll mention the prices for rooms at the **Chan-Kah,** at km. 31 on the road to the ruins, because you'll wonder what they are if I don't tell you. The very nicely done little bungalows, made of wood and stone, rustic but at the same time modern and comfortable, are fitted with ceiling fans and cost 1200 pesos single, 1500 pesos double. They're nice, but that's a lot to pay.

Last of all, the **Motel Nututum** (or Nututun; tel. 934/5-0101) is about three kilometers (two miles) from the Mayan statue along the road to the ruins, and then left on the road through the jungle to Ocosingo, Agua Azul, and San Cristóbal. The setting is beautiful, right on the Río Usumacinta, but accommodations are primitive. The manager plans to build 40 new luxurious, air-conditioned units, but whether they'll get the business to sustain them out here is another question. Check and see. At present, prices are fairly high for what you get: 575 pesos single, 675 pesos double, 825 pesos triple. If you've got your own car and camping equipment, you can camp on the riverbank (no hookups at all) for 120 pesos.

PALENQUE RUINS: Palenque is one of the most spectacular of the Maya ruins with its roof-combed temples ensconced in lush vegetation high above the savannahs. It was a ceremonial center for the high priests during the Classical period (A.D. 300–900), with the peak of its civilization being somewhere around A.D. 600–700. Pottery found during the excavations shows that there was a very early, pre-Classic people living here as early as 300 B.C. Alberto Ruíz Lhuillier, the archeologist who directed some of the explorations, states that because of "the style of its structures, its hieroglyphic inscriptions, its sculptures, its works in stucco and its pottery, Palenque undoubtedly fell within the great Maya culture. Yet its artistic expressions have a character all their own which is evident in the absolute mastery of craftsmanship, turning the art of Palenque into the most refined of Indian America." As you enter the ruins, the building to the right is the Temple of the Inscriptions, named for the great stone hieroglyphic panels found inside (most of them are now in the Archeological Museum in Mexico City) and famous for the tomb which was discovered in its depths in 1949. It took four seasons of digging to clear out the rubble that was put there by the Mayas to conceal the crypt. The crypt itself is some 80 feet below the floor of the temple and was covered by a monolithic sepulchral slab ten feet long and seven feet wide. You can visit the tomb, and so long as you're not a claustrophobe, you shouldn't miss it. The way down is lighted, but the steps can be slippery due to condensed humidity—watch it! This is the only such temple-pyramid (resembling the Egyptian pyramids) in the Americas! Besides the Temple of the Inscriptions, there is the Palace with its unique watchtower, the northern group (Temple of the Count and Ball court) and the group of temples beyond the Palace (Temple of the Sun, Temple of the Foliated Cross). The official guidebook has a detailed description of this site and is well worth the money. (For a summary of pre-Columbian history, see the Introduction of the book you're now reading.)

Plan to spend a whole day in these wonderful surroundings. When you're tired of looking at ruins, grab your bathing suit and head for the gorgeous stream and falls near the tiny museum at the end of the dirt track which goes past the "Grupo del Norte" complex of structures. A sign by the stream informs you (in Spanish) that there is no bathing allowed, but downstream a ways is a large pool out of view.

The small museum (open 8 a.m. to 5 p.m.) has a chronological chart of Maya history, and a modest collection of votive figurines, pieces of statuary, and stones with calendar glyphs. Entrance is free once you have paid for access to the ruins.

The Palenque ruins are open from 8 a.m. to 5 p.m. The entrance fee is 15 pesos, on Sunday 10 pesos, and it will cost you another 10 to park your car. By the way, a quarter mile back toward town from the parking lot, on the right-hand side (as you approach from town) is a path leading into the Cascada Motiepa, a cool, beautiful waterfall good for cooling the feet and resting the soul. Watch the mosquitos, though.

A Note on Bonampak

The ruins of Bonampak, southeast of Palenque on the Guatemalan border, were discovered in 1946 and constituted a very important find. Reproductions of the vivid murals found here, deep in the jungle, are on view in the Regional Archeology Museum in Villahermosa. To see the real thing at Bonampak you'll have to hire a small plane to buzz you in, or else hire a sturdy car or Jeep to take you the five hours into the jungle. You can visit nearby Yaxchilan on the same trip. Plan to camp overnight, or go and return in a day.

For airplane charters, try contacting the **Sociedad Cooperative Transporte Aereo de Tabasco,** S.C.L. (tel. 934/4-0035 or 4-2023), at the little Palenque Airport on the road in from Highway 186.

SWIMMING AT MISOL-HA AND AGUA AZUL: Steamy Chiapan jungle doesn't seem a likely place to discover Tahiti-type swimming spots, but you can find them at Misol-Ha and Agua Azul. Head out of Palenque on the road to San Cristóbal, and after 20 kilometers you'll arrive at **Misol-Ha.** Pay 30 pesos admission, and jump with a shout under the huge waterfall. What a way to cool down after climbing up the Temple of the Inscriptions!

Farther along at **Agua Azul** (65 kilometers, 1½ hours by bus from Palenque), you're a third of the way to San Cristóbal. The road to this spot is tricky, lacking many signs. It doesn't matter if you're on a bus, but if you're driving you must ask the way frequently. When in doubt at a fork, *always bear right.* This seems to work.

You'll pay 40 pesos admission to Agua Azul, after which you can desport yourself in the clear, blue, icy-cold waters of innumerable falls, a magnificent sight! Two little cheap restaurants and innumerable vendors keep your alimentary needs supplied.

FROM PALENQUE TO SAN CRISTÓBAL DE LAS CASAS: There is daily bus service between Palenque village and San Cristóbal de las Casas provided by the second-class lines Autobuses Lacandonia and Autobuses Tuxtla. The road is still under construction, and work was hampered by the eruption of El Chichonal volcano some years ago, but you can get through in about five or six hours. During the rainy season it might take a little longer—ask when you buy your ticket, which you should do a day in advance. The distance is about 130 miles.

Little bush airlines used to fly between Palenque and San Cristóbal, but nowadays the only scheduled flights are by Aviación de Chiapas, daily between Palenque and Tuxtla Gutierrez. You can usually get to Tuxtla in time to catch the midafternoon Cristóbal Colón bus to San Cristóbal, if the bus is not full up. Expect to pay about 1500 pesos for the entire trip, including taxis to and from airports, flight, and bus ticket. For information on flights from Palenque, go to the airport on the road from town toward the main highway.

4. Tuxtla Gutierrez

Tuxtla (alt. 1838 feet; pop. 180,000) is a boom-town capital of the state of Chiapas, long Mexico's coffee-growing center, but more recently an oil prospector's mecca. The mammoth reserves discovered in this wild, mountainous state several years ago have brought people, business, and wealth to Tuxtla. It's not an unpleasant town, but it's modern, hectic, and business oriented, so you'd best stop here only if necessary, as it offers little in the way of tourist sights.

ORIENTATION: It's a 40-minute ride into town from Tuxtla's new, main airport; driving or coming by bus from Oaxaca or Veracruz, you enter the same way, along Highway 190. From Villahermosa or San Cristóbal, you'll enter at the opposite end of town. Either way, you will end up at the big main square, Plaza Belisario Dominguez, with its gleaming white church (note the clockwork figures in the tower!) and modern buildings.

Tuxtla has another airport, a small one called the Aeropuerto Francisco Sarabia, in the suburb of Terán only 15 minutes from the center. You'll fly in here if you take Aviación de Chiapas (downtown office: 4a Calle Poniente and 1a Avenida Norte).

The street system bears a note of explanation. The city is divided by two "Central" streets: Calle Central, running north to south; and Avenida Central, running east to west—the main highway is the Avenida Central, also named Boulevard Dominguez (west of downtown). Streets are numbered from these central arteries, with the suffix *norte, sur, oriente,* or *poniente* designating the direction of progress from the central arteries.

The **Tourist Office** (tel. 961/2-0732) is at the western end of town on the Avenida Central (Boulevard Dominguez), just near the Hotel Bonampak Tuxtla, mentioned below. It is usually manned by someone who speaks little English and who is unfamiliar with the region.

The Cristóbal Colón bus terminal is at 2a Avenida Norte and 2a Calle Poniente, two blocks west of Calle Central.

WHERE TO STAY AND EAT: As Tuxtla booms, the center of the hotel industry has moved out of town, west to Highway 190. As you come in from the airport you'll notice the new motel-style hostelries, all of which charge rates out of our range: the Hotel Flamboyant (it's just that, too), the Palace Inn, Hotel Laganja, La Hacienda, and the older Hotel Bonampak Tuxtla.

Those driving can splurge at the **Hotel Bonampak Tuxtla** (tel. 961/2-0201), Avenida Central, Boulevard Dominguez 180, on the western edge of town. The Bonampak's a lavish layout with over 100 rooms, air conditioning, swimming pool, barbershop, beauty parlor, and restaurant. Rooms are not cheap at 1000 pesos single, 1250 pesos double, but in booming Tuxtla that's about the norm. The hotel's cafeteria is open from 6 a.m. to midnight (air-conditioned), and has hotcakes, sandwiches, and hot entrees. Prices are better, the food as good, and the air conditioning just as cool at the Flamingo Cafeteria downtown, which is described below.

Of the older downtown hotels, only a few are suitable, the rest being "hoteles de paso," or establishments which (ahem!) rent rooms by the hour.

Two small places right across the street from the Autobuses Cristóbal Colón terminal on 2a Avenida Norte, the **Hotel Santo Domingo** and the **Hotel Maria Teresa** (no phones), are strictly for emergencies only. Rooms are overpriced at 550 pesos double.

About your best bet in booming Tuxtla is the older **Gran Hotel Humberto** (tel. 961/2-2080), very near the plaza at Avenida Central 180 Pte., corner of 1a Calle Pte. Enter from Avenida Central (the entrance on 1a Calle is for another—unsuitable—hotel). Over 100 rooms here, all with air conditioning, adequate bathrooms, and elevators. The double rooms cost 900 pesos; single rooms, just a few dollars less.

The **Flamingo Cafeteria** is the place to eat downtown. Not far from the Plaza B. Dominguez, it's modern, air-conditioned, open almost all the time, and features a wide selection of dishes (and prices) served with dispatch. It's located in the Zardain Building, Calle 1 Poniente no. 17 (go down the passageway to the Flamingo's entrance). From the bus station, turn left, then take the first right. Walk up and across the Avenida Central, and the Zardain Building is on the right-hand side. At the Flamingo, Mexican dishes cost anywhere from 100 to 200 pesos, with sandwiches below this range and meat entrees above it. Seafood specialties are flown in frequently, so the oysters, shrimp, and fish may even be sort of fresh here. The daily comida corrida costs less than 200 pesos.

A Peripatetic Breakfast

Up early to catch a bus or plane? Before the Flamingo opens at 8 a.m., you can grab something to eat by visiting the panadería (bakery) farther up the same street (1a Calle Pte., up from the Avenida Central). Sweet rolls and danish in hand, walk back down toward the Flamingo and stop at the Jugos California stand for a huge glass of fresh-squeezed orange juice.

For Coffee Purists

There's not much to do in Tuxtla, but whenever I'm in town I drop by the **Cafe Avenida,** Avenida Central 226 at 1a Calle Pte., for a cup or two of the only thing they serve: freshly ground and brewed Chiapan coffee. Huge sacks of beans lean against the counter, the grinder hums away, producing wonderful coffee aromas. The Formica tables have been cleaned so often that the decorative pattern is wearing off. No tea, no sweets, just coffee, dark roasted (almost burnt), rough-flavored, and hearty, at 25 pesos the cup.

WHAT TO DO: It's possible to take a couple of out-of-town excursions, one being to the small town of **Chiapa de Corzo,** a 30-minute, eight-mile ride by bus from the main square (buses leave every 15 minutes in the morning, every 30 minutes in the afternoon), or 10 to 15 minutes by taxi. Those going on to San Cristóbal or over the mountains to the Yucatán (see below) will pass through Chiapa de Corso on their way.

Chiapa has a small museum dedicated to lacquered wood items, and also a small pyramid, pretty well restored and visible from the road.

Another more spectacular trip is to the canyon of **El Sumidero,** ten miles from the center of town along a country road. The canyon can be reached by taxi—you must strike a bargain with a driver, who will want about 800 to 1000 pesos a carload for the round trip.

Eleven blocks east of the central plaza on the way to El Sumidero is **Madero Park** which harbors the **Regional Museum of Anthropology,** the **Regional Zoo,** and the **Botanical Gardens.** In one short stop you can pick up lots of information here on Chiapas's past civilizations, her flora, and her fauna (including jaguars, monkeys, and other creatures native to the area). The museum is open from 9 a.m. to 2 p.m. and 4 to 7 p.m. Monday through Friday, 9 a.m. to noon on weekdays; the zoo is open from 7 a.m. to 7 p.m. daily. As the Parque Madero and these attractions are on the way to El Sumidero, you can see it all in the course of one trip.

Other than these, the best thing you can do in Tuxtla is go to the Cristóbal Colón bus station and book passage for San Cristóbal de las Casas or Villahermosa, gateway to the Yucatán.

SHORTCUT TO THE YUCATÁN: A road is being built between San Cristóbal and Palenque, and although it's open, it's rough; see Section 3 of this chapter for full details. Otherwise, you don't have to go all the way back to Tehuantepec to cross the mountains as Highway 195 is open and completely paved from Chiapa de Corzo (near Tuxtla) to Pichucalco, near Villahermosa. It's a winding mountain road that can't be taken fast, and shouldn't be anyway as the road meanders through some of the most gorgeous scenery in all Mexico: emerald-green mountains, thick banana groves, citrus trees growing wild by the roadside, quaint villages, and breathtaking vistas come one after the other as you wind along. It's important to get an early start on this road, especially if you're driving from San Cristobal, for patches of fog often slow traffic until you climb above the clouds. The trip from Chiapa to Pichucalco takes about six hours by car, seven by bus—the bus going on to Villahermosa, as Pichucalco is not a suitable place to stay (hotels strictly for dire emergencies). Autobuses Cristóbal Colón runs two daily buses from Tuxtla to Villahermosa.

BUSES FROM TUXTLA: Besides the two buses mentioned above going to Villahermosa, the Cristóbal Colón line also runs four daily buses to San Cristóbal, one to Oaxaca, and two to Comitán, on the way to the Guatemalan border at Ciudad Cuauhtémoc.

5. San Cristóbal de las Casas

The highway between Tuxtla and San Cristóbal de las Casas climbs almost 7000 feet in a matter of 50 miles and the scenery is spectacular. San Cristóbal itself (alt. 6855 feet; pop. 40,000) is a colonial town set in a lovely valley. (Note: It's chilly every evening of the year there, so bring a sweater.) The town is the major market center for Indians of various tribes from the surrounding mountains, chiefly the Chamulas, who wear baggy thigh-length trousers and white or black serapes; the Zinacantes, who dress in light-pink blouses and extremely short pants, whose hat ribbons are tied on the married men and dangling loose on the bachelors; and the Tenahapa, with knee-length black tunics, and flat straw hats. In a way, Indian life in Chiapas is an introduction to that of Guatemala, for San Cristóbal is deep in Mesoamerica where the Mayas flourished. In fact, nearly all the Indians around these parts speak languages derived from ancient Mayan. Some don't come into town at all, ever, and one group, the Lacandons (who number only 450), live so far off in the forests of eastern Chiapas that it takes six days on horseback to get to their territory. There are some Indian villages within access of San Cristóbal by road—Chilil, a Tuixtan village, where the Indian Institute maintains a clinic, reached via a drive through a beautiful forest; Amatenango del Valle, whose inhabitants make pots without a potter's wheel; Zinacantan, whose men weave hats; Contehuitz, Arcotete, and Tenajapa, the last village accessible only by Jeep. Without a guide who knows the area, however, there's not much to see. Most Indian "villages" consist of little more than a church and the municipal government, with homes scattered for miles around and a general gathering only for church and market days (usually Sunday).

In recent years San Cristóbal has become a popular vacation spot for Mexicans, not to mention North Americans and Europeans in search of a charming, cool, "unspoiled," traditional town to visit or to settle down in for a few years. Hotels and restaurants do a good business, but in general they're not very well run—a reminder that San Cristóbal is in fact a small country town high in the mountains.

ORIENTATION: Highway 190, the Pan American Highway, runs through the southern reaches of San Cristóbal. The first-class (Cristóbal Colón) bus station is right on the highway. The street which intersects the highway in front of the bus station is the Avenida de los Insurgentes, and nine blocks north along Insurgentes (a 10- or 15-minute walk) will bring you to the main plaza, complete with cathedral. Another nine blocks along the same street, in the same direction, will bring you to the public market, at the northern edge of town. From the market, minibuses trundle to outlying villages.

The second-class bus stations (Tuxtla and Lacandonia) are on Calle Pedro Moreno, three or four blocks from the first-class terminal. Walk east along Moreno to get to Insurgentes, then turn left (north).

Take note that this town has at least three streets named "Dominguez." There's Hermanos Dominguez, Belisario Dominguez, and Pantaleón Dominguez. Maybe more, who knows?

The municipal tourism office (tel. 967/8-0533), on the main square in the town hall next to the cathedral, is well organized, with a friendly, helpful staff.

WHERE TO STAY: San Cristóbal is no longer the quiet little village of ten years ago; in fact, it is presently at the boom stage when new hotels and restaurants spring up overnight.

The **Hotel Ciudad Real** (tel. 967/8-0187), on the zócalo, is one of the snazzier hotels in town, but the prices are still pretty reasonable: 475 pesos for a single, 625 pesos double. The rooms are new and rather small, but you are paying for the quite elegant decor and the central courtyard complete with a large fireplace, which is always blazing away on those cold (or cool) evenings.

Next door to the Ciudad Real is the **Hotel Santa Clara** (tel. 967/8-1140), a very similar establishment which tends to charge slightly more for its rooms: 500 pesos single, 675 pesos double.

SAN CRISTÓBAL DE LAS CASAS

The **Hotel Fray Bartolomé de las Casas,** on the corner of Niños Héroes (no. 2) and Insurgentes, next to the Pemex station (tel. 967/8-0932), is a nice old colonial inn with 18 rooms. If you are looking for a quiet abode this is the place, and although the rooms are plain, they are clean and in good condition with tile showers. The courtyard has numerous planters and bentwood furniture as well as parking. Singles are 350 pesos; doubles cost 500 pesos. *Note:* Hot water is only available between 6:30 and 10 in the morning and 6 and 10 in the evening.

At Avenida Juarez 16, corner of León, is the **Hotel Palacio de Moctezuma** (tel. 967/8-0352), a modern, clean, and neat hostelry with small rooms arranged around a central, glassed-in courtyard with a pretty fountain. Rooms are small and somewhat expensive: 600 pesos single, 750 pesos double. It's a decent place to stay.

The **Hotel San Martín,** Calle Real de Guadalupe 16 (tel. 967/8-0533), is a family-run operation, and is thus very clean. The rooms are on three floors in the long, narrow building with balcony-type walkways. Each room has a private tiled bath and a firm bed. Rates are 350 pesos single, 450 pesos double, 550 pesos triple. Ask about hot water availability before you register.

Students staying in San Cristóbal for any length of time find basic but acceptable hospedajes which charge 200 pesos per person per day or less. Usually these places are unadvertised, and were I to include names and addresses here the prices would surely skyrocket. If you're interested in a cheap, cheap hospedaje, ask around in a restaurant (try the Casa Blanca) or café and you're sure to find one.

To get you started, I suggest looking on Calle Real de Guadalupe, east out of the main square. Some of the best hospedajes are here. Other ones, on Insurgentes near the bus stations, tend to be noisy.

A Quiet Place on the Outskirts

The **Hotel El Molino de la Alborada** (tel. 967/8-0935), Apdo. Postal 50, San Cristóbal, Chiapas, is about 1½ miles from the center of town on the dirt road called, grandiosely, the "Periferico" ("Ring Road"). When San Cristóbal grows to the point where the Periferico is paved and in heavy use, this hotel might be subject to noise. But right now its eight very fine rooms are blissfully quiet, perched on a hillside backed by forest overlooking the town. The management is North American, and the price for a room is high but certainly not unreasonable: 700 pesos single, 800 to 950 pesos double. When you start out in search of El Molino, look for white stones spelling out "hotel" on the hillside. The hotel car makes several trips a day into town.

READERS' HOTEL SELECTIONS: "We stayed at **Posada del Abuelita,** Tapachula 18 (tel. 967/8-1741), near the market about 20 minutes from the bus station. The Posada is rather a youth hostel. They rent rooms around a patio and have dormitory space for 80 pesos per person. They have lots of clean showers and toilets and a kitchen with open chimney" (Dr. Hugo Lanz, Munich, W. Germany). . . . Another reader with words of praise for La Posada del Abuelita: "Run by a young man named Armando Alfonzo who speaks fluent English and French and knows the area well and is willing to help his guests in finding places. There are a total of eight rooms for 175 pesos single, 125 pesos per person for a double, and a dormitory" (Patricia Brid, Miami, Fla.). . . . "The **Posada Tepeyac,** on Calle Real de Guadalupe, has no bath or water in the rooms, but it's a friendly and inexpensive place: 275 pesos double, or 350 pesos for a room with bath. Down the street is the **Posada Margarita,** closer to the zócalo, same price" (Maren Sagvaag and P. H. Keim Börresen, Bergen, Norway).

WHERE TO EAT: Remember now, this is a country town, and so service may be fairly slow.

There's a double treat waiting at **La Galería,** Calle Dr. Navarro 1, between Utrilla and B. Dominguez. Open daily from 10 a.m. to 10 p.m., La Galería has exhibits of folk art, weaving, pottery, and painting. The little two-room café-restaurant upstairs thrums to cool, hip music while the efficient staff serve up chiles rellenos (stuffed green peppers), hamburgers, big fruit salads, and the like for 80 to 100 pesos—good place.

Ernest Hemingway called Paris "a moveable feast." San Cristóbal has its own, in the shape of the **Restaurant Normita,** at the corner of Juarez and Flores. The Normita has moved no fewer than three times in the past few years, and I keep following it around because the food and the prices are good. For 80 to 100 pesos you can get a Mexican specialty such as enchiladas which is sure to fill you up. Pozole, the thick, rich hominy stew, is also a good choice, or perhaps the cochinita (suckling pig) appeals to you. Come to the Normita from 1 to 11 p.m. daily, 6 to 11 p.m. on Sunday.

La Parroquía, Guadalupe Victoria 3, is a large restaurant with lots of tables on both main floor and mezzanine. The sumptuous set-price lunch here costs 135 pesos and gives you a choice of six entrees. Other things to have are meats for 130 to 195 pesos, drinks, and ice cream. Open daily from 7 a.m. to 8 p.m.

On my last visit, I discovered a new vegetarian restaurant and food shop named **El Trigal.** A pretty courtyard in an old house has been furnished with tables, plants, and a pyramid (to furnish digestive powers?), all at Calle 1 de Marzo no. 13, corner of 20 de Noviembre, on the north side of the Cine Las Casas. For breakfast, have granola with milk and bananas; for lunch, an alfalfa-and-lettuce salad with a bowl of lentil soup; for dinner, perhaps cream of carrot soup and chilaquiles made with tomatoes and cheese. The bill will be only 80 to 100 pesos, only 35 pesos more for a glass of wine (the only liquor served). When I tried it out, the food was excellent, the service inexperienced but very friendly.

A San Cristóbal standby is the **Restaurant Casa Blanca,** a very well-used place on Real de Guadalupe between Utrilla and B. Dominguez, half a block off the main plaza. It's a compliment to say the decor is undistinguished; the food is better, and there's often a good selection. Besides the soup, egg dishes, sandwiches, and meat courses on the à la carte menu, the Casa Blanca offers a daily comida corrida for 90 pesos, but some days it's better to order à la carte.

The **Restaurant Olla Podrida,** Mazariegos 24 at the corner of Allende, is a meeting and greeting point for the foreign vagabond set. They come for the food, for the pretty decorations of local crafts, and to read and leave messages on the useful message board. As for food, there's chile con carne that's not overly spicy, ham and eggs, good guacamole, and authentic hamburgers, all priced from 50 to 115 pesos. It's open long hours, from 8 a.m. to 11 p.m.

READERS' RESTAURANT SELECTION: "There is a café on Diego de Mazariegos / Francisco Madero between Insurgentes, Utrilla, and Juarez that's a real local hangout for young people. It's like a student café in Europe. Coffee is okay; people play cards, dominoes, or read and talk. It's a good place to go when it rains!" (Ruth Amernick, Berkeley, Calif.).

WHAT TO DO: Although San Cristóbal is a mountain town, it has drawn more and more visitors. They come to enjoy the scenery, the air, hikes in the mountains, and to look at the Indians in the zócalo. I have no doubt that the Indians come down from the mountains to look at them. In any case, the town is now showing signs of "progress." There is a new language center à la San Miguel de Allende called CIELO: Centro para Intercambio de Estudios Linguisticos Occidental. Students and professors seem to be drawn by beautiful colonial towns, and I can't blame them. CIELO features not only intensive Spanish courses, but also instruction in arts and crafts such as weaving and pottery. The courses are programed for winter and summer, but you can make arrangements for other times. For more information write to CIELO, Apdo. Postal 109, San Cristóbal de las Casas, Chiapas, México.

A recently built **Bellas Artes building,** on Hidalgo three blocks south of the plaza to the arch), is one of the more active centers in San Cristóbal. There is an enthusiastic director who is sponsoring all types of concerts, lectures, and art exhibits. Be sure to check in if you are interested in the arts. I recently saw a fine show of batiks and painting here. There should be a schedule of events and shows posted on the door, if the Bellas Artes is not open. By the way, there's a public library right next door.

Just being in San Cristóbal is good for mind and body, but for those who want the restoration afforded by a mineral bath, try the **Baños de Vapor Mercedarios,** at 1 de Marzo no. 55. For the soul I can recommend heartily a hike to some of the churches throughout the town. Very near the Bellas Artes, where the arch towers over Avenida Hidalgo at the intersection of Hermanos Dominguez, is the **Templo del Carmen.** It's a favorite of the townspeople despite its rather plain interior (some gilded work, paintings, and statues). It's over two centuries old. At the other end of town is the **Templo de Santo Domingo** (1560), on Avenida 20 de Noviembre, five blocks from the zócalo. The carved stone facade is in a style called "Plateresque," and there's a beautiful gilded wooden altarpiece inside. The **Templo de San Francisco** is near the aforementioned Carmen church, at the corner of Insurgentes and Callejon Libertad. During Holy Week you might walk through the pleasant square, enter the church with its dark, somber oil paintings and softly glowing gilt altarpieces, and hear the exquisitely simple sounds of a primitive flute and bells breaking the silence at intervals.

Get your wind up, because the next church visit takes stamina. From the hill which holds the **Templo de San Cristóbal** you will have a very fine panorama of the town—but you pay. Leave the zócalo on Avenida Hidalgo, turn right onto the third street (Hermanos Dominguez), and there at the end of the street are the steps you've got to climb. Take it slowly.

An easier church to visit is the **cathedral,** right on the zócalo, dating from the 1500s and boasting some fine timberwork and a very fancy pulpit.

FESTIVALS: San Cristóbal explodes with lights, excitement, and hordes of visitors during Holy Week, when the annual **Fería de Primavera** (Spring Festival) is held. Carnival rides, food stalls, handicraft shops, parades, and band concerts fill an entire week. Hotel rooms get hard to find, and room prices rise accordingly.

Another spectacular is staged **July 24th,** date for the annual fiesta. The steps up to the San Cristóbal church are lit with torches at night.

MARKETS AND SHOPS: Because of the many Indian villages near San Cristóbal where traditional crafts are still practiced, this is a good town in which to shop for pottery and woven goods. One of the best selections I've seen is at **Sna Jolobil,** in the former convent (monastery) of Santo Domingo, Avenida 20 de Noviembre between Navarro and Nicaragua. It's a cooperative store operated by groups of Tzotzil and Tzeltal craftspeople, with about 3000 members who contribute products, help in running the store, and share in the moderate profits. Their works are simply beautiful; prices are set, and are moderate, and quality is high. Be sure to take a look.

Sna Jolobil also has displays in **La Galería** (see the "Where to Eat" section, above), at Navarro no. 1 and Hidalgo.

San Cristóbal's **central market** is farther along Avenida Gral. Utrilla from the Santo Domingo church, about nine blocks from the zócalo. The market buildings, and the streets surrounding them, offer just about anything you'd have need of.

Market day in San Cristóbal is every morning except Sunday (when each village has its own local market), and you'll probably enjoy looking at the sellers as much as the things they sell. This area is especially good for woven and leather products. They make and sell beautiful serapes, colorful native shirts, and rebozos in vivid geometric patterns. In leather they are craftsmen of the highest rating making the sandals and men's handbags indigenous to this region. There are numerous shops up and down the streets leading to the market, all of them willing to sell you anything from string bags and pottery to colorfully patterned ponchos. Shop here: the products are good and the prices are right.

Those interested in the anthropology of this region will want to visit the museum and library called **Na Bolom**. The home, and headquarters, of noted anthropologists Franz and Trudy Blom for many years, it is now a focal point for serious study of the region. You can take a tour of the house from 8 a.m. to 1 p.m. any day but Friday; the museum is open from 4 to 6 p.m. every day but Monday. (For the museum, a donation is asked.) Na Bolom offers limited accommodations to serious visitors, with all meals included. Prices are well out of our range, though. Na Bolom is nine blocks from the zócalo. Leave the square on Real de Gaudalupe, walk four blocks to Avenida Vicente Guerrero, and turn left. Five and a half blocks up Guerrero, just past the intersection with Comitan, is Na Bolom.

SIDE TRIPS: A side trip to the village of **San Juan Chamula** really gets one into the spirit of Chiapas. The village, eight kilometers northeast of San Cristóbal, is the cultural and ceremonial center of the Chamula Indians. Activity centers on the huge church, the plaza, and the municipal building; each year a new group of citizens is chosen to live in the municipal center as caretakers of the saints. Carnival, just before Lent, is the big annual festival, and turns out to be a fascinating mingling of the Christian pre-Lenten ceremonies and an ancient Maya celebration of the five "lost days" which arise at the end of the 360-day Maya agricultural cycle. The Chamulas are not a very wealthy people as their economy is based on agriculture.

Buses to San Juan Chamula leave the municipal market in San Cristóbal at 7 and 11 a.m., 12:30, 2, and 4 p.m.

Zinacantan is another small village in the region where visitors are required to observe certain local customs: before seeing the church, one must ask permission of the Presidente Municipal, seated to the right of the church. Once permission is granted, an escort will show you the church, after which you are expected to drop a respectable number of coins into the offering box. Note also that no cameras are allowed in the town at any time.

HORSEBACK RIDES: Tired of riding buses? You can make arrangements to rent a horse at various places in town, including across the street from the Na Bolom Museum. Cost is about 500 pesos for an afternoon, more if you want to have a guide accompany you. Reserve your steed after 7 p.m. at least a day before you want to ride. You could, for instance, ride over to San Juan Chamula, or just up into the hills.

NIGHTLIFE: I think of San Cristóbal as a do-it-yourself nightlife town. Friendly conversation at several of my recommended restaurants, particularly the Olla Podrida with its international clientele, is a favorite evening pastime. The Normita frequently has a guitarist at night. And if it's just a cozy fire and a comfortable chair you crave, have a drink by the blaze in the Hotel Ciudad Real.

Otherwise, hang around one of the two movie theaters in town. There's a slim chance they'll be showing a film in English, or one that you might not mind watching in Spanish; and even if you don't want to see the movie, that's where many of the local citizens will be hanging out, for better or worse.

SAN CRISTÓBAL MISCELLANY: The **post office** *(Correos),* open from 9 a.m. to 1 p.m. and 3 to 6 p.m., is on Avenida 16 de Septeimbre, one block south of the main square. The **telegraph office** is on Calle Diego de Mazariegos, just past Avenida 5 de Mayo.

COMITÁN: Comitán (alt. 5018 feet; pop. 40,000) is a pretty town on a hillside whose chief distinction, apart from the production of a sugarcane-based fire water called *comitecho,* is that it's the last big town along the Pan American Highway before the Guatemalan border. It'd be best, considering Comitán's comely position but meager virtues, if you planned to go straight from San Cristóbal to the border; but should unforeseen circumstances drop you in Comitán, head for the **Hotel Internacional** (tel. 963/1-10), Avenida 11 and Calle 20, about a block off the zócalo. It's quite suitable and priced all right: singles are 350 pesos, doubles are 525 pesos. Lots of hot water. A breakfast of orange juice, coffee, toast, and jam is 105 pesos. Another place is the **Hotel Delfin,** next to the first-class bus stop. Prices are 250 pesos per person; they do have a few much cheaper rooms, but I'll bet you any money that after a look you won't want to rent them.

What do you do with a free day in Comitán? You take a side trip to the **Monte Bello National Park** and enjoy the multicolored lakes and exuberant tropical vegetation. Buses run out to the park, but schedules change with the seasons so check for latest information at the office of Transportes Montebello, on 5a Avenida Sur. Plan to see the park in a day as there are no places to stay overnight.

6. Tapachula

Although I prefer entering Guatemala via San Cristóbal (see above), you can go via the Mexican town of Tapachula (El Carmen on the Guatemalan side), a pleasant enough town of 120,000 people at the base of a 13,000-foot volcano. This is the Pacific Slope of Middle America, covered with plantations growing sugarcane, coffee, rubber, and bananas, many of them run by Germans or German-speaking people; the Slope is much the same in both Mexico and Guatemala. The drive to Tapachula is a long, hot one from Tehuantepec—

354 MEXICO ON $20 A DAY

almost 300 miles—and even longer and hotter from Coatzacoalcos or Veracruz. When you arrive, take refuge in Tapachula's main square, shaded by fine trees.

Tapachula's layout is logical if a bit confusing, so take a moment to consider it. Two central streets divide the town, the Avenida Central which goes from north to south, and the Calle Central which goes from east to west. All streets parallel to Avenida Central are also called avenidas, and are numbered (Avenidas 1, 3, 5, etc., are *east* of the Avenida Central; Avenidas 2, 4, 6, etc., are *west* of Avenida Central). The same arrangement applies for the calles: Calles 1, 3, 5, etc., are *north* of Calle Central; Calles 2, 4, 6, etc., are *south* of Calle Central.

WHERE TO STAY AND EAT: Most people will only stay one night in Tapachula, then head for Guatemala. You can do this one-night stand in comfort at the **Motel Kamico** (tel. 962/6-2640), a 53-unit motel on Highway 200 just south of town. Rooms are perhaps the best in Tapachula, at the most daunting prices: 1100 pesos single, 1250 to 1500 pesos double, but this gets you use of the swimming pool too—no mean privilege here in sweaty Tapachula. The **Loma Real Motor Hotel** (tel. 962/6-1440), on Highway 200 at the other end of town up on a hill, is slightly larger, slightly snazzier, and slightly more expensive.

Down to earth again, there's the **Hotel Puebla**, just off the main square, where clean and comfortable double rooms cost an affordable 750 pesos. Contact the hotel through its owner, Sr. Tizoc Perez G., who operates a pharmacy at 3a Poniente no. 31. Sr. Perez has two other small hotels, the Monaco and the Colonial, as well.

At 4th Avenida Norte no. 19 is the 51-room **Hotel Fenix** (tel. 962/6-1464), a slightly snazzier place than nearby hotels, featuring its own restaurant and bar, plus a tobacco stand and a parking garage. About a third of the rooms are air-conditioned. Rates are 450 pesos single, 600 pesos double (one bed), 650 pesos double (two beds); add 100 pesos for air conditioning.

Near the Railroad Station

Those arriving by train should look at the **Hotel San Francisco** (tel. 962/6-1454), Avenida Central Sur 94 (at the corner of Calle 12). You pay for the tiled bathrooms and piped-in music, but after a night on the train you might want to spend a little more for luxury. Of the 40 rooms, all are air-conditioned doubles and go for 700 to 950 pesos; rooms for one person cost just a bit less. The hotel has a restaurant pretty much at the top of our budget range, and a parking lot, which can be locked, for guests' cars.

ONWARD TO GUATEMALA: If you're not traveling on to Guatemala, there's no reason to come to Tapachula. Unfortunately, I can't really recommend travel in Guatemala as of this writing. The political situation—and civil order—are just too uncertain. I hope that in the next edition of this book I'll be able to recommend Guatemala once again.

Chapter XV

THE YUCATÁN AND MEXICO'S CARIBBEAN

1. Merida
2. Uxmal and Nearby Ruins
3. Campeche
4. Chichén-Itzá and Valladolid
5. Cancún
6. Isla Mujeres
7. Cozumel
8. Xel-ha, Tulum, and Cobá
9. Carrillo Puerto and Chetumal
10. Travel to Belize and Guatemala

CONTRARY TO POPULAR BELIEF, which places the Yucatán in the extreme southeast of Mexico, the land of the Mayas forms the far east-central part of the Republic. A look at the map reveals that the Yucatecan capital, Merida, is north of such major population centers as Mexico City, Guadalajara, Puebla, and Veracruz. Merida is also surprisingly close to the tip of Florida: from Mexico City to Merida it's about 600 miles as the crow flies, and from Merida to Miami it's a mere 675 miles.

Actually there are two Yucatáns—the peninsula and the state. The peninsula is the piece of land north of Highway 186 which extends from Francisco Escárcega to Chetumal, and includes part of the state of Campeche and all of the state of Yucatán, plus most of the new state (formerly a National Territory) of Quintana Roo. The Yucatán state is a wedge-shaped entity which includes Merida and many of the best archeological sites.

Merida is like a boom town these days, packed full in July and August, mostly because of the hordes of visitors, who come to Mexico for history and archeology rather than for beaches and sunning. Many visitors, however, do both: using Cozumel or Cancún as a base, they spend half their time on the beach and the other half touring the ruins. No matter what you may have heard about Mexico's Caribbean, it is quite possible to find a budget-priced room in this jet-set haven. Transportation is good, and the clear skies combine with the vivid blue water and white sand to make this a perfect base for Yucatecan explorations.

It's 900 miles from Mexico City to Merida by road, but there's frequent bus service from points along the way, and from Merida buses run to Puerto Juarez (for Isla Mujeres) and down the Caribbean coast for Cozumel, Tulum, and Chetumal; from Chetumal there's bus service to Belize City. Trains of the Ferrocarriles Unidos del Sureste line run daily from Coatzacoalcos to Palenque, Campeche, and Merida. And as for air service, besides the Mexican domestic services to Campeche, Merida, Isla Mujeres, Cozumel, and Chetumal, there's also international service connecting Yucatán directly with Miami, Los Angeles, Houston, and Guatemala City.

CHANGING TIME ZONES: The Mexican government has decreed that the Yucatán peninsula (the states of Campeche, Yucatán, and Quintana Roo) is to run on Eastern Standard Time, all year. Coming from Mexico City or Villahermosa, set your watch *ahead* one hour; coming from Miami or New York in winter, no change is necessary, but in summer you must set your watch *back* an hour, as Mexico does not observe Daylight Saving Time.

TOURING YUCATÁN: Today most visitors head directly for Merida, Cancún or Cozumel, and use those places as home base for further explorations. We'll start our Yucatecan tour in the Yucatecan capital—Merida—using that city as a base to explore the ancient Maya cities of Uxmal, Mayapan, Kabah, Sayil, Xlapak and Labná, plus the walled Spanish city of Campeche. Then we'll head east, passing Chichén-Itzá and Valladolid on our way to Puerto Juarez, Cancún, and Isla Mujeres. Finally, we'll head down the Caribbean coast for a tour of Cozumel, Tulum, Cobá, Lake Bacalar, and the brash new city of Chetumal, on the Belizean border.

I'd like to thank Prof. Stephen Althouse, of Miami's Barry University, for helpful insights into Mayan artistic and cultural practices, particularly at Chichén-Itzá and Uxmal.

1. Merida

Merida (pop. 300,000) is the capital of Yucatán, and has been its major city ever since the Spanish founded it in the mid-1500s on the site of the defeated Mayan city of Tiho. Although it's changing due to general growth and increased tourism, you'll still see examples of its ancient culture around.

Known for their general cleanliness, the Yucatecos stress this in their cooking. You'll want to sample the succulent, indigenous pork dishes, especially turkey stuffed with pork and sauce (pavo relleno negro), or suckling pig (cochinito).

In the market and elsewhere, you'll notice items woven of a sisal fiber called **henequen.** The raising of henequen is Yucatán's main industry, apart from tourists, and it is used to make hammocks, baskets, shoes, tablemats, twine, and hats. Panama hats are made here rather than in Panama, in damp caves near the city; they're amazingly resilient, and can be rolled, folded, jumped on, or crammed into a suitcase without losing their shape.

The tourist season is busiest in July and August, but most pleasant in December, January, and February; trade winds keep Merida's temperature comfortable most of the time. You'll need a light coat for winter, cool clothes for summer days, a sweater or jacket for summer evenings. Light raingear is suggested for the brief showers of late May, June, and July.

The major attractions of the Merida area are, of course, the Mayan ruins of Chichén-Itzá and Uxmal. But you will find that the town of Merida can easily be your base of operations for such visits, so first I'll deal with the problem of finding accommodations in the city itself.

A word of warning about street numbers: What with unnumbered dwellings and -A, -B, and -C additions, these progress agonizingly slowly. Example: I wanted to get from 504 to 615D on Calle 59 and did—after walking 12 blocks! Otherwise, the street grid is fairly easy to find your way in. Odd-numbered streets run east-west; even-numbered ones go north-south.

WHERE TO STAY: Merida's line-up of hotels is a budget traveler's dream-come-true. From the very expensive to the very low-priced, from the modern to the romantically old-fashioned, everyone can find a place that suits. Most hotels offer at least a few air-conditioned rooms (and current weather reports will tell you whether or not you'll need this), and a few of the places in the budget line-up even have swimming pools! Although Merida, and the Yucatán in general, are in the midst of a tourism boom, it is only in August that you may find absolutely every room taken. If you cannot find exactly what you want when you first arrive, take an available room for a night or two, and spend an hour the next morning pinpointing and reserving your chosen room.

For the price and location, it's hard to beat the **Hotel Colonial (4)** (tel. 992/3-6444), at Calle 62 no. 476, corner of Calle 57. This bright and modern five-story hotel has over 50 rooms, a swimming pool, and central air conditioning. But the prices are the best part: singles cost 880 pesos, and doubles go for 1100, representing good value for what you get. Here you're right next door to Merida's university.

The spanking-new **Hotel del Gobernador (24)** (tel. 992/1-3514 or 3-7001), Calle 59 no. 535 at the corner of Calle 66, qualifies as Merida's most modern. Sleek but small (43 rooms and 16 junior suites), the hotel features air conditioning and telephone in each room, a swimming pool, cafeteria, bar, laundry, and parking lot for guests' cars. Rooms cost 990 pesos single, 1210 pesos double, 150 pesos for each extra person. As for the junior suites, they have two double beds each, and cost about 250 pesos more per room than the standard accommodations. These rates are at the high end of our range, but the rooms are worth the money.

I'm very fond of the hotel **Posada Toledo (10)** (tel. 992/3-2256), Calle 58 no. 487 (at the corner of Calle 57), once a private mansion but now run as an inn with 19 rooms and a rooftop deck, good for sitting and viewing the city in the cool of the evening. The place seems to be a cross between a garden and a museum with well-kept antique furnishings and lots of verdure. Rates are 660 pesos single and 825 pesos double with ceiling fan, 825 pesos single and 990 pesos double with air conditioning.

At the corner of Calles 59 and 60 is a small park, and facing the park is the 43-room **Hotel Caribe (2)**, 59th and 60th (tel. 992/1-9232), with two floors of large, plain rooms and a third floor of near-luxurious rooms arranged around a huge central courtyard. Surprisingly, the furnishings and tiled baths are fairly modern, even in the old rooms, but they sometimes seem a bit damp. The new ones, furnished with beautiful natural wood, glass-globe wall lamps, cheerful red spreads, telephones, and equipped with ceiling fans or air conditioners, rent for 550 pesos single, 680 pesos double, with fan. Add 150 pesos for air conditioning. There's a tiny rooftop swimming pool, and a restaurant named El Rincon in the lobby.

Right down the street from the Posada Toledo, and much less expensive, is the **Hotel Mucuy (5)**, Calle 57 no. 481 (between Calles 56 and 58; tel. 992/1-1037). The hotel is named for a small dove said to bring good luck to

358 MEXICO ON $20 A DAY

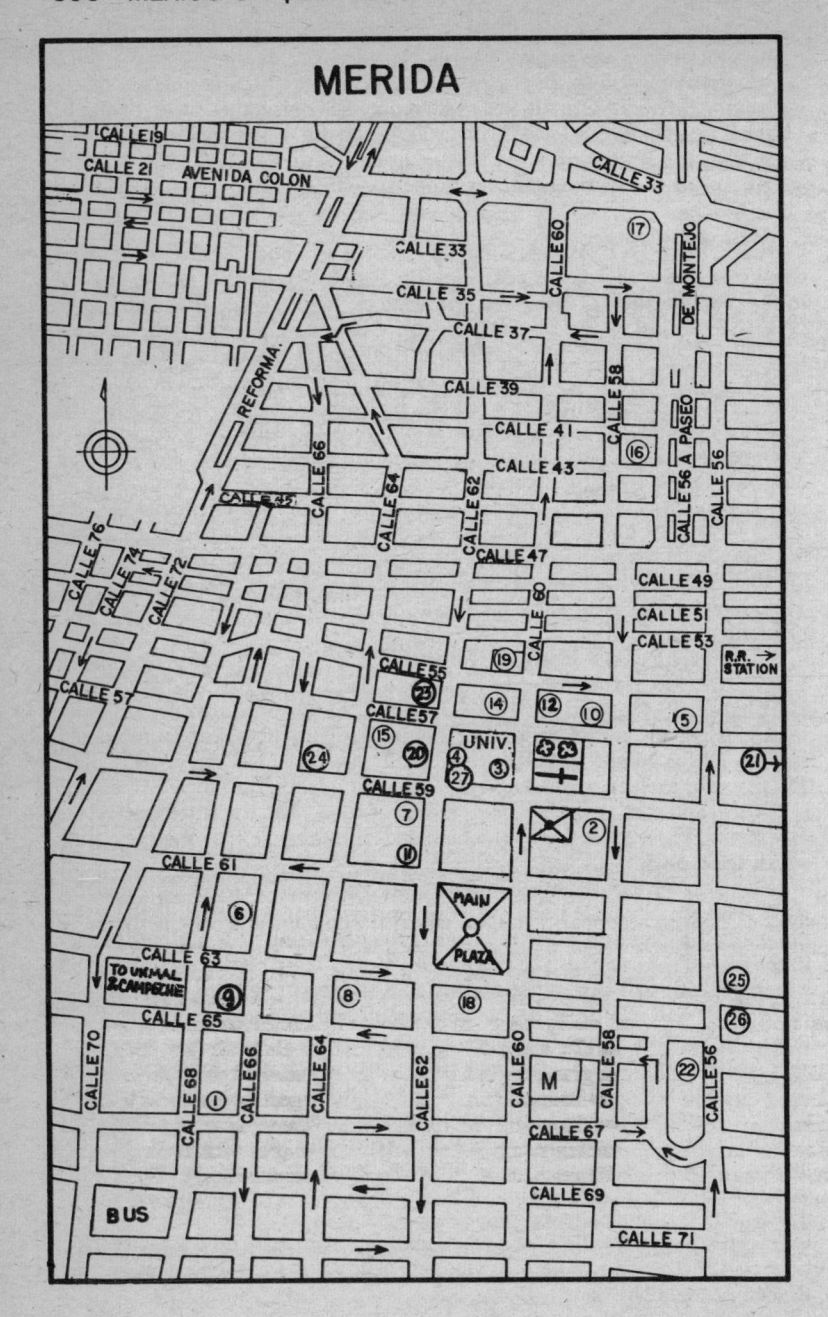

places where it alights, and you should have good luck, as many alight here. The 12 rooms, all with window screens, tile showers, and ceiling fans, are lined up on one side of a garden with fine grass and bougainvillea; you can park your car within the hotel gates for free. The owners, Sr. Alfredo and Sra. Ofelia Comin, give that kind of personal, friendly service that you find only in small hotels. Señora Comin speaks English. Rates are 275 pesos single, 385 pesos double, 440 pesos for three persons. A laundry sink and clothesline are available for guests' use. The roses and bougainvillea seem to be in bloom all summer here, and from the scented peacefulness of the Mucuy's courtyard it's only a few minutes' walk to the center of Merida.

The **Hotel Dolores Alba (25)** (tel. 992/1-3745), Calle 63 no. 464 between Calles 52 and 54, is an old Merida house converted to receive guests. Fifteen rooms here come with ceiling fans and showers, plus decorations of local crafts. A big open court and another court with a nice clean swimming pool give a sense of space. You'll pay 484 pesos for a double room with fan, or 605 pesos for a room with air conditioning. The Dolores Alba is run by the Sanchez family, who also have the Hotel Dolores Alba at Chichén-Itzá. Make reservations at one hotel for space at the other hotel, if you like.

The **Hotel Chac-Mool** (tel. 992/1-8578 or 3-0720), at Calles 54 and 55 (Apdo. Postal 433), is very near the railroad station, but is not what one thinks of as a "railroad hotel." Small, modern, neat and clean, the Chac-Mool has a friendly staff, lots of bright colors, and a few mod-colonial touches. The 26 rooms come with fans, or with air conditioning at the higher price. Singles cost 440 to 550 pesos and doubles are 550 to 660 pesos. Free parking. This is a good choice for any traveler, whether coming by rail or not.

The **Casa Bowen (9)** (tel. 992/1-8112), long lauded in this book as Merida's finest guest house, has been slipping in recent years. The original old building, with small, bare rooms around a courtyard, has been supplemented with a big new addition next door. Rooms in the addition come with kitchenettes, tile showers, and ceiling fans for 550 to 650 pesos. Rooms in the old building are cheaper, but not all that suitable. Service, once a strong point, has suffered greatly. The location is still good, though: Calle 66 no. 521-B, near Calle 65.

Another budget hotel is the **Hotel Latino (6)** (tel. 992/1-4831), Calle 66 no. 505, between 61 and 63. Inside, all 25 rooms have private baths, hot and cold water, built-in headboards and bed tables, the only furniture in the rooms being the beds themselves and a chair. Nevertheless, it's comfortable. Singles are 360 to 550 pesos, doubles are 425 to 645 pesos, and air conditioning is included in the higher priced rooms. This makes the Latino the best choice for low budget readers who really want the comfort of a cooled room.

The **Hotel Reforma (7)**, Calle 59 no. 508, just off Calle 62 (tel. 992/1-7920), is another of those grand old establishments embellished with flowered tiles and tortured wrought-iron staircase. The high-ceilinged rooms, most with ceiling fans, open on two floors off the central patio where there are rubber plants in huge pots. Furnishings are old but well kept: singles with ceiling fan are 370 pesos; double, 610 pesos. Add 150 pesos for air conditioning. The few rooms upstairs in the back around a separate little court are among the nicest in the hotel. A small swimming pool is open for guests' use.

The **Hotel Lord (8)**, a block out of the zócalo on Calle 63 at no. 516 (tel. 992/3-9371), is a rather sterile place which somehow looks as if it should be a barracks, except that it's painted a cheerful yellow. Although it's a newish building, the rooms are arranged in several tiers around a central court which serves as a parking lot for guests. All rooms have screens and ceiling fans, and cost 700 pesos single, 825 pesos double. Rooms with air conditioning rent for

125 pesos more. Don't let the hotel's architecture fool you: it's a fine place to stay, with a very friendly management.

Near the Bus Station

The **Hotel Posada del Angel (1)** (tel. 992/3-2754), Calle 67 no. 535 between Calles 66 and 68, is a mere 1½ blocks from Merida's main bus station, and thus a good choice for late arrivals. It's a tidy, modern white place with red tile accents and semicircular windows, two floors, and 16 rooms—more a-building. The few rooms on the front are very noisy due to the bus thrumming, but most rooms are in the back. Make sure yours is. Prices are 440 pesos single, 550 pesos double, for a room with bath and fan. There's free parking, if you've come by car, not bus.

The Big Splurge

Although the Yucatán is unquestionably one of Mexico's great delights, there's no denying that it can be hot and even frustrating to travel here, now and then. When you get the feeling you owe yourself a bit of luxury, head for the **Hotel Casa del Balam (12)** (tel. 992/1-0600), Calle 60 no. 488, at the corner of Calle 57. Thoroughly modern, the Casa del Balam has used the best of colonial decorations to construct a clean and attractive decor—lots of tiles and tasteful wood furniture—and has added to the charm by liberal use of Yucatecan handicrafts such as hand-woven bedspreads and colorful wall hangings. The entire place is air-conditioned, of course, all except for the garden swimming pool, where the sun is hot and good for tanning. You will pay 1375 pesos single, 1650 pesos double.

Merida's old **Hotel Colón (20)** (tel 992/3-4355), with a spa thrown in. In the rear is a private yard with a garden and swimming pool open to the sky. Steambaths offer an exotic kind of relaxation, and you can enjoy the soporific vapors in either the colorful public baths or—if you choose your room right—in the privacy of your own bathroom. In a fully modernized and centrally air-conditioned portion of the hotel, 19 rooms have wall-to-wall carpeting and some have private steambaths for 800 pesos single, 1000 pesos double—these rooms are your best buy. The dozen newest rooms are pretty luxurious, with all the modern touches and individual air conditioning units for 1300 pesos single, 1500 pesos double. Remember that for these prices you're getting free use of the steambaths and the swimming pool. You'll find the Hotel Coló at Calle 62 no. 483, between Calles 57 and 59, not at all far from the town's main plaza.

READERS' HOTEL SELECTIONS: "If you want to stay for three or four days, we can recommend **Hotel del Mayab**, Calle 65 no. 50. We paid 289 pesos double and enjoyed the pool very much" (Rüdiger Heim and Marion Schemnitzer, Münster, West Germany). . . . "I recommend the **Hotel Marguerita**, Calle 66 no. 506 between Calles 61 and 63. They charge 190 pesos single, 260 pesos double, for a clean bed, fan, and shower; extra for air conditioning" (Paul Traves, England, and Nora Solis, U.S.A.)."

WHERE TO EAT: As with hotels, Merida is a budget-traveler's delight when it comes to mealtime. American, Mexican, and Yucatecan meals from snacks to banquets are all easy to find. Some of the best dining you'll experience during your Mexican trip will be had here in the capital of Yucatán, and it will cost you anywhere from 25 pesos for a sandwich to 500 pesos for a complete and embarrassingly bountiful repast.

Probably the most popular meeting place in town is the **Restaurant Express (3)**, on the small plaza at Calles 59 and 60. Here, hordes of townspeople—mainly men—sit and ogle the hours away, totally devoid of atmosphere, with all attention focused on the sidewalk or at least a newspaper. The menu is vast—lengua à la Mexicana (Mexican-style tongue), pollo pibil (the chef wraps and marinates the chicken in banana leaves before cooking), hauchinango milanesa (red snapper). Top off whatever you choose with pasta de guayaba con questo (guava paste with cheese). Or simply while away some time here with coffee. Plan to spend 135 pesos for breakfast, about 175 pesos for the set-price lunch, and 250 pesos for dinner. Open 6 a.m. to 1 a.m. every day.

I used to recommend a number of restaurants on Calle 62 just north of the main plaza, but in recent years the traffic noise and fumes (particularly from the buses) have become overwhelming. Nowadays one is much better off dining right on the plaza, at the **Restaurant Nicte-Ha**, for instance. Although very plain, the Nicte-Ha is pretty quiet and pollution free, and prices are low: tacos, hamburgers, even carne asada and chicken dishes cost only 75 to 125 pesos. As of this writing, they do not offer a set-price lunch, though.

Keyed to the local and Stateside health-food fans, **Los Balcones (3)** advertises itself as a *"restaurante naturista,"* offering a variety of healthful comestibles such as brown rice, or a brown rice paella with bean sprouts, or maybe you'd like a vegetarian burger. The *licuadora* (blender) is whirring constantly to make drinks concocted of yogurt, fruit, nuts, raisins, and honey—almost meals in themselves. Despite its purist leanings, Los Balcones also serves such unhealthful but tempting items as beer, wine, coffee, Coke, and tequila. The restaurant is entered at Calle 60 no. 497, between Calles 57 and 59—that's right, go straight through the shirt store and up the steps to the rear. Tune in on the plain but funky decor, listen to the soft recorded music, and try for one of the few tables set out on the minuscule balconies which overlook the Parque Hidalgo and the church. The daily set-price meal costs 90 pesos, and is served from 1 to 7 p.m.

As Yucatecan cuisine spreads throughout Mexico, the fame of poc-chuc pork goes with it. The dish, a delectable concoction of grilled pork, tomatoes, onions, *cilantro* (fresh coriander leaves), and salt, was created in Merida at **Los Almendros (21)**, Calle 59 no. 434, between Calles 50 and 52. Actually, the first Los Almendros was deep in the Maya hinterland, at Ticul, but the branch in Merida has become the favorite spot to sample local delicacies. The restaurant has several low-ceilinged rooms, and a high-ceilinged *palapa*, or thatch roof supported by tall stripped poles. Start with venison broth (sopa Mestiza), then have poc-chuc, pollo pibil, or pavo relleno negro (baked turkey with a black stuffing of ground pork, roasted peppers, and Yucatecan spices). You'll find lots of similarly exotic and delicious entrees, all for about 170 pesos—with descriptions in English! The daily special plate, always a good bargain, costs about 210 pesos and constitutes a full meal.

For a light lunch, try **Pop (14)** on Calle 57 between Calles 60 and 62, next to the university. The little place is clean, bright, and modern, and seems to be where the gilded youth of Merida have their afternoon snack. Apple pie, Bavarian fudge cake, the best hamburgers in town, and air conditioning are the attractions. Prices are okay: 65 pesos for a hamburger, 100 pesos for a fruit salad with ice cream. Highly recommended. "Pop," by the way, is the first month of the 18-month Maya calendar.

If you'd like to go semi-elegant on dinner, drop in at the **Restaurant La Carreta (27)**, Calle 62 no. 484 between Calles 57 and 59, more or less across the street from the Hotel Colón. The owners have decorated this small, bright restaurant with tiles, pieces of old carved woodwork (including a big old headboard with delightful primitive figurines, probably from a hacienda bedroom), and local crafts. Start your meal with fruit cocktail à la xtabentun ("shta-ben-TOON," the Yucatecan honey liqueur), then a local dish such as pork chops Yucatán style, or poc-chuc pork, or cochinita pibil (suckling pig), and perhaps coconut ice cream for dessert. With wine, tax, and service, you might pay 400 pesos for such a meal, and your wine (or beer) can be ordered by the glass or the bottle. Open every day for lunch and dinner.

For after-dinner ice cream or Mexican pastries and cakes, **Colón** sets out bent-wire café tables and chairs in the portico on the zócalo (Calle 61 side). Besides serving dessert at budget prices (30 pesos for ice cream, 25 pesos for cakes), it provides the best vantage point for people-watching in the late afternoon or evening. Try some of their exotic tropical fruit ice creams such as coconut or papaya. Open 8 a.m. to midnight daily. Try to pick a time of day when auto traffic (with its noise and smelly fumes) is not so heavy in the square.

For Breakfast

A good breakfast choice, particularly if it's hot, is the aforementioned **Pop**, which has set breakfasts priced at 55 pesos (for a continental breakfast), 85 pesos with two eggs, and 115 pesos with two eggs plus bacon or ham.

To make your own breakfast, feast your eyes (and later your appetite) on pastries and sweet rolls from the **Panificadora Montejo**, at the corner of Calles 62 and 63, which is the southwest corner of the main plaza. It's hard not to overeat with your eyes as you choose from a dozen or more delectable breakfast treats. With a hot drink a suitable light breakfast can be thrown together for about 40 pesos.

For those (like me) who simply cannot start a day without fresh orange juice, here's good news. In recent years juice bars with the name of **Jugos California** have sprouted up all over Mexico, including all over Merida. Three of these thirst-quenching establishments are on or just off the main plaza: one on Calle 62 near Calle 61, one on the Calle 63 side of the plaza, and another just across the corner from it on Calle 62! Demand is brisk, and prices are not high for what you get: a tall ice cream soda-glass of juice squeezed right before your eyes for 40 pesos.

Starvation Budget Restaurants

Cafeteria Erik's (11), Calle 62 no. 499A just off the main plaza, among the various other Erik's restaurants in town belonging to the chain, has the reputation for the best tortas—fried sandwiches stuffed with ham and cheese, turkey, roast pork—for 20 to 28 pesos apiece. A few of these are very filling. A pleasant wood-paneled place with tablecloths, it features smooth jazz in the background.

Totally different, **El Louvre (11)**, right next door to Erik's off the main plaza at Calles 61 and 62, is rather inaptly named unless you consider it a gallery of people. Open 24 hours a day, this big open place probably feeds everybody who comes to Merida at one time or another—chicle workers, laborers from the sisal fields, planters, and townspeople. Prices are low: sandwiches for 18 to 32 pesos, eggs motulenos (Yucatán style on a fried tortilla with fried beans and chopped ham) for 36 pesos, lots of combination plates for 60 pesos and less. Calle 62 between the main plaza and Calle 57 is a riot of such small, rock-bottom food shops offering everything from chalupas to chow mein. Starvation-budgeteers are sure to find things to fit the appetite and the wallet all along the street.

One of the least discovered restaurants in town is a tiny spot called the **Cafe Alameda (26)**, Calle 56 no. 518, between Calles 63 and 65, which looks like absolutely nothing at all. But this is a popular rendezvous for local aficionados of Lebanese cookery. The food is good, clean—and very cheap. A skewer of shish kebab, a dish called berengena (barbecued eggplant), and quebbe, a sort of oval-shaped Arab hamburger are all offered, as is cafta entomatada (kefta with tomatoes), for 58 to 99 pesos. Closes early, around 7:30 p.m.

Where the Students Eat

Merida is the home of the Yucatán's university, and thus of student throngs deep into plain living and high thinking. Living plainly does not mean badly, however, for the humble torta (sandwich) always provides tasty and nutritious fare at a rock-bottom price. The mecca for this time- and budget-saver is **Las Mil Tortas (23)**, on Calle 62 between Calles 57 and 55. Very small, this shop-of-a-thousand-sandwiches sports a long list of sandwiches priced from 22 to 35 pesos. The few small tables are often filled with the student crowd, but you can get your tortas and *refresco* (soft drink) to go, all for less than 50 pesos. By the way, Las Mil Tortas is branching out now, and you may see similar shops in other parts of the city. There's one on Calle 56 near Calle 57, around the corner from the Hotel Mucuy.

The Big Splurge

Housed in a long low, stone mansion at the corner of Calles 64 and 57 (tel. 1-2298) is **Alberto's Continental Patio (15)**, where several large rooms open off a plant-filled patio and an occasional guitarist strums. The big menu's in both Spanish and English, with Lebanese dishes, such as cabbage rolls and the popular shish kebab. Turkish coffee is served. Two enormously popular house specialties are red snapper stuffed with shrimp and a Lebanese plate (shish kebab, kafta, kibby, and other savories). You can play it safe (in terms of cost) and order the set-price dinner, from soup to nuts, for 450 pesos, or you can order à la carte for slightly more. Alberto's is open for lunch and dinner (after 6:30 p.m.) daily.

Another place to try if you're feeling wealthy is the **Restaurante Portico del Peregrino (14)**, Calle 57 no. 501, right next door to the ever-popular Pop and across the street from the university. The restaurant aims to recapture the 19th century in Mexico, and does this rather well. You enter through a little garden court—a good place to take a bench seat and wait for laggers in your party—then through a cross-topped gateway into another little courtyard set with tables and shaded by vines and trees. If the weather is too warm for outdoor dining, escape to the air-conditioned bliss of the two enclosed dining rooms which are well stocked with antique bevelled mirrors and elegant sideboards. Table settings are done with white cloths and decent crystal. For less than 440 pesos you can have soup, berenjenas al horno (baked eggplant with layers of chicken, cheese, and savory spices), a brochette of venison, or pollo pibil, plus rum raisin ice cream for dessert. The Peregrino is open for lunch and dinner, noon to 3 p.m. and 6 to 11 p.m., every day of the week.

READERS' RESTAURANT SELECTIONS: "The **Fontana Cafeteria**, at the corner of Calles 59 and 66, is connected with the new Del Gobernador Hotel. The restaurant rates #1 with me in Merida. The service is personable, the prices reasonable, and the food excellent. Moreover, the hotel-restaurant bar makes the best mixed drinks in town" (Luverne Olson, Rochester, Minn.). . . . "**Luigi's**, an Italian restaurant next door to the

Casa Bowen at Calle 65 and 66, is a nice change. No fluorescent lights, no plastic tablecloths, no typical menu! Very clean, very polite, good prices: spaghetti and big salads for under 100 pesos, fish dinners for twice that much. It's a nice treat for those of us who religiously follow a *$20-a-Day* budget!" (Jody Kosack, Miami, Fla.).

WHAT TO DO: Even if your major reason for coming to Merida is an interest in the Mayan ruins nearby, you'll want to spend some time on the more mundane sights of the city.

Take the short walk down Calle 60 to Calle 65, then turn left for a couple of blocks to the **market (M)**. As this is the henequen center of the world the market is full of excellent quality hammocks, Panama hats, and bags. Be careful when choosing a hammock as there are certain things to look for, and the prices vary considerably from vendor to vendor. First of all, make sure that the hammock is long enough; it should be at least as long as the person who is going to use it, *not* including the end strings. There are three sizes of hammocks: single, double, and matrimonial. This is where you must be careful, because the vendors will try to sell you a matrimonial which is actually only a double. To know for sure you should count the number of end strings: a single hammock should have no less than 50 pairs of end strings, a double about 100, and a matrimonial about 150 to 175. The prices range from 450 pesos for a single to 1000 pesos for a matrimonial, although I did manage to get a beautiful matrimonial for 775 pesos.

A shop which specializes in hammocks, to the extent of having a private air-conditioned "testing room" where you can try before you buy, is **La Poblana, S.A.**, at Calle 65 no. 492, in the market area. Run by the irrepressible, even zany Sr. William Razu C., the shop is a major exporter of hammocks to the U.S., hammocks which turn up in department stores and boutiques selling for $60. Sr. Razu does not mind at all if you take the time to check each item carefully—in fact, it's clear that he positively loves dealing with *gringoes*. Prices are as mentioned above; some bargaining is possible if you plan to buy more than one or two. Ropes and mosquito nets are also for sale.

For those marvelous Panama hats, try **La Casa de los Jipis**, a *sombrería* at Calle 56 no. 526 run by a phlegmatic señora who will fit you with a fine hat for about 525 pesos.

The regional museum, or **Museo de Arqueología**, is in the **Palacio Canton (16)** on the Paseo de Montejo, open from 8 a.m. to 8 p.m., Tuesday through Saturday, 8 a.m. to 2 p.m. Sunday; closed Monday. Admission is 10 pesos. As you enter the grand old palace, built by a general, you begin your tour on the right with prehistoric exhibits. From fossilized mastodon teeth, the displays take you down the ages through all of Yucatán's history, giving special attention to what the daily life of the inhabitants was actually like. You'll see how the Maya tied a board to a baby's skull so the forehead would slope (a sign of beauty), how they filed teeth to sharpen them (talk about painful dentistry!), and what sorts of jewelry they wore. Enlarged photos show archeological sites, and a modern sand painting provides a vivid portrait of Maya daily life.

While you're in this neighborhood, take a stroll up the wide boulevard, **Paseo de Montejo**, to see some of the elegant colonial houses. The **American Consulate (17)** (tel. 992/7-7011) is four blocks north of the Palacio Canton on Montejo at Calle 33 on the left.

The **Palacio de Gobierno**, on the north side of the main plaza, houses a collection of large murals painted between 1971 and 1974. The paintings are of Maya and Mexican history and are exhibited on the upper level. Over the stairway is one of the murals which shows the Maya spirit intertwined with ears of corn, "the sunbeams of the gods." Nearby is a painting of the benevolent mustached dictator, Lázaro Cárdenas, who in 1938 expropriated 17 oil companies and was hailed as the new Mexican liberator. At the south end is another room with more paintings, a cool place to rest your feet and to have a look over the zócalo below. You can see the paintings in the palace almost anytime.

Overlooking the main plaza on Calle 63 is **Casa de Montejo (18).** Originally built in 1546 by Don Francisco de Montejo, founder of Merida, and still the home of his descendants, this huge house was only recently opened to the public. The original structure was quite primitive, but over the years the family made it into a showplace, and you can still see the central garden, formal portraits of the family's beautiful women and handsome men, rich furniture, and white plaster angels carved baroquely over the doors and windows. Upon leaving, walk across the street for a good view of the massive entrance, topped by the coat-of-arms. Open 9 a.m. to 1:30 p.m.; closed Sunday. Admission is 10 pesos.

Take a look inside the massy rockpile which is Merida's **cathedral,** on the main plaza. Begun in 1561, it is said that stones from the conquered Maya city of Tiho were used in its construction. It was finished 37 years later, in 1598. Inside, to the left of the main altar, is a smaller shrine with a curious burnt cross, recovered from a church nearby which burned to the ground. Also, don't miss the chance to look in the curious side chapel (open 8 to 11 a.m. and 4:30 to 7 p.m.), which has a life-size diorama of the Last Supper. The Mexican Jesus is covered with prayer crosses brought by supplicants asking for intercession. Fascinating!

A visit to **La Casa de la Cultura,** Calle 63 no. 513 between Calles 64 and 66, allows you to see one of Merida's most nicely restored monasteries, and to shop for regional crafts at the same time. No obligation to buy, but you may enjoy looking at the pottery, blankets, and woven goods. There are also two galleries here: the last time I visited, one had an exhibition of photographs, the other held regional crafts and weaving.

The Casa de la Cultura has a fine and extremely inexpensive cafeteria, plus a nice bookstore, and a useful bulletin board listing cultural events, near the main entrance.

READERS' SHOPPING TIPS: "Panama hats, when bought, should be checked for the smoothness and fineness of the weave as well as flexibility and stitching around the edge and inside the crown of the hat. Little circles of straw ends face the inside of the hat, and the more the better. Truly superb hats are 1000 pesos or more, but you can get good ones for less" (July and Lewis Leibovich, Santa Rosa, Calif.).

READER'S SIGHTSEEING TIP: "The main industry of Yucatán is henequen. On the northern outskirts of Merida is a large **henequen processing plant** of Cordemex. They provide an interesting guided tour of the facility during which you can see the various twine and rope products being made. From downtown it is about a 240-peso taxi ride to the plant, or you can take one of the frequent city buses.

"Also, 14 kilometers north and 7 kilometers east of Merida are the ruins of **Dzibilchaltún.** It's less well known than Uxmal or Chichén-Itzá, but since 1956 some buildings have been restored near the large cenote. The trip by car takes a half hour, and one can easily visit the ruins in a half day. Small admission charge" (Luverne Olson, Rochester, Minn.).

A Side Trip to Progreso

Want to zoom out to Progreso for a day? There's a good beach, not touristy but very Mexican, a fantastically long *muelle* (MUWEY-yeh, or pier) that shoots out into the bay to reach water deep enough for ocean-going ships, and lots of little seafood restaurants.

To get there, go to the special Progreso bus station on Calle 62 at no. 524, between Calles 65 and 67. Buses leave every five or ten minutes during the day, starting at 5 a.m. The trip takes 45 minutes.

Once in Progreso, Calle 19 runs along the beach. The bus station is about four blocks south of this street. The beach seems endless, and is crowded with coconut palms (and on weekends, with Mexican families). Calle 30 has lots of little seafood restaurants and souvenir shops. The **Restaurant Carabela**, for instance, will serve you a huge conch cocktail for 150 pesos, a fish platter for 250 pesos, shrimp for just a bit more.

MERIDA NIGHTLIFE: There are band concerts every Sunday at 9 p.m. in the zócalo. Every Thursday in **Santa Lucia Park (19)**, on the corner of Calles 60 and 55, you can hear some festive music and serenades by different mariachis. They begin at 9 p.m. and stop when their enthusiasm turns to thirst. Speaking of thirst, for a pre- or post-prandial drink, visit the very attractive bar of the **Hotel Merida**, Calle 60 no. 491, corner of Calle 57 (tel. 1-4456), or the bar of the new **Hotel Maria del Carmen**, Calle 68, between Calles 63 and 65. The former used to have the atmosphere of a gothic novel, but has been glazed with the chic of the Balsa hotel chain in recent years. The latter is a dark modern place where you ooze into a low chair and sip your drink off a low table floating in thick carpeting. Both have music during the evening from cocktail hour on . . . and on . . . until the wee hours.

A typical Yucatán club, **Tulipanes**, Calle 43 in Colonia Industrial, offers a nice but casual atmosphere. The club has a thatched roof and lots of open-air space. Dancing is possible, and shows fill the hours in between, including typical Yucatecan dancers. Below the club is a cenote or underground reservoir, by which they stage a Maya sacrificial dance—very impressive. The cover charge is 275 pesos, but this experience is well worth the cost.

MISCELLANEOUS: The **Tourist Office** (tel. 922/3-0123) is inconveniently located out of town at Avenida Itzaes 490 on the corner of Calle 59 (but there is a little booth in the arcade of the Palacio de Gobierno, on the main plaza, where you may get some help). The hours are 9 a.m. to 2 p.m. and 5 to 7 p.m. Monday to Friday, 9 a.m. to 1 p.m. on Saturday, and 9 a.m. to noon on Sunday. If you are driving from Campeche the office is on the main road (Highway 180, which becomes Avenida Itzaes) just after the large zoo and **Parque Centenario** on the right. If you are coming from town take the C. Centenario bus which leaves from the corner of Calle 61 on Calle 64. This bus makes the circuit from town to the Centenario Park and back again, so the same bus can be caught from in front of the park on Calle 59 for your return trip.

The AeroMéxico office is at Paseo de Montejo 460 (tel. 7-9000), or you can go to **AeroExpress** at Calle 58 no. 485 (tel. 1-7975). **Mexicana's** offices are at Paseo de Montejo and Calle 56-A no. 493 (tel. 1-0621 or 3-0508), or at Calle 58 no. 500 (tel. 3-2802 or 3-1031).

For the **post office (22)**, go to the corner of Calles 65 and 56. . . . A popular way to see the ruins at Chichén-Itzá and Uxmal is to rent a car for a few days to do the circuit. For sample rates, see Chapter XVI, "Car Rentals." **National Car Rental** is at Calle 60 no. 481 (tel. 1-0808), **Hertz** is at Calle 55 no. 479 (tel. 1-9333 or 1-8020) and at several of the snazzy hotels; a local outfit is **Mayaways Rent a Car** in the lobby of the Hotel Paseo de Montejo (tel. 1-9033).

(See also the Reader's Suggestion below.) Much more reasonable are the **daily tours** to both sites run by various companies. An all-day tour to either site, including bilingual guide, lunch, admission, and transportation to and from the site, should cost about 1200 pesos. Picking a good tour company is tricky, so I'd suggest asking other guests or the manager of your hotel for a recommendation; or go to one of the expensive hotels and see what they recommend for their guests.

The **American Consulate (17)**, as noted a few paragraphs above, is at Paseo de Montejo no. 453 (tel. 992/7-7011); it's open for business Monday through Friday from 8:30 a.m. to 1 p.m. and 2 to 5:30 p.m.

Tintorería Escalante (tel. 1-3567), Calle 56 no. 469, between Calles 55 and 53, will do your laundry quickly and inexpensively. This is not a coin-op, but an honest-to-goodness laundry that's inexpensive.

READER'S SUGGESTION—RENTAL CARS: "I rented a nice little Volkswagen Beetle from **Mexico Rent-A-Car** (tel. 992/1-7840), Calle 60 no. 495, in the lobby of the little Hotel del Parque. The man was so nice, and the price so much lower than the big firms' prices, that I came out way ahead. It seems to be a small, family operation with only a few cars. I was lucky because I got my car the same day, but it's probably a good idea to reserve a car days in advance if you can. Total cost for a four-day, 1100-kilometer rental—gas included—was 6500 pesos, or about $32.50 a day, which we split among three friends" (Jody Kosack, Miami, Fla.).

GETTING TO AND FROM MERIDA: Lots of choices are available to this popular destination.

By Bus

Merida's modern Union de Camioneros de Yucatán bus terminal on Calle 69 between Calles 68 and 70 handles most of the city's buses, first and second class. The ticket windows are pasted thick with exotic Mayan village names, there is a little air-conditioned cafeteria (open 5 a.m. to midnight), telephones, a telegraph office, even a Fotomat where you can take your own picture. You must pay a small fee to enter the boarding area.

Other services you might find useful are a shoeshine stand, a travel agency, a bank (9 a.m. to 1 p.m. only, weekdays), newsstands, and snack stands.

The special round-trip bus to Chichén-Itzá (2½ hours, one way) departs each morning at 8:30, and returns from Chichén at 3 p.m.

To Puerto Juarez and Cancún, buses depart every two hours or so, sometimes even more frequently; the trip takes between five and six hours.

Buses to Uxmal depart six times a day, with five return trips. The sound-and-light bus departs late each afternoon, and returns after the show. The one-way journey takes about an hour. For a while Transportes del Sur operated a special excursion bus which took passengers to Uxmal, Kabah, Sayil, Xlapak, and Labná, with time to explore each site, returning to Merida in the evening. Service has been suspended (as of this writing), but if they decide to start it up again, you'll be able to save hundreds and hundreds of pesos over the price of a comparable guided tour sold by a travel agency.

To Puerto Morelos there are three buses a day, four a day to Playa del Carmen (ferry for Cozumel), and six per day to Chetumal, on the border with Belize. There's also service to Labná, Sayil, and Kabah.

To Mayapán: Are you planning to go to the ancient Maya capital of Mayapán? The local trundle-bus leaves from a bus stop on Calle 56 between Calles 59 and 61. It'll be a slow trip.

By Train

See Veracruz and Palenque sections for specifics on trains coming to Merida; trains leave Merida's railroad station at the corner of Calles 55 and 48 daily at 8 p.m. for the junction with the main line at Coatzacoalcos. Rail service east of the Isthmus of Tehuantepec—and that includes Yucatán—is not very good in any way.

By Air

There are seven to eight flights daily between Merida and Mexico City, and daily flights to Cancún, Isla Mujeres, Cozumel, and Campeche. You can also fly directly to Acapulco, Veracruz, Villahermosa, and Monterrey. Eastern runs to and from Miami; AeroMéxico and Mexicana have one to two daily flights between Merida and Los Angeles. Taxis and mini buses are expensive, running about 170 pesos per person if you fill a cab and split the fare. If you're willing to wait a bit and suffer some bumps and bangs, turn right as you leave the air terminal, look for the sign that says "Autobuses Urbanos," and pick up a no. 79 "Aviación" bus to the center of town (corner of Calles 60 and 67); if your destination is the bus terminal, alight from the ancient machine at the corner of Calles 66 and 69.

See above under "Miscellaneous" for the addresses and telephone numbers of the two Mexican air carriers.

2. Uxmal and Nearby Ruins

The closest impressive ruins to Merida are those at Uxmal ("oosh-MAHL"), about 80 kilometers (50 miles) to the south. Uxmal and Chichén-Itzá (see below) are the two must-not-miss sites in Yucatán, but there are many smaller sites of beauty and significance. Depending on how you travel, you may be able to visit some of these other sites on your way to Uxmal.

Want the full rundown? First there's Mayapán, the ancient Maya capital city, badly ruined now but in a lush setting. It's difficult to reach, but thrilling to consider yourself walking among the ruins of the great Maya capital. Then there's Uxmal, with several of the most beautiful and awe-inspiring buildings ever constructed by man. Then 27 kilometers (17 miles) southeast of Uxmal is Kabah, with a unique palace, several other grand buildings, and a decorative style very different from that at Uxmal. From Kabah it's only a few kilometers to Sayil, with its immense palace reminiscent of Minoan structures. Xlapak (shla-PAHK) is almost walking distance (through the jungle) from Sayil, and Labná just a bit farther east. A short drive east from Labná brings you to the caves of Loltun. Backtrack to the main road (Highway 180) and you can head west to spend the night in Campeche.

Those with only a little time and/or money will have to limit themselves to seeing Uxmal on a day-trip by bus (see above, "Getting To and From Merida" for details). The ideal but more expensive way to tour the ruined cities south of Merida is to rent a car, plan to stay the night in a fairly expensive hotel at Uxmal (that's all there is), and allow two full days to sightseeing before hitting Campeche or returning to Merida, or driving on toward Tulum and Cancún. How interested are you in Mayan archeology? If you enjoy it as much as I do, then find some friends to share expenses, rent a car in Merida, ignore your daily hotel budget in Uxmal, and enjoy yourself. You can save money on hotels at Chichén, where you'll find an assortment of inexpensive and moderate hostelries. At Uxmal, there's no such choice. Figure $30 to $40 per day for the car, all in.

Another way to do it is to ignore Mayapán, get an early start in your rental car, and head south on Highway 180 directly to Uxmal. Spend the morning there, and the afternoon at Kabah, Sayil, Xlapak, and Labná, and then head on to find an inexpensive hotel in Campeche, or return to Merida. This tour would be about 250 kilometers (155 miles) round trip.

Here, then, is a stone-by-stone description of the ruined Maya cities south of Merida, starting with Mayapán.

MAYAPÁN: Founded by the semilegendary Quetzalcoatl (Kukulcán in Maya) in about 1007, Mayapán ranked in importance with Chichén-Itzá and Uxmal. It was a vast city, and for almost two centuries it was the capital of a Maya confederation of city-states which included Chichén and Uxmal. But before the year 1200 the rulers of Mayapán put an end to the confederation by attacking and conquering Chichén, and by forcing the rulers of Uxmal to live as vassals in Mayapán. For almost 250 years Mayapán was the center of power in Yucatán.

You can take a village bus to the Ruinas de Mayapán (not to be confused with the village of Mayapán, about twice as far from Merida; see above, "Getting To and From Merida," for details). But the easiest way is to drive. Ask directions frequently—it's very easy to take wrong turns or to get onto unmarked roads by mistake.

Head out of Merida toward Kanasin and **Acanceh** ("ah-kahn-KEH"), about 20 kilometers. In Acanceh there's a pyramid overlooking the main square. Turn right in the main square (around that statue of a smiling deer) and head for Tecoh (9 kilometers) and Telchaquillo (11 kilometers). This route takes you past several old Yucatecan haciendas, each complete with its big house, chapel, factory with smokestack, and workers' houses. Shortly after the village of Telchaquillo, a beat-up sign on the right-hand side of the road will point to the entrance of the ruins, on the right.

A hundred yards in from the road, after passing the guards' hut, are the remains of Mayapán. The main pyramid is ruined but still lofty and impressive. Next to it is a large cenote (natural limestone cavern, used as a well), now full of trees, bushes, and banana plants. A small temple with columns and a fine high-relief mask of Tlaloc, the hook-nosed rain god, are beside the cenote. Other small temples, including El Caracol, with its circular tower, are in the nearby jungle, reached by paths.

These piles of stones, though impressive, give one no idea of what Mayapán must have been like in its heyday. Supplied with water from 20 cenotes, it had over 3000 buildings in its enclosed boundaries of several square miles. Today, all is covered in dense, limitless jungle.

Mrs. Magdalena Canché, who you may meet as you enter the ruins, will sell you the requisite admission ticket for a few pesos, and help you with any bits of information you may need.

Heading onward, continue along the main road to Tekit (8 kilometers), turn right and go to Mama (7 kilometers), turn right again for Chapab (13 kilometers), and finally you'll reach **Ticul** (10 kilometers), the largest town in the region. Ticul has banks, restaurants, gas stations, and shops.

It's 22 kilometers (14 miles) from Ticul to Muna. At Muna, turn left and head south on Highway 180 to Uxmal, 16 kilometers away.

UXMAL: Although the ruins of Uxmal are visible from the highway, the impressiveness of this site will not strike you until you enter the archeological zone and walk around. Coming from the north along Highway 180, you'll pass the three hotels—all expensive—before you reach the ruins proper. Here's what to expect.

Where to Stay and Eat

Unlike Chichén-Itzá, which has several classes of hotels from which to choose, Uxmal has only one: comfortable, but expensive. But at Uxmal, "expensive" doesn't mean prices like at the Ritz, so you should be able to absorb a night's stay in your budget without too much pain.

Each of these hotels is willing to offer you room-with-meals plans, and you should look into them. Buying your dinner and breakfast—and perhaps even lunch—with your room in a package will ultimately save you money, because there's nowhere to eat but at the three hotels. Buying the meals separately adds up to more than buying the package. For savings, pack a box lunch in Merida and bring it along.

My favorite of the hotels here is the oldest one, the **Hotel Hacienda Uxmal** (for reservations, contact Merida Travel Service in the Hotel Casa del Balam, Calle 60 no. 488; tel. 992/1-9212). Right on the highway across from the ruins, the Hacienda Uxmal was built as the headquarters for the archeological staff years ago. Rooms are large and airy, with equally large bathrooms, screens on the windows, ceiling fans, and blocky, substantial furniture. The rambling building groups many rooms around a central garden courtyard complete with fine swimming pool and bar. A dining room and gift shop fill out the spare rooms. Singles cost 1320 pesos; doubles are 1540 pesos; huge triple rooms are 1870 pesos. For dinner and breakfast, add 500 pesos per person to these prices. You should definitely take the meal package here, as dinner alone costs almost 500 pesos if you buy it separately. In effect, you get a full breakfast for no extra charge when you take the meal plan. It's a five-minute walk to the ruins from the hotel. Check-out time is 2 p.m., so you can spend the morning at the ruins and take a cooling dip (you'll need it!) before you check out and head out on the road again.

Even closer to the ruins is the **Villa Arqueológica** (no phone)—the hotel driveway starts at the ruins parking lot. A Club Med operation, the Villa Arqueológica has a swimming pool, tennis court, library, audio-visual show on the ruins in English, French, and Spanish, and 40 air-conditioned rooms that are fully modern. The layout is posh and tasteful—it's the "designer" version of the Hacienda Uxmal. Room prices here are slightly higher than at the Hacienda Uxmal.

Farther out, north of the ruins several kilometers on the highway is the **Hotel Misión Uxmal**, a new and modern 40-room hotel which you can't help but notice as you drive. Same services here: restaurant, bar, pool, etc. The comfortable, air-conditioned rooms sell for slightly more than those at the Hacienda Uxmal.

You can't even buy so much as a sandwich at the ruins proper, and so for sustenance you must trek to one of the two hotels within walking distance. The Hacienda Uxmal has a little lunchroom and bar called the **Posada Uxmal, Cafe-Bar Nicte-Ha,** in a building right across the highway from the turnoff to the ruins. A ham-and-cheese sandwich costs about 100 pesos, a fruit salad only slightly less. This is a lot for what you get, but it's less to spend than the 300 pesos or so you'd spend on the set-price full lunch in the hotel. The café-bar is open from 12:30 p.m. to 7 p.m.

Seeing the Ruins

The ruins of Uxmal are open from 8 a.m. to 5 p.m. every day. Admission is 15 pesos (parking costs 10 pesos); on Sunday and holidays admission is 10 pesos.

A sound-and-light show is staged each evening, in Spanish (50 pesos) at 8 p.m., and in English (200 pesos) at 9 p.m. The special sound-and-light bus from Merida only stays for the Spanish show. If you stay for the English, you've got to find your own ride back to Merida. These arrangements do a lot to discourage attendance at the English-language show.

The Pyramid of the Magician: As you enter the ruins, you'll be confronted with Uxmal's dominant building, the Pyramid of the Magician. Legend has it that a mystical dwarf who had hatched from an egg built this pyramid in one night, which is where it gets it name. Actually, there are several temples underneath the one you see. It was common practice for the Maya to build new structures atop old ones, even before the old structures were ruined.

The pyramid is unique because of its oval shape, its height and steepness (wait till you see the steps on the other side!), and its odd doorway. The doorway is on the opposite (west) side near the top, and is actually a remnant of the fourth temple built on this site (what you see today is the fifth). In contrast to the clean, simple style of the rest of the pyramid, the doorway is in Chenes style, with elaborate decoration featuring stylized masks of the rain god Chac. In fact, the doorway is a huge Chac mask, with the door as mouth.

The View from the Top: It's a tiring and even dangerous climb, but what a view! You're now in an ideal position to survey the rest of Uxmal. Next to the Pyramid of the Magician, to the west, is the Nunnery Quadrangle, so called because it resembles a monastery or convent. To the left (south) of the Nunnery is the ruined ball court, and south of that are several large complexes. The biggest building, with a 320-foot-long facade, is called the Governor's Palace. Near it is the small House of the Turtles. Behind the Governor's Palace is the Great Pyramid, only partly restored, and beyond that the Dovecote, a palace with a lacy roofcomb that looks as though it'd be a perfect apartment complex for pigeons.

These are the main structures you'll notice from atop the Pyramid of the Magician, but there are others. For instance, the small ruined pyramid directly south is called the Pyramid of the Old Woman, which may be the oldest building at Uxmal. Due west of the pyramid is the Cemetery Complex, a temple with roofcomb that's pretty ruined. There's also a Northern Group, mostly covered with jungle and in ruins.

Uxmal is special among Maya sites because of the broad terraces or platforms constructed to support the building complexes—look closely, and you'll see that the Governor's Palace is not on a hill or rise, but on a huge square terrace, as is the Nunnery Quadrangle.

Now that you've got your breath, prepare for the climb down. If you came up the east side, try going down the west.

The Nunnery: No nuns lived here. It's more likely this was a military academy or a training school for princes, who may have lived in the 70-odd rooms. The buildings were constructed at different times: the northern one was first, then the southern one, then east, then west. The western building has the most richly decorated facade, with interesting motifs of intertwined snakes. Masks of the rain god Chac, with his hooked nose, are everywhere. The richness of the geometric patterns on the facades is one of the outstanding features of Uxmal.

As you head toward the archway out of the quadrangle to the south, notice that above each doorway in the south building is a motif showing a Maya cottage, or *na*, looking just like you see them today. All of this wonderful decoration has been restored, of course—it didn't look this good when the archeologists discovered it.

The Ball court: The ball court is ruined, and not so impressive. Keep it in mind, and compare it to the magnificent restored court at Chichén-Itzá.

The Turtle House: Up on the terrace south of the ball court is a little temple decorated with colonnade motif on the facade, and a border of turtles. It's small, but simple and harmonious—one of the gems of Uxmal.

The Governor's Palace: This is Uxmal's masterwork, an imposing edifice with a huge mural facade richly decorated in mosaic designs of the Puuc style. "Puuc" means "hilly country" and Uxmal has many examples of this rich decoration. The Puuc hills, which you passed over coming from Merida, are the Mayan "Alps," a staggering 350 feet high! Mayan towns near the hills favored this style of geometric patterns and masks of Chac, giving the style its name.

The Governor's Palace may have been just that: the administrative center of the Xiú principality, which included the region around Uxmal. The Xiú rulers later conquered the emperors at Mayapán, and became supreme in the region. The fall of Mayapán allowed Yucatán to split up into smaller principalities. It was just great for the conquistadores, who arrived less than a century after the fall of Mayapán and mopped up the principalities one by one. The great princes of Xiú, as it turns out, did the Maya people no favor by breaking up the hegemony of Mayapán.

Before you leave the Governor's Palace, note the elaborate stylized headdress patterned in stone over the central doorway.

The Great Pyramid: A massive structure partially restored, it has interesting motifs of birds, probably macaws, on its facade, as well as a huge mask—the Uxmalians went in for masks in a big way. The view from the top is wonderful.

The Dovecote: It wasn't built to house doves, but it could well do the job in its lacy roofcomb. The building is remarkable in that roofcombs weren't a common feature of temples in the Puuc hills, although you will see one (of a very different style) on El Mirador at Sayil if you visit that site.

Leaving Uxmal

It can give you quite a thrill to ponder what Uxmal must have been like in its heyday: great lords and ladies clad in white embroidered robes and feathered headdresses moving here and there; market day, when the common people would come from their thatched huts and gather nearby in a tumultuous scene of barter and brouhaha. Uxmal flourished in the Late Classical period, about A.D. 600 to 900, and then became subject to the Xiú princes (who may have come from the Valley of Mexico) after the year 1000. Four and a half centuries later, the Xiú conquered Mayapán (1440s). The conquistadores moved in shortly after, ending forever the glories of Mayan cultural independence.

If you're off to Kabah, head southwest on Highway 180 to Santa Elena (14 kilometers), then south to Kabah (13 kilometers).

KABAH: The ancient city of Kabah sits astride the highway, but you turn left into the parking lot. Buy your ticket (8 a.m. to 5 p.m. daily), 5 pesos to get in, the same to park your car.

The most outstanding building at Kabah is the one you notice first: that huge palace up on a terrace. It's called the Palace of Masks, or **Codz Poop** ("rolled-up mat") from a motif in its decoration. Its outstanding feature is the facade, completely covered in masks of the hook-nosed rain god Chac. All those eyes, hooked noses, and grimacing mouths, used as a repeated pattern on a huge facade, have an incredible effect. There's nothing like this facade in all of Maya architecture.

Once you've seen the Palace of Masks, you've seen the best of Kabah. But you should take a quick look at the other buildings, and follow the paths into the jungle, for a look at the **Tercera Casa** ("Third House"), or "Las Columnas." This temple has fine colonnaded facades on both front and, even better, back.

Across the highway, you'll pass a conical mound which was once the **Great Temple**, or Teocalli, and past it a great arch. This triumphal arch was much wider at one time, and may have been a monumental gate into the city. For all their architectural achievements, the Maya never discovered the principle of the true arch made of many small fitted stones and a keystone. Instead, they used this corbelled arch, which is simply two flat stones leaned at an angle against one another. Compare this ruined arch to the one at Labná, which is in much better shape.

SAYIL: Just short of five kilometers south of Kabah is the turnoff (left, east) to Sayil, Xlapak, Labná, Loltun, and Oxkutzcab. Four kilometers along this road are the ruins of Sayil, just off the road. The ruins are open from 8 a.m. to 5 p.m., and the admission cost is 10 pesos, half price on Sunday and holidays. Sayil is famous for **El Palacio**, the tremendous hundred-room palace which is a masterpiece of Mayan architecture. The rows and rows of columns and colonettes give the building a Minoan appearance. There are some nice decorative details, but for the most part El Palacio impresses one by its grandeur and simplicity.

Off in the jungle past El Palacio is **El Mirador,** a small temple with a slotted roofcomb, an odd structure. Beyond El Mirador, a crude stele has a phallic idol carved on it, with greatly exaggerated proportions. The Maya didn't normally go in for this sort of thing, and this crude sculpture may well be unique.

Climb to the top of El Palacio if the heat is not too intense. The breeze up here is cooling, and the view of the Puuc hills delightful. Sometimes it's difficult to tell which are hills and which are unrestored pyramids, as little temples and galleries peep out at unlikely places from the jungle foliage. That large circular basin on the ground below the palace is a catch basin for a cistern. This region has no natural cenotes (wells) to catch rainwater, so the natives had to make their own.

XLAPAK: Back on the road, it's 5½ kilometers to Xlapak ("shla-PAHK"), a small site with one building. The Palace at Xlapak bears the inevitable rain god masks. If you do this tour of the ruins in the summer rainy season, it may be at this point that Chac responds to your earnest pleas for a break from the heat. When I was there, Chac let loose a downpour. It soaked through. Cool, though.

LABNÁ: Labná is only three kilometers past Xlapak, open 8 a.m. to 5 p.m. (no charge). The first thing you should look at here is the monumental arch.

CAMPECHE

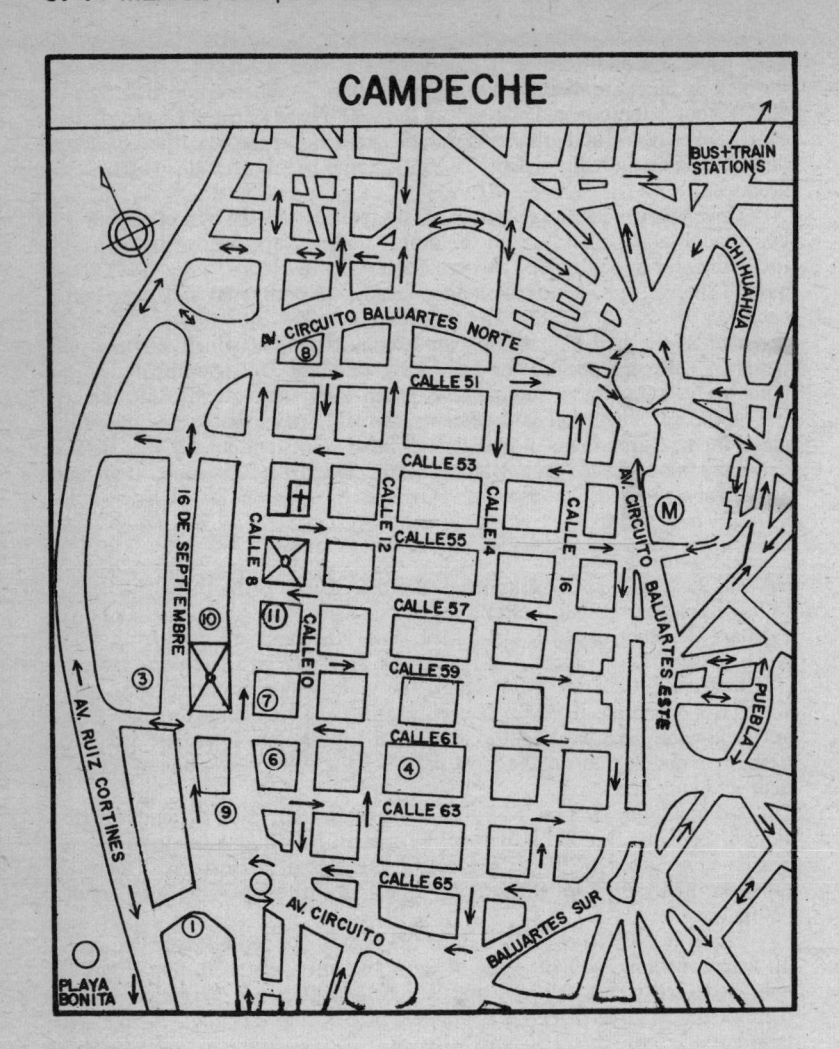

Good old Chac takes his place on the corners of one facade, and stylized Mayan huts are fashioned in stone above the doorways. El Mirador, or **El Castillo** as it is also called, stands near the arch, with its roofcomb towering above it.

The **Palacio** at Labná is much like the one at Sayil: huge, restrained, monumental. It's not in quite as good shape as that at Sayil, but still impressive. In the decoration, find the enormous mask of Chac over a doorway, and also the highly stylized serpent's mouth, out of which pops a human head.

LOLTUN: About 30 kilometers (18½ miles) past Labná on the way to Oxkutzcab (that's "oaks-kootz-KAHB") are the caverns of Loltun, on the left-hand side of the road. Besides being huge, the caves are important as an archeological site. Down in the depths you can see *chaltunes* (cisterns), carved glyphs, and paintings by Maya artists. You must take a tour here. The schedule says that tours are conducted at 9:30 a.m., 11:30 a.m., and 1:30 p.m., but in fact it depends on how many people are around.

HEADING NORTH, SOUTH, EAST, WEST: From Loltun, you can drive the few kilometers to Oxkutzcab, and from there north on Highway 184 to Ticul, Muna, and Merida (100 kilometers, 62 miles). Or you can head back past Sayil, then south on Highway 180 to Campeche. Those intrepid souls out to do a circuit of the northern peninsula can strike out southeast toward Tekax, Tzucacab, and Polguc on Highway 184. After about 200 kilometers (124 miles) you'll arrive in the town of Felipe Carrillo Puerto, where there are restaurants, hotels, banks, and gas stations. Carrillo Puerto thus serves as your jumping-off point for the tour north to Tulum, Xel-ha, Cozumel, and Cancún. See below for more information.

For the purposes of this book, let's assume you've decided to spend a night in the old walled city of Campeche, now known as a center of the Gulf of Mexico seafood trade. From Loltun or Uxmal, it's about 175 kilometers (109 miles) to Campeche.

3. Campeche

Campeche (pop. 100,000), capital of the state bearing the same name, is a pleasant coastal town with a smooth, leisurely pace. Founded by Cordoba in 1517 and officially claimed for the Spanish crown by the soldier Francisco de Montejo the Elder in 1531, Campeche was hounded for years by pirates who plied the gulf. To protect themselves, the townspeople finally built a wall around the city in the late 1600s. Ten or eleven remnants of these walls, called *baluartes* ("bulwarks"), are among the city's proudest links with the past. The town's modern monuments are on the shore near the big Hotel Baluartes: the new Town Hall with its auditorium (which looks like a square clam) next door, a municipal park, and the Tourism Office between the Town Hall and the water. Most of this modern construction is of the "you can't get there from here" school: stairways end in walls or precipitous drops; the sunken city park has no convenient entrance (you always find yourself jumping the grassy "moat"); and the ramp curves up to a "Turismo" sign, although in fact the **Tourism Office (1)** is in the bulwark *underneath* the ramp, and you must enter by jumping down from the path at the beginning of the ramp and walking around to the right! Once you get there, the staff is extremely helpful.

FINDING AN ADDRESS: Unlike most towns in Mexico, Campeche boasts a systematic street-naming plan whereby streets which run roughly north to south have even numbers, and those running east to west have odd numbers. Thus along Calle 14 you will cross in succession Calles 51, 53, 55, 57, etc., and if you turn right off Calle 14 onto Calle 51 you will cross Calles 12, 10, 8, etc., in your course down 51. Not to confuse you further, but the streets are numbered so that numbers ascend toward the south and west. After you get downtown and walk around for five minutes you'll have the system down pat. Bus, train, and airport terminals are all a good distance from downtown, and as Campeche is hardly a good town to negotiate by bus, I would recommend a taxi to get you from the various depots to the center.

WHERE TO STAY AND EAT: Campeche now has a Hotel El Presidente that siphons off the carriage trade from the older and once-elegant **Hotel Baluartes (3)** (tel. 981/6-3911), Avenida Ruíz Cortines. So you can almost afford to stay at this modern, waffle-fronted hotel overlooking the water, as rooms cost 1100 pesos single, 1250 to 1350 pesos double (the higher prices are for rooms with air conditioning). In the Baluartes's restaurant, you can enjoy a full-course dinner for 500 pesos.

More realistically, and still with air conditioning, try the **Hotel Lopez (4)**, Calle 12 no. 189, between Calles 61 and 63 (tel. 981/6-2527), where some of the staff speaks English and the rest are adept at reading your mind. The lobby is warmed by bright paint and strawberry-patterned tiles, and the three floors (no elevator) of 39 rooms circle a long, plant-filled center courtyard. The rooms themselves, all with telephones and showers, are clean and neat, and quite comfortable. Rates at the Lopez: singles are 650 pesos and doubles are 900 pesos, but this includes air conditioning. There are still a few rooms without cooled air which are 100 pesos cheaper.

The **Hotel America**, Calle 10 between Calles 59 and 60, is a three-story colonial house now turned into a hotel. All the rooms come with bath, and overlook a central, marble-paved courtyard complete with wishing well. Nice modern rocking chairs (Campechanos are great sitters and rockers) add to the courtyard's attraction. A double here costs only 770 pesos.

At the **Hotel Castelmar (6)**, Calle 61 no. 2, between Calles 8 and 10 (tel. 981/6-2186), you fully expect to find a pitcher and washbowl in each of the 20 rooms. You don't, but you do find very high ceilings, tiled walls, elderly plumbing, and the kind of furniture that might have been drafted into service from somebody's attic. For all that, the Castelmar is somehow quaintly charming, and its rates are a minimal 200 pesos single, 400 pesos double, with fan.

The best all-round restaurant choice in Campeche is the **Restaurant Miramar (7)**, Calles 8 and 61, very near the town hall building. The decor is simple but pleasant, with lots of light-colored stone and some dark wood and ironwork. The menu offers typical Campeche seafood dishes: fried, breaded shrimp for 210 pesos (ask for "camarones empanizadas"), ceviche or fish and vegetable cocktail for 145 pesos, arroz con calamares (squid and rice) for slightly more, and for dessert queso napolitana, a sort of very rich, thick flan.

The **Restaurant del Parque (11)**, overlooking the zócalo on Calle 57, is a beautifully white, cool, open place with a cozy air about it, due in part to use of incandescent (nòt fluorescent) lighting. Stereo music, caned chairs, and a tempting menu add to the attractions. Have soup, a fish dinner, and dessert for about 450 pesos; or dine for less on enchiladas or crêpes. Shrimp platters are available, but they'll run your meal tab up a hundred pesos or so.

WHAT TO DO: Besides visiting the museums, the most enjoyable pastime is to walk around the streets (especially Calles 55, 57, and 59), for the structures are in typical Mexican-colonial style. A glance through the large doorways will give you a glimpse into the colonial past with high-beamed ceilings, Moorish stone arches, interior courtyards, and lots and lots of peeling paint. Even the most luxurious establishment seems to give in to the humidity and accept the flaking walls.

As mentioned in the introduction, there are about ten bulwarks. The most interesting is the **San Carlos (9)**, now a library but originally it served as a lighthouse, watchtower, and church. You can take a look inside Monday through Friday from 9 a.m. to noon and 5 to 6 p.m. It's on the corner of Calles 10 and 63.

The **Historical Museum (10)**, on the ocean side of the zócalo, is small with only five rooms, but the displays are good. You enter via a small garden with several Maya stelae and the sacrificial Toltec statute of Chacmool. The admission fee is 6 pesos; hours of operation are Tuesday through Saturday from 9 a.m. to 2 p.m. and 3 to 8 p.m., on Sunday from 9 a.m. to 1 p.m.; closed Monday.

Campeche's history is one of swashbuckling romance, to say the least, and the Historical Museum will bring it all back to you. An exquisite ebony figurehead, made in Florence in the 1500s to grace the prow of a ship; old maps to speed the navigators on their way; weapons with which to fend off pirates (or to become a pirate); fine art objects in ebony and ivory; even Crusaders' swords shipped along for good luck and military blessing—this is the place to get the feel for colonial Campeche.

For colonial glitter with a touch of modern art, drop in at the **Museo de Campeche,** entered from Calle 10 at the corner with Calle 63. The museum is actually the nicely restored Templo de San José (1640), a fine place in which to display traveling exhibits of Mexican art. I saw one made up of the works of Mexican painter Joaquin Clausell (died 1935). The museum is free to all, open from 10 a.m. to 1 p.m. and 5 to 9 p.m. daily.

For Campeche's ancient lore, you must hop a "Playa Bonita" no. 55 bus from the center of town, and head out to the **Baluarte de San Miguel,** a little fortress on a hill on the left-hand side about half a mile out. In the Baluarte is the state's Archeological Museum, open daily from 9 a.m. to 2 p.m. and 3 to 8 p.m., charging 10 pesos to enter. Artifacts from Mexico's ancient history fill the exhibit rooms, including Olmec, Totonac, and Huasteca figurines and ceramic vessels. As one might suppose, Maya figures have a prominent place, including a nice statue of the sun god with crossed eyes (because the sun is so bright?) and large earplugs.

You'll probably hear about **Playa Bonita,** about four miles west out of town, but unless you're in need of some cooler air I recommend going to the Caribbean for your swimming. The last time I was there the beach was pretty dirty and the water not so appetizing.

4. Chichén-Itzá and Valladolid

The fabled pyramids and temples of Chichén-Itzá are Yucatán's best-known ancient monuments. You can't really say you've seen Yucatán until you've gazed at towering El Castillo, sighted the sun from the Maya observatory called El Caracol, or shivered on the brink of the gaping cenote which served as the sacrificial well. Luckily for travelers on a budget, Chichén-Itzá is well and frequently served by buses, as it's on the main highway (no. 180) between Merida and Cancún. Also, being on the main highway, Chichén-Itzá has a decent selection of hotels in all price ranges, so you needn't bend your budget here as you may have done at Uxmal.

An attractive, and money-saving, alternative to staying at Chichén is to stay in the sleepy town of Valladolid, 40 kilometers (25 miles) east of the ruins. You can get an early bus from Merida, spend the day at the ruins, then trundle on to Valladolid in a half hour. In recent years Valladolid has acquired some nice, modern hotels, and since they're a distance from the ruins, prices are very reasonable and crowds are not a problem.

Speaking of crowds, it's possible (but not probable) that your chosen hotel at Chichén-Itzá might be booked up. If you want to make a reservation, be advised that it is difficult to reach Chichén by phone; however, most hotels have a means by which you can make reservations in Merida. Read the hotel descriptions for details.

378 MEXICO ON $20 A DAY

ON THE ROAD: See the section above, "Getting To and From Merida," for bus information. Once you're on the road, it'll take between 1½ and 2 hours to reach Chichén (120 kilometers, 75 miles).

Along the way, tiny Maya hamlets with thatched houses (called *na*) dot the highway. Sometimes the frames of sticks are covered in mud plaster and whitewashed. The women take pride in wearing the traditional white *huipil,* which always has embroidery around the neckline, and several inches of lacy slip showing at the hem.

This is henequen country, and you'll pass a big Cordemex plant which gathers in the leaves from the surrounding fields. Tied in bundles, the leaves form huge piles by the plant, waiting to have the sisal fibers extracted and made into rope and cloth. Henequen has been the principal industry of Yucatán for centuries, and the vast henequen haciendas were owned by absentee landlords and worked by peasants who were little better than slaves. The great haciendas have been split up in recent yeras, but the hacienda complexes—house, smokestack, factory, chapel, workers' houses, gateway, narrow-gauge railways—still stand along the road. In every direction stretch the numberless stone-walled fields where the spiny henequen plants grow, taking years to reach maturity.

After an hour's musing on antique economics, you pass through the village of Pisté, which is only a mile or so west of Chichén-Itzá. Now there's a new sidewalk all the way from Pisté to the archeological zone. As long as you don't do it in the heat of the day, the walk is a comfortable 15 or 20 minutes.

CHICHÉN-ITZÁ: The archeological zone at Chichén is open from 8 a.m. to 5 p.m. daily. Admission costs 15 pesos, 10 pesos on Sunday and holidays. Hold onto your ticket as you will need it to enter and reenter the two parts of the zone.

Also note this: Two sights are open at special hours. If you'd like to visit the passage inside El Castillo, you can do it only from 11 a.m. to 1 p.m. and from 4 to 5 p.m.; the Camara de los Tigres is open only from 10 to 11 a.m. and 3 to 4 p.m.

This Mayan city was absorbed by the Toltecs in A.D. 987, when, as legend has it, a man named Kukulcán, who was the same as Quetzalcoatl from the Toltec capital of Tula, arrived from the west "for the redemption of his people." Here he built a magnificent metropolis combining the Maya Puuc style with Toltec motifs of the feathered serpent, warriors, eagles, and jaguars. There are actually two parts of Chichén-Itzá: north of the highway which is distinctly Toltec, and south of the highway which is of an early period with mostly Puuc architecture. A day is needed to see all the ruins here, and that means from 8 a.m. until 5 p.m. Begin with the beautiful 75-foot **El Castillo** temple, built with the calendar in mind: there is a total of 364 stairs plus platform, which makes 365 (days of the year), 52 panels on each side which represent the 52-year cycle of the Maya Vague Year Calendar, and nine terraces on each side of the stairways, a total of 18 terraces to represent the 18-month Maya calendar. If this isn't proof enough of the mathematical precision of this temple, come for the spring equinox (March 21), and when the sun goes down you'll see the seven stairs of the northern stairway plus the serpent head carving at the base touched with the last rays of the fading sun; within a 34-minute period the "serpent" formed by this play of light and shadow appears to descend into the earth as the sun leaves each stair, going from the top to the bottom, ending with the serpent head. To the Maya this is a fertility symbol: time to plant the corn.

CHICHÉN-ITZÁ

This is only one of the many fascinating things you will see at Chichén. Visit the **Temple of the Warriors:** at the top is a Chacmool (reclining sacrificial figure) and two columns of the feathered serpent; on the lower platform there are square columns carved on all four sides with intricate Toltec warriors. North of the plaza is a pathway which leads to the cenote or **sacred well,** where numerous sacrifices took place (archeologists have recovered skeletons and jewels from the depths). Then there is the **ball court,** the finest and largest in Mesoamerica, with its parallel walls and two stone rings through which the ball was thrown. The acoustics here are quite unbelievable: stand in the playing field and speak normally to your friends at the other end; they'll hear you. East of the ball court is the **platform of the tigers and eagles** with some interesting frescoes and bas reliefs, and behind this there is a temple of carved skulls (the Tzompantli), all different. There is more, but by this time you may need a cool *refresca,* so go to the highway where several stands offer you a place in the shade to sit and rest. Don't forget to visit the south side of the highway and the older Puuc-style architecture, including the famous **Caracol** or Observatory, where the priests made astronomical calculations.

Where to Stay and Eat

You can see all there is to see at Chichén-Itzá in a day, but you may not want to continue your journey after a tiring round of the ruins. Because rooms at Chichén are sometimes difficult to find in the busy season, here is a rundown on all the hotels near the ruins, whether budget priced or not.

A good place to stay overnight is the **Hotel Dolores Alba,** 1½ miles past the ruins on the road going east to Puerto Juarez. (If you go to Chichén-Itzá by bus from Merida, ask for a ticket on a bus that is going *past* the ruins—to Valladolid or Puerto Juarez—and then ask the bus driver to stop at the Dolores Alba; he will be glad to do so. Or take a taxi from the ruins to the hotel. Sra. Joaquina Comin de Sanchez, who runs the Dolores Alba, speaks English and is enthusiastic in her work: the 12 rooms are kept clean and neat, and several of them have been equipped with air conditioners to help the ceiling fans. Besides the motel-style rooms, which are older, you'll find two modern, air-conditioned rooms and a separate cottage which sleeps four in two bedrooms. Prices are 440 pesos single, 550 pesos double, 660 pesos triple, and 770 pesos for four (in the cottage). All rooms have showers, of course, and there's a pretty little swimming pool besides. Good meals are available here at decent prices, but you should realize that when it comes to dining you have little choice—the nearest alternative restaurant, or tienda to buy your own supplies, is several miles away. For your trips to the ruins, the Dolores Alba provides free transportation to guests without cars. By the way, this hotel is run by the same family that runs the Dolores Alba in Merida (tel. 992/1-3745) at Calle 63 no. 464. Either hotel will help you to make reservations at the other one.

The **Hotel Cunanchen,** right next to the church on the village square in Pisté, has a standard motel-style layout with little rooms grouped around a swimming pool. It's been under construction for two decades, and charges 420 pesos single, 480 pesos double, ceiling fan included.

The **Hotel Hacienda Chichén** is a short walk from the ruins, and guests stay in the bungalows built for those excavating the ruins some years ago. There's a fine pool (which, by the way, is open also to those who drop in for the 380-peso lunch), and all is quite plush—it should be for 1100 pesos single, 1500 pesos double. If I had to "upgrade" for a night, this romantic and sympathetic place is where I'd stay. Each cottage is named for an early archeologist working at Chichén. You can make reservations for the Hacienda by contacting the Merida Travel Service, in the Hotel Casa del Balam at Calle 60 no. 488, corner of Calle 57 (Apdo. Postal 407, Merida, Yucatán; tel. 922/1-9212).

Of the various hostelries at the ruins which are out of our price range, the **Piramide Inn** is among the least far out. Less than a mile past the ruins on the road to Puerto Juarez, the Piramide boasts near-luxurious large rooms equipped with king-size beds, air conditioning, wall hangings of local handicrafts, plus the bonuses of a pool and absolutely gorgeous landscaped gardens and grounds. A number of people on the staff speak English. For all this comfort one pays 792 pesos single, 842 pesos double. Besides the 42 rooms, the Piramide has ten bungalow suites, priced higher. You can make reservations in Merida by contacting the Piramide's sister hotel, the Principe Maya Airport Inn, Avenida Aviación km. 4.5, Apdo. Postal 433 (tel. 992/1-4050 or 4-0411).

The **Hotel Misión Chichén-Itzá** (tel. 4) is a fancy, deluxe establishment that's very new and very Holiday Inn, right in the town of Pisté. With two floors of rooms, a pretty pool, a shopping arcade, and a restaurant-bar, the Misión is the compleat place to stay, but it's not cheap: double rooms cost 1650 pesos. Meal plans are available, or you can drop in for breakfast (195 pesos), lunch (350 pesos), or dinner (480 pesos). For reservations in Mexico City, go to Florencia 15-A in the Pink Zone, or call 533-5953 or 533-3560.

The **Villa Arqueológica** is part of the Club Méditerranée operation, as you might guess by a glance at the lavishness of the layout: tennis courts, a pool, and garden-like grounds. On my last inspection tour I was quoted rates of 1440 pesos for two—a very reasonable price, for what you get. Meals are more expensive here than at the nearby Hacienda Chichén or at the Hotel Misión. For reservations in Mexico City, contact the office at Leibnitz 34, or telephone 514-4995 or 511-1284.

The **Hotel Mayaland,** sister hotel to the Hacienda Chichén and very close to it, is perhaps the most genteel and sumptuous of Chichén-Itzá hotels. Built positively to reek of jungle adventure, it boasts such subtle touches as a front doorway which frames perfectly El Caracol (the observatory) as you walk from the lobby outside. It has a swimming pool and restaurant-bar, of course, and very attractive rooms at these prices: 2200 pesos double, or 3600 pesos double with two meals per day. Make reservations as at the Hacienda Chichén.

The budget choice in the village of Pisté, next to the Pyramide Inn, is the very basic **Posada Novelo,** with adequate if bare rooms, all with showers, for 330 pesos single, 440 pesos double.

Food is available near the ruins in the expensive hotels, but for the budget traveler I recommend the little restaurants in the town of Pisté, or cheaper still, the eateries right by the ruins. Actually, these days Pisté's restaurants are pushing their prices up and standardizing their fare so that there is little difference among them. Expect to find your silverware encased in a plastic bag, and mood music (old Swingle Singers records, etc.) pulsing in the background —whether you like it or not. In any of the restaurants—El Carrusel, La Picuda, or the Poxil—they'll try to sell you an entire lunch of four or five courses, and will balk at à la carte orders. The cost will be anywhere from 275 to 325 pesos; that's a bit high, considering that the Hotel Misión, also in Pisté and very posh, charges only 350 pesos for lunch. About the cheapest of the town's restaurants are the Carrusel and the Poxil.

Luckily for us, Pisté still retains a few operating **loncherías,** where sandwiches, bowls of soup, and similar light-lunch fare are offered at low prices. One lonchería is right next to the Fiesta restaurant, another is in the small arcade by the highway, across from the church. Shops in the same arcade sell biscuits, drinks, and similar supplies. And the soft drink stands near the ruins will serve you a rough-and-ready comida for 150 pesos or so.

Nearby Sites

Spelunkers take note: the **Grutas** (caves) **de Balankanché** are 4½ kilometers from Chichén-Itzá on the road to Puerto Juarez. You can see them with a guide only. Guides begin their tours according to a schedule posted at the ticket office in Chichén-Itzá ruins.

Note that the caves are very humid and claustrophobic. If these conditions don't bother you, by all means explore.

VALLADOLID: Heading east from Chichén-Itzá, the next town along Highway 180 is Valladolid (that's "bai-ah-doh-LEET"). Not much happens here, although the tourist boom in Chichén-Itzá and Cancún has brought Valladolid newfound wealth and activity. It should take only half an hour to cover the 25 miles between Chichén and Valladolid.

The highway goes right past the main square in town, and it's here, or very nearby, that you'll find good hotels and restaurants.

Although it remained untouched by tourism for centuries, Valladolid is no newcomer to Yucatán. It was founded in 1543 near the site of a Maya religious center called Zací. The Franciscans built an impressive monastery here, called the **Convento de San Bernardino de Siena** (1552), and the town can boast of half a dozen colonial churches and two cenotes.

The main square is called the **Parque Francisco Cantón Rosado**, and when you find your way there, you'll be just a few steps from a variety of acceptable hotels and restaurants.

Where to Stay and Eat

Walking around the main square, here's what you'll find: El Parroquía de San Servasio (the parish church) on the south, the Palacio Municipal (Town Hall) on the west (with a little tourism information desk out front, open from 9 a.m. to noon daily).

Near El Parroquía, at the southwest corner of the square, is the **Hotel San Clemente** (tel. 985/6-2208 or 6-2065), a modern, colonial-style building covered in white stucco. The 64 rooms, each with air conditioning, ceiling fan, and tidy bath, are located on two floors around a central garden quadrangle complete with swimming pool. Rates, compared to those at Chichén or Cancún, are very low: 550 pesos double, all included.

On the west side of the square is the **Hotel Maria de la Luz** (tel. 985/6-2070), which is well known for its breezy restaurant overlooking the square. A daily set-price lunch is featured for only 175 pesos, beverage included. The food is hearty rather than delicate, but filling. A heaping fruit salad and a cold soft drink costs less than 100 pesos. The rooms at the Luz are similar to those of the aforementioned hotel in accoutrements and price, although they're a bit more worn. The swimming pool at the Luz is definitely not crystal clear.

The north side of the square holds the **Hotel El Mesón del Marqués** (tel. 985/6-2073), a nice old colonial building. Signs in English advertise the restaurant (very tidy) and gift shop. The rooms are in a modern addition, however, and come with air conditioning for 660 pesos double. The addition (two floors completed, the third under construction) is behind the pretty tree-shaded courtyard, and therefore away from street noise.

To the right of El Mesón del Marqués is a **market patio,** with little stalls grouped around it. Here's where to go for light meals, sandwiches, and snacks. Sit outside at one of the Coca-Cola folding tables for an inexpensive breakfast or lunch. You can assuage your hunger for less than 100 pesos for sure.

About the most popular restaurant on the square with local people is **El Papillon,** on the west side near the Hotel Maria de la Luz. It's close and dark inside, but the tables always seem to be busy with locals chowing down on enchiladas, frijoles, carne asada, and other *antojitos.* A three-course lunch here will set you back less then 150 pesos.

My favorite hotel in Valladolid is not on the main square proper, but just a block off of it. It's the brand-new **Hotel Don Luis** (tel. 985/6-2024), Calle 39 no. 191. From the north side of the square (which is Calle 39) go east (that's away from the Hotel Maria de la Luz) one block, and the Hotel Don Luis is on the left-hand side: you'll spot the sign. Despite its being on a busy street, the Don Luis's rooms are quiet, big, and air-conditioned. All are doubles, many with two double beds. A thoughtful touch is that the washbasin is located *outside* the bathroom, so one can wash while another showers. The swimming pool in the courtyard is attractive and very clean, and prices are good: 520 pesos double. Try it.

Tinum, a Mayan Village

Valladolid is the jumping-off place for a visit to a unique adventure: a stay in a real Mayan village. This is only for the intrepid, but if you're one, read on.

Some years ago, Ms. Bettina McMakin left Miami to settle in the tiny village of Tinum, to get away from it all. She learned the Mayan language, got to know many of the villagers, and soon had visitors. At first they were just friends from back home, but later her "visitors" included those interested in discovering exactly what it's like to live as the Mayas did—and do.

Ms. McMakin doesn't spend a lot of time in Tinum anymore, but the tradition of hospitality survives, carried on by her village friends, especially Don Chivo.

Here's what you do: twice daily, buses run from Valladolid to Tinum in 40 minutes. Or you can take the daily 3 p.m. train from Merida to Tinum, arriving at 7:15 p.m. (or thereabouts). Bring a hammock with you, or write ahead to arrange to have one made and waiting for you in Tinum. Don Chivo will arrange for you to board with a Maya family in their *na* (house of sticks with a thatched roof), and to eat with them and share their daily life. The cost, paid directly to the family, is 250 pesos per day, nonprofit. Be sure you realize that this is the real thing: you sleep in your hammock, live with a dirt floor, cook on a fire, and use one of the two bathrooms in Dona Bettina's house. You're welcome for two or three nights.

ONWARD TO CANCÚN: Having refreshed yourself with a stop in Valladolid, you're ready to head onward to Cancún and Isla Mujeres. These two favorite resort destinations are only a handful of miles apart in distance, but worlds apart in ambience. The 160-kilometer (100-mile) ride from Valladolid to Cancún or Puerto Juarez will take about two hours.

5. Cancún

Less than a decade ago, the name Cancún would have meant little to anyone. Perhaps a resident of Puerto Juarez or Isla Mujeres would have linked the name to a hook-shaped sandy island a few hundred feet off the Yucatecan coast, a desert island of powdery limestone sand, surrounded by coral reefs. Today Cancún is the magic word in Mexican vacations.

Looking to expand tourism, the Mexican government had done a study to find the best location for a new jet-age resort, and Cancún came out on top. From a tiny mainland hamlet, Ciudad Cancún soon grew to a city of 30,000; its projected size is 70,000, to be reached in a few years. Engineers, construction crews, shopkeepers, and restaurateurs all flocked to the new development, and as the luxury hotels began to increase on the deserted sand island, so did the vacationers in search of warm sun and cool waters. Although Cancún is already well on the way to world fame, it is not yet completed. You may still see advertisements for condominiums which boast that "construction on our project is completely finished!"

What makes Cancún the perfect site for a resort? The land is the beautiful Yucatecan jungle, the long sand spit is perfect for seaside hotels, the beaches are covered in a very fine sand which has been called "air-conditioned" by its ingenious promoters. Mayan ruins at Tulum, Chichén-Itzá, and Cobá are a short drive away, and for a change of scene the older resorts of Isla Mujeres and Cozumel are close at hand. The Caribbean waters are incredibly blue and limpid, temperatures (both air and water) are just right, and the coral reefs and tropical climate guarantee brilliant underwater life, good snorkeling, and fine scuba diving. All these pleasures do not come cheap, however, and the price structure in Cancún's *Zona Turística* (out on the sand spit, also called the Zona Hotelera) is not geared to the budget traveler. In fact, Cancún was developed for the visitor coming by air directly to the resort for a stay of a week or two, and the price structure reflects this market. It may sound strange for me to give such a tip, but I recommend that those coming to Cancún for a few weeks on the beach in a fancy hotel buy a package trip which includes air fare, hotel, some meals, and amusements, with perhaps a few days of car rental included. This will not be cheap, but it will be a lot cheaper than walking into the Aristos or the Cancún Caribe and asking for a room—the highest room rate is the one applied to the casual single visitor.

That having been said, let me move on to the good news that it is quite possible to enjoy the pleasures of Cancún *without* taking a package trip or spending $100 a day. The trick is to follow the recommendations of this book and *not* stay in the Zona Turística, but rather in one of the more modest but comfortable hotels in Ciudad Cancún, on the mainland.

GETTING AROUND: Special minibuses (called Combi's) run from Cancún's international airport into town for 150 pesos per person. As of this writing, minibus service is one way only, and you'll have to hire a taxi for twice that amount to get back to the airport.

In town, almost everything's within easy walking distance. The only places you need take buses to are the beaches near the luxury hotels in the Zona Turística, and to Puerto Juarez/Punta Sam for ferries to Isla Mujeres. City buses will trundle you from your in-town hotel out to the beaches of the Zona Turística for a ridiculously low fare. These "Ruta 1" buses operate every 15 minutes or so along the Avenida Tulum, Ciudad Cancún's main street, all the way to Punta Nizuc at the far end of the Zona Turistica.

As for Puerto Juarez/Punta Sam, catch a Ruta 1 (to Puerto Juarez) or Ruta 3 (to Puerto Juarez and Punta Sam) bus along Cancún's main street, Avenida Tulum, and the bus will take you straight to the ferry docks.

384 MEXICO ON $20 A DAY

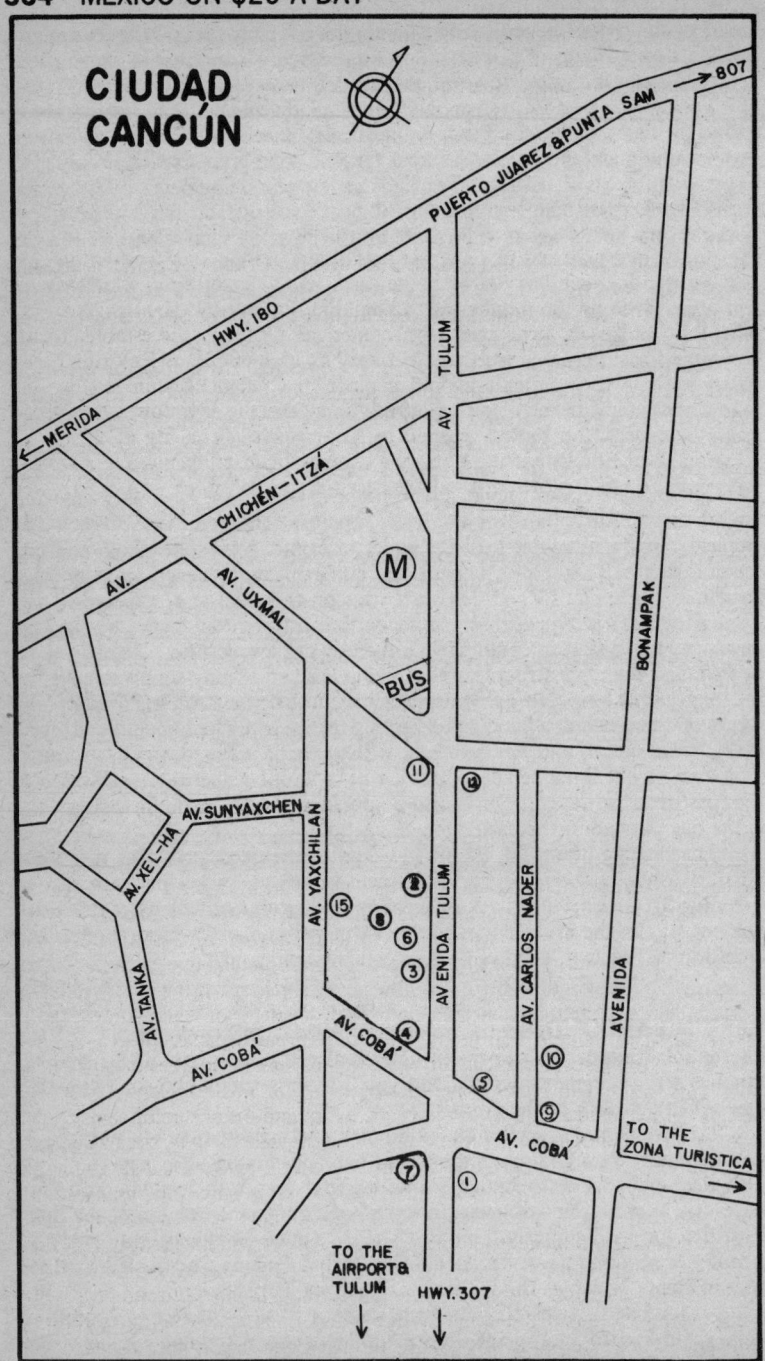

CIUDAD CANCÚN

The city fathers have instituted an authorized table of taxi fares, but in any case it's best to make a deal on a fare in advance. From Ciudad Cancún out to, say, the Hotel Camino Real should cost 250 pesos; a short ride between two of the big hotels, less than 140 pesos; from Ciudad Cancún to the airport, about 300 pesos. Drivers will probably ask a good deal more for a fare to the airport.

A Note on Addresses

Starting with a clean slate, one would think the city fathers of Ciudad Cancún would have laid out a street-numbering system that was simple and easy to use, but such has not been the case. As of this writing, addresses are still often given by the number of the building lot and by the *manzana* (city block). Some streets have signs with names on, although the establishments along the street may refer to the street only by its number, as Retorno 3, etc. In short, it is very difficult to find a place in Ciudad Cancún just by the numbers. Luckily, the city is still relatively small and the downtown section can easily be covered on foot. I've tried to be very specific in my directions to recommended establishments. Your best companion in confusing Cancún is the map in this book, with numbers keyed to places I mention.

WHERE TO STAY: Ciudad Cancún has a good collection of moderate- and budget-priced hotels, just as does Acapulco, Cozumel, or any other Mexican resort town. Prices are a bit higher than in, say, Merida, which is not right next door to a fabulous resort, but you can stay overnight comfortably and inexpensively in Ciudad Cancún. Off-season (April and November), bargain for a price reduction.

Right on the main thoroughfare of Avenida Tulum, at the corner with Claveles, is the three-story **Hotel Tulum (3)** (tel. 988/3-0503). Look for a modern white edifice with orange bands running around the building and the name painted high on the facade—there's no street-level sign. The very fine modern rooms here have beige walls, dark-wood trim on light fixtures and windows, bambooish lamps and wicker-back chairs, plus other "decorator" touches. Air conditioning is in all rooms, and the price of 775 pesos single, 895 pesos double is about right for what you get, if a bit high for our budget.

Just off Avenida Tulum, entered from Calle Claveles 37, is the new **Antillano Hotel (6)** (tel. 988/4-1021 or 4-1244). Modern wood-and-stucco in design, the Antillano has air-conditioned rooms that overlook the busy Avenida Tulum and also the side streets. Being one of the newer hotels downtown, it's decidedly a bit fancier, and includes a swimming pool. Consider that when you study the prices: 875 pesos single, 950 pesos double, 1150 pesos triple, all in.

The seafood restaurant chain of Soberanis has both a restaurant and a hotel in Cancún. The **Hotel Soberanis (4)** (tel. 988/3-0109), Cobá 5 (near the corner with Avenida Tulum) has a bright white-and-orange color scheme and some of the touches normally found only in high-priced hotels, such as elegant table lamps, two double beds to a room, and little balconies. All rooms are air-conditioned, of course, and are priced at 800 pesos single, 900 pesos double with one double or two twin beds, 1000 pesos double with two double beds.

Every now and then one comes across a hostelry which is unusual because it brings an air of country life to the city. Such a place is the **Novotel (11)** (tel. 988/3-0999), Avenida Tulum at Avenida Uxmal. Behind the modern white stucco hotel are small buildings of wood and thatch resembling traditional Maya houses scattered among small but very fine lawns and gardens, and shaded by four grand palm trees. Morning glories blare along a fence, and ducks—perhaps also a tiny lamb on wobbly legs—ramble about here and there. The rooms leave nothing to be desired in the way of city comforts except perhaps air conditioning: all come with table fans, bottled water, good baths covered in colored tiles, and bedspreads done in fancy patterns. The price for a double is 990 pesos; a bit less for a single if a room's available. Rooms in the big modern building out front cost about 200 pesos more.

Carrillo's (6) (tel. 988/3-0849) is on a side street called Calle Claveles which meets Avenida Tulum at two places (Claveles forms a loop). Look for the intersection of Claveles and Tulum that's right across from the Banco Nacional de México and its large statues of Tula's Atlantean men; official address is Retorno 3, Manzana 22. Now that you're there, you'll find Carrillo's to be one of the strangest places in Cancún. Although a few of the hotel's rooms are older and more standard, most are finished—walls and ceiling—in a nubbly white stucco which gives the entire place a troglodytic quality. Add plywood vanities, tiled showers, and individual air conditioning units and you have the standard room at Carrillo's which rents for 660 pesos single, 748 pesos double. Besides the two-story hotel, Carrillo's building houses a seafood restaurant (see below).

The **Hotel Cancún Randall (7)** (tel. 988/3-0972) opened in 1980. Two wings of two floors each hold a variety of single rooms, doubles, and suites, and a pool awaits your pleasure outside. Most of the modern rooms have two double beds, and cost 950 pesos single, 1100 pesos double, and 1350 pesos triple. The Randall is at the intersection of Avenidas Tulum and Cobá.

On the Avenida Tulum right downtown is the **Hotel Rivemar (8)** (tel. 988/3-0671 or 3-0833), a modern but heavily used establishment right in the midst of downtown. Rooms are air-conditioned, of course, with private baths, and are priced at 770 pesos single, 990 pesos double, 1200 pesos triple.

The Big Splurge

Were I to upgrade in pricey Cancún, it wouldn't be to one of the skyscrapers out on the beach, but to the new **Hotel America (1)** (tel. 988/3-1500) on Avenida Tulum at Avenida Brisa. From here you can walk into the center of town and yet stay in a top-class, luxurious, air-conditioned hotel. The America has its own beach club, with a free shuttle bus to take you there, plus its own swimming pools right in the hotel. Prices are moderate, for what you get: 1300 pesos single, 1700 pesos double, 1900 pesos triple.

A Different Kind of Place

The **Suites Residencial "Flamboyanes" (10)** (tel. 988/3-0450; reservations in Merida, call 992/1-0603 or go to Calle 65 no. 514) is a different, and delightful, place run by people who definitely know what they're doing. Here on Avenida Carlos J. Nader, just off Avenida Cobá, are 80 suites in a number of attractive two-story buildings surrounded by grass and trees, and equipped with a private swimming pool. All suites are air-conditioned and include a bedroom, a living room with couches to sleep two more people, fully equipped kitchen with dining area, bathroom, and terrace/porch. A suite for one or two persons costs 1400 pesos, plus 280 pesos for each additional person. From time to time the Flamboyanes make special offers on rates and you might be able to stay for three days (two nights) for, say, 2400 pesos double. The daily rate goes down for extended stays, of course. Remember that you are renting an *apartment* here, and not just a hotel room, and thus the prices are very reasonable for what you get.

WHERE TO EAT: One must be cautious in accepting the extravagant claims made by the luxury hotels for their own restaurants. The very economics of the situation are against them: package tours must be offered at a competitive low price, and so the meals included in the tour must be fancy but not expensive to prepare. Guest must go away satisfied, but it must be remembered that guests have prepaid their meals, which puts them in a difficult position if they don't like the food! I've had letters from readers who have stayed at the fancy hotels and have found the food so mediocre they made the trip into Ciudad Cancún every day and paid extra just to have tasty meals.

Living by the philosophy of this book does away with the luxury hotel reataurant problem, as I'll recommend only small independent restaurants in downtown Cancún which must compete nightly for clients, and which therefore are careful that price *and quality* are competitive. Besides full restaurants offering a comprehensive menu and wine list, note also my choices of places offering set-price lunches (called comida corrida), and snack stands for a quick bite.

The popular **Restaurant Pop (12)**, famous in Merida for a number of years now, has a branch in Cancún at Avenida Tulum 29, corner of Avenida Uxmal. As in Merida the fare tends to the light, simple, and delicious rather than the elaborate and expensive. Breakfast or a light lunch can be had in the cool comfort of Pop's air-conditioned dining room for 80 to 150 pesos, a more substantial dinner should be in the range of 250 pesos. Wine and beer are served.

Carrillo's Restaurant (6) (tel. 3-0849), in the hotel of the same name (see above), is a good place to dine for almost any occasion, whether you want to put together a light lunch for a couple of dollars, or to go all-out and have lobster for about 700 pesos. A nice filet of red snapper (huachinango) will cost 200 to 350 pesos, depending on style of preparation, while a steak will cost a few dollars more. For a full meal, with wine, tax, and tip, expect to pay 450 to 600 pesos per person. The big bonus at Carillo's, fairly rare in Cancún restaurants, is air conditioning. In winter it's fun to sit at one of the outdoor tables, but in the heat of summer almost everyone opts for the cool indoor dining room.

A very popular sidewalk restaurant on Avenida Tulum is popular for its food, its ambience, and its clientele—all three. It's **Blackbeard's Taberna (2)**. The food might consist of ceviche, the marinated fish cocktail, followed by a brochette (the specialty) of beef, chicken, shrimp, lobster, or all of the above. Finish with cheesecake, or ice cream topped with a liqueur, accompany your meal with a full carafe of the house wine, and the entire bill for two people might come to 1600 pesos. You can dine for less, though: say, 600 pesos per person. The decor is rustic Mexican wooden shanty, the clientele mostly international sun-seekers. Open every day.

Is there no place to get a good, inexpensive (under $4) meal in Cancún? There is. At **Pizza Rolandi (5)**, Avenida Cobá between Tulum and Nader, you can get the basic cheese-and-tomato pizza for 125 pesos which, with a drink, will satisfy your hunger very pleasantly. The super-special pizza costs 300 pesos, which isn't bad, and Italian specialties like spaghetti and fettucine cost about that, as well. Italian desserts are offered. Pizza Rolandi is usually crowded, its outdoor patio tables busy with the hungry, thirsty (beer is served), thrifty set.

Across the street from the aforementioned Carrillo's is **Chocko's (8)**, a ramshackle, semi-open-air collection of brightly lit dining rooms where the noise level is high, but the fun level is even higher. Something is always going on here—mariachis, a lasso-twirling *charro* (cowboy), or a solo guitarist—to liven up the already-lively crowd. The food seems to be of second interest here, and the service is, well, casual. But you can have soup, main course, dessert, and a bottle of beer, tax and tip included, for 575 pesos. And don't forget all that free entertainment.

If you've enjoyed restaurants of the Carlos Anderson chain in other cities, you can in Cancún, too. **Carlos & Charlie's** is out in the Zona Hotelera, on the right as you ride out the peninsula. Same upbeat atmosphere, same menu, and price that will put you out about 500 to 600 pesos per person for a full evening.

Restaurant prices in Cancún tend to be high, as this is a ritzy beach resort, but I wouldn't even aim you in the direction of **Hugo's (9)**, at Avenida Cobá 89, corner of Nader, if I didn't think it was extraordinary. Here seafood is the specialty, and you can get red snapper done properly, the way it should be: the whole fish is carefully baked or grilled. It's a comfortable but somewhat formal place which you should save for a special evening. Figure to spend a total of 1600 pesos for two, wine, tax, and tips included.

The local incarnation of the Soberanis seafood restaurant group is at Avenida Cobá 5 and 7, in the **Hotel Soberanis (4)**. The patio dining area is shaded by large awnings, and although you're not far from Avenida Tulum here, it's fairly quiet. Service is attentive, and prices are moderate considering the general range of prices in Cancún for seafood. Fish entrees are a moderate 220 pesos, and are the best things to have—avoid the soups and cocktails. Soberanis opens about 9 in the morning (good for breakfast), and closes at 11 p.m. or midnight.

A Steakhouse Splurge

One of Ciudad Cancún's more luxurious dining establishments is **El Potrero (15)**, Avenida Yaxchilan 50, a steakhouse with a Wild West decor and American-style arctic air conditioning. Surrounded by wine racks, mementoes of *charro* life, and rough wood, you drink wine or beer from large metal goblets and dine on various cuts of steak. Access to the salad bar included, a meal here will be in a typically Cancún range: 600 to 800 pesos per person. Open 1 p.m. to midnight.

WHAT TO DO: First thing to do is to explore the sandy, once-deserted island (now actually a peninsula) which is this billion-dollar-resort's reason for being. Perhaps the best thing to do is to take a ride to the end of the line just to see the fabulous resort and get your bearings. On the return trip, get off the bus at El Parian Centro Comercial, next to the Convention Center, and wander along the beaches from there. The best stretches of beach are dominated by the big hotels, of course, but all beaches are public property in Mexico. Note well, though: on the sea (as opposed to the lagoon) side of the sand spit, *undertow* is a potentially deadly problem. Swim where there's a lifeguard.

If you'd rather not insinuate yourself onto a hotel beach, the public beach called **Playa Tortuga** is a short walk from the Convention Center bus stop. Both swimming and underwater observation are fine from Playa Tortuga, "Turtle Beach."

Day-long excursions, or perhaps even an overnight stay, are easy using Cancún as a base. The Mayan ruins at Tulum should be your first goal, then perhaps the *caleta* (cove) of Xel-ha, and later to nearby Isla Mujeres. By driving fast or catching the buses right, one can get to Chichén-Itzá, explore the ruins, and return in a day, but it's much better to make a trip of several days

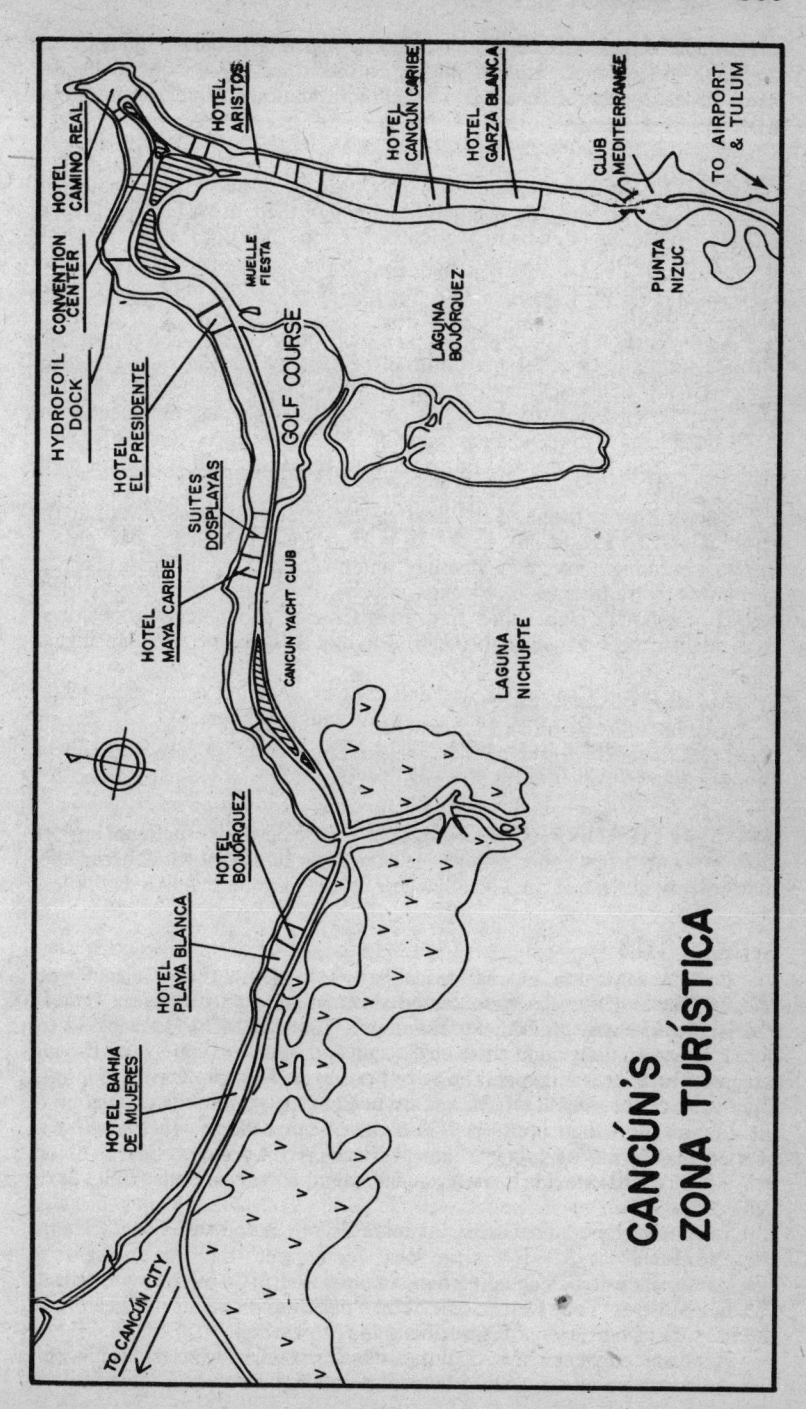

CANCÚN'S ZONA TURÍSTICA

and include Merida and Uxmal on the same trip. If you plan to go south to the island of Cozumel, think of staying on the island at least one night. See below for transportation details and further information on all of these destinations.

NIGHTLIFE: Ciudad Cancún has hardly been in existence long enough to have developed an indigenous nightlife, although there are a few lively spots which are offshoots of clubs in Merida or Mexico City. But the real action is in the Zona Turística at the big hotels. Part of the thrill of getting away to the Caribbean is the intrigue of meeting new people either on the beach or in the cool, dark depths of a disco or nightclub.

All the big hotels have night places, usually both a disco and a supper club with a floor show or at least live music for dancing. Expect to pay a cover charge of about 250 pesos per person in the discos or show bars, or be subjected to a 200-peso minimum (since drinks cost 125 to 175 pesos, this means that you'll actually have to spend a minimum of 250 pesos to cover your "200-peso" minimum). Add 10% tax and tip to these prices, and you'll see that a night out in fabulous Cancún is not all that cheap.

Believe it or not, one of the least expensive evenings can be had at the deluxe **Hotel El Presidente,** in the Zona Hotelera. In the lobby bar, groups entertain each night except Wednesday, and no cover or minimum is charged. The music is traditional—mariachis, jarocho, etc.—and changes every half hour. In the hotel's club, called **Bum Bum Cancún,** the thatched roof shivers every night except Monday to the cool jive of salsa music, for dancing, of course.

At the **Hotel Cancún Caribe,** dancers can work out every night of the week except Monday. Look for a two-drink minimum here.

The posh **Camino Real Hotel** hosts a Mexican Music Night each Friday, and lays on as much rhythm as anyone could handle.

GETTING TO AND FROM CANCÚN: With its own international airport, Cancún is only a few hours' flying time from anywhere in North America. For shorter trips, buses will run you anywhere in the Yucatán in half a day or less.

By Air

Both AeroMéxico and Mexicana have several flights to Cancún from Mexico City and Merida. AeroMéxico also operates flights between Cancún and Houston, Paris, Madrid, Montréal, and Toronto. Mexicana runs a very popular nonstop daily flight between Cancún and Miami; if you live on the east coast of North America, a good way to begin your Mexican travels is to take a bus or train (or a flight) to Miami, fly to Cancún, explore the eastern tip of the country, and then head via Merida and Campeche to other sections of Mexico, making an "open-jaw" route. Mexicana is at Avenida Uxmal 8–10 (tel. 988/3-0700); AeroMéxico is on Avenida Tulum, corner of Nader (tel. 988/3-0361 or 3-0335).

Local Carriers: AeroCaribe, Avenida Tulum at the corner with Uxmal (tel. 988/3-0394 or 3-0403), is the local "commuter" outfit, with flights to Merida, Chichén-Itzá, Villahermosa, Chetumal, Belize City, Cozumel, Tulum, and Isla Mujeres. They feature special tour packages as well, such as a day at the ruins of Chichén, or a Scuba-diving tour to Cozumel.

A smaller carrier is Aero Cozumel, which sometimes runs day tours from Cancún to its home base, the island of Cozumel. This procedure may not survive, now that a high-speed hydrofoil service has been initiated to that destination. Ask your hotel or a travel agent for details.

By Hydrofoil

A hydrofoil service has been instituted by the Secretaría de Turismo, operating from a dock near the Convention Center (see map, "Cancún's Zona Turística") to Isla Mujeres and Cozumel. The service is brand new at this writing; check with your hotel for latest details on service, times, and prices.

By Bus

Both the A.D.O. line and Autobuses del Caribe have their Cancún terminal across the street from the Hotel Plaza Caribe, at the intersection of Avenidas Uxmal and Tulum in Ciudad Cancún. Ten buses a day head for Merida, three a day go to Mexico City, seven a day run to Tulum and Playa del Carmen (for boats to Cozumel), and four of these last buses continue to Chetumal. The Merida bus will drop you in Chichén-Itzá.

To get to Isla Mujeres, take a Ruta 3 city bus along Avenida Tulum to Puerto Juarez or Punta Sam (six miles away) to get the boat. For full details, see below under "Getting to Isla Mujeres."

6. Isla Mujeres

There are two versions of how Isla Mujeres got its name. The more popular one states that pirates used the island as a place to park their women while they were off buccaneering on the Spanish Main. The other account attributes the name to conquistador Francisco Hernandez de Cordoba, who was reportedly struck by the large number of female terracotta figurines he found in temples on the island.

Although the more prosaic version is probably correct (aren't they always?), incurable romantics such as myself continue to nurse the forlorn hope that the tale about pirates and their women might have some vestige of authenticity.

Modern Isla Mujeres has happily displayed a healthy immunity toward the latter-day pirate whose prey is American green rather than Spanish gold. While there are a few expensive hotels (notably the Zazil-Ha and the Posada del Mar), you'll encounter a satisfying number of facilities for budget travelers and even beachcombers.

The booming development at nearby Cancún has trickled down to people on Isla Mujeres: the fishermen sell more fish, the workmen have more work, and tourist facilities do a good business with visitors over for the day, or a night or two, from Cancún. Not only that, Isla Mujeres is now enjoying its own mini-boom, which brings me to an important point:

GET THERE EARLY: In the busy seasons, June to August and December through February, Isla Mujeres can literally fill up with overnight visitors. Making reservations at the island's small hotels does not always go smoothly and reliably, so the best thing you can do is to get to the island as early in the day as possible. You may even have to stay a night in Cancún so that you can arise early for the first ferry. Check-out time in most hotels is 1 or 2 p.m. Plan to arrive no later than that in February, July, and August.

See below for information on reaching the island from all points.

WHERE TO STAY: Isla Mujeres has a varied assortment of places to put up for the night, in all price ranges. Quality of housekeeping seems to be on a rollercoaster, however: if a hotel fills up, the manager tends to sit back on his laurels, fire the housekeeping staff, put off repairs, and take it easy. When business drops off, he gets back to work. That's life in these island towns.

The island's newest hotel—and thus the one in the best state of repair—is the **Hotel Rocas del Caribe** (tel. 988/2-0011). Right on the surfy eastern beach near town, all rooms have fans and marvelous sea views, plus private shower-baths. The charge for a room, single or double, is 990 pesos. The address, although it's of little practical value, is Madero 2.

The older **Hotel Rocamar** (tel. 988/2-0101) is perched on the higher ground at the opposite side of town from the ferry dock, and thus has a commanding view of the sea. Everything's done in nautical style here, with every conch shell ever opened in the restaurant going to line the garden walkways; ropes and hawsers are employed as trim; even the bathroom sinks are mounted in Lucite tops, and the Lucite is chock full of small seashells. The sea breezes keep the rooms cool, assisted by ceiling fans. Although definitely among the most well-used rooms on the island, the Rocamar's collection of *quartos* has the breeze and the view. Prices are 1050 pesos single, 1300 pesos double. If they're not busy, you can make a deal for a lower price.

The **Hotel Martinez** (tel. 988/2-0154), two blocks from the ferry dock (turn left as you debark, go two blocks, and turn right), has been around for years and years, and satisfied guests keep returning because here the basics are rigidly observed: rooms are spotless, sheets and towels are gleaming white (although perhaps a bit frayed here and there), and little luxuries such as soap are provided. Prices are fair, at 500 pesos single, 600 pesos double per day, ceiling fans (but no air conditioning) included.

Just up the street from the Martinez is the **Hotel Osorio** (tel. 988/2-0018), which is even a better bet at lower prices, like 575 pesos double, with fan.

A new addition to Isla Mujeres's collection of small, basic hotels is the **Hotel Caribe Maya**, on Avenida Madero (tel. 988/2-0190), where the showers are tiled, although a few bits and pieces of furniture (the bedside tables, for instance) may have seen service in some older and now long-gone establishment. The three floors are set up motel style, and rooms rent for an exceptionally high 800 pesos single, 1000 pesos double. Come here as a last resort only.

The **Hotel Berny** (tel. 988/2-0025), Avenidas Juarez and Abasolo, is not very old, and yet it manages to look as though it served as a bivouac for the army of Pancho Villa. It was built nicely, with white stucco walls and red tile floors, and a pretty swimming pool in the courtyard. But upkeep is bad, and prices are too high: 875 pesos single, 1250 pesos double, including continental breakfast.

Even more basic than the above choices is the **Hotel Caracol**, just off Avenida Madero, which charges 600 pesos single, 850 pesos double for its spartan rooms with ceiling fans. An inexpensive restaurant in the Caracol's lobby (right next door to the infinitely more plush Ciro's) draws customers from hotel guests and the general public alike.

The **Autel Carmelina**, on Avenida Guerrero, gets its strange name from the combination of "auto" and "hotel." But there is little strange about the place itself: two floors of plain, clean rooms, very basic, with private baths and ceiling fans. Prices are 500 pesos single, 600 pesos double. A parking lot in front of the hotel adds to the "Autel" theme, although few guests come by car.

For Beachcombers

When it finally happened, people wondered why no one had thought of it before. **Poc-na** (tel. 988/2-0090) bills itself as "a basic clean place to stay at the lowest price possible," and it's just that. The reception desk just inside the door stocks such items as toothpaste, soap, pens, and paper, and will rent you a sheet, towel and soap, or blanket, and a canvas bunk or nylon hammock (plus you get your own private locker). The open bunk rooms are arranged around a central palapa-shaded dining area provided with picnic tables and served by a small kitchen. Meals are served cafeteria-style, with a breakfast of eggs, juice, toast, and coffee costing a high 130 pesos. The location is excellent, only a short walk from the beaches at the northern tip of the island. I must note that Poc-na can be cheap, but it's not necessarily so. If you have your own hammock or sleeping bag, the basic charge is 195 pesos per person per night. But here's what Frank Jablonski, of Madison, Wisconsin, writes: "After the basic charge, we had to pay 150 pesos each for a pad to put over the uncomfortable nylon rope-bed—and that's paid for *each night*. You also have to rent sheets and a pillow (at a flat rate for your entire stay). The cost for two people who came without hammocks or sleeping bags averaged out to 650 pesos—as opposed to 600 at the Hotel Martinez. Also, two of us had to put down a hefty deposit to secure a place to stay." That pretty much makes Poc-na for campers with some of their own equipment.

Poc-na is not the only place for campers. Walk north on Avenida Hidalgo all the way to **Playa Cocoteros** (beach), and you'll spy a primitive but sympathetic group of palapas (thatched shelters) in which you can hang your hammock for 75 pesos, or rent a hammock from them for 100 pesos. Little beachfront eateries are close at hand to provide sustenance.

Just So You'll Know

Wonder what it costs to stay at El Presidente's newest and most dramatic addition to their hotel chain? Well, the daringly designed **Hotel Zazil-ha**, which you admired during the voyage to the island by ferry boat, rents its air-conditioned rooms for 1850 pesos single, 2550 pesos double, with a junior suite even more. These are off-season (summer) prices, and in the prime winter months you must pay, well, somewhat more. Rush to your phone and make a reservation by dialing 988/2-0147.

WHERE TO EAT: Dining on Isla Mujeres is not wildly cheap, but it is certainly easier to keep to a budget here than in, say, Cancún or Cozumel. The first thing you must learn is the password: **Avenida Hidalgo**. Going north out of the town's main square, this street is lined with small and inexpensive or moderately priced places to have a meal. With the coming of Cancún's prosperity, Avenida Hidalgo has undergone a facelift and now boasts lots of trees and shrubs. Many houses have rustic gardens in pseudo-Caribbean style. All these decorations were laid out by a landscape architect to make Isla Mujeres "more authentic," and although authenticity may in fact have been driven out, beauty and quaintness have been ushered in. It's a pleasant street.

I will start our culinary excursion in the main square, head north on Avenida Hidalgo, and then afterward mention some places for waterfront dining.

Among Isla Mujeres's most dependable old standbys is the **Restaurant Gomar**, which has two outdoor tables on Avenida Hidalgo and about 16 indoors. Decor is modern, warm, and nice, with lots of natural wood and the quaint touch of hand-woven tablecloths (protected under glass). In general, prices here are among the highest on the avenida, but this means soups cost 75 pesos, a serving of succulent sea turtle is 225 pesos. Full meals come to about 375 to 500 pesos, complete.

Of the other restaurants on Hidalgo, most are very similar in price and atmosphere to the **Restaurant La Mano de Dios,** on Hidalgo at the corner of Matamoros. A family operation, one suspects the family beds down for the night right in the dining room after the last dish has been washed. You can have lentil soup—delicious—and the filet of fish, plus a large fruit salad and a soft drink for a total bill of 250 pesos, although in the hot weather you might not have the appetite needed to finish it all. Shrimp cocktail, fried bananas, and other such delicacies are offered, along with the regulation chicken tacos, omelets, and breakfast huevos rancheros. Tablecloths are of plastic, the air is moved by ceiling fans, the whole front of the restaurant is open to the street, and the long fluorescent tubes are painted red and green for "atmosphere."

Right next to the plain Hotel Caracol is the fancy restaurant called **Ciro's,** very much like the aforementioned Gomar in decor, and also in price: various omelets cost 80 pesos; turtle, shrimp, or roast meat as an entree will cost about 240 pesos; chicken dishes cost a bit less as a rule. At Ciro's, the bonus is air conditioning.

More modern, spacious, and airy than most other eateries on Hidalgo is the **Restaurant Boca del Río,** across the street from La Mano de Dios at the corner of Matamoros. Prices at the Boca del Río are similar to those at La Mano, even a few pesos less on some items. They may have set out a few sidewalk tables, also.

The **Restaurant Estrellita Marinera,** on Hidalgo, always has a collection of café tables enclosed by groups of ardent people-watchers. In the afternoon, it's usually a busy spot as the comida costs a mere 95 pesos and comprises fried fish, rice, frijoles, and salad.

Across the street from the Estrellita Marinera is that essential establishment for fixing your own breakfast and picnics, the **Panadería La Gloria,** filled with fresh bread and sweet rolls.

Near the Ferry Dock

The **Restaurant Tropicana,** directly opposite the car-ferry dock, has a heavy patronage of local people. You couldn't call its Formica furniture romantic, nor its fluorescent lights, but the prices aren't bad: sopa de pollo costs 55 pesos, the island favorites of beef, turtle, or chicken go for 145 to 195 pesos, and lobster (the spiny variety) is about 425 pesos. Note that the Tropicana is open from 7 a.m. to 10 p.m. daily.

WHAT TO DO: Isla Mujeres is a sun and sea haven with all the attractions: snorkeling, swimming, fishing, or just plain relaxing. There are two beautiful beaches, one in town called the **Playa Cocos,** to your left as you get off the boat, and **Garrafon Beach** about five kilometers to your right. Playa Cocos is quite shallow and is better for swimming, while Garrafon beach with its coral reef is excellent for snorkeling.

There are several agencies which offer tours around the island as well as lessons in scuba diving and deep-sea fishing. The best tours I've found are those run by the **Union de Lancheros,** to the left as you get off the boat. Included in this adventure is a visit to the large turtles, and the biological station, swimming and snorkeling at Garrafon Beach, and a lunch of fish or shrimp from the day's catch at the little Idios Beach. The whole trip, including lunch, is 650 pesos per person and well worth it. (**Note:** Make your boating arrangements a day in advance as they like to get an early start at about 8 a.m.) Getting to Garrafon Beach on your own is difficult as there are no buses. You can walk (takes 1½ hours), hitch, rent a bicycle (150 pesos per day) or a moped (180 pesos for two hours), or take a taxi. The price for the last method will be high (160 pesos) even if you split the cost. Rent your snorkeling equipment before heading out of town for the beach. It should cost no more than 125 pesos for snorkel, mask, and fins. While at Garrafon you might like to take a walk to the south end of the island and its lighthouse. Just beyond the lighthouse is a Maya ruin believed to have been an observatory built to the moon goddess Ix-Chel.

The **Fortress of Mundaca** is about four kilometers in the same direction as Garrafon, off about half a kilometer to your left. The fortress was built by the pirate Mundaca Marecheaga who in the early 19th century arrived at Isla Mujeres and proceeded to set up a blissful paradise while making money from selling slaves to Cuba and Belize. The fortress is set in a pretty, shady park, and is a nice trip if you are suffering from too much sun.

Playa Lancheros, south of town a few miles, has shady palapas, a snack stand, and a good sandy beach.

Ask around at the docks, and you'll find a boatman who is willing to ferry you over to **Isla Contoy,** an uninhabited National Park island north of Isla Mujeres where the beaches are very fine, the bird life rich and colorful, and life is blissfully peaceful.

GETTING TO ISLA MUJERES: The island's position at the heart of the Mexican Caribbean's resort area, and its location just a few miles from the mainland, makes it easily accessible.

From Merida

Buses leave from the bus station several times a day, and you can travel either first or second class depending on the bus. Your destination is Puerto Juarez, from which you take a ferryboat to the island. You can also fly from Merida to Cancún, and proceed from there (see below).

From Cozumel

Aerocaribe operates daily flights between Cozumel and Isla Mujeres; contact them for schedules and rates at 2-0386 in Cozumel, 2-0064 in Isla Mujeres, 3-0394 in Cancún. If you don't fly, you must take a ferry to the mainland, then a bus to Puerto Juarez, then another ferry to Isla Mujeres (see below, and also in the Cozumel section). The new hydrofoil may make a trip between Cozumel and Isla Mujeres as service expands—check and see.

From Cancún

Aerocaribe operates a few flights, but it's hardly worth it to fly when you're so close. Take a Ruta 3 city bus to Puerto Juarez or Punta Sam to get the boat. Buses can be caught along the Avenida Tulum or Cancún, running about every 15 minutes.

The new hydrofoil service from the dock near the Convention Center in Cancún's Zona Turística has service to Isla Mujeres, but schedules are still in flux as the service is new. Check for current schedules at your hotel, or at a travel agency.

From Puerto Juarez

Puerto Juarez is the dock for the more expensive passenger boats to Isla Mujeres. Boats run at various times to the island; in busy seasons, boats run hourly. Fare is 25 to 50 pesos per person, and the trip takes about half an hour. Buy your ticket from the booth on the right just before the dock.

From Punta Sam

To save a bit of money, stay on the Ruta 3 bus from Cancún past Puerto Juarez to the end of the line at Punta Sam, a few miles north of Puerto Juarez. This is the car-ferry dock for Isla Mujeres, and a passenger ticket costs only 10 pesos; cars cost 85 pesos. Boats run from Punta Sam at 6, 8:30, and 11 a.m., and 2, 4, and 6 p.m. From Isla Mujeres, the return trips run at 5, 7, and 10 a.m., and 1, 3, and 5 p.m. In good weather, the car-ferry trip takes about 40 minutes one way.

7. Cozumel

In Mexico's Caribbean resort area, if Cancún is the jet-set's port of call and Isla Mujeres belongs to the beachcombers, Cozumel, 44 miles south of Cancún, is a little bit of both. More remote than either of the other two resorts, this island (pop. 30,000) becomes more of a world unto itself, a place where people come to get away from the day-tripping atmosphere of Isla Mujeres or the megadevelopment feeling of Cancún, a place to take each day as it comes for a week or more without moving very far from the hotel or the beach. There is actually little reason to leave the island as all the necessarys for a good vacation are here: excellent snorkeling and scuba places, sailing and water sports, fancy hotels and modest hotels, elegant restaurants and taco shops, even a Mayan ruin or two. If, after a while, you do get restless, the ancient Maya city of Tulum and the lagoon of Xel-ha provide convenient and exciting goals for excursions.

GETTING TO COZUMEL: Daily bus service from Merida via Puerto Juarez and Cancún provides easy access to Puerto Morelos, the dock for the car ferry to Cozumel, and to Playa del Carmen, the dock for the strictly passenger boat to the island. Both A.D.O. and Autobuses del Caribe have buses that arrive in time to catch departing ferries, and to meet returning ferries. In addition, there's now a hydrofoil service direct from Cancún.

The Hydrofoil

A new daily hydrofoil service has been started by the Secretaría de Turismo between Punta Cancún and Cozumel. The Cancún dock is near the convention center in the Zona Turística. Ask at any travel agency or hotel travel desk for the latest schedules and fares.

The Car Ferry

Car ferries leave from Puerto Morelos, 21 miles south of Cancún, daily at 6 a.m. for the 2½- to 4-hour voyage; be at the ticket office by 5 a.m. to buy your ticket. Passenger cars and small campers have preference over larger vehicles, and so there's hardly ever a problem getting a ticket if you're there on time. The return voyage from Cozumel leaves the new car-ferry dock, south of town near the Hotel Sol Caribe, at 10 or so, but be there by 9 a.m. to buy your ticket and get in line. The fares are 80 pesos per person, 425 pesos per vehicle. Of course, you don't have to have a car to use this ferry (which is closer to Cancún than is the strictly passenger boat from Playa del Carmen). Passengers on foot are welcome aboard, but it is inconvenient to get to the docks by bus at that early hour. For hints on a place to stay and eat, see "Heading South," below.

The Passenger Boat

Three boats a day in each direction ply the waters between Cozumel's downtown dock and Playa del Carmen, 44 miles south of Cancún. From Playa del Carmen, times are 6 a.m., noon, and 6 p.m.; from Cozumel, times are 4, 7, and 9:30 a.m., and 4 p.m. The trip takes 45 minutes and costs 110 pesos. If you must wait overnight at Playa del Carmen, there is one (expensive) hotel, the **Hotel Molcos,** which will rent you a room with bath, air conditioning, and a sea view for 1300 pesos double; meals in the restaurant are on the comida corrida plan, and cost 400 pesos for lunch or dinner. Make reservations by calling Turismo Aviomar in Merida at 992/1-6661 or 1-6620. Several parking lots in Playa del Carmen will take care of your car while you're on Cozumel for about 50 pesos per day.

The Hotel Molcos is located conveniently near the dock. But up in the village of Playa del Carmen, on the road into town from the highway on the right-hand side, is the **Posada Lily,** a small hostelry offering rooms for 650 pesos, bath-equipped, of course. You can walk the mile to the dock in 15 or 20 minutes if your bags aren't impossibly heavy.

Near the Posada Lily, on the other side of the street, is a little **Motel** (so-called), with no other name. Simple rooms in this new structure cost 725 pesos, all in.

Flights

Both Mexicana and AeroMéxico operate daily flights to and from Cozumel and Merida and Mexico City; one or the other also runs planes from the following cities: Houston, Miami, Villahermosa, Oaxaca, and Acapulco.

Aerocaribe operates small planes in the eastern Yucatán, connecting Cozumel with Cancún, Chetumal, Isla Mujeres, Chichén-Itzá, and Merida. Their office in Cozumel is on Avenida Rafael Melgar south of the main square (tel. 2-0386).

Aero Cozumel, located at Playa del Carmen's fledgling airstrip and at Cozumel's airport, operates an air shuttle service in modern eight-seat planes between Playa Del Carmen and Cozumel. Flights leave about every half hour during the day, take only eight minutes to make the trip, and cost 550 pesos one way. It's nice to have this alternative to the ferry ride, which can be noisy, windy, and fraught with the dangers of seasickness. Aero Cozumel runs day trips to and from Cancún, as well.

WHERE TO STAY: These days Cozumel has a good selection of hotels in all price ranges. In summer there is usually little trouble finding a room. In the high-season months of December, January, February, and March, it's good to write ahead for reservations. Prices are higher in those months as well.

398 MEXICO ON $20 A DAY

First I'll detail the better, moderately priced hotels, and then move on to the very low-priced places.

You can hardly do better than the **Hotel Vista del Mar** (tel. 987/2-0545), on the shoreline promenade called Avenida Rafael Melgar at no. 45. Large rooms here shine with white paint and a joyful decor, which includes, in many rooms, a sea-view wall entirely of glass opening onto a small balcony from which you can gaze at the public beach just across the street, and far out to sea. Each room has its own air conditioner, and prices are set according to the season and whether or not the room has a view: off-season the rooms cost 900 pesos double without the view, 975 pesos with; during high-season months of mid-November to mid-April prices are slightly higher. If you can afford it, try this place first.

Whether or not you will feel "Comfortable as In Your Own Home," as advertised in the brochure, you are certain to admire the **Hotel Elizabeth** (tel. 987/2-0545), Calle Dr. A. Rosado Salas no. 3-A, for their cleanliness and the helpfulness of the staff. A minute and manicured garden plot adds a splash of green. You have two choices for accommodations: suites come with kitchen, living room, and bedroom, a refrigerator and all utensils, and cost 1350 pesos double; the double rooms (no kitchen) cost 925 pesos.

A downtown hotel with great appeal is the **Hotel Mary-Carmen** (tel. 987/2-0581), 5a Avenida Sur 4, half a block from the zócalo (main square). Watched over by a conscientious collection of matronly señoras, the hotel specializes in cleanliness and some elegant touches: brocade couches in the lobby, extra decoration in the rooms, screens on the windows, and a mammoth *mamey* tree in the courtyard. The two-story structure harbors 27 rooms priced at 800 pesos single, 990 pesos double (with two beds). All rooms have beautiful tile baths and also air conditioning.

On the waterfront drive, the **Hotel Bahía** (tel. 987/2-0209; Apdo. Postal 286), Avenida Rafael E. Melgar 25, is the perfect answer to a budget hotel seeker's dream. A sky-blue and sea-blue color scheme is 100% appropriate here, and the rooms are modern, quite clean, and all have good tiled showers. The help is friendly. All 18 rooms have air conditioning and cost 660 pesos single, 770 pesos double. A few rooms have a smidgen of sea view—nothing panoramic.

The **Hotel Barracuda** (tel. 987/2-0209; Apdo. Postal 163) Avenida Rafael E. Melgar Prolongación Sur, is a bit expensive for our budget but will be of special interest to divers. The rooms are tiny, but each has a tiny sea-view balcony and is clean, modern, and cheerful. Lack of size in the rooms is made up by the palm-tree-and-beach view. You get a small refrigerator in your room, and also air conditioning. The hotel has its own beach, snorkel-renting place, scuba school and boats, waterskiing gear, etc.—in short, everything for the water-sports freak. Continental breakfast and cold drinks are available, but no meals—you'll have to walk five or ten minutes into town for those. Prices are 1200 pesos single, 1850 pesos double. Rates are the same year round.

A modern hotel which looks as if it should be expensive—but isn't—that's the **Hotel Maya Cozumel** (tel. 987/2-0011), Calle 5a Sur no. 4. The upbeat rooms are painted in white and orange and have odd triangular showers. Comfy leather deck chairs add another touch of class. In the rear court is a small swimming pool surrounded by thick lawn and bougainvillea; a small restaurant/bar looks onto the lawn and pool. Housekeeping standards could be a bit better, but the price is right: 790 pesos double.

The **Hotel El Marques** (tel. 987/2-0537), 5a Avenida Sur no. 12, right downtown, has several surprising touches which make it a delight. The rooms have quaint formal-ish touches such as ersatz gold trim and Formica-marble countertops, but the air conditioning is genuine, the baths are kept quite clean, and the staff is attentive. The big surprise is the tiny swimming pool (you won't expect the hotel to have one when you see it) and the ingenious wall-waterfall behind it, next to a minuscule bar. Rates are 750 pesos single, 895 pesos double. A great place!

Right across the street from the El Marques is a mini-mall of shops, and also the **Hotel Suites Bazar Colonial** (tel. 987/2-0506), Avenida 5 Sur no. 9. Prices at this nice, new hostelry might seem high at 1500 pesos double in the junior suites, and 1850 pesos double in the master suites, but you get a nicely appointed studio or one-bedroom apartment, with complete kitchenette, for the cost. It's certainly one of the few hotels on the island to have an elevator, which serves its four floors. Rooms are quiet, and air-conditioned.

The **Posada Letty** (no phone) is hard to find because there's nothing to tell you it's a hotel except for a tiny sign: no lobby, reception desk, potted palms. But the rooms are there, each with louvered wooden shutters on the windows to let in the breeze and ceiling fans to whirl it around. All rooms have tiled showers and ceiling fans, and single travelers pay 440 pesos, two persons pay 550 pesos for any of the eight rooms on two floors. To get to the Letty, walk from the main square up Calle 1 Sur past the Banco del Atlantico until you see the small sign on the right-hand side of the street. The man who runs the Letty works in the little store on the corner just past the pension. Official address: Calle 1 Sur at 15a Avenida Sur.

The **Hotel Pepita** (tel. 987/2-0098), 15a Avenida Sur no. 6 (or no. 120, by a later numbering system), corner of Calle 1 Sur, is more like a pension than a hotel. Rooms, some old, some new, some abuilding, have been fixed up with ceiling fans and tile baths and rent for 625 pesos single, 850 pesos double, 975 pesos triple, but this may include such luxuries as a mammoth bottle of purified water *in the room,* as well as a small refrigerator to keep it cool. It's very quiet here on the back street, and if your room gets stuffy you can relax in the very beautiful garden terrace to one side of the hotel. For reservations, write to Apdo. Postal 56.

A quiet downtown choice is the **Hotel El Pirata** (tel. 987/2-0051), 5a Avenida Sur no. 3-A, a small place with quite acceptable standard rooms going for 550 pesos single, 630 pesos double with ceiling fan, or 630 pesos single, 720 pesos double with air conditioning. Here you're only two blocks from the ferry dock and a stone's throw from the main square.

WHERE TO EAT: Cozumel is well provided with places to dine, but one must be careful in choosing a place because "resort food" is a problem here, as it is in most seaside resorts. Proprietors think that hungry customers will show up whether the food is good or not, and they're not far from wrong. A number of places rise above this level of thinking, though, and here they are:

Best all-around is a restaurant suitable for breakfast, lunch, dinner, or just a late-night dish of ice cream. The **Restaurant Las Palmeras** is only a few steps from the zócalo at the corner of Avenidas Juarez and Rafael Melgar, very near the ferry dock. Las Palmeras is open to the four winds, although tables are shaded from the sun. Always busy, service is nonetheless fairly efficient, and prices are moderate. A set breakfast of bacon, eggs, and strong coffee will cost 160 pesos, a light lunch of enchiladas suizas followed by guayaba con queso (guava paste with a slice of cheese, and crackers—delicious!) will be only about 220 pesos. Dinner can be light as lunch, or can run to seafood (250 to 450 pesos per plate) or even lobster (550 pesos).

Right across the street from Las Palmeras is the **Restaurant El Portal,** a bit more formal a place, at least in appearance. The "portal" is a Spanish-style brick arcade, and the colonial theme is pursued throughout the one huge dining room. Service tends to be a bit slow, but prices are moderate: filete de pescado (fish filet), served either amandine or Yucatecan style, is 200 pesos, other entrees a bit more.

Pepe's Plaza Restaurant, 5a Avenida no. 2, just around the corner from the main square, is an old favorite of mine which is fast approaching the limits of our budget. With care, though, you should be able to enjoy a delicious lunch here. A nice club sandwich, for instance, with a bottle of beer and ice cream for dessert, costs about 250 pesos. At dinnertime, prices go up: onion soup, a charcoal-grilled steak or a fish, and dessert, may set you back 700 to 1000 pesos, all in, which is too much.

Pepe has other restaurants in town. **Pepe's Grill,** south of the main square on the waterfront drive (Avenida Rafael Melgar), is deluxe compared to Pepe's Plaza: low lights, soft music, solicitous waiters. Tables are open to sea breezes; failing that, ceiling fans move the air. The menu is short and not cheap, with most meat and fish courses costing 600 pesos, although a Mexican combination plate is 400 pesos. Despite the prices, it's a very popular place.

BBQ Pepe's Place, on Melgar north of the square between Calles 4 and 6 Norte, is the newest Pepe place. The specialty is barbecued spare ribs, chicken, and roast beef. The decor and service is beach-bum hideaway, with high-volume rock music accompaniment: old wagon wheels, plants, funky-posh design of wood beams and paraphernalia. There's a view of the bay, and a menu (in English) with prices similar to those at other Pepe places.

For a semi-elegant meal, my favorite place is the **Restaurant Bar La Langosta,** down at the south end of Avenida Melgar near the post office and that funny lighthouse. It's a nice big open palapa by the sea, good service, lower prices than most restaurants right in town, and a short, sweet menu. A New York-cut steak is priced at 400 pesos, a lobster at 500 pesos, and all main courses come with rice and vegetable. Add a bowl of soup and a bottle of beer or glass of wine, and you'll pay 700 to 800 pesos for dinner here. The restaurant is open from 2 p.m. to midnight.

The **Soberanis** chain is opening a new, large restaurant on the southern reaches of Avenida Melgar. In fact, they'll probably be serving by the time you arrive, having closed their small location right on the main square. Soberanis specializes in seafood, but in recent years quality has suffered. Let's hope this new place can resurrect the old reputation.

The ubiquitous Carlos & Charlie's has an eatery in Cozumel, upstairs one flight near the AeroMéxico office and the new Cine Cozumel on Avenida Melgar north of the square. Called **Carlos & Charlie's and Jimmy Kitchen,** it's got the requisite antique photos and posters, rock music, ceiling fans, brash waiters, etc. Have an oyster cocktail or crema de langosta (cream of lobster soup) as an appetizer, then pescado pibil (Yucatán-style fish) or even pescado borracho ("drunken" fish, stewed in beer), plus one of the creative desserts. With beverage, tax, and tip, expect to pay 500 or 600 pesos. You can drop in just for a drink in the little lounge overlooking the water, perfect for a sunset.

Less Expensive Fare

Although Cozumel does have resort prices, there are also some places at which to have a low-priced meal. For an inexpensive burger, head south along Melgar to **Pancho Burger,** more or less across from the post office. A brightly lit, modern stand-up or take-out place, Pancho Burger serves up American-style hamburgers and cheeseburgers for 65 pesos or so, depending on the one you order. Cold drinks are sold as well.

When Cozumel has a pizza joint, it's no dive, and so **Pizza Rolandi,** four blocks north of the main square along Avenida Rafael Melgar, is about as elegant a pizzeria as you're likely to run into anywhere. Deck chairs and red-and-white checkered tablecloths make the interior garden very mod, and candle lamps add romance. The Four Seasons pizza, at 225 pesos, is eight inches in diameter and serves only one person, but what a serving: it comes topped with black olives, tomatoes, asparagus, cheese, and ham. The pizza margarita costs only 200 pesos, but others (six kinds) are all priced the same as the Four Seasons. Wine, beer, and mixed drinks are all served. Rolandi is open from noon to midnight daily.

Starvation Budget Restaurants

Although you may doubt it, there are possibilities for dining on Cozumel which will leave your budget not only intact, but robustly healthy. On Calle 2 Norte, half a block in from the waterfront, is the **Panificadora Cozumel,** excellent for a do-it-yourself breakfast, or for picnic supplies. Right across the street from the panificadora is the **Cocina La Económica,** a tiny family-run *fogata* ("cookfire"). Were it not for the plastic-covered tables and chairs you might think you were wandering into somebody's kitchen. Well, that's about what it's like as the señora cooks up daily comidas corridas (set-price lunches) for lowly sums such as 80 to 100 pesos for four or five courses. À la carte dishes are equally cheap, but it's best to avoid the menu and just ask the señora what's cooking today. The Económica is a holdover from the days when sleepy Cozumel had lots of these mama-run eateries. Let's hope it survives a good many more years.

For informal outdoor starvation-budget dining, head up Avenida Juarez 3½ blocks from the zócalo to the **Jardín Cristal,** a small *taquería* on the right-hand side very near the Hotel Meson del Peregrino. Open usually only in the evenings from 6 to 11 p.m.; the señora and señoritas at the Cristal will bring you plates of panuchos (tortillas with frijoles inside, sort of like tortilla-size ravioli) for 18 pesos per panucho. With shredded chicken, lettuce, and tomato on top, a few of these make a good light supper. Various tacos are also 18 pesos apiece, as are soft drinks. The Jardín Cristal is Cozumel's answer to the neighborhood snackbar.

WHAT TO DO: What is there to do on Cozumel? Tour the island, swim, snorkel, scuba-dive, that's what. Let's start with a tour so you can get the lay of the land.

Touring the Island

The question of tours brings us to rentals, as there is no good reason to take an organized tour. You can rent a bicycle, motorbike, or car, and the motorized vehicles will take you around the southern part of the island easily in a half day, although it will take all day to cover the 70 kilometers (42 miles) on a bicycle.

Lots of places in town rent vehicles, but one of the oldest established places is **Ruben's Renta de Vehiculos** (tel. 2-0258), Calle 1 Sur no. 21. Ruben's will rent you a bicycle for 250 pesos per day, a motorbike for 125 pesos an hour or 1000 pesos a day, a car (VW Safari) for a few hundred pesos more. Arrange your rental a day in advance, and get there early in the morning if you want to get the best vehicle—the one on which most of the gadgets (horn, lights, starter, seats, etc.) work.

Be aware that all of these vehicles are open to the sun, and that you can get burned easily. There's a tendency to forget that riding in the sun is just as much exposure as lying in the sun.

Now that you've rented your vehicle, perhaps packed a lunch, you're ready to start off on a tour of Cozumel's beaches and snorkeling spots.

The Beaches

Head south along Avenida Melgar out of town, past the Hotel Barracuda. The Hotel La Perla is next, then the Villa Blanca. Remember that no hotel in Mexico "owns" the beach—by law, all beaches are public property, so feel free to use a "hotel" beach. On Cozumel this public ownership is more important than ever, as most of the island is surrounded by coral reefs difficult to walk across (that coral is sharp!) let alone lie on.

About eight kilometers (five miles) south of town you'll come to the big Sol Caribe and La Ceiba hotels, and also the car-ferry dock, for ferries to Puerto Morelos. Go snorkeling out in the water by the Hotel La Ceiba, and you might spot a sunken airplane. No, it's not the wreckage of a disaster; it was put there for an underwater movie.

A mile past the hotels is famous **Chancanab,** recently fixed up by the tourism authorities. Chancanab has a reputation for fine swimming and underwater scenery.

Next beach you'll come to heading south is **Playa Maya.** The beach is nothing special, but it's a beach (and on Cozumel that counts for a lot). A small restaurant will provide sustenance. The **Playa San Francisco,** 16 kilometers from town, is much nicer, with several little eateries and a beach club.

After Playa San Francisco, the drive becomes boring as you plough through the jungle on a straight road for miles. The only distraction is the turnoff (on the left) to Cedral, a tiny market hamlet which is deserted most of the time. Otherwise, all you see is jungle until you're 28 kilometers (17½ miles) from town.

Finally, though, you emerge near the southern reaches of the island on the east coast. The lighthouse you see to the south is at **Punta Celarain,** the island's southernmost tip. The sand track is not suitable for motorbikes, but in a car you can drive to the lighthouse in about 25 minutes.

The road along the east coast of the island is wonderful. Views of the sea and the rocky shore, surf pounding into it, on the land side are little farms and hamlets. Exotic birds take flight as you approach, and monstrous (but harmless) iguanas skitter off into the undergrowth. Most of the east coast is unsafe for swimming because the surf can create a deadly *undertow,* which will have you far out to sea in a matter of minutes. But at a few places on this coast there are headlands and breakers which create safe swimming areas. At **Chan Río** you can swim, and also at **Punta Morena,** where there is even a small motel and restaurant. **Playa Chiqueros** is also safe, and has a little restaurant.

Halfway up the east coast, the paved road meets the transversal road back to town, 15 kilometers (9½ miles) away.

Continuing On . . .

Not ready to go back to town yet? For adventure, start out on the sand track that continues north from this junction. Follow this road for 18 very rough and rocky kilometers through the jungle, past little abandoned farms, along the rocky shore to **El Castillo Real,** an unimpressive but authentic Maya ruin in the middle of nowhere. The trip from the paved road to the Castillo takes 1½ hours, and then the same amount of time to return, but the time is spent watching hermit crabs scutter through the sand, watching lizards watch you, and listening to pairs of parrots squawk as they wing overhead. Don't attempt this trip in a large or a low car, or on a motorbike. Best thing to have is a VW Safari.

Back in Town

The adventure over, spend some time strolling along the Avenida Rafael Melgar admiring the unique black coral which is found in Cozumel's waters, and which is made into all sorts of fanciful jewelry.

At night, check out what's playing at the Cine Cozumel, Avenida Rafael Melgar between 2 Norte and 4 Norte. It's probably in Spanish, but when it comes to the light melodrama usually offered here, that's just as well.

North of Town

Head north of town along the west coast and you'll pass a yacht marina and several older hotels as well as some new condominiums. A few of the hotels sit atop nice beaches. Feel free to use them (the beaches, not the hotels).

Snorkeling and Scuba-Diving

Anyone who can swim can go snorkeling. Rental of the snorkel (breathing pipe), goggles, and flippers should only cost about 100 pesos for a half day. The brilliantly colored tropical fish provide a dazzling show for free.

Various establishments on the island rent Scuba gear—tanks, regulator with pressure gauge, buoyancy compensator, mask, snorkel, and flippers. Many will also arrange a half-day expedition in a boat complete with lunch for a set price. Sign up the day before, if you're interested.

Boat Excursions

Another popular Cozumel pastime is the boat excursion, by yourself or as part of a group, with snorkeling or Scuba-diving or without. Various types of tours are offered, including a glass-bottom boat tour lasting 1½ hours and costing 300 pesos per person. You can make arrangements, among other places, at the **Sociedad Cooperativa de Producción de Servicios Turísticos San Miguel** (whew!), on Avenida Melgar between Calles 4 and 6 Norte (tel. 2-0080).

HEADING SOUTH: From Playa del Carmen it's possible to catch a bus heading south past Xel-ha, Tulum, and Felipe Carrillo Puerto to Chetumal. If you're going to Xel-ha, Tulum, and Cobá, you'll have to take your chances catching buses as no routes terminate or originate in those places.

8. Xel-ha, Tulum, and Cobá

The ruins of the walled Mayan seaside city of Tulum are among the major archeological attractions in the Yucatán, and the incredibly beautiful cove of Xel-ha is a timeless bit of paradise. As of this writing, both are best approached by means of a guided tour or rental car (find others, and split the cost) as there are few lodging places, and only very basic or very expensive restaurants, nearby. Little shack loncherías at the entrance to Tulum ruins sell the makings of light meals at rather high prices. You can get cold drinks here, too.

Pemex gasolines are on sale at the Tulum turnoff; the next station is at Felipe Carrillo Puerto, a two-hour drive to the south. Buses will stop to pick up passengers at the Tulum turnoff if there are vacant seats available on the bus.

HEADING SOUTH: Starting at Puerto Juarez or Cancún, your car or bus passes the Cancún airport before heading out onto the open road. About 36 kilometers (23 miles) south of Puerto Juarez is **Puerto Morelos,** the dock for the car ferry to Cozumel. Those planning to visit that island, and to take their cars, will have to get up very early in order to get to the dock in time (see above, "Getting to Cozumel"). An alternative would be to stay overnight at the little **Posada Amor,** on the inland road to the ferry dock, on the right-hand side. Simple rooms with screens on the windows and one common bathroom rent for 400 pesos double. The restaurant is rustic and very amusing: a big thatched hut decorated with painted wooden masks, craft items, and a motorcycle helmet in each corner. Ask what they have—the menu is liable to be limited to one or two items. Prices are reasonable, and an entire meal need cost only 150 pesos or so. No alcohol is served.

The village of Muchi is the next landmark after Puerto Morelos: and soon you're in **Playa del Carmen,** 32 kilometers (20 miles) south of Puerto Morelos. Playa del Carmen, being the dock for the passenger boats to Cozumel, has several places to stay and to eat. See "Getting to Cozumel" for details.

Continuing south, your journey will bring you to **Akumal** (36 kilometers, 22½ miles), which has a fine beach and two resort-type expensive hotels, the Club Akumal Caribe and the Hotel Villa Maya & Casitas; then Aventura, a beach being developed by the tourism authorities (it has a long way to go yet); Chemuyil, a similar beach development; X-Cacel, yet another beach; and Xel-ha.

XEL-HA: The Caribbean coast of the Yucatán is carved by the sea into hundreds of small *caletas* (coves) which form the perfect habitat for tropical marine life, both flora and fauna. Many caletas remain undiscovered and pristine along the coast, but one caleta 117 kilometers south of Cancún is enjoyed daily by snorkelers and scuba-divers who come to luxuriate in its warm waters, palm-lined shore, and brilliant fish. Xel-ha (that's "SHELL-hah") is a bit of paradise for swimming, with no threat of undertow or pollution. Being close to the ruins at Tulum makes Xel-ha the best place for a dip when you've finished clambering around the Maya castles. The short 8½-mile hop north from Tulum to Xel-ha is hard to do by bus, but you may have luck hitchhiking. Those who don't have a car and who don't want to chance missing Xel-ha can sign up for a tour: most companies include a trip to Tulum and a swim at Xel-ha in the same journey.

The entrance to Xel-ha is half a mile in from the highway. You'll be asked to pay a 22-peso "contribution" to the upkeep and preservation of the site.

Once in the park, you can rent snorkeling equipment, buy a drink or a meal, change clothes, and take showers—facilities for all these are available. When you swim, be careful to observe the "swim here" and "no swimming" signs. (*Hint:* In the swimming areas, the greatest variety of fish are to be seen right near the ropes marking off the "no swimming" areas, and near any groups of rocks.) Xel-ha is an exceptionally beautiful place!

TULUM: At the end of the Classic period in A.D. 900 the Maya civilization began to decline and most of the large ceremonial centers were deserted. The Postclassic period (A.D. 900 to the Spanish Conquest) in the Yucatán is one of small rival states, Maya in culture but with some imported traditions from the Mexicans. Tulum is one such city-state, built in the tenth century as a fortress city overlooking the Caribbean. Aside from the spectacular setting, Tulum is not otherwise an impressive city. There are no magnificent pyramidal structures as are found in the Classic Maya ruins. The most imposing building in Tulum is the large stone structure on the cliff called the **Castillo** (castle), actually a temple-cum-fortress. At one time this was covered with stucco and painted. The view from on top of the Castillo is quite grand. From here you get a good view of the city walls which are constructed of limestone. In front of the Castillo are several palace-like buildings: unrestored stone structures partially covered with stucco. The **Temple of the Frescoes** is directly in front of the Castillo and contains some 13th-century wall paintings, which are quite interesting. They are inside the temple and the lighting is bad, so if you have a flashlight it would be helpful to bring it along. Most of the frescoes are hard to see, but they are distinctly Maya in content: representing the gods Chac (rain god) and Ix Chel (the goddess of the moon and of medicine). On the cornice of this temple is a relief of the head of a god. If you get a slight distance from the building you will see the eyes, nose, mouth, and chin. Notice the remains of the red-painted stucco on this building—at one time all the buildings at Tulum were painted a bright red.

Much of what we know of Tulum at the time of the Spanish Conquest comes from the writings of Diego de Landa, third bishop of Yucatán. He wrote that Tulum was a small city inhabited by about 600 people, who lived in dwellings situated on platforms along a street. The town commanded a strategic point on the Caribbean and thus supervised the trade traffic from Honduras to the Yucatán. Tulum survived about 70 years after the Conquest, when it was finally abandoned.

The ruins are open 8 a.m. to 5 p.m. Admission is 10 pesos.

Where to Stay and Eat

The turnoff to the Tulum ruins (left), at the Pemex station, is the first point you hit coming south from Xel-ha. At this turnoff you'll find a small airstrip (to the right, northwest), two moderately priced restaurants, and the small two-story **Motel El Crucero**. It's very simple and basic, but rooms have hot and cold water, ceiling fans, and prices of 750 pesos double. Get a room downstairs if possible, as these are the cooler ones. For food, you have El Crucero's thatched restaurant, or **El Faisan y El Venado** across the road. El Faisan y El Venado, "The Pheasant and the Deer," is a translation of the Mayan word Yucatán, meaning "the land of pheasants and deer."

In at the entrance to the ruins are small soft-drink stands and eateries serving up things at resort prices. Not much you can do about it, though, if you're hungry. The **Centro Chac Mool**—it's that modern palapa on the beach north of the ruins—gives more, but charges more as well.

About a mile south of the turnoff to Tulum is the road to Cobá, another fascinating Maya city. Less than a mile past the Cobá road is Tulum village, with little to offer the tourist. If you're driving, turn right when you see the signs to Cobá, and continue on that road for 50 kilometers (30 miles).

COBÁ: The Yucatán is rich in breathtaking Mayan cities, but in its time, fewer were grander than Cobá. Linked to important cities many miles distant by excellent, straight roads through the jungle, Cobá itself covered numerous square miles on the shores of two Yucatecan lakes.

Today the city's principal monuments are on display again, but unless you take a tour or rent a car, they're difficult to reach.

Pay the 10-peso admission fee at the little entrance shack, and stroll into the ruins. Keep your bearings as it's very easy to get lost on the maze of dirt roads in the jungle.

The Grupo Cobá boasts a large, impressive pyramid just in the entry gate to the right. Were you to go straight, you'd pass near the badly ruined *juego de pelota* (ball court).

Straight in from the entry gate, walk for 10 or 15 minutes to a fork in the road. The right fork leads to Nohoch Mul group, which contains El Castillo, the highest pyramid in the Yucatán (higher than the great El Castillo at Chichén-Itzá and the Pyramid of the Magician at Uxmal). The left fork (more or less straight on) goes to the Conjunto Las Pinturas. Here, the main attraction is the Pyramid of the Painted Lintel, a small structure with traces of the original bright colors above the door. You can climb up to get a close look.

Throughout the area, intricately carved stelae stand by pathways, or lie forlornly in the jungle underbrush.

It can be hot here deep in the jungle. You'd be well advised to visit Cobá in the morning, or after the heat of the day has passed.

9. Carrillo Puerto and Chetumal

From the Cobá turnoff, the main highway (no. 307) heads southwest through Tulum village. About 23 kilometers south of the village are the ruins of **Chunyaxche**, on the left-hand side (look for the little restaurant). The ruins aren't very exciting, but the price is right: admission is free after you sign the register. In exploring Chunyaxche, I was virtually eaten alive by mosquitos in the beautiful jungle. You may have better luck, though.

After Chunyaxche, the highway passes 72 kilometers (45 miles) of jungle-bordered road with few distractions. Then comes an oasis of sorts.

FELIPE CARRILLO PUERTO: Felipe Carrillo Puerto (pop. 15,000) is the only oasis in the jungle along the road to Ciudad Chetumal, and has this to offer: several banks (off the zócalo), gas stations, a market, a small ice plant, a bus terminal, the intersection with the road back to Merida, and a presentable handful of modest hotels and restaurants to serve the traveler's needs. Carrillo Puerto is the turning point for those making a "short circuit" of the Yucatán Peninsula, as Highway 184 heads west from here to Ticul, Uxmal, Campeche, and Merida. It is quite possible you may have to spend the night here, and very probably that you will arrive in town hungry.

Where to Stay and Eat

The highway goes right through the town, becoming Avenida Benito Juarez in town. Coming from the north, you will pass a traffic circle with a bust of the great Juarez. The town market is here. Just south of the traffic circle you can observe the following: a modest establishment on the left called **Tortas y Hamburguesas La Avenida.** For all its modesty, this little señora-run eatery is extremely popular with local people because the delicious tortas (sandwiches) and hamburgers are sold at bargain prices of about 18 to 28 pesos.

Past Tortas y Hamburguesas is **El Faisan y El Venado**, on the left, a typically F.C.P. restaurant with those high-backed plastic kitchen chairs you've now become familiar with, plus ceiling fans, child waiters, and meal prices of about 200 pesos. Want a venison steak? They may have some in, so ask. More attractive restaurants are just a few steps down the street.

With a Pemex gas station on your right, the **Restaurant 24 Horas** will be on your left. Tidier than El Faisan y El Venado, but priced about the same, the 24 Horas has long hours—24 of them, in fact—to recommend it, plus decent food at moderate prices. Also, it has a breathtaking Mayan glyph picture stone gracing the wall of its dining room. Be sure to take a look. This is the place to come for breakfast especially, as it'll be the only place in town open early. Scrambled eggs, ham, instant coffee, and watermelon slices will cost 150 pesos. For cheaper fare, you can wait until the little café across the street opens up.

The aforementioned restaurant is not bad, although it tends to fill up in the evening with beer drinkers rather than diners. For a nice dinner, the pillars of local society go to the place right next door, the **Restaurant Zona Maya**. Open for lunch and dinner only, the Zona Maya is wonderfully air-conditioned, be-Muzak'd, and supplied with provisions. A good hamburger or sandwich, with a soft drink, will cost 100 pesos, a pizza big enough for two people will be 200 pesos, a plate of roast chicken with french fries 175 pesos. Decor (as though it mattered, with that heavenly air conditioning) is a leopard skin, some crossed machetes, and a bug zapper. And double-knit table cloths. Felipe Carrillo Puerto, it has been noted by this observer, is a town dedicated to the creative use of double-knit synthetic fabrics. By the way, beer—and wine!—are served, and the beer-only crowd is kept at bay by a sign that says "We reserve—strictly—the right of admission."

Just pass the Restaurant Zona Maya is the small **Hotel San Ignacio**, a simple place with an interior court (for parking), and clean if very bare rooms. Prices are 300 pesos single, 600 pesos double, 800 pesos triple, with private bath and ceiling fan. Get to bed early—this town wakes with the dawn.

The street which crosses Avenida Juarez at the Hotel San Ignacio is Calle 67. Turn right onto it, go up past the banks (Banobras and Banrural), and you will see the main square. Turn right just before the square for the **Hotel Chan Santa Cruz**, located more or less behind the bank buildings. The plain rooms here, grouped around a courtyard in older buildings, cost slightly less than at the San Ignacio.

On the main square, diagonal to the church, is an old Caribbean-style building—look for the wooden gallery on the second story. This houses the **Hotel Esquivel**, an odd collection of rooms, many with added-on showers, all neat and well kept if basic. Ceiling fans keep you cool; in some cases, double-knit sheets and pillowslips keep you hot. The lamp tables are sections of Mayan columns from temples. Original oil paintings decorate some walls. As for prices, the Esquivel is similar to the other places in town: 300 pesos single, 550 pesos double, 750 pesos triple. Parking in the rear.

Lake Bacalar

From Carrillo Puerto to Chetumal is another 2½ hours' ride. About 100 kilometers (64 miles) past Carrillo Puerto you'll sight the limpid waters of Lake Bacalar, a crystal-clear body of water fed by swamps and streams. It's a heavenly place to swim, and the perfect place for a resort, but so far progress in building facilities has been painfully slow. If you're in your own car, take a detour through the village of Bacalar and down along the lakeshore drive.

You'll pass the **Hotel Laguna,** which has been under construction for a decade, and will probably be that way for another decade. Rooms here (there are only a few complete) are overpriced at 900 pesos for two, but this is all there is. Past the Laguna a way is a small, extremely primitive camping area on the shore.

As you approach the end of the lake, Highway 307 intersects Highway 186. Turn right, and you're headed west to Escárcega, Palenque, and Villahermosa; turn left, and you'll be going toward Chetumal. The turnoff to Belize is on the road *before* you enter Chetumal, but you may need to stop in the town for a meal or a bed.

CHETUMAL: The territory of Quintana Roo recently surpassed the minimum population requirements for statehood in the Mexican union, and so Chetumal (pop. 50,000) is now the capital of the new state of Quintana Roo. While a territory, it was a free-trade zone to encourage trade and immigration, and as the free-trade regulation is still in effect, much of the town is given over to small shops selling a strange assortment of imported junk and treasures of pretty inflated prices. The old part of town, down by the river (Río Hondo), preserves a Caribbean atmosphere with its wooden buildings (and sticky heat), but the newer parts are modern (and rather raw) Mexican. Lots of noise and heat, so your best plan would be not to stay—vacant rooms are difficult to find—but if you must, here are some hints.

Where to Stay and Eat

Behind the Central Bus Station is the **Hotel Real Azteca** (tel. 983/2-0666), Calle Belize 186. Walking out the front door of the bus station, turn left and walk past the market (on your left), turn left again (so the large CFE plant is on your right), and go down a block to the Calle Belize. Turn right, and the hotel is on the left-hand side of the street. It's modern, clean, and all airconditioned, and costs 600 pesos single, 875 pesos double. This is your first choice. If it's full, the **Hotel Continental Caribe** (tel. 983/2-1100), across the street from the bus station entrance, at Avenida Héroes 71, has recently been rebuilt into a luxury palace, a modern Sheraton-type establishment with central air conditioning, a series of swimming pools in the courtyard, a restaurant large as a basketball court (and cold as a cave), and prices to match: 1600 pesos single, 1800 pesos double. It rents a lot of rooms though, even at those prices, because Chetumal is booming and rooms are scarce, particularly comfortable, air-conditioned rooms.

Down the hill from the bus station on Avenida Héroes, 1½ blocks in toward the center of town, is the Continental Caribe's competition. The **Hotel El Presidente** (tel. 983/2-0542 or 2-0544) has similar central air, pool, and restaurant, and is presently attempting to swipe the Continental's business by charging 1500 pesos single, 1700 pesos double.

Still farther down along Avenida Héroes at the corner of Avenida Obregon four longish blocks from the bus station, is the **Hotel Jacaranda** (tel. 983/2-1155), a modernish two-story hostelry which is undistinguished except for its prices, which are a pleasure to relate: 250 to 375 pesos single, 400 to 550 pesos double, the higher prices being for rooms with that blessed air conditioning. Many similarly priced hotels are right nearby.

Another budget choice is the **Hotel San Jorge** (tel. 983/2-1065), Avenida Juarez 87. (Juarez is the street which runs *behind* the bus station. From that point, walk down the hill 2½ blocks and the hotel will be on your left.) The two floors of rooms here are well located around a breezy central airspace, which means you might be able to get along with just a fan and pay 360 pesos single, 575 pesos double, or 650 pesos triple. If you want air conditioning, it'll cost you 200 pesos more per room.

As for places to dine, there are many little market eateries (and indeed the produce-filled market itself) right next door to the bus station. Across the street from the station, the **Hotel Continental Caribe's** immense restaurant puts out a mammoth breakfast buffet until 11 a.m. for 385 pesos a head; after that, the high-quality comida corrida costs 650 pesos—hardly cheap. For better prices, you'll have to walk a ways.

Two blocks down the hill on Avenida Héroes is the **Restaurant Grijalva,** just past the Hotel El Presidente on the left-hand side of the street. Three señoras bustle about, one hands you an impossibly inclusive menu, and then chirps ¡*No hay!* ("We don't have it!") to most of your selections. Nevertheless, they always have the makings for enchiladas or quesadillas, and the charge will be only 55 to 90 pesos. Chicken and fish dinners cost twice that figure.

Strolling along Avenida Héroes is an adventure in Chetumal's recent history. As a National Territory, tax and Customs laws were relaxed to encourage immigration, and so the sidewalks are lined with import shops selling everything from pickled asparagus to Minoltas, usually on the same shelf. Prices are quite high by U.S. standards.

The **Restaurant Baalbek,** in the middle of the block past 9a Calle (or Calle Plutarco Elias), demonstrates by its name that some of the immigrants were Lebanese—not unusual in the Yucatán. Prices are a bit high here, but the bills must pay for the wrought-iron café furniture out front and the tablecloths inside. A big refrigerator keeps the food fresh until it's served. A plate of eggs or a fruit salad costs only 65 pesos, but heartier fare—fried chicken, grilled meat, fish—in in the 200- to 260-pesos bracket. Tacos and enchiladas are in between.

All the way down by the Río Hondo, in the old Caribbean section of town, is the incongruously modern **Restaurant Chetumal,** on Calle 5 de Mayo a block northwest of Avenida Héroes, on the riverbank. Open to cooling sea breezes from the Bay of Chetumal, it's a fine place for a refreshing salad of chicken or fruit (90 to 135 pesos), or a big Mexican combination plate (195 pesos). Look around at the quaint wooden buildings nearby before hiking back to the bus station.

TRANSPORTATION FROM CHETUMAL: Lots of bus service, a few flights.

By Bus

From the bus station in Chetumal you can get a seat to Tulum, Playa del Carmen, or Puerto Juarez to the north; Villahermosa, Veracruz, and Mexico City to the west; or to Belize City in the country to the south, once called British Honduras but (since 1973) officially named Belize.

Three direct first-class buses a day go to Cancún via Tulum, Playa del Carmen, and Puerto Morelos. With changes en route, four first-class buses a day go to Mexico City, seven a day go to Villahermosa.

Second-class bus service includes routes daily to Tulum and the coast (two buses), Merida (four buses), Campeche (two buses), Villahermosa (four buses), San Andres Tuxtla, Veracruz, and Mexico City (one bus).

To Belize, a bus runs daily, departing at 4 p.m. and making the run through Corozal, Orange Walk, and roadside villages to Belize City. If you're coming from Puerto Juarez, get an early bus (before 10 a.m.) in order to make this connection.

By Air

Daily flights link Chetumal with Mexico's major cities. If you're looking for flights to Belize City, the thing to do is cross the border to Corozal, and there you'll discover that Maya Airways operates at least two flights daily to the capital. In Corozal, contact Mr. A. Liborio Ayusa (tel. 04-2005, office; or 04-2024, home).

Aerocaribe, the regional carrier with offices in the Hotel El Presidente (tel. 983/2-2690 or 2-0544) in Chetumal, has plans for a route from Chetumal to Belize City. Check with them for current status. Flights between Chetumal and Cozumel, Cancún, and Isla Mujeres are operational as of this writing.

Leaving Chetumal

From Chetumal you can make the long, hot trip due west to Escárcega and Palenque; you can cut diagonally across the peninsula to Merida; you can retrace your steps to Cancún; or you can go on south to Belize and even Guatemala.

10. Travel to Belize and Guatemala

Belize is a fascinating country, which I have enjoyed visiting during the revision work for successive editions of this guidebook. However, this once-placid country has undergone many changes since independence from Great Britain, and I cannot recommend that you travel there at this time. Reports of robbery, especially of tourists, are common. For an up-to-date assessment of the situation in Belize, call the U.S. Department of State's Citizens' Emergency Center in Washington, D.C. (tel. 202/632-5225) and ask if there is a Travel Advisory issued for that country.

If you have a car, and if you're planning just to drive through Belize without stopping in Belize City, you might not run into problems. But then you're faced with the situation in Guatemala, which isn't so hot nowadays, either. (And, incidentally, relations between Belize and Guatemala are horrible.)

Since the Ríos Montt government came to power in Guatemala, the situation for tourists in that country seems to have gotten a fraction better. But I still can't recommend that you go there now, especially if you plan to visit the northwestern portion: Chichicastenango, Quezaltenango, and Huehuetenango. Believe me, it is a very sad day when I must urge readers *not* to visit this beautiful and hospitable country (in the past I have done just the opposite), but so it is today. Check with the Citizens' Emergency Center (see above) if you're in doubt.

I look forward to visiting Belize and Guatemala in the next few years, if conditions improve, and to including full coverage of these countries in this book, as I have in the past. Let's hope for the best.

Chapter XVI

LATIN LISTINGS

1. The ABCs of Life South of the Border

WHENEVER I HAVE found myself in some foreign country, dozens of questions have always come up that guidebooks neglected to answer. Often these questions concerned very minor things—how to make a phone call—except that no question is minor when you don't have the answer to it.

In this section, I have tried to anticipate some of the questions that you may find yourself asking. You will probably think of many other listings yourself; if so, I would appreciate hearing about them. Such listings will be included in future versions of this book. For the present, here's my own collection of vital statistics, from A to Z.

ABBREVIATIONS: Dept.—apartments; **Apdo.**—post office box; **Av.**—Avenida; **Calz.**—calzada or boulevard. C on faucets stand for *caliente* (hot), and F stands for *fría* (cold). It's not uncommon, however, to see faucets made in the U.S. and marked H and C. Yet because the plumbers don't understand English, the C faucet will be on the left *(caliente)* side, and will dispense *hot* water; the H faucet will be on the right and, in this case, will signify *cold* water. In elevators, **PB** *(planta baja)* means "ground floor."

ALTITUDE: Remember as you stroll around Mexico City that you are now at an altitude of 7240 feet—almost a mile and a half in the sky—and that there is a lot less oxygen in the air here than what you're used to. If you run for a bus and feel dizzy when you sit down, that's the altitude; if you think you're in shape, but all the same you puff and puff getting up Chapultepec hill, that's the altitude. It takes about ten days or so to acquire the extra red blood cells you need to adjust to the scarcity of oxygen.

At very high-altitude places such as Ixta-Popo Park outside Mexico City (13,000 feet), your car won't run very well, you may have trouble starting it, and you may not even sleep well at night.

AMERICAN EXPRESS: The Mexico City office is at Hamburgo 75 (tel. 905/533-1680 or 525-3159), in the Zona Rosa. It's open for banking, the pickup of clients' mail, and travel advice from 9 a.m. to 2 p.m. and 4 to 6 p.m. Monday through Friday, and also 9 a.m. to 1 p.m. on Saturday. If it's mail you're going for, remember that they charge $1 if you have no American Express credit card, travelers check, or tour ticket to prove that you're a client of theirs.

The Acapulco office is at Costera Aleman 709A (tel. 4-1095).

AUTO MECHANICS: Your best guide is the **Yellow Pages**. For specific makes and shops which repair them, look under *Automoviles y Camiones: Talleres de Reparación y Servicio;* auto parts stores are listed under *Refacciones y Accesorios para Automoviles.*

I've found the Ford and Volkswagen dealerships in Mexico to give prompt, courteous attention to my car problems, and prices for repairs are, in general, much lower than in the U.S. or Canada. I suspect that other big-name dealerships—General Motors, Chrysler, and American Motors—give similar, very satisfactory service. Oftentimes they will take your car right away and service it in a few hours—a thing almost unheard of at home.

Mexico imports lots of American cars of all makes, and the country manufactures a tremendous number of Volkswagens (using the old 1600 engine).

BANKS (See also "Money"): In Mexico, banks tend to be open from 9 a.m. to 1:30 p.m., Monday through Friday.

Large airports have currency-exchange counters which stay open as long as flights are arriving or departing.

Many banks south of the border have an employee who speaks English.

For the fastest and least complicated service, travelers checks or cash are the best things to carry. You can usually get a cash advance on your credit card if you wish. Personal checks may delay you for weeks—the bank will wait for it to clear before giving you your money. For money by wire, see "Money."

READERS' BANKING SUGGESTIONS: "**Banco del Atlantico** in Mexico City has started keeping some of its branches open seven days a week. Saturday they are open morning and afternoon; Sunday, morning only" (Lawrence Hughes, Berkeley, Calif.). . . . "**Banamex** changes money at the official rate without a service charge" (Tobah M. Gass, Berkeley, Calif.).

BOOKSTORES: In Mexico City, **Sanborn's** and **Woolworth's** always have books in English, as well as magazines and newspapers. So does the **American Bookstore,** Madero 25 off Bolívar (tel. 512-7284). The **American Benevolent Society's Caza Libros** (tel. 540-5123) at Monte Athos 355, 2½ blocks off of Reforma *west* of Chapultepec Park in the section called Lomas Barrilaco, has used books in Spanish and English, hardback and paperback, plus magazines, records, and prints. All profits go to charity projects of the society.

French and English books and magazines, especially those dealing with Mexico, its history, archeology, and people, are the specialty of the **Cia. Internacional de Publicaciones,** or Libererías C.I.P. for short. Branches of this firm in Mexico City are located at Serapio Rendon 125 (just off Sullivan Park, near the Hotel Sevilla), at Avenida Madero 30 not far from the House of Tiles, and also in Polanco, San Angel, Guadalajara, and Merida.

About the most convenient foreign- and Spanish-language bookstore in Mexico City, with a good selection of guides and books on Mexico, is **Central de Publicaciones—Librería Mizrachi,** Juarez 4 near Avenida Lázaro Cárdenas, right across from the Bellas Artes. Another shop, nearby, is the **Librería Británica,** Madero 30-1 (tel. 521-0180). The Museo Nacional de Antropología in Chapultepec Park also has a shop with a good selection of books on Mexico, particularly special-interest guides (birds, flowers, geology and mineralogy, cuisine, etc.).

BRIBES: Called *propina* (tip), *mordida* (bite), or worse, the custom is probably almost as old as mankind. Bribes exist in every country—as one sees upon picking up a daily newspaper—but in Third World countries the amounts tend to be smaller and collected more often. You will meet with bribery, so you should know how to deal with it.

At the Mexican border, the Customs officials have it down to an art. If you don't offer a tip of a few dollars to the man who inspects your car (if you're driving), he'll come right out and ask for it, as in "Give me a tip." Some officials, at the Mexican, Guatemalan, and Honduran borders, will do what they're supposed to do (stamp your passport or birth certificate, inspect your luggage, etc.) and then say, "Two dollars, please." If it's an official fee, you'll get a receipt. If you get no receipt, you've paid a bribe.

You can avoid some bribes, and after paying the umpteenth one, you'll want very badly to do so. Here's how: officials don't put the touch on everybody, and they don't always put it on in the same amount. Those dressed in suit-and-tie formality, with pitch-black sunglasses and a scowl on the face, rarely get touched at all. Those who are dressed for vacation fun, seem good-natured and accommodating, are touched every time and for ever-larger amounts. You may not want the bother of dressing up for border crossings (in that heat!), but you should at least act formal, rather cold and businesslike, perhaps preoccupied with Important Affairs on your mind. Wear those dark sunglasses. Scowl. But whatever you do, avoid impoliteness, and *absolutely never insult a Latin American official!* When an official's sense of *machismo* is roused, he can and will throw the book at you, and you may be in trouble. On the other hand, you must stand your ground (although always politely). Various means by which I, in my long experience, have cut down the high cost of bribing is by ignoring completely a request for "one dollar, please" (the request was not repeated); by plunking down less than the desired amount; or by politely requesting a receipt (in which case the request was dropped). Remember, only certain people pay bribes. What you want to do is be among that group who do not. The border official will request a bribe only after he has sized you up. Make him think you're dignified and important.

BUSES: Bus travel is the most popular form of transportation in Mexico. More and more foreign tourists are choosing to travel this way, and so here's a glossary of bus terms you'll find useful:

Autobus	Bus
Camion	Bus or Truck
Directo	Nonstop
Equipajes	Baggage (claim area)
Foraneo	Intercity
Llegadas	Gates
Local	Bus which originates at this station (see "Paso")
Paso, de paso	Bus originating somewhere else which will pass through this station; stops if seats are available.
Primera	First (class)
Recibo de Equipajes	Baggage claim area
Sala de Espera	Waiting Room
Sanitaríos	Toilets
Segunda	Second (class)
Sin Escala	Nonstop
Taquilla	Ticket window

When traveling by bus, it's best to buy your ticket (and thus reserve your seat) a day in advance, or even more than a day in the case of very long-distance and international buses, and those running on holidays.

CAMERAS AND FILM: Both are more expensive than in the States; take full advantage of your 12-roll film allowance, and bring extra batteries. A few places in resort areas advertise developing for color film, but it might be cheaper to wait till you get home.

If you're really into the sport, bring an assortment of films at various ASA/DIN speeds as you will be photographing against glaring sand, in gloomy Mayan temples, in dusky jungles, through hazy humidity. The proper filters are a help, as well.

CAMPING: It's easy and relatively cheap south of the border if you have a recreational vehicle or trailer, a bit less easy if you're tenting. Some agencies selling Mexican car insurance in the U.S. will give you a free list of campsites if you ask. The AAA has lists of sites. The *Rand McNally Campground & Trailer Park Guide* covers Mexico.

Campgrounds here tend to be slightly below the standards of northern ones (with many attractive exceptions to this rule, though). Remember that campgrounds fill up just like hotels during the winter rush-to-the-sun and at holiday times. Get there early.

CAR RENTALS: The car-rental business in Mexico is as far flung and well developed as in Europe and the U.S., with the usual problems and procedures. As elsewhere, it's good to reserve your car in advance in Mexico, an easy task when you fly into the country, as most airlines will gladly make the reservations for you. Mexico City and most other Mexican cities of any size have several rental offices representing the various big firms and some smaller ones. Rent here/leave there arrangements are usually simple to make.

With a credit card (American Express, VISA, MasterCard, and so forth) rentals are simple if you're over 25, in possession of a valid driver's license, and have your passport with you. Without a credit card you must leave a cash deposit, usually a big one.

Driving in Mexico City, and especially in and out of it (to sights a day's drive out of town) is a pretty big hassle, and parking's certainly a problem, so I can't recommend a rental car. But if you have enough people to fill one and to share the cost, and this is your preference, the information below may help you out.

You can save yourself some money by renting only as much car as you *need:* make sure that the company you select offers the VW Beetle or Datsun—usually the cheapest car—if that will do, and make sure they will have one on hand to rent you. (Sometimes they'll say they do over the phone, but when you arrive at the office the cheapest cars will be "all booked up" for two weeks, etc.)

Don't underestimate the cost of renting a car. The total amount you'll be out-of-pocket for a short one-day trip to, say, Cuernavaca (85 kilometers, or 50 miles, from Mexico City) might be in the range of $40. Take your time when you look over the company's brochure, estimate the distance and time, allowing a generous margin for wrong turns, side trips, etc.—those kilometers are expensive!—and then add up *all* the charges you'll have to pay *before* the clerk starts filling out an order form.

Your completed estimate should look something like this, based on a total of 170 kilometers for the very cheapest car offered:

Basic daily charge	$12.00
Kilometers, 170	13.60
Full nondeductible insurance	5.00
Subtotal	$30.60
IVA tax @ 10%	3.06
Gas @ 10 pesos per liter	4.50
Tolls and parking	2.00
Grand Total	$40.16

This estimate is for Mexico City; in a resort, a one-day rental would be slightly cheaper as the custom there is to include 200 free kilometers in every rental deal. But longer rentals in resorts turn out to be even more expensive than in Mexico City. An average three-day rental in a resort might be $125, a few dollars cheaper in Mexico City. For a week, the figures might be $300 for a resort, $275 for Mexico City—and these are for the very cheapest car offered, Group "A." Add about 15% to these estimates for Group "B" cars (VW Caribe—that's the Mexican version of the Rabbit, VW Safari), about 30% for Group "D" cars (Jeep, Ford Fairmont, VW Bus or Combi).

Recently, the larger firms in the big cities and resorts have been offering weekly unlimited-mileage rates. If you plan to do a lot of traveling, these can be great bargains. Plan your route, work out the mileage, then add about 15% to your mileage total to compensate for wrong turns, detours, and side trips. The unlimited-mileage price, plus the insurance charges, should then be compared to the "subtotal" above; remember, gas, 10% tax, tolls, and parking will still come out of your pocket.

Once you've made up your mind to rent a car, finding a rental office is a snap. Rental desks are set up in the airports, in all major hotels, and in many travel agencies. The large firms like Avis, Hertz, National, and Odin have rental offices on main streets as well.

CLOTHES FOR TRAVEL: Mexico tends to be a bit more conservative in dress (except for the capital) so shorts and halter tops are not generally acceptable except at seaside resorts. Cool clothes are needed at all times for the lowlands (the Yucatán, and coastal areas). In the highlands where you reach 7000 or so feet you will need warmer clothes (a warm sweater and jacket). A raincoat is a good idea (a fold-up plastic one will do) for the rainy season (middle of May through September) and at all times for Mexico City where it rains almost every afternoon for an hour or so. For more hints on clothing, see the Introduction to this book.

CONSULATES: See "Embassies," below.

CRIME: It's getting to be more of a problem in Mexico—which is to say that there was not much of a crime problem before. Although you will feel physically safer in most Mexican cities than in comparable big cities at home, you must take some basic, sensible precautions.

First, remember that you're a tourist, and a tourist is a mark. Beware of pickpockets on crowded buses, the Metro, in markets. Guard your possessions very carefully at all times; don't let packs or bags out of sight even for a second (the big first-class bus lines will store your bag in the luggage compartment under the bus, and that's generally alright, but keep your things with you on the less responsible village and some second-class buses on country routes).

Next, if you have a car, park it in an enclosed or guarded lot at night. Vans are a special mark. Don't depend on "major downtown streets" to protect your car—park it in a private lot with a guard, or at least a fence.

Women must be careful in cities when walking alone, night or day. Busy streets are no problem, but empty streets (even if empty just for afternoon siesta) are lonely places.

As to the police, in the past they have been part of the problem, not part of the solution. Although Mexico no doubt has dedicated and responsible officers, the general impression is that police have little training and fewer scruples. If you have the misfortune to be robbed, you should go to the police and report it, and get them to certify a report of the loss (you may have to write up the report yourself). But don't expect much sympathy, and even less action.

All these warnings having been stated, let me repeat that the prudent person need feel no more danger in Mexico than at home; most of the time you'll feel in less danger.

CUSTOMS AND DUTY-FREE GOODS: Coming to Mexico, Customs officials are very tolerant as long as you have no drugs (that is, marijuana, cocaine, etc.) or firearms. You're allowed to bring two cartons of cigarettes, or 50 cigars, plus a kilogram (2.2 pounds) of smoking tobacco; the liquor allowance is two bottles of anything, wine or hard liquor.

Reentering the U.S., you're allowed by **federal law** to bring in a carton (200) of cigarettes, *or* 50 cigars, *or* two kilograms (total, 4.4 lbs.) of smoking tobacco, or proportional amounts of these items, plus one liter of alcoholic beverage (wine, beer, or spirits). If you bring larger amounts of these things, you will have to pay federal duty and internal revenue tax. *But wait!* Your quotas will also be subject to **state laws** (i.e., of the state in which you reenter the U.S.). The state law may not allow you to bring back *any* liquor, which means *you will have to pour it out.* It's not simply a matter of paying duty, it's a matter of absolute quotas—or no quotas at all—for some states. This liquor quota is most strictly applied at the border posts, less strictly at airports not near the border.

Here are the limits for liquor in the states which border Mexico, from information supplied by the Distilled Spirits Council, Washington, D.C.:

Arizona: You may not import more than the federal duty-free limit; any amounts over the limit will be destroyed.

California: You may bring in a "reasonable amount" of liquor for each adult, for personal use only (not for resale or as gifts).

New Mexico: You may bring in a reasonable amount duty-free.

Texas: All liquor brought into Texas is subject to state tax; for amounts of hard liquor over one quart, you must have a permit from the state liquor authorities.

Canadian returning-resident regulations are similar to the U.S. ones: a carton of cigarettes, 50 cigars, two pounds (not kilos) of smoking tobacco, 1.1 liters (40 oz.) of wine or liquor, *or* a case of beer (8.2 liters). All provinces except P.E.I. and the Northwest Territories allow you to bring in more liquor and beer—up to two gallons (9 liters) more—but the taxes are quite high.

DOCTORS AND DENTISTS: Every embassy and consulate is prepared to recommend local doctors and dentists with good training and up-to-date equipment; some of the doctors and dentists even speak English. See the list of embassies and consulates under "Embassies" (below), and remember that at the larger ones a duty officer is on call at all times. See also "Hospitals," below.

DRUGSTORES: The word is *farmacía,* and they will sell you just about anything you want, with prescription or without. Most are open every day but Sunday from 8 a.m. to 8 p.m. The Sanborn's chain has a drug counter in many of their establishments.

If you need to buy medicines outside of normal hours, you'll have to search for the *farmacía de turno*—pharmacies take turns staying open during the off hours. Find any drugstore, and in its window should be a card or sign with the word "Turno" and the name and address of the establishment that's open that night (or Sunday). Local newspapers very often carry a schedule of which farmacía will be open at what time.

ELECTRICITY: Current in Mexico is 110 volts, 60 cycles, as in the U.S. and Canada, with the same flat-prong plugs and sockets. Light bulbs may have bayonet bases, though.

EMBASSIES: They provide valuable lists of doctors, lawyers, regulations concerning marriages in Mexico, etc. Contrary to popular belief, your embassy cannot get you out of a Mexican jail, provide postal or banking services, or fly you home when you run out of money. Consular officers can provide you with advice on most matters and problems, however. Here's a list.

Canada

The Canadian Embassy in **Mexico City** (tel. 905/533-0610) is at Melchor Ocampo 463-7, right near Reforma. Hours are Monday through Friday from 9 a.m. to 1 p.m. and 3 to 5 p.m.; at other times the name of a duty officer is posted on the embassy door. In **Acapulco,** the Canadian consulate is in the hotel El Mirador, La Quebrada 74 (tel. 748/3-7291); hours are 9 to 1 and 3 to 5:30. In **Guadalajara,** go to Vallarta 1373 (tel. 36/25-9932).

United Kingdom

The British Embassy in **Mexico City** is at Río Lerma 71, at Río Sena (tel. 905/511-4880 or 514-3327). There are honorary consuls in the following cities: **Acapulco,** Hotel Las Brisas, Apdo. Postal 281 (tel. 748/4-6605); **Guadalajara,** Lerdo de Tejada 2264-102 (tel. 36/15-1406); **Merida,** Calle 58 no. 450 (tel. 992/1-6799); **Monterrey,** Privada de Tamazunchale 104 (tel. 83/56-9114); **Veracruz,** Avenida Morelos 145 (tel. 293/2-4323).

United States

The American Embassy in **Mexico City** is right next to the Hotel Maria Isabel Sheraton at Paseo de la Reforma 305, corner of Río Danubio (tel. 905/553-3333). There are U.S. Consulates in **Guadalajara** at Progreso 175 (tel.

36/25-2998); in **Mazatlán** at Circunvalación 6, corner of Carranza (tel. 678/1-2685 or 1-4488); and in **Monterrey** at Avenida Constitución 411 Poniente (tel. 83/43-0650). In addition, consular agents are resident in **Acapulco** (tel. 748/2-1906); **Cancún** (tel. 988/3-0178); **Oaxaca** (tel. 951/6-0654); **Puerto Vallarta** (tel. 322/2-1143); **San Luis Potosí** (tel. 481/2-5327); and **Veracruz** (tel. 293/2-6921).

HOLIDAYS, PUBLIC: Banks, stores, and businesses are closed on national holidays, hotels fill up quickly, and transportation is crowded. Here are the holidays celebrated in Mexico:

January 1	New Year's Day
February 5	Constitution Day
March 21	Birthday of Benito Juarez
March-April (moveable)	Holy Week (closures usually Good Friday through Easter Sunday)
May 1	Labor Day
May 5	Battle of Pueblo, 1862 (Cinco de Mayo)
September 1	President's Message to Congress
September 16	Independence Day
October 12	Columbus Day (Mexico: Day of the Race)
November 20	Mexican Revolution Anniversary
December 24-25	Christmas Eve (evening); Christmas Day

HOSPITAL: In Mexico City there is a hospital staffed by English-speaking personnel. It's the **American-British Cowdray ("A.B.C.") Hospital,** located at Calle Sur 132-136, corner of Avenida Observatorio ("Sur 132" is the name of the street; tel. 905/515-8500). Take the Metro (Line 1) to "Observatorio," and the hospital is a short ride from there. Have your insurance up to date as the hospital bills at Stateside prices.

Clinics and hospitals with English-speaking doctors exist in other major areas visited by tourists. Call your consulate (See "Embassies") for a list of telephone numbers.

INFORMATION: Before you leave home, you can get tourist information from any of the Mexican National Tourism Council offices listed in the Introduction to this book. Once you're in Mexico, drop in to the tourism information offices mentioned in the text for each city or area.

The **Secretariat of Tourism,** once located right downtown at the intersection of Juarez and Reforma, is now at Avenida Presidente Masaryk 172, north of Chapultepec Park in the section called Polanco. To replace their handy downtown info booth there is now a special Tourist Information telephone number (the person on the other end will speak English): dial 905/250-0123.

LAUNDRY: All hotels can make some arrangements to have your laundry taken care of. Small laundries can be found in all but the tiniest villages. Coin laundries exist in all cities of any size—just ask at your hotel or a tourism information office.

LIBRARIES: Mexico City has several libraries of English-language books connected with her diplomatic missions. Check out the **Benjamin Franklin**

(American) Library, on Niza between Londres and Liverpool. The **Canadian Library** (English and French books and periodicals) is at Melchor Ocampo 481, near the intersection with Reforma, open Monday through Friday from 10:30 a.m. to 1 p.m. and 2 to 5 p.m. The British Embassy, Consular Section, has British periodicals in the waiting room. See also "Bookstores," above.

MAIL: Mail service south of the border tends to be slow (sometimes glacial in its movements) and erratic. If you're on a two-week vacation, it's not a bad idea to buy and mail your postcards in the Arrivals lounge at the airport to give them maximum time to get home before you do.

For the most reliable and convenient mail service, have your letters sent to you c/o the **American Express** office at Hamburgo 75, México, D.F. (open Monday through Friday from 9 a.m. to 2 p.m. and 4 to 6 p.m., on Saturday from 9 a.m. to 1 p.m.), which will receive and forward mail for you if you are one of their clients (a travel club card, or an American Express travelers check is proof). They charge a small fee if you wish them to forward your mail.

General Delivery (Poste Restante)

If you don't use American Express, have your mail sent to you care of *Lista de Correos,* (City), (State), (Country). In Mexican post offices there may actually be a "lista" posted near the Lista de Correos window bearing the names of all those for whom mail has been received. If there's no list, ask, and show them your passport so they can riffle through and look for your letters.

You'll have to go to the central post office—not a branch—to get your mail, if the city has more than one office.

Post Offices

The main one in **Mexico City** is located at the corner of Tacuba/Hidalgo and Lázaro Cárdenas, across the street from the Bellas Artes. It's open from 8 a.m. to midnight weekdays, 8 a.m. to 8 p.m. on Saturday, 8 a.m. to 3:45 p.m. on Sunday. On the third floor is an interesting philatelic exhibit, open for free from 9 a.m. to 1 p.m. weekdays, 9 a.m. to noon on Saturday.

Branch post offices in Mexico City are located at the following places you might find yourself: **Zócalo**—Beneath the Hotel Majestic, in the arcade running along the west side of the square, at no. 7, down the passage bearing a sign, "Almacenes Nacionales de México"; **Plaza de la República**—Just north of the Monument to the Revolution at the corner of Arriaga and Mariscal; **Insurgentes/Reforma Intersection**—Off Sullivan Park on Río Lerma near the intersection of Río Marne, almost across the street from the Hotel Maria Angelo's; **Buenavista Railroad Station**—In the railroad office building adjoining the station to the east; **Zona Rosa**—At the corner of Londres and Varsovia.

Parcel Post

In Mexico City you'll have to take parcels to the special parcel post office called Correo Internacional no. 2, Calle Dr. Andrade and Río de la Loza (Metro: Balderas or Salto del Agua), open Monday through Friday from 8 a.m. to noon. Don't wrap up your package securely until an inspector examines it.

Glossary

Words you'll need to know include these:

Spanish	English
Aduana	Customs
Buzon	Mailbox
Correo Aereo	Airmail
Correos	Postal Service
Entrega Immediata	Special Delivery, Express
Estampillas	Stamps
Giros Postales	Money Orders
Lista de Correos	General Delivery, Poste Restante
Oficina de Correos	Post Office
Paquetes	Parcels
Por avion	Airmail
Registrado	Registered Mail
Seguros	Insurance (insured mail)
Sellos	Stamps (sometimes rubber stamps)
Timbres	Stamps

MONEY (See also "Banks"): The dollar sign ($) is used to indicate pesos in Mexico. As many establishments dealing with tourists also quote prices in dollars, confusion is cleared up by the use of the abbreviations "Dlls." for dollars, and "m.n." *(moneda nacional*—national currency) for pesos, so "$20.00 m.n." means 20 pesos. Banks often charge a fee for changing travelers checks, or give a rate of exchange below the official daily rate. Hotels usually exchange below the official daily rate as well. The bank which writes your travelers checks (American Express, First National City, etc.) will give you the best rate of exchange.

In recent years it has been normal for the exchange rate on travelers checks to be better than that for cash dollars—you actually get something back for your penny-on-the-dollar investment in safety.

Canadian dollars seem to be most easily exchanged for pesos at branches of Banamex and Bancomer.

Credit Cards

You'll be glad to know that Mexico is well into the age of living on the little plastic card, and that you will be able to charge some hotel and restaurant bills, almost all airline tickets, and many store purchases. You can get cash advances of several hundred dollars on your card. You can't charge gasoline purchases in Mexico at all.

VISA, MasterCard (which is "Carnet" in Mexico), American Express, and their affiliates are the most widely accepted cards. You may not see your card's logo in a shop window or on a travel agency door, but don't worry—the Mexican equivalents such as Bancomer and/or Bancomatico will do just as well.

Money by Wire

If you need to get money from your bank at home, don't try to clear a check through a Mexican bank—it takes too long. Instead, go to the office of **Telegramas Internacionales** in Mexico City (tel. 905/519-5920), Balderas 14-18, near Colón and just off the west end of the Alameda, any day but Sunday from 8 a.m. to midnight. Have the money remitted to that office, and pick it up about four days later with your passport and Tourist Card. If there's any chance you'll leave Mexico City before the money arrives, try to get cash somewhere else. It takes up to six months for your home bank to track down an unclaimed international money order.

NEWSPAPERS AND MAGAZINES: For American travelers in Mexico the English-language newspaper *The News* is an excellent buy. It carries many Stateside columnists as well as newsworthy commentaries, and a calendar of the day's events including concerts, art shows, plays, etc. A Spanish-language paper, *Excelsior,* has a daily partial page in English. Most hotels carry the *Mexico City Daily Bulletin,* a free throw-away sheet in English with a list of events in the city and environs. Note: Not all the information is correct (e.g., museum hours). Sanborn's carries many United States papers, usually a day old.

Newspaper kiosks in larger Mexican cities will carry a selection of English-language magazines—*Time, Newsweek,* and the like.

POST OFFICE (See "Mail").

RADIO STATIONS: There are lots of stations in Mexico City, on both AM and FM, all in Spanish. Station XELA, 800 kH AM and 98.5 mH FM, broadcasts classical music, as do several university stations.

RELIGIOUS SERVICES: Services in English in Mexico City are at the following times and places:
  Baptist: Capital Baptist Church, Bondojito corner of Calle Sur 136 (tel. 516-1862), across from the American School and A.B.C. Hospital. Services 10:45 a.m. Evening worship 6 p.m.
  Catholic: St. Patrick's Church, Bondojito 248, Colonia Tacubaya (tel. 515-1933), Sunday mass given at 10 and 11 a.m. At the Church of la Votiva, Reforma 290, confessions in English are heard.
  Christian Science: First Church of Christ Scientist, Calle Dante 21, Colonia Anzures. Service 11 a.m. Bilingual meeting Wednesday, 7:30 p.m. Reading room open Monday to Saturday, 4 to 7:30 p.m.
  Church of Christ: Central Church of Christ, Calle 13 de Septiembre 26 in Colonia Condesa (tel. 562-2344 or 529-7385). (It's on a one-block, one-way street between Tacubaya and Chapultepec.) Worship and communion 9 a.m.; Bible classes for all at 10 a.m.
  Episcopal: Christ Church Episcopal, Articulo 123 no 134 (tel. 521-0389), Communion 8 a.m. Morning prayer or Communion and sermon 10 a.m. St. Andrews at San Jeronimo 117 in San Angel.
  Greek Orthodox: St. Sophia, Agua Caliente corner of Saratoga, Colonia Lomas Hipodromo (tel. 540-0080), Orthros 10 a.m.; liturgy (in Greek and Spanish) 11 a.m.
  Interdenominational: Central Church, Balderas 47 at Independencia (tel. 560-9223), special worship service for tourists 8:30 a.m. Sunday. (Held in sanctuary of Messiah Methodist Church.)
  Jewish: Hebrew Synagogue, Justo Sierra 71 (tel. 522-48-28), Saturday services at 7 and 9 p.m. Beth Israel Community Center, Virreyes 1140, Lomas (tel. 520-8515), services 8:30 p.m. Friday, 10:30 a.m. Saturday.
  Lutheran: Lutheran Church of the Good Shepherd, Paseo de las Palmas 1910, Colonia Lomas (tel. 596-1034), services 10:30 a.m.

Methodist: Messiah Methodist Church, Balderas 47 (tel. 560-92-23), service at 8:30 a.m.

Mormon: Church of Jesus Christ of Latter Day Saints (tel. 540-2790 or 540-3797), Cerro de Jesus 75, Colonia Campestre Churubusco (same block as Taxqueña Metro station on Tlalpan Line 2); SS and Sacrament 9:30 a.m. to 1 p.m.

Presbyterian: Gethsemane Presbyterian Church, Allende and Cuauhtémoc in Coyoacan (tel. 524-49-28), services in English 9 a.m. Sunday.

Quaker: The Quaker Center is at I. Mariscal 132 (tel. 535-2752). Meetings are Sunday at 11 a.m.

Union Evangelical Church: Located at Reforma 1870, in Lomas (tel. 520-0436). Sunday services at 9:15 and 10:30 a.m.

Unitarian Church: Herodoto 46 (tel. 531-7166), meetings at 11 a.m. on Sunday and 8 p.m. on Wednesday.

SIESTA: The custom of having a copious, long lunch and taking a rest during the heat of the day is still well entrenched south of the border. You may notice it less in mountainous areas and in the big cities, where life seems to plow onward from morning to evening without a break. But in coastal towns and hot climates, expect banks, offices, consulates, and museums to take a somewhat lengthy break for lunch. You'd be well advised to do the same.

SPANISH LESSONS: A dozen towns south of the border are famous for their Spanish-language programs. In Mexico City, there's the **Mexican–North American Institute of Cultural Relations,** Hamburgo 115 and Varsovia 43 (tel. 905/511-4720) in the Pink Zone. You can sign up for courses in University City as well. Also, consult Mexican National Tourist Council offices (listed in the Introduction to this book) about schools in Cholula, Cuernavaca, Guadalajara, Merida, and San Miguel de Allende.

STUDENT INFORMATION OFFICES: Students traveling on a budget may want to contact the student headquarters in the various cities which can supply information on student hostels, organized tours, charter flights, as well as free maps and printed materials about the area. The office in **Mexico City** is at Hamburgo 273 (tel. 905/514-4213 or 511-6691); in **Guadalajara,** it's Pedro Moreno 1328 (tel. 36/25-3226), and in **Monterrey,** at Plaza Zaragoza (tel. 83/40-5236).

TAXIS: Taxis are dealt with in each separate section of this book.

TELEGRAMS: Note that the telegraph office may be in a different place than the post office in many cities. For the address of the international telegraph office in Mexico City, see "Money."

TELEPHONES: Local calls in Mexico cost 20 centavos for three minutes. There are two types of coin phones: in one the slot at the top holds your coin in a gentle grip until your party answers, then it drops; if there's no answer or a busy signal you can pluck your coin from the slot. The other type is the sort where you insert a coin which disappears into the bowels of the machine, and drops into the cashbox when your call goes through, or into the return slot if it doesn't (after you hang up). This type of phone is often jammed, and your coin won't drop, so that when your party answers you will hear them but they won't hear you. Try from another pay phone.

Long Distance

Long-distance calls in Mexico are as expensive as local calls are cheap. And international long distance calls tend to be outrageously expensive, unless you are calling collect to the U.S., Canada, or Britain. To find out estimated charges *(tarifas)* and area codes *(claves)* you don't know, dial 07 in Mexico City.

To call the U.S. or Canada collect, dial 96 + Area Code + number, and tell the *operadora* that you want *una llamada por cobrar* (a collect call), *telefono a telefono* (station-to-station), or *persona a persona* (person-to-person).

If you don't want to call collect, you'll have to go to a *caseta de larga distancia*, or call from your hotel, as it's impracticable to load hundreds of 20-centavo pieces into a pay phone. Your hotel will levy a service charge—perhaps a percentage!—on top of the already exorbitant rate. Ask in advance what they'll add on. At a caseta you pay just the call charge.

From a caseta or hotel, dial 95 + Area Code + number for the U.S. and Canada, or 98 + Area Code + number for anywhere else in the world. If you need the international (English-speaking) operator after all, dial 09 in Mexico City. Casetas in Mexico City are at the airport (two), Buenavista Station, Terminal Norte de Autobuses, in the Insurgentes and Merced Metro stations, at Donceles 20, and at Sullivan 143.

To call long distance (abbreviated "lada") within Mexico, dial 91 + Area Code + number. Mexican area codes *(claves)* are listed in the front of the telephone directories, and in the hotel listings for each area in this book. For Mexico City, it's 905/; for Acapulco, 748/.

Calling to Mexico from Abroad

I've included Mexican Area Codes in all important telephone numbers so that you can call long distance within Mexico, or to Mexico from the U.S. and Canada (and, for that matter, from the rest of the world). Mexico's *claves* (Area Codes) and numbers are sometimes shorter than those up north, but they work just as well. Until the Mexican system is fully integrated with that in the U.S. and Canada, you may have to ask the operator for assistance in calling. Good news: her help is free, and the rate you pay is the direct-dial rate.

Saving Money in Mexico

You can save up to 29% by calling in off-peak periods. The cheapest times to call are after 11 p.m. and before 8 a.m. any day, and all day Saturday and Sunday; the most expensive times are 8 a.m. to 5 p.m. weekdays.

TIME: Central Standard Time prevails throughout the most of Mexico. The states of Sonora, Sinaloa, and parts of Nayarit on the western coast are on Mountain Standard Time. The state of Baja California Norte is on Pacific Standard Time, but Baja California Sur is on Mountain Time.

The Yucatán peninsula runs on Eastern Standard Time (that is, the states of Campeche, Yucatán, and Quintana Roo).

Note that Daylight Saving Time is *not* used in Mexico, except in Baja California Norte (late April to late October).

TIPPING: When it comes to tipping, you should throw out the iron 15% rule right away south of the border, no matter what other travel literature may say. Do as the locals do: for meals costing $2 to $3 or under, leave the loose change; for meals costing around $4 or $5, leave from 6% to 10%, depending on service. Above $6 to $7, you're into the 10% to 15% bracket. Some of the more crass high-priced restaurants will actually add a 15% "tip" to your bill. Leave nothing extra if they do.

Bellboys and porters will expect about 25¢ per bag. You needn't tip taxi drivers unless they've rendered some special service—carrying bags or trunks, for instance.

TURISTAS: This is the common name for diarrhea from which many tourists suffer, although others seem immune. It's not only unclean food or water that's to blame, but also the change of eating habits and environment. If your condition becomes serious—fever and chills, stomach pains—do *not* hesitate to call a doctor. To neglect a potentially serious stomach ailment, because of the belief that turistas is painful but not dangerous, could be an unhappy mistake. Also, it is advisable, no matter how serious your illness, to consult a doctor before buying or taking any kind of drug. For more information on turista, refer to the Introduction to this book, Section 3, "Health and Medicaments."

WATER: Most hotels have decanters or bottles of purified water in the rooms and the snazzier hotels have special taps marked *"Agua Purificada."* Virtually any hotel, restaurant, or bar will bring you purified water if you specifically request it.

Appendix

FOR YOUR INFORMATION

1. **Shopping Guide**
2. **Basic Vocabulary**
3. **Useful Phrases**
4. **Menu Terms**

1. Shopping Guide

The charm of Mexico is no better expressed than in arts and crafts. Hardly a tourist will leave these countries without having bought at least one of these hand-crafted items. Mexico is famous for textiles, ceramics, baskets, onyx and silver jewelry, to mention only a few.

This guide is designed to help the traveler know some of the crafts and the regions where they can be found. I have listed the cities or villages where the item is sold (and often crafted), the first place listed being the best place to buy. The larger cities, especially Mexico City and Oaxaca, will have many crafts from other regions but, in general, a greater variety and better prices are still to be found in the areas where the items are made. Also included at the end of the shopping guide is a table of metric conversions and clothing sizes. I have not listed any prices for the crafts since this is really dependent on one's bargaining ability. For some hints on bargaining see Chapter IX, Section 3 under "Markets." I would add that it is very helpful to visit a government fixed-price shop (every major Mexican city has one, usually called the **Artes Populares** or **FONART**) before attempting to bargain. This will give you an idea of the cost versus quality of the various crafts. Following, now, are the various crafts, in alphabetical order.

BASKETS (woven of reed or straw): Oaxaca, Guanajuato, Mexico City. Cost depends on the tightness of the weave and the size of the basket.

BLANKETS: Oaxaca and Mitla (made of soft wool with some synthetic dyes; they use a lot of bird motifs). Make sure that the blanket you pick out is in fact the one you take since often the "same" blanket in the wrapper is *not* the same.

CERAMICS: Tlaquepaque, Guadalajara, Mexico City (hand-painted dishes and bowls); Puebla, Oaxaca, Mexico City (clay figurines and scenes—glazed, unglazed, and painted); Coyotepec and Oaxaca (black pottery, especially bells and animal jars); Puebla and Izupa de Matamoras (colorful folk-art earthenware candelabras, hand-painted and unglazed).

GLASS (hand-blown and molded): Monterrey; Mexico City at the Avalos Brothers glass factory, Carretones 5 (Metro: Pino Suarez).

GORANGOS (knited wool pullover ponchos—hip length): Santa Ana Chiautempan, 49 kilometers north of Puebla near Tlaxcala. A good selection for a slightly higher price can be found in Puebla and Mexico City; Chiconcoac, one hour's drive northeast of Mexico City, a few miles east of Texcoco.

GUITARS: Made in Paracho, 25 miles north of Uruapan on Highway 37.

HAMMOCKS AND MOSQUITO NETTING: Merida, Campeche, Mazatlán. See market section in Merida (Chapter XV) for details on buying.

HATS: Durango (woven straw); Merida (Panama), made of sisal from the Maguey cactus; finest quality weaving; easy to pack and wash.

HUARACHES (leather sandals with rubber-tire soles): San Blas, Merida, Mexico City, Hermosillo, and in fact most states.

HUIPILS (hand-woven and embroidered blouses indigenous to Yucatán and Chiapas): Huipils can also be found in most major towns in these states, with a good selection in Merida and San Cristóbal de Las Casas. Most of the better huipils are in fact used ones that have been bought from the village women and cleaned. The new huipils that are made for the tourist are often of inferior quality since they are made with synthetic dyes and a coarser weave. Note that huipils can be distinguished by villages; for instance, in Chiapas the pattern is very floral using bright colors, while in San Antonio, Guatemala, the predominant color is red with interesting lattice and geometric designs. Look around before buying; you'll be amazed at the variety.

LACQUER GOODS: Uruapan, 300 miles west of Mexico City, where they are made; also can be bought in Morelia and Patzcuaro.

LEATHER GOODS: Mexico City along Calle Pino Suarez, San Cristóbal de Las Casas, Oaxaca.

ONYX: Puebla (where onyx is carved), Querétaro, Mexico City

REBOZOS (woman's or man's rectangular woven cloth to be worn around the shoulders or waist, similar to a shawl): Oaxaca, Mitla, San Cristóbal de Las Casas, Mexico City, Patzcuaro. Rebozos are generally made of wool or a blend of wool and cotton. Nowadays they are using synthetic fibers, so check the material carefully before buying. Also, compare the weave from different cloths since the fineness of the weave is proportional to the cost.

SERAPES (heavy woolen or cotton blankets with a slit for the head, to be worn as a poncho): Santa Ana Chiautempan (49 kilometers north of Puebla near Tlaxcala), San Luis Potosí, Santa Maria del Río (25 miles south of San

Luis Potosí), Chiconcoac (one hour's drive northeast from Mexico City, near Texcoco), Saltillo, Toluca, Mexico City.

SILVER: Taxco, Saltillo, Mexico City. Copper and tin masks are found in Oaxaca and Mexico City. Sterling silver is indicated by "925" on the silver, which certifies that there are 925 grams of pure silver per kilogram, or that the silver is 92.5% pure. In Mexico they also use a spread-eagle hallmark to indicate sterling. Look for these marks for otherwise you may be paying a high price for an inferior quality that is mostly nickel, or even silver plate.

STONES (chalcedony, turquoise, lapis lazuli, amethyst): Querétaro, San Miguel de Allende, Durango, Saltillo, San Luis Potosí. The coast of turquoise is computed by weight, so many pesos per carat.

TEXTILES: Oaxaca, Santa Ana, and Tlaxcala are known for their excellent weaving, each culturally distinct and different. The Oaxaqueños are famous for their hand-loomed woven tablecloths. See the reader's suggestion in Puebla section (Chapter XIV) for textiles in Santa Ana.

TORTOISE SHELL: Veracruz, Campeche.

METRIC CONVERSIONS:
   1 inch = 2.54 centimeters
   1 foot = 30.5 centimeters
   39.37 inches = 1 meter
   1 mile = 1.6 kilometers
   .62 miles = 1 kilometer
   1 pound = .4536 kilograms
   2.2 pounds = 1 kilogram
   1 U.S. gallon = 3.79 liters
   .26 U.S. gallons = 1 liter

Clothing Size Conversions
Women's

	U.S.	Mexican
dress	6,8,10,12,14,16,18	36,38,40,42,44,46,48
blouse	30,32,34,36,38,40,42,44	same
shoes	5,5½,6,6½,7,7½,8,8½,9	35,35½,36,36½,37,37½,38 38½,39

Men's

collar	14,14½,15,15½,16,16½,17	36,37,38,39,41,42,43
shoes	8,8½,9,9½,10,10½,11,12	41,41½,42,42½,43,43½,44,45
jackets	38,40,42,44,46,48	48,50,52,54,56,58

2. Basic Vocabulary

Let me now deal with the omnipresent, unavoidable, unfortunate fact that not everyone in Mexico speaks English (this isn't as silly as it sounds; these days, English is taught in most Mexican schools).

428 MEXICO ON $20 A DAY

Berlitz's *Latin American Spanish for Travellers,* available at most bookstores for $4, cannot be recommended highly enough. But for added convenience, I've included a list of certain simple phrases for expressing basic needs, followed by some menu items presented in the same order in which they'd be found on a Mexican menu.

		Pronounced
Hello	Buenos dias	bway-nohss dee-ahss
How are you?	Cómo está usted?	koh-moh ess-tah oo-sted
Very well	Muy bien	mwee byen
Thank you	Gracias	grah-see-ahss
You're welcome	De nada	day nah-dah
Goodbye	Adiós	ah-dyohss
Please	Por favor	pohr fah-bohr
Yes	Sí	see
No	No	noh
Excuse	Perdóneme	pehr-doh-neh-may
Give me	Déme	day-may
Where is?	Dónde está?	dohn-day ess-tah
the station	la estación	la ess-tah-see-own
a hotel	un hotel	oon oh-tel
a gas station	una gasolinera	oon-nuh gah-so-lee-nay-rah
a restaurant	un restaurante	oon res-tow-rahn-tay
the toilet	el baño	el bahn-yoh
a good doctor	un buen médico	oon bwayn may-dee-co
the road to ...	el camino a ...	el cah-mee-noh ah ...
To the right	A la derecha	ah lah day-ray-chuh
To the left	A la izquierda	ah lah ees-ky-ehr-dah
Straight ahead	Derecho	day-ray-cho
I would like	Quisiera	keyh-see-air-ah
I want	Quiero	kyehr-oh
to eat	comer	ko-mayr
a room	una habitación	oon-nuh hab-bee-tyah-nay
Do you have?	Tiene usted?	oos-ted
a book	un libro	oon lee-bro
a dictionary	un diccionario	oon deek-see-own-ar-eo
How much is it?	Cuánto cuesta?	kwahn-toh kwess-tah
When	Cuando?	kwahn-doh
What	Qué?	kay
There is (Is there?)	Hay	eye
Yesterday	Ayer	ah-yer
Today	Hoy	oy
Tomorrow	Mañana	mahn-yawn-ah
Good	Bueno	bway-no
Bad	Malo	mah-lo

VOCABULARY

Better (best)	(Lo) Mejor	meh-hor
More	Más	mahs
Less	Menos	may-noss
No Smoking	Se prohibe fumar	seh pro-hee-beh foo-mahr
Postcard	Tarjeta postal	tahr-hay-tah pohs-tahl

1 **uno** (ooh-noh)
2 **dos** (dose)
3 **tres** (trayss)
4 **cuatro** (kwah-troh)
5 **cinco** (seen-koh)
6 **seis** (sayss)
7 **siete** (syeh-tay)
8 **ocho** (oh-choh)
9 **nueve** (nway-bay)
10 **diez** (dee-ess)
11 **once** (ohn-say)
12 **doce** (doh-say)
13 **trece** (tray-say)
14 **catorce** (kah-tor-say)
15 **cuince** (keen-say)
16 **dieciseis** (dee-ess-ee-savys)
17 **diecisiete** (de-ess-ee-see-ay-tay)
18 **dieciocho** (dee-ess-ee-oh-choh)
19 **diecinueve** (dee-ess-ee-nway-bay)
20 **veinte** (bayn-tay)
30 **treinta** (trayn-tah)
40 **cuarenta** (kwah-ren-tah)
50 **cincuenta** (seen-kewn-tah)
60 **sesenta** (say-sen-tah)
70 **setenta** (say-ten-tah)
80 **ochenta** (oh-chen-tah)
90 **noventa** (noh-ben-tah)
100 **cien** (see-en)
200 **doscientos** (dos-see-en-tos)
500 **quinientos** (keen-ee-ehn-tos)
1000 **mil** (meel)

3. Useful Phrases

Do you speak English?	¿Habla usted Inglés?
Is there anyone here who speaks English?	¿Hay alguien aquí qué hable Inglés?
I speak a little Spanish.	Hablo un poco de Español.
I don't understand Spanish very well.	No lo entiendo muy bien el Español.
The meal is good.	Me gusta la comida.
What time is it?	¿Qué hora es?
May I see your menu?	¿Puedo ver su menú?
What did you say?	¿Mande? (colloquial expression for American "Eh?")
I want (to see) a room	Quiero (ver) un cuarto (una habitación)
for two persons	para dos persones
with (without) bath	con (sin) baño
We are staying here only one night (one	Nos quedaremos aqui solamente una noche

week) (una semana).
We are leaving tomorrow. Partimos mañana.
Do you accept travelers ¿Acepta Usted cheques de
checks? viajero?
Is there a laundromat ¿Hay una lavandería cerca
near here de aquí?
Please send these clothes to Hágame el favor de
the laundry. mandar esta ropa a la
lavandería.

4. Menu Terms

almuerzo	lunch	frito	fried
cena	supper	poco cocido	rare
comida	dinner	asado	roast
desayuno	breakfast	bien cocido	well done
el menu	the menu	milanesa	breaded
la cuenta	the check	veracruzana	tomato and green olive sauce
tampiqueña	thinly sliced meat		
cocido	boiled	pibil	roasted
empanado	breaded		

BREAKFAST (desayuno)

jugo de naranja	orange juice	huevos motuleños	egg on ham with tortilla, cheese, and tomato sauce
cafe con crema	coffee with cream		
pan tostado	toast		
mermelada	jam	huevos poches	poached eggs
leche	milk	huevos fritos	fried eggs
te	tea	huevos pasados al agua	soft-boiled eggs
huevos	eggs		
huevos rancheros	fried eggs on a tortilla, covered with tomato sauce	huevos revueltos	scrambled eggs
		tocino	bacon
huevos cocidos	hard-boiled eggs	jamón	ham

LUNCH AND DINNER

| antojitos | Mexican specialties | caldo de pollo | chicken broth |
| caldo | broth | frijoles refritos | refried beans |

sopa	soup	menudo	tripe soup
sopa de ajo	garlic soup with egg	médula	bone marrow soup
sopa clara	consommé	salchichas	knockwurst
sopa de lentejas	lentil soup	taco	filled fried tortilla
sopa de chicaros	pea soup	torta	sandwich
sopa de arroz	rice pilaf (not soup!)	tostada	crisp fried tortilla
		enchilada	filled tortilla
pozole	meat-hominy stew	tamales russos	cabbage rolls

SEAFOOD (mariscos)

almejas	clams	merluza	hake (type of cod)
anchoas	anchovies	ostiones	oysters
arenques	herring	pescado	fish
atún	tuna	mojarra	perch
calamares	squid	pez espada	swordfish
camarones	shrimp	robalo	sea bass
caracoles	snails	salmon	salmon
caviare	caviar	salmon ahumado	smoked salmon
corvina	bass		
huachinango	red snapper	sardinas	sardines
jaiba	crab	solo	pike
langosta	lobster	trucha	trout
lenguado	sole		

MEATS (carnes)

ahumado	smoked	callos	tripe
alambre	shish kebab	venado	venison
albondigas	meatballs	conejo	rabbit
aves	poultry	cordero	lamb
bistek	steak	costillas de cerdo	spare ribs
cabeza de ternera	calf's head	faisan	pheasant
cabrito	kid (goat)	filete milanesa	breaded veal chops
carne	meat		
carne fria	cold cuts	filete de ternera	filet of veal
cerdo	pork	ganso	goose
chiles rellenos	stuffed peppers	pavo	turkey
chicharrón	pigskin cracklings	higado	liver
chorizo	spicy sausage	jamón	ham
chuleta	chop	lengua	tongue
chuleta de carnero	mutton chop	lomo	loin
chuletas de cordero	lamb chops	mole	chicken in spicy bitter chocolate sauce
chuletas de puerco	pork chops		

432 MEXICO ON $20 A DAY

paloma	pigeon	**pollo**	chicken
pato	duck	**res**	beef
pechuga	chicken breast	**riñones**	kidneys
perdiz	partridge	**ternera**	veal
pierna	leg	**tocino**	bacon

VEGETABLES (legumbres)

aguacate	avocado	**espinaca**	spinach
aceitunas	olives	**frijoles**	beans
arroz	rice	**hongos**	mushroom
betabeles	beets	**jicame**	sweet yellow turnip
cebolla	onions		
champiñones	mushrooms	**lechuga**	lettuce
chicharos	peas	**lentejas**	lentils
col	cabbage	**papas**	potatoes
col fermentada	sauerkraut	**pepino**	cucumber
coliflor	cauliflower	**rabanos**	radishes
ejotes	string beans	**tomate**	tomato
elote	corn (maize)	**verduras**	green
entremeses	hors d'oeuvres	**zanahorías**	carrots
esparragos	asparagus		

SALADS (ensaladas)

ensalada de apio	celery salad		
ensalada de frutas	fruit salad	**guacamole**	avocado salad
ensalada mixta	mixed salad	**lechuga**	lettuce salad
ensalada de pepinos	cucumber salad		

FRUITS (frutas)

chavacanos	apricots	**higos**	figs
ciruelas	yellow plums	**limon**	lime
coco	coconut	**mamey**	sweet orange fruit
duraznos	peaches	**mango**	mango
frambuesas	raspberries	**manzanas**	apples
fresas	strawberries	**naranjas**	oranges
con crema	with cream	**pera**	pear
fruta cocida	stewed fruit	**piña**	pineapple
granada	pomegranate	**platanos**	bananas
guanabana	green pear-like fruit	**tuña**	prickly pear fruit
		uvas	grapes
guayabas	guavas	**zapote**	maple-sugary fruit

DESSERTS (postres)

arroz con leche	rice pudding	helado, nieve	ice cream
brunelos de fruta	fruit tart	macedonia	fruit salad
coctel de aguacate	avocado cocktail	nieve	sherbet
		pastel	cake or pastry
coctel de frutas	fruit cocktail	queso	cheese
compota	stewed fruit	torta	cake
flan	custard	leche tipo bulgar, lavin	yogurt
galletas	crackers or cookies		

BEVERAGES (bebidas)

agua	water	leche	milk
brandy	brandy	licores	liqueurs
cafe	coffee	manzanita	apple juice
cafe con crema	coffee with cream	refrescas	soft drinks
		ron	rum
cafe negro	black coffee	sidra	cider
cerveza	beer	sifon	soda
ginebra	gin	te	tea
hielo	ice	vaso de leche	glass of milk
jerez	sherry	vino blanco	white wine
jugo de naranja	orange juice	vino tinto	red wine
jugo de tomate	tomato juice	refresco	soft drink
jugo de toronja	grapefruit juice		

CONDIMENTS AND CUTLERY

aceite	oil	pan	bread
azucar	sugar	bolillo	roll
copa	goblet	pimienta	pepper
cilantro	coriander	sal	salt
cuchara	spoon	taza	cup
cuchillo	knife	tenedor	fork
epazote	Mexican tea	tostada	toast
mantequilla	butter	vinagre	vinegar
mostaza	mustard	vaso	glass

PREPARATION AND SAUCES

asado	roasted
cocido	cooked
bien cocido	well-done
poco cocido	rare
empanado	breaded
frito	fried
al horno	baked
milanesa	Italian breaded
mole poblano	hot red peppers and cocoa sauce with raisins and spices
a la parilla	grilled
pibil	sauce of tomato, onion, red pepper (hot), cilantro, vinegar; wrapped in a banana leaf
poc chuc	pork leg cooked with onions, cilantro, sour oranges, and served with black beans
relleno negro	stuffed ground pork, pimento, olives, eggs, epazote, salt, vinegar and tomato stuffing
blanco	the above with raisins, cinnamon, and capers
queso	ball of cheese stuffed with ground pork, capers, onions, raisins, almonds, and eggs served in a white sauce
tampiqueño	thinly sliced meat
veracruzana	tomato and green olive sauce

NOW, SAVE MONEY ON ALL YOUR TRAVELS!
Join Arthur Frommer's $15-A-Day Travel Club

Saving money while traveling is never a simple matter, which is why, almost 20 years ago, the **$15-a-Day Travel Club** was formed. Actually, the idea came from readers of the Arthur Frommer Publications who felt that such an organization could bring financial benefits, continuing travel information, and a sense of community to economy-minded travelers all over the world.

In keeping with the money-saving concept, the membership fee is low—$14 (U.S. residents) or $16 (Canadian, Mexican, and foreign residents)—and is immediately exceeded by the value of your benefits which include:

(1) An annual subscription to an 8-page tabloid newspaper *The Wonderful World of Budget Travel* which keeps you up-to-date on fast-breaking developments in low-cost travel in all parts of the world—bringing you the kind of information you'd have to pay over $25 a year to obtain elsewhere. This consumer-conscious publication also provides special services to readers:

Traveler's Directory—a list of members all over the world who are willing to provide hospitality to other members as they pass through their home cities.

Share-a-Trip—requests from members for travel companions who can share costs and help avoid the burdensome single supplement.

Readers Ask . . . Readers Reply—travel questions from members to which other members reply with authentic firsthand information.

(2) The latest edition of any TWO of the books listed on the following page.

(3) A copy of *Arthur Frommer's Guide to New York*.

(4) Your personal membership card which entitles you to purchase through the Club all Arthur Frommer Publications for a third to a half off their regular retail prices during the term of your membership.

So why not join this hardy band of international budgeteers NOW and participate in its exchange of information and hospitality? Simply send U.S. $14 (U.S. residents) or $16 (Canadian, Mexican, and other foreign residents) along with your name and address to: $15-A-Day Travel Club, Inc., 1230 Avenue of the Americas, New York, NY 10020. Remember to specify which *two* of the books in section (2) above you wish to receive in your initial package of members' benefits. Or tear out this page, check off any two books on the opposite side and send it to us with your membership fee.

FROMMER/PASMANTIER PUBLISHERS Date _____
1230 AVE. OF THE AMERICAS, NEW YORK, NY 10020

Friends, please send me the books checked below:

$-A-DAY GUIDES
(In-depth guides to low-cost tourist accommodations and facilities.)

☐ Europe on $20 a Day $9.25
☐ Australia on $20 a Day $7.25
☐ England and Scotland on $25 a Day $7.95
☐ Greece on $20 a Day $7.25
☐ Hawaii on $25 a Day $8.95
☐ Ireland on $25 a Day $7.95
☐ Israel on $25 & $30 a Day $6.95
☐ Mexico on $20 a Day $8.95
☐ New Zealand on $20 & $25 a Day $6.95
☐ New York on $25 a Day $5.95
☐ Scandinavia on $25 a Day $7.95
☐ South America on $25 a Day $7.95
☐ Spain and Morocco (plus the Canary Is.) on $25 a Day $7.95
☐ Washington, D.C. on $25 a Day $7.25

DOLLARWISE GUIDES
(Guides to tourist accommodations and facilities from budget to deluxe, with emphasis on the medium-priced.)

☐ Egypt $6.95
☐ England & Scotland $7.95
☐ France $7.95
☐ Germany $6.25
☐ Italy $7.95
☐ Portugal (incl. Madeira) . $7.25

☐ Canada $8.25
☐ Caribbean (incl. Bermuda & the Bahamas) $8.95
☐ California & Las Vegas ... $7.95
☐ Florida $6.25
☐ New England $6.95
☐ Southeast & New Orleans .. $6.95

THE ARTHUR FROMMER GUIDES
(Pocket-size guides to tourist accommodations and facilities in all price ranges.)

☐ Amsterdam/Holland $3.95
☐ Athens $3.95
☐ Boston $3.95
☐ Hawaii $3.95
☐ Dublin/Ireland $3.95
☐ Las Vegas $3.95
☐ Lisbon/Madrid/Costa del Sol . $3.95
☐ London $3.95
☐ Los Angeles $3.95
☐ Mexico City/Acapulco $3.95

☐ Montreal/Quebec City $3.95
☐ New Orleans $3.95
☐ New York $3.95
☐ Orlando/Disney World/ EPCOT $3.95
☐ Paris $3.95
☐ Philadelphia/Atlantic City . $3.95
☐ Rome $3.95
☐ San Francisco $3.95
☐ Washington, D.C. $3.95

SPECIAL EDITIONS

☐ How to Beat the High Cost of Travel $3.95
☐ New York Athlete (NYC sports guide for jocks & novices) ... $8.95
☐ Where to Stay USA (Accommodations from $3 to $25 a night) $6.25
☐ Speak Easy Phrase Book (Fr/Sp/Ger/Ital. in *one* vol.) $4.95

☐ The Adventure Book: 237 Adventure Trips Throughout the World (8½ × 11 Premier Edition with 115 full color photographs) $14.95
☐ Museums in New York (Incl. historic houses, gardens, & zoos) $8.95

In U.S. include $1 post. & hdlg. for 1st book over $3; 75¢ for books under $3; 25¢ any add'l. book. Outside U.S. $2, $1, and 50¢ respectively.

Enclosed is my check or money order for $ _____

NAME _____

ADDRESS _____

CITY _____ STATE _____ ZIP _____